PERSUASION IN THE MEDIA AGE

PERSUASION IN THE MEDIA AGE

SECOND EDITION

TIMOTHY A. BORCHERS

Minnesota State University Moorhead

Boston   Burr Ridge, IL   Dubuque, IA   Madison, WI   New York
San Francisco   St. Louis   Bangkok   Bogotá   Caracas   Kuala Lumpur
Lisbon   London   Madrid   Mexico City   Milan   Montreal   New Delhi
Santiago   Seoul   Singapore   Sydney   Taipei   Toronto

The McGraw·Hill Companies

Mc Graw Hill **Higher Education**

Some ancillaries, including electronic and print components, may not be available to
customers outside the United States.

This book is printed on acid-free paper

3 4 5 6 7 8 9 0 DOC/DOC 0 9 8 7 6

ISBN: 978-0-07-286291-1
MHID: 0-07-286291-2
Publisher: *Phillip A. Butcher*
Sponsoring editor: *Nanette Giles*
Developmental editor: *Josh Hawkins*
Senior marketing manager: *Leslie Oberhuber*
Media coordinator: *Christie Ling*
Senior project manager: *Rebecca Nordbrock*
Senior production supervisor: *Carol A. Bielski*
Designer: *Cassandra J. Chu*
Associate photo research coordinator: *Natalia C. Peschiera*
Art editor: *Emma C. Ghiselli*
Art director: *Jeanne M. Schreiber*
Interior and cover design: *Linda Robertson*
Cover photos (clockwise from upper left): © *Richard T. Nowitz/CORBIS;*
   © *AFP/CORBIS;* © *Reuters NewMedia Inc./CORBIS;* © *Photodisc*
Typeface: *10/12 Plantin Light*
Compositor: *Thompson Type*
Printer: *R. R. Donnelley and Sons, Inc.*

Library of Congress Cataloging-in-Publication Data
Borchers, Timothy A.
      Persuasion in the media age / Timothy A. Borchers.
         p. cm.
      Includes bibliographical references and index.
      ISBN 0-07-286291-2 (softcover: alk. paper)
      1. Persuasion (Rhetoric)   2. Mass media.   I. Title.
P301.5.P47B67 2005
302.23'01—dc22
                                                              2003070606

www.mhhe.com

To Jack, Bernie, George, Susanne, and Oliver

Brief Contents

Preface   xxi

Part I: Concepts of Persuasion   1

1   Persuasion in Contemporary Society   3
2   Theories of Persuasion   31
3   Persuasion and Ethics in the Media Age   63

Part II: Variables of Persuasion   93

4   Media Influences on Persuasion   95
5   Audiences and Attitudes   129
6   Persuasion and Visual Images   157
7   Persuasion and Language   186
8   Persuasion and Culture   214
9   The Persuasiveness of the Source   242
10   The Reasoning Process   272
11   Motivational Appeals   302

Part III: Contexts and Applications of Persuasion   323

12   Persuasive Campaigns and Movements   325
13   Advertising   357
14   Interpersonal Persuasion   383
15   Creating Persuasive Presentations   415

References   R-1   •   Credits   C   •   Index   I-1

Contents

Preface   xxi

Part I: Concepts of Persuasion   1

1   Persuasion in Contemporary Society   3

A Glimpse at the Media Age   6

Media and Consciousness   7
- *Orality 8 • Literacy 9 • Electronic Media 10 • Hypermedia 11*

Persuasion and Culture   12
- *Media and Knowledge 13 • Postindustrial Culture 15*

The Postmodern Condition   16

Defining Persuasion   16
- *Selected Perspectives 16 • Persuasion and Related Terms 20*
- Internet Activity: International Identification   20
- Thinking Critically: Defining Persuasion   21

Persuasion in the Media Age 22
- *Persuasion Is Audience Oriented 22 • Persuasive Effects Are Overdetermined 22 • Much Is Left Unsaid 24 • Persuasion Is Ubiquitous but Invisible 24 • Persuasion Variables Are Reflexive 25*

Objectives for Persuaders   25
- *Forming Relationships 26 • Repetition 26 • Electronic Eloquence 26 • Commoditization 27*
- Internet Activity: Persuasion on the Internet   27

Implications for Audience Members   27
- *Evaluating Information 28 • Understanding the Persuasion Process 28 • Self-Concept and Persuasion 29*
- Ethical Insights: Ethics and the Persuasion Process   29

Summary   30

Key Terms   30

2 Theories of Persuasion   31

The Nature of Theory   32

Functions of Theories   34

Early Rhetorical Theory   35

> *Aristotle 36*

> ▪ Internet Activity: Presidential Persuasion   39

> *The Five Canons 39*

Semiotics   41

Audience-Oriented Theories   44

> *Cognitive Dissonance Theory 45 • Problematic Integration Theory 46 • The Elaboration Likelihood Model 48*

The Social Construction of Reality   51

> ▪ Thinking Critically: Processing Persuasive Messages   52

> *Symbolic Convergence Theory 53 • An Example 54*

Media Theories   54

> *One-Shot Model 55 • Two-Step Flow of Information 55 • Uses and Gratifications Research 56 • Cultivation Analysis 57 • Agenda Setting 58*

> ▪ Ethical Insights: Ethics and Violent Entertainment   59

> ▪ Internet Activity: Setting the Internet News Agenda   60

Summary   61

Key Terms   62

3 Persuasion and Ethics in the Media Age   63

Ethics and Persuasion   64

Ethical Challenges of the Media Age   65

> *Deception 66*

> ▪ Ethical Insights: Ethical Responsibilities of Persuaders and Audience Members   66

> *Access 67 • Oppression 68 • Privacy 69 • Conflict of Interest 69*

> ▪ Internet Activity: Protecting Your Privacy Online   70

Approaches to Ethical Decision Making   70

> *Universal versus Situational Ethics 71 • The First Amendment 71 • Richard Johannesen 72*

The Making of Ethical Judgments   73

> ▪ Internet Activity: Resolving Ethical Issues   76

Persuasion and the Public Sphere   76
  ■ Thinking Critically: Ethics and the Ideal Speech Situation   80

Visual Images and Ethics   81
  National Press Photographers Association's Code of Ethics   81

Political Persuasion   82
  American Association of Political Consultants' Code of Ethics   83

Advertising   83
  American Association of Advertising Agencies' Creative Code   84

Organizational Advocacy   85
  Public Relations Society of America's Statement of Professional Values   85

Journalism   86
  Society of Professional Journalists' Code of Ethics   87

NCA Credo for Ethical Communication   87

Five Guiding Principles   88

Ethics and Audience Members   89
  Being Informed 90 • Keeping an Open Mind 90 • Being Critical 90 • Expressing Ethical Judgments 90

Summary   91

Key Terms   91

Part II: Variables of Persuasion   93

4 *Media Influences on Persuasion*   95

Defining Media   96
  Media Sources 96 • Media Channels 99 • Media Content 99 • Media Audiences 100 • Putting It Together 101

Assumptions about Media   101

How Media Persuade Us   103
  ■ Internet Activity: Identifying Media Influence   104

The Sensory Experience of Media   104
  Visual Symbols 104 • Music and Auditory Symbols 105 • Subliminal Persuasion 105

Media Channels   106
  Newspapers 106 • Radio 108 • Television 110 • Internet 113
  ■ Ethical Insights: Ethics and the Digital Divide   115
  Convergence: The Blurring of Media Boundaries 115

▦ Internet Activity: Analyzing Media Convergence   119

News   119

What Is News?   120

▦ Thinking Critically: Analyzing a News Article   123

News Decisions 123 • Presentation 125 • Audience Empowerment 125

Entertainment Media   126

Summary   128

Key Terms   128

5 *Audiences and Attitudes*   *129*

The Audience in the Media Age   130

Size 130 • Anonymity 132 • Taking Control 132

Audiences and Attitudes   134

Defining Attitude 134 • Attitude Formation 134 • Changing Attitudes 137

Audience Analysis   138

Adapting to Audiences 138 • Creating Audiences 139

▦ Thinking Critically: Adapting to Audiences   140

Polling   140

What Is Polling? 140 • Functions of Polling 142 • Assessing Polling 143

▦ Internet Activity: Assessing a Poll   143

Audience Segmentation   144

Demographics 144 • Psychographics 145

▦ Internet Activity: Take the VALS Survey   147

Geodemographics 149 • Segmenting Internet Audiences 149 • Other Methods of Audience Segmentation 150

▦ Ethical Insights: Ethics and Audience Analysis   151

Ratings   152

Television 153 • Radio 154 • The Print Media 154 • The Internet 155

Summary   155

Key Terms   156

6 *Persuasion and Visual Images*   *157*

Attributes of Visual Symbols   159

Color 159 • Form 160 • Lighting 162 • Spatiality 163 •
Movement 163

Media Influences on Images   164
Typography 164 • Photography   165 • Motion Pictures 166
▪ Internet Activity: Evaluating Photographs   167
Television Images 168 • Computer-Generated Images 168 •
Interactive Multimedia 169
▪ Ethical Insights: Ethics and Visual Images   170

How Visual Images Persuade   171
Image as Representation of Reality 171 • Image as Proof 173 •
Image as Argumentative Claim 177

Applications of Visual Communication   178
▪ Internet Activity: Identifying Claims in Political Cartoons   179
Visual Spectacles 179 • Logos 179 • Architecture 182

Evaluating Images   183
▪ Thinking Critically: Evaluating Images of Status   184

Summary   185
Key Terms   185

7 *Persuasion and Language*   186

Using Language Strategically   187
*Language Intensity 187 • Powerful Language 188 • Language
and Imagery 188 • Rhetorical Figures 189 • Metaphor 190*

Contested Meanings   191

Creating Social Reality   193
Symbol Use 194 • Naming 196 • Framing 197 •
Dramatistic Redemption   198
▪ Ethical Insights: Ethics and Spin Control   199

Electronic Eloquence   201
*Personification 201 • Self-Disclosure 202 • Conversational Style
202 • Verbal Distillation 203*
▪ Thinking Critically: Memorable Slogans   205
Visual Dramatization 205
▪ Internet Activity: Presidential Eloquence   208

Language and Power   208
*Ideology 209 • Power 209 • Power and Language: A Feminist
Perspective 210*
▪ Internet Activity: Gender, Power, and Cyberspace   212

Summary   212

Key Terms   213

8   *Persuasion and Culture*   *214*

Defining Culture   215

> *Beliefs, Values, and Behaviors 216 • Mainstream Cultural Beliefs, Values, and Behaviors 217 • Culture and Conflict 218*

Cultural Trends   219

> *Buzz 219 • Culture Scanning   220*
>
> ▪ Internet Activity: Culture Scanning   221

Cultural Beliefs   221

> *Primary Beliefs 222 • Immigrant Beliefs 222 • Frontier Beliefs 223 • Religious and Moral Beliefs 224 • Social Beliefs 224 • Political Beliefs 225 • Beliefs on Human Nature 225*

Cultural Values   226

Cultural Behaviors   228

Maintaining Culture   230

> *Hegemony 231*
>
> ▪ Thinking Critically: Hegemony and Advertising   232
>
> ▪ Internet Activity: Managing Power in *The Simpsons*   233
>
> *Patriarchy   233*
>
> ▪ Ethical Insights: Protecting the Interests of Minorities   235

Transforming Culture   236

> *Consumer Culture 237 • Multiculturalism 239*

Summary   240

Key Terms   241

9   *The Persuasiveness of the Source*   *242*

The Source in the Media Age   243

Defining Credibility   244

> *Ethos 245 • Source Credibility 246*

The Image of the Source   248

> ▪ Internet Activity: Judging Credibility   249
>
> *Characteristics of Images 249 • Effects of Images on Audiences 251*
>
> ▪ Internet Activity: Describing Images   252

Creating an Image 253 • Media and Images 254 • Choosing Meanings for an Image 255 • Evaluating Images 255

Institutional Sources   256

    ■ Thinking Critically: Martha Stewart's Image   257

    Organizational Image   258 • Spokespeople 258

    ■ Ethical Insights: Ethics and Organizational Image   259

Individual Persuaders   261

    Nonverbals 261 • Delivery 264 • Impression Management 264

Image Repair   266

Covert Persuasion: Propaganda   268

    Entertainment Media 269 • News Media 269

Summary   270

Key Terms   271

10 *The Reasoning Process*   272

Reasoning in the Media Age   273

Toulmin's Model of Reasoning   274

    Claims 274 • Data 276 • Warrant, or the Reasoning Process 280

    ■ Ethical Insights: Ethics and Reasoning   283

    Additional Components of the Toulmin Model 285 • Toulmin's Model in the Media Age 286

    ■ Internet Activity: Reasoning in Everyday Life   287

Narratives   289

    Evaluating Narratives 290 • Using Narratives 291

Evaluating a Persuader's Reasoning   292

    Tests of Evidence   292

    ■ Thinking Critically: Evaluating Web Pages   296

    Argument Fields   297 • Fallacies 298

    ■ Internet Activity: Identifying Fallacies   300

Summary   300

Key Terms   301

11 *Motivational Appeals*   302

The Power of Motivational Appeals   303

Emotion   305

    Defining Emotion   305

    ▦ Ethical Insights: Ethics, Advertising, and Self-Esteem   308

    Fear 308

Needs   311

    ▦ Internet Activity: Fulfilling Safety Needs   312

Values   314

The Nature of Motivational Appeals   317

    ▦ Thinking Critically: Values and Business Presentations   317

    ▦ Internet Activity: Appealing to Values   318

    *Narrative Form 318 • Humor 319 • Visual Communication
319 • Media 320*

The Social Construction of Affect   320

Summary   321

Key Terms   322

Part III: Contexts and Applications of Persuasion   323

12 *Persuasive Campaigns and Movements*   325

Media and Persuasive Campaigns and Movements   326

    ▦ Ethical Insights: Ethics and the Boundaries of Persuasion   327

Verbal Symbols   329

    Slogans 329 • Songs 330

Visual Images   331

    Images 331 • Image Events 332

Political Campaigns   335

    How the News Media Cover Politics 335

    ▦ Thinking Critically: Alternative Voting Methods   337

    *Political Consultants 337 • The Message 338 • Managing the
Meaning of the Message 340*

    ▦ Internet Activity: Watching Debates   347

Persuasive Movements   347

    *Types of Persuasive Movements 348 • Media Framing and
Persuasive Movements 348*

    ▦ Internet Activity: Understanding Media Frames   350

*Understanding the Persuasion of Movements 350 • Outcomes 352
• An Example 352 • Expressive Persuasive Movements 354*

Summary   355

Key Terms   356

13 *Advertising*   357

Advertising in the Media Age   358

Researching Audiences for Advertising   360

Targeting Audiences 360 • Measuring Audiences 361

Media Selection   361

*Television 362 • Newspapers 362 • Radio 363 •
Magazines 363 • Out-of-Home Advertising 363 •
Internet 364 • Direct Mail 364*

Challenges to Advertisers in the Media Age   364

*Media-User Behavior Challenges 364 • Audience Demographic
Challenges 365 • Advertisement Environment Challenges 366*

Responding to the Challenges   368

Branding 369

▪ Thinking Critically: Creating the Krispy Kreme Brand   370

Cross-Promotion   371

▪ Ethical Insights: Ethics and Cross-Promotion   373

*Product Placement 373 • Relationship Marketing 375 •
Internet Advertising 377*

▪ Internet Activity: Exploring Internet Communities   379

▪ Internet Activity: Exploring Internet Advertising   380

Advertising's Effects   380

Summary   382

Key Terms   382

14 *Interpersonal Persuasion*   383

Interpersonal Persuasion in the Media Age   384

Interpersonal Persuasion Variables   385

*Attraction 385 • Dominance 386 • Involvement 386 •
Situation 386*

Compliance Gaining   387

*Techniques 387 • Situation 388 • Power 391 • Compliance
Gaining in the Media Age 392*

Sequential-Request Strategies   393
Foot in Door 393
▨ Ethical Insights: Ethics and Lowballing   395
Door in Face 395
▨ Internet Activity: Using Sequential Request Techniques   396
Personal Selling   397
Personal Selling in the Media Age 397 • A Model of Personal Selling 399
Interviewing   401
Characteristics 402 • Goals of the Participants 402 • Types of Questions 403 • Types of Interviews 404
▨ Internet Activity: Persuasive Interviewing   406
Conflict Resolution   408
Causes of Conflict 408 • A Model of Dispute Resolution 408
▨ Thinking Critically: Climate and Conflict Resolution   410
Methods for Resolving Disputes 410
Detecting Deception   411
Summary   413
Key Terms   414

15 **Creating Persuasive Presentations   415**
Presentations in the Media Age   416
Topic and Thesis Statement   416
Audience Analysis   417
Creating the Audience 418 • Direct Analysis 418 • Segmentation 419
▨ Thinking Critically: Speaking to Multiple Audiences   420
Other Audience Analysis Factors 420
Analysis of Topic   421
Supporting Ideas   423
Premises and Evidence 423 • Locating Premises and Evidence 424
▨ Internet Activity: Evaluating Evidence   425
▨ Ethical Insights: Ethics and Plagiarism   426
Arrangement   426
Elements Common to All Persuasive Speeches 426 • Organizational Patterns for Fact/Value Topics 428 • Organizational Patterns for Policy Topics 428

Using Verbal Symbols   430

Delivery   430
> *Modes of Delivery   430 • Vocal Cues   431 • Gestures and Body Movements   432*

Sample Persuasive Presentation   432

Making Strategic Decisions   435
> *Forewarning   436 • One-Sided and Two-Sided Messages   436 • Ordering Effects   437 • Primary versus Recency Effects   437 • Inoculation   438*

Multimedia Presentation Aids   438
> *Functions   439 • Design   440 • Use   441*

Creating Mediated Persuasive Messages   442
> ■ Internet Activity: Using Multimedia   443

Print Advertising   443 • Video Advertising   444 • Websites   445

Presenting via Mediated Channels   446

Summary   447

Key Terms   448

References   R-1
Credits   C
Index   I-1

Preface

We are constantly bombarded by persuasive messages. Everyone from advertisers and politicians to our friends and colleagues seek to gain our support for their ideas, products, or services. In today's world, persuaders use increasingly sophisticated ways of exerting influence over the attitudes, beliefs, and behaviors of their audiences. It is essential, therefore, that we develop an ability to critically analyze the myriad of persuasive messages we encounter. Consider two brief examples:

A television commercial for a new car tells us much more than how many miles to the gallon the car gets or which safety features it includes. Automobile advertising tells us what kind of cars we should drive, the cultural importance of driving particular cars, and why it is important to have the freedom of mobility that driving affords. We often don't even realize how the implicit messages of advertisers affect our attitudes and, ultimately, our buying behavior.

Politicians—in combination with news media sources—use public opinion polling to shape the public's agenda, telling us which issues are important and which are not. While this agenda may be reflective of some people's priorities, it is just as likely to exclude the priorities of many others. In fact, politicians purposely create agendas that ignore many members of the public, instead targeting smaller, more influential groups that can help them win re-election.

As persuaders begin to target individuals through direct-broadcast satellites, direct mail, and narrowcasting television programming, the challenge of making informed decisions is even greater.

Persuasion in the Media Age explores the nature of persuasion today and offers strategies for critically evaluating persuasive communication. This text provides a contemporary response to an age-old problem: understanding and adapting to the technological advances in our society. Today's world demands a new perspective of persuasion: one that is grounded in the assumption that human consciousness has been forever altered by communication technology. In order to respond to this fast-paced change, we must move beyond traditional theories to better understand how to respond to and evaluate persuasive communication in this era of technological advances.

APPROACH

Persuasion in the Media Age provides a contemporary, interdisciplinary approach to the study of persuasion. In addition to teaching the basic principles of persuasion, the goal of the text is to emphasize the role that media and technology play in contemporary persuasive practices and to teach strategies for developing critical responses to persuasion.

The challenge in creating such a text is in drawing from a wide variety of theorists, including many who have not been featured in traditional treatments of persuasion. The content in this book draws heavily from Kenneth Burke's theory of identification, as well as from the work of such theorists as Walter Ong, Neil Postman, Kathleen Hall Jamieson, Michael Calvin McGee, and others. Together, these scholars contend that persuasion in a society constantly adapts to its cultural beliefs and values, as well as to the economic and social structures that govern the society.

FEATURES

An Emphasis on the Media Age   There is an emphasis throughout on how persuasion has been changed by electronic media. Starting with the view that human consciousness, culture, and epistemology have been forever changed by electronic media, the text details how persuaders have altered their strategies in order to identify with today's audience members.

Interdisciplinary Approach   *Persuasion in the Media Age* presents a theory of contemporary persuasion that is informed by the work of scholars in many disciplines. The disciplines of anthropology, cultural studies, sociology, management, political science, history, women's studies, marketing, human communication studies, and rhetorical studies are represented in the text. This interdisciplinary approach seeks to bring together the latest thinking on persuasion, while also drawing on foundational concepts, such as attitudes, rhetoric, and human motivation.

Emphasis on Audience and Visual Images   Chapters on audience and visual images are unique to this treatment of persuasion. Today's persuaders use sophisticated methods to understand and target audiences. These methods are explored in Chapter 5. Likewise, persuasion today uses the powerful symbolism of visual images to identify with audiences. Chapter 6 addresses how visual images suggest meaning and how persuaders use them.

Emphasis on Ethics   Chapter 3 is devoted to ethics, and all chapters include a discussion of ethics as it relates to that chapter's subject matter, found in boxes entitled "Ethical Insights." The text uses the National Communication Association Credo for Ethical Communication as one touchstone for ethical issues. The ethics discussions are framed in a way that allows for discussion about the case study featured and the ethical issues involved.

Contemporary Examples   Throughout the text, many contemporary examples of persuasion are used to augment the concepts discussed. These examples come from popular culture, advertising, politics, and organizational life. Students will be able to identify with these examples and form meaningful connections between the content and their lives.

Specific Contexts   The last section of the text provides separate chapters covering a variety of specific, persuasive contexts, including politics, social movements, advertising, and interpersonal persuasion.

CHANGES IN THE SECOND EDITION

Increased Use of Social Science Research   The latest social science research about persuasion has been included to complement the existing discussion of the book. New topics include deception, problematic integration theory, message effects research, and language strategies.

Enhanced Web Pedagogy   The book now features Internet-based activities for each chapter. This change allows for better integration with the website to bring alive the study of persuasion for contemporary students.

Updated Examples   Each example in the book has been reviewed and updated as needed to provide the most timely illustrations possible of the book's theoretical concepts.

Updated Theory Discussion   New theories have been added to the book's discussion, and existing theories have been reworded, as necessary, so students can better understand the concepts.

Revamped Pedagogical Features   Several changes have been made to the book's pedagogical features to make it easier for students to use them. Glossary entries and discussion questions have been moved to the margins, and each chapter includes a list of learning objectives at the beginning of the chapter. Lists and boxes have been used to make reading the text more accessible.

Organizational Changes   Chapter 12 now addresses both political campaigns and movements, where previously these had been discussed in separate chapters. Other chapters have been reorganized to provide a more effective narrative.

ORGANIZATION

This book is organized into three main parts. Part I examines the core concepts in persuasion. Chapter 1 presents an overview of persuasion in the media age and a definition that will guide our study. Chapter 2 surveys the range of theories that have been used to examine persuasion. Chapter 3 examines the relationship between ethics and contemporary mediated persuasion.

Part II analyzes the key variables in the persuasion process. Chapter 4 examines the media while Chapter 5 discusses the audience. Chapters 6 and 7 examine the visual images and language strategies that persuaders use to communicate their message. Chapter 8 studies the interaction between persuasion and culture. Chapters 9, 10, and 11 reflect the Aristotelian concepts of ethos, logos, and pathos, focusing on the source, the reasoning process, and motivational appeals.

Part III discusses how persuaders use the variables of the persuasion process in various settings. Chapter 12 examines political campaigns and persuasive movements. Chapter 13 discusses how persuaders identify with audiences through advertising. Chapter 14 looks at the ways individuals use persuasion theory in their daily interactions with others. Finally, Chapter 15 surveys how persuaders create persuasive presentations.

INSTRUCTOR'S RESOURCES

The text is fully supported by an online learning center for students and faculty, which can be found at http://www.mhhe.com/borchers2. The site contains activities, relevant links, study guides, and teaching resources. The website is designed to allow readers to explore in more detail issues identified at certain points in the text.

In addition to the online learning center, there is an instructor's resource CD available for this text. It includes pedagogical tips, detailed chapter outlines, media suggestions, sample syllabi, suggested exercises, and test questions designed to assist in teaching.

ACKNOWLEDGMENTS

I wish to thank many individuals for their enthusiasm, insight, and encouragement during my work on this project. My effort has been sustained by colleagues, students, mentors, friends, and family.

My colleagues and students at Minnesota State University Moorhead have been extremely supportive of this project since its inception. I am fortunate to work in an environment that nurtures both teaching and research, which I think this project brings together in a unique way. In particular, I wish to acknowledge the support of Jim Bartruff, Theresa Carson, Rusty Casselton, Craig Ellingson, Virginia Gregg, Dave Gaer, Lynn Harter, Theresa Hest, Ted Larson, Scott Titsworth, David Wheeler, Virginia Klenk, and Peter Quigley.

I am indebted to the staff at the MSUM library. They filled my every request and sent constant reminders about overdue books. Peg O'Neill and Dianne Schmidt have been especially helpful.

My students—too numerous to name—have been a constant source of ideas, inspiration, and patience.

My parents, Glenn and Carole Borchers, and my extended family have been incredibly supportive of this project, as well.

The individuals at McGraw-Hill have been instrumental in guiding this project to its completion. Joshua Hawkins and Nanette Giles have been insightful, supportive, and helpful.

A great deal of credit goes to the reviewers of the first edition, including William N. Denman, Marshall University; Michael E. Eidenmuller, University of Texas at Tyler; Emilie Falc, Winona State University; Linda Ferguson, Virginia Wesleyan College; Thomas Hobbs, Chapman University; Scott Moore, California State University, Fresno; Charles J. Stewart, Purdue University; and Frederick H. Turner, Rider University. Their praise encouraged me, and their criticism sharpened the analysis and coverage of the book. I thank them for their insightful and thorough comments.

Finally, I wish to acknowledge the support of my wife, Susanne Williams. She was, and is, a constant source of support, encouragement, and inspiration to me. My son, Oliver, has put up with the presence of the laptop in his sandbox and playroom. He is a constant lesson to me that even at the youngest age, we are easily susceptible to persuasion's influence.

PART I
Concepts of Persuasion

The three chapters that make up Part I of this text explore fundamental concepts of persuasion. Chapter 1 presents the framework for the book. Its central argument is that the medium a culture uses to transmit its messages—be it spoken words, printed words, radio, television, or other electronic means—forever changes the members of that culture as well as what is communicated by that medium. Electronic media (radio, television, the Internet) dominate our culture today, influencing the methods of persuasion used in our culture.

Chapter 2 provides a theoretical framework for the book. The chapter discusses a variety of theories that all lend to our contemporary understanding of persuasion. Each theory focuses on some aspect of the persuasive process, and together, these theories orient our study of persuasion.

Chapter 3 discusses the ethical implications of persuasion today. Electronic media have created new ethical dilemmas for persuaders and audience members alike. We survey these dilemmas and offer several ideas for how audience members and persuaders can understand what is appropriate in today's world.

1

Persuasion in Contemporary Society

Learning Objectives

After reading this chapter, you should be able to:

1. Trace the influence of media on culture and persuasion.

2. Explain various approaches to studying and defining persuasion.

3. Identify characteristics of persuasion in the media age.

4. Name the objectives for persuaders.

5. Recognize the implications of contemporary persuasion for audience members.

Consider three contemporary examples of persuasion: one a political speech, the second an Internet site, and the third a recent television commercial.

Colin Powell, speaking before the United Nations Security Council on February 5, 2003, commanded international attention when he sought to justify war against Iraq. With United States and other world citizens divided about the potential war, Powell mustered his credibility to present the Bush administration's case for war. Using photographs, video clips, and a PowerPoint presentation, Powell forcefully argued that war was necessary to remove Saddam Hussein and his weapons of mass destruction. Powell was effective. Following the speech, the percentage of the American public who believed war was justified rose from 58 percent to 63 percent, according to a *USA Today*/CNN/ Gallup Poll (Benedetto, 2003). Clearly Powell used his credibility, authority, and an international platform to persuade the world community that war with Iraq was justified.

3

Powell's speech to the United Nations exemplifies several important aspects of persuasion in the media age. First, persuaders have the ability to command large audiences. Powell's speech was heard, seen, or read by millions around the world. News coverage of the speech dominated world newscasts and newspapers. Additionally, this example illustrates the significance of the media in shaping how we see, hear, and think about world events. Second, Powell's speech made use of several photographs and video clips. Images have become an important means by which persuaders are able to convince audiences to change their beliefs. You can view the images from Powell's presentation at several Internet sites that are linked from the Web page for this book. Finally, Powell's speech shows that persuasion has consequences. Despite the opposition of U.S. citizens and several prominent world nations, the United States was able to gain enough support to lead a war against Iraq and depose Hussein.

The world followed the events of the Iraq War through the eyes, cameras, and laptops of the embedded journalists who traveled with the coalition troops. Journalists of another sort, "bloggers," also brought the war to the people of the world. Blogging is the posting of personal journals to Web pages. Throughout the war, Iraqi bloggers were persuasive, shaping people's perspectives about the war and providing their own firsthand account of the war as could no other conventional journalist. One blogger, Raed, wrote this about his observations of Baghdad in the first days of the war:

> Half an hour ago the oil filled trenches were put on fire. First watching Al-jazeera they said that these were the places that got hit by bombs from an air raid a few miniutes [sic] earlier but when I went up to the roof to take a look I saw that there were too many of them, we heard only three explosions. I took pictures of the nearest. My cousine [sic] came and told me he saw police cars standing by one and setting it on fire. Now you can see the columns of smoke all over the city. (Monday, March 24, 2003; Pax, 2003).

Blogging is a new form of persuasive communication that is significant for several reasons. First, blogging gives considerable power to single individuals. Bloggers are able to easily write about their experiences while commanding an international audience of readers. Bloggers such as Raed don't need the credibility or resources associated with large news organizations. At the same time, blogging strips power from the journalism industry. Instead of watching CNN, world citizens interested in the war could instead read Raed's account to get a firsthand view of the war. Additionally, blogging suggests that the Internet has emerged as a persuasive medium which has international access and appeal. It is a medium, however, that sometimes makes it difficult to question the identity and ability of information sources, such as Raed. Many readers have questioned whether he actually exists or if an imposter created Raed's Web log.

Let's now consider an example from the world of advertising. If you watched the 2003 Super Bowl, you may remember seeing an advertisement for Pepsi Twist, featuring the Osbournes. Ozzy Osbourne, the famous musical performer and star of the reality-based television series based on his family, is depicted in his kitchen, in a scene reminiscent of the hit television series. His children confront him with what appear to be cans of Pepsi and announce that they aren't drinking Pepsi, but instead Pepsi Twist, a new brand of soft drink. Then, Ozzy's children announce that they aren't really his children, but instead are the Osmonds, Donny and Marie. After tearing off masks, the Osmonds launch into their hit song, "I'm a Little Bit Country," to which Ozzy screams in fear. Next, we see Ozzy waking up, thinking he's had a bad dream and seeking comfort in his wife, only to find Florence Henderson in bed with him. The commercial fades to images of Pepsi Twist and Diet Pepsi Twist and a voiceover asking, "Like twists? Try Pepsi Twist and Diet Pepsi Twist."

The Intermedia Advertising Group found that the Pepsi ad had the highest recall of all the Super Bowl ads that year (Ad Age). Recall rates for the ad were 150 percent higher than for an average ad (Ad Age). The ad was effective for several reasons. First, the ad featured the Osbournes, the popular family who was featured in the MTV television series about their life. Pepsi relied on audience members to know and understand who the Osbournes were. Second, the ad used humor—juxtaposing the hard-rock Osbournes with the more family-oriented country style of the Osmonds. Humor is an effective tool to help audiences remember a persuasive message. The ad was also ironic; it did not say much at all about the product being sold. Finally, the advertisement was effective because of when it aired and who the audience was. Pepsi aired the ad during the 2003 Super Bowl, a time when millions of viewers from the targeted demographic groups would be watching television.

Many theorists say that we are living in a time of chaos, instability, and upheaval. A confluence of forces—technological and cultural—influences how we communicate with others. We live in a time when television dominates how we experience the world. A medium such as the television is often viewed only as a channel, or way, of transmitting information. It is important to realize, though, that television, like any medium, does more than serve as a pipeline for information to our homes. The medium brings information to us, to be sure, but it also changes that information—and it changes those who receive the information, those who send it, and the culture in which the information is transmitted. We'll explore this somewhat controversial claim in more detail shortly.

Specifically, the three examples we have just discussed—Powell's speech, the Iraqi blogger, and the Pepsi commercial—suggest some new ways of thinking about the components of the persuasive process. Audiences today are actively involved—as indicated by the blogging example—and they often behave in ways that belie traditional methods of prediction. The sources of today's persuasive messages can be very powerful, such as Powell, or they can lack traditional sources of power, such as the blogger. The message of today's persuasion is often implicit and ironic—as in the Pepsi commercial. Finally, the media-dominated culture in which we live requires different mental processing skills—the ability to "decode" the Pepsi commercial—and the medium influences the direction and flow of messages—as in the case of the blogger. We will refer to these examples throughout the book to further illustrate these points.

The central argument of this book is that contemporary culture presents us with a complex web of influences, many of which we cannot ignore and many of which we do not consciously choose. Persuasion is vastly different today than it has been for centuries. Media, and other forms of technology,

mediated world
an environment in which media serve as intermediaries in the communication process, coming between audiences and persuaders and affecting the information that passes between the two

Think about a persuasive message you recently encountered that was successful—that is, one that made you alter your thinking or behavior in some way. What form did the message take? What aspects of it did you find convincing? Did the message appeal to you emotionally, analytically, or both? In general, why do you think the message was successful?

have altered individuals and cultures and consequently the ways we produce and receive persuasive communication. Because in today's world the media serve as intermediaries in the communication process, coming between audiences and persuaders and affecting the information that passes between the two, we can be said to live in a **mediated world.** We refer to this changed environment as the media age throughout our discussion.

This book explores the ways media technologies have influenced the study and practice of persuasion. By examining the variables of persuasion and the contexts in which persuasion takes place, we will gain a better understanding of how persuasion occurs today. As an audience member, you will be better able to assess the influences you encounter in your life.

In this introductory chapter, we take a closer look at media and contemporary society. We then consider a definition of persuasion that will guide our study of the topic. Finally, we explore in greater detail the characteristics of persuasion today, as well as the impact of these characteristics on persuasive messages and the people who receive them.

A Glimpse at the Media Age

We live in a media age. Media surround us, permeating our every waking moment. In Chapter 4, we explore in detail the presence and implications of media in our lives. Here, let's examine how media shape our world. Consider your experiences with media today. The music you may have listened to on your way to school is influential in setting standards for how you dress, talk, and behave toward others. The hip-hop movement, for example, introduced baggy pants, floppy hats, and unique words to our culture. The movie you saw last night influences your perceptions of yourself and your culture. If you watched a murder thriller, some researchers argue, you may have a heightened fear of crime as a result.

Likewise, entertainment programs on television influence us. We emulate the characters we see on these shows, and we relate to each other in ways that are defined by the influence of these programs. We are constantly exposed to advertising as well. From commercials on the radio and television to advertisements on bus-stop benches to flyers posted on classroom bulletin boards, someone is almost always trying to persuade us to believe something different or behave in a certain way. We may think we can avoid its influence by not purchasing a particular product, but advertising has a profound influence on our lifestyles. We define who we are by the clothes we wear, the food we eat, and the car we drive. Each of these attributes has certain values assigned to them by advertising. The mediated, technological environment of contemporary society has influenced even our interpersonal communication. Our idea of who we are is developed, in part, by our interaction with media. Self-concept is a very important feature of our interpersonal communication with others. Truly, we cannot escape media or their influence. With this glimpse of how media pervade our lives in mind, let's explore how media influence how we understand our world and our culture.

Media and Consciousness

Walter Ong (1982) is a scholar who has written a great deal about the impact of a communication medium on its users and their culture. A central argument in his work is that each medium creates different ways of thinking, different ways of feeling, and different states of awareness. That is, a medium alters the consciousness of its users. Ong identifies three major types of media in the world's history: oral, written, and electronic. We'll also discuss another: hypermedia. Ong contends that for a given culture, one form of communication will be dominant. Electronic media—specifically, television—today dominate U.S. culture.

The implication of living in a culture dominated by electronic media is that even our face-to-face interaction with others is influenced, in some way, by our media environment. Although the persuasion may not be mediated, the affect of our media culture is profound. Consider three typical face-to-face persuasive encounters and ways that each is influenced by our mediated environment:

- The practice of preaching is changing, due to the use of PowerPoint and electronic media in communicating with parishioners. Many churches are using PowerPoint in their services, to provide visual cues to an audience that is saturated with visual images and has grown accustomed to having an image to reinforce the spoken word. Woodland Hills Church in St. Paul, Minnesota, for example, posts PowerPoint slides from each week's sermon to the Web. Additionally, many churchgoers are accessing sermons and other religious resources on the Web. The Christian Internet Broadcasting Network streams sermons from its website to users worldwide. One pastor in Germany recently broadcast his sermon to more than 1,300 young people on their cellular phones. The sermon was altered to accommodate the different medium.

- The face-to-face interaction of a city council meeting is also influenced by our media environment. City council members must be sensitive to how their comments are portrayed in news media, since city council deliberations are usually important news items for a community. Additionally, city council members are influenced by voters who have used electronic resources to gain support for particular positions, such as an e-mail petition or website. Needless to say, campaigning for public office, whether for the presidency, city council, or local school board, is dominated by mediated advertising and visual images, in addition to door-to-door campaigning.

- Finally, let's consider a personal and intimate decision that two people often make. The decision to marry someone is influenced by a variety of factors, not the least of which is our idealized conceptions of the perfect spouse created through our exposure to media. As we'll see, it is difficult to detach ourselves from the images we see of couples on television sitcoms, in movies, or in the news media. These conceptions inherently influence our choice of a spouse (or even someone we might consider dating) and how we communicate with that person. Of course, the whole concept of marriage is today a media issue. Advocates for gay marriages,

Table 1.1 Characteristics of Media Cultures

Culture	Media	Sender-receiver relationship	Thinking style
Oral	Face to face	Immediate	Cannot conceive of ideas outside immediate experiences
Literate	Printing	Separated	Linear thought Abstract thought
Electronic	Television Radio	Sense of participation	Vicarious experience Participate via media
Hypermedia	Internet	Interactive	Nonlinear

for instance, have used the media and mediated channels of communication to influence legislators and opinion-leaders about the subject.

Having briefly surveyed how our media environment influences many different types of persuasion, let's now survey various media cultures to learn more about the influence of media on a culture. Each culture is briefly outlined in Table 1.1.

ORALITY

The oral medium relies on face-to-face communication between source and receiver and was first used by *Homo sapiens* some 4 to 5 million years ago (Chesebro & Bertelsen, 1996). The oral medium relies exclusively on vocalizations and body movements to express thought. Early communication by humans was probably limited to crude gestures and oral sounds that signified events and relationships that were immediately present in the communication context. Only for the past 4,000 to 5,500 years have humans used symbols, or words and images, to communicate. Researchers contend that changes in the brain and the vocal system allowed humans to begin using what we might call words at that time. Oral communication takes advantage of the immediate presence of speaker and listener to make sense of what is being discussed. In fact, it is impossible to isolate one aspect of the communication situation—speaker, message, and receiver—from its relationship to the other components. It is important to keep in mind that 700 million people around the world still rely primarily on the oral medium of communication (Chesebro & Bertelsen, 1996). Most people living in the United States today do not use this form of communication exclusively.

Ong (1982) contends that orality creates a certain kind of consciousness. He explains that people who communicate only via the oral medium must develop memory aids to help them recall complex thoughts. You probably learned some of these as you developed the ability to write. For example, the phrase, "*i* before *e*, except after *c*" helps you spell such words as *receive*. Oral communicators also lack the ability to use abstract thought. A hammer is only a hammer, it is not a "tool." Oral communicators don't think about larger categories of objects; they refer only to the specific object that is present in time and space. Oral communication is also redundant; speakers constantly repeat themselves so that their audience understands their message. Finally, oral communicators have a close relationship to their audience. In fact, oral communicators know their audience, share certain characteristics with their listeners, and identify with them.

Persuasion in oral societies takes the form of storytelling, in which one communicator relates a traditional story to an immediate group of listeners. The poet Homer is a good example of an oral persuader. His poetry, including the *Iliad* and the *Odyssey*, are actually stories that were finally put into written form after years of being recited by ancient storytellers. The stories provide lessons to listeners and persuade them to adopt particular perspectives of the world.

LITERACY

Humans were forever changed when they first put their ideas into written form on paper. It took three thousand years after they developed language before communicators transferred their ideas to writing. The first alphabet probably consisted of simplified Egyptian hieroglyphics, where each symbol represented an object. The first complete alphabet is thought to have been that of the ancient Greeks, which first appeared in 1500 B.C., well before the days of Plato and Aristotle. With an alphabet, communicators could now write their ideas on paper and did not have to rely on their memories or various memory devices to express their thoughts. Still, widespread dissemination of written communication was impossible because of the work it took to manually copy texts. It was not until the invention of the movable-type printing press in the mid-1440s that writing became a dominant form of communication: between 1450 and 1500, the number of books in print surged from several thousand to more than 9 million (Chesebro & Bertelsen, 1996).

Once communicators used written language, Ong says, their consciousness was forever altered. In literate cultures, the sender and the receiver of communication messages are separated, and the context in which the message was initially created is not readily apparent to the receiver of the message. As a result, the receiver cannot immediately question the sender of the message. Printed words are arranged in a linear fashion, providing for a different type of cognitive processing than that used in oral cultures. We can now consider such concepts as logic. The use of clichés, an important memory device used in oral cultures, now becomes a sign of shallow thought and expression. Writing makes abstract thought possible. Ideas can be grouped into categories, allowing for subordination of some ideas to others. We can now understand the concept of a "tool" as referring to a set of objects including hammers, saws, and chisels. As you can see, using alphabets and printing presses creates a very different orientation to the world.

In literate societies, persuaders use evidence to support their claims, to create logical relationships between their ideas, and to call upon their audiences' emotions. In Chapter 2, we discuss Aristotle's theory of persuasion, which describes, in detail, how persuaders can create their messages. As you read about

Aristotle's theory, keep in mind that he is writing in a society that is just beginning to use writing, but one that does not yet have access to printing presses.

ELECTRONIC MEDIA

Today, literacy still exerts its influence on our consciousness. We still tend to think in ways that resemble how the ancient, literate peoples thought. We cling to our traditional ideas about persuasion, which include evidence, reasoning, and organized thoughts. Yet, our consciousness more often reflects that of the electronic media to which we are exposed. In our country, the medium of television dominates how we communicate and see the world. Worldwide, however, only 3 percent of the world's people rely on electronic communication to the extent that we do in the United States (Chesebro & Bertelsen, 1996).

Just as spoken and written media changed the consciousness of the world's citizens, so too have electronic media. Electronic media reunite the sender and receiver, but differently than in oral cultures. Ong (1982) explains that electronic media create a *sense* of participation for receivers, but that those listeners are still physically separated from the source. The receivers resemble the audiences of ancient times, but they are larger in size and more diverse in composition. Listeners have a great deal of control over the communication situation. We can easily change the television station when we want to watch something else, for instance. Information is decontextualized—it exists without history and background—and visual images are commonplace. Our written communication often looks less like writing and more like the electronic media that it imitates. Think of the newspaper *USA Today*. With colorful images, charts, and vending machines that resemble a television set, the newspaper belies its written format to appeal to the electronic consciousness of its readers.

Joshua Meyrowitz (1985) argues that electronic media change their users' sense of time and place. He explains that electronic media have decreased the importance of physical presence in the experience of people and events. We can "experience" social events without being present. When a political candidate gives a speech to an audience in Austin, Texas, those of us who do not live in Texas can still "participate." Communicators now penetrate a family's home, once a shelter from the external world. Interactive media, such as chat rooms and videoconferencing, blur these boundaries even more. Meyrowitz contends that electronic media have redefined our ideas about audiences, who are not physically present with communicators, and communicative "arenas," which often do not exist in physical space (for instance, chat "rooms"). Meyrowitz argues that individuals change their behaviors to adapt to these new situations created by our mediated world. At the core of his analysis is how electronic media have reorganized social settings. As a result, he explains, individuals create new identities for themselves and learn new forms of social behavior. You'll see throughout this book how persuaders make use of electronic media to restructure their audiences' sense of place and identity.

Electronic media also allow us to vicariously experience events. Through television or the Internet, we can have "real" experiences that aren't real. We experience the joys and sadnesses of the individuals who fill our media. These "people" may be real-life individuals or fictional characters. While watching the news, we may see a story about someone who has been victimized by a crime. We feel empathy toward the person and may be able to put ourselves in their position. We may also feel empathy toward a character on our favorite soap opera. In either case, electronic media allow us the sense that we are experiencing real events when, in fact, we are not. We'll explore the implications of this phenomenon throughout this book.

A good example of persuasion in the electronic age is the political town hall meeting. The town hall meeting looks like a persuasive event of ancient days. A political candidate addresses a physically present audience and discusses with them the important issues of the day. The meeting has the appearance of being a rational (literate) discussion about issues and policies. If we take a step back, however, we realize that the event is usually staged for a television audience. The vast majority of audience members are not physically present, but are distant from the event. If the speaker is savvy enough, however, members of the distant audience can be made to feel as if they are part of the studio audience. Instead of evidence and reasoning, the persuader uses strategic visual expressions and carefully planned slogans and narratives to respond to audience questions.

HYPERMEDIA

Complicating our discussion of electronic communication is the emergence of a new form of electronic communication. The Internet is a good example of interactive media, or **hypermedia.** In some ways, we are on the cusp of yet another media period. Like new media before it, the Internet will forever change those who use it. Price and Price (2002) explain that hypermedia fundamentally change the relationship between persuader and audience member. With hypermedia, there is no longer one persuader who provides information to a mass audience. Instead, "many individuals exchange information with each other, aided by some people who do more writing than others" (p. 4). Additionally, the linearity of more traditional forms of communication is disrupted by the use of hyperlinks, which allow users to jump from one topic to another.

hypermedia
a category of interactive electronic media that includes the Internet and interactive CD-ROMs

What remains to be investigated is the effect that hypermedia have on our consciousness and culture. In some ways, hypermedia reflect the consciousness of the electronic age. But in other ways, these media are vastly different. In reality, it is probably too soon to tell what impact hypermedia will have on the consciousness of its users. We can, though, make a few observations about the Internet and how it is similar to, yet different from, other forms of electronic media, such as television and radio.

One characteristic of the Internet is its interactivity. Audience members become users in a way that is quite different from how we use television or radio. The creator of a website, for instance, does not usually know how users will travel through the site. Users have a great deal of discretion in determining the length of time they spend on a page and what page they look at next. Quite often, users leave the site without having looked at every page on it. Thus, users, or audience members, have a great deal of power to manipulate and control the communication setting.

The Internet allows us to communicate with people from all over the world. Our reach extends, not through real time and space, but through virtual time and space. We also form relationships with groups of people who we know only virtually. In fact, we form virtual communities with other people. The distortion in time and space that Meyrowitz associates with television is even more pronounced with the Internet. The growth of wireless networks will only heighten the virtual connections between people.

Consider again the town hall meeting. If we add an interactive component, such as allowing viewers to e-mail their questions to the show, we have a completely different persuasive situation. Audience members are no longer relegated to being observers. Instead, they become participants, influencing the questions that are asked and the direction of the discussion. Whether or not the candidate actually addresses their questions, audience members have a sense that they can influence what is happening.

Persuasion and Culture

culture
a set of beliefs, values, and practices that sustains a particular people; also, the products those people produce

We have been discussing the effect of the medium on individuals and their consciousness. As groups of individuals use the same medium, they share a common way of perceiving the world. In other words, they share a **culture.** James W. Carey (1988) explains that "communication is a process through which a shared culture is created, modified, and transformed" (p. 43). Media have profound influences on what communities of individuals believe, value, and practice. Chesebro and Bertelsen (1996) explain that media inherently select, emphasize, or encode certain stimuli, but not all of the available stimuli. Media are limited in the number of understandings they can convey. When you watch or read the news, for instance, you don't see all the news of the day—only what can fit in the time or space allowed for news. You share with other audience members similar perspectives about the news you see. Likewise, many of us watch entertainment programs such as *Friends.* When we do so, we share with the other viewers the beliefs and values expressed in the show. Users of a particular media, then, view the world from a common understanding. Likewise, people who use different media shape their world around different assumptions and understandings. Culture is, at least in part, dependent on the medium of communication that its members use. Because it is so widespread, electronically mediated communication provides members of our culture with a common set of values and beliefs that is transmitted via that media.

This book details how persuasion occurs in a culture whose consciousness has been influenced by electronic media. Although we know a great deal about persuasion as it occurred in the oral and literate cultures of ancient times, we are just beginning to come to terms with persuasion as it occurs today. We now turn our attention to two striking features of mediated culture. First, we examine how mediated information creates a new type of knowledge, or truth, in a culture. Second, we discuss how the people of our contemporary culture are fragmented as never before. We also discuss the implications of these features for persuasion.

MEDIA AND KNOWLEDGE

Marshall McLuhan (1964) argues that the "medium is the message." McLuhan was saying that the medium of the message—face-to-face, print, electronic—is more than a simple transportation device for the message. It is a transportation device that alters what is being transported. Television news, for instance, shapes public opinion and attitudes in different ways than does news coverage in newspapers. Watching a presidential debate causes us to form different ideas about the candidates than does reading about the debate in a magazine. In fact, McLuhan later wrote that the medium is the "massage," indicating that it transforms viewers in subtle ways that seem pleasurable at the time. Living in an electronic culture, as we in the United States do, we have a different view of the world than do many of the world's citizens, who live in an oral culture.

Consider as an example four experiences you may have with music. If you go to a live concert, you experience the performance firsthand. The concert provides you with a great deal of information—its setting, the performers, the audience, the music—that comes together to form your conception of the concert's meaning. If you cannot go to the concert, you may instead read about it in the paper the next day. The newspaper reviewer's description of the concert would, no doubt, differ from your response had you been there. Maybe you watch the concert on television instead of attending it. Although you hear the sounds and see the images of the concert, you don't truly "experience" the performance. Perhaps you purchase a CD recording of the concert so that you can hear the music and the audience's reaction. Perhaps you order the performer's music from a website such as CDNOW, where you can create your own collection of the performer's songs, some that were performed at the concert and some that were not. You might even create a CD that has music from other performers. With each different type of media, the meaning of the event to you changes. In each case, the medium alters the content it conveys.

Compare how a similar persuasive message is delivered by two different media—for example, a print versus a televised ad for the same product or public service campaign or a radio versus a televised report of the same news story. How does the medium affect the content and meaning of the message? Does your response to the message vary from one medium to the other? If so, how and why? What implications do you think your responses have for producers of persuasive messages and for your own role as a receiver of such messages?

In exploring the implications of McLuhan's famous phrase, Neil Postman (1985) argues that media create different ideas about what is "true" in a given culture. He writes, "As a culture moves from orality to writing to printing to televising, its ideas of truth move with it" (p. 24). Truth arises in how we communicate about and through particular media. Intelligence is often seen as determining what is true, so it follows, says Postman, that a culture's measures of intelligence are derived from the nature of the media that penetrate that culture. To be intelligent in an oral culture, for instance, means that one can memorize a great deal of information. In a print culture, says Postman, being knowledgeable means being able to objectively and clearly evaluate the strength of arguments conveyed in words. In an electronic culture, being able to use slogans and project compelling images are seen as marks of intelligence.

Postman's Observations about Media and Knowledge

1. Knowledge is fragmented.
2. Knowledge appears in forms most suitable to television.
3. Knowledge requires specific processing skills.
4. Knowledge is produced by invisible technologies.

Postman's (1985) point is that each new medium creates a body of discourse in a culture that privileges certain types of intellect. The intellect produced by television, he argues, is inferior to that produced in literate cultures. In fact, Postman goes so far as to argue that a television-based knowledge system pollutes public communication today. One reason for this is that television-based knowledge is *fragmented*. Television juxtaposes short, unrelated events and fails to present a logical, ordered view of the world. We get, instead, a fragmented view of the world in which ideas have no relationship to each other. The communication we receive lacks a context: It is decontextualized. Kathleen Hall Jamieson (1988) explains that in past times speakers provided historical background for the subject they were discussing. Today, she says, history is used sparingly. We are exposed to images and ideas that are disconnected from one another. Instead of hearing or seeing the complete story, we see only bits and pieces of several stories. Recall that in oral cultures, both sender and receiver had to be physically present for communication to occur. The context of the communication event was known to all.

In addition, Postman (1985) argues that as a result of television's influence in society, politics, religion, education, and other matters of public business must appear in *forms most suitable to television*. Television requires that our communication be short and to the point. Jamieson (1988) maintains that such communication ignores complex ideas and favors assertion over argument. Television also causes us to give preference to that which is theatrical or flashy. In fact, scholars contend, flashy and theatrical become the standards by which we evaluate communication. We do not judge a discourse for its logical appeal, but rather for its aesthetic appeal. Jean Baudrillard (1983) says that audiences are seduced by communicators who project stylized appearances. Baudrillard goes so far as to suggest that we do not want seriousness today, but rather spectacle. Bruce Gronbeck (1995) argues that politics, for example, often takes the form of the telespectacle. The political nominating convention, held every four years by each political party, showcases the party's unity, optimism, and ideology with catchy songs and slogans, colorful balloons, and inspirational speeches. Voters take part in the spectacle through their television sets.

Images, because they are so powerful and because they can be readily created and reproduced, have had a profound impact on how we communicate. Sonja K. Foss and Marla R. Kanengieter (1992) argue, "We no longer live in a logocracy—a culture based on verbal texts—but in a culture characterized by omnipresent visual images in forms such as television, film, billboards, architecture, and dress" (p. 312). Advertising often does not even feature the product that is being sold. Instead, we see images of objects and people who may or may not appear to be related to the product. A common complaint about our political system is that political leaders are elected based on the image they present, not for the policies or ideas they espouse. Use of images presents challenges, not only to persuaders, but also to those of us who must determine the meaning of those images.

The sheer *amount of information* present in an electronic culture also requires special skill for receivers of that information. Postman (1992) argues that the vast amount of information has demanded new methods of controlling information, methods that give modern persuaders a great deal of power when they communicate with audiences. According to Postman, it is difficult to judge the information we receive. Information, he says, is "not only incapable of answering the most fundamental human questions but barely useful in providing coherent direction to the solution of even mundane problems" (1992, p. 70).

Finally, Postman identifies the presence of *"invisible technologies"* in our lives—technologies that persuaders use frequently. Whether we realize it or not, we are surrounded by technology. Postman uses the example of the technology of language. Language, he argues, is a technology, much like a machine, that carries with it a specific ideology and way of seeing the world. Language "give[s] direction to our thoughts, generate[s] new ideas, venerate[s] old ones, exposes[s] facts, or hide[s] them" (1992, p. 127). Statistics are another technology that we accept without questioning. Persuaders today make widespread use of public opinion polling, which relies on the science of statistics. Despite questions about the accuracy of such polling, political leaders, entertainment industry executives, and many advertisers put their faith in polling, creating what Postman calls "information-trivia," which places "all information on an equal level" (1992, p. 137). The point of this is that persuaders today use many of these invisible technologies in an attempt to support their claims. As citizens in a media culture, we are often unable to evaluate the claims made by persuaders because we are unaware of these invisible technologies.

POSTINDUSTRIAL CULTURE

Our discussion thus far has focused on media's role in creating a certain kind of culture that contains a certain kind of person who uses, and is used by, a certain kind of information. In fact, media may be the one thread that unites our postindustrial culture today. The term **postindustrial culture** refers to the fragmentation of society that has resulted from economic, social, and technological changes (Bell, 1973). Economically, our society has moved from an emphasis on manufacturing to more specialized service industries. Whereas in the past, all of your neighbors worked for the same company and did the same kind of work, today everyone on your block performs a different job at a different company—and for different pay. People today work in careers that did not exist until recently.

> **postindustrial culture** a society that is fragmented due to the economic, social, and technological changes that have accompanied its maturation from a manufacturing to a services orientation

As a result, society is stratified along different lines than it was in the past. People have formed new social relationships. You might know your coworkers, for instance, better than you do your next-door neighbor. Although electronic media did not cause the widespread fragmentation of society, they have done a great deal to enable audience diversity. We no longer think of ourselves as living in a unified world. When advertisers can target their products to individuals, as opposed to groups, they foster the idea that each person is an autonomous consumer. Technology has allowed us to replace the face-to-face interaction that characterized past communities with mediated interactions. When I read the *New York Times* on the Internet and my neighbor reads the *Los Angeles Times* and we both live in Minnesota, our concept of community is at least partially altered. Persuaders, then, are faced with the demand of targeting unique messages to specific individuals. In addition, audience members struggle to define themselves in a postindustrial world.

The Postmodern Condition

postmodern condition
a breakdown in the accepted understanding of the world, marked by questioning of accepted theories, assumptions, and views of reality and by power struggles among persuaders for control of the meaning of events, images, and symbols

We have discussed various ways that electronic media have brought about certain ways of thinking, relating, and knowing that dominate contemporary society. Some scholars have called this set of symptoms the **postmodern condition** (see Jameson, 1991; Lyotard, 1984; McGee, 1990). The postmodern condition is marked by a breakdown of common ways of understanding the world. There are many voices today that desire to be heard, and electronic media allow this discussion to occur. Inherent to the postmodern condition is a struggle for power as persuaders attempt to control the meaning of events, images, and symbols. Truth, knowledge, and certainty are all questioned in a postmodern culture. Postmodernism is often seen as a reaction to our culture's mindset during the Industrial Revolution of the late 19th and early 20th centuries. As new industries, media, and ways of knowing emerged, people began to question taken-for-granted theories, assumptions, and views of reality. Today we are faced with a struggle among various interests to manage power in our culture. Persuasion and media are central features of this struggle today.

With this understanding of how our contemporary world and its inhabitants are influenced by media, let's turn our attention to the specific nature of persuasion within this electronic world. In short, persuasion in the media age is different from persuasion in years past because of its increased attention to using technology to reach specific audiences, because of differences in consciousness that exist among audience members, and because of the type of information that is used to persuade audiences.

Defining Persuasion

In most textbooks, considerable time is spent in the first chapter defining the subject to be studied. This is important for several reasons. First, definitions establish limits. As the previous scenarios indicate, there is much that we could call persuasion—far too much for a single course. Viewed broadly, the term loses some of its meaning. It is important to differentiate the subject of "persuasion" from its broader relation "communication."

It is also necessary to define what we mean by persuasion to provide a common base for understanding. Starting with a shared definition will make the discussion more productive.

Perhaps the most important reason we begin by defining terms is so that you understand the perspective from which we will approach our subject. Persuasion has different meanings for different communication scholars. Some take a social scientific approach to its study; others are more humanistic in their approach. We will draw on both traditions. No matter what you study, your perspective largely determines what you see and how you interpret what you see.

SELECTED PERSPECTIVES

Humans have studied persuasion for centuries and have offered many definitions for the word. Aristotle provided one of the earliest when he defined *rhetoric,* a term that is often used interchangeably with *persuasion,* as "an ability, in each [particular] case to see the available means of persuasion" (trans. 1991, p. 36). Like many of the early teachers of rhetoric, Aristotle was concerned with describing how various tools can bring about persuasive effects in audiences. Among these tools are proof, use of emotion, organization, and style. Early definitions of persuasion focused on the sender and how the sender could more effectively create a persuasive message. Aristotle's definition reflects the principles of the literate period. His approach has often been called "rational" because it assumes a systematic approach to teaching and using persuasion.

Other definitions of persuasion focus on the receiver and how the receiver's motives and attitudes affect the success of a persuasive message. Among the scholars taking this approach is Wallace C. Fotheringham, who defined persuasion as "that body of effects in receivers, relevant and instrumental to source-desired goals, brought about by a process in which messages have been a major determinant of those effects" (1966, p. 7). Fotheringham shifted the focus from producers to receivers and emphasized the psychological effects of persuasive communication.

Kenneth Burke provides a definition of persuasion that focuses on the strategies discussed by Aristotle, the effects embodied in Fotheringham's definition, and a modern understanding of the power of symbols in communication. In short, his theory of persuasion includes many aspects of the persuasive process and can be thought of as systemic. Burke wrote in *A Rhetoric of Motives* (1969b) that persuasion is "the use of symbols, by one symbol-using entity to induce action in another" (p. 46). His theory focuses on the words and images that constitute persuasion and also on how persuader and receiver both contribute to the persuasive process.

Our definition of persuasion draws on Burke's theory and makes use of his notion of identification: ***Persuasion*** *is the coproduction of meaning that results when an individual or a group of individuals uses language strategies and/or other symbols (such as images, music, or sounds) to make audiences identify with that individual or group.* Let's look more closely at this definition (Figure 1.1).

First, both the sender (persuader) and the receiver (audience member) are participants in the persuasive process. Persuasion is, thus, the **coproduction of meaning.** That is, our study of persuasion is concerned not just with the tools used by persuaders or the attitudes of receivers, but rather with how both sender and receiver come together to create a shared reality. The audience plays an active role in persuasion; persuasion is a process instead of a simple one-way transmission. Persuaders create messages, to be sure, but the persuasive process is incomplete until the audience becomes involved.

The audience, Michael Calvin McGee (1990) writes, constructs the persuasive message from the "scraps and pieces of evidence" that the persuader provides. Audience members filter, so to speak, the ideas of the persuader and give their own meaning to what is being communicated. Audience members use the experiences they have within their culture to create these meanings. We use what we know about the world to make sense of persuasive messages. Thus, we cannot study only a persuader's words. We must also address the culture in which the persuasion occurs, as well as the attributes of the audience that shape

persuasion
the coproduction of meaning that results when an individual or a group of individuals uses language strategies and/or other symbols (such as images, music, or sounds) to make audiences identify with that individual or group

coproduction of meaning
the process by which persuaders and audience members arrive at mutually agreed upon meanings for words and visual images

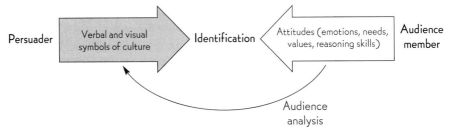

Figure 1.1 Definition of Persuasion   In our definition of persuasion, the persuader uses verbal and visual symbols of culture—as well as audience analysis—to affect the attitudes of an audience member. The result of persuasion is a state of identification between persuader and audience member.

how they process the persuader's ideas. Persuasion is not a simple cause-effect process, in which a persuader combines evidence in a way that changes how an audience thinks. It is far more complicated today. Our definition acknowledges that complexity by including the audience member as an important component. Jesse Ventura, a former actor and professional wrestler, surprised everyone when he was elected governor of Minnesota in 1998, over more traditional and well-respected candidates. His election hints at the complexity of the persuader-audience relationship today. Despite the polls, voters responded to the former professional wrestler in ways that traditional models of persuasion could not explain.

Figure 1.1 uses the word *identification* to depict the coproduction aspect of persuasion, placing the term between the persuader and the audience member. Persuaders want audience members to join them in producing meaning that is beneficial to them—the persuaders. Burke (1969) calls this sharing of similar "sensations, concepts, images, ideas and attitudes" (p. 21) **identification:** "You persuade a man [*sic*] only insofar as you can talk his language by speech, gesture, tonality, order, image, attitude, idea, identifying your ways with his" (p. 55). Burke further explains, "A is not identical with his colleague, B. But insofar as their interests are joined, A is identified with B. Or he may identify himself with B even when their interests are not joined, if he assumes that they are, or is persuaded to believe so" (1969, p. 20). Gary C. Woodward (2003) offers some additional ways to help us understand the concept of identification. He equates identification with terms such as *common ground, associating,* and *connecting.* That is, persuaders seek to find common ground with, associate with, or connect with audience members. Later in this chapter, we'll say that persuaders seek to build relationships with audience members. This idea stems directly from the theoretical construct of identification.

Burke explains that persuaders can identify with audience members by using language in one of three ways. The first type of identification is obvious and direct. "It flowers in such usages as that of a politician who, though rich, tells humble constituents of his humble origins" (Burke, 1972, p. 28). Democratic presidential candidate Joe Lieberman used this method of identification when he announced that he was running for the presidency:

identification

a state of alignment that exists with another when we share a similar way of viewing the world

It was here that my parents Henry and Marcia—themselves children of immigrants—worked their way into the America's middle class and gave my sisters and me the opportunities they never had. It was here that I first understood the power of the promise of America—that no matter who you are or where you start, if you work hard and play by the rules, you can go as far in this country as your God-given talents will take you. (Lieberman, 2003)

The second type of identification uses antithesis, creating an us versus them distinction. That is, persuaders can unite with audience members by demonizing some other person, group, or idea. The audience is then forced to make a choice between the persuader and the "other" that has been demonized. In his 2003 State of the Union Address, President George W. Bush sought to identify with the Iraqi people by portraying Hussein, not the United States, as their enemy: "And tonight I have a message for the brave and oppressed people of Iraq: Your enemy is not surrounding your country—your enemy is ruling your country" (2003).

The third type of identification "derives from situations in which it goes unnoticed" (Burke, 1972, p. 28). For instance, using the word *we* to unite audience members with the persuader is a powerful, yet subtle type of identification. Notice how many times first-person words are used in the mission statement for Microsoft: "At Microsoft, we see no limits to the potential we all might reach because we see no limits to human imagination. That is what inspires us. And that is why we create software that helps people and businesses reach their potential. It's not just our purpose. It's our passion." This statement is clearly designed to unite all Microsoft employees, creating identification with the company and its mission. As we continue our discussion in this book, consider how persuaders use each of the three methods of identification to build relationships with their audiences.

In addition to the linguistic methods of achieving identification, Woodward (2003) clarifies that sight, sound, smell, and touch are other resources we use to "consider another person's experiences and recognize them as our own" (p. 2). In the media age, persuaders use these resources to cause us to recall experiences that will lead to identification. Music, for instance, can cause us to recall past experiences that are either pleasant or unpleasant. Persuaders who then use this music can cause us to identify with their message. The same can be said of art, photographs, other types of sounds, and movies. We'll discuss how music, sound, images, and video are used by persuaders in later chapters of this book. Woodward and Burke both demonstrate that the concept of identification is a useful approach to persuasion in the media age. Let's turn our attention now to some of the additional components of our definition of persuasion.

Our definition of persuasion uses the phrase "language strategies and/or other symbols" to indicate the content of persuasion. **Symbols** stand for, or represent, something else. The word *tree*, for example, is a symbol for an idea that we all share. It is not the physical object itself but is instead a representation of that object. Words, images, sounds, and gestures can all be symbolic. A wave represents a greeting. A stop sign represents the law that says one should stop at an intersection. A cloud pictured on a televised weather forecast means

symbol
a word, image, gesture, or sound that stands for (represents) a physical object, an idea, or a feeling

INTERNET ACTIVITY

International Identification

We have discussed Powell's speech to the United Nations at the beginning of this chapter. Powell sought to identify with world citizens to gain support for going to war against Iraq. Read the transcript of Colin Powell's speech to the United Nations on February 5, 2003. You can find the speech on the White House website, http://www.whitehouse.gov/news/releases/2003/02/20030205-1.html. As you read the speech, consider how Powell sought to identify with his American audience. How did he identify with his international audience? Be sure to consider not only the three ways of using language to identify with an audience, but also the ways Powell used images and video to identify with his audience. Using what you have read about identification, evaluate Powell's speech.

that the day will be cloudy. It may be less obvious for you to consider how music and other sounds can also be symbolic. As we have just discussed, though, music often conjures images in our minds that cause us to have association with certain ideas or meanings. If you have ever seen a movie or commercial that effectively uses music, you can appreciate the symbolic power of sound to communicate meanings to us. We will next discuss how symbols are used to foster identification. Complete the Internet Activity: International Identification to learn more about how political leaders create identification.

Finally, we should note that the persuader can be a single individual, such as a political candidate, or a group of individuals, such as an organization. Persuaders "perform" symbols for audience members. Performances can take many forms. We usually think of these performances as speeches, but they can also be advertisements, entire events, photographs, architecture, or dramatic television shows, to name just a few forms. We usually think of persuaders as powerful individuals capable of generating wide interest for their topic. In the past, this may have been true. Throughout this book, however, you will learn about influential individuals who lack traditional sources of power. The Iraqi war blogger discussed earlier demonstrates this new kind of persuasive power. In this book, we take a broad view of the ways in which persuaders attempt to identify with audiences. Think about the definition of persuasion we have just discussed as you read Thinking Critically: Defining Persuasion.

PERSUASION AND RELATED TERMS

The concept of identification allows us to distinguish persuasion from other terms. You may have thought about persuasion as coercion or use of force to accomplish some objective. For example, holding a gun to someone's head and asking for his or her money may certainly produce the desired response. However, the person would turn over the money due to sheer force, not persuasion. Use of persuasion to obtain money would involve stating reasons or appealing to emotions to obtain a monetary donation from another. Many theorists distinguish between persuasion and coercion on the grounds that coercion does not involve free choice, whereas in persuasion the receiver has some choice as to

THINKING CRITICALLY

Defining Persuasion

Given what you now know about persuasion, consider these situations and determine whether persuasion is involved in each case:

- You approach a bus stop where someone is waiting for the bus to arrive. The other person has taken up a large section of the bench with books and other personal effects. As you approach, he or she gathers the personal effects, making room for you to sit down. Have you "persuaded" this person to move the belongings for you?

- You read an editorial in the school newspaper that explains why it is important to vote in the upcoming student council elections. You find the article interesting and think that it would be a good idea to vote in the elections. When election day arrives, however, you forget to vote. Did the article persuade you?

- You enjoy watching a particular television show, as do many of your friends. When it comes time for you to get a new hairstyle, you choose the style of one of the characters on the show you most enjoy watching. After all, the style is one of the most popular today. Were you "persuaded" to style your hair in this manner? Who persuaded you to do so?

The first scenario does not fit our definition of persuasion because you did not make a conscious at-

tempt to get the person to move his or her belongings. You simply approached the bus stop, without indicating that you wished to sit down. The second scenario meets our definition. Although you did not actually vote, you identified with the editorial's writer that voting was important. Thus, overt behavior is not necessary for persuasion, or identification, to occur. This situation resembles what we have called the rational approach to persuasion.

The third scenario easily fits our definition because you have identified with the symbolism of the hairstyle worn by one of your favorite television stars. The producers of the show, the star, and other viewers who wear that hairstyle have all persuaded you that you should do so as well. They have established a standard of beauty that includes wearing your hair in a certain way. They have made it "cool" to do so. The third scenario reflects the systemic approach to persuasion that we discuss in this book.

Consider what we have discussed, and think about these questions:

1. What examples of persuasion have you encountered today?

2. What instances of communication that are not persuasion have you experienced recently?

whether to accept the proposed ideas. For identification to occur, the receiver must consciously choose to align himself or herself with the message and/or its sender. Thus, we do not include acts of force in our definition of persuasion.

Having excluded force and coercion from our definition, it must be said that in the media age, it is sometimes difficult to determine whether receivers consciously choose their actions or beliefs. You might picture a continuum, with persuasion/identification on one end and force/violence on the other. Often, we fall prey to what Postman (1992) calls the "invisible technologies" of language or statistics or other aspects of popular culture, and we fail to see that we can reject what the persuader says. We may feel compelled to wear a particular type of clothing without fully realizing that we can reject the lifestyle prescribed by advertising and popular culture. Thus, there is a large gray area surrounding the concepts of persuasion, coercion, and choice.

Persuasion is a broader concept than another related term, *argumentation.* You may be familiar with the study of argumentation, which is usually defined as the process of comparing claims in support of and in opposition to a proposition. The study of argumentation is included in the study of persuasion, but persuasion typically makes use of a greater variety of visual symbols, language strategies, and audience appeals than does argumentation.

Persuasion in the Media Age

Apply the model of persuasion in Figure 1.2 to a specific mediated persuasive message, such as an advertisement, a political speech, or a television show. Identify the various components—persuader, audience member, medium, language, and visual images. Can you identify ways in which the medium may have affected the format and content of the message? As an audience member, how would you respond to the persuader in this specific situation?

Having defined persuasion, we can now place our definition in the context of today's media culture, individuals who have particular ways of seeing the world and who value certain types of information. Figure 1.2 illustrates how our definition of persuasion fits within the context of the media age. We have added two more persuaders—representing the many who persuade us in the media age—and a shaded circle to represent the mediated context of contemporary persuasion. This shaded region represents the "filter" of media on how we communicate. Even interpersonal communication must be considered in light of the mediated context of our culture today. Next we consider what this model suggests about contemporary persuasion. The main characteristics of persuasion today are illuminated in Table 1.2.

PERSUASION IS AUDIENCE ORIENTED

First, our model suggests that persuasion today is audience oriented. The source (or persuader) does not necessarily have an authority position. The source uses language strategies and visual images to suggest meaning to an audience, but the audience, using its own attitudes and reasoning skills, constructs its own meaning. Persuaders provide us with a range of responses from which to choose. A website is a good example of this situation. The hypertextuality of websites allows users to experience them in different ways. Users often follow different paths through a website. In fact, the website's creator often loses control when the site provides interactive elements, such as search devices. Links allow users to leave the website. It is difficult, then, for persuaders to control the experience of audience members. Persuaders attempt to do so, however, by using sophisticated tools of audience analysis. By understanding their audiences, persuaders can attempt to influence how those audiences identify with them. Yet there is no guarantee that persuaders will succeed in doing this. We discuss the audience further in Chapter 5.

PERSUASIVE EFFECTS ARE OVERDETERMINED

Persuasion today does not occur through a simple cause-effect relationship. We say that persuasive effects are *overdetermined*, meaning that a variety of factors influence how we construct meaning from a persuader's symbol use. It is difficult to isolate the single variable that predicts how an audience member will respond to a persuader. Rarely does only one persuader attempt to persuade us. Figure 1.2 uses three arrows to represent the many persuaders who influence us on a particular issue. In reality, we never really know how many persuaders are attempting to identify with us. Whether they are political candidates, com-

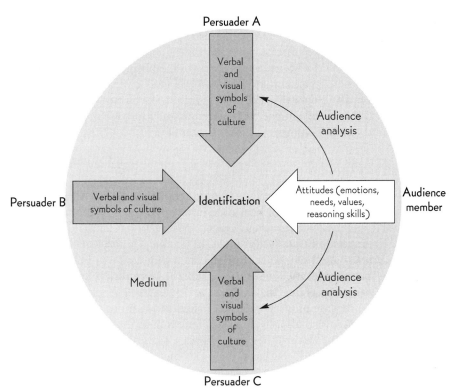

Persuader A

Verbal and visual symbols of culture

Audience analysis

Persuader B

Verbal and visual symbols of culture

Identification

Attitudes (emotions, needs, values, reasoning skills)

Audience member

Medium

Audience analysis

Verbal and visual symbols of culture

Persuader C

Figure 1.2 Persuasion in the Media Age Our model includes two more persuaders to indicate the presence of multiple persuaders in contemporary persuasive situations. The shaded circle represents the influence of the medium in the persuasive situation.

Table 1.2 Characteristics of Persuasion in Media Age

Characteristic	Example
Persuasion is audience oriented.	Websites allow users to navigate in ways of their own choosing.
Persuasive effects are overdetermined.	The success of *The Bachelor* can't be explained by any single reason.
Much is left unsaid.	Advertisements rely on audience members to know certain pieces of information.
Persuasion is ubiquitous but invisible.	People are surrounded by the Nike logo but don't always realize its power.
Persuasion variables are reflexive.	We are persuaded to accept standards of credibility by credible persuaders.

panies that produce soft drinks, or organizations that seek our time and loyalty, persuaders constantly seek to identify with us. We often identify with persuaders, not because of something they communicate to us, but because of how others talk about them or because of how they appear to us in mediated images. When you consider that culture also plays a role in how we identify with persuaders, you can appreciate even more the statement that persuasive effects are overdetermined. Our culture is full of influences about what we should believe and value. In addition, persuaders seek to create, maintain, and transform culture in ways that serve their interests. In the Pepsi commercial, the ad did not explain why Pepsi Twist tasted better than another similar soft drink. (It would have been difficult even to do so.) Instead, Pepsi used the Osbournes to send the message to audiences that it was "cool" and trendy to try something different, drinking Pepsi Twist. Of course, you had to know who Ozzy Osbourne was in order to make the desired association. We fully explore the importance of culture to persuasion in Chapter 8.

MUCH IS LEFT UNSAID

In today's world of mediated persuasion, much is left unsaid. M. C. McGee (1990) explains that we cannot possibly say all there is to say about a subject. As a result, a persuader's argument usually relies less on data and reasoning and more on the claim he or she advances. In Chapters 6 and 7, we address the nature of symbols and how they communicate a wide range of possible meanings to us—meanings that extend beyond what is communicated. Researcher David Slayden (1999) argues that what we are really experiencing is the end of persuasion and the rise of information. Persuaders are more often in the business of providing information to their audiences than they are of convincing their audiences to take a certain action. Slayden argues that persuaders today attempt to remove barriers that keep their audiences from acting on their message. They often accomplish this simply by telling the audience about their idea. Slayden points to the use of irony by today's persuaders. Advertising today often does not state claims about the product or service being advertised. The audience already knows the proposition the advertiser will advance. Although Powell's UN speech was effective, a majority of Americans probably had many reasons to support the war against Iraq: fear of terrorism, fear of Hussein, loyalty to the president and troops, and other reasons. It is difficult to pinpoint the single reason a majority of Americans supported the war.

PERSUASION IS UBIQUITOUS BUT INVISIBLE

Researchers indicate that we see about 3,000 advertisements a day. This figure is just part of the total number of persuasive messages to which we are exposed daily. From architecture to apparel, persuaders reach us in numerous ways. Yet much of this persuasion occurs in ways of which we are unaware. We have already discussed how the medium of communication changes what is communicated. We often think of a medium as a transportation device that simply brings information to us. Instead, media create a particular view of the world. In addition, visual images and words carry with them meanings that we have learned through our culture but don't think much about. We tend to think that being "efficient," for instance, is a good characteristic. This belief comes from our culture, but the process by which we have come to believe this is usually obscured from our view. Finally, we are studied, tracked, and evaluated by persuaders as never before. When you shop at the grocery store and use a "preferred customer card," for instance, you are telling the store—a persuader—what you like to purchase and where it can find you. The store uses this information to target you with persuasion that it thinks you will identify with.

PERSUASION VARIABLES ARE REFLEXIVE

Finally, each element in our model of persuasion in the media age is itself a product of the persuasive process. For example, our cultural beliefs influence how we identify with persuaders, but they are themselves products of previous persuasion. Persuaders seek to influence how we construct our culture: what we believe to be true and what we value. If we think it is important to look nice, we will be likely to purchase expensive clothing from a particular store. Thus, by first influencing our ideas about appearance, persuaders can subsequently influence our ideas about changing that appearance. Likewise, we think of some persuaders as being more "credible" than others and are consequently more likely to identify with them. Yet what being "credible" means is determined through our interactions with other persuaders. As a result, our study of persuasion and what it means to be persuasive can never be complete. Our standards for evaluating persuasion shift from time to time.

Using what we have discussed in this chapter, create an alternative model of persuasion. Be sure to include the persuader, audience member, medium, language, and visual images, and any other elements you think are necessary. How is your model similar to the one shown in Figure 1.2? How is it different?

Objectives for Persuaders

The characteristics of persuasion in the media age that we have just discussed have implications for both persuaders and audience members. As audience members, we must be aware of how persuaders adapt their messages to overcome the challenges to persuasion today. If we were to summarize the strategies used by effective persuaders today, we would say that *effective persuaders create an intimate, ongoing relationship with their audience in order to communicate the value of their product, service, or idea.* Persuaders in the media age have four objectives: forming relationships, repetition, "electronic eloquence," and commoditization. Each may be thought of as a way in which persuaders identify with us. Let's examine these four objectives, as outlined in Table 1.3.

Table 1.3 Objectives for Persuaders

Objective	Example
Forming relationships	Websites are able to customize their appearance and appeals to your preferences.
Repetition	Brand logos are placed wherever possible, so that people are constantly surrounded by them.
Electronic eloquence	Politicians speak in ways that will attract media coverage.
Commoditization	Wearing designer brands has more value than wearing generic brands.

FORMING RELATIONSHIPS

A primary goal for persuaders today is building relationships with audience members. Persuaders have to do more than "cut through the clutter" of today's world. They have to communicate to identify with us. For identification to occur, we must think that we share similar characteristics with those who wish to persuade us. Persuaders seek to show that they share our concerns and beliefs and that we should identify with them and their message. Persuaders construct relationships through their language and their use of images. Politicians, for instance, frequently show us that they are one of us. They tell us and show us that they come from a humble background, that they are concerned with our values, and that they are worthy of our vote. Large organizations seek to form relationships with potential customers and clients, but also with their own employees or members. Forming relationships with audience members may seem natural to you, but Jamieson (1988) contends that this has not always been the case. For some time, persuaders used communication to wage war on their opponents, and audiences were left to judge who the "winner" was. The winner received the loyalty of the audience. Today, it is different. The intimate medium of television has made it necessary for persuaders to relate to audience members in new ways. The idea that persuaders today attempt to foster relationships with audience members plays a key role in our later discussions.

REPETITION

Persuaders today often use repetition to identify with us. Given the amount of persuasion to which we are exposed, persuaders think that we will be more likely to identify with them if we encounter them more frequently. In Chapter 6, we discuss the Nike logo, the swoosh symbol. Think of how often you encounter this symbol. Chances are you see it throughout your day: on caps, on T-shirts, on billboards, in magazines, and, of course, on shoes. By making us aware of its image, Nike is hoping that we will attend to its message and identify with it. Repetition is also accomplished through such strategies as using brand names and advertising. As we continue our discussion, look at the ways the objective of repetition plays a key role in how persuaders communicate with us.

ELECTRONIC ELOQUENCE

Postman (1985) argues that we place greater value on those ideas that are expressed in a form suitable to television. Thus, the form of expression influences our perceptions of what is true and important. Persuaders must communicate in ways that reflect the consciousness, culture, and knowledge expectations of their audiences. Persuaders today adopt a style of using symbols that Jamieson (1988) calls "electronic eloquence." She argues that in past times, persuasive discourse featured a confrontational metaphor. Speakers delivered fiery orations in front of large, public audiences to defeat their opponents. Television, she explains, brought persuasion to the intimate setting of the living room. Television also provided close-ups of persuaders, allowing us to learn a great deal of information about them. As a result, the style used by persuaders changed as

INTERNET ACTIVITY

Persuasion on the Internet

The Internet has emerged as an important tool to help businesses build relationships and identify with consumers. Visit the website for a large corporation, such as McDonald's, Nike, or Coca-Cola. Explore the site for a few minutes, clicking on links and reading the information that is provided. Pay particular attention to ways that you can customize your experience on the site. Evaluate the degree to which the website fulfills the objectives for persuaders that are listed in the book. Overall, how effective is the website?

well. Jamieson explains, "In the quiet of our living rooms we are less likely to be roused to a frenzy than when we are surrounded by a swarming, sweating mass of partisans" (p. 55). Jamieson also claims that one way we judge the credibility of a persuader is by who the persuader is as a person. Audiences look to persuaders who are open-minded, compassionate, and have conviction. We like to know that persuaders hold dear to their heart those ideas they state publicly. Using the principles of electronic eloquence that we discuss in Chapter 7, persuaders can communicate effectively through the electronic medium.

COMMODITIZATION

A final objective for persuaders today is creating value for their products or ideas, turning those products into commodities that can be sold to audiences. This process is often called **commoditization.** We identify with persuaders when they can provide something valuable to us. Today, information is all around us. It is not difficult to obtain. Thus, persuaders must somehow make the information they communicate seem valuable to us. Power today lies not in producing information, but in giving value to communicated information. This is obviously true in the case of advertising, where consumers today purchase clothing as much for the brand name on the label as for any other reason. A company like the Gap tries to create value in its name so that clothing carrying its label is more valuable to consumers than is generic-label clothing. Similarly, organizations make it valuable to be a part of the group, as an employee or a donor. The central goal of persuasive speaking today is to give value to information. Complete the Internet Activity: Persuasion on the Internet to gain experience with persuasive strategies in the media age.

commoditization
a strategy used by persuaders to create value for their products or ideas

Implications for Audience Members

Our previous discussion of persuasive objectives should cause some concern for audience members. Persuaders have developed sophisticated ways of communicating to us. If they are effective at building relationships, for example, we might not even know that we are being persuaded. Thus, it is important that audience members be aware of how persuaders operate so that they can defend themselves from those efforts if they wish. In this section, we discuss some of the ways audience members can prepare themselves to deal with persuasion in the media age.

Tips for Audience Members

1. Acquire and evaluate information necessary to make important decisions.
2. Understand the nature of influence and how persuasive sources seek to influence us.
3. Think carefully about how persuaders influence how we think about ourselves and others.

EVALUATING INFORMATION

Information overload is a term used to describe the vast amount of information in our culture today. We often do not sufficiently process the information to which we are exposed. Instead, we form relationships with those persuaders who seem to be the most like us, sometimes without evaluating what they have to say. Quite often we do not know the source of a persuasive message. In oral cultures, the receiver knew who the source was and more than likely had a personal relationship with the source. In the media age, we often do not come face-to-face with those who attempt to persuade us. In addition, the vast amount of information that is available to us can seem to be of relatively equal importance. It is important that we distinguish the trivial from the meaningful, even when it is not easy to do so. Each chapter in this book contains a discussion entitled Thinking Critically to help you develop the skills you need to evaluate the information of the media age. Each chapter also addresses the subject of ethics. Here, you're asked to consider the ethical challenge posed by spam, the subject of Ethical Insights: Ethics and the Persuasion Process, and answer the questions in the box.

UNDERSTANDING THE PERSUASION PROCESS

Persuasion today is often invisible. We do not see how persuaders are attempting to identify with us. We may see the outward manifestations of the forms of persuasion, but we seldom think about how persuaders create their persuasive messages. The newspaper you read this morning and the television programming you watched are the products of numerous decisions made by persuaders. News programming, for example, may not always be determined by the most important news events of the day, but instead by the news that will help the station or the newspaper sell advertising. News, we will see, is often dramatized and personalized to have an entertaining effect on its readers and viewers. Advertising, which constantly surrounds us, has probably been tested on samples of viewers to gauge its effectiveness.

Our political leader's words have been carefully considered, not only by the politicians, but by their staffs of consultants as well. In fact, the clothing the political figure is wearing may have been the subject of a heated debate among his or her advisors. Politicians are often accused of making policy decisions based on audience polling. We often do not realize the extent of polling's influence on public policy and may be misled about how the political process works. This book provides you with a look into the persuasive process. We examine how persuaders make decisions about what strategies to use and what message to communicate.

ETHICAL INSIGHTS

Ethics and the Persuasion Process

If you have an e-mail account, then you probably have at some point received spam, which is unsolicited e-mail selling some product or service. E-mail users today frequently receive offers for business opportunities or new products. If you have seen an e-mail that begins with the words "Would you like to earn hundreds of dollars working at home?" then you have received spam. Frequently companies mail spam to thousands of computer users. These companies often do not make their names known to those who receive their messages. In some cases, companies send so much spam that it overwhelms a computer network's capacity and the system crashes. For now, let's consider the ethics of spam.

On one hand, spam can be seen as unethical because it is an unwanted intrusion by a persuader who is not known to you. Especially troublesome are the methods used by spammers to identify your e-mail address. Spammers often purchase information about you from companies with whom you do business. Or spammers get your e-mail address from you when you visit their website. One ethical concern we discuss in greater detail in Chapter 3 is privacy. Persuaders must take great care to protect the privacy of their audience members today. On the other hand, spam

can be seen as a simple invitation, or advertisement, for you to read or delete from your computer. In some cases, reading what an unsolicited e-mail message has to say may be beneficial to you.

In Chapter 3, we discuss persuasion, ethics, and the media age in greater detail. As part of that discussion, we consider codes of ethics that have been created by various organizations concerned with persuasion and ethics. One such code is the National Communication Association (NCA) Credo for Ethical Communication. One statement of the NCA Credo posits, "We advocate sharing information, opinions, and feelings when facing significant choices while also respecting privacy and confidentiality" (NCA, 1999).

What do you think about spam? Is spam ethical? Consider the use of spam, and answer the following questions:

1. What are some guidelines that could be used to govern the sending of spam?

2. Does spam create a hardship for you as a computer user?

3. Are there ethical ways for companies to advertise their products or services without using spam?

As they do so, persuaders face a multitude of ethical decisions. Chapter 3 focuses exclusively on ethics and persuasion. With insight into the persuasive process, you will be a better consumer of the persuasion you encounter.

SELF-CONCEPT AND PERSUASION

Finally, we should be aware of how our self-concept is influenced by persuaders. Persuaders communicate the very essence of who we are to us. Woodward (2003) argues that the essential function of communication is to help us determine where we fit within a community. The same could be said specifically of persuasion. Through persuasion we come to understand who we are and how we should interact with others. Our discussion of culture indicates that persuaders attempt to create values and beliefs that foster identification with them. Persuaders often do not have our best interests in mind, though. Our culture's obsession with consuming products, for instance, makes us feel that, if we do not have the latest styles or fashionable brands, we are somehow inferior to those who do. Ideas about what is beautiful often cause us to question our sense of self. As you read the chapters in this book, watch for ways in

Where do your ideas about such things as ideal body shape and ideal interpersonal relationships come from? Do you compare yourself and your life to models or standards that you have encountered in daily interactions with real people or to those presented in advertisements, magazine articles, television programs, films, and other media?

which persuaders seek to influence how we think of ourselves. It is important to our health and our well-being that we understand how we conceive of ourselves in the face of a heavily mediated world that is filled with persuaders telling us what *they* think we should be.

Summary

We live in a media age that has changed many aspects of our existence, including the means through which individuals persuade each other. Specifically, media has changed human consciousness, our cultural orientations, and our ideas about what is true.

Theorists such as Walter Ong argue that the dominant medium in a given culture influences the consciousness of the people within that culture. In an electronic culture, such as ours today, there is only an illusion of closeness between persuader and audience. Our ability to employ and interpret slogans, jingles, and spectacles defines contemporary intelligence. We value information that comes to us in a theatrical format, argues Postman.

With the changes brought about by today's media, we must adapt our methods of thinking about persuasion. We might think of persuasion as the coproduction of meaning that results when individuals or groups of individuals use language strategies and/or visual images to make audiences identify with them. This definition allows us to appreciate the power of the audience in the persuasive process. Central to this definition is the idea that persuasion is a form of identification.

This definition of persuasion alludes to several characteristics of persuasion today. Persuasion is audience oriented, its effects are overdetermined, much is left unsaid, it is ubiquitous but invisible, and it is reflexive. These characteristics lead persuaders to form relationships with audience members, use repetition to ensure that their message is heard, communicate using the principles of electronic eloquence, and create value for their ideas and products. As a result, audience members must carefully evaluate the information they encounter, understand the persuasion process, and have a good sense of their self-concept because it is under constant attack from persuaders.

Key Terms

WWW: Visit the book's website at http://www.mhhe.com/borchers2 for multiple-choice quizzes, Internet activities, and key terms flashcards.

mediated world 6	persuasion 17
hypermedia 11	coproduction of meaning 17
culture 12	identification 18
postindustrial culture 15	symbol 19
postmodern condition 16	commoditization 27

2
Theories of Persuasion

Learning Objectives

After reading this chapter, you should be able to:

1. List the five functions of communication theories.

2. Describe Aristotle's theory of persuasion and the five canons of rhetoric.

3. Describe semiotics and the different ways that symbols have meaning.

4. Describe cognitive dissonance theory, the elaboration likelihood model, and problematic integration theory.

5. Describe symbolic convergence theory.

6. Describe various theories of media, including the two-step flow of information, uses and gratification research, cultivation analysis, and agenda setting.

Oprah Winfrey has enjoyed a great deal of success as a talk show host in recent years. We can attribute her success to many factors. Unlike other talk show hosts, who often rely on sex and violence to attract viewers, Oprah enjoys a high degree of credibility with the audience. Those who watch her show trust what she has to say, and her guests are knowledgeable about their subject matter. Viewers are also attracted to Oprah's show because she is a dynamic speaker and often hosts guests who are just as dynamic. In addition, Oprah's fans watch her show to gain valuable information. Oprah's show fulfills some need for her viewers. Whether viewers tune in to Oprah for her advice or for entertainment, her show's success can be explained through persuasion theory.

Table 2.1 Chapter 2 Theories

Theory	Focus
Aristotle's Theory of Persuasion	Message generation and source
Five Canons of Rhetoric	Message generation and presentation
Semiotics	Meaning
Cognitive Dissonance Theory	Audience reception and processing
Problematic Integration Theory	Audience reception and processing
Elaboration Likelihood Model	Audience reception and processing
Symbolic Convergence Theory	Social interaction and meaning
Uses and Gratification Theory	Media use
Cultivation Analysis	Media effects
Agenda Setting	Media effects

This chapter introduces you to a group of theories that have been used to describe persuasion. We will refer to these theories in our future discussion, after providing the basic ideas of each theory here.

You'll note that the theories in this chapter are grouped according to the main components of the persuasive process that we discussed in the previous chapter: persuasive source, audience, message, and medium. For each component, we'll discuss some of the major theories that help us better understand this component. These theories also help to provide the "big picture" for our future study. An outline of the theories and their focus is contained in Table 2.1.

We also discuss some of the weaknesses of each approach in describing persuasion as it occurs in the media age. These general theories of persuasion help explain the persuasive process across a variety of contexts. As you continue to read this book, you will encounter additional theories that explain how persuasion operates in specific contexts. These theories and research topics are identified in Table 2.2.

Theories are human constructions, and no one theory completely or accurately describes the concept it sets out to explain. You will find some theories more useful than others, and we will use some of these theories more frequently than others in later chapters. But all of the theories presented enjoy a rich tradition in communication research, and all offer the potential to explain to students of persuasion today's mediated world. We first discuss the nature of theory and then examine several specific persuasion theories. Keep in mind what we said in Chapter 1: that persuaders today create an intimate, ongoing relationship with their audience in order to communicate the value of their product, service, or idea. As you read about each theory, consider the degree to which it is useful in understanding the objectives of contemporary persuaders.

The Nature of Theory

We use theory virtually every moment of every day. When you choose what to wear in the morning, you theorize about the impression your appearance will

Table 2.2 Additional Theories and Research Topics

Theory/Research topic	Theorist/Researcher	Chapter
Universal Pragmatics	Habermas	Chapter 3
Attitude Formation	Fishbein and Ajzen; Zanna and Rempel	Chapter 5
Rokeach's Belief Hierarchy	Rokeach	Chapter 5
Functions of Visual Images	Messaris	Chapter 6
Dramatism	Burke	Chapter 7
Electronic Eloquence	Jamieson	Chapter 7
Ideographs	McGee	Chapter 7
Language Intensity	Hamilton and Hunter	Chapter 7
Powerful Language	Burrell and Koper	Chapter 7
Rhetorical Figures	Various	Chapter 7
Metaphors	Various	Chapter 7
Muted Group Theory	Kramarae	Chapter 7
Hofstede's Cultural Orientation	Hofstede	Chapter 8
Cultural Beliefs	McElroy	Chapter 8
Cultural Values	Various	Chapter 8
Cultural Behaviors	Hammond and Morrison	Chapter 8
Consumer Culture	Lears	Chapter 8
Aristotelian Ethos	Aristotle	Chapter 9
Source Credibility	Berlo, Lemmert, and Mertz	Chapter 9
Impression Management	Goffman; Leathers	Chapter 9
Image Repair Strategies	Benoit	Chapter 9
Nonverbal Communication	Leathers	Chapter 9
Toulmin's Model of Reasoning	Toulmin	Chapter 10
Narrative Paradigm	Fisher	Chapter 10
Maslow's Hierarchy of Needs	Maslow	Chapter 11
Fear	Mangeau	Chapter 11
Values	Rokeach	Chapter 11
Life Cycle of Persuasive Movements	Stewart, Smith, and Denton	Chapter 12
Rhetoric of Agitation and Control	Bowers, Ochs, and Jensen	Chapter 12
Branding	Various	Chapter 13
Product Placement	Various	Chapter 13
Relationship Marketing	Peppers and Rogers	Chapter 13
Compliance Gaining	Marwell and Schmidt	Chapter 14
Sequential Request Strategies	Dillard (and others)	Chapter 14
Deception	Buller and Burgoon	Chapter 14
One- and Two-Sided Messages	Allen	Chapter 15
Ordering Effects	Various	Chapter 15
Primacy vs. Recency	Hovland and Mandell	Chapter 15
Inoculation	Pfau and others	Chapter 15

have on your friends, instructors, or employers. As you search for a parking spot on campus, you theorize about where you might be most likely to find a space at that time of day. When you seek to resolve a conflict with your roommate, you theorize what you should say and how you should say it. In short, theories help us interpret our world and predict the behavior and responses of others.

In these examples, we use a rather broad definition of *theory*. Communication professors use a more specific definition of the term when they engage in the research process. Stephen Littlejohn has defined a theory as "any attempt to explain or represent an experience" (1996, p. 2). Dominic A. Infante, Andrew S. Rancer, and Deanna F. Womack define a theory as a "set of related statements designed to describe, explain, and/or predict reality" (1993, p. 7). A **theory** is an answer to a question. It explains why people do what they do. A theory of persuasion is a set of statements designed to describe, explain, and/or predict persuasive communication. Keep in mind that researchers define persuasion in different ways: We surveyed a couple of approaches in Chapter 1. Because they define persuasion differently, researchers formulate theories that take different approaches to persuasion as well. To more fully understand the idea of theory, let's identify five functions of theories.

theory

an answer to a question; an explanation of why people do what they do

Functions of Theories

Theories should explain data, predict future events, express ideas in a simple manner, identify testable hypotheses, and be useful (Griffin, 2000). First, theories clarify a confusing situation by *explaining data*. Theories focus our attention on particular aspects of a situation, and they help us ignore information that is unimportant. Theories explain why events happen as they do. A theory of credibility can help us to explain why Oprah Winfrey is a popular talk show host. As we will discuss shortly, a credible speaker has the attributes of dynamism and trustworthiness, which we have said characterize Winfrey. A good theory of persuasion should focus our attention on the important aspects of the persuasive process that we discussed in Chapter 1: the role of media, aspects of the persuasive message, the influence of culture, the image of the persuader, and the role of the audience.

Theories also help us *predict future events*. Theories identify patterns in events to determine their underlying causes. Thus theories establish cause-effect relationships that allow us to predict future events. Cognitive dissonance theory, for example, predicts that if individuals experience tension between two ideas, they will seek to reduce that tension. We should observe that theories are not always perfect at prediction, especially when human action is involved. Humans sometimes, if not usually, behave in ways that defy prediction. An individual experiencing cognitive dissonance, for instance, may not try to reduce the tension. As we will see, prediction becomes difficult in the media age. Voters in the Minnesota gubernatorial election in 1998—which we discussed in Chapter 1—acted in ways that political experts could not understand. Events change rapidly, and people often act in ways that defy logic. We will, however, seek to explore some of the key relationships involved in persuasion, such as culture and beliefs, visual images and perception, and attitude and behavior.

Third, a good theory *expresses its ideas simply*. Theoretical statements should follow smoothly from each other. Those who design theories should avoid overly complex frameworks. The rule of parsimony states that when given two possible explanations for an event, we should accept the simpler explanation (Griffin, 2000). Once again, we can turn to cognitive dissonance theory as an example. In its simplest form (when individuals experience psychological tension, they seek to reduce that tension), cognitive dissonance theory offers an easy-to-understand explanation of how persuasion occurs. There is the temptation to oversimplify, however, when it comes to persuasion. We will explore the argument that a variety of factors are necessary to explain the persuasive process in the media age.

A fourth objective of a theory is to *identify testable hypotheses*. A good theory has the possibility of being proved wrong. A theory that cannot be proved wrong offers us no real guidance about how to understand a confusing situation. It does not help us to predict because its predictions cannot be proved false. There must be some way for future researchers to evaluate a theory. The elaboration likelihood model (ELM), which we will examine later in this chapter, states that individuals use one of two routes when processing persuasive messages. But what if there are *three* routes of processing persuasive messages? There is nothing in the ELM that precludes researchers from one day observing other possibilities. As we examine theories of persuasion, we look for the regular patterns that emerge when persuaders interact with audiences in the media age.

Finally, theories are *practical*. They have utility. Theories are useful to our lives in some way. As you study communication theory, keep in mind that not everyone considers all theories useful. We pick and choose those theories that help us make sense of communication. The theory of interpersonal deception, for example, helps us to determine whether we should believe certain individuals. By observing certain characteristics of a persuader, we can make an assumption about that person's honesty and thus choose to believe what the persuader says or discard the proposed ideas. Theories of persuasion should be immensely practical, both for persuaders and for audience members. As audience members it is important that we be able to identify and recognize the strategies used by persuaders when they try to sell us a product or gain our vote.

Early Rhetorical Theory

The first theories of persuasion focused on oratory in literate cultures, which we refer to as rhetoric. For many centuries, we equated persuasion with rhetoric. Now, however, traditional public speaking is no longer seen as the dominant form of persuasion. Today we consider many more types of persuasion, including advertising, persuasive movements, and organizational identification practices. We'll explore the implications of these differences in what we consider persuasion later. For now, let's explore the contributions of ancient theorists to our understanding of contemporary persuasion. Specifically, we'll

Table 2.3 Key Aristotelian Concepts

Concept	Terminology	Definition	Example
Types of persuasion	Deliberative	Determine future action	Legislative debate
	Forensic	Prove past action	Court proceedings
	Epideictic	Praise or blame a person or event	Eulogy speech
Artistic proof	Ethos	Proving the persuader's credibility	"I have the experience necessary to be your mayor."
	Pathos	Appealing to audience emotion	"Purchase a cell phone to keep yourself safe when traveling."
	Logos	Using logical reasoning	"Because wearing a condom can reduce the likelihood of getting a sexually transmitted disease, you should wear a condom."

examine the work of Aristotle and Cicero and the ideas from a book called the *Rhetorica ad Herennium*.

ARISTOTLE

Aristotle was among the first theorists to present a unified theory of persuasion. Trained as a biologist, he was interested in classifying the elements of persuasion. Much of what Aristotle said about persuasion was recorded in *The Rhetoric*. His theory has served for centuries as a useful account of persuasion. If you have taken a class in public speaking, there is a good chance that you have relied on the wisdom of Aristotle in preparing and presenting your speeches. In subsequent chapters of this textbook, we discuss how persuaders use Aristotelian concepts in the media age. For now, let's examine some of the basics of his theory, as outlined in Table 2.3.

Aristotle initially identified three types of persuasive speaking situations: deliberative, forensic, and epideictic. **Deliberative speeches** are designed to prove that some future action should be taken. They are similar to speeches made in a legislative assembly. Your city council engages in deliberative persuasion when it debates whether to hire more police officers. The council members in favor of such a proposal may argue that hiring more police officers will reduce future crime. Deliberative speeches have as their ends the advantageous or the harmful. Speakers try to convince an audience that a future action will produce some advantage or prevent some harm. **Forensic speeches** attempt to prove that some past action occurred. Attorneys in a court of law engage in judicial persuasion. A prosecutor attempts to persuade the judge or jury that some criminal action took place in the past and that the defendant was responsible for the action. Defense counsel may dispute that the event took place, or if it did, the defense may argue that the defendant was not responsible for the event. Judicial speakers aim at the just or the unjust. **Epideictic speeches** praise or blame some person or event. These speeches focus on the morals or

deliberative speech
a speech designed to prove that some future action should be taken

forensic speech
a speech that attempts to prove some past action occurred

epideictic speech
a speech praising or blaming a person or event in order to comment on the community's values

virtues of the person or event in question. The speaker praises some individual because the individual displays virtues that are important to the community. A funeral eulogy usually praises an individual for his or her virtuous life.

Persuaders use proof to persuade audiences, said Aristotle. There are two categories of proof: artistic and inartistic. Inartistic proof is controlled by the situation and simply used by the persuader. Examples include statistics, photographs, or examples of past situations. Today, we find inartistic proof in the library, in the form of studies, newspaper coverage of events, or photographs. Aristotle was more interested in artistic proof, proof that is created, or invented, by the persuader. There are three types of artistic proof: ethos, or character; pathos, or emotion; and logos, or logic.

The study of **ethos,** or the **credibility** of the speaker, is very important because audiences are persuaded not only by the argument presented, but by the speaker as well. A speaker's ethos, according to Aristotle, is composed of three qualities: practical wisdom, virtue, and goodwill. Practical wisdom concerns making decisions and having knowledge of what one is speaking about. Virtue refers to the qualities of compassion expressed by a speaker. Goodwill is having the audience's best interests at heart. A speaker who has these three traits is persuasive, according to Aristotle. Secretary of State Colin Powell—a former army general and volunteerism spokesperson—is a persuader who exhibits all three of these characteristics. He demonstrated practical wisdom during his military career, his work with volunteerism displays virtue, and he conducts himself in a way that shows concern for his audience. In Chapter 9, we examine credibility in greater detail, but Aristotle's words provide a good framework for understanding the persuader. We will refer to his ideas of ethos throughout the book.

Effective speakers not only have credibility (or ethos), but they use pathos as well. **Pathos** is a form of proof that appeals to an audience's emotions. Aristotle believed that effective speakers understand an audience's emotions and use those emotions to persuade them. Aristotle argued that the persuader must answer three questions regarding emotion. First, what is the audience's state of mind? Second, against whom are their emotions directed? Third, why do audience members feel the way they do? Without knowing the answers to all three questions, Aristotle argued, it is impossible to bring about a desired emotion in an audience. Emotions discussed by Aristotle include anger, calmness, friendliness, enmity, fear, confidence, shame and shamelessness, kindliness, pity, indignation, envy, and emulation.

John Kerry, 2004 Democratic presidential candidate, used the emotion of empathy to describe the plight of a construction worker from Iowa in a May 16, 2003, speech in Des Moines:

> And they're caught in a trap. They're people like Robert Giles from Indianola. He's a member of the Painter's Union and the father of a two-month-old girl. He usually works all day and goes to classes in the evening. But in this economy, construction jobs are few and far between. He can't find work, he's about to lose his health coverage, but he's nowhere near able to afford to buy health insurance on his own. Those who claim to care about family values should care more about families like Robert Giles's.

ethos
a persuader's credibility

credibility
the degree of character, competence, and trustworthiness audience members perceive a persuader to have

pathos
a form of proof (a persuasive strategy) that appeals to the audience's emotions

Kerry's use of a specific example and the narrative style of this example lends to its emotional impact. Aristotle argued that a speaker must understand emotions to persuade his (or her) audience. We discuss emotions further in Chapter 11, adding to Aristotle's treatment of the topic.

logos
a persuader's use of logical reasoning (induction and deduction) to persuade an audience

The third type of artistic proof is **logos,** or the use of logical argument. Aristotle wrote that there are two types of logical argument: induction and deduction. One form of **inductive reasoning** is argument by example: reasoning from particular cases to a universal conclusion. A persuader might use examples of three school shootings to argue that school violence is a serious problem that should be reduced. **Deductive reasoning,** on the other hand, involves reasoning from generalizations to structurally certain conclusions. An example would be these three statements: All people are mortal. I am a person. Therefore, I am mortal. If the first premise is true—that all people are mortal—then the conclusion is certainly true. In some cases, persuaders do not state all three statements because they are assumed true. In this case, we could leave out the statement "All people are mortal" because this is widely known. Roger Aden (1994) contends that arguments in the media age typically leave out statements, relying on the audience's previous knowledge and experience to supply the missing information. We discuss reasoning in detail in Chapter 10. Having discussed ethos, pathos, and logos, complete the Internet Activity: Presidential Persuasion.

inductive reasoning
the synthetic process used to reason from particulars to probable conclusions

deductive reasoning
the analytic process used to move from generalizations to structurally certain conclusions

Persuasion relies on commonplaces, or *topoi.* A commonplace is a standard argument that can be used in a variety of persuasive situations. Aristotle defined 28 commonplaces, or lines of argument, that may be used. Speakers may employ any of these strategies to persuade their audiences. One of Aristotle's most famous lines of argument is the "more and less": If something is good, then more of it is better. If something is bad, then less of it is better. A recent advertisement for Intel stated, "Now everyone gets to hog the Internet." The product being advertised was a computer interface that lets multiple users access the Internet from one phone line in a home or business. The premise is that if the Internet is good for one person, then the more who can use it, the better.

Aristotle also discussed the arrangement of persuasive speeches. Aristotle claimed there were really only two necessary parts to persuasive communication: stating the claim and then demonstrating, or proving, it. The statement of the claim can be implicit or explicit. Aristotle also noted that listeners do not believe that which is not proved. Although Aristotle was writing for speakers, his ideas can be applied to mediated forms of persuasion as well. An advertisement for Chrysler illustrates Aristotle's suggested arrangement. At the top of the ad is the claim: "Sixteen years ago the minivan was unchartered territory. Today we're still leading the way." The ad then shows a Chrysler minivan. Proof for the claim that Chrysler is still "leading the way" appears at the bottom of the ad: "We were the first with carlike handling, a driver's side sliding door, Easy Out Roller Seats and Dual Zone Temperature Control. With all of our inventive ideas, it's no surprise the competition is still following our lead." The ad first states its claim and then demonstrates why its claim is true.

Pick an advertisement in a magazine, and consider Aristotle's three types of artistic proof. How does the ad appeal to your emotions? How does the ad establish the persuader's credibility? How does the ad use logical reasoning to communicate its point? How is the ad arranged? Is the ad effective?

Aristotle also taught that a persuasive speech might include an introduction and a conclusion in addition to the body. The introduction attracts the

INTERNET ACTIVITY

Presidential Persuasion

Aristotle's theory of proof and his concepts of ethos, pathos, and logos are still useful ways of creating and evaluating persuasive messages. Throughout his presidency, George W. Bush used ethos, pathos, and logos in his speeches. Visit the president's website at http://www.whitehouse.gov. Click on the "Current News" link and read a transcript of one of the president's speeches. Evaluate the speech based on how well it uses ethos, pathos, and logos. If the speech lacked any of these forms of proof, how might it have been improved?

audience's attention, establishes goodwill with the audience, and states the claim. The conclusion reviews what was said and parts company with the audience. A television commercial might also use an introduction, a body, and a conclusion.

Style, or the manner in which ideas are communicated, is important to the persuasive effect of communication as well. Aristotle summarized style by saying a communicator should "be clear." If a speech is not clear, it has not served its function. Aristotle was also interested in metaphor as a stylistic device. A **metaphor** associates a new idea with an idea the audience already understands. A metaphor can be used to make something seem greater or lesser than it really is. Aristotle also observed that connectives, such as transitions, signposts, previews, and reviews, should be used to tie one thought to the next. A *transition* links what was just discussed with what will be discussed next. A *signpost* uses words such as *first, next,* or *finally* to let the audience know the persuader is moving to another idea. *Previews* list ideas that will soon be discussed, whereas *reviews* relate what has been discussed recently. We will complement Aristotle's discussion of style with a view of style more appropriate to the media age in Chapters 6 and 7.

style
the manner in which ideas are communicated

metaphor
a linguistic device that associates a new idea with an idea the audience already understands

THE FIVE CANONS

The anonymous author who wrote the ancient book *Rhetorica ad Herennium* identified the **five "canons" of rhetoric**—the components of the persuasive process. The book, which first appeared in ancient Rome, was the first comprehensive textbook on speechmaking. Although earlier theorists, such as Aristotle, had discussed the topics of the *Rhetorica ad Herennium,* this anonymous book is the first complete handbook of persuasion theory (Kennedy, 1963). The book describes five canons of rhetoric: invention, arrangement, style, delivery, and memory. By examining these five canons, we can understand the major issues involved in the art of public speaking. Despite the age of these concepts, they remain relevant today. Each is highlighted in Table 2.4.

five "canons" of rhetoric
the principal elements of persuasive oratory: invention, arrangement, style, delivery, and memory

Invention refers to the creation of the ideas around which a speech is based. Our previous discussion of inartistic and artistic proof concerns ways of inventing arguments for a persuasive message. In Chapter 16, we discuss stock issues, another method for inventing arguments.

Table 2.4 Five "Canons" of Rhetoric

Canon	Description
Invention	Creation of ideas around which a speech is based
Arrangement	Ordering of ideas so they will be persuasive to the audience
Style	Use of language to create an impression on the audience
Delivery	Use of voice and gesture in the presentation of the speech
Memory	Remembering the speech to maximize eye contact and credibility

Arrangement deals with how the speaker arranges the ideas so that they will have the maximum effect on the audience. Aristotle's discussion of the parts of a speech can be placed in the category of arrangement. We discuss more specific ways of organizing speeches in Chapter 15. In the meantime, keep in mind Aristotle's ideas of statement and proof, although in the media age we often see or hear only the statement without the proof.

The third canon, *style,* refers to the method by which the speaker uses language to create an impression on his or her audience. Since the ancient Greeks, theorists have identified particular ways of using language to maximize its persuasive effects. Persuaders take great care to choose the right words and arrange them carefully so as to produce the maximum effect on the audience. A speaker's style can be influential in persuading his or her audience.

The fourth canon is *delivery,* the use of voice and gesture to communicate. Throughout the history of rhetoric, theorists have at times praised delivery and at other times condemned it for its ability to sway audiences to accept poorly supported arguments. In the media age, delivery, for better or worse, has become an important aspect of a speaker's effectiveness. Successful politicians, lawyers, and sales representatives are able to communicate in a conversational style to their audiences (Jamieson, 1988). As Postman (1992) argues, we expect them to look, act, and sound like movie stars. As such, we expect eloquence on the part of persuasive speakers.

Memory, the fifth canon, has, at times, played an important role in persuasion. Great orators of the past could remember whole speeches and deliver them to several different audiences. Memory was a sign of intelligence in oral cultures. Today, speakers are able to communicate to large audiences electronically and do not need to remember entire speeches for repeated speaking occasions. In addition, TelePrompTers allow speakers to appear as if they are saying a speech from memory. Yet, memory is important for persuaders. Politicians must remember large amounts of information to have at the tip of their tongue in political debates. Sales representatives must remember information about their audience to customize their sales pitches. Producers of television shows must remember cultural events and beliefs to incorporate them in their shows. Memory has a function in today's persuasion, even if that function is somewhat different than it was in the past.

The ancient theorists have provided us with a rich framework from which we can understand persuasion. Yet, the usefulness of this framework for us today must be tempered by several observations. First, persuasion today occurs in many forms, not just public speaking. We consider advertising, events, images, and culture to be persuasive. Second, the source of persuasion today is just as often institutional as it is individual (Sproule, 1988). Persuasion occurs within a framework of economic, social, and institutional forces. The ancient theorists were mostly concerned with political speeches given in public assemblies. Third, persuasion today makes use of images, which the ancient theorists do not specifically discuss. Our understanding of persuasion must account for the ways in which images are persuasive. Fourth, persuasion today is usually mediated by literate or electronic media. The mediated nature of persuasion introduces new variables to the process that were not present in the persuasion of past cultures. Although the ancient theories of oratory offer us considerable help in understanding persuasion, they are limited in their explanative value for the media age.

Semiotics

The ancient theories that we have just discussed assumed that words had more or less concrete meaning. Words were not seen as ambiguous. It was important, the ancients believed, that persuaders use the correct word in order to communicate clearly. Years later, theorists observed that words are more or less arbitrary—and that our language system is symbolic. That is, the words we use represent our ideas. Words are a type of **sign,** a term used to describe something that designates something other than itself. Most signs do not carry a meaning themselves, but instead are given meaning by those who use them and those who receive them. Although a red, octagonal stop sign may have almost universal meaning in our culture, other signs, such as the word *chair*, for example, have multiple meanings. You might think of a soft recliner, and I might be thinking about the gray, ergonomically correct desk chair in which I am sitting when we each hear the word *chair*. Words and images have many meanings. This gives them persuasive power. Many scholars have studied how signs come to represent something else. To better understand language as a persuasive tool, we will examine the ideas of several theorists who study **semiotics,** the theory of the meaning of signs and symbols.

sign
something that designates something other than itself

semiotics
the theory of meaning

C. K. Ogden and I. A. Richards (1923) challenged earlier thinking about words and their meanings. Previously, theorists believed that words had "correct," or "proper," meanings. That is, a word had one commonly agreed upon meaning. Ogden and Richards, however, said that meaning does not depend on the word, but rather on the people who use the word. Meaning relies on the personal context: the experience individuals have with objects. Ogden and Richards proposed that meaning has three dimensions: words, or symbols; thoughts, or references; and objects, or referents. One of Ogden and Richards's lasting contributions to the study of semiotics is the semantic triangle (Figure 2.1). The triangle describes the relationships between the three dimensions of meaning. Between the symbol and the thought, there is a direct relationship, and between the referent (object) and the thought, there is a direct relationship. Yet, between

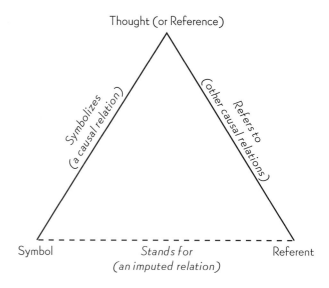

Figure 2.1
Ogden and Richards's
semantic triangle
From Ogden and Richards
(1923, p. 14)

Thought (or Reference)

Symbolizes
(a causal relation)

Refers to
(other causal relations)

Symbol

Stands for
(an imputed relation)

Referent

the object and the symbol, there is an indirect relationship. A group of theorists called the General Semanticists explained this aspect of language by saying, "The map is not the territory." They implied that the words we use do not accurately reflect the reality they represent. You might also think about the phrase "The word is not the thing" to help you understand this concept.

Suzanne Langer (1960) uses the word *concept* to refer to the shared ideas we have about an object. We are able to communicate because we share certain concepts of objects and ideas. We often think of the concept as the *denotation*. Yet, Langer wrote, "As quickly as the concept is symbolized to us, our own imagination dresses it up in a private, personal conception" (1960, p. 72). Thus, a *conception* is an individual's private idea of what a word means. We think of this as *connotation*. Langer allows for private meanings for words, but she also acknowledges that words have common meanings as well.

We have so far used *sign, symbol,* and *word* more or less interchangeably. To semioticians, these words have very different meanings. *Sign* is the broader term, which includes *signals*—natural signs—and *symbols*—more or less arbitrary signs. Footprints in the snow, for instance, are a natural sign—a signal. The word *stop* is an arbitrary sign that means "halt." It is a symbol. Charles Sanders Peirce makes a further distinction, when he explains that there are three types of signs: iconic, indexical, and symbolic (Buchler, 1940). Iconic and indexical signs are natural signs, whereas symbolic signs are arbitrary. Throughout the book, we mostly concern ourselves with how signs function as symbols—and use the terms *symbol* or *symbolic* to refer to this function. It is important to be aware of the differences in how signs obtain meaning for audiences.

Iconic signs resemble what they represent. The words *boom, splat,* and *drip* are examples of words that sound like what they mean. A photograph can also be iconic because it resembles what it represents.

Indexical signs get their meaning because of the association they have with another object. Smoke, as a sign of fire, is an example of indexical mean-

iconic sign
a sign that gets its meaning because of a resemblance to what it signifies; examples include photographs and drawings

indexical sign
a sign that gets its meaning because of the association it has with what it signifies; smoke as a sign of fire is one example

ing. If you watch soap operas, you know that characters often obtain their meaning because of their association with other characters (Brummett, 1994). Viewers know, for instance, that a certain character was once married to another character. Peirce suggests thinking of an index finger pointing at another object as an aid to remembering the concept of indexical meaning.

The third type of sign, **symbolic,** is much more ambiguous and makes language and other signs confusing and rich with meaning at the same time. These signs have a purely arbitrary relationship with what they mean. The word *stop,* for instance, has an agreed-upon meaning that has no relationship to the idea it represents. We have simply decided to use the word *stop* to mean "halt." We could have just as easily used the word *go* to mean "stop," and *stop* to mean "go." Peirce argues that because these words have an arbitrary relationship with what they mean, they could mean many things.

symbolic sign
a sign that gets its meaning in a purely arbitrary way; a flag is an example of a symbolic sign

Although the meanings of iconic and indexical signs are often apparent or evident, we must understand how symbolic signs come to have meaning. To make sense of symbols, we use **codes,** or correlations between words and the objects they represent. Arthur Asa Berger defines a code as "a system of conventions that enables one to detect meaning in signs (in other words, permits 'decoding' them)" (1984, p. 189). The English language, for example, is a code that helps us determine what words in our language mean. You might think of a dictionary as a "codebook" that helps you break the code for words you encounter in your reading that you haven't seen before.

code
a set of rules that enables us to understand the meaning of signs and symbols

A number of theorists have discussed codes. One is Umberto Eco (1979), who offers a comprehensive system for discussing codes. Eco's focus is on the role culture plays in creating codes. If you think about the culture of a particular group of people, it is full of rules for determining what things mean. In my home state of Nebraska, people take great interest in the University of Nebraska football team. As you drive through the state on a fall Saturday, you are likely to see red flags with a white "N" being flown from people's homes. An outsider would not know the code to understand what the flag means. If you are from Nebraska, though, you know that the flag is a sign that can be understood to mean school spirit, or "Go Big Red!"

We live life switching between various codes to determine the meanings of the signs we encounter. Language codes permit us to understand that the word *dog* means "a four-legged mammal." Scientific codes allow us to make sense of chemical symbols, such as H_2O and CO_2. Insignia codes help us to understand flags (such as my red Nebraska flag), uniforms, and shop signs. Etiquette codes help us to function in various social and interpersonal settings. Fashion codes enable us to understand the meaning of the clothing we wear. Ritual codes allow us to make sense of weddings, funerals, and graduations. Our lives are full of codes. In fact, one theorist has identified more than 100 types of codes. We learn codes in school, at home, and through popular culture.

Examine an ad in a magazine. What are some of the signs that comprise an ad? What codes are necessary to understand the ad? What is the overall message of the ad?

When words mean different things to different people or when a word can have several meanings, codes do not help us make sense of the signs we encounter. A. A. Berger calls this *code confusion,* which results in a struggle to determine meaning, and identifies several causes for this confusion. Meanings for signs can change, so that it is no longer apparent what the signs mean.

Birkenstock sandals used to be worn by "granola" types, or people not interested in high fashion or extravagant living. Birkenstocks were a sure sign that the wearer was somehow "different" from the mainstream. As the popularity of the shoe grew because of its durability and comfort, however, more and more people began wearing the shoe. Today, it is difficult to tell anything about the beliefs or lifestyle of someone wearing Birkenstocks. Likewise, signs can be ambiguous in their meaning. A sign may have several meanings, or several signs may mean the same thing. In any case, codes are not easy to use. As media bring us a greater number and variety of signs, confusion about which code to use becomes more common in our lives.

This code confusion, or breakdown in meanings, has led scholars, such as Jacques Derrida, to argue that signs actually prevent us from understanding our world. Derrida uses the word *differance* to indicate the differences between a word and the referent it supposedly represents. There is always a difference between a sign and what it signifies. We use the "detour of the sign" when we cannot show the thing to which the sign refers (Derrida, 1982). Signs are thus removed from that which they represent. Words cannot represent reality because they do not accurately reflect the object they indicate. Not all scholars agree with Derrida's view of signs and meaning, but his ideas have influenced how we think about language in the media age.

As we have seen, signs represent some object, and they acquire meaning through the individuals who use them. Signs mean different things to different people because of differences in context and culture. It is this openness of meaning that allows signs to have different degrees of persuasive power. Some signs have stronger meanings associated with them than do others. Persuaders choose their words carefully so as to have the maximum effect on their audience. If there were no question about what words mean, persuaders would not have to study how words should be used. Semiotics is the study of how symbols have meaning.

When we use signs, we do so to represent some idea or object. Although signs do not have universal meaning, we do share similar interpretations of what they mean because of denotative meaning. In addition, signs achieve meaning for receivers in one of three ways: iconic, indexical, and symbolic. In subsequent chapters, we will see how persuaders manage the meaning of language and visual images for their audiences. How the meaning of signs is managed has implications for power, ideology, and ethics.

Audience-Oriented Theories

The symbols we use to communicate are powerful. Yet individual audience members do not always act as persuaders think they will. In fact, sometimes individuals act in ways quite different from those suggested by persuasive messages. In this section, we examine persuasion from the perspective of the audience member. We explore how individuals process messages so as to better understand how they may respond to a persuader's message. We examine cognitive dissonance theory and the elaboration likelihood model.

COGNITIVE DISSONANCE THEORY

Cognitive dissonance theory, developed by Leon Festinger (1957), proposes that individuals seek balance, or consistency, in their lives. When we experience inconsistency between two beliefs, we find ways to restore balance. Persuaders, then, seek to disrupt the balance in our lives and then to offer us a way to restore that balance. Or persuaders convince us that if we use their product or service, we will maintain the balance in our lives. Either way, the compelling force that we feel to remain balanced drives us to seek remedies and solutions in a wide variety of ways. Let's look more closely at Festinger's theory.

Festinger (1957) explains that individuals try to maintain consistent relationships between their ideas. Two cognitive elements, or ideas, can be related in one of three ways, he says. First, the two ideas can have an irrelevant relationship. For instance, you might believe that a particular candidate would make a good president, and you might think that driving a particular make of car is a good idea. These two thoughts are not related in any way, and believing both ideas does not cause you any psychological discomfort. Second, the two ideas can be consonant with each other. You might think a particular candidate would be a good president, and then that person announces that he or she supports a law that you also favor. Because you support the candidate and the law, your beliefs have a consonant relationship, and your support for the person is strengthened.

However, Festinger (1957) also identifies a third type of relationship—**dissonance**—which describes the relationship between inconsistent ideas. If you are planning to purchase a particular car brand and model and then hear that the car's manufacturer has recalled that model, you experience dissonance. You thought the car was safe, but then learned that it was not. Or you might prefer a candidate for political office and then learn that he or she supports a law you oppose. You would have to choose between your belief about the candidate and your belief about the law. Festinger argues that we seek to avoid believing two inconsistent ideas, that we look for some way to reconcile the two beliefs. Festinger associates dissonance with hunger; when we are hungry, we seek food.

dissonance
the result of the relationship between two inconsistent ideas

Cognitive dissonance can be reduced in one of several ways as outlined in Table 2.5. First, the individual can *change one of his or her ideas* to bring it in line with the other. A smoker, for example, may quit smoking when he or she hears that smoking causes lung cancer. You might drop your support for the candidate who opposes a policy you support. Second, an individual may *seek information to support one of the ideas.* The smoker may seek information that contradicts the study he or she read about smoking causing cancer; this would let the smoker continue smoking because he or she could believe the new idea to be false. Third, an individual might *avoid information* that results in dissonance. The smoker might change the television channel when the evening news discusses research related to smoking and cancer. You might avoid discussing politics with friends with whom you disagree on political issues. Fourth, an individual can *reduce the importance of one* of the cognitive elements. You might persuade yourself that the policy you had previously supported is not that

Table 2.5 Cognitive Dissonance Actions

Action	Example
Change one of the ideas	"I have been persuaded that smoking is harmful, so I'll stop smoking."
Seek more information	"Another study found that smoking isn't harmful, so I'll continue to smoke."
Avoid contrary information	"I'll just stop reading the health section of the newspaper so I don't have to read about new scientific studies."
Reduce the importance of one of the cognitive elements	"The chance that smoking will be harmful to me is so small that I'll continue to smoke."
Introduce a third cognitive element to reconcile the two dissonant elements	"Scientific studies are so confusing that you can't really trust anything you read."

important an issue. You might come to believe that supporting this candidate outweighs your previous ideas about the policy he or she opposes.

The final way an individual can reduce dissonance is to *use a third cognitive element to reconcile* the two dissonant elements. Festinger (1957) provides an interesting example of a culture that believes people are good—not just that people *should be* good, but that they *are* by nature good. Yet, contrary to this belief is the fact that children in this culture experience a period of aggression and hostility. The culture has introduced a third belief—that supernatural forces sometimes invade a person—so that they can continue to hold on to their belief that people are good. Another example comes from the world of politics. The news media often portray candidates as dishonest, incompetent, or unworthy of office. If you support a candidate who has been portrayed negatively by the media, you experience dissonance. A popular way for candidates to reduce this dissonance is by blaming the media for wrongly characterizing them. Thus, they introduce a third idea that allows voters to support them despite negative media coverage.

Cognitive dissonance theory was first developed in the 1950s, but it remains a good way to explain persuasion in the media age. As we turn to media more frequently to learn who we are, dissonance caused by media sources affects us in new and different ways. Our self-concept, as discussed in Chapter 1, is influenced by media messages that contradict how we think and feel about ourselves. We discuss this point further in Chapter 11. Yet cognitive dissonance is a receiver-oriented theory that does not consider the wide range of variables involved in the persuasive process.

PROBLEMATIC INTEGRATION THEORY

Austin Babrow's (1995) theory of problematic integration (PI) is emerging as an excellent way to understand how audience members use communication to choose from among a range of behaviors. Essentially PI states that when we experience problems integrating two diverse ideas, we turn to communication to

Table 2.6 Problematic Integraton Matrix

		Evaluation	
		Positive	**Negative**
Probability	**High**	No problem integrating ideas	Problematic integration (divergence)
	Low	Problematic integration	No problem integrating ideas

help resolve our discomfort. Babrow explains that audience members tend to make two kinds of judgments: probabilistic and evaluative. A *probabilistic judgment* is a "subjective judgment of the likelihood of an association between the two objects of thought" (p. 283). Imagine, for instance, that you are considering going to graduate school. Part of your decision would be determining if graduate school would be useful to obtaining a job in your chosen profession. If you want to be a college professor, then there is a high probability that graduate school is necessary to fulfill your career goals. If you want to work in sales, however, there is a low probability that graduate school is necessary to be successful in this field. We also make *evaluative judgments* about ideas, says Barbrow (1995). He explains that we judge the "goodness or badness of a given object or relation between objects" (p, 283). Returning to the example of your graduate school decision, you will also decide if graduate school would be a positive or negative experience. You consider if you will enjoy it, if you will be successful, and how much sacrifice it may take.

The two judgments we have discussed—probabilistic and evaluative—can be related in four ways (see Table 2.6). Specifically, Babrow, (1995) identifies *divergence* as a form of problematic integration that arises when evaluative and probabilistic judgments are at odds. Consider again the graduate school example. If you know that you have to go to graduate school because you want to be a professor and you think that graduate school will be a positive experience, you have no difficulty integrating these beliefs and you will probably apply to graduate school. On the other hand, if you know that you need to go to graduate school but think it will be a negative experience, you will experience problematic integration. However, if you don't need to go to graduate school and think it would be a negative experience, you won't have difficulty making the decision not to go to graduate school.

Lets consider another example of divergence before exploring some additional types of problematic integration. An advertisement from the Sun Safety Alliance asks, "What will your kids bring home from the beach this summer?" The answer: "11 seashells, 3 pockets full of sand, 1 piece of driftwood, 2 times the risk of developing skin cancer." The ad then states, "Fact: Just one blistering sunburn as a child can double the chance of developing skin cancer later in life." Readers of the ad at this point experience problematic integration: There is a high probability that something bad will happen to their children at the beach. So, how does a parent believe this problem and make sure that nothing bad happens at the beach? The ad replies, "Fact: You can significantly reduce your family's risk by following a few simple steps." The ad lists applying sunscreen, wearing protective clothing, and staying out of the sun between 10 A.M. and 2 P.M. The admonition is then given to talk to a health professional for more advice.

In addition to divergence, Babrow (1995) identifies three additional forms of problematic integration. At times, we are unable to clearly make judgments about probability and evaluation. In these situations, *ambiguity* is the form of problematic integration. If you don't know much about graduate school or the expectations of future employers, you would be unable to make the judgments we have discussed and could experience tension because of the ambiguity. Additionally, Babrow explains that *ambivalence* results when a single idea provokes opposite feelings. You might, for instance, give a positive evaluation to receiving a graduate degree but at the same time dread the tests and papers you would have to complete before earning the degree. A final type of problematic integration would occur if your desire is *impossible* to achieve. If you would like to go to graduate school, but known that you can't—due to cost, location, or conflicting career or family obligations—you would experience problematic integration, according to Babrow.

The advertisement we discussed previously hints at how persuaders may use communication to create and relieve problematic integration. Communication, says Babrow (1995), is a *source* of problematic integration. We use communication to form probabilistic and evaluative judgments. From the advertising example, you can see how persuaders strategically use communication to influence the judgments that audience members make. In some cases, persuaders strategically use communication to influence the judgments that audience members make. In some cases, persuaders purposely present information in a way that creates problematic integration. Communication is also the *medium* through which problematic integration spreads. Babrow explains that our culture, implicitly, contains many kinds of probabilistic and evaluative statements that we have come to know. For instance, we evaluate highly relaxing at the beach and spending time outside in the summer. Thus it is natural for an audience member to consider taking children to the beach, and we see this a positive experience. Finally, communication is a *resource* for dealing with problematic integration. Babrow explains, "We might warn, chide, advise, encourage, or otherwise use language as a resource to help another person deal with PI" (p. 286). The advertisement we have discussed clearly uses communication to warn and advise readers to take proper precautions when going back to the beach. Additionally, your advisor might be able to help you determine if graduate school is right for you. Babrow's theory is a new way of thinking about how persuaders influence audience members and holds much promise for communication theory about persuasion.

THE ELABORATION LIKELIHOOD MODEL

Richard E. Petty and John T. Cacioppo's theory of persuasion is called the elaoration likelihood model (ELM). Their theory states that persuasion occurs

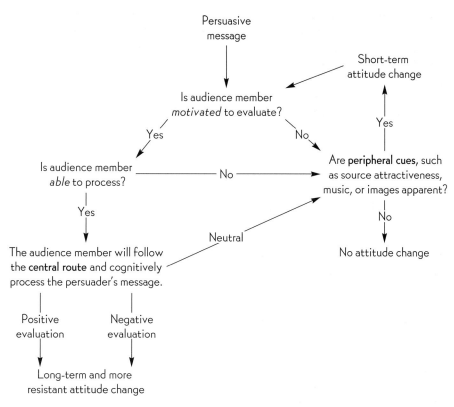

**Figure 2.2
Diagram of the
Elaboration
Likelihood Model**
Adapted from Petty and
Cacciopo (1986)

through one of two routes: the central route or the peripheral route. The *central route*—which uses logical processing—produces more permanent persuasion, whereas the *peripheral route*—which makes use of contextual cues—results in temporary attitude change. Let's explore more closely Petty and Cacioppo's view of how audience members process persuasion. Review Figure 2.2 as you read this section.

Individuals process persuasive messages through one of two routes, claim Petty and Cacioppo (1986), depending on the type of message they are processing. **Central-route processing** requires "careful and thoughtful consideration of the true merits of the information presented" (p. 3). Individuals therefore process logical, content-based messages through the central route. **Peripheral-route processing** makes use of "some simple cue in the persuasion context (e.g., an attractive source)" (p. 3). In other words, the peripheral route relies on a message's spokesperson, background music, or flashy computer graphics. A televised car commercial, for example, may provide persuasive cues along both routes. It may provide logical information concerning gas mileage, engine size, and safety features. Peripheral cues would include images of the car racing through the mountains, the smiling faces of the driver and the passengers, and fast-paced music highlighting the "sporty" nature of the car.

As you watch the car commercial, you may or may not pay attention to the logical information. The route an individual uses to elaborate on a message is

central-route processing
attending to persuasive messages on the basis of the logical information they contain; audience members must be both motivated to attend to the message in this way and able to do so

peripheral-route processing
attending to persuasive messages because of the cues they contain, such as images, sound, or spokespeople

determined by two factors: motivation and ability. *Motivation* refers to such factors as personal relevance, need for understanding, and personal responsibility. If you are shopping for a new car and are on a tight budget, you'll probably pay attention to information about the car's price and gas mileage. If you are shopping for a car and have a family, you'll probably tune in to the safety features of the car. You must also have the *ability* to process the information. When we can't understand what is being communicated, we use the peripheral route. Sometimes, information about the size of the engine or other features of the car is stated in technical terms that not everyone can understand. If you don't know what a "V-6, dual-overhead-cam" engine refers to, you cannot use the central route to process that message.

Central route processing involves two stages, according to Petty and Cacioppo (1986). First, the audience member will evaluate the initial quality of the arguments and his or her attitude toward the variables presented by the persuader. If the audience member has strong feelings toward the message at this point, he or she will generate new beliefs about the subject and store them in memory. By doing so, the audience member will adopt a new attitude, either positive or negative, that is resistant to future persuasive attempts. The new attitude, say Petty and Cacioppo, is also predictive of behavior. It is also important to point out that audience members may not always process messages by the central route objectively. Their biases may influence how they respond to the message, and they may develop counterarguments to what is presented.

If you are not motivated or able to process the ad's information via the central route, you use the peripheral route. If you are not shopping for a car, for instance, you probably will not pay attention to the car's gas mileage or its safety features. If you know nothing about car engines, you will not be able to understand the unique features of a particular model. You still may be persuaded by the advertisement, though. The flashy images of the car racing through the mountains may inspire you to investigate the car. The spokesperson used or the layout of the advertisement may capture your attention. Thus, you use peripheral processing as you watch the ad.

Petty and Cacioppo (1986) theorize that persuasion resulting from central-route processing is more permanent than that fostered by peripheral-route processing. Attitude changes created through the central route are more resistant to future messages as well. The reason: "Attitude changes induced via the central route involve considerably more cognitive work than attitude changes induced under the peripheral route" (p. 21). Central-route processing requires that individuals compare new information to what they know to be true before adopting the new information. Information obtained through the peripheral route may be assessed only once. In addition, peripheral-route processing is usually based on some affective response to stimuli. Finally, the perception that thoughtful consideration is given during central-route processing leads to greater confidence in one's decision and a more lasting commitment to the decision.

Apple computer effectively used advertising that featured both central- and peripheral-route processing in their recent Switch campaign. In an effort to win users from Windows-based computers, Apple told the stories of a variety of famous and everyday people who switched to Apple. One commercial featured skateboarder Tony Hawk. In terms of logical, cognitive messages, Hawk talked about how simple it was to edit video on an Apple. Peripheral cues in the ad include Hawk, a popular spokesperson, as well as images of skateboarding, a popular sport for Apple's target audience. Because the ad featured both logical and peripheral cues, it was effective in winning support from a wide audience. Thinking Critically: Processing Persuasive Messages addresses how the two theories we have just discussed can be applied to another persuasive message.

Petty and Cacioppo (1986) help us to visualize the way audiences process persuasive messages. Since audience members are different, they will use different ways of processing messages, depending on their motivation to attend to a persuasive message and their ability to process the information. Like cognitive dissonance theory, and problematic integration theory, the ELM provides us with a good view of how receivers may process persuasive messages. But the ELM does not tell us much about other variables of the persuasive process.

Look at an advertisement in a magazine. How does the ad create dissonance for its audience? What methods does the advertisement suggest for reducing dissonance? How does the ad encourage central- or peripheral-route processing?

The Social Construction of Reality

Another group of theorists, including Kenneth Burke, Walter Fisher, George Herbert Mead, Herbert Blumer, Peter L. Berger, Thomas Luckmann, and Ernest Bormann, suggest that we create what we know of our world through the language we use to describe it. Although these theorists differ somewhat in their approaches to this topic, as a whole they suggest that what we know of reality is the result of our interactions with society and other individuals. The way we act toward other people, ideas, and objects is based on what they mean to us. That meaning is not based on something innate to the person, idea, or object, but is instead based on the interaction we have had with that object or with other people. As we go through life, we constantly interpret our surroundings and can change the ideas we have about people, ideas, or objects.

For example, when you entered college, you may have had no interest in the sport of football. You may have avoided going to the football games at your high school because doing so meant sitting in the hot sun (or cold autumn wind) watching players run up and down the field for a few hours. The meaning you assigned to football was established through your previous interaction with the sport. As you interacted with your classmates at college, however, you may have come to learn that going to college football games had nothing to do with the game of football. Your friends went to the games purely for social interaction. As a result, you went to a game and enjoyed the time you spent with your friends. The meaning of a football game changed based on your interactions with others. We repeat this process throughout our lives as we constantly adjust the meanings we have for objects in our world through our encounters with those objects and with other people. Burke summarized the social construction of reality with this phrase: "And however important to us is the tiny sliver of reality each of us has experienced firsthand, the whole overall 'picture'

THINKING CRITICALLY

Processing Persuasive Messages

We have just discussed two theories that help explain how audience members process persuasive messages. Cognitive dissonance theory and the elaboration likelihood model both provide psychological explanations for how persuasion occurs. Think about these theories as you consider this advertisement for the National Flood Insurance Program.

The advertisement creates cognitive dissonance with the headline: "There's a chance of flooding in your area. Are you willing to bet the house on it?" The beginning of the second paragraph increases that dissonance: "The sad fact is that floods are a night-

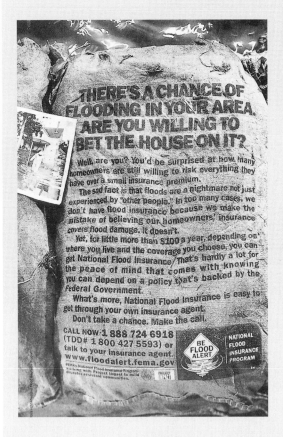

mare not just experienced by 'other people.'" The picture of a flooded house accompanies these words and effectively enhances the dissonance. The desired audience response to this dissonance is for receivers to choose to pay a "small insurance premium" for flood insurance. Since the advertisement was placed in *This Old House* magazine, there is a good chance that readers are home owners. The advertisement was also created for people who live in particular geographic areas and was placed in magazines distributed in these areas. The advertisement may not, however, create dissonance for those who live in apartments or in areas that don't experience flooding.

The ELM can also help us to understand the persuasiveness of the advertisement. Those who are motivated to view the ad and to respond to it would use the cognitive route (central-route processing). These receivers would include home owners in areas threatened by flooding. The cognitive route would help readers understand the cost of flood insurance and know how to purchase it. The peripheral route would be used by those who do not own homes or do not perceive themselves as threatened by flooding. The ad offers peripheral cues, though, in an attempt to attract unmotivated viewers. Two such cues are the sandbag design and the photograph of the flooded house.

Consider the explanations offered by these two theories as you answer these questions:

1. Which theory—cognitive dissonance or the elaboration likelihood model—seems to you to better explain the National Flood Insurance Program ad?

2. How might the flood insurance ad be modified to increase the level of dissonance it creates for audience members?

3. Consider your response to the ad. Are you motivated or able to use the central route to process the advertisement's message? If not, do the peripheral cues entice you to read the advertisement? Why or why not?

is but a construct of our symbol systems" (1966, p. 5). Persuaders use language to structure a reality that is favorable to their message.

SYMBOLIC CONVERGENCE THEORY

A specific theory that describes this process is symbolic convergence theory. Ernest Bormann and his colleagues found that groups of people often dramatize past or future actions in the form of puns, analogies, fables, or narratives. These dramatizations are called **fantasies,** creative interpretations of events by group members to fulfill some need (Bormann, 1985). People engage in fantasy sharing in informal settings, such as hallway discussions, and in formal settings, such as meetings. The fantasies are told in response to some need and use characters and plotlines. Some are told so often that only a word or two from the story is needed for the group to burst into laughter or understand what is meant. These fantasies serve important functions for the group. The stories allow group members to reduce tension or resolve conflict. The stories also help the group create a shared culture, or way of seeing the world. Thus, the simple act of storytelling is an important tool for group communication. In other words, the conversations of employees at the bar after work, in the hallway during office hours, or during formal meetings and seminars are important in bringing about convergence in the group's way of thinking.

> **fantasy**
> the creative interpretation of an event by group members to fulfill some need

Bormann hypothesizes that group fantasy sharing can be used to explain how larger groups of people create shared visions of reality based on stories told by media. Events such as political campaigns can be viewed as a set of stories that "chain out" among voters. Members of the public view an unfolding fantasy much as they would a movie or a play. **Fantasy themes** are the contents of stories that are retold by group members. Sometimes, the group develops particular fantasies that have similar plot outlines, scenes, and characters (Bormann, 1985). These repeated patterns of exchange are called **fantasy types.** As the fantasy themes chain out among group members, the group forms a **rhetorical vision,** which is a common way of seeing the world based on the process of sharing fantasies. Bormann explains, "When a number of people come to share a cluster of fantasy themes and types, they may integrate them into a coherent rhetorical vision of some aspect of their social reality" (p. 133). Some rhetorical visions are so powerful for people that they live their lives according to them. Bormann calls this phenomenon a *lifestyle rhetorical vision;* religion is an example.

> **fantasy themes**
> contents of stories that are retold by group members
>
> **fantasy types**
> fantasies that have similar plot outlines, scenes, and characters; they are repeated patterns of exchange
>
> **rhetorical vision**
> a similar way of understanding reality shared by members of a culture, community, or group as the result of fantasy sharing

As the news broke of a bombing in Oklahoma City in 1995, the nation engaged in fantasy sharing. The fantasy theme that terrorists from the Middle East had bombed the building chained out through the media and soon served as the rhetorical vision. The story had a plotline—the bombing—and characters—alleged Middle Eastern terrorists. The fantasy made use of a fantasy type: the stereotype that foreign terrorists seek to bomb the United States. Soon, the nation learned that the bombing was the result of domestic terrorists. But the degree of acceptance the initial story received indicates the power of fantasy sharing to shape how we view the world.

AN EXAMPLE

Margaret Duffy (1997) uses symbolic convergence theory to explain the persuasive strategies used by a public relations firm hired to persuade the Iowa legislature to allow riverboat casino gambling in Iowa in 1989. She argues that whereas past lobbying attempts to bring riverboat gambling to the state had failed, the CFM&Z public relations firm succeeded because its campaign used a more sophisticated persuasive strategy. The campaign cast the riverboat industry, and its attendant gambling component, as a way to save the struggling Iowa economy. The riverboats would bring tourists to the state and create jobs for Iowans. To downplay the gambling component even more, the campaign focused on the historical importance of riverboats in Iowa. In fact, the press conference at which the developers announced their plans was held at the Iowa State Historical Building.

For the plan to work, however, the Iowa State Legislature had to approve gambling, which previously it had not done. Those who opposed gambling were portrayed as "foes to be vanquished" (Duffy, 1997, p. 123). The two developers were portrayed as heroes. Media response to the campaign was excellent. The fantasies created by the public relations firm chained out with little resistance from the opposition. Duffy concludes, "The skillful public relations–created messages chained through mass media and contributed to fantasy themes that engaged journalists and larger audiences" (p. 128). Her description of this persuasive movement is a good example of how symbolic convergence theory can be useful not only for those studying persuasion, but also for those who create persuasive messages.

Consider a current event in the news, and describe it from the perspective of symbolic convergence theory. What is the fantasy theme? Who are the characters? How does the fantasy sharing create a rhetorical vision? Who benefits from how the rhetorical vision is created? Who is hurt by how reality is constructed?

Duffy claims that the public relations firm took advantage of the journalistic practices of the modern media. Indeed, symbolic convergence theory is a good way to view persuasion in the media age. Mass media are important variables in the chaining-out process. If you have ever received a chain letter via e-mail that has been sent to hundreds of other people, you have witnessed firsthand the power of the Internet to chain out stories. The Oklahoma City example provides insight into how media perpetuate fantasy themes and how we as a culture come to believe what we see and hear. Media foster a common way of seeing the world. As we continue our discussion of persuasion in the media age, we use symbolic convergence theory as a lens to understand the persuasive process and to explain how ideas and beliefs spread throughout a community.

Media Theories

Much of the persuasion we encounter today is through media channels. In Chapter 4, we discuss in greater detail the institutional, economic, and cognitive effects of media on our perception of persuasion. Here, we survey several theories to understand how researchers understand media and persuasion.

ONE-SHOT MODEL

Initially, media researchers thought that persuasion occurred simply through the transmission of symbols. The one-shot model assumed that media have a powerful effect on their audiences. Most theorists today do not subscribe to this model. It is useful, however, to understand why early theorists assigned it such power.

Initial assumptions about the power of media were based on the success of propaganda during the world wars. In 1917, immediately following the United States' entry into World War I, President Wilson established the Committee on Public Information. More than 150,000 employees created an immense amount of information designed to convince Americans to support the war effort, while at the same time attempting to weaken the resolve of the German people. In all, more than 100 million posters were distributed, 75,000 people spoke in movie theaters in support of the war, and millions of leaflets were dropped on Germany. These efforts apparently were successful, leading psychologists to conclude that exposure to mediated messages is an effective way of changing attitudes. Further research, such as that conducted by sociologists Paul Lazarsfeld, Bernard Berelson, and Hazel Gaudet, moderates the claims of early media theorists.

TWO-STEP FLOW OF INFORMATION

In the 1940s and 50s, researchers began to study real populations of people to understand the effects of media. What they found was a more complicated pattern of symbol sharing than the single-shot model indicated. A study conducted by Lazarsfeld, Berelson, and Gaudet, called *The People's Choice* (1944), questioned four groups of 600 persons each from the entire population of Erie County, Ohio, during the summer and fall of 1940. The study sought to determine what factors accounted for a person's decision to vote for a particular candidate. Interviewers assessed the socioeconomic status (SES) of the subjects, and the subjects were asked a variety of questions, including political party identification, religion, attention to print and radio media, time of decision, and interpersonal influences. The authors found that media played a minimal role in voters' decisions. Primarily, social and interpersonal factors played a more persuasive role with voters than did media.

The authors found that social pressure was very influential in determining a person's vote. Using statistical analysis, the researchers sought to determine which *socioeconomic variables* accounted for the voter's decision. For example, Protestants of high SES were more likely to vote Republican than were Catholics of lower SES, who often voted Democratic. Specifically, the investigators found that voter attitudes are fairly stable. Seventy-seven percent of the panel voted in the 1940 election for the party that their parents and grandparents had voted for. The authors found that voters insulate themselves from information that may run contrary to their predisposition. Change does occur, but it is more likely to be seen in those people who face considerable cross pressures. For example, a woman of lower SES who is Protestant is drawn by her

SES to vote Democratic, but her religion influences her to vote Republican. As a result, the woman may choose a candidate from a party different from her parents and different from the party she voted for in the last election.

The researchers also identified a multistep flow of information. They identified *opinion leaders,* who learned about the political candidates and then, in turn, shared this information with other members of the community, who did not otherwise use media. "This suggests that ideas often flow *from* radio and print *to* the opinion leaders and *from* them to the less active sections of the population" (Lazarsfeld, Berelson, & Gaudet, 1944, p. 151). In short, interpersonal influence was more persuasive to the voters of Erie County, Ohio, than was media influence. The symbols that opinion leaders shared with voters were seen to be highly persuasive. Thus, the study tempered the early one-shot model. Not only did media play less of a role in determining voting patterns than did socioeconomic variables, but media's influence was diffused by opinion leaders.

USES AND GRATIFICATIONS RESEARCH

The theories we've just discussed focus on the role of media in shaping the attitudes of audiences. A body of research called the uses and gratifications perspective argues that instead of being used by media, audiences actively select from among media to gratify their needs. In this sense, uses and gratifications research suggests that media have only a limited influence on us. That is, audience members engage in symbol sharing only when they have a need to do so.

Uses and gratifications is not a unified body of research, however. J. G. Blumler (1979) notes, "There is no such thing as *a* or *the* uses and gratifications theory, although there are plenty of theories about uses and gratifications phenomena" (p. 11). Despite the disparity in approaches, several general statements can be made about the uses and gratifications perspective. The theory, as outlined by Elihu Katz and colleagues (1974), is concerned with "(1) the social and psychological origins of (2) needs, which generate (3) expectations of (4) the mass media or other sources, which lead to (5) differential patterns of media exposure (or engagement in other activities), resulting in (6) need gratifications and (7) other consequences, perhaps mostly unintended ones" (p. 14). Let's discuss these propositions in greater detail.

There are several antecedent conditions that motivate behavior. People have basic needs that must be fulfilled. These include food and shelter. People with these needs may or may not use media to fill them. For example, people who are experiencing a natural disaster, such as a flood, tornado, or hurricane, may turn to media to meet their basic survival needs. Social situations also motivate our behavior. During elections, for example, people are motivated to use media to learn about the candidates running for office. Or, people may be motivated to use media to relax after a day at work.

Researchers have identified several motives for using media. *Surveillance* involves learning about the world. We typically use news media to survey our world. *Curiosity* is the desire to learn something new about the world. Reality-based shows, such as *The Bachelor* or *Survivor,* are good examples of media

Table 2.7 Uses and Gratification Table

Gratification sought	Description	Example
Curiosity	Learn something new about the world	Watch reality-based television shows
Diversion	Need to escape the reality of life	Watch *Friends* or *All My Children*
Personal identity	Comparing ourselves with media characters to learn who we are	Watching *Trading Spaces* to learn your preference for interior design styles
Correlation	Finding information that confirms our beliefs	Reading editorials with which we agree
Cultural transmission	Discovering what it means to be an American	Reading fashion magazines

that cater to our curiosity motive. *Diversion* is the need to escape the reality of life by being entertained by media. Thursday night programming on NBC has become a way for many Americans to escape from the workweek and prepare for the weekend. *Personal identity* is the need to learn who we are. We can do this by exposing ourselves to a variety of media characters. We identify with some of them; we do not identify with others. However, by comparing ourselves with them, we learn about who we are. *Correlation* is the need to affirm what we know or believe. We read editorials in newspapers to fulfill this need. *Cultural transmission* is our need to learn about what it means to be an American. When we use media to learn about the latest fashion styles, for example, we are motivated by our desire to learn about our culture. Table 2.7 summarizes our motives for using the media.

When audiences are motivated to behave in a certain way, they assess ways media can satisfy their needs. If media are available to satisfy those needs, the audience member uses them. Finally, the person receives effects from his or her action. The effects can be subjective, such as gratifications received, or objective, such as knowledge obtained. Many unintended consequences result from media exposure as well. Uses and gratifications research has made an important contribution to our understanding of media use. Specifically, this body of literature suggests a very different, and more active, role for the audience than do other media theories.

Choose a popular television show. For what reason do you think viewers watch the program? What purpose(s) do(es) the show serve? What view of the world does the show cultivate?

CULTIVATION ANALYSIS

Cultivation analysis examines the relationship between extent of television viewing and conception of reality. The theory is based on work developed by George Gerbner and the Cultural Indicators research project, which began in the 1970s. Cultivation analysis hypothesizes that "heavy viewers will be more likely to perceive the real world in ways that reflect the most stable and recurrent patterns of portrayals in the television world" (Signorielli & Morgan, 1990, p. 10). Gerbner and his colleagues Larry Gross, Michael Morgan, and Nancy

Signorielli wrote that television is a form of storytelling and that from our infancy, television determines how we see the world through these stories. That is, television is seen to cultivate a certain perspective or belief system among all of its viewers. This theory is interested in the cumulative effects of a mass media culture.

Morgan and Signorielli (1990) explain that cultivation analysis seeks to identify and assess patterns in television content. Researchers focus on the images, portrayals, and values that "cut across" program genres (p. 16). For example, researchers might determine to what degree television shows women playing roles that are equal to those of men. Then, researchers determine if heavy television viewers see the world in ways that are similar to the way it is portrayed on television. The assumption is that heavy television viewers do not get as much varied information about the world as do light television viewers. In other words, those people who watch a great deal of television, it is assumed, are more likely to see the world as television portrays it. Light viewers, on the other hand, form their opinions about the world from a variety of sources and do not readily accept the portrayals of television.

Cultivation theorists advance some interesting claims. Heavy viewers of television, they claim, believe in the reality that is depicted on television, even if that reality is different from the reality of their world. By studying television viewers over a six-year period, researchers using the cultivation analysis theory found that heavy viewers tend to see the world as meaner than do light viewers and that heavy viewers mistrust people more than do light viewers. Other research has found that sex role, age role, and political and religious stereotypes can be attributed to television viewing. Cultivation analysis argues that television and other media have a powerful cumulative effect on their users. The process of symbol sharing, then, has implications for how we view our world. In addition, the common experiences of symbol sharing that we all have predispose us to see the world in particular ways. Consider recent allegations that the entertainment industry markets violence to young viewers as you read the ethics discussion for this chapter in Ethical Insights: Ethics and Violent Entertainment.

AGENDA SETTING

agenda-setting theory
the observation that the media may not be able to tell the public what to think, but that they are effective at telling the public what to think about

The **agenda-setting theory** assumes that media may not be able to tell the public what to think, but that media are effective at telling the public what to think about. In a sense, media set the agenda for the public, for politicians, and for other media. Maxwell E. McCombs (1981) explains, "The idea of agenda-setting influence by the mass media is a relational concept specifying a positive—indeed causal—relationship between the emphases of mass communication and what members of the audience come to regard as important" (p. 126). The agenda-setting theory rests on the fact that media cannot possibly cover all the news of the day. Even with daily newspapers and entire cable networks devoted to the news, decisions must be made about what stories get attention on a given news day. An important aspect of the agenda-setting theory is the notion of gatekeepers. A gatekeeper regulates the flow of information to the public. Edi-

ETHICAL INSIGHTS

Ethics and Violent Entertainment

You have just read about cultivation analysis and its argument that our perception of the world is related to our media consumption. In recent years, advocacy groups and government agencies have argued that violent and sexual programming in the entertainment media should be scrutinized more closely. Following incidents where children engaged in violent acts while making popular culture references, former President Clinton ordered a study of the entertainment industry. In 2000, the Federal Trade Commission reported that movie studios, music companies, and video-game makers target children with violent products. The report, which received a great deal of support in Washington and from the presidential candidates of the time, found that entertainment companies advertised R-rated movies in high school newspapers and on shows watched heavily by children. The companies countered by arguing that these same media also reach the adult market. The report prompted state attorneys general to proclaim that they would sue entertainment companies for their content.

The First Amendment is often used by members of the media to defend their practices. But some ethicists argue that the First Amendment does not guarantee that children have the same rights to purchase or view media content as adults do. The National Communication Association Credo for Ethical Communication (NCA, 1999) explains, "We condemn communication that degrades individuals and humanity through distortion, intolerance, intimidation, coercion, hatred, and violence." Based on this statement, we might consider violent entertainment programming to be unethical.

As you think about the ethics of the entertainment media, consider these questions:

1. What should be done, if anything, to control violent entertainment content?

2. Do you agree with cultivation theory that media consumption influences our view of the world? Does this influence extend to behaviors that media consumers might take, such as killing or other acts of violence?

tors are often seen as powerful gatekeepers when they decide what story will lead and which stories will be excluded from the day's news.

Agenda setting is a three-part process, according to Everett M. Rogers and James W. Dearing (1988). First, the *media agenda* is set. The media agenda includes the stories and articles that are broadcast or printed in various media outlets. The type of coverage they provide is determined in several ways. As we have discussed, media are part of a larger social system that has many players, including advertisers, political leaders, and popular figures. Four types of relationships, according to Stephen D. Reese (1991), may exist between media and these external forces, or sources:

- *High-power source and high-power medium:* In this relationship, media and their sources may agree on what the media agenda should be or they may disagree, in which case a struggle to set the media's agenda occurs. Your city's mayor and a local television station are examples of a high-power source and a high-power medium. Wayne Wanta and Yu-Wei Hu (1994) found that the higher the credibility of news coverage, the more susceptible the public is to media's messages.

- *High-power source and low-power medium:* In this case, the source uses the medium to reflect his or her views. The president of the United States communicating with a local newspaper is an example of this type of relationship.

Setting the Internet News Agenda

Although agenda-setting theory was first developed with print and broadcast media in mind, its findings hold true in the Internet age as well. Visit the websites for several news organizations. You might visit your local newspaper or television station as well as some national networks, such as CNN or Fox News. Compare the articles that are featured on the site. How are they similar? How are they different? Is there an agenda for the day's news? If there is, who do you think has set the agenda?

- *Low-power source and high-power medium:* In this case, the medium sets its own agenda and minimizes the voices of others. A news story on your local television station about a small community activist group is an example of this type of relationship.

- *Low-power source and low-power medium:* In this situation, the events of the day control the media agenda. The relationship between a small community activist group and the local college's newspaper is often determined by what happens in the community, not by the persuasive power of either party.

The media agenda creates the *public agenda,* the second step in the agenda-setting process. The media agenda and the public agenda are related in one of three ways. The public may already have the same agenda as the media. In this case, the media agenda is representative of the public agenda. Second, the public may hold a differing agenda. In this case, media are limited in their effect on the public. The scandals in the Clinton White House were met by a public that did not care. The public, in that case, did not accept the media's agenda. A third relationship, the focus of the agenda-setting theory, is described as persuasion, when media are effective at setting the public's agenda.

The final step in the agenda-setting process is the creation of the *policy agenda,* which is created by the public agenda. Ideally, our representatives in government enact the laws that are of concern to the public. If media have established the public's agenda, however, then our leaders enact the media's agenda, minimizing the voice of the public in determining policy.

Think of a recent persuasive encounter. Choose a theory from this chapter that helps you understand the encounter. How does the theory explain what happened? How does the theory help you predict what will happen in the future?

There are many scholars who argue that it is difficult to determine whether media set the public agenda or whether they merely reflect the public agenda. That is, there are some who argue that media are simply providing the information that we want to hear about. We set our agenda, and media fulfill that agenda. Numerous factors explain why media cover certain news stories and why they ignore others. We discuss these factors in Chapter 4. The Internet Activity: Setting the Internet News Agenda asks you to consider this theory.

The media theories highlighted here provide us with a view of the channel of persuasion and how audiences use that channel to communicate, fulfill needs, and learn about their world. These theories do not address all the variables of persuasion, such as content and the nature of the persuader.

Summary

A variety of theories can help us understand persuasion in the media age. Individually, these theories are incomplete in their analysis of the persuasion process; yet when their critical insights are combined, they provide a more complete understanding of the persuasion process.

Theories of persuasive oratory provide us with a historical perspective from which we can understand how persuasive messages have been constructed. Much of the insight provided by Aristotle and the *Rhetorica ad Herennium* helps us understand persuasion today. In fact, this book is organized, in part, around Aristotle's principles of ethos, pathos, and logos. Yet these theories take as their point of departure the clearly defined speech presented by a male persuader in an oral/literate culture. Today's culture forces us to make different assumptions about the speaker, about the occasion, and about media and audiences. For instance, persuaders are seldom in the direct physical presence of their audiences.

Semiotics helps us to understand how words have meaning for audiences. There is no natural link between a word and its meaning. Instead, meaning is determined through a culture's use of codes. The fluidity of meaning makes it difficult for audience members to understand persuasive messages today. Persuaders strategically take advantage of ambiguity in meaning when they communicate to us.

Festinger's cognitive dissonance theory and Petty and Cacioppo's elaboration likelihood model explain how audience members process persuasive messages. Cognitive dissonance says that we seek balance in our lives and take steps to restore balance when our cognitive elements are disrupted. The ELM explains that audience members process persuasive messages via one of two routes: the central route or the peripheral route. Persuasion that occurs via the central route is more permanent and more resistant to change than is that obtained through the peripheral route.

Symbolic convergence theory is one example of a theory that explains how reality is socially constructed. Through words and images, persuaders create widespread meaning for their messages. When a culture comes to have a similar interpretation of reality, we say that its members share a rhetorical vision.

The media theories discussed in this chapter all seek to explain the effect media have on their audience members. The single-shot model claimed a great deal of influence initially, but current theory has refuted it. The two-step flow of information moderated the single-shot theory, but again does not provide an accurate picture of media today. The uses and gratifications approach contends that instead of being acted upon by the media, individuals actively seek to use the media to fulfill certain needs. On the other hand, cultivation analysis argues that heavy media use results in a sense of the world that is similar to what is depicted in the media.

Key Terms

WWW: Visit the book's website at http://www.mhhe.com/borchers2 for multiple-choice quizzes, Internet activities, and key terms flashcards.

theory 34	semiotics 41
deliberative speech 36	iconic sign 42
forensic speech 36	indexical sign 42
epideictic speech 36	symbolic sign 43
ethos 37	code 43
credibility 37	dissonance 45
pathos 37	central-route processing 49
logos 38	peripheral-route processing 49
inductive reasoning 38	fantasy 53
deductive reasoning 38	fantasy themes 53
style 39	fantasy types 53
metaphor 39	rhetorical vision 53
five "canons" of rhetoric 39	agenda-setting theory 58
sign 41	

3

Persuasion and Ethics in the Media Age

Learning Objectives

After reading this chapter, you should be able to:

1. Understand the importance of studying ethics and persuasion.

2. Identify specific ethical challenges of the media age.

3. Describe various approaches to ethical decision making.

4. Assess the openness of a culture to persuasion by using the theory of universal pragmatics.

5. Recognize the importance of codes of ethics in several persuasive contexts.

When Internet users download the Alexa toolbar software program, they can receive helpful advice while shopping online. Alexa offers price comparisons and more information about the product the user is considering. At the same time, the software records information about its users and provides information to the company that developed the software, Alexa, a subsidiary of Amazon.com. Alexa collects its user's address and information about purchases the user has made or is considering. Alexa also collects information about you when you register for its software. It uses this information to understand how consumers shop online. Alexa contends that it does not link personal information about you—your name, for instance—to your Web surfing habits—which sites you visit and what products you purchase. Please read Alexa's privacy policy, which can be accessed from the link on this book's Web page. Consumer advocates fear that although Alexa may not correlate this information now, the company has the capability to do so and that its privacy policy may change. If you use the Internet and products like the Alexa toolbar, you place your faith in persuaders to protect personal information about you. These companies have an ethical obligation to safeguard your privacy.

Privacy is just one of many ethical issues that confront contemporary persuaders and audience members. Since humans first began to persuade each other, they have been concerned with doing so ethically. **Ethics** has been described as "the study of right or good conduct as it affects the individual (character) and society" (Limburg, 1994, p. 11). Richard L. Johannesen (1996) explained that ethical judgments focus on "degrees of rightness and wrongness, virtue and vice, and obligation of human behavior" (p. 1). Generally, the standards we may use to make ethical judgments include "honesty, promise-keeping, truthfulness, fairness, and humanness" (1996, p. 1). Ethics is concerned with whether actions are desirable and good for the individual and the community at large. Ethics is the study of how we should act when faced with equally compelling choices (Patterson & Wilkins, 1998). At the basis of ethics is a value system that helps members of a culture to understand which actions the culture believes to be good and which it believes to be wrong. Rationality is an important aspect of ethics. We must be able to explain ethical decisions to others. That is, reasoning underlies the ethical choices that we make. In our study of ethics in this chapter, we make explicit some of the fundamental values that help us to make ethical decisions about persuasive communication. We also examine how individual persuaders and our culture arrive at ethical judgments.

In this chapter, we explore the relationship between ethics and persuasion. We also identify some of the unique ethical challenges the media age poses to persuaders. Our discussion also focuses on how persuaders and audience members make ethical judgments in light of these challenges. We make ethical judgments by using philosophical arguments, public debate, and codes of ethics. At the end of the chapter, we highlight the specific ethical responsibilities of audience members. In short, this chapter discusses the appropriateness of the strategies used by persuaders to form relationships with audience members.

ethics

the study of which actions individuals and society consider desirable and undesirable, as well as of the rationale for their judgments when they are faced with equally compelling choices

Ethics and Persuasion

Before we examine the ethics of persuasion, let's recall our definition of persuasion from Chapter 1. There, we defined persuasion as *the coproduction of meaning that results when an individual or a group of individuals uses language strategies and/or visual images to make audiences identify with that individual or group.* Recall from our discussion of this definition that choice is necessary for a persuader and an audience to identify with each other. Persuasion also makes use of a wide range of behaviors, such as reasoning and feeling.

Richard Johannesen (1996) argues that it is important to discuss ethics and persuasion together for three reasons. First, when we engage in persuasion, we have an impact on others. The persuader attempts to get audience members to believe something new or engage in some kind of behavior. Thus, the persuader influences what audience members do or think. Audience members put their trust in what the persuader says. We like to think that those who persuade us are being truthful when they do so. Thus trust, which is an ethical value, is important in the persuasion process.

Because persuasion requires the conscious choice of ends and means, it involves ethics (Johannesen, 1996). The idea of choice requires that the persuasive process be conducted ethically. Communication that denies choice to audience members or to the persuader, then, becomes something else, such as coercion or violence. **Coercion** is the use of force to compel an audience member to do what a persuader desires. Persuaders who use coercion deny audience members the opportunity to freely identify with them. Fundamentally, coercion denies audience members the opportunity to exercise such basic human actions as reasoning, feeling, and thinking. **Violence** is the use of physical action to force compliance with a persuader. Again, violence removes thinking, feeling, and reasoning from the interaction and denies audience members the opportunity to utilize basic human characteristics. If we consider ethics to be grounded in the concept of choice, then persuasion is the best way to achieve the goal of identification.

coercion
the use of force to compel someone to do something

violence
the use of physical action to compel someone to do something

Finally, persuasion and ethics are linked because persuasion involves behavior that can be judged (Johannesen, 1996). The inclusion of language strategies and visual images in our definition of persuasion raises the issue of judgment. Persuasion is also a social process that involves more than one individual. Thus, the potential is present for one individual to judge the words and actions of another individual.

As the persuasion industry becomes more sophisticated, the lines between persuasion, coercion, and violence are becoming increasingly blurred. In this chapter—and throughout the book—we look at where the ethical lines are being drawn and how they have become blurred in the media age. The value guiding our discussion in this chapter and throughout the book is *choice:* Persuasive communication that allows individuals to consciously choose their beliefs and behaviors is ethical, whereas that which denies choice is unethical. Consider the discussion in Ethical Insights: Ethical Responsibilities of Persuaders and Audience Members as you think more about persuasion and ethics.

Who do you think plays a more significant role in ethical persuasion: the persuader or the audience member? Who is the more accountable?

We begin this chapter by exploring several ethical challenges for persuaders and audiences in the media age. Each of these challenges in some way impairs the audience member's ability to choose a course of action or a belief.

Ethical Challenges of the Media Age

The media age presents unique challenges to persuaders in the ethical arena. New technology, coupled with enhanced methods of reaching audiences, has created situations in which persuaders must closely examine their actions to determine if they are communicating ethically. In this section, we outline several specific challenges to persuaders and audience members in the media age. The concerns that we discuss here cut across a variety of persuasive contexts. Later in this chapter, we focus on ethical concerns that relate to specific contexts, such as advertising.

ETHICAL INSIGHTS

Ethical Responsibilities of Persuaders and Audience Members

As you consider these two scenarios, think about the ethical implications involved.

Imagine that you are shopping for a new car. You know very little about how to buy a car or what features may be useful in a new car. Therefore, you go to a dealer to learn something about the new cars on the market. The sales representative shows you a top-of-the-line model and explains why the car's features will be useful for you. The leather seats, for instance, will make the car worth more when you resell it in a few years. Convinced that the dealer has identified a good car for you, you purchase the automobile.

It could be argued that the dealer acted unethically by selling you a car that may include features that you do not need. The National Communication Association Credo for Ethical Communication (NCA 1999) states: "We promote communication climates of caring and mutual understanding that respect the unique needs and characteristics of individual communicators." In this instance the dealer may not have created a climate of "caring and mutual understanding." Likewise, failing to research available cars and to articulate what features you need may be an ethical lapse on your part.

Or imagine that today is election day. You feel that you should vote. You don't know much about the candidates, although you have seen television commercials and read newspapers articles about those running

for office. One candidate, in particular, has used a lot of advertising to sell his or her image. The commercials haven't discussed the candidate's policy proposals at any length. Because of the heavy advertising, you feel that this person should be elected. You go to the polls to vote for the person, despite knowing very little about where the candidate stands on the issues.

We could argue that it was unethical for this politician to inundate voters with image-based advertising without discussing his or her stand on policies. Likewise, we could argue that voters have a responsibility to investigate all of the candidates before they vote. The NCA Credo for Ethical Communication discusses the responsibilities of audience members for their communication. By not investigating the candidate fully, you may have failed your ethical duty.

As we will see in this chapter, ethical decisions are seldom without question. As you think about these scenarios, answer these questions:

1. Do you think the sales representative acted ethically in this situation? Or did the sales representative take advantage of your lack of knowledge about cars?

2. Was it ethical for this candidate to overwhelm you with advertising? What ethical responsibilities do you think voters have?

DECEPTION

For us to make sound decisions, it is important that the information on which we base our decisions be sound. Thus, persuaders who attempt to deceive their audiences undermine the persuasive process because they deny their audiences the information they need to make a choice. In the media age, persuaders can potentially deceive audiences as never before. By using digital imaging techniques—using computers to edit and print photographic images—or by taking advantage of an audience member's "information overload," persuaders often obscure the true meaning of their claims. It should be stated that this is sometimes not done intentionally, but the effect is that audience members are often confused by a persuader's message. Let's study some examples to understand a few of the ways in which persuaders mislead audiences in the media age. We discuss digital image manipulation in a later section of this chapter.

Technology can make it difficult for audience members to fully comprehend a persuader's message. In 2000, Mazda was fined $5.25 million by the

Federal Trade Commission (FTC) for misleading advertising about leasing of its cars. The information Mazda provided about leasing its cars was judged to be too small and shown on the television screen for too short a time for audience members to understand the leasing terms. The FTC also determined that sounds and images distracted viewers from the terms of the lease agreement. In the media age, it is important that persuaders not use technology to obscure important parts of their message.

Ethical implications also arise when persuaders seek to prove their arguments for audiences. When they use proof or language that is ethically suspect, persuaders do not provide audience members with the proper means by which to evaluate their message. Many weight-loss programs, for instance, use examples of individuals who lost weight by following the program. In recent years, the sandwich shop Subway used Jared S. Fogle as an example of someone who lost weight by eating Subway sandwiches. Fogle, who lost more than 200 pounds by eating Subway sandwiches, was shown to be an example of how others could lose weight by eating at Subway. As we'll discuss in a later chapter, proper use of examples requires that examples be representative and typical. Jared is not a typical example and although Subway noted in its advertising that other people may not experience the same results, their "Jared" campaign was clearly designed to promote the subs as a way for people to lose weight. Consequently, Subway's use of Jared is ethically questionable because the company relied on faulty reasoning that could potentially mislead consumers.

ACCESS

Persuasion can be a liberating experience for audience members. We form ideas of who we are through persuasion, and we come into contact with new ideas and ways of thinking. Mediated persuasion enables us to make political and personal decisions about matters that are important to us. Many of us may take mediated persuasion for granted. We are surrounded by televisions, radios, newspapers, and computers connected to the Internet. Yet, not all members of society have access to the media that bring us the important information on which we base our decisions. This unequal access to communication resources is often called the **digital divide.** When not all have access to media resources, a disparity develops between those who have technology and those who do not. Those who have access to communication technologies are more aware of their choices in the persuasion process. Those without access are not fully aware of their choices. Promotion and use of media resources are ethical concerns for this reason. We examine this topic in greater detail in Chapter 4. For now, let's examine two instances in which lack of access raises ethical problems for persuaders and audience members.

digital divide inequality of access to communication resources, such as telephones, computers, and the Internet

Although political candidates are not required to debate their ideas in front of large audiences, it has become customary for them to do so. In fact, the audience for a presidential debate is often the largest of any television show for the year. In 2000, presidential candidate George W. Bush's initial position on participating in campaign debates was that he would debate Al Gore three times, but only once in a format that would be televised by all the major networks. The other two debates would be held on single networks—NBC and

CNN. Bush, in effect, tried to limit the audience for the debates. In the case of the CNN debate, only those people who had access to cable—primarily voters in the upper and middle classes—would be able to hear the candidates discuss the important issues of the campaign. Bush's initial debate stance could be considered unethical because he sought to limit access to important political ideas. He later agreed to three debates sponsored by the Commission on Presidential Debates that were broadcast on all television networks.

The American Library Association (ALA) has taken steps to ensure that libraries that receive public funds, such as your local library, provide all users with equal access to information resources. ALA policies, for example, oppose the charging of user fees for the provision of information services (Chapin, 1999). That is, your local library should not charge you to use the Internet at its facility. In addition, libraries should not limit access to content that some may deem controversial. Betty Chapin argues, "Information retrieved or utilized electronically should be considered constitutionally protected unless determined otherwise by a court with appropriate jurisdiction" (p. 21). The ALA has created ethical standards by which librarians can help to ensure equality of access for all audience members.

OPPRESSION

Some ethicists have argued that the very nature of persuasion creates certain ideas about what is normal or acceptable in society. In Chapter 1, we said that one of the objectives for persuaders today is to make their products or ideas valuable. The result is that some other product or idea is seen as less valuable. Those individuals who use products or have ideas that do not meet the persuaders' definitions are then marginalized because they do not fit in with society. In this sense, all of us are denied information from which to make decisions and choices. When persuasion determines our values and beliefs, it is difficult to step outside of those values to make careful choices.

Advertising, for instance, is most effective when it creates and maintains cultural values. Jean Kilbourne (1999) discusses advertising's effects on how we see ourselves and our world. She writes, "Advertising often sells a great deal more than products. It sells values, images, and concepts of love and sexuality, romance, success, and, perhaps most important, normalcy. To a great extent, it tells us who we are and who we should be" (p. 74). Kilbourne traces specific effects of advertising on audiences, focusing on such subjects as relationships, eating disorders, and cigarette smoking. She directly addresses the ethics of power and advertising when she discusses advertising's relationship to sex and violence. Kilbourne writes, "Sex in advertising is pornographic because it dehumanizes and objectifies people" (p. 271). Advertising fosters a culture, says Kilbourne, that creates and maintains certain attitudes and values, such as that women are valuable only as sex objects.

In another way, persuasion is fundamentally related to power. Persuaders seek to use words and images in a way that will give them power over an audience and other persuaders. Often, they disempower some group to achieve success. Discrimination and sexual harassment in the workplace remain ethical problems related to power and persuasion. In 1996, Texaco officials, in closed-door meetings that were secretly tape-recorded, referred to African American employees as "black jelly beans" and "niggers." When the tapes were made public, Texaco faced a public backlash, suspended the managers involved, and instituted diversity programs. Equal opportunity laws and sexual harassment laws have been designed to force compliance with ethical standards related to language, persuasion, and power.

PRIVACY

When persuaders obtain information through audience analysis, they have ethical responsibilities to protect that information from others who would use it without discretion. Our discussion in Chapter 5 reveals the extent to which persuaders delve into the attitudes of audience members. When persuaders obtain information about us without our knowledge, they may ingratiate themselves with us in a way that undermines our decision-making ability. In other words, we lose our ability to choose actions and beliefs when persuaders target us with highly sensitive personal information. We are often persuaded without knowing that we are being persuaded. In Chapter 5, we consider an example of a company that lost control over information about its clients. For now, let's consider several ways that audience members lose their privacy in the media age.

In September 2000, Amazon.com announced a new privacy policy that would view consumer information—such as credit card information, addresses, and consumer preferences—as a "business asset" that it might sell or transfer to other businesses. In the event that Amazon.com is acquired by another business, the consumer information it has collected would likely be transferred to the acquiring business. Under the new policy, consumers no longer have the choice to "opt out" of sharing information with another business. Consumer groups, such as TRUSTe, reacted negatively to the new policy because they believe that businesses must provide choice to consumers with regard to their personal information. Amazon.com insists that its new policy provides more information to consumers about what it might do with their information, but ethical questions remain over how persuaders should protect the information they obtain about their audiences. Investigate the privacy of your personal information by completing the Internet Activity: Protecting Your Privacy Online.

CONFLICT OF INTEREST

The vast web of influence that we have said characterizes persuasion today also makes it difficult for audience members to fully appreciate the role of persuaders in the persuasive process. The news media depend on sources for stories. These sources, such as politicians, depend on news reporting for publicity. As a result, each has a vested interest in how reporting takes place. We are not always aware of these interests. In addition, the large media mergers in recent years have made it difficult to understand who is controlling news and entertainment programming.

INTERNET ACTIVITY

Protecting Your Privacy Online

When you shop online, you turn over a great deal of personal information to the online retailer. At some point, you probably click on a button to accept the terms of use for the company. Without realizing it, you may be giving that company a great deal of discretion in what they do with your personal information. Visit your favorite online retailer or the website for a store where you'd like to shop. Or, check out the website for Amazon.com. Find a link to the company's privacy policy and read their policy. Did anything in the policy surprise you? Will you take any precautions the next time you use the company's online services? Are you generally comfortable that the company will protect your privacy?

During the Iraq war, the Department of Defense and the major news organization developed a plan to embed reporters with frontline troops. The reporters would train, sleep, and eat with military troops while reporting on the war's developments. In return, the reporters agreed not to report exactly where the troops were stationed and their mission. You probably remember seeing images of troops engaged in gunfights or of the troops traveling across the desert. Skeptics of the plan feared that the reporters would become too friendly with the troops and fail to provide honest coverage of the war. Others worried that the reporters would report troop movements, endangering their lives and mission. Although there will be much analysis of the program, CNN's Wolf Blitzer (2003) reports that his initial skepticism about embedded reporters "wasn't justified." He argues that the arrangement "worked rather well for all concerned." Still, it's important to remember to closely analyze news coverage so that you understand the relationships between reporters and their subjects.

Medical reporting, too, faces the danger of hiding potential conflicts of interest. Recent reporting about Celebrex, a drug developed to treat osteoarthritis and rheumatoid arthritis, relied on the expert opinions of several doctors. The doctors downplayed the side effects of the drug on such shows as *Today* and *Dateline NBC*. What viewers did not fully appreciate from the coverage was that the doctors who were interviewed had been paid by G. D. Searle, the company that produces Celebrex, to test the drug. Other media sources, including the *Wall Street Journal*, found that Celebrex had been linked to 10 deaths and 11 cases of gastrointestinal hemorrhages during the first three months the drug was on the market (Lieberman, 1999). The point is not that NBC reporters or the doctors they interviewed lied about the drug, but rather that their bias was neither questioned nor fully exposed. Persuaders should have an ethical responsibility to disclose their association with the ideas they communicate.

Think of additional examples of the ethical challenges of the media age. What do you think the persuader in each of your examples could have done to be more ethical?

Approaches to Ethical Decision Making

Given the challenge posed by persuasion practices, theorists have identified several criteria, or sets of standards, by which persuaders and audience members can make ethical judgments. It is important that when they make ethical judgments, persuaders and audience members justify their reasons to others. The approaches that we examine here have been used by philosophers, scholars, and practitioners to make ethical decisions about persuasion. Each approach specifies a value or set of values that should guide an ethical decision. Often these approaches become operationalized in a **code of ethics,** which is a formal statement by an organization of its ethical standards. We'll examine codes of ethics later. For now, let's understand some of the guiding principles by which persuaders make ethical decisions and attempt to justify those decisions. First, though, we must explore the various arguments for universal and situational ethical perspectives.

code of ethics
an organization's formal statement of its ethical standards

UNIVERSAL VERSUS SITUATIONAL ETHICS

The philosopher Immanuel Kant argued that ethical standards are categorical imperatives—that is, that ethical standards are universal and do not vary with the person, situation, or context. By "categorical imperative," Kant meant that there are some acts that are always right and some acts that are always wrong. In the media age, people have a variety of beliefs about which ethical standards are valid and which are not. Members of contemporary culture have many different, and often conflicting, values. The use of rigid, universal ethical standards is not readily accepted in today's world. Yet the appeal of such standards is strong. As we examine the National Communication Association's Credo for Ethical Communication later in this chapter, you will see that certain ethical standards, such as honesty, respect, and human dignity, are widely accepted within the communication discipline.

John Stuart Mill provides us with a different view of ethical standards. Where Kant's standard is universal, Mill's standard is determined by the situation. Mill's principle of utility suggests that what is ethical is that which produces the greatest public good. Ethical standards may vary depending on the situation. For instance, in many cases, the president of the United States should not lie to the American people. In particular, when running for office, presidential candidates should not lie about their record or the records of their opponents. Likewise, when trying to have new legislation passed, the president should not lie about its presumed effects. In some situations, however, it may be desirable for the president to lie. In times of war, for instance, we do not expect our president to be forthright about the timing of attacks. To be honest at these times would endanger the lives of those involved in the mission as well as jeopardize the mission and the good that might come of it. Mill's principle of utility, then, acknowledges ambiguity as to what is ethical. It provides opportunity for public discussion about what is ethical.

THE FIRST AMENDMENT

One universal ethical standard that we recognize today is the freedom of speech guaranteed by the First Amendment to the United States Constitution. The nation's founders viewed this amendment as a way to protect our democracy.

This amendment influences how we think about news reporting, political communication, persuasive movements, and other manifestations of persuasion. The First Amendment is used by persuaders to justify unpopular communication.

News reporters argue that the First Amendment gives them the power to make ethical decisions about how they present the news to the public. This protection allows the news media to aggressively question government officials about corruption; at the same time, this freedom allows the news media to determine the news of the day. Politicians use their First Amendment rights to speak openly about issues that may not be popular with the current government or with the people. Freedom of speech allows political persuaders the opportunity to question the nature of our government. Freedom of speech has been an important way for members of persuasive movements to petition the government for changes in voting, employment, and housing laws. By holding legal protests, such as the Million Mom March—in favor of gun control—or the civil rights March on Washington—a motivator of sweeping changes to U.S. voting laws in the 1960s—persuaders gather large numbers of people in support of change.

This is not to say that freedom of speech is guaranteed in every communication situation. The Supreme Court has ruled that freedom of speech should be seen as subordinate to other ethical standards, such as respect for human life. It is illegal, for instance, to shout "Fire" in a crowded theater because such a statement would cause harm to individuals. Likewise, selling or obtaining child pornography is illegal because this type of communication infringes on the rights of children. Thus, although freedom of speech is often seen as a universal ethical standard, there are instances in which other values are determined to be more important.

RICHARD JOHANNESEN

Johannesen (1996) provides one of the most comprehensive discussions of ethical standards in the communication discipline. He identifies a set of standards that is often used to make ethical decisions. We will survey his discussion of three ethical standards.

Political Perspective   One way that we can make ethical decisions is by assessing the degree to which a behavior reflects the values and procedures of a culture's political system. Johannesen (1996) outlines several characteristics of the American political system that serve as guides for ethical decisions. Our political system relies on the rationality of its citizens to make decisions, cast votes, and govern effectively. That is, reason and logic are fundamental tenets of our system. Thus, persuasion that undercuts the rationality of decision making can be judged unethical. Consider the political scenario described earlier in the box Ethical Insights: Ethical Responsibilities of Persuaders and Audience Members. From it, you might conclude that an overwhelming amount of political advertising is an unethical attempt to short-circuit people's rationality. That is, a candidate who structures a campaign knowing that people base their vote more on name recognition than on consideration of the issues is not promoting the public's ability to make a rational electoral choice.

Johannesen outlines a set of procedures inherent to our political system that reflects the ethical concerns we have just discussed. For instance, unrestricted debate and discussion ensure that all who wish to influence the political process have the opportunity to speak and be heard. In addition, legal procedures exist to protect those who wish to influence the political system. The press also has the freedom to question our political leaders and the decisions they make. From the political perspective, ethical persuasion upholds and reflects the values and procedures of the American political system.

Human-Nature Perspective   The human-nature perspective on ethical standards focuses on the essence of human nature. This approach argues that the characteristics that separate us from animals can serve as the basis for making ethical judgments. Thus, communication that reflects the importance of reasoning, symbol use, and value judgments is ethical. Communication that denies the importance of these concepts is unethical. Persuasion that dehumanizes an individual is judged to be unethical. The use of sexist or racist language is often seen as unethical because such language dehumanizes its subject. Persuaders who refer to women as "chicks," "foxes," or "babes" view them as something less than thinking, rational, mature adults. Labeling African Americans "mud people" strips them of their humanity.

Dialogical Perspectives   The dialogical perspective argues that ethical human communication should reflect the values of a dialogue, instead of a monologue. Johannesen (1996) explains that honesty, inclusion, confirmation of the worth of the other individual, mutual equality, and a supportive climate characterize a dialogue. A monologue, on the other hand, focuses on the needs of one communicator and reduces the opportunity for feedback from the audience. A dialogue, Johannesen argues, encourages audience member and persuader to make a choice, which we have said is an important part of ethical persuasion. In the media age, we are too often confronted with persuaders who seek to have a monologue with us. Advertising that is repetitive and mindless, for instance, does not encourage a response from us. The most ethical, and perhaps the most effective, persuasion involves the audience member in the coproduction of identification.

Which of Johannesen's ethical standards are most persuasive to you? Which do you use most regularly to make ethical judgments?

The Making of Ethical Judgments

Although we have just discussed several ethical standards, ethical decisions are seldom clear-cut. We are often forced to make ethical decisions because two value systems, or ethical standards, conflict. For instance, cigarette companies have the right to advertise their product because of First Amendment guarantees and the value our culture places on free-market capitalism. On the other hand, tobacco advertising may be seen as unethical when it targets children, who cannot legally purchase tobacco products. When such a conflict arises, we use persuasion to convince others that some behavior is ethical or that it is not. Like other concepts in our study of persuasion, ethical standards are created and ethical judgments are often made through the persuasion process, as illustrated in Figure 1.2. Ethical judgments are made on a variety of levels: at the cultural level, organizational level, and personal level. As with other aspects of persuasion today, media play a large role in shaping public discussions of ethics. Persuaders often decide for themselves what they consider ethical and unethical. In some cases, organizations make unilateral decisions about what each considers appropriate; in other cases, some organization that has the power to enforce ethical judgments determines the outcome. At other times, court decisions determine the final outcome. In the examples that follow, we will see how persuaders make ethical judgments.

In some cases, persuaders make ethical judgments on their own without resorting to public debate. In 1999, Calvin Klein decided to drop advertising for children's underwear after New York City Mayor Rudy Giuliani and other critics complained that the ads looked pornographic. The ads featured two boys sitting on a couch, one wearing boxers, the other briefs. Critics complained that the ads would appeal to pedophiles. Klein pulled the ads, acknowledging that the public response raised issues the company had not considered.

Organizations of persuaders often adopt codes of ethics to help their members, and the public at large, understand the various interests involved in ethical decisions. Although grounded in ethical theory, codes of ethics such as these are at best guideposts and cannot serve as the final answer for those making ethical judgments. However, such codes do have the power to influence *how* organizational members make ethical decisions. We discuss several specific codes of ethics in later sections of this chapter, concluding by examining the Credo for Ethical Communication created and adopted by the National Communication Association.

When persuaders make ethical judgments that others believe are wrong, they are often called upon to change their position. Ethical decisions are often discussed widely throughout culture, with many people offering their ethical judgments. Individuals, organizations, and government agencies are the persuaders in these situations. The news media often facilitate the discussion, influencing how the public thinks about ethics. Although there is usually no formal vote on the question, public opinion polling, boycotts, or organizational decisions often determine the outcome of these discussions. Let's examine an example to better understand how our culture passes judgment on ethical decisions.

Critics of Dr. Laura Schlesinger, a self-help radio talk show host, made ethical challenges against her following statements she made on her radio show regarding homosexuals. Dr. Laura called homosexuals "deviants" who are "biological errors." At the time, Schlesinger was one of today's most popular talk show hosts, being heard on more than 400 stations. Her newspaper column appeared in more than 100 papers. The protests against Dr. Laura became louder when she was signed to host a television talk show beginning in September 2000.

Gay and lesbian organizations have been the major opponents of Dr. Laura and her show. The organization GLAAD (Gay and Lesbian Alliance against Defamation) led the protests. The group picketed Paramount Studios, the company producing Dr. Laura's television show, and took out advertising in trade journals urging companies not to advertise on the show. A website called StopDr.Laura.com received more than 3 million hits a week in early 2000. As a result of the public outcry against Dr. Laura, advertisers, including Proctor and Gamble, pulled their advertising—$2 million worth—from the television show. United Airlines, Xerox, and Toys "R" Us canceled advertising on her radio show. Formal organizations also weighed in with their judgments. The Canadian Broadcast Standards Council determined that Dr. Laura's claims regarding homosexuals violated the Canadian Association of Broadcasters' code of ethics. As a result, radio stations airing her show also had to air announcements notifying the public of the council's decision. The show was dropped from Canadian stations. Dr. Laura later apologized for her word choice in referring to homosexuals as "deviants." Dr. Laura's career (her television talk show was canceled in early 2001) and credibility suffered from what some perceive to be unethical communication on her part.

When public protest is not successful at influencing an organization's judgment, critics of the organization can pursue a variety of avenues to bring about the decision they want. In some cases, a regulatory agency, such as the Federal Trade Commission or the Federal Election Commission, determines what is ethical. In other situations, a lawsuit may be brought against the ethically suspect organization.

The FTC is charged with regulating trade in the United States. Thus, its responsibilities include identifying ethically suspect persuasive practices used in commerce, such as in advertising. The FTC recently warned retailers Buy.com, Office Depot, and Value America that advertising computers with a $400 rebate was potentially misleading (Teinowitz, 2000). The advertising did not make clear that the rebate was valid only when consumers signed up for three years of Internet service. The ads also did not make clear when consumers could expect their rebate. In some cases, the rebates took 17 weeks to arrive. In this situation, the FTC simply warned the ethically suspect organizations. The FTC also has the power to fine organizations that do not comply with ethical communication practices, as was the case in the Mazda example discussed earlier.

In some cases, lawsuits filed against a persuader cause ethical decisions to be made in court or to be settled before the case reaches trial. In recent years, tobacco companies have been accused of using unethical advertising to target cigarettes at children and youth. State attorneys general banded together in 1999 to sue tobacco companies for this advertising. The result was a $206 billion settlement between the major tobacco companies and 46 states. In addition to the monetary settlement, tobacco companies agreed not to target their advertising to youth, to stop sponsoring certain athletic events, and to remove billboard advertising.

At the most fundamental level, every audience member is involved in ethical decision making. We may choose to vote for a candidate we determine is

Describe an ethical judgment that you have made recently. How did you express your judgment? What was the result?

INTERNET ACTIVITY

Resolving Ethical Issues

As we have just read, resolving ethical issues takes place on several levels by many individuals. One of the best ways that you can take part in discussions about ethical issues is to read media coverage of ethical topics. Read an issue of the Ethics Newsline, published by the Institute for Global Ethics, http://www.globalethics.org. Choose a persuasion-related ethical issue discussed in the newsletter, and read the coverage of that issue. Describe how you think the issue will be resolved. Will an individual or organization take action? Will the government intervene? How will the public be involved?

ethical and against someone who we believe is unethical. We may give our business to an organization that we think is ethical or avoid businesses we believe are unethical. The Internet Activity: Resolving Ethical Issues, has you think more closely about ethical decision-making.

Persuasion and the Public Sphere

As you can see, ethical decisions are often disputed in the public arena. Some theorists lament the state of mediated persuasion because it does not allow for the free and open expression of ideas. One such theorist is the German philosopher Jurgen Habermas. He set out to develop a theory that would lead to a vibrant "public sphere," in which all members of society could openly and rationally discuss issues that were important to them. This open discussion would result in symbol sharing, which would maximize the possibilities for choice and identification. Habermas was critical, however, of the domination of public discussion by particular interests—namely, the interests of capitalism. He saw this domination as inhibiting the audience's ability to choose whether to identify with a persuader or not. Let's examine Habermas's theory more closely.

Habermas explains that society is a mix of three interests: work, interaction, and power. *Work* produces goods or services. It is a technical interest, says Habermas, in that technology is used to accomplish practical and efficient results. *Interaction* is the use of language and other symbolic communication systems to achieve social cooperation. Examples of interaction include conferences, family relations, and speeches. The third interest is *power,* or the ability to be free from domination. Each of the interests somehow mediates between human experience and the natural world. Ideally, society is a mix of all three interests, with each influencing individuals equally. Habermas is concerned that in capitalistic societies, technical interests dominate discussions in the public sphere. That is, our political and social discussions are dominated by the ideology of those who produce goods and services.

To free ourselves from the domination of the technical interests, we must be competent in our use of communication, says Habermas. His theory of universal pragmatics describes how individuals can reflect on their language use and use rational argument to emancipate themselves from the technical interests. Habermas writes, "The task of universal pragmatics is to identify and reconstruct universal conditions of possible understanding" (1979, p. 1). Habermas focuses on how persuaders can identify with their audiences through the use of rational discourse.

At the core of universal pragmatics are speech acts and how those speech acts can be challenged to come to rational understanding. A **speech act** is a statement that accomplishes something or does something. A promise is an example of a speech act. When you make a promise, you enter into an implicit contract by which you agree to do something in exchange for something else. Habermas (1979) outlines three types of speech acts: constatives, regulatives, and avowals. *Constatives* are used to assert the truth or falsity of something. When you say that it is cold outside, you are using a constative. Constatives reflect the cognitive use of language because they describe something that is happening in the world. *Regulatives* are used to influence someone else. You use regulatives when you make a promise or issue a command. Regulatives are examples of the interpersonal dimension of language. We use regulatives to manage the interpersonal relationships in our lives. *Avowals* express the speaker's feelings or emotions. The statement "I am happy" is an example. Avowals reflect the expressive use of language. We use first-person sentences to disclose our internal condition to others (Habermas, 1979). Table 3.1 outlines the types of speech acts in this theory.

> **speech act**
> a statement that accomplishes something or does something

Let's consider an advertisement that is part of the "got milk?" campaign to understand the speech acts involved. You may be familiar with this campaign. Usually, a celebrity is featured wearing a milk moustache. A memorable caption that reflects the celebrity is used, and the got milk? slogan is displayed at the bottom of the page. Usually a factual statement is used to persuade the reader to drink milk. One particular ad featured actress and model Andie Mac-Dowell. She is pictured in a country scene with the words "Beauty mark" printed next to her face. Toward the bottom, readers are advised, "Milk has vitamin A and niacin to help keep skin looking smooth and healthy." The famous slogan, "got milk?" is again used to entice readers to drink milk.

We can say that the ad contains each of the speech acts identified by Habermas. The ad uses a *constative,* or truth claim, when it says that "Milk has vitamin A and niacin to help keep skin looking smooth and healthy." The ad also uses a *regulative,* or command, when it asks the reader "got milk?" The overall tone of the ad is also making a command of readers to drink milk, or at least to consider doing so. Finally, the image of MacDowell suggests an *avowal,* that she is happy and content. Although she doesn't explicitly make a statement about her internal state, readers are expected to imply her feelings from her facial expressions and body posture.

Constatives, regulatives, and avowals must meet thematic validity standards for accurate communication to occur (Habermas, 1979). Constatives must be *truthful*. Habermas (1979) says that the intention of the speaker does not matter. What matters is the "truth of the proposition" (p. 58). In the case of the milk ad, we should ask if milk really does help keep skin looking smooth and healthy. Regulatives must be *appropriate* given the interpersonal relation-

Table 3.1 Types of Speech Acts

Speech act	Definition	Evaluation standard
Constative	Assert truth or falsity	Truthfulness
Regulative	Use to influence	Appropriateness
Avowal	Express internal state	Sincerity

ship between the speaker and the listener. A student, for example, cannot demand that an instructor give a certain grade for an assignment. Such a command is not appropriate to the relationship. In the milk ad, we might question the command that we drink milk. Is this command appropriate for the nation's milk providers to ask of the general population? Avowals must be *sincere* expressions of a speaker's feelings. If I say that I am happy, that statement must be a genuine reflection of my mood. Since we will never be able to tell if MacDowell is indeed happy in the milk ad, we might read some more about her to learn if she is, generally, happy and if she drinks milk.

Habermas fears a society in which audience members take a persuader's words for granted. He argues that audience members should question what a persuader says and does. To question the statements of a source, we engage in **discourse.** There are different types of discourse, depending on which type of statement—constative, regulative, or avowal—is being questioned. Sincerity is usually not resolved through discourse, but rather through continued communicative action. When we doubt the sincerity of a speaker, for instance, we examine nonverbals or we ask questions that probe sincerity. Habermas (1973) argues, "It will be shown in time, whether the other side is 'in truth and honestly' participating or is only pretending to engage in communicative action and is in fact behaving strategically" (p. 18). In the case of constatives or regulatives, however, we turn to discourse.

Constatives, or truth claims, are resolved through theoretic discourse, which uses evidence to support arguments. *Theoretic discourse* is the search for arguments to support a statement concerning truth; it is a "claim of validity" (Habermas, 1973, p. 18). The milk ad, as we have said, claims that drinking milk, because it contains Vitamin A, will lead to smooth and healthy skin. A variety of studies contradict this claim by saying that drinking milk may lead to acne, in teenagers especially, and bone fractures. Theoretic discourse would use these contradictory studies to refute the truth claim presented in the ad. Additionally, we might point out that the picture of MacDowell—which is used to support the claim about drinking milk and smooth skin—is potentially retouched, so it does not provide an accurate form of support for the claim.

Practical discourse is used when appropriateness is questioned. Habermas wrote that practical discourse offers justifications for the use of regulatives, statements that are used to influence others. We might question the appropriateness of the milk ad's command to drink milk by pointing out that many readers of the ad are lactose intolerant and drinking milk will make them sick. According to the National Digestive Diseases Information Clearinghouse,

discourse
a statement that challenges a speech act

Table 3.2 Types of Discourse

Related speech act	Discourse type	Definition
Constative	Theoretic discourse	Evidence for a claim
Regulative	Practical discourse	Justifies statement of influence
Avowal	None—use direct communication action	

30 to 50 million Americans are lactose intolerant, including 75 percent of African Americans and Native Americans and nearly 90 percent of Asian Americans. If we were to use discourse, we would question the appropriateness of the ad's request that we drink milk because it does not make the side effects of drinking milk known to its audience. Table 3.2 outlines the basic types of discourse.

As arguers attempt to resolve their differences over truth claims, they may not agree on standards for their discussion. Thus, they turn to *metatheoretical discourse* to argue about what constitutes good evidence or reasonable standards. There is a great deal of evidence about drinking milk. The perspective of universal pragmatics seeks to have discussion about which standards are appropriate to use in discussions about truthfulness and reasonableness. If we were to discuss drinking milk, we would want to discuss the source and methods of research used to generate evidence about milk. For instance, we might agree that studies done of diverse populations by unbiased third-party researchers would be the best to use to establish what is true about drinking milk.

Finally, speakers may resort to *metaethical discourse* to argue about the nature of knowledge itself. Metaethical discourse is a philosophical argument about how knowledge is generated. Thomas A. McCarthy (1978) explains, "For here we must consider the question, what should count as knowledge?" (p. 305). Traditionally, knowledge is produced by scientific inquiry. We might assume that evidence from scientific study is the most reliable, but Habermas would caution us to also consider other ways that knowledge is created. You might be lactose intolerant and know from personal experience that drinking milk makes you sick. No scientific study would be necessary to prove this and, to you, scientific analysis of the benefits of drinking milk would be a flawed way to generate knowledge about the topic.

The point of this example is not that drinking milk is good or bad or that the got milk? campaign is unethical. What is important, from the perspective of universal pragmatics, is that we are able to freely discuss and debate the truth claims, reasonability of making requests, and sincerity of advertising in contemporary culture.

Keep in mind that Habermas's goal is a vibrant public sphere that fosters ethical communication. To achieve this goal, communication must meet the three standards of the **ideal speech situation,** a theoretical construct that helps us envision a society free from controlling interests. First, the ideal speech situation requires freedom of speech. All individuals must be able to freely express their ideas. Second, all individuals must have equal access to speaking. Finally, the norms and obligations of society must be equally distributed. One group in

ideal speech situation a theoretical construct that helps us envision a society free from controlling interests

THINKING CRITICALLY

Ethics and the Ideal Speech Situation

A teacher at Naperville North (Illinois) High School was recently fired for sexually abusing a female student of the school. Student reporters for the school newspaper judged the event to be newsworthy, researched the story, and wrote a 385-word article for the school newspaper. School administrators, however, told the students that they could not print the story. A large blank space was instead left in the paper, and the paper's editor wrote an editorial criticizing the administration's decision. The students soon gained national media attention for the issue and the administration allowed the article to be printed. The article was also displayed on www.bolt.com, an Internet site that prints banned articles from school newspapers. Following discussions with the district's school board, a committee established guidelines for what could and could not be printed in the school newspaper. Although the final result may allow students at Naperville North to exercise their voices, student reporters at colleges and high schools often encounter resistance from school administrators when making editorial decisions.

Jurgen Habermas might claim that the interests of school image and reputation dominated other interests at this school, including the students' right to free speech. Initially, the situation did not appear to reflect Habermas's theory of the ideal speech situation. In a few pages, we will discuss the Society of Professional Journalists ethics guidelines, which include this statement: "Journalists should be free of obligation to any interest other than the public's right to know" (SPJ, 1996). This statement reflects Habermas's ideal speech situation, but in practice, this guideline may sometimes be difficult to follow. Student journalists like those at Naperville North High School may find it particularly difficult to free themselves from other interests.

Consider Habermas's ideas as you answer the following questions:

1. What responsibilities do student reporters have to cover school news? What responsibilities do administrators have to protect privacy and the school's reputation? What should be done when these interests compete with each other?

2. How does the Internet help to realize Habermas's goal? How might the Internet reflect the interests of the dominant group in a society?

3. Using Habermas's theory, what are some guidelines you would suggest to the Naperville North school board as it considers boundaries for the student newspaper?

Consider a current discussion that is occurring in society. Does the discussion resemble Habermas's goal of the ideal speech situation? Do all parties have an equal chance to communicate? Can they do so freely? Are expectations about what is true and false shared by all involved in the discussion? How might the discussion be improved to give more voices the opportunity to participate?

society must not dominate the speaking situation. Habermas calls for us to use rational communication, in the form of universal pragmatics, to restore the public sphere and allow individuals to make free choices concerning identification with a persuader. As you read about the school newspaper at Naperville North High School in Thinking Critically: Ethics and the Ideal Speech Situation, consider Habermas's theory and how students and administrators at the school can work together to serve the interests of the school population.

Postman (1985) argues that although there are distinct shifts in a culture's preference for one medium over another, the existing media are never completely displaced. Thus, new forms of media challenge the knowledge base of existing media. The intellect produced by television, for instance, is contradicted by that produced by writing, for instance. Jurgen Habermas's theory helps us to understand how we can use language, or discourse, to challenge the reality created by electronic media. For example, the organization Adbusters asks us to question the relationships we have with advertisers. (The website for this organization can be found by looking on this book's website.)

We next discuss the specific ethical challenges posed by several persuasive contexts and examine ethical codes that are relevant to these contexts. Following this discussion, we look at the integrated Credo for Ethical Communication developed by the National Communication Association. We will refer to these codes throughout this book as we discuss relevant ethical issues in each chapter.

Visual Images and Ethics

The use of images by persuaders has raised ethical concerns. With today's digital technology, images can easily be manipulated to serve the ends of unscrupulous persuaders. Experts believe that it is possible to digitally alter a photograph without leaving any sign of what has been done (Grumet, 1997). In 2000, officials at the University of Wisconsin–Madison digitally inserted an image of an African American student into a picture of Caucasian students on the cover of the school's admissions booklet. The student's photograph was inserted to give the appearance of diversity. When students found out about the digital insertion and raised questions, the school pulled the booklet and reprinted it at a cost of $64,000.

In Chapters 6 and 10, we address the use of digital image insertion in advertising and other programming. This practice alters an image so that readers or viewers see a new product. In Chapter 6, we look at how CBS digitally inserts its logo on buildings and other backgrounds for its news shows. In Chapter 10, we examine how Dannon manipulates photographs of celebrities to make it look as if they are holding Dannon yogurt containers. Before we consider these examples, let's examine the code of ethics of the National Press Photographers Association (n.d.). The code addresses these and other areas of image use.

National Press Photographers Association's Code of Ethics

1. The practice of photojournalism, both as a science and art, is worthy of the very best thought and effort of those who enter into it as a profession.

2. Photojournalism affords an opportunity to serve the public that is equalled by few other vocations and all members of the profession should strive by example and influence to maintain high standards of ethical conduct free of mercenary considerations of any kind.

3. It is the individual responsibility of every photojournalist at all times to strive for pictures that report truthfully, honestly and objectively.

4. As journalists, we believe that credibility is our greatest asset. In documentary photojournalism, it is wrong to alter the content of a photograph in any way (electronically or in the darkroom) that deceives the public. We believe the guidelines for fair and accurate reporting should be the criteria for judging what may be done electronically to a photograph.

5. Business promotion in its many forms is essential, but untrue statements of any nature are not worthy of a professional photojournalist and we condemn any such practice.

6. It is our duty to encourage and assist all members of our profession, individually and collectively, so that the quality of photojournalism may constantly be raised to higher standards.

7. It is the duty of every photojournalist to work to preserve all freedom-of-the-press rights recognized by law and to work to protect and expand freedom-of-access to all sources of news and visual information.

8. Our standards of business dealings, ambitions and relations shall have in them a note of sympathy for our common humanity and shall always require us to take into consideration our highest duties as members of society. In every situation in our business life, in every responsibility that comes before us, our chief thought shall be to fulfill that responsibility and discharge that duty so that when each of us is finished we shall have endeavored to lift the level of human ideals and achievement higher than we found it.

9. No Code of Ethics can prejudge every situation, thus common sense and good judgment are required in applying ethical principles.

Political Persuasion

Politicians and political consultants face ethical challenges as they persuade voters to support a particular candidate. Because the stakes are so high in a political campaign, it is necessary that political persuaders act ethically when they communicate with the public. Let's highlight some of the ethical challenges faced by political persuaders.

Political consultants must decide whether to work for a particular candidate or issue. Consultants often must choose whether they should work for someone with whom they do not agree. It is not uncommon, for instance, for a pro-choice consultant to work for a pro-life candidate. In these situations, consultants must choose between their personal ideas of what is right or wrong and their need to work to support themselves and possibly a family. Consultants often address this ethical dilemma by concluding that the candidate for whom they will work is the best one in the campaign and will make a good leader, despite the differences of opinion between them on some matters.

A second ethical gray area in politics is that campaign laws are ambiguous or nonexistent. Dennis W. Johnson and Edward P. Grefe (1997) say there are no real penalties for lying in a campaign. If caught, the consultant and the candidate may both lose credibility and the candidate may lose the election, but no criminal or civil penalties are imposed on those who lie in political campaigns, except when rules against libel or slander apply. Further, many election laws are ambiguous, such as current laws regarding "soft money." In recent years, the line between political party–sponsored advertising for a candidate (which is illegal) and advertising for or against an issue (which is legal) has been fuzzy. As a result, candidates and consultants are forced to rely on their own ideas about ethics to make campaign decisions. Legislators have passed reforms that would clarify the soft money issue, but the usefulness of this legislation is uncertain.

Finally, the American public questions the relationship between consultant and candidate because political consultants have no accountability to the voters (Johnson & Grefe, 1997). The candidate can be voted out of office or impeached, but the influence of the consultant on public policy goes unchecked.

For instance, consider the example of former President Bill Clinton's advisor Dick Morris. Although many members of Clinton's administration had to be approved by Congress, Morris was simply hired by Clinton. Many observers believe that Morris exercised a great deal of influence over Clinton—influence that was difficult to detect and difficult to question. We like to know what forces influence political decisions. Morris's involvement slipped under the radar of many political observers, causing them to question whether he was influential in several Clinton administration policies. In fact, Morris used the codename "Charlie" to conceal his identity when he called Clinton.

To respond to some of the ethical challenges we have discussed, the American Association of Political Consultants (n.d.) has established a code of ethics for its members:

American Association of Political Consultants' Code of Ethics

- I will not indulge in any activity which would corrupt or degrade the practice of political consulting.
- I will treat my colleagues and clients with respect and never intentionally injure their professional or personal reputations.
- I will respect the confidence of my clients and not reveal confidential or privileged information obtained during our professional relationship.
- I will use no appeal to voters which is based on racism, sexism, religious intolerance or any form of unlawful discrimination and will condemn those who use such practices. In turn, I will work for equal voting rights and privileges for all citizens.
- I will refrain from false or misleading attacks on an opponent or member of his or her family and will do everything in my power to prevent others from using such tactics.
- I will document accurately and fully any criticism of an opponent or his or her record.
- I will be honest in my relationship with the news media and candidly answer questions when I have the authority to do so.
- I will use any funds I receive from my clients, or on behalf of my clients, only for those purposes invoiced in writing.
- I will not support any individual or organization which resorts to practices forbidden by this code.

Advertising

Each year, the National Advertising Division (NAD) of the Better Business Bureau investigates 100 to 150 cases of potentially unethical advertising. Many companies comply with the decisions made by the NAD, but the Federal Trade Commission is the ultimate enforcement authority concerning unethical advertising. Advertising is fraught with ethical decisions and dilemmas, in part because rules regarding ethical advertising are themselves vague. Let's examine a few ethical issues related to advertising.

Advertisers often use a spokesperson to endorse a product, service, or idea. When we see someone saying that he or she uses a product and that it works well, we may be persuaded to purchase the product. Quite often, however, the actor or actress in the commercial does not use the product—and does not have to. The FTC requires only that celebrities who endorse a product or service actually use what they are selling. Anonymous actors or actresses do not have to use the product they sell to us, a practice that is potentially misleading.

puffery
use of a claim that has no substantive meaning but that may nonetheless be persuasive

Puffery, use of a claim that has no substantive meaning but that may nonetheless be persuasive (Savan, 2000), is another ethical concern in advertising. The FTC cannot take action against advertisers who use puffery despite the fact that it may mislead audience members, because the claims these advertisers make don't mean anything. When an advertiser claims its sports car is "sexy," consumers may be persuaded to purchase the car because of this image, but the advertiser cannot be held responsible because "sexy" doesn't mean anything substantive. Likewise, use of the term "state of the art" requires little proof on the part of advertisers. Puffery may be persuasive, but this type of language also gives advertisers an ethical defense against their critics.

On a more fundamental level, advertising creates images of an ideal life that many of us will never achieve. Advertising shows us perfection: perfect skin, perfect families, perfect homes. We often measure ourselves and our accomplishments by the advertising we encounter. When we do not achieve the standards idealized in advertising, we feel marginalized and oppressed, an aspect of ethical persuasion we discussed earlier. In addition, Americans spend billions of dollars each year trying to achieve the perfection we see in advertising. We contaminate the environment, exploit workers in other countries, and objectify members of our culture. In Chapter 11, we examine how ideas of the perfect body image contribute to the presence of eating disorders in our culture. Most formal codes of ethics or rules governing advertising do not address these issues.

Fundamentally, there are few legal requirements for ethical advertising. Three rules help the FTC make ethical judgments: (1) An ad cannot be deceptive; (2) objective claims must be supported by competent studies; and (3) advertisers are responsible for the reasonable implications of their ads to consumers (Savan, 2000). Thus, advertisers and those who make decisions regarding ethical advertising have few hard-and-fast rules for determining what is ethical. In Chapter 10, we examine how advertisers use digital imagery to make a deceptive correlation between their product and a celebrity spokesperson. Such imagery is potentially unethical. For now, let's consider the American Association of Advertising Agencies' Creative Code, its Code of Ethics, which is contained in its Standards of Practice (AAAA, 1990).

American Association of Advertising Agencies' Creative Code

Specifically, we will not knowingly create advertising that contains:

a. False or misleading statements or exaggerations, visual or verbal
b. Testimonials that do not reflect the real opinion of the individual(s) involved
c. Price claims that are misleading

d. Claims insufficiently supported or that distort the true meaning or practicable application of statements made by professional or scientific authority

e. Statements, suggestions, or pictures offensive to public decency or minority segments of the population

Organizational Advocacy

An **organization** is a "social collectivity (or a group of people) in which activities are coordinated in order to achieve both individual and collective goals" (K. Miller, 1999, p.1). Organizations include corporations, nonprofit groups, churches, universities, and other collective entities. Organizations persuade their members as well as the public about a variety of issues. Whether an organization wants to influence the community's vote on building a new performing arts center or to persuade the community that it is not to blame for a recent tragedy involving its product, organizations use persuasion. Because the public has a stake in the actions of organizations, it is important that organizations communicate ethically. Several ethical issues face organizational persuaders.

organization
a social collectivity (or a group of people) in which activities are coordinated to achieve both individual and collective goals

One fundamental challenge for organizational persuaders is combining loyalty to the organization with truthfulness to audience members. A corporate spokesperson, for example, must be truthful with the public while also portraying the organization in the best possible way. Often, it may be impossible to carry out these competing interests.

Another challenge for organizational persuaders is whether to be forthright about the identity of their client. Public relations practitioners, for instance, may be more effective in a given situation if they do not reveal their association with an organization. When persuaders are not honest about this relationship, however, the public can be misled.

To provide guidance to organizational persuaders, the Public Relations Society of America (2000) has developed a code of ethics for its members. As you think about organizational persuasion, consider the ideas contained in the society's Statement of Professional Values:

Public Relations Society of America's Statement of Professional Values

Advocacy

- We serve the public interest by acting as responsible advocates for those we represent.
- We provide a voice in the marketplace of ideas, facts, and viewpoints to aid informed public debate.

Honesty

- We adhere to the highest standards of accuracy and truth in advancing the interests of those we represent and in communicating with the public.

Expertise

- We acquire and responsibly use specialized knowledge and expertise.

- We advance the profession through continued professional development, research, and education.
- We build mutual understanding, credibility, and relationships among a wide array of institutions and audiences.

Independence
- We provide objective counsel to those we represent.
- We are accountable for our actions.

Loyalty
- We are faithful to those we represent, while honoring our obligation to serve the public interest.

Fairness
- We deal fairly with clients, employers, competitors, peers, vendors, the media, and the general public.
- We respect all opinions and support the right of free expression.

Journalism

Journalists, who we have said often function as persuaders in the media age, also face ethical issues. Because they have enormous power to influence what their audience believes and what it does, journalists must exercise careful ethical judgment. In Chapter 4, we discuss how the news media are often constrained in their coverage by economic factors. The news media, for better or for worse, are in business to earn a profit. Because of the profit orientation of their employers, journalists often find themselves in situations calling for ethical judgment. Let's survey some of the ethical issues journalists face.

In the media age, it is important that journalists check their sources carefully and use discretion. When broadcasting live, reporters sometimes use sources they have not fully checked, or the reporters do not themselves have the facts of the situation straight. The Internet has forced news reporters and editors to make quicker decisions about what to print and broadcast. They fear being scooped by a competitor if they are not the first to run a story. In addition, some online news sites do not use the same editorial standards as more established news organizations. The *Drudge Report*, which we discuss in Chapter 4, is an example of a website that does not employ the checks and balances of a typical newsroom. Matt Drudge, the site's author, does not use editors to check his information, and he freely posts unsubstantiated rumors. Mainstream news media will face continued pressures to compete with information sources that do not subscribe to the same code of ethics to which traditional media adhere.

History is also replete with examples of journalists who have fabricated sources for their stories or given a false impression from the evidence that exists. The summer of 2003 saw at least three such cases. In May 2003, *New York Times* reporter Jayson Blair was found to have fabricated and plagiarized numerous stories for the paper. As a result, Executive Editor Howell Raines and Managing Editor Gerald Boy resigned their positions with the paper. Later that month, Rick Bragg, Pulitzer Prize–winning reporter, resigned from the *Times* for not crediting a freelance reporter on a story he wrote. A month later, sportswriter Michael Kinney was fired by *The Sedalia* (Missouri) *Democrat* for plagiarizing portions of columns he had written. It is important that the public be able to trust what they read and hear in the news media. Occurrences such as these jeopardize the trust the public puts in the news media.

Finally, the profit motive of journalism raises ethical issues. Because most news media rely on advertising for revenue, they may try to avoid negative stories about their advertisers. When reporters or editors fail to give the same scrutiny to their advertisers that they would to nonadvertisers, they fail in their ethical responsibilities to provide fair reporting to the public. Blake Fleetwood, a reporter for the *New York Times*, uncovered the fact that Tiffany's—the upscale Fifth Avenue New York jewelry store—received $4.5 million from the New York state government in a program designed to keep New York businesses in the city. Fleetwood uncovered many other businesses that also benefited from the program, despite the fact that businesses like Tiffany's, Fleetwood alleged, could not afford to do business elsewhere, making this an unnecessary outlay of government funds. Yet Tiffany's was one of the *Times*'s largest and oldest advertisers. Consequently, editors rewrote Fleetwood's story and moved the mention of Tiffany's to the 19th paragraph (Fleetwood, 1999). Fleetwood's editors were attempting to placate both the public's need for the article and their advertiser's need for public support. Editors at the *San Jose Mercury News* published an article telling readers how to negotiate lower car prices. The article exposed scams in the car dealership industry. Because of the article, dealerships in San Jose boycotted advertising in the paper for four months, costing the paper more than $1 million (Fleetwood, 1999).

Given the ethical demands placed on the news media, journalists have adopted a set of ethical standards to help them determine what is right and wrong. Examine the standards maintained by the Society of Professional Journalists (1996):

Society of Professional Journalists' Code of Ethics

- Seek truth and report it: Journalists should be honest, fair and courageous in gathering, reporting and interpreting information.
- Minimize harm: Ethical journalists treat sources, subjects and colleagues as human beings deserving of respect.
- Act independently: Journalists should be free of obligation to any interest other than the public's right to know.
- Be accountable: Journalists are accountable to their readers, listeners, viewers and each other.

NCA Credo for Ethical Communication

The National Communication Association (NCA) is an organization composed of more than six thousand communication educators. NCA members have a variety of interests, ranging from public address to organizational communication to mass communication. The NCA Credo for Ethical Communication was developed and passed by the organization in 1999. The 10 principles of the Credo are designed to instruct educators, practitioners, and the general public about ethical communication. The NCA Credo synthesizes many of the ideas contained in our previous discussion of codes of ethics. Consider the NCA's 10 principles:

- We believe that unethical communication threatens the quality of all communication and consequently the well-being of individuals and the society in which they live.
- We endorse freedom of expression, diversity of perspective, and tolerance of dissent to achieve the informed and responsible decision making fundamental to a society.
- We are obligated to be just as respectful and responsive to other communicators as we expect them to be respectful and responsive to us.
- We believe that access to communication resources and opportunities is necessary to fulfill human potential and contribute to the well-being of families, communities, and society.
- We promote communication climates of caring and mutual understanding that respect the unique needs and characteristics of individual communicators.
- We believe that truthfulness, accuracy, honesty, and reason are essential to the integrity of communication.
- We advocate sharing information, opinions, and feelings when facing significant choices while also respecting privacy and confidentiality.
- We are committed to the courageous expression of personal convictions in pursuit of fairness and justice.
- We condemn communication that degrades individuals and humanity through distortion, intolerance, intimidation, coercion, hatred, and violence.
- We accept responsibility for the short- and long-term consequences for our own communication and expect the same of others.

How valuable are codes of ethics such as those we discussed? What codes of ethics are you bound by as a student? Do you consider those codes as you write papers, attend classes, and live as a student on campus? How might the NCA Credo for Ethical Communication influence your academic career?

Five Guiding Principles

We have discussed a variety of ethical standards, codes, and principles in this chapter. Each is useful within specific contexts and some of what we have discussed, such as the NCA Code of Ethics, is useful across a variety of persuasive situations. Baker and Martinson (2001) present a more concise, easily remembered set of ethical standards that are useful for all persuaders to consider. The five standards can be easily remembered by the acronym, TARES:

- Truthfulness (of the message)
- Authenticity (of the persuader)
- Respect (for the persuadee)

- Equity (of the persuasive appeal)
- Social responsibility (for the common good)

Lets discuss these five standards and their applicability to some of the situations we have discussed in this chapter.

The first standard is the *truthfulness* of the message. We have discussed deception earlier in this chapter. Baker and Martinson (2001) explain further: "People rely on information from others to make their choices in life, large or small. Lies distort this information, alter the choices of the deceived, and injure and lead him or her astray" (p. 160). To achieve truthfulness, the persuader's intent is important, as is factual accuracy, completeness, and fairness.

The second standard is *authenticity* of the persuader. This standard focuses on attributes of the persuader including his or her integrity and personal virtue, genuineness and sincerity, and the independence and commitment to principle. Persuaders should make sure that they do not sacrifice their principles when communicating to audiences, they must personally believe in the product or service being promoted, and they must consider how they feel about the message.

Respect for the persuadee is the third standard proposed by Baker and Martinson (2001). This standard "requires that professional persuaders regard other human beings as worthy of dignity, that they not violate their rights, interests, and well-being for raw self-interest or purely client-serving purposes" (p. 163). Persuaders should ask if their message has the potential to benefit the audience, if the quality of the information is adequate for the audience needs, and if the message facilitates informed decision making on the part of the audience member.

The standard of *equity* of the persuasive appeal addresses messages that are unjust or manipulated. For this standard to be fulfilled, there must be an equity between the persuader and audience member, vulnerable audiences must not be targeted, and persuasive claims must be made within the abilities of the audience members to understand those claims. Baker and Martinson (2001) explained that persuaders should abide by the Golden Rule, "do unto others as you would have them do unto you."

The final standard, social responsibility, "focuses on the need for professional persuaders to be sensitive to and concerned about the wider public interest or common good" (Baker & Martinson, 2001, p. 167). We discussed this point previously with the idea of oppression and we will return to this subject many times in our study of persuasion. The messages, products, and services promoted by persuaders should be beneficial, not harmful, to the community or culture. Persuaders should take into consideration the ethics of the community or culture. They should also strive to promote cooperation and understanding between people. Baker and Martinson also point out that stereotyping and other forms of discrimination should be avoided because they are harmful to the public good.

Ethics and Audience Members

So far in this chapter, we have focused on the ethical challenges facing persuaders in the media age and how persuaders make decisions about ethics. In the final section of this chapter, we focus on the ethical responsibilities of audience members. You'll remember that, in our definition of persuasion, both persuader and audience member share equally in the outcome of the persuasive situation. Thus, audience members have ethical responsibilities as well.

BEING INFORMED

It can be difficult to be informed in the media age because so much information is available. In addition, much of the information we receive is inaccurate or biased by some persuasive force. Audience members must seek to educate themselves as much as possible about issues that are important. We should do what we can to learn where political candidates stand on the issues. We should consult several sources for news, instead of relying on only one television network, one newspaper, or one magazine. We should investigate the value of the products and services we use. We must be active consumers of information so that unscrupulous persuaders do not mislead us.

KEEPING AN OPEN MIND

We must also keep our minds open to all sides of an issue or idea. The media age is marked by a diversity of viewpoints and opinions. Yet we are often conditioned to see the world as conforming to a very narrow set of norms and standards. In fact, persuaders often seek to show us that one idea or one product or one way of life is more valuable than all others. We should celebrate differences in perspectives and seek to learn from those persuaders who are different from us. Doing so will help us to make sound decisions, and it will provide equal opportunity to all involved in the persuasive process.

BEING CRITICAL

We should not accept the ideas of others without question, however. We should constantly use critical-thinking skills to question the logic and reasoning of persuasive messages. We should question whether the emotions, needs, and values persuaders use to influence us are legitimate. Taking this course is a positive step toward being a critical consumer of persuasion. Using critical-thinking skills, you will learn how persuaders seek to give value to their ideas. You will learn how to test the evidence and reasoning they use. You will understand the many forces that make the persuasive process what it is today.

EXPRESSING ETHICAL JUDGMENTS

Earlier in this chapter, we noted that all of us make ethical judgments on an individual basis each day. As you listen, read, and see the persuasive messages that surround you, consider the various ethical standards we have discussed. Think about how you can use those standards to understand the persuasion you encounter. Then, when you discuss persuasion with others, express your ethical judgments and your reasons for making them.

Summary

Ethics and persuasion are linked on several levels. It is important that both persuaders and audience members exercise and express ethical judgments.

Challenges facing persuaders and audience members in the media age include deception, access, oppression, privacy, and conflict of interest. In each case, the mediated nature of the persuasive process introduces factors that all involved in the process must consider.

Ethical decisions can be made based on several standards, including Kant's categorical imperative, Mill's utilitarian principle, the First Amendment to the U.S. Constitution, or Johannesen's ethical standards. Ethical judgments are made at various levels, including the cultural and the individual.

Habermas argues that a vital public sphere of discussion requires communication competence, which makes use of universal pragmatics. When we take assumptions about persuasion for granted, we fall victim to controlling interests in society and cannot freely discuss issues that are important to us.

Persuaders and audience members face ethical challenges that reflect the context in which the parties function. Persuaders involved in specific persuasive contexts have developed codes of ethics tailored to their particular situations. The NCA Credo for Ethical Communication is a broad ethical statement that integrates many of the concerns common to these contexts.

By assessing the truthfulness, authenticity, respect, equity, and social responsibility of a persuasive message, we can evaluate its ethical dimensions.

The ethical responsibilities of audience members include being informed, keeping an open mind, being critical, and expressing ethical judgments. Audience members play an important role in ethical persuasion.

Key Terms

Visit the book's website at http://www.mhhe.com/borchers2 for multiple-choice quizzes, Internet activities, and key terms flashcards.

ethics 64	speech act 77
coercion 65	discourse 78
violence 65	ideal speech situation 79
digital divide 67	puffery 84
code of ethics 71	organization 85

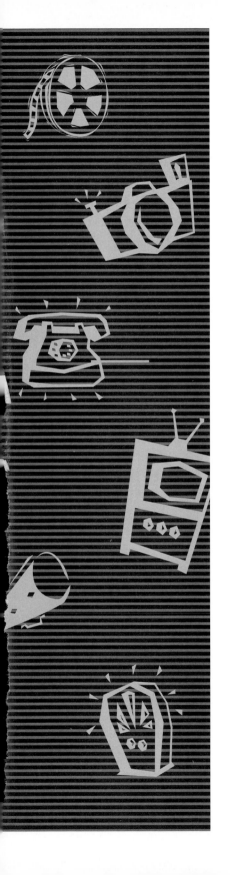

PART II
Variables of Persuasion

Chapters 4 through 11 explore the variables involved in the persuasion process. Each of these variables is highlighted in the model of the persuasion process presented in Chapter 1. It is important to observe that although each variable is isolated for the purposes of our discussion, they are often indistinguishable from one another in practice. Reasoning and motivational appeals, for example, often cannot be separated as neatly as they are in the discussion that follows. In addition, our discussion in Chapter 4 should be seen to extend throughout subsequent chapters because media influence all variables of the persuasion process. Finally, keep in mind that each variable we discuss is itself a product of the persuasion process and is therefore highly dynamic.

Chapter 4 explores how media influence persuasion. The chapter focuses on media audiences, sources, and channels. The chapter also discusses the nature of news because news is an important source of persuasion today. Chapter 5 examines the audience and how persuaders seek to understand their audiences. It also addresses how audiences can take control of the persuasion process.

Chapters 6 and 7 focus on the symbolic nature of persuasion. Chapter 6 addresses visual images and how they are persuasive to audiences. Chapter 7 looks at language. The central discussion in this chapter revolves around Jamieson's (1988) concept of electronic eloquence.

Chapter 8 examines how culture plays an integral role in the persuasion process. Not only do persuaders use cultural beliefs, values, and behaviors to persuade audiences, but persuaders also seek to maintain and transform certain aspects of culture.

Chapters 9, 10, and 11 address the Aristotelian constructs of ethos, logos, and pathos. Chapter 9 discusses the persuasiveness of the source and the characteristics that we use to judge sources of persuasive messages today. Chapter 10 examines the reasoning process and how it is often minimized in the media age. Chapter 11 explores the range of motivational appeals that persuaders use, including emotions, needs, and values.

4

Media Influences on Persuasion

Learning Objectives

After reading this chapter, you should be able to:

1. Understand the various components of the modern media industry.

2. Identify the impact and influence of media on persuasion.

3. Describe the influence entertainment media and news media have on our culture.

Think for a moment about how you have been persuaded today. You probably awoke to the music of a radio, read the newspaper, watched television, and selected from among a host of consumer products as you went about your daily business. From the moment we awaken until we go to bed, we are bombarded with persuasive messages. Most of us think that we make conscious choices about the persuasive messages we choose to accept and those we ignore. Lurking beneath the surface, though, are persuasive forces beyond our knowledge or control.

Consider, for instance, your decision to purchase a particular brand of clothing. There is a good chance that you have purchased clothing from a store such as Old Navy, Abercrombie and Fitch, or the Gap. Brand-name clothing purchased at these and other stores provides consumers with benefits that extend beyond comfort and value. Advertising, for instance, shows us attractive people wearing particular brands of clothing. When characters in movies or television shows wear particular brands, those brands take on added significance. In fact, some companies pay to have their products used in entertainment media to give them wide popular exposure. Thus, although you might think you purchase a pair of jeans from Old Navy because they look good, there is a good chance that you are also aware of the added meaning and value associated with wearing the jeans. It is the job of persuaders, in this case, to make you aware of that meaning and value.

In Chapter 1, we discussed how the medium used to transmit a message changes the message, its sender and receiver, and the culture in which it is communicated. In this chapter, we explore in greater depth how media influence persuasion today. Whether the message involves advertising in a newspaper or magazine, political campaigning on the evening news, or developing a corporate image on the World Wide Web, media present a challenging intermediary between persuaders and receivers. In addition, members of the media—journalists, programming directors, and editors—are themselves persuaders. In Chapter 1, we discussed how changes in media have sparked changes in individual consciousness, culture, and knowledge. Thus, it is imperative that we start our discussion of the persuasive process with media because media influence all that we study. Throughout this chapter, we examine how media influence how persuaders create intimacy with their audiences and how media are used to give value to persuaders' products, services, and ideas.

This chapter defines media, offers three assumptions about media, and discusses how media persuade us. Then we turn our attention to specific media channels. Finally, we explore the nature of mediated news and entertainment programming. News is a mediated filter that causes us to view the world in certain ways. News helps us to make decisions about political candidates, it creates presumptions about the guilt and innocence of suspects accused of crimes, and it facilitates discussions about culture. For these reasons and more, the news deserves our attention as a specific kind of media content. Likewise, entertainment programming shapes our beliefs and values in powerful ways.

Defining Media

Media is a term that describes a variety of people, structures, technologies, and relationships. Traditional definitions of media focus on messages that originate from some institutional source, travel through some channel, and reach a large, anonymous audience. Although these basic components of media are present today, their nature has changed with the advent of new electronic forms of communication. The current media environment does not always fit this description. Although previously constrained by cost, individuals can now offer messages inexpensively via the Internet. Audiences for media messages are sometimes small and on occasion make themselves known to the producers of the messages. To better understand the nature of today's media, let's discuss the various components of media.

media source

the specific person or groups of people who produces messages for audiences

MEDIA SOURCES

Media source refers to the specific person or group of people who produces messages for audiences, including news, advertising, and entertainment programming. A news journalist, a graphic designer, and a magazine photographer are all examples of media sources. Media sources, write Jamieson and Karlyn Kohrs Campbell (1997), have traditionally been institutional and impersonal. Traditionally, we think of media content as originating from *institutional sources*. Large organizations are responsible for the production of much of the media content today. Producing a film or publishing a newspaper usually requires money and a large staff. The financial burden of producing media content has encouraged media organizations to become larger, to reduce costs and streamline operations. AOL Time Warner Inc. is a striking example of the magnitude of media consolidation. The 2001 merger of America's largest Internet service provider—AOL—and one of America's largest media companies—Time Warner–Turner—has created a company that not only has a great deal of content, but that also has many ways of delivering that content. This media giant owns a variety of magazines, including *Time, Sports Illustrated,* and *People*. It also owns the Warner Bros. broadcast television network and the cable networks CNN, TBS, TNT, and HBO. It owns four film studios: Warner Bros., Turner Pictures, Castle Rock Entertainment, and New Line Cinema. It publishes books through the companies Time-Life, Little, Brown & Co., and Bookspan (formerly Book-of-the-Month Club). AOL Time Warner owns Atlantic Recording, Elektra Records, and Warner/Chappell Music. Finally, it also owns the CNN Interactive and Turner New Media multimedia companies. As you can see, AOL Time Warner is a huge company that controls much of what you see, hear, and read. Recent rule changes will potentially cause an increase in media ownership consolidation.

In addition, many media organizations have become the property of large companies that have nothing to do with media. NBC, for example, is owned by General Electric. Dean Alger (1998) argues that megamergers such as these reduce the numbers of voices that are heard in media and raise questions about fair competition. In addition, large media outlets sometimes face conflicts of interest when a news branch must report on the activities of another division owned by the same company. Media mergers raise questions about how we, as audience members, are to evaluate information when it all comes from the same source. Knowing this, we need to question the willingness of media to put a positive spin on self-serving stories. We can also seek to obtain information from a variety of sources.

In addition to being institutional, media sources are also *impersonal*. The consolidation of radio stations means that the local disc jockey no longer selects which records to play. Marketing experts who live many miles from the local radio audience determine what that audience hears. Similar practices occur in the news world as well. Instead of using their own reporters, local radio stations are increasingly turning to national companies such as Metro News to provide their news feeds. A reporter for Metro News often tapes a news story for two or three different stations in the same market. The stories are slightly different, depending on the client station's format, and the reporter uses a different name for each station. Listeners have no idea that the reporter they are listening to has created the same story for different stations or that the reporter does not work for the radio station. Local radio stations make similar arrangements with companies that provide traffic and weather reports. In fact, radio stations that use the "AccuWeather" forecast rely on meteorologists who work in Pennsylvania. Rifka Rosenwein (1999) reports that with the economic realities of consolidation, use of anonymous news and weather reporters will soon be commonplace.

At the same time, technology offers the potential for more and more voices being heard by and made known to the public. Although clearly at a disadvantage when compared with the large media organizations, any individual can potentially establish a World Wide Web presence and disseminate information to a large audience. A good example of this phenomenon is the *Drudge Report,* a news report e-mailed to subscribers and posted to the Web by Matt Drudge, a former CBS gift shop manager. In July 2003, Drudge's website reported 1.5 billion hits in the previous year. Sources from around the country e-mail Drudge their news tips. He assembles them and posts a daily report to the World Wide Web at www.drudgereport.com. His news has been influential— and often inaccurate. He takes credit for breaking the news of Monica Lewinsky's affair with President Clinton. He was also the first to report that Connie Chung would be fired from CBS and that Jack Kemp would be Bob Dole's running mate in 1996. Yet on other issues, Drudge has been wrong. For instance, he once incorrectly reported that White House aide Sidney Blumenthal had a history of spousal abuse (Poland, 1997). Drudge later retracted the story. He admits that his stories are sometimes wrong and that he has no editor to review his reporting.

One of the problems posed by this new type of journalism, which may be ideologically biased or inaccurate, is that it can be difficult to differentiate it from reporting that has been put through a series of checks and that meets the standards of an editor and a publisher. As media present new opportunities to online publishers, we, the public, must carefully evaluate the information we read and hear. This increase in the number of media sources presents ethical challenges to both producers and consumers of media.

Media sources are also trying to become more familiar with their audiences. The most striking example is the morning news show. NBC started the trend of broadcasting from a street-level studio in June 1994 (Figure 4.1). (Actually, NBC's *Today* show simply moved back to its original 1950s studio, which was also at street level and in full view of the public.) From Studio 1A, the *Today* show hosts can be seen through glass windows as they read the news and interview guests. In fact, the hosts typically mingle with the live audience during the broadcast. Audience members pay nothing to see the show. They simply stand on the sidewalk outside the studio during filming. Attending the broadcast of the show has become a major tourist attraction in New York, and audience members go to great lengths to get on television. Since NBC began broadcasting in front of a live audience, other networks have followed, including CBS, ABC, and MTV. The *Today* show hosts have become friendly faces to millions of viewers because of their seemingly personal relationships with audience members. Numerous local stations use live, remote feeds from county fairs, conventions, or community events to further develop the relationship be-

Figure 4.1
Weather reporter Al Roker talking with the *Today* show audience
Chatting with the audience lets Roker and the other *Today* hosts give the illusion that they are familiar with the audience.

tween media source and audience. We must keep in mind that although we may think we have a relationship with Katie Couric or Matt Lauer, we really do not. We must still critically evaluate the news they provide.

MEDIA CHANNELS

Media channel, or **medium,** refers to the means used to transmit a message. The oral medium is still an important means of transmitting persuasive messages. If you recall our discussion of media cultures from the first chapter, you'll remember that many cultures in the world are still dominated by oral communication. The United States, though, is more influenced my electronic media, so we'll discuss here the implication of electronic media for persuasion, focusing on radio, television, and Internet. We'll also address the print medium because it has, and still does, influence persuasion as well in our current culture. An important point to remember—no matter the medium discussed—is that the medium of a message does more than simply transmit the message to the audience. The medium changes the content it carries, the people who send and receive it, and the culture in which the transmission takes place. We'll discuss each medium in greater length later in the chapter.

MEDIA CONTENT

Media content refers to the programming carried by a media channel and produced by a media source or organization. The evening news or an episode of a television program are examples of media content. **News media** designates a specific type of media organization that is concerned with reporting on the state of current events. **News** refers to the content produced by news

media channel
the means used to transmit a message, including spoken words, print, radio, television, or the Internet; also called the medium

medium
the means used to transmit a message, including spoken words, print, radio, television, or the Internet; plural: media

media content
the programming carried by a media channel and produced by a media source or organization

news media
a specific type of media organization that is concerned with reporting on the state of current events

news
the content produced by news media

entertainment media
organizations primarily
concerned with non-
news programming, such
as motion picture studios
or the entertainment
divisions of the major
networks

**entertainment
programming**
non-news programming,
including motion
pictures; radio and
television talk shows;
and television dramas,
sitcoms, "reality" TV,
and game shows

media. **Entertainment media** refers to organizations, such as motion picture studios or the entertainment divisions of the major networks, that are primarily concerned with non-news programming, or **entertainment programming.** We'll discuss the persuasive effects of news and entertainment media later in this chapter.

Media content is transmitted rapidly to a vast audience and is available for only a short period of time, according to Jamieson and Campbell (1997). Mediated messages are *instantaneous.* News reports from around the world, sports updates the minute something happens, and instant stock market prices are all examples of the power of media to bring instant information to us. The *Starr Report,* which made public allegations of sexual misconduct by then-President Bill Clinton, was released to the world via the Internet in September 1998. President Clinton, along with members of Congress and the general public, were able to read the report moments after it was released. Although copies of the report were printed—and sold in paperback form—the fastest way to get the report was via the Internet. Although some Web servers experienced overload, millions of people were able to download the report and read it that afternoon.

The rapid release of information, though, is also cause for concern. Messages that are released before they have been thoroughly checked run the risk of being erroneous. News producers do not have the luxury of waiting until their deadline to decide whether to publish a story or not, because constant updates are made to Internet news sites and cable news networks such as CNN Headline News. The instant release of information has changed the landscape for acquiring and evaluating knowledge in our society.

Messages transmitted via media are also *ephemeral.* They appear on the airwaves or on the front pages of our newspapers today, and tomorrow they are gone. We focus our attention on a particular issue for a short period and then move on to something else. Electronic media do not have the permanence associated with printed material. With the Internet, some news articles are archived online for only a short period of time. The permanence of communication has changed with the advent of the Internet and other electronic media.

MEDIA AUDIENCES

media audience
the group of people who
can potentially receive
media content

Media audience refers to the group of people who can potentially receive media content. We discuss the audience in greater detail in Chapter 5. For now, let's briefly consider several aspects of media audiences. First, media audiences are potentially *large.* Movies draw hundreds of millions of viewers, special television events like the Super Bowl attract nearly 40 million viewers, and many magazines boast circulation rates of more than 1 million. Media audiences are also *anonymous.* Media sources usually do not know the members of their audience. Media audiences are *heterogeneous* as well, made up of people with different beliefs, attitudes, and values. Finally, media audiences are able to use technology to *circumvent* the persuasive messages of producers. Using technology such as ReplayTV, which we discuss later, audience members can pause live television broadcasts and skip commercials. They can also compare various messages by, for example, visiting a selection of websites advocating different positions on an issue. Media audiences today are active processors of information and present many challenges to persuaders.

PUTTING IT TOGETHER

The product of the interaction between media sources, channels, content, and audience is called **media.** The term refers to the web of sources, channels, and content. It includes broadcast signals, media personalities, and the words and images of media content. This definition is important. People make three mistakes in discussing media. First, they use the word *media* to refer to any or all of the dimensions just listed, obscuring what exactly it refers to. Second, they use the term to refer to a singular, monolithic set of people, channels, and effects, as in, "Media has an influence on how we relate to the world." Not only does this statement fail to designate one aspect of media, but it views media as one body acting alone. In fact, there are hundreds of media organizations, which produce thousands of media messages, transmitted through several media channels. To reinforce this idea, we use *media* in the plural. Third, people tend to view media organizations as nameless, faceless entities that create programming based solely on economic or political factors. We must keep in mind, however, that it is individuals—working within organizations and responding to corporate pressures—who make decisions concerning media content. We must also recognize the artistic elements involved in the creation of media content and that individuals, not machines, create art.

Assumptions about Media

With this definition in mind, let's look at three assumptions concerning media:

1. Media persuade us.
2. Media sources, channels, and content present us with mediated realities.
3. Media sources are profit-making businesses.

First, *media* sources, channels, and content *persuade us* by creating knowledge about products and people and their place in our culture. We purchase cars, toasters, cereal, and other consumer goods and services based on the words and images selected for us by advertising professionals. We select political leaders based on the impression we get of them through various media channels. We learn what is important in our culture from media content. Because we are constantly exposed to the persuasive appeals of media sources, channels, and content, it is crucial that we spend some time uncovering how knowledge about people, places, and events is created. For instance, we will discover how a political figure's image is created to maximize his or her media appeal. We will learn how advertisers segment their audiences in order to target their persuasive

Go onto the World Wide Web and a website that you have not visited before. Who do you think the audience for that website is? How large is the audience?

media
the web of message transmission means (channels), sources, and content; includes broadcast signals, media personalities, and the words and images of media content

messages to the most receptive ears. We will study how language, images, emotion, and logic function in a mediated world. This book will equip you to understand the multitude of ways in which persuasion occurs in our mediated society.

Second, *media* sources, channels, and content *present us with "mediated realities."* The pictures we have in our heads of the world, of people, and of corporations are not usually based on our real experiences with them (Nimmo & Combs, 1990). Instead, these pictures are formed through our interactions with media images. Some theorists argue that the symbols we use create reality. You may never have been to Fargo, North Dakota. Yet you have probably heard about Fargo and the Upper Midwest in the media. You may have seen news reports of terrible snowstorms in the area, or you may have seen the Academy Award–nominated film *Fargo* a few years ago (which, ironically, was neither set nor filmed in Fargo). Some media images of Fargo are not that flattering. Yet people who visit Fargo usually remark that it is quite nice and not at all what they had pictured. It is a large city with warm summer weather. People who have never been to Fargo have in their minds a picture of Fargo that has been created through media.

Media are very powerful in shaping our responses to images of people, places, and things. Although it may be inconsequential that you will never visit Fargo because of what you think it is like, it is another matter when we elect our political leaders based on the same type of information. We may think we know something about a particular candidate, but we must keep in mind that we really have only an image of that person—an image that has been created and transmitted via media channels. The same holds true for the images we have of what the ideal marriage or friendship should be like. We form ideas about how we should relate to others based on how we see fictional characters relating to other fictional characters. Media, then, provide a constant source of information about who we are and how we should act.

Third, it is important to observe that *media sources are profit-making businesses.* The function of media is to attract audiences for advertisers (Jamieson & Campbell, 1997). It is impossible to separate media sources and content from the economic and political system in which they operate. The news we read and the television programs we watch are "products" designed to attract audiences, resulting in higher ratings that are used to sell advertising. As a result, we do not always receive the most "objective" coverage of a particular issue. We may not even be exposed to the most important issues of the day. Instead, we are held hostage to what media sources think will help them sell the most products.

The profit orientation of media sources affects virtually every decision media companies make. Often we are unaware of these decisions and the powerful influence they have on how we see the world. The freedom of news media to pursue their own agenda does have its benefits. That the media industry is privatized, not public, ensures that the government cannot control what we see. However, with the merging of large media organizations, it becomes difficult for us to determine whose interests are being served: the media source's or our own. The profit orientation of media sources influences much of what we study in this textbook. Knowing that media are interested primarily in profit helps make important aspects of mediated persuasion visible.

How Media Persuade Us

t assumption about media was that they persuade us. Let's examine
mption a bit more closely. Media have three effects on persuasion: as
as gatekeeper, and as advocate. We will first examine media as *channel*.
dium is never simply a pipe through which information is sent. Recall
n's (1964) idea that the form of media influences our perception of its
McLuhan suggests that even the form of media content, whether a
y or a sitcom episode, persuades us to adopt a particular way of see-
ontent. For instance, we have come to expect news to be told to us in
form. We expect news reporters to tell us stories. Thus, the nature of
um influences our perception of its content.
ere are times, though, when the channel exerts only minimal influence
content of the message. Such is the case in advertising, direct mail, and
narketing. In the case of advertising, media sources—the advertising agen-
es—create messages to be broadcast to audiences. In most cases, these messages are broadcast without modification by the channeling media. The
exception would be when the advertisement fails to conform to community
standards for taste or decency. In the case of direct mail or telemarketing, the
media source—the advertiser—uses printed material and the U.S. Postal Service or the telephone to disseminate the message. In this case, the medium is
involved only as a channel. In these cases, media exert minimal influence on
message content.

In other cases, media sources serve as *gatekeepers* for information. Media
not only broadcast the message, but they interpret the message in some way.
The news is a good example of how media sources serve as gatekeepers. Because news media cannot possibly show us everything that happens each day,
editors must determine which of the day's events should receive public attention, thus prioritizing events for the audience. Journalists produce content and
present the content in a way that gives meaning to it. Another example is entertainment programming. In a media source's attempt to attract audiences to sell
advertising, it often creates a particular type of content. The content it produces carries with it implicit messages of what is important in our culture. It is
said that "sex sells," and shows about sex can be used to generate large audiences. By using sex to sell their programming, media focus society's attention
on sex and its importance. In all of these ways, the profit focus of the media
source requires that it act as a gatekeeper.

Provide an example of an article or advertisement from a newspaper in which media served as channel. Provide an example of media as a gatekeeper. Provide an example of media as persuasion source.

Finally, media sources themselves become *advocates*. The media source
generates persuasive messages with the stated intent of persuading audiences.
Editorials are prime examples. Editorial pages give news editors a chance to influence public opinion by presenting arguments for or against a particular
issue. Columnists use their space to influence attitudes and beliefs as well. The
proliferation of shows such as ABC's *20/20* and *Primetime Live* are additional
examples of how media attempt to influence their audiences directly. As we
talk about media and media sources, keep these distinctions in mind. Internet Activity: Identifying Media Influence will help you understand these
influences.

INTERNET ACTIVITY

Identifying Media Influence

We have just discussed the three ways that media persuade audiences. The media channel influences audiences indirectly and media personnel influence audiences directly as gatekeepers and advocates. Visit the website for one of the leading news organizations, such as www.cnn.com or www.msnbc.com. Identify how the site influences audiences in each of the three ways we have discussed. How does reading news on the Internet differ from reading a newspaper or watching television? How does the news site regulate the information the public receives? Does the news organization take a position on an issue? How effectively does the site communicate its position?

The Sensory Experience of Media

Electronic media provide several avenues for persuasion, including words, sounds, and visual images. Contrast today's media of persuasion with that of ancient Greece, where persuaders could only use their voice, body, and words to communicate. Today's channels of persuasion are truly multimedia in nature, which create a great number of outlets for a persuader's ideas. These cues reach us on emotional, and perhaps even subconscious, levels, which make them significant to study. We'll discuss here the sensory experience of media and its impact on persuasion.

VISUAL SYMBOLS

One of the most striking senses appealed to by media is that of sight. We are surrounded by photographs, logos, and other images. Messaris (1997) explains that visual images are persuasive because they seem realistic, serve as proof for arguments, and suggest arguments to audiences. We'll explore a great variety of images, learn more about Messaris's theory of visual persuasion, and examine film and video in Chapter 6. Each of these media has ways of being "read" by viewers. The transition in a film, for instance, can suggest the passage of time. By using techniques such as editing, camera angle, transitions, and special effects, persuaders are able to use film and video to persuade audiences. As we watch these media, we automatically understand what they are communicating. Additionally, film and video, like other visual images, can elicit emotions in audience members. If you've ever cried during a movie, you realize how powerful media can be in affecting our emotions.

The computer—the Internet, in particular—has created new ways of appealing to an audience's senses. The graphical design of the Internet features visual imagery, often at the expense of words. The Internet is capable of broadcasting multimedia, such as audio and video. Additionally, the Internet allows us to extend our sensory experience through time and space. We can experience—through pictures, sound, and video—events that take place a world away from us. We can communicate with other individuals in real time through either e-mail, messaging, or video conferencing. We'll explore the Internet in more detail later in this chapter.

MUSIC AND AUDITORY SYMBOLS

Music, and other auditory cues, are another significant part of experiencing media. If you've watched a scary movie, you know how significantly the music affects how you think and feel about the film. The music is a symbolic cue that something good or bad is about to happen. Television commercials, too, use music to stimulate us to make purchasing decisions. In some cases, the musical score alone is persuasive; in other situations, the music, along with the lyrics, communicate messages to audiences.

Deanna Sellnow (1996) explains that a musical score is related to emotion. Music, she writes, can "symbolize patterns of musical feeling" (p. 48). In particular, the intensity and release patterns of a musical score are related to the emotional tensions and releases we feel in our everyday life. For instance, a quick tempo, or speed, relates to feelings of intensity, while a slower tempo is a release. A dissonant harmonic chord structure intensifies, while a consonant harmonic chord structure releases. Sellnow explains that these variables (tempo, harmonic chord structures, and others) should be viewed as working together throughout the score to reflect emotions. The next time you watch a television commercial, pay careful attention to how intensity is created and released within the commercial. If done effectively, the rising and falling action in the score will mirror the feeling desired by the commercial. Sellnow (1996) explains that the musical score influences how we feel about the lyrics of a song. The musical score functions "to enrich the lyrical message by communicating an emotional dimension or attitudinal stance" (p. 49). At times, the score intensifies the lyrical message or the score may contradict the lyrics and present different meanings to different audience members. Ultimately, Sellnow argues for viewing the score and lyrics as equally compelling aspects of music.

Woodward (2003) takes a slightly different approach toward music. You'll recall that in the first chapter, we drew on Woodward's work to explain the concept of identification. Music, he explained is translated into visual terms that reflect prior experiences we've had. He wrote, "Our senses are constantly feeding us impressions that prompt memories of the past: moments we consciously reconstruct to be better or worse than the original experiences" (p. 3). A persuader either seeks to use music to associate a product or service with a past experience that was positive or tries to call upon the audience's negative feelings toward some topic. Woodward's view is in line with the popular notion of the "theater of the mind," in which our sensory experiences create virtual theaters in our minds. Yet, we react to these images and "theatrical productions" as if they are real.

SUBLIMINAL PERSUASION

Finally, we address how the media create so-called extrasensory experiences for audiences. There has been a great debate about whether subliminal messages are used in persuasion or not. Recent debate about the topic was sparked in 1957 when market researcher James Vicary claimed that subliminal messages to eat po[ ]drink Coca-Cola flashed on a movie screen and resulted in an increa[ ]s of the concession stand products. After much skepticism, Vicary cl[ ]results were fabricated (Merikle, 2000).

Wilson Bryant Key's work in subliminal persuasion also received a great deal of attention in the 1970s and 80s. In a 1981 book, *Subliminal Seduction,* he asserts, "Every person reading this book has been victimized and manipulated by the use of subliminal stimuli directed into his unconscious mind by the mass merchandisers of media" (p. 1). Key argues that the techniques of subliminal persuasion were a well-kept secret and that "the average citizen, as well as most social and behavioral scientists, simply do not know what is going on" (p. 1), or they "appear not to want to know what's going on" (p. 1).

In particular, Key focuses on subliminal sexual messages. For instance, he identifies a particular advertisement for Gibley's London Dry Gin, that appeared in a 1971 edition of *Time* magazine. Research subjects, Key reports, apparently had feelings of "sexuality," "satisfaction," or "romance" after seeing the ad, even though they simply reported seeing pictures of a gin bottle and collins glasses. Key explains that the ad contains the word *sex* subliminally hidden in three ice cubes pictured in the ad. He attributes the sexual feelings experienced by the viewers to the subliminal message contained in the ice cubes. "Incredulous though you might be at this point, these subliminal SEXes are today an integral part of American life—even though they have never been seen by many people at the conscious level" (1981, p. 5). Our popular culture is filled with other examples of such hidden messages.

Kazdin (2000) explains that many people think that subliminal perceptions are more powerful than the perceptions of which we are aware. Research studies, he argues, have found that subliminal messages—if, indeed, they exist—are processed in the same way as other stimuli. Further, psychological studies have been unable to detect any kind of persuasive effect of subliminal messages (Kazdin, 2000). Despite claims to the contrary, however, many experts and audience members continue to believe that subliminal messages have a powerful persuasive force. The next time you page through a popular magazine, examine the ads closely to see if you can detect any kind of hidden messages.

Media Channels

Having discussed the various components of media and their function in persuasion, we can turn our attention to a more detailed discussion of media channels: newspapers, radio, television, and the Internet. Although we examine the popularity and persuasive significance of each of these media channels separately, keep in mind that today the boundaries between media channels are not so distinct. This blurring of media channels is called convergence, a subject we look at more closely at the end of this section.

NEWSPAPERS

Newspapers are read by 79.3 percent of the population for an average of 24 minutes a day. Circulation rates have decreased steadily in recent years as well

Table 4.1 Newspapers: Total Number and Circulation

Year	Number of newspapers	Circulation (in millions)
1970	1,748	62.1
1975	1,756	60.7
1980	1,745	62.2
1985	1,676	62.8
1990	1,611	62.3
1995	1,533	58.2
1997	1,509	56.7
2001	1,468	55.6

From U.S. Bureau of the Census (2002, p. 700)

(Table 4.1). Richard Campbell (1998) attributes this decline to the availability of new media that compete for our time. In addition, the total number of newspapers in existence (see Table 4.1) has declined. In 1970, there were 1,748 newspapers with a combined circulation of 62.1 million readers. By 2001, the number of papers had decreased to 1,468, with a combined circulation of 55.6 million (Census, 2002). R. Campbell (1998) notes that the number of newspapers has declined because of consolidation among large newspaper companies. In cities that once had two or three newspapers, there is now one.

Interestingly, circulation for Sunday newspapers has increased, from 49.2 million in 1970 to 59.1 million in 2002. Mark Fitzgerald (1997) explains that people are concentrating their time on the Sunday paper instead of weekday papers. The Sunday paper usually discusses a wider variety of topics—such as travel and entertainment—that appeal to more readers than does the limited coverage of the weekday paper. In many foreign countries, newspapers are far more popular than they are in the United States. In Sweden, for instance, newspaper companies sell 500 newspapers for every 1,000 people.

Three important variables influence how today's newspaper contributes to the persuasion process. First, the use of wire services has shaped and continues to shape newspaper coverage. Smaller newspapers can cover national and international news by subscribing to stories written by reporters working for wire services, such as the Associated Press or Reuters. Thus, a small newspaper, such as the *Des Moines Register,* can provide its readers with coverage of national events in the same way that a larger newspaper, such as the *New York Times,* does for its readers. In fact, the *New York Times* has its own wire service: Many local papers reprint articles that appear in the *Times.*

As a result, wire services homogenize much of the news and exert a powerful agenda-setting influence on newspaper coverage. Stories that are transmitted by wire services are typically picked up by a substantial number of local newspapers. Thus, no matter which newspaper you read, you may find the same story in each one. If you have ever been exposed to newspapers from several different cities on the same day, you know that what is on page 1 in Omaha might also be on page 1 of the Detroit paper. We discuss agenda setting in greater detail in Chapter 2.

Compare today's printed newspaper with the paper's website (if available). Compare the printed newspaper to another newspaper's website. How are the stories similar? How are they different? Do both news sources use wire service stories?

A second variable that shapes the newspaper industry is consolidation of ownership. In the past, newspapers were locally owned, much as were neighborhood grocery stores and restaurants. But just as national chains now dominate the grocery and restaurant businesses, so, too, do they predominate in the newspaper industry. The Gannett Corporation, for example, owns 74 daily U.S. newspapers with a combined circulation of 6.7 million. The company also owns 22 television stations covering 17.4 percent of the country. Chains, such as Gannett, own 75 percent of all newspapers in the country today (DeFleur & Dennis, 1998). Critics charge that chain ownership decreases the importance given to local news and limits the number of independent local voices (DeFleur & Dennis, 1998). Critics also assert that given the profit orientation of large newspaper and media chains, they will sacrifice news quality and sensationalize the news for profit.

A final variable that influences our study of persuasion is the widespread presence of newspapers on the Internet. Many, if not most, newspapers now have an Internet site at which viewers can read the local news from anywhere in the world. If you are curious about events in Boston or Little Rock or Los Angeles, you can read that city's local newspaper each day. Much of the national news will be the same because its basis is wire service stories, but the local news from each city will be different. In this respect, audiences are becoming larger and more heterogeneous. The speed at which news is produced is another Internet-related factor. Many online newspapers offer constant updates to their printed news during the day. The speed of news transmission may promote errors in reporting, as reporters and editors sacrifice fact checking for fast online publishing. In fact, Jules Whitcover (1998) argues that news organizations that wait to publish stories until they can check them adequately may find themselves scooped by less scrupulous sources.

RADIO

Radio is the second most popular media source today, next to television. Ninety-nine percent of all households have a radio. There are 4,685 AM radio stations and 5,892 FM stations in the United States. Approximately 84.4 percent of all Americans listen to the radio, and we spend an average of 2.63 hours a day listening to it. Teenagers, in particular, tune in to the radio. Ninety-five percent of the nation's youth listen to the radio for an average of 10 hours a week. Radio offers teens music, and they listen to the radio wherever they are: at home, in the car, at school, or at work. For advertisers, the radio is an effective marketing tool because teens are loyal to their radio stations and radio stations usually segment their audiences neatly for advertisers (Zollo, 1999).

Our discussion of persuasion considers three types of radio: talk radio, Internet radio, and satellite radio. It also looks at source consolidation. *Talk radio* is the most popular radio format in the United States. Prior to 1987, a federal law called the Fairness Doctrine restricted blatantly ideological radio programming. With its repeal, however, the airwaves opened to talk radio and to hosts such as Rush Limbaugh, who makes no secret of his ideological leanings. More than half of talk radio today is devoted to politics. Limbaugh, the most popular talk-radio show host attracts a target audience that advertisers consider ideal: 25- to 54-year-old males, with college degrees and household incomes of more than $50,000 (Paige, 1998). More than 90 percent of talk radio listeners vote (Paige, 1998).

Researchers have identified several reasons for talk radio's prominence. Some contend that talk radio fosters a sense of community for its listeners and provides audience members with the opportunity to say what is on their minds. Paige (1998) describes talk radio as an antiestablishment medium. It allows callers to voice their displeasure with the nature of current events. For example, in recent years when the Democrats were in control of the White House, conservative hosts and callers dominated talk radio. Whatever its function in the lives of listeners, talk radio has a profound influence on American political and social life. Future talk radio will seek to attract more diverse audiences, including Christians, younger listeners, and Hispanics.

Second, technology has altered the radio industry and changed radio's role in the persuasion process. On the production side, computer and satellite technology allows local stations to give the illusion that they are being responsive to local demands for programming and news. In reality, "New satellite and Internet technology allows a technician at a small station literally to cut and paste bits of local news, weather and chatter into piped-in programming with a click of a mouse on a computer screen" (Polgreen, 1999, p. 9).

Equipped with Internet access and the appropriate software, computer users can receive radio broadcasts from around the world over *the Internet*. *Satellite radio* allows users to receive radio broadcasts beamed from a satellite. Although satellite radio is available at home and in the workplace, the most significant application is in cars. You can drive from Florida to Washington and listen to the same radio station the entire way. Direct-to-consumer satellite broadcast presents new challenges for local radio stations while allowing consumers to receive entertainment options specifically suited to their tastes. Advertisers will have to adapt to both Internet and satellite radio as they attempt to reach consumers.

Finally, *consolidation* in ownership of radio stations influences the type of programming available. The 1996 Telecommunications Act changed the limitations on how many and what type of radio stations a company could own. In a big market, a company can now own as many as eight stations. In smaller markets, a company may now own between five and seven stations. In some small cities, it is possible for one company to own all the local radio stations. The programming that results from such consolidation is specifically tailored to reach certain demographic target audiences. In fact, "playlists are strategically selected by teams of market researchers who often live and work hundreds of miles away from the people that will actually hear the music" (Polgreen, 1999, p. 9). As a result, new and unique programming options are unavailable for local listeners and emerging artists.

A countermovement to the rapid consolidation of radio station ownership is a provision in Federal Communications Commission rules that allows for low-power FM stations (LPFMs), which are far less expensive to operate than a high-power station. The programming options of LPFMs could be much

Table 4.2 Television Viewing by Demographic Group, 2002 (in percent)

Group	Television viewing	Prime time TV viewing	Cable viewing
18–24	90.5	73.5	67.4
25–34	92.3	80.3	72.0
35–44	92.7	80.8	75.4
45–54	94.3	85.4	76.1
55–64	95.3	86.7	76.5
65+	96.9	88.6	70.1
Male	94.1	81.9	74.1
Female	93.1	83.1	72.1

From U.S. Bureau of the Census (2002, p. 699)

narrower, aimed at a specific community or neighborhood. Critics of radio ownership consolidation contend that LPFMs would allow a wider variety of voices to be heard and would restore emphasis on local news and programming.

TELEVISION

Today, television is the dominant medium in the United States. In 1948, there were 17 stations broadcasting to a mere 102,000 television sets in the United States. By 1960, 90 percent of U.S. homes had a television, and by 1978, more than 98 percent of homes had at least one television. Today, the average house has 2.4 television sets, 68 percent of homes have cable television, and 85.1 percent of homes have a videocassette recorder (VCR). There are 1,663 television stations and more than 10,000 cable television systems. More than 90 percent of all Americans watch television, and we spend an average of 4.55 hours a day doing so, which makes television our most significant media source. More than 90 percent of the public in each major demographic group reports watching television. Table 4.2 breaks down television viewership by age group. Women and men are relatively equal in their viewing. It is clear that television's influence on persuasion is profound. We will divide our discussion of its influence into three categories: technological advances, cognitive effects, and social implications.

Technological Advances   Technological advances in the television industry primarily affect how a persuader communicates with an audience. Persuaders today have more opportunities to reach narrowly defined audiences, and they do so using "lifelike" imaging technology. Technology has rapidly changed television from the small black-and-white images of the 1960s. One of the first technological advances in television was color. Although color broadcasting technology was available as early as 1946, most network broadcasts were not transmitted in color until 1967 (DeFleur & Dennis, 1998). Color dramatically changed the way viewers saw their world. Color images were more lifelike than black-and-white images, eliciting an emotional response from viewers. High-definition television (HDTV) is the next major technological change in the television industry. HDTV allows the viewer greater control over the type of image broadcast and provides an enhanced picture quality. HDTV images have a three-dimensional quality to them. With HDTV, pictures of real events may be sharper and more lifelike than the event itself, blurring the line between experience and simulated experience even more.

Three innovations have changed how audiences receive television images: cable, videocassette recorders, and direct-broadcast satellite systems. These innovations have at the same time changed the nature of the television audience. Initially, television viewers used large antennae on their rooftops to obtain the broadcasts. Cable television was developed in the 1950s to overcome physical barriers to over-the-air broadcast signals (DeFleur & Dennis, 1998). Cable allows many users to share a large antenna owned by the cable company. In 1997, 69 million homes were cabled, which is 68 percent of all homes. Cable television has decreased traditional network television viewing and increased market segmentation. Viewers are able to watch programming tailored more specifically to their tastes. Persuaders have new, and more efficient, avenues for the distribution of their messages. VCRs provide a means for audiences to fast-forward through commercials on programs they have recorded to watch at a later time. As we will see later in this book, advertisers are being forced to adapt to consumers' media use habits.

Direct-broadcast satellite (DBS) systems offer viewers an alternative to cable. By mounting an 18-inch satellite dish on or near their house, installing a receiver near their television set, and subscribing to a monthly service, viewers can receive television programming beamed directly to them from satellites in space. By 2003, 20.36 million Americans subscribed to direct-broadcast satellite (Cuprisin, 2003). This number is expected to grow as regulations concerning broadcasting of local programming by satellite change. DBS gives even more control to viewers, allowing them to watch pay-per-view movies, commercial-free television shows, and a wider range of programming options than are available on local cable systems. As viewers gain more control, persuaders lose power and their ability to reach audiences.

Technology is currently being developed that will give viewers even more control over what they see on the television screen. Sprint has developed an interactive television system that allows viewers of sports programs to control certain production elements, including camera angle. Called the "Den of the Future," the system allows viewers to access game statistics and even interact with other viewers who have similar systems. Digital television recorders allow viewers to "pause" live TV, fast-forward through commercials, and record up to 30 hours of programming on a built-in computer hard drive. The devices also allow viewers to rewind a show while it is being recorded to review something that happened or was said earlier. Digital television recorders can identify specific programs that viewers may find interesting. However, these recording devices are also able to track the viewing habits of their owners and report this information to the service provider. NBC is one broadcast company that has invested in the technology to allow it to gain this information. With more information about their audiences, persuaders can more narrowly target their messages. You may receive different advertising than your neighbor while you both watch the same program. Such technology also raises privacy concerns. When persuaders can track what we watch and when we watch it, the possibility exists that they will use this information to exploit their relationship with us.

As the viewer gains more control over television programming, persuaders must adapt their methods of reaching audiences. In the past, persuaders could bank on the fact that there were few programming options for viewers, that viewers had to move from their chairs to change the channel, and that, short of turning off the television, viewers had little choice but to watch commercials. At the same time, technology allows persuaders to more specifically target their messages to audiences.

Cognitive Effects   In Chapter 1, we explored Ong's (1982) theory about the cognitive effects of television on its audience. Television has changed the way we view time and space. We can view live events taking place many miles from where we live. We are thus transported, by television, to those places. The impact of the electronic media on our culture is profound, according to Joshua Meyrowitz (1985): "Many Americans may no longer seem to 'know their place' because the traditionally interlocking components of 'place' have been split apart by electronic media" (p. 308). He continues, "Our world may suddenly seem senseless to many people because, for the first time in modern history, it is relatively placeless" (p. 308).

Television has also changed the way we process information and thus see the world. Recall our discussion of media cultures from Chapter 1. The introduction of television to our society created subcultures of individuals who perceived the world differently than did those who primarily used print or radio media sources. The world became fragmented when individuals began to view society in different ways. With numerous cable channels, audiences are subdivided into many distinct units. Advertisers must deal with these smaller, more fragmented audiences in new ways.

Television has firmly established the role of images in society. Because television is the dominant medium in society, other media have been forced to copy its visual nature, creating a visual orientation throughout our culture. Newspapers such as *USA Today* use a visual, television-like layout and design in order to give readers a quick look at the day's news. *USA Today* has also gained attention for its sales stands, which are shaped to look like television sets.

Social Influences   Television is a profound socializing force that persuades us to accept a certain view of the world. We find television sets in many locations around the house: the family room, the living room, the kitchen, and the bedroom (Morgan & Signorielli, 1990). Televisions are now standard features in some automobiles, and we can receive television broadcasts on our workplace computers, meaning we are potentially exposed to television during all of our waking hours. Michael Morgan and Nancy Signorielli (1990) further explain the influence of television: "Television has become our nation's (and increasingly the world's) most common and constant learning environment. It both (selectively) mirrors and leads society" (p. 13). No matter what we watch, the medium of television creates messages with a certain type of meaning. Specifically, the narrative form of television dominates how we think, communicate, and perceive others. Television has forced persuaders to use a style appropriate to it. We discuss this style in greater detail in Chapters 6 and 7.

INTERNET

Persuaders design messages exclusively for the Internet as well as use the Internet to disseminate messages traditionally conveyed through other media. For instance, in addition to being published in print form, many newspapers and magazines are published in electronic form on the Internet. Thus, the Internet is a unique type of media and signals a shift to the concept of convergence, discussed in the next section.

The Internet actually began in the 1960s as a way for military leaders to communicate in times of crisis. After commercialization was allowed in the 1990s, the Internet exploded, providing a fast, inexpensive method for communicating with others. Educators use the Internet to obtain research. Businesses use the Internet to advance their image. Private individuals use the Internet to do just about anything, from chatting with their friends to posting pictures of their latest vacation to shopping for hard-to-find items. The Internet has no central control, and no one owns the Internet. The Internet includes the popular World Wide Web and its graphic interface, e-mail, news groups, and chat rooms.

In 1997, the Internet was used by 15 percent of the population. In 2001, 53.9 percent of the population used the Internet. The average number of visits from home during July 2003 was 31—about once per day; from work, the average number of times users logged on the Internet was 67—about twice per day; and, the average Internet session from both home and work lasted 33 minutes. Interestingly, users stayed on a web page for only 1 minute, whether they accessed it from home or work (Nielsen/NetRatings, 2003).

Although other media sources are fairly constant in their use by members of different demographic groups, Internet use varies greatly by group. Higher income groups are much more likely to use the Internet than are lower income groups, younger groups more likely than older groups, and Caucasians more likely than African Americans. (Table 4.3 breaks down Internet use by demographic group.) This disparity in use reflects the digital divide, the fact that some people have greater access to the Internet than others. This digital divide has ethical considerations for persuaders, which we discuss in Ethical Insights: Ethics and the Digital Divide.

Four important features of the Internet influence our study of persuasion. First, the Internet, more so than other media, has erased the boundaries of time and space. We can instantly communicate with other individuals in faraway places. Using videoconferencing technology, we can even see the individual with whom we are communicating. We can access overseas newspapers, gaining exposure to the views and perspectives of other cultures. As a result, society becomes more fractured, meaning that persuaders must adapt their traditional methods of reaching audiences.

Second, the Internet's use of hypertext—which lets users "jump" from one spot in a text to another—has given audiences of persuasive messages more

Table 4.3 Internet Use by Demographic Group, 2001

Group	% of group that uses Internet
9–17	68.6
18–24	65.0
25–49	63.9
50+	37.1
Male	53.9
Female	53.8
White	59.9
Black	39.8
Asian American and Pacific Islander	60.4
Hispanic	31.6
Less than $15,000 family income	25.0
Income of $50,000–74,999	67.3
Income of $75,000 and over	78.9
Less than a high school education	17.0
High school diploma	39.8
Bachelor's degree	80.8

From U.S. Bureau of the Census (2002, p. 713)

control over how they process information. Instead of reading an entire article, Internet viewers can use hyperlinks to skip around in the article. We can pick and choose which information we want to receive by clicking on the hyperlinks provided on a site. Providers of Internet content must design their pages so that users can gain information quickly. Persuaders must also create ways of keeping viewers on their sites for longer periods of time, so that they are exposed to advertising and other information. Hypertext gives users the ability to rearrange information and construct documents of their own design. Hypertext, more than any other technology, allows audience members to participate fully in the creation of persuasive messages. The powerful influence of the persuader is minimized to an extent by hypertext.

Third, the technology of the Internet allows for interactivity. Although newspapers and magazines have always had the ability to print readers' letters to the editor, the Internet greatly enhances the ability of persuasive message sources to hear and respond to their users. MSNBC reporter Kari Huus (1998) explains: "While watching the drama unfold in Indonesia I had dozens of readers writing to me every day—many of them Indonesians in Jakarta or living abroad. Human rights groups were sending statements. Individuals were sending accounts of looting in other towns around the country" (p. 63). She continues, "Not all of these comments are useful or can be verified, but some lead to story ideas, angles or contacts" (p. 63). Today, we can e-mail talk show hosts, log our votes on instant surveys, and read the *Starr Report* along with the entire world.

Finally, the Internet has greatly enhanced the ability of persuaders to target specific audiences. Marketers can accurately pinpoint potential customers by

ETHICAL INSIGHTS

Ethics and the Digital Divide

The digital divide is a growing problem in our society. Although many Americans have access to the Internet and its wide range of information—much of which is potentially empowering—many others do not. A 1999 report issued by the U.S. Department of Commerce found that while more Americans than ever have access to telephones, computers, and the Internet, there is still a significant "digital divide" separating those who "have" from those who "have not." In the nation's poorest high schools, for instance, only 39 percent of classrooms have Internet access, which is 24 percent below the national average (Revenaugh, 2000, p. 38). Likewise, a household with two Caucasian parents who earn less than $35,000 a year is three times as likely to have Internet access as is a similar African American household and four times as likely as a similar Hispanic household (Revenaugh, 2000, p. 38).

The digital divide threatens to marginalize even further those who do not have access to technological resources. As we depend more and more on media such as the Internet to bring us news, information, and educational resources, it is easy to see how equality of access is a significant goal for which we should strive. Consider how often you use the Internet and for what reasons. You probably do research

for papers, purchase goods and services, read the news, and communicate with your friends via the Internet. Now consider how difficult these tasks would be for someone without access to the Internet. In addition, think about how difficult it would be to get a job today without knowing how to use the Internet.

In Chapter 3 we discussed the National Communication Association's Credo for Communication Ethics (NCA, 1999). One of its principles is this: "We believe that access to communication resources and opportunities is necessary to fulfill human potential and contribute to the well-being of families, communities, and society." A variety of initiatives have been taken to provide Internet access to all people, yet the struggle continues. Consider the ethics of equality of access to media resources as you answer these questions.

1. What are some of the problems that arise from inequality of access to communication resources? What implications does the digital divide have for those who are already marginalized in our culture?

2. Assess the equality of access to communication resources in your community. Who are the haves? Who are the have-nots? What impact does the digital divide have on your community?

---

tracking those customers' travels on the Internet. Say, for instance, that as you surf the Internet, you access websites about video games. Later, as you check your e-mail at one of the free e-mail services, an advertisement appears for a particular video game. Clicking on the ad takes you to a site that is selling the game you want. Another few clicks and you've ordered the game. Or you do a search on Yahoo! for "automobiles." When the list of hits appears, the advertising at the top is for Ford or Chrysler or some other car company. Internet marketing targets users who are ready to buy a particular product or service. In fact, technology has appeared that can track your every move on the Internet. Advertising on television or in magazines cannot target audiences as precisely. We explore these themes more fully in subsequent chapters.

How do you use each of the media channels discussed? How often and for how long do you use each type?

CONVERGENCE: THE BLURRING OF MEDIA BOUNDARIES

Convergence describes the integration of voice, video, and data technologies. In the past, radio, television, and print media sources were separate entities.

convergence
the networking of various media sources through the integration of voice, video, and data technologies

Audiences would obtain information separately from each medium. Development of the Internet and the Telecommunications Act of 1996, however, facilitated the development of new broadband systems (Baldwin, McVoy, & Steinfeld, 1996). Now, different media sources, and even telephone, are combined into a vast network. Television and radio networks broadcast on the Internet. Newspapers and magazines are published online. R. Campbell (1998) explains, "It is no longer very useful to discuss print media and electronic or digital media as if they were completely segregated forms" (p. 53). As the equipment with which we access media becomes a single unit, such as Ultimate TV, the possibilities will be virtually limitless. Imagine watching television programming aimed specifically at your demographic group. An advertisement appears for a product that interests you. With a few mouse clicks, you can order the product and have it shipped to your house. Two examples will help to further define convergence.

Oxygen Media is a multimedia company seeking to educate and sell goods and services to women. Gerry Laybourne, founder of Oxygen Media, sees a day when women will watch television programming on an issue that concerns them, like financial success for new divorcées. Something on the program will catch the viewer's interest and she will turn on her computer and access a financial Web page provided by Oxygen Media. The user might then order a book on investing or she might use an Oxygen Media financial service and purchase shares in a mutual fund. Later, the same woman might watch a travel show on the Oxygen Media network and book her trip using an Oxygen Media travel site. The goal is to "trap viewers with decent programming" and then keep them tuned in for the commercials or else switch them to their computers to access information from the show's website (Post, 1999, p. 112). Oxygen Media is one company that is capitalizing on media convergence. Log on to the website for this textbook to access Oxygen Media.

MSNBC, which debuted in July 1996 as a joint venture between NBC television and Microsoft, the computer software company, is another example of convergence. MSNBC's experiences in the years since serve as a glimpse into the present and future of media convergence. Alicia C. Shepard (1997) describes MSNBC as one brand with two operations, an NBC cable studio in Fort Lee, New Jersey, and a multimedia website operated from Redmond, Washington. MSNBC programming is developed simultaneously for cable and the Internet. The goal of MSNBC is "cross-pollination," or the use of one medium to foster viewership of another. MSNBC journalists search for ways to make television and the Internet compatible.

Viewers who switch to MSNBC on their cable television or satellite systems see regular programming like *Time and Again,* talk format programming, and news shows. Internet users who access www.msnbc.com see a Web page that looks like any other major news company's Web page: links to news stories, video clips, and real-time video and audio feeds. Figure 4.2 shows an image from the MSNBC website.

Cross-pollination is achieved in several ways. MSNBC on-air personalities, such as Jane Pauley, host of the show *Time and Again,* often suggest that viewers access MSNBC's Internet site for more information on the stories

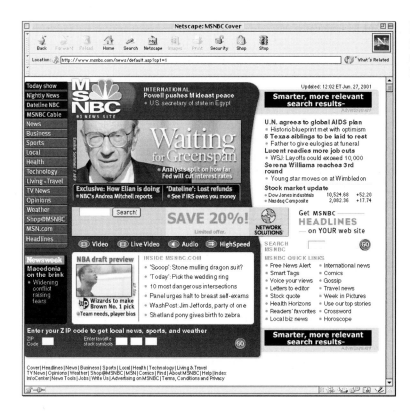

Figure 4.2 The MSNBC Web page presents a variety of examples of convergence. Which can you identify?

being aired. MSNBC has integrated video and software in other ways as well. During President Clinton's second inauguration, MSNBC viewers on the Internet could manipulate a camera focused on the ceremony. Viewers could zoom in on audience members or change the angle of view. Viewers can also rank pro football teams and receive an immediate vote tally that includes the viewer's own rankings. Concurrent chat rooms allow viewers to communicate with other viewers in real time.

MSNBC is pioneering the way that breaking news is covered in the media age. MSNBC reporter Kari Huus (1998) writes of her experiences covering political unrest in Indonesia. As a reporter for the cable television/Internet network, she had more options, and thus more choices, for how to cover the breaking news event halfway around the world than some other journalists did. She recounts: "I was carrying a digital recorder, digital camera, regular SLR camera, and a cell phone" (p. 63). "I could use the cell phone to call in periodic updates to the story so that MSNBC news editors could publish bare-bones text stories within minutes. Or I could use the time to instead record digital sound and still pictures. Then I could jump on a motorcycle taxi to return to the hotel, process the sound and images, and send them by Email for immediate publication" (p. 63).

In the end, Huus used a combination of these options. She called in the story from the scene, so that MSNBC could publish it immediately. She recorded sound and pictures for later use. When the president of Indonesia resigned, MSNBC immediately published a banner on its website with the news.

Later, Huus did a phone interview for the television station and wrote an in-depth analysis for Internet publication. Without the printing process to slow them down, MSNBC reporters are able to quickly disseminate news to the world. Huus is quick to point out that the process is not perfect, but: "Internet news can be rich and timely. However, the results can also be confusing, incomplete or overwhelming. It may be gratuitous to point out that those of us who report news for the Internet are still working on the formula" (1998, p. 63).

The impact of convergence for persuaders and audience members is three-fold. First, convergence allows users *immediate access to vast libraries* of information. Users have the potential to learn many different sides to a news story, but only if they so choose. Audience members can get their news and information from media sources that have a decidedly different perspective than that of their local newspaper or television station. Elizabeth Hilts (1998) contends that broadcast television often sparks public discussion about an issue, whereas newspapers provide deeper coverage.

At the same time, as Postman has argued, the vast amount of information available creates a situation in which we lose the ability to judge the validity of the information we see. All information appears to be equal. Hoaxes perpetuated by e-mail are good examples of the information overload Postman discusses. E-mail users frequently receive messages that appear genuine. These messages promise a free trip to Disneyland courtesy of Bill Gates, warn against people who steal internal organs from drugged victims, or mobilize e-mail users against certain social movements. One such hoax warned e-mail users that the U.S. Postal Service was attempting to charge e-mail users 5 cents for each e-mail sent. Many recipients took the message seriously. The Postal Service received complaints from e-mail users across the country. The e-mail even prompted a viewer question in a debate between New York U.S. Senate candidate Hillary Rodham Clinton and Rick Lazio. Yet the entire message was fabricated. There was no pending legislation in Congress, no Virginia lawyer who had supposedly initiated the crusade, and no U.S. Representative named Tony Schnell who was allegedly pushing for a tax on e-mail. Check out this textbook's website for a link to a site that evaluates Internet e-mail hoaxes. For audience members, the information potential of the Internet is both a blessing and a curse.

Second, convergence allows for what Campbell (1998) has called "*mass customization,* whereby product companies and content providers can customize a Web page or media form for an individual consumer" (p. 53). Audience members can receive the news they want to read. Advertisers can pinpoint audience members who will be receptive to their product or service. Satellite broadcasters can transmit television or radio programming to specific households that have specific interests and needs. Mass customization has also been referred to as one-to-one marketing or relationship marketing, as opposed to the traditional marketing approach of one-to-many. We discuss new forms of marketing based on this idea throughout the book.

Finally, convergence emphasizes the *symbolic, mediated nature of our environment.* When we purchase books and music, read the day's newspaper, and watch the nightly news from our computer, we lose our sense of place in the

Bennett (1996), summarizing scholarly critiques of the news, argues that news has four characteristics that make it palatable as a product for consumers. These characteristics, common to much news coverage, affect the public's ability to obtain an accurate account of the day's events. News is personalized, dramatized, fragmented, and normalized, writes Bennett. Although these characteristics are true of many news media organizations, not all news media exhibit these features. We discuss exceptions to these generalizations later.

Personalized   The news tends to focus on the individual actors in news events, as opposed to the institutional factors involved in the story. Bennett (1996) explains that the news directs public attention to scandals, careers, personal wins and losses, and prestige and status. Personalized news omits the context necessary for the public to fully understand the personal struggles being portrayed. Personalized news is appealing to the public because we feel strongly about the people involved. The news, then, allows us to feel we are playing a role in this personal struggle. For example, the 2000 presidential campaign was covered as a personal battle between the various candidates. During the primaries, the news carefully documented each attack and counterattack. Of particular interest to news media was John McCain, the Arizona senator who had been a prisoner of war during the Vietnam War. We choose sides in the personal battles we see in the news, but lose sight of the context of the news story.

Bennett argues that this leaves us with an egocentric view of the world in which our view of news events is controlling; we can see no other perspective. Bennett also contends that the world of "personalized politics" is a fantasy world in which we focus not on issues and context, but on the current hero. Finally, personalized news tends to privilege the views of those who are featured, usually upper-class Caucasian men. The personalized nature of the news hides the lives and experiences of women and minorities. As a result, audiences form stereotypical views of women and minorities. Julia Wood (1998) argues that personalized news creates two images of women: good women and bad ones. Good women stay at home and take care of the family. Bad women are cold, aggressive, and evil. Minorities are viewed similarly. Personalization of the news has implications for how we view ourselves and others.

Dramatized   The news is also dramatized, which is to say that it is presented in the same way as a television program, movie, or theatrical production. In an oft-quoted statement, NBC's Reuven Frank told his correspondents in 1963, "Every news story should, without any sacrifice of probity or responsibility, display the attributes of fiction, of drama. It should have structure and conflict, problem and denouement, rising and falling action, a beginning, a middle, and an end. These are not only the essentials of drama; they are the essentials of narrative" (quoted in Patterson, 1994). As a result, news media tend to focus on conflict, personalities, and a "stock of plot formulas" to make the story interesting for the audience. Dramatic weather reports, for example, often border on fiction, especially when they do not come to fruition. Bennett (1996) also argues that the dramatic focus of the news is done poorly. In good theater, we get a glimpse of the history, context, and role of institutional pressures on the dramatic action. Contemporary news coverage does not provide these cues.

As a result of the dramatic focus of news, Bennett (1996) argues that it is difficult to draw the line between "journalists as reporters of fact and as creators of fiction" (p. 37). Thus, although journalists are perceived to be providing "just the facts," they color the story in a certain way that removes it from the reality it is pretending to portray. This prevents us from fully understanding the issue, although we think we have grasped the important points of the story. As a result, we are not able to act on the issue, and democracy suffers because its citizens are uninformed. Bennett also argues that the public sees dramatized news as trivial. Finally, Bennett says that dramatized news creates false impressions about the severity of problems in society. Because dramatic issues like crime receive a lot of attention, we tend to think they are more widespread than they are (Morgan & Signorielli, 1990).

Fragmented   The news is also fragmented, claims Bennett (1996). It is a "jigsaw puzzle that is out of focus and missing many pieces. When focus is provided it is on the individual pieces, not on how they fit into the overall picture" (p. 58). Fragmentation occurs because media focus on current events, the current crisis around the world, the latest act of violence at home, or the current political campaign. Bennett argues that long-term patterns and trends are ignored. We watch a story about war in another country, but we learn little about the history of the country and its people. We see stories about violence in the United States, but fail to grasp the full weight of the institutional factors that led to that violence. The result of fragmentation is that "image, illusion, and stereotype are the only messages that can be communicated" (Bennett, 1996, p. 61). Our view of the world is not complete because we see only a small portion of it. When the audience is uninformed on an issue, it has difficulty making sense of news fragments.

Normalized   Finally, our news is normalized. Bennett (1996) defines normalization as "the tendency to filter new information through traditional values, beliefs, and images of society and to deliver the filtered information through the reassuring pronouncements of authorities charged with returning things to normal" (p. 65). In other words, the news tends to cast as deviant those members of society who do not fit the "norm."

Bennett (1996) argues that the normalizing character of the news creates a narrow set of values and expectations. When we see protestors, we view them as harmful to the democratic system. When we hear stories about the unique customs of immigrants, we view these individuals as "different" and therefore bad. Bennett argues that news media have a conservative effect on our society because change is constantly cast as not normal and, therefore, wrong. News media, then, carry with them values about how society should be. Consider how the article excerpt in Thinking Critically: Analyzing a News Article displays one or more of the characteristics we have examined.

Exceptions   Typically, news transmitted by large organizations exhibits the characteristics we have just discussed. Smaller news organizations often pro-

THINKING CRITICALLY

Analyzing a News Article

Bennett (1996) argues that the news is dramatized, personalized, normalized, and fragmented. Look for examples of each characteristic as you read this excerpt from an article published in the *Fargo Forum* on August 17, 2000 (Campbell, 2000).

Richard Taylor strolled the railroad tracks north of Main Avenue in Fargo Wednesday. Taking the usual route toward his residence, he discovered his home was not in its usual spot.

A few yards away, the scuffed white dairy truck—sans wheels—that Taylor, 53, has lived in since 1993 sat in a grassy-turning-muddy field behind a fleet of used cars at Ness Auto Sales and The Budget Lot.

"This was my home," Taylor laughed, nervously.

Taylor's cramped living quarters—replete with clothes and books and a small stove—had to be moved from its niche in the ditch along the train tracks. A bulldozer was clearing the area, a former auto salvage yard site. The old cars and spare parts were taken away a few years ago. Except for Taylor's abode.

"It was the only thing they left," Taylor said.

It was unclear Wednesday afternoon exactly why the lot was being bulldozed. Budget Lot General Sales Manager Donnie Olson said the adjacent lot was recently cleaned up for weed control purposes. He thought the same thing was being done around Taylor's living space.

The article exemplifies each characteristic of Bennett's theory. It features conflict (drama), a homeless person facing the forces of city bureaucracy. In fact, the story fits the common news stereotype of innocent victim versus large, faceless organization. The article is personalized, focusing on Taylor and his personal struggle to find a place to live. The article is normalized in the sense that it portrays Taylor as somehow "different" from the rest of society because he lives in a dairy truck instead of a house. The article is also fragmented because its relationship to long-term issues is sketchy. The article does not discuss issues facing the homeless or why people such as Taylor are homeless. It appeared in the paper only because Taylor's home had been moved. The next day, the paper made no mention of Taylor or the issues facing him and millions of other people.

Think about Bennett's ideas of news, and answer these questions about the excerpt:

1. Who is not featured in this story? What events and ideas are featured? Does the article's emphasis on personality overwhelm a discussion of ideas and events?

2. What beliefs and values are portrayed as normal? What beliefs and values are portrayed as being deviant?

duce news that does not reflect the standards used by the large organizations. Examples may include minority-owned newspapers that attempt to offer a different view of the news than their larger competitors. Many cities also have arts-oriented newspapers that provide a different perspective on current events. Gay-lesbian-bisexual-transgendered newspapers also exist to offer a different viewpoint. Although not all of these sources are able to avoid the characteristics identified by Bennett, they do attempt to place current events in a different framework in order to empower their readers.

NEWS DECISIONS

The characteristics of news that we have just discussed arise due to how news organizations make decisions about what is newsworthy. News media must constantly decide which stories to run. Graber, McQuail, and Norris (1998) explain that there is simply too much information to cover in one day, making selection of what to cover necessary. Decisions about what to feature are based on a number of factors, many of which involve the nature of the news media as a profit industry. News organizations are constantly concerned with being "scooped" by other news organizations. News organizations want to be the first to report on a particular story or to get a particular interview. News organizations also face time and resource limitations. This section surveys the nature of news decision making and the impact these decisions have on the public's perception of its world. Several factors influence the decision making of news media: access, cost, time and space, and competition.

First, news organizations must have *access* to an event in order to cover it (Jamieson & Campbell, 1997). News events that happen in distant places or at undesirable times are often not covered. The U.S. news media have been decreasing the quantity of foreign news coverage for years. International news coverage is usually limited to the current "hot spot" because that is where the news personnel are located. As news consumers, we fail to realize that events are taking place in other parts of the world because we do not see news about those areas.

Cost is a second constraint on media (Jamieson & Campbell, 1997). It is expensive to send reporters to events and to hire enough reporters to cover all the news. Thus, news media are turning to national organizations such as Metro News to help them cover news events. In fact, many news organizations are decreasing the number of reporters covering foreign news because of the cost involved. Persuaders are mindful of the fact that media organizations are limited in their ability to cover stories and will create newsworthy events at times and places conducive to inexpensive media coverage. In Chapter 7, we discuss how persuaders use pseudoevents to overcome this constraint.

Time and space for stories is a third constraint (Jamieson & Campbell, 1997). Traditional media have a very small amount of time to cover news stories. The traditional half-hour newscast, for instance, contains only about 22 minutes of news. In fact, all the words said in a televised newscast could easily fit on half a page in a newspaper. For print media, space is a concern. Advertising determines how much space is devoted to news. Without advertising, news coverage decreases. The Internet opens the possibility for expanded news coverage.

Finally, *competition and deadlines* affect news decisions. Editors must decide whether to run a story as it is or wait until it can be further researched and substantiated. News organizations want to be the first on the scene and often "go live" to report breaking news. The result is that reporters may not have researched the story fully before airing it to thousands, or millions, of people. As media converge and news can be provided to the public instantly, the demands for speedy reporting will increase.

The tragic deaths of John F. Kennedy, Jr., his wife, Carolyn Bessette Kennedy, and her sister Lauren Bessette in 1999 offer a dramatic example of how media competition and deadlines influence news coverage. Kennedy, his wife, and his sister-in-law were killed when their small plane crashed into the ocean off Martha's Vineyard late one summer Friday evening. Initial news reports were sketchy about whether the plane had crashed and who was on board.

Many media organizations covered the search-and-rescue attempt live for several days following the plane's disappearance. As each new detail emerged, news media were quick to report it and to get responses from those close to the investigation and from the Kennedy family. Despite the fact that almost nothing new emerged for several days, news media continued to cover the story, almost to the point of absurdity. It was clear that news media were still learning to negotiate the rules of news-on-demand that media convergence had made possible.

PRESENTATION

The presentation of the news affects viewers in several ways. *Breaking news,* for instance, presents numerous problems for media. When they are "live" on the scene, reporters do not have the chance to interview sources beforehand to find out if they are credible. Many times, reporters will talk to whomever they can in these situations. Sometimes those sources are credible, and sometimes they are not. Also, it is difficult for reporters to carefully check the accuracy of the information they are receiving in a breaking-news situation. But by not going live, a news organization would let its competitors be first on the scene.

Reporters often cite *anonymous*—unnamed—*sources.* You often hear a reporter say, "Sources in the White House confirm that. . . ." Because the person who provided the information to the reporter is not named, the source cannot be questioned about what he or she has said. We'll discuss anonymous sources further in Chapter 9.

Finally, there is the possibility of *bias* in the news. A great debate continues to rage about whether media have a conservative or a liberal bias. Studies have been inconclusive on this question. There is no question, however, that some members of media have particular biases or that certain news organizations tend to favor one political party or the other. The *Wall Street Journal,* for instance, is usually considered to be a conservative media organization. The *New York Times,* on the other hand, is usually seen as liberal.

AUDIENCE EMPOWERMENT

Given the rather dismal view of the news we have just presented, you may be thinking that it is impossible to become an informed citizen in today's world. Being informed is possible, but it requires knowledge of the constraints on news media and the ability to locate credible news information. First, it is important to be aware of how economic, social, and political forces constrain news media and to appreciate the effect these constraints have on news coverage.

In addition, it is important to learn how to seek out credible news information. National Public Radio (NPR) has long been considered one of the most credible news sources. NPR provides regular citizens an opportunity to express their views on topics and it provides more in-depth analysis of issues than other media sources. You might also search for news from a variety of sources to determine the degree to which a story is significant. You can check the website for this textbook to learn of some informative news sources. Keep in mind that finding the same news in several locations does not necessarily mean that

Listen to a radio broad-cast on National Public Radio. How are radio broadcasts on NPR different from those on your local commercial station? How are they similar?

the story is credible: Wire service stories are often reprinted in several newspapers. Knowing about the limitations on news media and understanding how to find and differentiate news will help you become a knowledgeable consumer of today's news.

Entertainment Media

We have just discussed the impact of the news media on persuasion. While much of what we experience and think about is based on the news, we are also exposed to a great variety of other media programming that is persuasive. We have previously defined entertainment programming as that which is non-news programming, including motion pictures, radio and television talk shows, and television dramas, sitcoms, reality-based shows, and game shows. In this section, we'll see how this type of programming can be persuasive.

Slater and Rouner (2000) explain that fictional messages—such as those contained in entertainment programming—can influence an audience member's beliefs about social groups and social issues. In particular, audience members naturally process narratives, which are stories about human relationships. In some cases, we are more likely to process narratives than we are factual information. Slater and Rouner write that this is possible because we seem to automatically process narrative information, and we can remember it more easily. We become invested in fictional messages and have emotional responses to them. In other words, fictional messages—like the plot on your favorite television drama—can engage us so much in their story about human relationships that we don't realize the persuasive messages we are hearing and seeing. As a result, we form specific beliefs and values.

Rosen (1986) explains, "Day after day, soaps encourage viewers to escape their own lives, to ignore the actual problems in their own community and nation, and to yearn for perfect love in a mythic community" (p. 66). In Chapter 11, we'll examine more closely how emotions and values are influenced by our interaction with our environment, which includes entertainment media.

What entertainment programming do you watch? What effect do you think this programming has on your beliefs and values?

In particular, Parenti (1992) argues that entertainment media often shape our political beliefs. Echoing the ideas of Slater and Rouner (2002), Parenti sees the narrative form of entertainment media being especially effective in conveying beliefs to audience members. Parenti explains, "Beliefs are less likely to be preached than assumed. Woven into the story line and into the characteristics, they are perceived as entertainment rather than as political judgments about the world" (p. 3). Parenti identifies a variety of beliefs that he argues are influenced by entertainment media. Saturday morning cartoons, for instance, often have messages that, using violence, we can defeat foreign invaders.

Entertainment media may also contribute to our stereotypes about other people in our culture. In this sense, it is persuasive by presenting us with vivid, yet unrealistic, pictures of individuals in our culture. The caricatures of individuals that appear in entertainment programming seem so real to us that we respond to them as if they are. Fiske (1987) notes that an obvious view of television is that it provides an "unmediated picture of external reality" (p. 21).

Our beliefs are then influenced by these images that we take to be accurate. Recall our discussion of cultivation analysis theory in Chapter 2. This theory states that heavy exposure to television, generally, leads to views of the world that are not necessarily accurate. For instance, if you watch a lot of television police shows, you are more likely to have a view of the world in which African American men are more frequently the perpetrators of crimes than they are really.

Tan, Fujioka, and Tan (2000) tested the hypothesis of cultivation theory. They studied television viewers to see what kind of stereotypes they formed toward African Americans. Additionally, they were interested in how these viewers felt about the political policy of affirmative action. The researchers tested a sample of 166 Caucasian college students who watched an average of 9.96 hours of television per week. When asked to compare African Americans and Caucasian Americans, the students rated African Americans as less positive than Caucasians on almost every trait surveyed. Additionally, the respondents could recall more negative stereotypes from television about African Americans than they could positive stereotypes. The respondents' views of African Americans correlated with their opposition to affirmative action policies based on their earlier observations. They summarized their study: "Perceived negative television portrayals of African Americans led to negative stereotyping which in turn predicted opposition to affirmative action" (p. 370).

Entertainment media also commodify the products, services, or ideas of persuaders as well. Remember that persuasion today often relies on commodification of some event, person, or object. In the first chapter, we discussed how persuaders seek to give value to their products and ideas. One way they do this is through the use of entertainment programming. By featuring their products or services in specific entertainment media, persuaders can make audience members aware of the product or service and make it seem valuable. Gauntlet and Hill (1999) note that television provides us with a common basis for discussions and that people enjoy talking about their experiences with television. For instance, in the Bravo reality series, *Queer Eye for the Straight Guy*, products from local businesses are often featured. Sales of a $2600 sofa and a $900 coffee table from New York furniture store Desiron quadrupled after they were seen on the hit television show. After seeing the furniture—and other items, such as personal grooming products—on the show, audience members may believe that the products have intrinsic value and seek to obtain them.

Fundamentally, entertainment programming may contribute to a change in the consciousness of a culture and its members. If you accept Ong's thesis from the first chapter—that the dominant media in a culture affect the thought process of the culture—then you can see how the very structure of entertainment programming creates certain kinds of thinkers. Postman, for instance, argues that *Sesame Street,* with its quick cuts and short segments, creates viewers who have short attention spans. Whether you agree that *Sesame Street* is responsible for a short attention span, Ong, and others, make the point that the dominant medium of a culture affects its consciousness. If nothing else, entertainment media force us to organize our lives in half-hour- or hour-long blocks of time. As we continue our study of persuasion, keep in mind the wide variety of ways that entertainment media may persuade us.

Summary

What we know of our world today is brought to us by media. A variety of terms help us understand the influence of media on persuasion. Specifically, media channel refers to the technological means used to communicate a message. Media source is the specific person or group of persons that communicates to an audience. Media content refers to programming. Media refers to the interaction between channels, sources, content, and audience.

There are three important assumptions about media that influence our study of persuasion. First, media persuade us. We act based on what media show us through programming, news, and advertising. Second, media create symbolic realities. We rely on these images to serve as knowledge. Third, media are in business to make a profit. As such, media serve as channels, gatekeepers, and persuaders.

The multisensory aspect of media makes it a powerful persuasive tool. Through visual images, music, and other auditory symbols, media appeal to our senses in ways that words alone cannot.

Media audiences are potentially large and impersonal, but their nature is changing due to changes in technology. Media content is fragmentary and ephemeral. Media sources are usually large organizations, but technology is making it possible for audience members to become sources. Media channels provide persuaders with numerous resources, but also limit their ability to communicate with us. Convergence of media sources is dramatically altering previous assumptions about media.

The news is our way of getting information about the world. News is dramatized, normalized, personalized, and fragmented, argues Bennett (1996). Because of this, many news media give us incomplete versions of our world. This has implications for how we perceive ourselves and others.

Finally, entertainment media shape our ideas about ourselves and our world. We get caught up in the narratives of entertainment programming and miss its persuasiveness.

Key Terms

WWW: Visit the book's website at http://www.mhhe.com/borchers2 for multiple-choice quizzes, Internet activities, and key term flashcards.

media source 96	entertainment media 100
media channel 99	entertainment programming 100
medium 99	media audience 100
media content 99	media 101
news media 99	convergence 115
news 99	

5
Audiences and Attitudes

Learning Objectives

After reading this chapter, you should be able to:

1. Describe characteristics of audiences in the media age.

2. Identify the components of an attitude.

3. Explain how persuaders use audience analysis in creating their messages.

4. Understand how audiences are measured using polling, demographics, psychographics, geodemographics, and ratings.

Consider two typical experiences you may have with media. As you surf the Internet, you perform searches, visit websites that interest you, and perhaps register to obtain special privileges from one or more of those sites. You might use the Internet to do research; to communicate with your friends and family; or to learn about the latest news, sports, and entertainment events. When you are done surfing the Net, you might watch some television. Perhaps you have a favorite night of the week for television viewing. If you are like millions of other Americans, you might tune into Thursday night's "Must See TV" on NBC. Whether you are online or watching television, you are using media to fulfill some need or experience.

In each instance, however, mediated persuaders are using you as well. When you use the Internet, you often leave a record of who you are, where you are, and what sites you visit. For instance, once you register at an online site, you are often greeted by a personal message when you return to that site. When you are online, you provide persuaders with a great deal of information about who you are. Persuaders also observe television viewers. Through various ratings systems, persuaders have a reasonable idea of the kinds of people who use media. Although you may not have been surveyed about your viewing habits, other viewers like you have been. On a deeper level, you, and others like you, are assembled by programmers and sold to persuaders. "Must See TV," for instance, is designed to attract 18- to 45-year-old viewers. By purchasing programs aimed at this group, NBC seeks to achieve high ratings—and consequently, large revenues—from advertisers interested in targeting their messages to just such viewers. Just as audiences use media, media use audiences.

Since the earliest days of persuasion, speakers have been concerned with affecting the attitudes of an audience. Before the use of media, a persuader spoke to an immediate audience, who relayed the persuader's message to others through word of mouth. Today, a persuader's message is broadcast to millions of people throughout the world in a matter of seconds. Not only do large audiences receive a persuader's message, but technology makes it possible for persuaders to understand their audiences as never before. Audience segmentation techniques make it possible to pinpoint ideal audiences for an advertiser's product. Telephone polling makes it possible for political candidates to receive instantaneous feedback from audiences. Video and Internet technology makes it possible to send immediate responses to readers and viewers. For these reasons, the audience plays an important role in persuasion, as we indicated in Chapter 1. At the same time, the audience often does not fully realize the strategies used by persuaders in an effort to identify with the audience. This chapter makes some of those strategies visible.

This exploration of the role of the audience in the persuasive process begins with a survey of the nature of the audience in the media age, examining its size, anonymity, and power. Next we explore audience attitudes, a primary variable in the persuasion process. Third, we discuss ways that persuaders learn about their audiences—through polling, segmentation, and ratings. This chapter explains how persuaders seek to understand their audiences so they can form intimate relationships with them. Knowledge of these strategies helps us, as audience members, to evaluate and judge the persuasive messages we encounter.

The Audience in the Media Age

Technology has made the audience a prominent feature in the persuasive process. As we discussed in Chapter 1, audiences play an active role in the cocreation of meaning. Persuaders use audience analysis to understand their audiences and adapt their messages. At the same time, technology makes it possible for audiences to circumvent the messages of persuaders and communicate directly with other audience members. In short, the audience for today's media is potentially large, anonymous, and able to circumvent the persuasive messages of producers.

SIZE

Media audiences are potentially very large (Jamieson & Campbell, 1997). While the ancient Greeks and Romans relied on vocal projection to reach audiences as large as several thousand, today's persuaders can reach millions through television, radio, print, or the Internet. The Super Bowl, for example, annually attracts television audiences of 40 million—usually the largest television audiences of the year. During a typical week, the top-rated television show is watched by 10 to 12 million viewers. On some rare occasions, such as televised presidential debates, as many as 70 million viewers tune in for some portion of the debate. Large audiences mean that a persuader's message must appeal to many different groups of people. Large audiences potentially give an enormous amount of power to the persuader. Persuaders can set the public's agenda for what it discusses, shape societal values and beliefs, and influence how we spend our time and money. Two important concepts—narrowcasting versus broadcasting strategies and primary versus secondary audiences—can help us better understand how audience size affects media persuaders.

Narrowcasting versus Broadcasting   Both traditional broadcast networks and smaller cable-only networks have taken advantage of narrowcasting to reach desired audiences. **Narrowcasting**—targeting programming at a small, narrowly defined audience—allows persuaders to reach ideal target audiences for their messages. Television shows such as *Trading Spaces, ESPN Sportscenter,* or *Sábado Gigante* are examples of narrowcasting programming. Advertisers who want to reach people who are interested in these subjects know that these programs will deliver the most receptive audiences. The advent of cable has brought about the creation of numerous television networks, some with very small audiences. The Golf Channel, the Food Network, and Comedy Central are examples of networks that appeal to audiences that are smaller than those enjoyed by the traditional networks of NBC, ABC, and CBS.

narrowcasting
a strategy used by persuaders to target a small, narrowly defined audience

The decreasing number of television viewers in recent years is causing networks to rethink this narrowcasting approach. Ed Martin (1999) reports that broadcasters are looking to attract more diverse audiences than in the past. Consequently, we are seeing a return to **broadcasting,** an attempt by network executives to attract a demographically more diverse audience. The hottest television show in 1999–2000 was the ABC game show *Who Wants to Be a Millionaire.* More than 75 percent of the American public watched at least one episode of the show, indicating its broad audience appeal. Broadcasting is effective for advertisers who are trying to create a highly recognizable brand, for instance. In any case, persuaders manipulate audience size through narrowcasting or broadcasting strategies.

broadcasting
a strategy used by network executives to attract a large and demographically diverse audience

Primary versus Secondary Audiences   Although the primary audience for a persuader's message may be large, secondary audiences make the total number of audience members even larger. Secondary audiences hear about, see, or read a persuader's message after it has initially reached the intended audience. Technology allows a persuader's message to be received by multiple audiences. Before paper was invented, ancient persuaders relied on the art of storytelling. The audience had to be immediately present to hear the speaker's words. Only after the story had been retold to others did its audience grow.

Today, it is rare that a persuader's message remains only in the eyes and ears of the initial audience. Through print and broadcast technology, the entire world is able to read, hear, and see persuasive communication. When the president delivers a message to a small audience of senior citizens in Florida, it takes only a few minutes for millions to hear and read those words or an account of the speech. Even courtrooms, once blocked from the view of television cameras, have become spectacles for public consumption of persuasive messages. Through rigorous reporting and Freedom of Information Act requests, journalists are able to obtain even the most secret of grand jury testimony, meeting reports, and political decisions. Even information from a one-on-one meeting in the corporate world may spread to others in the organization and beyond. In essence, the words of a persuader are almost always broadcast to a larger audience than is initially present for the communication. It is important for persuaders to create their messages for multiple audiences.

ANONYMITY

Whether large or small, audiences today are usually anonymous (Jamieson & Campbell, 1997). Media sources cannot see their audience, creating distance between the source and the receiver. Writers for wire services do not know their readers. Actors and actresses have never met those who spend countless hours with them over the course of a year. Quite often, interpersonal persuaders also do not know their audiences. An attorney, for instance, may know the names of the trial jurors, but almost never knows them personally. Salespeople often do not know their clients personally, although developing a personal relationship with them can be an important persuasive strategy.

Audiences are becoming less anonymous today than in the past, however. When audience members can e-mail the host of a news show while the show is airing, the audience becomes an active part of the program. The MSNBC network regularly features chat sessions during which audiences can have their calls or e-mails aired as part of the show. MSNBC reporter Kari Huus says that when she receives letters or e-mail from her viewers, it reminds her that "the subjects of the stories and the readers—who are sometimes one and the same—are real people" (1998, p. 63). It is impossible for persuaders reaching millions of people to know each audience member. Yet the appearance of knowing their audience is a powerful way for persuaders to foster identification. Likewise, by making themselves personally known to persuaders, audience members can influence the nature of a persuader's message.

TAKING CONTROL

The media age provides audience members with the opportunity to create their own messages, independent of media organizations. Channel surfing is a prime example of how audience members create their own programming by shifting between the carefully arranged messages of producers (Chesebro & Bertelsen, 1996). Likewise, the hypertext layout of Web pages allows users to create their own structure for Internet text. Two more examples further illustrate the power of audience members to circumvent the traditional media producers.

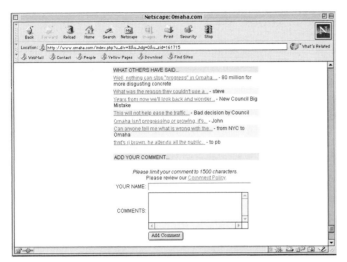

Figure 5.1   The *Omaha World-Herald* gives the readers the opportunity to interact with the stories it publishes in its online version. How do those who comment influence how other readers respond to the content of the article? Does reader involvement empower or disempower viewers? Does reader involvement improve journalism?

Amazon.com has become one of the largest e-commerce sites on the Web. The company relies only on its website to sell books, music, and other products to consumers. Users can log on to the Amazon.com site, order a book or CD, and wait for it to arrive in the mail. One reason Amazon.com has been so successful is because of the way it allows audience members to interact with each other. As you read about a book that interests you, you can click on a link to find what other books have been purchased by readers of your chosen book. You do not need to rely on book review editors to make additional suggestions; you can immediately tell what other books might interest you. In addition, you can read reviews posted by others who have read the book. Again, there is no need to rely on "experts" to review the book for you. Instead, you can turn to the impressions of other audience members like yourself.

Reading what others have to say about books may help you make your book purchasing experience more efficient, and the same technology has the potential to change the nature of journalism. Many news sites feature links to other news stories related to the story you are reading. When you follow these links, you create your own news story. Online newspapers allow readers to add their comments to particular stories. Figure 5.1 gives you an idea of how readers reacted to one story in the *Omaha World-Herald*. Readers can, in essence, add to the ideas of the reporter. In other words, the role of editor is being taken over by readers, who are creating a structure for and determining the content of the online news gathering experience. The potential this holds for how we process the news is staggering.

We have explored some ways that audiences can circumvent the messages of persuaders today. To what extent do you think audiences have more or less power in the media age? How can audience members take more advantage of empowering technology?

As we have seen, media audiences are potentially large, although their size can be determined, in part, by how persuaders create messages. Media audiences are also anonymous, although persuaders seek to know their audiences and form relationships with them. Audiences can also circumvent or alter the messages of persuaders in several ways.

So far, we have discussed audiences as a group of individuals. In the next section, we focus on individual audience members and how they think about persuasive messages.

Audiences and Attitudes

James Price Dillard (1993) contends that all of the questions central to persuasion examine how messages relate to audience *attitudes*. Like Dillard, a great number of researchers see attitude as a central part of the persuasion process. You'll note that in our model (Figure 1.1) the audience's attitude plays an important role in how persuaders and audience members achieve the coproduction of persuasion. Let's look more closely at the important concept of attitudes.

DEFINING *ATTITUDE*

attitude

a learned response to some person, object, or idea; an attitude has a positive or negative dimension; also, a way of seeing the world that is reflected in our language

Martin Fishbein and Icek Ajzen (1975) provide what is perhaps the most widely accepted definition of **attitude:** "a learned predisposition to respond in a consistently favorable or unfavorable manner with respect to an object" (p. 6). Let's look more closely at this definition. First, attitudes are *evaluative*. They help us to feel or think about an object in a favorable or unfavorable way. You might say that attitudes have a positive or negative dimension, or direction. An attitude toward a political candidate, then, would be positive or negative. The statement "I think this candidate would be a great president" reflects a positive attitude.

Second, attitudes are *learned*. We use our past experiences and the knowledge that has been given to us by others to form attitudes. We are not born with attitudes. When considering which make of automobile to purchase, you form attitudes about the various manufacturers and models from your interactions with friends, parents, or previous encounters with a particular company. We learn how we should feel toward particular brands of products.

Third, attitudes are are *predispositions*. Attitudes do not correspond directly with behavior. Instead, attitudes simply direct us to respond in a certain way to a particular stimulus. Just because you support a particular candidate for office does not mean that you will actually go to the polls to vote for the candidate. Thus, your attitude toward a candidate or a type of car is not an accurate predictor of your behavior. You might have a positive attitude toward a particular car, but might not necessarily purchase that car.

Finally, attitudes have are *flexible stability* (Dillard, 1993). They are consistent from one situation to the next, but they are not entirely rigid. They can be adapted to accommodate changes in the environment. Thus, a positive attitude toward Republicans might generally predispose you to support a Republican politician. However, your attitude would not be so rigid that you would fail to support a Democrat on occasion. Or you might generally favor domestic cars, but might, at times, consider foreign models as well. Let's look, now, at how attitudes are formed.

ATTITUDE FORMATION

Attitudes are based upon or generated from three types of information: cognitive information, affective/emotional information, and past behaviors (Zanna & Rempel, 1988). That is, an attitude is caused by or results from information provided to an audience member by a persuader. Let's look more closely at the types of information that create attitudes.

Cognitive Information   Cognitive information is often called a belief. A **belief** is an idea we have about what is true or false. You may believe that the earth is a sphere, you may believe that a particular make of car is a better value than another, and you may believe that you look attractive when wearing the color blue. Milton Rokeach (1968) writes that beliefs cannot be observed; instead, we observe a person's words and actions to infer their beliefs.

belief
an idea we have about what is true or false

By the time we reach adulthood, we have thousands of beliefs that are organized into some kind of psychological structure. Beliefs are thought to be arranged along a central-peripheral continuum. Beliefs that are central are more resistant to change and, when changed, result in widespread changes in the individual's cognitive system. Beliefs on the periphery are inconsequential and can be changed easily. Rokeach identified five types of beliefs, and his model will help us better understand the idea of cognitive information and how it influences attitudes.

The first type of belief, "Type A: Primitive Beliefs, 100 Per Cent Consensus," represents "'basic truths' about physical reality, social reality, and the nature of the self" (Rokeach, 1968, p. 6). Type A beliefs are shared by all and are rarely subjects of controversy. They are highly resistant to change and central to the person's belief system. Examples of Type A beliefs include "I believe that the sun rises in the east," "I believe that winters in Wisconsin are cold," and "I believe that the earth is round."

"Type B: Primitive Beliefs, Zero Consensus" are incontrovertible and learned by direct experience with the object of belief, but they are not shared by all. In fact, Type B beliefs refer to the self-image of the person who holds the belief. Because they are not shared, they are usually impervious to persuasion and thus are central to the individual's belief system. Examples of Type B beliefs include "I am a smart person," "I believe in God," and "The world is a friendly place." Our interactions with media sometimes influence Type B beliefs. Cultivation theory, for instance, suggests that our ideas about safety are, in part, influenced by our exposure to crime and violence on television. Likewise, our ideas of what it takes to be popular or happy are formed from our media experiences.

Rokeach's third type of belief, "Type C: Authority Beliefs," refers to the faith individuals put in authority figures, such as parents, religious groups, or friends. We learn to trust certain individuals or groups. As we go through life, we learn which authority figures share our beliefs and can be trusted. Examples of Type C beliefs are "My parents have my best interests in mind," "My instructor is knowledgeable," and "Democrats have concern for the working person."

The fourth type of belief is "Type D: Derived Beliefs." Rokeach explains that Type D beliefs are "ideological beliefs originating with religious or political institutions, and derived secondhand through processes of identification with authority rather than by direct encounter with the object of belief" (1968, p. 10). That is, we accept the ideas and beliefs of authority figures without having direct experience with the object of belief. *Type D beliefs can be changed by persuasion.* Examples of Type D beliefs include "I believe that gun control legislation keeps guns away from criminals," "I believe that free trade is good for the U.S. economy," and "I believe that war with Iraq was justified."

"Type E: Inconsequential Beliefs" are the fifth of Rokeach's belief types. Type E beliefs represent "more or less arbitrary matters of taste" (Rokeach, 1968, p. 11). They are incontrovertible because they derive from direct experience with the object of the belief, but they are inconsequential to the person's total belief system because they are not related to other beliefs. Examples of Type E beliefs are "My favorite color is blue," "My favorite flower is a rose," and "I like vanilla ice cream."

In short, a person's belief system consists of inconsequential beliefs, beliefs derived from authorities, pre-ideological beliefs about authorities, and primitive beliefs held only by the individual as well as primitive beliefs shared by all (Rokeach, 1968). "Taken together," Rokeach explains, "the total belief system may be seen as an organization of beliefs, varying in depth, formed as a result of living in nature and in society, designed to help a person maintain, insofar as possible, a sense of ego and group identity, stable and continuous over time" (1968, pp. 11–12). Type A beliefs are the most central to one's belief system; Type E beliefs are the most peripheral. Type D beliefs are the most subject to persuasion.

Affective/Emotional Information   The second type of information that creates attitudes is affective/emotional information, including emotions, needs, and values. That is, you may form your attitude toward a political candidate, not based on the candidate's position on an issue, but based on how the candidate makes you feel. You might feel secure with a candidate and thus have a positive attitude toward the candidate. We don't always make decisions based solely on our rational beliefs. Sometimes, perhaps even to a greater extent, our attitudes are formed based on feelings that are independent from our beliefs (Zanna & Rempel, 1988). In short, we often form our attitudes based on our feelings. We discuss this topic in greater length in Chapter 10.

Which type of information—cognitive, affective, or behavioral—do you think most people use to form attitudes? Which type do you use most frequently?

Past Behaviors   Attitudes are also comprised of information about past behaviors. Our direct experience with something causes us to have an attitude toward that object, person, or idea. For instance, if you go to a new restaurant in town, you are likely to form an attitude about that restaurant based on the experience you have there. The attitude might be positive or negative, but your experience with the restaurant will likely lead to an attitude on your part. Voting for a particular candidate would likewise form an attitude about that candidate or another candidate from the same party in future elections. Persuaders often try to get us to commit to a particular action because once we do so, we form a positive attitude toward that action, which might lead to our carrying out the action. Thus, taking a pledge or an oath is a behavior designed to create a positive attitude toward the action that is promised. To some degree, persuaders can manipulate our experiences in order to form attitudes toward those experiences.

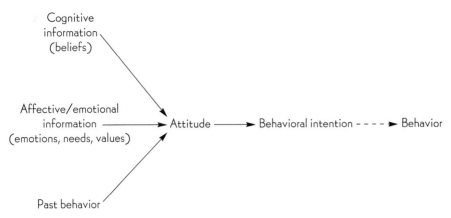

Figure 5.2
Components of an Attitude
Attitudes are comprised of cognitive information, affective/emotional information, and past behavior. An attitude is simply a behavioral intention. It may or may not lead to an actual behavior on the part of the audience member.

CHANGING ATTITUDES

As the model of an attitude in Figure 5.2 shows, an audience member's attitude is the linchpin to changing audience behavior. If a salesperson wants to close the sale, he or she must change the attitude of the audience member toward the product or service in question. If advertisers want an audience member to purchase a product, they must change the audience's attitudes toward that product. Attitude researchers provide us with some general theories about how persuaders can change attitudes. In short, persuaders change attitudes by changing the information on which we base attitudes.

Murray G. Millar and Karen U. Millar (1990) found that attitudes formed by cognitive information were more easily changed by affective information than by new cognitive information. Your belief that a particular candidate is smart is more easily changed by your negative feelings toward the candidate than it is by information that contradicts your belief about the candidate's intelligence. Likewise, affectively formed attitudes were more easily changed by cognitive information than by new affective information. Your positive feelings toward a particular candidate are more easily swayed by logical, contradictory information about the candidate than by contradictory feelings about the candidate. The researchers contend that use of cognitive information to alter cognitively based attitudes results in counterarguing from the audience member. The same is true of affective information that targets affectively based information. When persuasion is based on different information than that used to form the attitude, the audience member is caught off guard and is unable to defend against the persuasion (Dillard, 1993).

Dillard (1993) argues that when attitudes are created by multiple sources of information, those sources of information may, at times, conflict with each other. You might, for instance, know logically that you shouldn't eat junk food, yet emotionally you might be drawn to it (Dillard, 1993). Individuals may also have attitudinal ambivalence toward an object or issue—that is, they might be evenly balanced toward it. Dillard contends that attitudinal ambivalence should not be confused with apathy, which is the absence of an attitude.

This book is about changing attitudes. It explores the variety of ways in which persuaders attempt to change the attitudes of audience members. In the next two chapters, we discuss the "building blocks" of persuasion: visual and verbal symbols. Then, in Chapter 8 we explore how our culture provides information to us that shapes our attitudes. In Chapter 9, we study how a persuader influences an audience's attitudes, and then we focus on persuaders' use of the type of information just described: cognitive in Chapter 10 and affective in Chapter 11. In Part 3 of the book, we explore how persuaders influence attitudes in a variety of contexts. First, though, it's important to examine how persuaders understand audience attitudes and how they target their messages to those attitudes.

Audience Analysis

audience analysis
the process by which persuaders break down their audience into small, observable units

As persuaders consider how to create messages, they first consider the attitudes of the audience for each message. Because attitudes aren't visible, persuaders must infer the audience's attitudes using audience analysis. **Audience analysis** is the process by which persuaders break down their audience into small, observable units. In some situations, the persuader can simply consider the occasion of the persuasive message, visually survey the audience, and then make adjustments to the message based on what is seen. At other times, the persuader must use sophisticated tools to identify the audience's makeup. Audience analysis serves two functions. First, persuaders learn about audiences in order to communicate effectively to them. In other situations, persuaders use audience analysis to create their audiences.

ADAPTING TO AUDIENCES

At times, a persuader must change the attitudes of the audience. For example, there may be times when a persuader wants to appeal to the widest possible American audience. When a president sends troops to war, for instance, he usually delivers a nationally televised speech describing the reasons for the military action and invites the support of the nation as a whole. Or the president of a company must explain to his or her workers the reasons for recent layoffs or budgetary cutbacks. In this situation, some audience members may be openly hostile to the words of the persuader.

In situations such as these, the persuader must adapt to the audience. There are a variety of ways for the persuader to learn about his or her audience and then provide information to change the audience's attitudes. The president often uses the arguments that public opinion polling has found a majority of audience members will accept. In many cases, our presidents have argued that military action is necessary to protect the interests of the country, a reason many Americans accept. The company president, after conducting interviews with small groups of employees to see what they are thinking, chooses those arguments that fit with the perceptions of the audience. We discuss how persuaders use audience analysis to adapt to their audiences in our later discussion of polling. For now, examine the two advertisements in Thinking Critically: Adapting to Audiences to better understand how persuaders adapt to their audiences.

CREATING AUDIENCES

In addition to tailoring their messages to audiences, persuaders often create audiences that have attitudes consistent with their messages. "The audience" is generally only some segment of the entire population. It may be a group of people who are of the same age or income level, for example. Assembling the right people to hear, read, and see the message is often crucial to the persuader's success. Advertisers, for instance, target their messages to audiences that are created for them by television networks, newspapers, and magazines (Ang, 1991). Knowing that an audience comprised of 18- to 34-year-old women will have attitudes that are attractive to certain high-paying advertisers, television production companies create shows that this audience will want to watch. Advertisers are willing to pay high advertising rates to networks that air these shows. In essence, the television network creates an audience for the advertiser. In this case, audiences are commodities that are bought by persuaders and sold by media organizations.

Politicians create target audiences as well. It has been said that the 2000 presidential election focused on middle-class working families. Anticipating that this audience would cast the crucial votes in the election, the presidential candidates campaigned on issues that would interest this group of voters: health care, social security, and targeted tax cuts. Although the candidates may have ignored the needs and concerns of the larger audience, voting patterns indicated that the middle-class working-family audience was crucially important to the outcome of the election.

Attorneys create audiences for their trials as well. In most jurisdictions, more jurors are called to jury duty than will eventually hear the case. In the jurisdiction in which I live, approximately 30 jurors are called for jury duty on the day on which a trial is to be held. Of those 30 potential jurors, 20 are randomly chosen to participate in the jury selection process. From this group, the final panel of 12 is seated. Attorneys use the voir dire process to choose from the larger group of jurors those who they believe will be sympathetic to their case and will fairly evaluate the evidence. Jury consultants help attorneys make decisions about which jurors to seat and, during the trial, how to appeal to the jury. Our judicial system is set up so that attorneys have some control over the creation of the jury panel, their audience.

We turn now to an examination of the specific ways persuaders learn about us, their audience. In some situations, persuaders use polling to directly assess audience attitudes toward a topic. Or persuaders use audience segmentation techniques to infer their audience's attitudes. Some persuaders also use ratings of media audiences to determine audience size and attitudes. In all of these instances, persuaders use audience analysis to more precisely target their message toward receptive receivers.

THINKING CRITICALLY

Adapting to Audiences

Persuaders use what they learn from audience analysis to adapt their messages to their audiences. Consider these advertisements for the Toyota Tacoma and the Lincoln Navigator. Each advertisement promotes a vehicle, but each takes a very different approach to doing so. You can probably guess that each advertiser is aiming to attract a different type of audience.

The advertisement for the Toyota Tacoma truck is aimed at a youthful, thrill-seeking, and budget-conscious audience. The ad depicts the Tacoma as generating a great deal of adrenaline—more than cuddling and Vegas, but still less than seeing someone wearing a thong. The advertisement is designed to help readers picture themselves racing through the mountains, seeking adventure and an adrenaline rush. The Tacoma advertisement appeared in *Rolling Stone* magazine, a publication that attracts readers who often seek thrills but do not have the financial resources for more expensive vehicles.

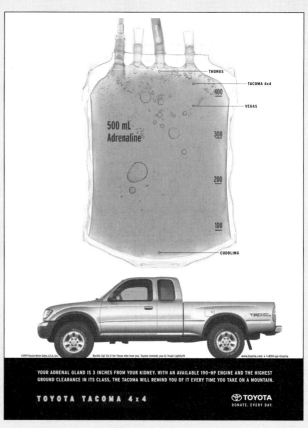

Polling

Polling has become an important dimension in the relationship between audience and message producer. From politics to business, constituents and consumers are being asked their attitudes. **Polling** is the use of statistical theory to assume some characteristic of a population based on a survey of a representative sample of that population. Quite often, polling helps persuaders determine audience attitudes and how to construct messages to change those attitudes. Polling is often conducted during the persuasive process to gauge the effectiveness of the message. Persuaders also use poll results as persuasive proof, to demonstrate the acceptance of the persuader's message by at least part of the target audience.

polling

the use of statistical theory to assume some characteristic of a population based on a survey of a representative sample of that population

WHAT IS POLLING?

The polling industry began in the mid-1930s. Before that, newspapers had conducted unscientific "on-the-street" surveys in which a few people revealed

Tread luxuriously.

Tread lightly *and* luxuriously in Lincoln Navigator, the world's most powerful full-size luxury SUV. Tread spaciously, too. Navigator has room for seven in three rows of leather-trimmed seats. Call 800-688-8898, visit www.lincolnvehicles.com or see an authorized Navigator dealer.

Lincoln Navigator. American Luxury.

The Lincoln Navigator advertisement attempts to attract a completely different type of audience. The Navigator does not promise thrill-seeking, but luxury. Instead of discussing engine horsepower, the Navigator ad boasts of leather-trimmed seats and room for seven passengers. The Navigator ad was placed in *Brill's Content,* a publication that attracts an older, more upscale audience than *Rolling Stone.*

As you consider the persuasive messages you encounter, think about how each has been manipulated to some degree to attract audience members like yourself. Take another look at the two advertisements and answer these questions:

1. How might the two advertisements be adapted for the opposite type of audience? To what extent is it possible to adapt the Navigator's advertisement to a younger, less upscale audience?

2. What do the two advertisements tell you about how persuaders view particular audiences?

their opinions on public matters. In 1935, George Gallup founded the Institute of Public Opinion, which published a syndicated newspaper feature disclosing the results of various samplings of public opinion. At the same time, Elmo Roper was commissioned by *Fortune* magazine to conduct similar surveys. The 1936 presidential election prompted similar surveys by marketing researcher Archibald Crossley. As the methods of statistical analysis developed in the 1950s and 1960s, so too did public opinion polling. Today, Americans are asked questions by professional pollsters on a variety of issues: from which toothpaste they prefer to which television station they watch to which presidential candidate they favor.

Polling uses statistical theory to gauge the opinion of a larger population based on a small sample. Polls are conducted by mail, by telephone, or face-to-face. For example, if a candidate for the city council wishes to know the most important issues in the minds of potential voters, he or she can call a small percentage of the city's population to learn their opinions. Or the council member can mail surveys to a sample of the population. It is not uncommon for pollsters to talk to people at public locations, such as shopping malls. If the survey is done correctly, a few hundred voters can provide an accurate picture of an entire city population.

Despite the science behind polling, there have been gross errors in the accuracy of polling results. Increasingly, the Internet is being used to conduct quantitative surveys. Online research is less expensive and faster than traditional survey formats, such as mail or phone. Another advantage of Internet surveys is that they tap a very particular audience—those who use the Internet. For example, Hilton Hotels recently teamed with several airlines to sponsor a travel survey conducted over the Internet. Within a year, 17,500 people responded to the survey. However, although targeting a sample of Internet users may be beneficial for some surveys, it is not for others.

FUNCTIONS OF POLLING

As previously noted, audience polling serves three purposes: to assess audience attitudes, to evaluate the effectiveness of a message, and to prove persuasive arguments. Politicians have long used public opinion polls to test public acceptance of issues and strategies. During recent presidential campaigns, polling was used extensively to test the messages of the candidates. Former President Clinton's researchers had compiled extensive data about the attitudes of the public nearly two years before the 1996 election. Clinton was able to use these data, counter negative opinions of himself, and re-create his image well before the 1996 general election. Many observers have declared the two Clinton campaigns to be groundbreaking in their use of public opinion polling. Clinton used polling to evaluate his message and to make changes when necessary.

Technology has made polling more accurate and affordable for persuaders, resulting in greater use of and reliance on polls. Computerized polling is used extensively in market research to have customers evaluate persuasive campaigns. Manufacturers test full-color and multimedia mock-ups of their products on consumers before mass production. Advertisers use polling to find the best advertisement among those being considered. Multimedia technology allows advertisers to create computerized surveys that include demographic and lifestyle questions for the respondents and mock-up versions of advertisements. The Carrier Corporation used this technology when considering a new ad campaign. After reviewing the results of its research, the company decided to stay with its old campaign because it was more appealing to the target audience. By testing mock-ups of potential ads before producing the actual advertisement, advertisers can save time and money.

Entertainment programmers also uses a type of polling to test their products before they are taped. Each episode of the television show *Friends*, for instance, is taped in front of a live audience. The show's producers will at times ask the audience if they think a particular joke is funny or if plot development is effective. Based on the audience's response, the most effective line is performed and taped.

Persuaders use poll results as proof for their arguments, giving the audience some power over persuaders. Polling is one way that audiences can provide feedback to media organizations. The Nielsens—which we discuss later in

INTERNET ACTIVITY

Assessing a Poll

We have just discussed four ways to evaluate a poll. Polls are widely reported in the news media, and we give much weight to the results of the polls. Even polls that are not conducted scientifically have a great deal of persuasive impact on society. Go to http://www.cnn.com and search the site using the word "poll." Read an article that is returned in the search results. Use the four criteria we have discussed in this chapter to evaluate the poll. How knowledgeable about the poll topic were the respondents? Did the poll contain loaded wording? Was the sample valid? How was the poll reported? Do you have enough information to evaluate the poll?

this chapter—are a way for the public to "vote" for certain types of television programming and against others. Media organizations make important decisions regarding programming based on Nielsen numbers. In addition, governments often take action based on public opinion polling. When news media show that a majority of the public are for some position or against another position, our political leaders are mindful of those findings.

ASSESSING POLLING

Because of the power given to polling in our society, it is important that we address several issues related to poll results. This discussion should help to make you a more critical consumer of the polling you encounter. Herbert B. Asher (1998) argues that we should approach polling with "healthy skepticism" (p. 171) and provides a list of topics to help consumers evaluate poll results.

First, we should assess the degree to which respondents are likely to be informed about the topic of the poll. It is important that the respondent has a genuine opinion about the matter at hand. In some cases, respondents will simply answer a poll question according to the social pressures of the interview situation. Polls should allow respondents to indicate that they have no real view on the subject.

Second, we should examine the wording of the question to assess the degree to which it contains loaded phrasing. The question "Do you favor building a new, $42 million convention center?" is potentially problematic because it includes information about price. Audience members should also examine the order in which questions are asked. Earlier questions can influence how respondents reply to later questions (Asher, 1998).

Third, consumers should assess the poll sample. Ideally, samples are chosen scientifically, using random sampling techniques. The poll should report that this is the case. Many polls, however, are "unscientific," meaning they did not use a scientific sampling procedure. Many of the polls conducted on Internet sites are not scientific because everyone in the population does not have an equal chance to participate.

Finally, Asher (1998) explains that we should examine the end products of the poll. We should identify who is reporting the poll results and determine

As a result of audience polling, some have speculated that persuaders today take action based not on what they think is right or wrong, but on what public opinion polls indicate is favorable or unfavorable. To what extent do you think this is true? What are the dangers of making decisions based on public opinion?

whether the entity might have an interest in reporting the results in a certain way. A political party, for instance, will be likely to report polling results in a way that favors the party. The Gallup Organization and the Roper Poll are respected polling agencies, but results from their polls can be interpreted in a variety of ways. Complete the Internet Activity: Assessing a Poll to gain experience using these evaluative criteria.

Audience Segmentation

segmentation
audience analysis technique that divides the audience into smaller groups to more precisely infer attitudes

Polling allows persuaders to directly assess audience attitudes. Yet audiences are mass groups of people, and it can be difficult to understand their collective attitudes. Thus, persuaders use audience **segmentation** to divide the population into more meaningful units to more precisely infer audience attitudes. These units are based on demographics, psychographics, and geodemographics. By using census data, surveys, focus groups, and a variety of other methods, persuaders can target an audience for their message and create their message in a way that appeals to that particular audience. Persuaders speaking to small groups of individuals as well as persuaders who reach millions with their mediated messages all use audience segmentation techniques.

DEMOGRAPHICS

demographics
an audience analysis technique that divides the audience into groups based on identifiable traits such as age, sex, race, income level, political party affiliation, and religious affiliation

Demographics divides an audience into groups based on such identifiable characteristics as age, sex, race, income level, group memberships, ethnicity, and religious affiliation. We briefly discuss the influence of several of these variables on current trends in the persuasion industry. We also examine how persuaders adapt their messages to target these groups.

Age   Age is one demographic factor persuaders must consider as they produce their messages. Youth, in particular, are a prime audience for persuaders today. There are 72.3 million Americans under the age of 18, which is 26 percent of the population. Youth today are active consumers who influence purchasing decisions—by themselves and their parents. Ed Keller (quoted in Roper ASW, 2003), CEO of Roper ASW, reports that "purchasing clout among today's kids has expanded beyond the traditional borders of snack food and video games. We are beginning to see children as young as eight having an impact on new, more sophisticated areas like home design."

The 2003 Roper Youth Report asked parents if their children have influence on spending decisions. The poll found that children influence their parents' decisions about purchasing food (84 percent), DVDs/videos (79 percent), music (73 percent), and books (66 percent). In each category listed here, the influence of children increased from the 2002 survey. Ninety percent of youth 8-17 say they go to the mall "occasionally." Of those, one-third say they go "fairly often" and 10 percent go "very often." Today's youth have a variety of products produced just for them and they are the target of many persuasive messages because of their spending power.

Sex   Journalist Shannon Dorch (1994) reports that men and women are increasingly buying products that have traditionally been purchased by members of the opposite sex. Women now make more than half of all new-car buying decisions, for instance, and the number of men who now help with indoor cooking has risen from 35 percent in 1975 to 50 percent in 1990. However, Dorch writes that advertisers have not figured out how to market products of this sort to the other sex. A recent advertisement for a sport-utility vehicle showed the truck towing a boat. Although women are increasingly involved in purchasing sport-utility vehicles, they are not interested in towing capacity. Neither are men, Dorch argues. Advertisers might instead look for health benefits, for instance, that both sexes receive from products and use appeals aimed at health. For example, Dorch says that men who cook can be persuaded to buy cooking products by touting the benefits of well-cooked foods. A recent ad showing a man and a woman with a low-fat product appealed to both groups of consumers.

Race   Although the United States has been labeled the "melting pot" for some time, the nation is only now becoming a nation of diverse peoples. Not only are minority populations in this country increasing in size, but so too are the numbers of mixed-race families and their children. In 1990, nearly 2 million children under the age of 18 had parents of different races. Youth today play with children of other racial backgrounds, eat ethnic foods, and have heroes from all races. The toy industry has capitalized on this changing demographic by producing dolls and action figures of many races.

Sexual Orientation   The Internet has provided marketers with an effective vehicle for reaching the gay market. More than 2 million people had created profiles at the news, culture, and chat site Gay.com by July 2003. In addition, gfn.com, the Gay Financial Network, offers its members the opportunity to sign up for annuities and mortgages online (Weissman, 1999b). The Internet is an ideal medium for reaching this market for several reasons, Weissman writes. First, television is too broad a channel, and thus too expensive, to reach the gay audience. In addition, television faces cultural pressure to avoid certain types of advertising, including ads aimed at gay men and lesbians. Print options are limited as well. Some gays and lesbians fear that subscribing to a publication will publicize their homosexuality (Weissman, 1999b). In addition, there are only two national gay magazines. The Internet, however, provides an audience that is larger than the circulation of both those magazines combined. Gay men and women are three times more likely than the general population to be online: 65 percent go online more than once a day, and 71 percent purchase goods or services over the Internet (Weissman, 1999b).

How might you use demographic analysis in your career? How might you use psychographic analysis in your career?

PSYCHOGRAPHICS

Knowing the demographic characteristics of the audience is not enough for persuaders because demographics does not always reliably predict an audience member's attitude. Using psychographics, however, persuaders can understand

psychographics

an audience analysis technique that combines demographic information about an audience with information about members' attitudes, opinions, and interests

how certain products and activities fit with an audience's lifestyle or self-image. **Pyschographics** combines demographic information about an audience with information about their attitudes, opinions, and interests (Heath, 1996). One of the more popular psychographic instruments is VALS, developed by SRI Consulting Business Intelligence. VALS divides the population into segments based on the personality types of individual audience members. VALS is used as products are developed, introduced to the market, and positioned for customers. The original VALS instrument was developed in the 1970s; it has been modified several times since then. Let's briefly examine the VALS profile and how persuaders use VALS to target audience members.

VALS is based on the idea that an individual's personality drives his or her behaviors. VALS uses psychology to understand and predict what actions people are likely to take as a result of their personality. The VALS profile refers to this idea as the *primary motivation*—the specific attributes that determine what is meaningful for a person. According to VALS, people have three primary motivations: ideals, achievement, and self-expression. When a person is motivated by knowledge and principles, they are said to be motivated by ideals. Those who desire to demonstrate their success to others are said to be motivated by achievement. Individuals who are motivated by self-expression desire social or physical activity, variety, and risk. The psychographic profile also considers a person's *resources*, or the age, income, education, energy level, self-confidence, and other attributes that enhance or constrain a person's expression of their personality. The two dimensions of primary motivation and resources can be charted to produce eight segment types: innovators, thinkers, achievers, experiencers, believers, strivers, makers, and survivors. See where you fit on this profile by completing the Internet Activity: Take the VALS survey.

- *Innovators* are people who have all three primary motivations—ideals, achievement, and self-expression. They also have the resources to express their motivations. Innovators are receptive to new ideas and technologies, are active consumers, and purchase upscale products and services. They are leaders in their occupation and seek challenges.
- *Thinkers* are motivated by ideals and have sufficient resources. They are mature, satisfied, and comfortable, and they desire order, knowledge, and responsibility. They are mostly conservative, but are open to new ideas. They seek products that are durable, functional, and valuable.
- *Achievers* are motivated by achievement and have the resources to purchase products that help create their image. They are goal-oriented and committed to family and careers. Achievers are politically conservative and respect authority. They favor status oriented and time-saving consumer products.
- *Experiencers* are motivated by self-expression and have resources to fulfill their need for excitement, variety, and the risky. They spend a great deal of their income on fashion, entertainment, and socializing.
- *Believers* are motivated by ideals but have fewer resources than thinkers. Believers are conservative, having firm beliefs in family, religion, commu-

INTERNET ACTIVITY

Take the VALS Survey

You have just read how persuaders use surveys such as VALS to understand and target audience members. You'll now have the chance to take the VALS survey to see where you fit in the VALS framework. Keep in mind that these categories are only tools of market researchers and that they can't reflect your true attitudes and feelings. Go to http://www.sric-bi .com/vals/surveynew.shtml and take the online version of the VALS survey. Are you surprised by the results? In what ways could persuaders target you and others in this group?

nity and the nation. They follow established routines and are predictable and loyal consumers, purchasing familiar brands and products.

- *Strivers* are motivated by achievement but, like believers, have a lower level of resources. They purchase products to emulate people that have greater material wealth. Shopping is seen as a social activity that demonstrates their ability to purchase consumer products. Often, they lack the skills or education to advance in their careers.

- *Makers* are motivated by self-expression, but lack the resources to live extravagantly. They focus on tasks such as raising children, fixing a car, and canning vegetables. They are respectful of authority, but oppose government intrusion on individual rights. They prefer value to luxury in consumer products they purchase.

- *Survivors* lack the resources and do not show a primary motivation. They are focused on fulfilling basic desires and are cautious consumers. Survivors are not a meaningful market for most persuaders.

Persuaders use VALS and other psychographic instruments, in several ways. VALS helps them to understand potential markets for new products or ideas. Persuaders can assemble focus groups of members of a particular segment to understand more clearly how their product or idea can appeal to this group. Persuaders can also choose media and strategies to appeal to their target segment. For instance, an automobile manufacturer used VALS to understand which audience would be most enthusiastic about advanced safety features in a new car line. A Japanese automaker used VALS to better understand its target group. The company was able to reposition its brands, resulting in an increase in sales. A medical company in Minnesota used VALS when it opened a cosmetic surgery clinic. By understanding the primary motivation and resources capabilities of its market segment, the clinic created an effective advertising campaign. Finally, a U.S. long-distance company used VALS to select a spokesperson with whom its target segment could relate.

VALS and other psychographic profiles use quantitative data—numbers— from consumer surveys to understand audiences. Persuaders also are increasingly using qualitative tools that examine a respondent's narrative about a product or an idea to understand their audiences. Qualitative research, which in the past suffered from questions of validity and reliability, today uses "tighter controls and computers aids" and a wider array of techniques (Heath, 1996, p. 40). Qualitative research is "useful for a variety of tasks, such as tweaking concepts and images for commercials, making packaging changes, and fine-tuning product development" (p. 41).

One reason for the change from quantitative to qualitative analysis is that consumers are changing. R. P. Heath reports: "Old psychographic dimensions such as attitudes toward work and leisure or health and fitness don't fit today's realities. People's involvement with media, and their responses to and skills at getting information, are the most important predictors today" (1996, p. 40). In addition, marketing and advertising companies are trimming their research divisions and operating under tighter budgets from their clients. As a result, quantitative measures, such as VALS, are becoming a luxury because they are expensive and time-consuming (p. 40). We'll briefly examine how qualitative tools such as focus groups, personification, concept mapping, and collages can help persuaders understand the psychology of their audiences.

focus group
a small group of systematically selected people whose attitudes about a product, image, or idea are probed by a trained facilitator using in-depth, open-ended questions

Focus groups have been used for some time to probe audience members' emotional connection to a product, image, or idea. While quantitative polling uses objective surveys to study large numbers of people, focus groups ask in-depth questions of a handful of people. A focus group is led by a trained facilitator, who asks several open-ended questions of group participants. Although the information obtained is not as generalizable as that gained through polling, focus groups provide rich data that are often used as the basis for a quantitative survey.

Personification is an exercise in which consumers are asked to picture what a company would "look like if it walked into the room" (Heath, 1996, p. 42). A respondent's answer indicates his or her attitudes toward the company. In a recent campaign for Sprint Business Services, a marketing agency found that when asked to picture long-distance companies as animals, consumers pictured AT&T as a lion, MCI as a snake, and Sprint as a puma (p. 42). Presumably, audiences felt that AT&T and MCI were dangerous animals interested in profit. Sprint, on the other hand, was pictured as a sleek, fast animal running ahead of the pack. Thus, Sprint uses the slogan that it can "help you do more business" (p. 42).

Concept mapping "asks consumers to rate products on dimensions such as popularity and quality" (Heath, 1996, p. 42). Consumers' responses are represented graphically as concentric circles, as grids, or in a hierarchy. A visual map is formed that depicts the consumer's ideas of how certain products and brands are related to each other. Heath writes, "The technique gathers a lot of information and sorts numerous brands quickly, highlights users' versus nonusers' perceptions, provides feedback on packaging issues, and encourages argument and discussion" (p. 42). Increasingly, researchers are using computers to organize the results of such mental mapping. One recent study asked consumers to respond to questions regarding concepts, products, scents, and tastes. Using a computer to record these responses, the Vlasic pickle company developed pickles with varying degrees of savoriness. You may have seen a Vlasic jar that rated its contents' degree of hotness.

Marketers also ask consumers to create *collages* and then discuss their creations in focus groups. One woman in a recent study created a collage out of broken glass to illustrate what she felt like when she had a migraine headache. Some marketers give focus-group participants disposable cameras to take pictures of objects that represent their feelings about concepts. In one study, reports R. P. Heath, focus group members used their photographs to create collages of "comfort" (1996, p. 42). Many of the participants took pictures of fluffy beige and white objects. The client then used these colors in its stores and product lines. Psychographic research such as that discussed provides insights into the minds of consumers.

GEODEMOGRAPHICS

Geodemographics takes psychographics one step further by showing where particular demographic groups live. Persuaders can divide counties and cities into one-block units and target their communication even more narrowly. The outdoor advertising industry has recently begun to use geodemographic information in sales of billboards. Billboards are an effective way to reach young, active adults who spend a lot of time driving and less time in front of the television. A research firm in Illinois takes pictures of car license plates as the drivers pass by its billboards. Each plate is then tracked to its owner's address, giving the billboard advertiser a great deal of information about who is exposed to particular billboards.

> **geodemographics**
> an audience analysis technique that shows where audiences with particular demographic characteristics live

Altoids, "the curiously strong peppermint," is a popular product among young adult consumers. Research found that most potential customers were not exposed to traditional advertising on television or radio. Using geodemographics, Altoids's ad agency determined where potential customers lived. The agency then placed ads in nontraditional locations, such as telephone booths, bus shelters, and on city buses—places potential customers visited each day. In each of the 12 markets tested, sales increased 50 percent.

New York City's public transportation system sells advertising on the back of its fare cards. The market is ideal for advertising. New Yorkers take more than 5 million trips each day, and 75 percent of riders carry fare cards. Most riders keep their fare cards four weeks or more, meaning they are exposed to ads on the cards at least twice a day for a month at a time. The fare cards are only the latest part of the Metropolitan Transportation Authority's overall advertising plan, which includes selling advertising on subway platforms, in bus shelters, and elsewhere. Future plans would allow users to present their fare cards in exchange for discounts at businesses that advertise.

SEGMENTING INTERNET AUDIENCES

Because of its data collection potential, the Internet offers persuaders many opportunities to understand and segment online audiences. Computer technology can easily record a great deal of information about users of Internet sites and determine what kind of users various sites attract. For instance, most websites can easily determine what type of software you are using, the location

cookie

a line of software code
placed in a file on your
computer that identifies
you to the site host
when you revisit the site

from which you are accessing the site, and how long you spend on the site. Cookies are also useful to Internet content providers. A **cookie** is a line of software code that is placed in a file on your computer when you access a site that uses cookie technology. Thus, the next time you visit the site, the site's software can read your cookie file to learn all about you. Neil Randall (1997) identifies three functions of cookies: retaining ordering information, tracking site navigation, and personalizing Web pages.

First, cookies are used to retain your ordering information. When you visit a site that sells something, you frequently fill a virtual shopping cart with your selections. If you leave the site without completing the purchase and then return later, your cart may still contain the items you previously identified. A cookie allowed the site to detect what items you had previously selected. Second, cookies allow Webmasters to track your navigation of the site. They can tell how long you visit the site, which pages you visit, and how frequently you log on. Cookies can also tell which other Internet sites you visit and customize information for you based on your previous travels. Finally, cookies allow Internet sites to customize their site for you. On your first visit to a site like My.Yahoo.com, you select which news you would like to appear on your customized homepage or which stock quotes you would like to view. Later, when you return to the page, your original preferences appear and the page is customized to your viewing needs. This also allows the site to advertise products on the page that appeal to your interests.

Although cookies are useful to persuaders and can be useful to Internet viewers, they also raise security questions. Some observers are concerned that information obtained from the Internet user is sold to third parties, who then market products to the individual. Some users are concerned that credit card and other sensitive information will fall into the hands of unscrupulous Internet content providers. Users can take steps to reduce the amount of information they provide when traveling the Web. Cookies can be turned off in the Preferences file of many navigators, although doing so may prevent the user from accessing certain Internet sites. In addition, the computer user can install software to prevent creation of cookies without notification. Legislation is also being considered to better ensure the privacy of the online audience. Ethical Insights: Ethics and Audience Analysis addresses questions related to online privacy.

OTHER METHODS OF AUDIENCE SEGMENTATION

We have so far discussed some of the common methods of audience segmentation. Information needs and resources may inhibit a persuader's use of these methods, and persuaders may segment particular audiences differently than we have discussed. Let's look at how a salesperson, a public health official, and an attorney might segment their audiences.

A sales representative might divide his or her audience into renewals and new accounts. The pitch aimed at renewal customers would be different from that aimed at new customers. For renewals, the salesperson would stress the positive aspects of the past relationship, the benefits of continued service, and

ETHICAL INSIGHTS

Ethics and Audience Analysis

The use of sophisticated audience analysis techniques on the Internet has raised questions concerning the privacy of audience members. When you use the Internet, for instance, you often leave a trail of information, including your name, address, Social Security number, and credit card information. This information can be sold by the persuaders who gather it or obtained by hackers who breach Internet security measures. A study sponsored by the California HealthCare Foundation found that most of the health-related Internet sites it surveyed do not protect your private information (Clausing, 2000). Advertisers on these sites were able to obtain the names and addresses of users, as well as any health data users may have provided to the site. In another situation, a hacker known as Maxus obtained credit card information from the website of CD Universe, a retailer of music and DVD movies. When the company refused to pay the hacker $100,000, he posted as many as 25,000 credit card numbers on his website. As we travel the Internet, we leave a great deal of personal information behind.

Legislators have called for tighter laws concerning Internet privacy rights. These laws would require that persuaders disclose the type of information they collect from audiences as well as tell audiences what they

will do with the information. Fundamentally, privacy is an ethical concern of persuaders in the media age. In its code of ethics the Public Relations Society of America (2000) charges its members "to protect the privacy rights of clients, organizations, and individuals by safeguarding confidential information." Likewise, the National Communication Association Credo for Ethical Communication (NCA, 1999) addresses this issue with the following statement: "We advocate sharing information, opinions, and feelings when facing significant choices while also respecting privacy and confidentiality." Consider these statements as you think about online privacy and answer these questions:

1. How should society balance the interests of online businesses with the privacy rights of online consumers? Should online businesses be allowed to gather personal information about users?

2. What kind of laws should be passed, if any, to protect online consumers?

3. How do you protect yourself when you use the Internet? (For some tips, consult the website for this book.)

4. What are some of the implications if consumers do not feel confident using the Internet?

new features that are available. For potential new customers, the salesperson would introduce the customer to the advantages of the company and compare the company with its competitors.

Public health officials also use segmentation. A study conducted by Jenifer E. Kopfman and Sandi W. Smith (1996) found that for organ donation campaigns, there are three primary segments of the audience: those who have signed a donor card, those who have a high intent to sign a donor card, and those who have a low intent to sign a donor card. Each group possesses certain attributes, such as altruism, knowledge, and fear. For example, a person high in intent to sign a donor card (but who has not actually done so) has limited knowledge about organ donation, a positive altruistic attitude, and a high level of fear about organ donation. Health communication professionals can target a campaign toward this segment of the audience by providing plenty of information about donation and calming their fears about donation.

Attorneys frequently use audience segmentation when they choose jurors for a trial. By asking questions that will identify prospective jurors as belonging to distinct segments of the public, attorneys are able to quickly eliminate those who will not be sympathetic to their case. At the same time, they are able to identify those who may be good jurors for their client. In a recent drug possession trial, the defendant's attorney asked potential jurors to rank marijuana on a scale of 1 to 10, with 10 representing cocaine, a harmful drug. As a potential juror in the case, I presumed that the attorney wanted us to compare the dangers of marijuana with those of cocaine. One by one, jurors gave a score for their perception of the danger of marijuana. Three distinct groupings emerged: the first group, which gave scores of 1 to 4; a second group, which ranked marijuana 5 to 8; and a third group, which said marijuana was just as dangerous as cocaine, giving it a score of 9 or 10. From this question, both attorneys were able to quickly identify the attitude of each juror toward marijuana. Not surprisingly, most of the jurors who were selected came from the middle group.

What are some of the dangers of classifying people according to the VALS categories? In which category do you fit?

As we conclude our discussion of audience segmentation, it is important that we make several observations. First, labels such as "White," "African American," "Asian," and "Hispanic" are misleading and do not truly identify those so labeled. As more and more Americans do not fit neatly into any one category, this type of labeling will become a greater problem. Controversy about which labels to include on the 2000 Census exemplifies the difficulty of accurate classification. A related concern of categorization is that persuaders will appeal directly to the most powerful groups and ignore the concerns of other groups. Much television programming today is aimed at individuals in the most lucrative demographic category, young people with college educations and high incomes. The needs and interests of other demographic groups, such as children or minorities, are ignored. In addition, persuaders do not always take into account subgroups within larger demographic groups. For years, political candidates have targeted women. Quite often, these appeals have been liberal in nature. Many women, however, are conservative; their concerns are not the same as those of the dominant subgroup.

Audience segmentation uses particular characteristics of individual audience members—observable traits, attitudes and lifestyles, and geography—to group them into smaller units. The final section of this chapter explores how persuaders combine this information with ratings to determine media audiences.

Ratings

ratings

measurements of media audiences by a third party

For persuaders who use media, ratings are an important aspect of audience analysis. **Ratings** are measurements of media audiences by a third party. For instance, the audience of your favorite radio station is measured periodically to determine how many listeners it has. Often, ratings companies also determine demographic and/or psychographic information about the audience as well. Television, radio, newspaper, magazine, and Internet advertising are all sold based on the audience for each media type as determined by an impartial third party who determines the ratings for each media organization. For example, advertisers who want to target the attitudes that they think a young, male audience will possess must select a media type that ratings have determined is dominated by that demographic group. Media producers and advertisers rely on several different organizations to learn about viewing, listening, or reading audiences.

TELEVISION

The Nielsen ratings are the primary way the television industry learns about its audiences. Through various data collections techniques, such as electronic meters and diaries, the Nielsen company tracks the television habits of millions of Americans. The majority of Nielsen ratings are computed based on diary entries by "Nielsen households." A small sample of households is used to estimate the national audience for a show. There are four "sweep" months during the year: February, May, July, and November. Ratings from these months are used to calculate advertising rates. The statistics Nielsen obtains are expressed in two ways: ratings and shares. A rating is the percentage of all households with televisions in the United States tuned to a particular show at a particular time. A share is the percentage of households *watching television* tuned to a particular show at a particular time. The final soccer match of the 1999 Women's World Cup between the United States and China on July 10, 1999, drew a 13.3 rating and a 32 share. This means that of all households with televisions, 13.3 percent saw the soccer match and that of everyone watching television at the time, 32 percent were tuned to the game. The estimated number of homes tuned to the soccer final that afternoon was 40 million.

The Nielsen company now provides additional information to networks and advertisers concerning how long and how often viewers watch a particular show. The information pits broadcast networks against cable companies in their competition to win advertising money. The Nielsen study divides the audience into four sections: "Gold Card viewers watch most of a show, and tune in often; Occasionally Committeds watch most of a show, but tune in less often; Silver Sliders watch only some of a show, but tune in often; and Viewers Lite only watch some of a show, and tune in less often" (Weissman, 1999a). Network shows such as *NYPD Blue* were found to draw the largest percentage of Gold Card minutes. Cable programs accounted for the most Viewers Lite.

Broadcasters argue that advertising placed on shows that draw large numbers of Gold Card viewers is more effective, because the viewers are more interested in the show. Loyal viewers are less likely to "channel surf" during commercials on their favorite shows. Cable companies complain that the survey was too small and that the conclusion that loyal television viewers watch commercials aired during their favorite shows is specious. Critics of the survey also contend that so-called Gold Card viewers may be "couch potatoes" who aren't selective about the type of programming they watch (Weissman, 1999a). While Nielsen will more than likely adapt the survey to better serve both broadcasters and cable companies, the study demonstrates that survey instruments are being developed to help persuaders better understand audiences and determine how to best direct their messages.

Nielsen is the most popular television ratings system, but it is far from perfect. Throughout the years, various reforms have been suggested for how the company gathers information about television viewers. A recent case in Albany, New York, illustrates the importance of accurate audience information. The July/August 1998 *Brill's Content* reported that of the 851 households who took part in the November 1997 Nielsen survey in Albany, one household submitted a diary stating that nine adults in the household had watched an average of 13.5 hours of television a day, most of it on one station, the local Fox affiliate. A competing station reviewed the Nielsen results and found, not only that the household had higher-than-normal averages, but that one member of the household worked for the Fox station—a direct violation of Nielsen rules, but one the company had missed. The Fox station received nearly $500,000 in undeserved advertising revenue because of the error.

RADIO

Radio stations rely largely on Arbitron ratings to determine their advertising rates. Arbitron measures radio audiences in 270 local U.S. markets, serving 2,300 stations. Abritron operates in much the same way as the Nielsen company. A small sample of radio listeners are provided with a small stipend to log their radio listening habits in a diary. The results are compiled at several times during the year, and radio stations are provided with the information about who is listening to their station. Advertisers then pay for time on the stations based on what Abritron finds.

Arbitron is experimenting with a personal portable meter (PPM), an electronic device that individuals in the sample would take with them throughout the day to record when they listen to the radio. The PPM measures a signal the radio station transmits in its broadcast (Patchen & Kolessar, 1999). Each night, the device logs into the Arbitron mainframe computer to record the individual's daily activities. A pilot study of the PPM in England found it to be user friendly, thus producing "an outstanding degree" of cooperation and compliance with the survey (p. 67). Like Nielsen, Arbitron is not perfect in its measurement of radio audiences, but it is the primary way that stations track their listeners.

THE PRINT MEDIA

Advertising rates for newspapers and magazines are based on circulation figures compiled by the Audit Bureau of Circulation (ABC). The ABC is a "self-regulatory auditing organization" that computes the circulation figures for printed media. While it might seem that circulation figures would be easy to ascertain, the ABC uses many guidelines when computing circulation rates. One area of controversy is discounted subscription rates provided to customers. Perhaps you have received an offer from a magazine to subscribe at a low rate, $1 an issue, for example. If this rate is less than half the normal subscription price, the magazine cannot consider you to be a subscriber. The ABC uses the "50 percent rule" to help it determine the number of inexpensive or free subscriptions the publication may count as subscribers. Another area of concern is when hotels or conventions purchase large numbers of a publication to give away to attendees. The ABC has specific rules for counting bulk subscriptions. Despite the complexity in figuring subscription rates, the ABC seeks to fairly count a publication's subscribers to provide fair competition for advertising dollars.

Not all in the newspaper and magazine industry are convinced that circulation rates are the best standards to measure the reach of printed media. When advertisers compare the reach of various media, they generally use different standards of measurement. A local radio station may reach 100,000 listeners, as based on Arbitron ratings, while the local newspaper may have only 50,000 subscribers. This does not necessarily mean that the newspaper ad will be seen by fewer people than will hear the radio spot. Newspaper and magazine publishers often consider the readership of their publications rather than the circulation rate. A family may have only one subscription to a newspaper, but the paper is often read by two or three or more people. In addition, a newspaper typically has online readers who do not pay for a printed version of the paper. The current method of counting subscribers does not consider these additional readers. As competition for advertising dollars continues, newspapers and magazines will continue to seek more equitable methods of measuring their reach.

THE INTERNET

The Nielsen/NetRatings is one method used to measure Internet audiences. The Nielsen company uses a panel of 15,000 Internet users to complete its survey of Internet use. The panelists record a variety of factors related to their use of the Internet: which sites they visit and how much time they spend on each one, as well as how often they go online during a given period. From these data, Nielsen calculates the total number of Internet users during a given period. Nielsen also determines which banner advertisements were the most successful. Nielsen is just one of many methods used by Internet advertisers and content providers to determine who is visiting a site and for how long. Most Internet content providers can log their users with software and then use the information to sell advertising space. As the Internet develops, methods of measuring online traffic will become more precise.

Summary

Whether you are selling a political candidate or pitching an idea to your superiors, understanding your audience is crucial. The audience for persuasive messages today is potentially large, anonymous, and able to circumvent the persuasive process. At the same time, mediated audiences can be quite small, known to persuaders, and powerless in the face of the persuasive process.

Audience members have attitudes, which are the central components in determining the degree of identification the persuader achieves. Attitudes are composed of cognitive, affective, and behavioral information and lead to behavioral intentions, which may lead to behaviors. It is important for persuaders to understand the attitudes of their audiences.

Americans today are polled, tested, and understood as never before by persuaders. Polling allows persuaders to directly assess audience attitudes. Using tools of audience analysis, such as audience segmentation and ratings, persuaders can infer the attitudes of their audiences and more effectively deliver messages aimed at a receptive audience.

Key Terms

WWW: Visit the book's website at http://www.mhhe.com/borchers2 for multiple-choice quizzes, Internet activities, and key terms flashcards.

narrowcasting 131	demographics 144
broadcasting 131	psychographics 146
attitude 134	focus group 148
belief 135	geodemographics 149
audience analysis 138	cookie 150
polling 140	ratings 152
segmentation 144	

6

Persuasion and Visual Images

Learning Objectives

After reading this chapter, you should be able to:

1. Identify the attributes of visual symbols and how those attributes give meaning to symbols.

2. Understand how media communicate visual images.

3. Describe three ways that visual images persuade audiences.

4. Explain how visual images communicate through visual spectacles, logos, and architecture.

5. Use theory to evaluate visual images.

Imagine yourself standing in New York's Times Square, which has often been called the Crossroads of the World. It is home to theaters, television studios, and flagship department stores. In recent years, Times Square has also become known for neon, billboards, and mammoth television screens. Examine the visual images in Figure 6.1. You cannot help but notice how many there are. Billboard advertisements feature photographs, large type, and the easy-to-recognize logos of major companies. Standing in Times Square, one cannot help but feel the persuasive power of images.

Study the images carefully. Each picture, logo, or symbol is designed to fulfill a number of persuasive functions. The Coca-Cola advertisement induces you to identify with the soft drink, its image, and its worldwide popularity. The Virgin, Kodak, and McDonald's signs are designed to build name recognition for those popular brands. The numerous signs for Broadway plays are

Figure 6.1
How many different types of visual images can you identify in this picture of New York's Times Square?

designed to make the shows seem important and worthy of your time and money. Images are powerful persuasive tools today and often take the place of words in our culture.

Like the verbal symbols we will study in Chapter 7, visual symbols are powerful ways of suggesting messages to audiences. Some theorists even contend that in the media age, visual signs are used more frequently and with more force than verbal signs. Mitchell Stephens (1998) maintains that "the image is replacing the word as the predominant means of mental transport" (p. 11). Jamieson (1988) agrees, saying that images often substitute for words in a persuader's message. Put simply, visual images dominate many forms of persuasion. Taco Bell, for instance, spends 20 times more money on its permanent media that display only its name and logo than it does on advertising (Henderson, 1998, p. 14).

This chapter explores the persuasive power of visual images, which are a primary tool used by persuaders as they form relationships with audiences. Before discussing three specific ways that images persuade, we need to understand how images suggest meaning and how the medium of an image often suggests particular meanings to audiences. At the end of the chapter, we explore how images are persuasive in three contexts: visual spectacles, logos, and architecture.

Attributes of Visual Symbols

Images are composed of a variety of symbolic elements that each suggest meaning to a viewer; when combined with other elements, images can portray a powerful single message or a variety of messages, often contradictory to one another. Thus, the meaning of images is not always easy to "read." In fact, in many cases, it is this ambiguity that gives images such power. In other cases, the elements of the image work together to create a powerful meaning for viewers.

To begin our discussion of persuasion and visual images, we examine some basic elements of image composition: the symbols that make up images. These symbols have particular meaning because of how we respond to them physiologically as well as because of how culture creates and transmits meaning for them. That is, the symbols that compose images are iconic, indexical, and symbolic, to use Peirce's terminology from Chapter 2. To clarify how visual images have meaning, we consider the attributes of color, form, lighting, spatiality, and movement.

COLOR

Donis A. Dondis (1973) contends that "color is, in fact, loaded with information and one of the most pervasive visual experiences we all have in common. It is, therefore, an invaluable source for visual communicators" (p. 50). There are three dimensions of color that are important for us to understand: hue, saturation, and brightness. *Hue* is the color itself (Dondis, 1973). There are three primary hues—yellow, red, and blue—from which other colors are created. *Saturation* refers to the "relative purity" of the color (Dondis, 1973). It is the difference between black and gray, red and pink. Saturation is affected when black, white, or gray is added to the pure color. Saturated, or pure, color is simple, primitive, and uncomplicated. The less saturated colors are more subtle and neutral. *Brightness* refers to the range of color from light to dark. By adjusting the three dimensions of color—hue, saturation, and brightness—it's possible to create millions of colors.

Each color, explains Dondis (1973), has certain meanings attached to it. These meanings are created and maintained by how we communicate about certain colors. Paul Martin Lester (2000) outlines some of the meanings that we have for various colors:

- In ancient Egypt, women who wore *red* fingernails were thought to be in the highest social class.
- *Purple* has been associated with dignity or sadness.
- Baby boys are dressed in *blue* because the color reflects the color of the sky, where the gods lived. The color is seen to give boys power and protect them from evil spirits.
- The color *green* is thought to be associated with fertility.

Our ideas about the meanings of particular colors relate to how persuaders communicate with us today. Dark blue, gray, and black are often seen as "power" colors, indicating that they convey authority and power. Brown, on the other hand, is seen as "a more friendly color." Rodney Jew and Martin Q. Peterson (1995) write that lawyers who do not want to intimidate a jury may wish to wear "friendly" browns instead of darker colors. Color preferences vary with age. Youth prefer warm, bright colors, whereas adults may prefer cool colors. In our culture, the colors red, white, and blue take on additional meaning. Virtually every political candidate uses these colors in his or her campaign, as do a variety of businesses, such as Pepsi.

FORM

Form is another quality of images that attracts attention and influences the meaning we assign to images. Form is composed of dots, lines, and shapes.

Dots   The most fundamental element of an image is a dot. A dot is a "filled-in circle made with a writing implement" (Lester, 2000, p. 31). Dots command our attention in several ways. Lester explains that a dot placed to one side of a piece of paper creates tension because it produces imbalance. Two dots on a page require that we divide our attention between them. With three dots, Lester maintains, we mentally draw a line to connect the dots. Pointillism is an art technique that consists of applying a series of dots that when viewed from a distance combine to form a clear image. In fact, a television screen is really a collection of differently colored dots that combine to form an image in the viewer's mind.

Lines   When a series of dots are placed so close together that there is no space between them, they form a line. A line, explains Lester (2000), has "an energy that comes from the sequence of individual dots" (p. 31). Lines evoke emotional responses from viewers. Straight lines, for instance, indicate stiffness or rigidity. Horizontal lines indicate space—either expansiveness if placed at the bottom of an image or confinement if placed at the top. Vertical lines create division for a viewer. Diagonal lines have a stimulating effect on the viewer. Curved lines communicate playfulness, suppleness, and movement (Lester, 2000). The thicker the line, the more confident is the message communicated by the line.

Shapes   Lines come together to form shapes. The three basic shapes are the triangle, parallelogram, and circle. The *triangle,* which is composed of three lines and angles, indicates action, conflict, and tension and is the most dynamic of the shapes. Triangles communicate tension because of the incongruity between the solid base and the point. Lester (2000) observes that triangles also make the eye follow the direction of the point. The *parallelogram*—squares and rectangles—are composed of four lines that meet at right angles. Parallelograms indicate dullness, honesty, and straightness. You may have heard someone called a "square," which indicates the person's dullness and lack of spontaneity. The rectangle is used most commonly to frame mediated images (Lester, 2000). The 35 mm photography format and the high-definition television screen and movie screen are all rectangular. The *circle,* a "continuously curved figure

Figure 6.2
Advertisement for Marvin Windows

whose outline is at all points equidistant from its center point" indicates end-lessness, warmth, and protection (Dondis, 1973). The wedding ring is a good example of how a circle communicates these ideas. Circles can overcome the other elements of an image because they are so powerful (Lester, 2000).

Shapes help to give an image its direction. The square corresponds to the *horizontal and vertical;* the triangle to the *diagonal;* and the circle to the *curve.* Horizontal-vertical direction relates to balance and stability. The diagonal is the opposite of balance. Dondis (1973) identifies the diagonal as "the most unstable directional force and consequently the most provoking visual formulation" (p. 46). The curve, like the circle, indicates "encompassment, repetition, and warmth" (p. 46).

Shapes also contribute to an image's sense of balance, which refers to how equally elements in the composition are distributed. Dondis (1973) contends that balance is the most important psychological and physical influence on our perception. He explains that we seek to have two feet "firmly planted on the ground" (p. 22). Thus, the presence or absence of balance in a visual design can have a stabilizing or destabilizing effect on its viewer. *Axial balance* means that "the elements of the composition are arranged equally on both sides of imaginary axes in the composition" (Berger, 1998, p. 56). Axial balance indicates formality, sophistication, and elegance. *Asymmetrical balance* conveys stress, energy, and excitement (Berger, 1998).

To see how the elements of form are used in persuasion, consider three ads, for Marvin Windows (Figure 6.2), Ford (Figure 6.3), and OnStar

Find an advertisement in a magazine. How does the advertisement use shape, direction, color, and balance to suggest meaning to the audience?

Figure 6.3
Advertisement for Ford

Linda begged Steve to log off the Internet for a day.

"How about we see the world in person this afternoon?" she challenged.

And before you could say "download," their Ford Expedition

took them to places so unreal and so far out there, Steve thought,

"Hey, the information superhighway is for wimps."

1999 Ford Expedition

Control-Trac system for automatic 4WD traction when needed.
Industry Exclusive: New available power adjustable pedals for improved driving comfort.
Standard removable fold-flat third-row seat with new roller system.   Available 5.4L Triton™ V8 engine.
Expedition is a Low Emissions Vehicle that runs cleaner than most passenger cars on the road today.

Comparison comparisons based on published 1998 competitive data.

(Figure 6.4). The Marvin Windows ad, depicting a bank of rectangular windows, uses the principles of vertical direction and axial balance to communicate that Marvin Windows are reliable, weather-tight, and secure. The Ford ad uses diagonal direction and the triangle shape to imply that the Ford Expedition is an exciting vehicle that will allow you to experience "places so unreal and so far out there," as the ad states. The asymmetrical balance in the ad—the Expedition on the left and the people on the right—shows that the demands of work are outweighed by the call of adventure. The OnStar ad, which promotes safety and security, makes use of curves and circles to demonstrate the comfort and security offered by the service. The OnStar ad also uses axial balance to expand the sense of comfort and stability.

LIGHTING

Arthur Asa Berger (1998) explains that our ability to see anything is a function of how light is used in the image. Lighting reveals shape, texture, and color. Berger notes, "Lighting is one of the tools that artists and photographers can control and is an extremely powerful aesthetic device" (p. 58). Berger describes two kinds of lighting: flat and chiaroscuro. *Flat lighting* attempts to eliminate all shadows in the image. The light is strong, indicating rationality and knowledge. Berger notes that soap operas typically use flat lighting. *Chiaroscuro lighting*

Figure 6.4
Advertisement for OnStar

creates strong shadows, typically associated with emotion or suspense. Horror movies typically make use of chiaroscuro lighting.

SPATIALITY

Another element of images is spatiality, the use of space in an image. *White space* refers to the blank space in a layout used to attract attention or communicate meaning. Designers generally use white space on the edge of the design to draw attention to copy or images used in the design. White space also makes a layout appear "exclusive" (Jewler & Drewniany, 1998, p. 140). Examine the use of white space on this page. Does it direct your attention to the copy on the page? Does it have any other meaning for you? Is there too much white space or not enough?

MOVEMENT

A final element of visual images is their degree of movement. We are naturally attracted to movement, and persuaders use this attribute of images to communicate to us. Lester (2000) describes three types of movement. *Apparent movement* is the movement we perceive in a film. When we watch a film, we do not see characters who are actually moving, but instead we see a series of still images of the characters projected at a rapid speed. The movement occurs because of how our brain remembers and processes the still images. *Graphic movement* is the movement of our eyes through some kind of layout. As you read this page, for instance, your eyes move in a particular direction as determined by the author and the graphic designer. *Implied movement* is motion that we perceive in some images that have been specially designed to provide the illusion of movement. Making lines wavy, for instance, allows them to appear as if they are moving.

We have discussed several basic elements of visual images. Some of these elements suggest a range of inherent meanings, whereas others acquire meaning by the ways they have been used in our culture. Because we are interested in how persuaders use visual images in the media age, let's next consider the impact of medium on how audiences attribute meaning to visual images.

Media Influences on Images

Today's media enhance the power of visual images to persuade us. When we see a photograph of a memorable event, the image lingers in our consciousness. Video of an event creates ideas about truth and knowledge. But even the way that words and images are displayed on a newspaper page, in an annual report, or on a Web page suggests how we should perceive the information as well as provides credibility for what we read. It is important, then, for us to consider how the nature of the medium affects how visual images persuade.

TYPOGRAPHY

The layout and the design of printed and Web materials have meaning for audiences. This enables persuaders to communicate a "philosophy, an ideology, and the spirit of [the] times" (Meggs, 1997, p. 3). We see thousands of messages each day. The appearances of these messages must attract our attention for us to process them. In this section, we discuss four graphic design elements—contrast, harmony, rhythm, and typeface—that affect how we perceive persuaders' messages.

Examine a recent newspaper. How does the layout invite you to read the rest of the paper? How does it indicate what is important to read? In what order are the various sections of the newspaper arranged?

Differences in color, type size, and texture all produce *contrast* in a design. Designers focus the audience's eye movements by using contrast in the layout. *Harmony* refers to the consistent use of colors, typeface, and shapes to produce a coherent layout. Harmony communicates to the reader which elements of the design should be viewed together. A layout has *rhythm:* There is a pattern in its use of design elements. Rhythm creates expectations for the reader about what is to come. It can also be used to lead audiences through the layout. This page's rhythm leads you to turn the page.

The *typeface(s)* the graphic designer chooses for the layout have distinctive meaning as well. There are two general categories of typeface: serif and sans serif (Table 6.1). Serif faces, such as Times and New York, have horizontal

Table 6.1 Typeface Categories and Examples

Serif faces	Sans serif faces
New York	Arial
Times	Helvetica
Palatino	Geneva
Courier	**Impact**

strokes at the tops and/or bottoms of each letter. These strokes guide the reader from word to word. Serif faces are used mostly in the body of the message. Sans serif faces, such as Helvetica, Arial, and Impact, do not have the additional strokes and are commonly used in headlines and logos because of their distinctive and simple design. Persuaders use typeface to communicate meaning to the reader, but also to guide the reader through the publication. Typeface and the other design features we have discussed make is easier for readers to follow the persuader's ideas. Colin Wheildon (1995) suggests that the physical burden of reading a newspaper, magazine, or advertisement is a key concern of those who use these media to communicate with audiences.

PHOTOGRAPHY

Photography is the dominant form of permanent image in the world (A. A. Berger, 1998). A photograph is "an image, in the form of a positive print, taken by a camera (a device with a lens and a shutter) and reproduced, permanently, on a photo-sensitive surface" (p. 74). Photographs are used for a variety of purposes, from capturing a family vacation to documenting historical events in international newspapers. It may be tempting to think that cameras do not lie. That is, we might believe that what we see is an accurate representation of reality, but in fact photographic images are subjective interpretations of events. We often treat these as if they were objective, and we react to them as if they were actual objects or persons, a point we discuss further in the next section. As audience members, we must consider several variables of photography to understand the persuasive power of its images. Three elements—framing, angle, and pose—influence how we perceive a photograph's meaning.

Framing refers to the composition of the photograph and what is excluded from the picture. By centering the subject in the photograph, the persuader communicates a sense of balance. By placing the subject to one side, the persuader creates a sense of imbalance. In addition, cameras capture only what is in the viewfinder. Photographers can exclude elements of a scene that they do not want to document.

The *camera angle* shapes our view of the subject by determining whether we see it from the top, bottom, side, or front. The angle the photographer uses can influence how we perceive the pictured subject. An upward-looking camera angle gives power to the subject; a downward-looking angle communicates weakness. A straight-on shot indicates that the subject is trustworthy. Examine

Figure 6.5 Oliver North Taking the Oath before Testifying in the Iran-Contra Hearings   How does the photographic medium suggest that North is powerful and heroic? How might our image of North be different had cameras not been allowed in the Senate chambers that day?

the picture of Oliver North from the Iran-Contra hearings (Figure 6.5). Because the picture was taken from below, North appears to have a great deal of power.

Pose is another element of photography that influences how we perceive what is pictured. Some photographs are taken without the subject's knowing exactly when the shutter will be snapped, whereas other subjects are well-prepared for the photograph. Fashion models, for instance, pose for their pictures; victims of war usually do not. When persuaders pose subjects, they can manipulate the props the subject uses, the subject's facial expression, and the activity the subject engages in. Refer, again, to the picture of Oliver North in Figure 6.5. Although it was taken as part of an actual proceeding, the photograph is posed, or at least North's appearance is manipulated in a way beneficial to him. His uniform, for instance, creates the perception that he is powerful, trustworthy, and heroic. Complete the Internet Activity: Evaluating Photographs to see how photographs communicate a subjective view of the world.

MOTION PICTURES

Moving images have captivated audiences for years. Today, moving images are presented to audiences through a variety of media. A *film* is a "succession of discrete frames, projected at a rate of twenty-four frames per second (normal speed) that offers the illusion of motion" (A. A. Berger, 1998, p. 96). Film traditionally is characterized by light being projected through a celluloid medium that contains discrete images. The term *video* is often used to describe a

INTERNET ACTIVITY

Evaluating Photographs

We have discussed how photographs—while appearing to offer an objective account of reality—are highly subjective. Framing , camera angle, and pose are three ways that photographs present only a selective version of an event. For this Internet Activity, go to http://www.cnn.com, http://www.msnbc.com, or your local newspaper's website and evaluate the photographs on the site using what we have discussed here. How does the photograph frame the event? What is left out of the photograph? What is included? What camera angle is used, and what does this suggest about the event? Finally, how is the subject posed? What meaning do you ascribe to the photograph?

medium used to show moving images on a television screen or a computer monitor. *Digital video* describes the use of digital, rather than analog, recording and editing hardware to create a computer file containing moving images. In this section, we'll focus on film. In later sections, we'll discuss moving images as they relate to television and computers.

The basic unit of film is a frame, which is similar to a photograph. Through editing, the frames are assembled in a way that tells the story of the film, even though those frames may have been recorded in a different order. For example, the last scene of a movie may be filmed first. A number of devices influence the meaning we take from a film and how we feel about the film.

One group of devices helps us to understand transitions in films. A *wipe* replaces a previous image with a new one by using a sharp vertical, horizontal, or diagonal line. A wipe produces a sharp break in the action of a movie. A *dissolve*, on the other hand, uses a slower process of gradually fading a previous image into a new image. A dissolve suggests that a good deal of time has passed between the two scenes. A *cut* stops the previous sequence and replaces it with a new image to indicate excitement. Music videos often use quick cuts to move from image to image. A. A. Berger (1998) explains that these devices function as punctuation in the movie, showing us the relationship between scenes. Through our experience with film, we have learned what many of these devices mean.

The camera action also influences how we think and feel about a movie. The *zoom* shot moves us closer and closer to the subject, intensifying the image and allowing us to inspect it closely (A. A. Berger, 1998). Directors use zoom shots to indicate importance or to reveal something. A *reverse zoom* moves away from the object and asks us to take a look at the larger picture. A *reaction* shot shows the face of a character reacting to something that has occurred. It influences our emotional connection to the action of the story. A *montage* combines visual elements in an ordered sequence to create meaning and an emotional response from the viewer. Film directors may use handheld cameras to provide shaky, jerky images that communicate realism and truthfulness. The 1999 *Blair Witch Project* used handheld cameras to achieve this effect.

Films have a powerful effect on us. Films provide us entrance to narratives, or stories, which often have heroes and villains, right actions and evil actions. When we immerse ourselves in the narrative, our attitudes are influenced by what happens on the screen. The scale of the images and the quality of the sound system are two variables that afford a very different experience for us in a theater than we have in our homes. Of course, as home theaters become more popular and more sophisticated, viewers will soon be able to experience the same effects of the theater in their homes.

TELEVISION IMAGES

Television images are quite different from film images, explains A. A. Berger (1998). A film uses a series of still images that are projected very rapidly on a screen. We only think the images are moving. Television images are made up of tiny dots that are constantly in motion. The smaller size of the television screen also influences the meaning we attach to the images we see. Horror movies, for instance, are scarier when we see them on a large movie screen than on our smaller television screen. Berger contends that the smaller size of the screen and the shorter distance we sit from the screen when we watch television give us the illusion that we are being with others when we watch television, that we have an "electronic intimacy" (p. 116). The smaller screen also means that the action moves toward and away from us. On a theater screen, the action moves from side to side. In short, television images draw us in because of the intimacy of our relationship with the screen and because of the direction in which the action takes place. Keep in mind, too, that as it does with photography, the camera angle influences what we see and how we relate to those images.

John T. Morello (1988) examined television's influence on the 1984 presidential debates. Morello explains that camera work provides visual clues as to who is winning a point during a debate. At one point in the 1984 debates, Walter Mondale made an inaccurate statement about Medicare spending, yet the camera angle prompted viewers to think his statement was accurate. Use of certain camera angles can help persuaders create relationships with their audiences. As we watch political candidates speak on television, we form a connection with them, not only because of what they say, but also because of how they appear to us on the screen. John F. Kennedy, in his 1960 debate with Richard Nixon, looked Americans in the eyes and talked to them about why he wanted to be president. Nixon did not use the camera to create the same connection. Camera angle is an important part of how persuaders identify with their audiences. Morello concludes, "Televised debates are mediated reality where argument content is altered in ways that may go unnoticed" (p. 287).

COMPUTER-GENERATED IMAGES

Computers have greatly changed how persuaders use visual images. Persuaders use computers both to create new images and to manipulate existing images, such as photographs or video. Computer graphics programs allow users to generate "pictures" of numerical data, such as charts or graphs. Persuaders also use computers to create multimedia presentational aids using software applications such as Microsoft PowerPoint. Using this software, persuaders can integrate images (photographs, charts, and video) with words and present the results to large audiences. Computers have also changed the motion picture industry. Since the use of computer animation in movies first gained prominence in 1982, with Disney's *Tron,* computers have enhanced the visual spectacle of current films. In recent movies, such as *Titanic* and *Eyes Wide Shut,* computer-generated actors and actresses have made it difficult to tell real characters from those that are made of pixels. The video game industry has also developed increasingly lifelike games. Computers can also perform complicated mathematical functions that can produce accurate animations that allow the audience to "experience" the persuader's idea. The Boston Red Sox baseball team used a Web-based animation to convince area residents that building a new baseball stadium would be a wise investment. By visiting the team's website, viewers can experience watching a game in the proposed stadium.

The future of computer-generated images may well lie in virtual reality. Lester (2000) explains that **virtual reality** refers to numerous formats that allow the user to enjoy the illusion of being a character within what appears to be a three-dimensional scenario. Virtual reality ranges from a computer screen that the user can control with arm movements to a complete body suit in which the user can see, hear, and feel a computer-generated "reality." With virtual reality, you can "fly" an airplane, "walk" through historic cities, or even "have sex" with a computerized "person." Virtual reality promises to reshape how we relate to persuaders.

virtual reality numerous formats that allow the user to enjoy the illusion of being a character within what appears to be a three-dimensional scenario

Persuaders use computers to alter existing images as well. Using computer hardware and software, persuaders can add to or delete from photographs people, objects, or events. As you'll read in Ethical Insights: Ethics and Visual Images, CBS has superimposed its logo on buildings and parks. Persuaders can also darken, lighten, or change the color of photographs. This practice is fraught with ethical implications. We discuss ways persuaders manipulate images later in this chapter.

INTERACTIVE MULTIMEDIA

Interactive multimedia, including the World Wide Web, is a medium that combines many of the elements that we have discussed in this section: typography, photography, video, and computer-generated images. A website such as CNN.com typically employs text, photographs, video, and charts. A CD-ROM that a company distributes to potential customers includes the same types of images. Yet there are some important differences in how viewers use these images. With interactive multimedia, the user controls which images to look at, the size of the images, and the camera angle. The user navigates the website or CD-ROM without the presence or direction of the persuader. Island Hideaways, Inc., a rental agency for vacation houses and boats in the Caribbean, has used CD-ROMs to advertise its services. Instead of sifting through pages of photographs looking for just the right information, potential customers of Island Hideaways can use the CD-ROM to search for precise information concerning location, budget, and room size (Seideman, 1996). On a standard

ETHICAL INSIGHTS

Ethics and Visual Images

Millions of *CBS Evening News* viewers on December 31, 1999, probably did not realize that a sign bearing the CBS logo in New York's Times Square that evening was not real. Instead, the sign shown behind anchor Dan Rather had been digitally created by the network. Using the same technology that placed a virtual image of a can of Coca-Cola in the UPN series *Seven Days*, CBS superimposed its logo over that of rival network NBC. CBS viewers saw the CBS eye, while those watching in person and on other networks saw the NBC peacock. The incident raises important ethical questions concerning the use of digital image placements in mediated persuasion.

CBS executives defended the company's use of digital placement techniques on its New Year's Eve news program and in other CBS news shows, including *The Early Show*. The network has "placed" its eye logo on carriages, ice skating rinks, and the sides of buildings in an effort to brand its studio's neighborhood, Times Square. Steve Friedman, executive producer of *The Early Show*, defended the practice by arguing that it does not change the content of the news program (Kuczynski, 2000). Andrew Heyward, president of CBS News, explained that he saw the digital placement as the use of graphics to change the news "set" (Carter, 2000). While admitting that there was potential to abuse the technology, Heyward also said the network would aggressively exploit its capabilities. Anchor Rather explained that he was not satisfied that CBS had used the technology ethically, calling it a mistake and saying it should not have been done.

Media critics argue that CBS's placement of its logo in this case was unethical. Harry Jessell, editor of *Broadcasting and Cable,* explains (in Kuczynski, 2000) that when people see live video, they should think that what they are watching is real. The Society of Professional Journalists code of ethics states, "Journalists should be honest, fair and courageous in gathering, reporting and interpreting information" (SPJ, 1996). Likewise, the National Communication Association (1999) asserts that "truthfulness, accuracy, honesty, and reason are essential to the integrity of communication." In this situation, it is easy to see how an audience member could have been misled by the digital insertion of the CBS logo. Superimposing the logo put the network's accuracy in question. In addition, NBC—which pays to have its peacock displayed in Times Square—was denied the opportunity to have its logo seen by some television viewers. CBS essentially stole from NBC the benefits of its advertising.

What do you think? Consider these questions as you think about the ethics of digital image placement:

1. Was CBS ethical in digitally superimposing its logo over the NBC logo in Times Square? Why or why not?

2. Do audience members have an expectation that when they watch live or taped video they are seeing an accurate representation of some event?

3. Would CBS's action have been ethical had it placed its logo on an empty building, without covering another company's advertisement?

4. Create three ethical guidelines that can be used to help advertisers use digital placement technology.

5½-inch CD, the company is able to fit 2,500 photographs, 30 minutes of music, 21 maps, 200 pages of text, and spreadsheets outlining 390 properties and 23 resorts (Seideman, 1996).

Our discussion so far has focused on the elements of visual images that serve to attract the viewer's attention and suggest what meaning the viewer should assign to the images. We have also explored how the medium influences the meaning we assign to visual images. In the next section, we address to a greater degree the "content" of images and, specifically, how images persuade viewers. To do so, we will refer to our discussion of semiotics from Chapter 2.

How Visual Images Persuade

Visual signs perform several functions for persuaders. The elaboration likeli-hood model (Chapter 2) indicates that audience members process messages through central and peripheral routes. Visual signs are important for both routes. It is easy to see how visual signs aid an audience member's peripheral-route processing, but we will also study how visual signs can produce central-route processing as well. That is, visual signs both attract attention to a persuader's message and offer cognitive arguments to audience members.

Drawing on Peirce's theory, Paul Messaris (1997) contends that visual signs obtain meaning in one of three ways: iconic, indexical, or symbolic. Based on Peirce's distinctions, Messaris identifies three functions served by visual signs:

1. Images represent reality.
2. Images serve as proof for a persuader's message.
3. Images suggest arguments to audiences.

IMAGE AS REPRESENTATION OF REALITY

Messaris (1997) argues that one function of images is to represent reality. Im-ages are able to represent reality because of their iconic properties. Images such as photographs and drawings resemble what they mean. We have just said that photography is an interpretive enterprise that does not accurately capture the "reality" of a situation. Messaris acknowledges this, but argues that the link is close enough for us to perceive the image as being a representation of some-thing "real." Messaris explains, "Nevertheless, all of these kinds of pictures are capable of capturing and conveying to our eyes the distinctive features that our brains need in order to be able to figure out what we are looking at" (p. 3). Messaris identifies two ways in which images represent reality. First, they at-tract attention to the persuader's message. Second, images elicit an emotional response from the audience. In both cases, images serve to provide peripheral cues to audience members. We next examine how images represent reality.

Attracting Attention   Messaris (1997) argues that persuaders must get the attention of the audience if they are to be successful. The use of celebrities who look into the camera and talk directly to us about a particular product is an ex-ample of the attention-getting function of images. This approach works be-cause we like to look at people who look at us. Images attract attention in several ways, contends Messaris: violating reality, using a metaphor, playing on a vi-sual parody, and using direct eye gaze.

First, images can *violate reality* in an attempt to get us to look at them. When an image appears to differ from reality, we are drawn to it. We expect one view of reality and the image provides another. That incongruity attracts our attention. An advertisement showing a sport utility vehicle impossibly perched high on a rock cliff draws your attention to the powerful engine and off-road performance qualities of the truck. With computer-generated video technology, it is quite easy for persuaders to create ads that violate reality.

Second, Messaris (1997) contends that images contain *metaphors* for what they are supposed to mean. We are again drawn to the image because it is different from what we would expect. A recent advertisement for computer modems showed a man who was trying to watch a baseball game but whose view was obstructed by a large column. The advertisement asked if your modem was coming between you and your enjoyment of the Internet. The paradox of the column obstructing the baseball fan's view implied a strong metaphor about Internet connection speeds.

Images also attract our attention when they make use of *visual parodies.* Visual parodies involve using well-known images in new ways. Grant Wood's painting *American Gothic* has been used in countless ways by advertisers trying to get us to take notice of their product. Visual parodies give audience members a "flattering sense of being hip and media conscious" (Messaris, 1997, p. 21). Look at the advertisement in Figure 6.6, a spoof from *Adbusters* magazine. It plays on the popular "got milk?" ad campaign to urge people to drink soy instead of milk. Because we think it is one of the popular milk ads, we pay attention to it, but then learn that it is not for milk—and we remember it.

Direct eye gaze is another way of attracting attention. We look at people who are looking at us. We give them our attention. The well-known poster of Uncle Sam calling to potential army recruits is a classic example of using direct eye gaze to attract attention. The covers of popular magazines often use direct eye gaze by featuring a model who is looking at us. We look back and are drawn to the magazine.

Making an Emotional Appeal   One benefit of the iconic properties of images is that they attract attention. Iconic images also elicit an emotional response from their viewers. Political campaign advertisements that feature an upward-looking camera shot are examples of emotion-eliciting ads because the camera encourages a reverent attitude toward the candidate. Messaris (1997) identifies four ways that visual images elicit emotion: camera angle, look of superiority, identification, and sexual appearances.

First, images use *camera angle* to communicate power and status. Camera angle can be used to look down on an object, to look up at an object, or to look at an object on a level view (Messaris, 1997). A low camera angle—looking up at the subject—makes the subject appear more powerful. A high camera angle—looking down at the subject—makes the subject less powerful. A level camera angle puts the subject on an even footing with the audience. Messaris (1997) contends that a low camera angle is rarely used in political images because the politician wants to identify with the voter and not appear to be a powerful figure. Examine the ad in Figure 6.7 for Chico's. The picture is shot from below, prompting us to view the woman as having a high degree of class and taste. Purchasing clothing from Chico's will let the audience member achieve this standing as well. Messaris notes that a high camera angle can be used to communicate nurturance and subservience.

Camera angle, combined with other visual elements, helps persuaders create a *look of superiority* with visual images. Messaris (1997) contends that producers of high-fashion items often use facial expressions to communicate that their products are superior to other products. In addition, the artifacts that sur-

I was raised to believe that milk was part of a healthy diet. Then I discovered that to increase production, many dairy companies inject cows with hormones and antibiotics that we end up drinking. And that cows are kept "artificially" pregnant so they'll produce milk all year long. So I scrapped my milk mustache for a soy one. It's healthier for me AND the cows.

WHY MILK?
Try soy instead.

Figure 6.6 An Advertisement Featuring Visual Parody   If you look closely, you'll see that this ad is not urging viewers to drink milk, but rather soy. What elements of the advertisement might lead you to conclude initially that this ad is part of the "got milk?" advertising campaign?

round the model communicate superiority. Again examine the advertisement for Chico's in Figure 6.7. In addition to the upward-looking camera angle, the woman's clothing, jewelry, and the stone wall in the background communicate superiority.

Images create *identification* with the audience as well. We feel some kind of bond to the person in the image. We see ourselves in that person. Messaris (1997) notes that identification is perhaps the strongest association that we make with the iconic properties of images. He explains, "By identifying with someone else, we turn the observed consequences of his or her actions into lessons for our own lives" (p. 44). Observe once again the advertisement for Chico's in Figure 6.7. The model exhibits characteristics of self-confidence and beauty. Viewers may identify with these characteristics and make the association that Chico's clothing can help them achieve those same characteristics.

Finally, images use *sexual appearances* to elicit a response from viewers. Messaris (1997) argues that both men and women are drawn to attractive images of models. In addition to sexual appeal, ads featuring naked or scantily clad human bodies communicate status and ideas about beauty. Usually we only see models who conform to a very narrow standard for beauty.

Find an advertisement in a magazine or on television. How does the ad attract attention? How does the ad make an emotional appeal to the audience?

IMAGE AS PROOF

Iconic images, as we have discussed, prompt us to perceive them as something real. When functioning iconically, then, images promote peripheral-route

Figure 6.7   This advertisement for Chico's features several photographic cues that suggest meaning. What is your impression of the woman pictured here? Why?

processing. On the other hand, indexical images prompt central-route processing. Indexical images point to or suggest that something has happened (Messaris, 1997). In that sense, they serve as "proof" for a persuasive statement. Footprints in the snow are proof that someone recently walked through the area. A photograph showing a representation of a particular time and place is proof of what happened at that time and place. It "testifies" about what has happened (Messaris, 1997, p. 130). Keep in mind, however, that these pictures can be deceptive, a point we discuss later.

In commercial advertising, images are used to demonstrate products (Messaris, 1997). Advertisers show how well their paper towel absorbs a spill or how well a certain laundry detergent cleans dirty clothing. When audience members see these demonstrations, they are persuaded. Images are also used to show products that are visual in nature. Seeing how good a new sofa looks in an advertisement assures us that it will look just as good in our house. When we see a model wearing a particular brand of clothing (see Figure 6.7), we think that we will look just as good in that clothing.

Political advertising also makes use of the indexical property of images. Political ads often picture a candidate's supporters as a mix of sexes, races, religions, and ages. By suggesting—through images—that all these people support the candidate, these pictures lead the audience to believe that the candidate is attracting a wide variety of voters. Thus, audience members who are undecided are potentially persuaded that this candidate represents all people's interests. In addition, picturing the candidate in advertising allows voters to get to know him or her. Voters feel they know the candidate because they recognize the candidate's appearance and mannerisms.

In the courtroom, images can be powerful forms of proof for the jury. Pictures of crime scenes, animations of accidents, and charts displaying statistical evidence are three examples. In some cases, live demonstrations are used. Such was the case in the criminal trial of O. J. Simpson. Simpson was asked by prosecutors to try on the disputed glove that he allegedly wore during the murder of which he was accused. When the glove didn't fit, the jury had a powerful image of a man accused of a crime he did not commit. The prosecution was unable to overcome this image.

Because we put so much faith in photographs or drawings as proof of a persuasive argument, it is important that we consider four ways in which images can deceive us: staging, editing, selectivity, and mislabeling (Messaris, 1997). *Staging* involves planning a visual image so that it appears spontaneous. Many visual images are staged to control for unplanned abnormalities. Whether it be posing homeless people for a news story or featuring plastic food in a restaurant advertisement, persuaders often stage images for audiences. So-called reality television is another example. Shows such as CBS's *Survivor* or MTV's *Real World* were popular because they appeared to be "real." Yet the shows' producers created situations in which the participants were forced to act in a certain way or say something that the other participants would find controversial. In many ways, reality television is staged to promote conflict and higher ratings for producers.

Second, persuaders often edit images to make them appear more persuasive. *Editing* is quite common in political campaign advertising. Ads for former President Clinton in 1996 spliced black-and-white images of crisis and Republican nominee Bob Dole with color images of prosperity featuring President Clinton. The ads pictured Dole as someone who would block Clinton's efforts to bring prosperity to the country. In addition, the Democratic ads used images of Dole with then–House Speaker Newt Gingrich to further associate the Republican nominee with gridlock in Congress. The ads were effective because of the editing that was used.

In some cases, persuaders do more than juxtapose images. With the proper software, photographers can easily manipulate photographs in a digital darkroom. The photographer may delete or enhance certain parts of a photograph for aesthetic reasons. Messaris (1997) reports that editors often dilate the pupils of models to make them appear sexually aroused, which creates emotional appeal. Electronic manipulation is commonly used to enhance the beauty of supermodels, as well. Cindy Crawford was once quoted as saying that not even Cindy Crawford looks like Cindy Crawford. The message that digitally perfected models send to members of society is potentially dangerous when viewers feel they have to live up to these unrealistic images.

One of the most controversial manipulations of a visual image occurred in 1994, following the arrest of O. J. Simpson. Both *Time* and *Newsweek* ran Simpson's mug shot on their covers. There were striking differences in the two "photos," however. The one on the cover of *Time* was a darkened version of the

**Figure 6.8
A Political Rally for
Howard Dean during
the 2004 Election
Campaign**
Does this photograph
"prove" Dean's popular-
ity? What elements of
the rally may this image
leave out?

original, a "photo" that *Time* had altered to make it appear more "artistic."
Numerous complaints were lodged against *Time*. Civil rights activists alleged
the altered image made Simpson appear darker, more "Black." *Time* apolo-
gized, saying that it had only wanted to soften Simpson's image. As audience
members, it is important that we be aware of the limitations of using images as
evidence. We must be aware that images can be manipulated to serve the interests of persuaders.

Third, photographs are always *selective representations* of reality. They always include some details and leave out others. As such, they are not true representations of a real situation. Audience members must constantly judge the
degree to which images are representative of their context, or if they were taken
out of context. Images of political campaign appearances are not only staged,
but often are selective. When we view footage on the news of a speech made by
a political candidate, it usually seems as if the candidate was speaking to a capacity crowd of waving and cheering supporters. The cameras are often positioned to give the impression of a large crowd. The most excited supporters are
placed between the cameras and the politician, and often behind the politician
as well. The picture of Howard Dean's rally in Figure 6.8 makes it look as if a
lot of people attended the event. In reality, there may not have been any more
attendees than are pictured. (We discuss pseudoevents, persuasive events such
as this rally that are selectively presented to the public, in Chapter 7.)

Finally, images can be misleading because of *mislabeling*. Advertisers and
news media often rely on stock (file) footage or pictures—generic photographs
or video—to provide visual images to accompany what is being said. Often,
what is being shown is not what is being described.

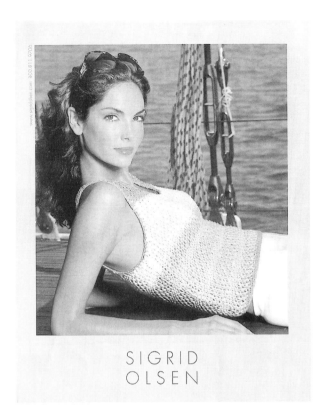

Figure 6.9   How does this advertisement for Sigrid Olsen communicate the value of its clothing? What is suggested by the woman's pose? By her eye contact? Does the ad's use of white space help the clothing label achieve high status?

IMAGE AS ARGUMENTATIVE CLAIM

Images function to attract our attention and make emotional appeals. They also serve as proof for a persuader's message, although we must view images used in this way with a suspicious eye. In other cases, images function as words for persuaders. Messaris (1997) contends that images can say things that words cannot. They do so because of the meanings that our culture has associated with particular images. We tend to equate particular images with particular meanings because we have learned the code of what images mean. Thus, images "show us the unspoken" (p. 221). Images are sometimes used instead of words when it is inappropriate to express the content of the message with words. Because images are ambiguous, they can be useful to persuaders in stating controversial claims.

Some persuaders may seek to appeal to an audience member's quest to achieve social status. Much luxury merchandise is aimed at society's upper classes. Messaris argues that both conspicuous consumption and conspicuous leisure can be used to communicate social status. Persuaders are reluctant, however, to appeal directly to these values. Instead, they let images speak for them. Examine the advertisement in Figure 6.9. How does the ad communicate social status? How does the ad create value for the company's apparel?

Figure 6.10 A political cartoon can communicate a great deal more than words can say. Consider the questions posed in the text as you think about this cartoon. TOLES © 2003 TheBuffaloNews. Reprinted with permission of UNIVERSAL PRESS SYNDICATE. All rights reserved.

Political cartoons have enjoyed a long history of using images to communicate arguments to audiences. In past generations, political cartoons have triggered revolutions, toppled political machines, and turned public opinion upside down (Marschall, 1999). Today, the voices of cartoonists are just one of many we hear offering us their opinions in media. Yet the power of images to communicate argumentative premises cannot be denied. Look at the cartoon in Figure 6.10 about the California budget situation. What does the cartoonist imply about the problem? Does the cartoonist imply that the governor can solve the problem? Examine the claims of additional cartoons in the Internet Activity: Identifying Claims in Political Cartoons.

In this section, we have examined the three functions of images. Iconically, images represent reality. Indexically, images are proof for a persuader's argument. Symbolically, images express ideas that are unsuitable for linguistic expression. We next explore how these images operate in particular persuasive contexts.

Applications of Visual Communication

The ideas about how visual signs communicate meaning to their audiences can be applied in a variety of contexts. Images constantly surround us; often we do not even realize their presence. From the magazine we read to the spectacle of shopping, from a company's logo to its storefront, images persuade us in untold ways each day. Let's examine these three contexts: visual spectacles, logos, and architecture.

INTERNET ACTIVITY

Identifying Claims in Political Cartoons

You have seen how political cartoons can communicate a wide variety of implicit meanings. Visit the website, http://cagle.slate.msn.com/politicalcartoons. Look at several of the cartoons on the site. In each case, identify the underlying claim or proposition of the cartoon. In other words, what is the cartoon implying, but not saying outright? How persuasive are political cartoons to you? What are the limitations of political cartoons and their persuasiveness?

VISUAL SPECTACLES

Sometimes images are combined with others to create a visual spectacle. **Visual spectacles** are persuasive events designed to appeal to the senses. Political campaigns often make use of visual spectacles. The scene of a political rally is one of color, patriotism, and excitement. The speaking platform is often draped in red, white, and blue bunting. American flags are everywhere, along with posters, bumper stickers, and buttons supporting the candidate. Bands play, entertainers perform, and political allies speak. The event is carefully orchestrated to look spontaneous. Crowds are positioned in a certain way in front of the cameras. Smaller crowds are consolidated in a confined area to make them look larger. Photo opportunities with the candidate are provided. All of these images combine to create the political spectacle. Bennett (1992) warns that such spectacles may distance voters from politics because audience members become mere props in a production staged by political professionals. Consider Figure 6.8 again. How does that image reflect our discussion of visual spectacles?

> **visual spectacle**
> a persuasive event utilizing a combination of images designed to appeal to the senses

Barry Brummett and Margaret Carlisle Duncan (1994) explore the use of visual spectacle in their analysis of shopping malls. What they conclude probably does not come as a surprise to anyone who has ever shopped in a large mall. On one level, the visual spectacle of the shopping mall—racks of shoes; large, tree-filled atriums; and the swirl of people—appeals to consumers who enjoy being part of the spectacle. Whether they purchase anything is not important. If they enjoy the visual spectacle, they will be back for more shopping. Shopping malls also provide a sense of empowerment. Shoppers can associate with new people who are unlike themselves. By engaging in "people watching," shoppers enter a new world. Finally, Brummett and Duncan argue that shopping malls give shoppers the opportunity to reinvent themselves. Wandering through Eddie Bauer, for instance, allows us to picture ourselves as "rugged outdoor types" (p. 197). As adults, we "play dress-up," figuratively or literally, when we view the displays in a mall. Ultimately, Brummett and Duncan argue that the visual spectacle of a shopping mall supports the capitalist system by ensuring that shoppers have a pleasing experience and will come back in the future.

> *Describe a visual spectacle that you have recently experienced. What symbols composed the spectacle?*

LOGOS

A **logo** is the graphic design used by a company or an organization to identify itself and its products (Henderson, 1998). (Do not confuse the plural form,

> **logo**
> the graphic design used by a company or organization to identify itself and its products

logos, with the Greek word *logos*, which means logical proof.) Logos are used repeatedly and consistently by organizations to reinforce their image. Contemporary logos trace their roots to the ancient Greek, Roman, and Egyptian craftsmen, who stamped their initials on their products. Medieval kings used royal seals to mark their possessions. By the 1400s, trades, such as medicine and masonry, used trademarks to identify their members as being well trained in a particular field. In the late 1890s, businesses adopted logos as a way to distinguish themselves from their competitors.

Today, virtually every business and organization uses a logo to create identification with their consumers or constituents. Logos are part of the organization's overall image, which we will discuss in Chapter 9. Logos are very important in creating both a company's cognitive and its affective image for consumers. In fact, Coca-Cola's logo is estimated to be worth $3 billion. As we discuss the functions and characteristics of logos, we will use the Nike logo of the swoosh stripe (Figure 6.11) to demonstrate how one company has used its logo to create a worldwide audience of followers.

Functions of Logos   "Logos are one of the main vehicles for communicating image, cutting through clutter to gain attention, and speeding recognition of the product or company" (Henderson, 1998). *Effectively communicating the organization's image* is one function of a logo. For Nike, the relationship between its corporate image and its logo became significant when it sought to increase sales in its non-U.S. markets. To foreign consumers, Nike was just one of many tennis shoe brands in terms of utility and value. Nike needed to create an image of its shoes that was unique from what the other shoe companies were offering. Nike sought to "transform the sneaker from a well-cushioned foot covering into a lifestyle badge, to turn the company's signature Swoosh logo into a trademark of the definitive Nike 'tude" (Grimm, 1993, p. 12). Thus, Nike marketed an attitude to go with its shoes in an attempt to persuade foreign consumers to purchase the shoes, and, more important, the Nike image. The logo became associated with this attitude and took on value.

A second function of a logo is to *cut through the clutter* of other advertising images to gain the consumer's attention. Nike capitalized on the recognition factor of its logo by creating "segments" that linked products together using the logo. For instance, its "Air Jordan" segment—named for basketball player Michael Jordan—linked its logo with shoes, clothing, colors, athlete, and television advertising to create packages of consumer goods that were instantly recognizable to shoppers (Katz, 1993). The logo was instrumental in providing a unifying link for the segment.

A very important function of a logo is to *help the consumer make selections rapidly.* The elaboration likelihood model we discussed in Chapter 2 identifies the importance of peripheral cues in helping audiences make decisions. The Nike swoosh has become a significant peripheral cue for Nike's advertising. Constant exposure to the swoosh has trained us to search for the logo when making purchasing decisions. Author Phil Patton (1997) once counted 28 exposures to the swoosh in a 30-minute time period in New York City. With this much saturation of our culture, it is easy to see how the Nike logo aids consumers in making decisions.

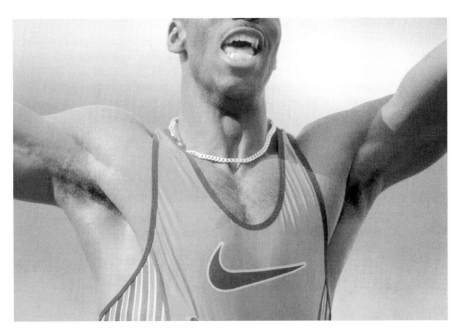

**Figure 6.11
Olympic Gold Medal-
ist Michael Johnson
Sporting the Globally
Recognized Nike
Swoosh**
What impact does a
celebrity spokesperson
have on the success of
a logo?

Characteristics of Effective Logos   Henderson identifies four characteristics of effective logos: recognition, affect, meaning, and subjective familiarity. Effective logos, he argues, promote *recognition and recall* by their viewers. Recognition means that the consumer remembers seeing the logo. It should stick in the consumer's mind even if the consumer sees the logo only briefly. Also, the logo should help viewers recall the name of the company with which it is associated. Nike has achieved both recognition and recall. The swoosh has a recognition factor of more than 90 percent in consumer surveys (Patton, 1997).

Effective logos also create *positive affective reactions* in consumers (Henderson, 1998). They promote formation of an emotional connection between the logo and the sponsoring organization. The diagonal direction of the swoosh, for example, evokes feelings of both movement and sound, as in the sound that one makes when moving quickly past some other person or object (Patton, 1997). The positive feelings associated with the symbol are easily transferred to athletes who promote the Nike organization and to the organization itself. Katz (1993) reports that schoolchildren in China named basketball player, and Nike spokesperson, Michael Jordan as one of the two greatest men in history.

Effective logos also have *meaning* for their audiences. The message of a logo should be easy to interpret (Henderson, 1998). All people who see the logo should come to the same conclusion about what it means. In 1995, Nike decided to drop its name from its logo and use the swoosh alone. Its intent was to create a logo that transcended language (Patton, 1997). Today, the swoosh stands as one of the few corporate logos that is free of words or letters. Katz (1993) argues that even most schoolchildren realize the meaning behind wearing a hat with the Nike swoosh. Nike's use of multiple-sport athletes, such as Bo Jackson and Deion Sanders, reinforces the idea that its shoes are versatile (Patton, 1997).

Think of a logo for a company and evaluate its effectiveness using the criteria discussed in this chapter.

Finally, effective logos have *subjective familiarity* for their audience, even if audience members have not seen the logo before. A logo should easily foster a relationship between the company and the viewer. The logo should be similar to other well-known symbols in order to evoke a feeling of familiarity (Henderson, 1998). Nike accomplished subjective familiarity by using a logo that looks like a check mark or a boomerang (Patton, 1997). The check mark, contends Patton, "serves as a stamp of approval" from the Nike corporation (p. 60). The Nike swoosh is both abstract and graceful (Patton, 1997).

Logos, such as the Nike swoosh, communicate an organization's image, help consumers cut through the clutter of contemporary advertising, and enable consumers to make rapid purchasing decisions. Logos accomplish these goals by being easily recognizable, creating positive affective feelings for the organization, constructing universal meaning for the organization, and having subjective familiarity for the audience. The logo an organization uses to communicate its image is a powerful persuasive tool.

ARCHITECTURE

Visual signs are used in another context as well: architecture. From the countertops of fast-food restaurants to the cultural experience of shopping in the flagship stores of hallowed brands, persuaders use visual images to communicate to us in the places where we work, shop, and play. Indeed, architects and designers have a keen sense of their role in the persuasion process. Designer Nancye Green (1998) contends, "But as designers of environments, we can formulate and shape narratives, drawing on the dimensions of space and time, to weave together the breadth of elements necessary to build a totally immersive experience" (p. 241). Architecture is persuasive in two ways: through the use of physical space and symbolism.

A persuader's use of space can attract or repel those audience members who use the space. Paco Underhill is a "retail anthropologist" who has observed 50,000 to 70,000 shoppers annually in person or on videotape. He provides some interesting observations about how the layout of a store influences shoppers (Labich, 1999). The entrances to stores should be free of elaborate displays, Underhill asserts, to give customers a chance to orient themselves to the store. Underhill has also observed that most U.S. shoppers turn right when they first enter a store. In Europe and other countries, shoppers turn left. The spacing of aisles is also important; shoppers often do not navigate narrow aisles. Placing shopping baskets at various places in the store encourages shoppers to purchase more. Providing chairs for tired shoppers and their sometimes unwilling shopping companions also increases sales.

Museum designers also use space to create a narrative for visitors. Enviroramas are museum exhibits that completely surround the visitor with exhibits in a particular room (Harvey et al., 1998). Visitors can interact with the exhibits and view movies and animations to complete their experience in a given envirorama. Exhibits can also be arranged in such a way that visitors experience a chronological story or a narrative told in an order the designer deems appropriate. Use of space also influences a visitor's immersion. For example, a geology museum used meandering, narrow, and darkened hallways to increase the average attention span of visitors at an exhibit (Harvey et al., 1998). Museums use space to control the actions of their visitors. In so doing, they achieve their goal of immersion.

Architecture also communicates through its use of symbols. It is a "text" for us to decode. The theory of semiotics is useful in examining buildings and spaces. Architecture can be "read" in much the same way as a written speech or a logo. Semiotics can help us uncover the symbolic meanings for various signs in the architectural "text." The NikeTown store in New York tells a story that invites customers to enter the store and purchase Nike products. The store's exterior looks like a gymnasium, with a brick facade and arched windows. Only half the space in the store is devoted to retail; the remaining portion is taken up by video screens, sporting equipment, and sports memorabilia. Visitors to the building experience the Nike image and are told a story about Nike and the role of sports in society. The building, then, is a narrative that visitors can decode in a way that builds support for the Nike brand.

Another example of how symbols communicate to audiences through architecture is the Vietnam War Memorial in Washington, D.C. The solemn black wall on which the names of those killed in the Vietnam conflict are inscribed draws 12,000 to 15,000 visitors a day. The wall's polished granite face serves to reflect those who look at it and their emotions (Blair, Jeppeson, & Pucci, 1991). The symmetry of the wall creates a sense of closure, conveying the message that the war—and controversy about the war—is over. In its granite composition, with its inscribed names, the wall resembles a gravestone. The wall is accessible to visitors and does not dominate its environment. It is black, a color of both sadness and shame, two experiences felt by our nation over the Vietnam conflict. Finally, the wall is open to interpretation, indicating that many people still cannot resolve their feelings about the war (Blair, Jeppeson, & Pucci, 1991).

We have seen that architecture communicates through its use of physical space and symbols. Architecture can be a rich source of visual communication through physical properties and symbolism. Green (1998) maintains that designers are "not simply designing stores and restaurants and shopping malls. Because we're impacting the total relationship between brand and customer. We are creating the experience of the brand" (p. 241).

Evaluating Images

Jamieson (1988) contends that visual images are not testable as arguments. Thus, we are vulnerable to their use by persuaders. She argues that audience members need to be vigilant when assessing the persuasive effects of visual images. Sonja K. Foss and Marla R. Kanengieter (1992) outline a procedure by which audiences can evaluate visual images. The basis of the approach is the function the image performs from the critic's (audience member's) perspective, not the intent of the creator/artist. Foss and Kanengieter propose that audiences make three judgments about visual images.

THINKING CRITICALLY

Evaluating Images of Status

Foss and Kanengieter propose a model of analyzing images in which the critic asks three questions: What is the function of the image? How is that function communicated? What are the implications of that function? We'll use this model to analyze the advertisement for Sigrid Olsen in Figure 6.9. When we determine the function of the advertisement, we could argue that Sigrid Olsen is attempting to portray itself as an upscale clothing line. The company is telling audience members that purchasing its clothing is important.

Sigrid Olsen communicates this message through its use of several symbols in the image. The woman is reclining restfully on the pier along water, indicating a relaxed and leisurely state. Her posture is indicative of people with wealth who have the time and resources needed to relax next to water. The clothing she is wearing is also significant. The textures, colors, and style are all fashionable and, seemingly, expensive. The woman's direct eye contact with the viewer is also a sign of power, as we will discuss in Chapter 9. Together, these symbols indicate the value of Sigrid Olsen clothing.

Finally, Foss and Kanengieter explain that critics should comment on the appropriateness of the image's communicative function. We could argue that Sigrid Olsen is promoting the cultural values of consumption and leisure. The company is attempting to define what is valuable in our culture. We might also argue that this viewpoint privileges certain people, but disempowers those who cannot afford to relax along the water in expensive clothing.

Foss and Kanengieter ask us to question what we take for granted in images. However, their model allows for multiple interpretations of an image. Consider these questions:

1. What other functions might the Sigrid Olsen advertisement serve? How does it communicate these functions?

2. Are some of the other functions communicated by the advertisement more appropriate than the function that we identified earlier?

3. How do audience members determine the functions of images they encounter?

First, the audience judges the "function communicated in the image, accomplished through the critic's analysis of the image itself" (Foss & Kanengieter, 1992, p. 216). The critic examines the physical data of the image and then judges its function. Wearing a baseball cap with the Nike swoosh stitched onto its front might be perceived to indicate loyalty to a particular brand of shoes. The same cap could be perceived to be hiding something—an unkempt appearance, for example.

Second, the critic asks "how well that function is communicated" (p. 216) based on the support available in the image. The critic considers the various "stylistic and substantive dimensions of the image" (p. 216). The swoosh on the cap may be enough for the critic to judge that the cap effectively communicates Nike's image.

Finally, Foss and Kanengieter (1992) say, the audience takes the evaluation process one step further: "scrutiny of the function itself—reflection on its legitimacy or soundness, determined by the implications and consequences of the function" (p. 217). If the function of the object is deemed to be problematic in terms of its consequences, "other functions may be suggested as more legitimate than the one communicated by the image" (p. 217). Returning to the cap, one could argue that the cap is problematic because of its association with a company that has recently faced controversy over the working conditions of its foreign employees. The cap might also signal to an audience member its wearer's desire to conform to social pressures. For a closer look at Foss and Kanengieter's theory, read the discussion in Thinking Critically: Evaluating Images of Status. Foss and Kanengieter's method helps us to recognize that the audience may receive a different message than the persuader intends, and to consider the range of possible meanings images may have.

Using Foss and Kanengieter's suggestions for judging visual images, choose one of the advertisements from this chapter and critique its effectiveness.

Summary

Images play a powerful role in the persuasion process. Like words, images are symbols that are the building blocks of persuasive messages. Images communicate in ways that words cannot.

The individual elements of an image suggest meaning to the viewer. Use of dots, lines, shapes, direction, and balance all serve to indicate stability or excitement. Space and proportion also communicate meaning to viewers. Color is one of our most profound visual cues, conveying many different ideas to viewers. Finally, camera angle and lighting can be used to represent reality in mediated images.

Images serve three primary functions for persuaders: as representations of reality, as proof, and as argumentative claim. As representations of reality, images attract attention and make an emotional appeal. Images also serve as proof of some real experience. In commercial advertising, images are used as proof that products achieve intended results. Political candidates use images to prove who they are and who supports them. However, persuaders sometimes manipulate images to serve their needs, so audience members must be aware of how images are manipulated. Images also say things to audiences that words cannot. Images communicate ideas about social status and sex and romance. Because they are ambiguous, images can "say" the unspeakable.

The persuasive functions of visual images are manifest in the contexts of visual spectacles, logos, and architecture. Visual spectacles combine images to form experiences for audience members. Logos are powerful tools by which persuaders identify with their audiences. Architecture communicates through physical space and symbolism.

It is difficult to "test" an image for truthfulness, yet visual images can be evaluated based on how well they communicate an idea and on the appropriateness of the idea.

Key Terms

Visit the book's website at http://www.mhhe.com/borchers2 for multiple-choice quizzes, Internet activities, and key terms flashcards.

virtual reality 169

visual spectacle 179

logo 179

7

Persuasion and Language

Learning Objectives

After reading this chapter, you should be able to:

1. Identify ways of using language strategically.

2. Understand how meanings are contested and that persuaders seek to determine the meanings of words and symbols.

3. Explain how language is used to create social reality.

4. Describe the influence of television on language and the characteristics of electronic eloquence.

5. Identify how language creates, transforms, and reinforces power relationships in society.

There's a good chance that you know the companies associated with the following slogans:

- Just Do It.
- Think different.
- Quality is job one.

Slogans such as these are repeated often enough that knowledge of their meaning comes naturally to us. Persuaders use slogans and jingles in the same way that they use logos, which we discussed in Chapter 6. In an electronic culture, persuaders often reduce their use of language to short, memorable phrases. Whether the persuader is a political candidate, an advertiser, or the angry demonstrators of a persuasive movement, the persuader uses language to suggest meaning to an audience. The use of language in this manner helps us to form relationships with persuaders as well. Not only do you likely know the companies behind the slogans just mentioned—Nike, Apple, and Ford—but you probably have some feelings toward those companies as well. Indeed, slogans are good ways for persuaders to build relationships with their audiences.

In this chapter, we look closely at another of the "building blocks" of persuasion: language. Persuaders use both visual images (Chapter 6) and language to identify with their audiences. Verbal symbols—the words used by persuaders—are a powerful means for influencing the attitudes of audience members and forming relationships with them. Language is one way in which we understand our culture, and as we will learn, culture is an important part of persuasion. Language also communicates ideas about the source of a message, evokes an emotional response from audience members, and provides reasons for audience members to identify with the source. As we discuss language, we will also use the words *verbal symbols* and *discourse* to describe it.

As we have noted, media have altered many aspects of contemporary society. Media have allowed the expression of multiple perspectives, changed our consciousness, and created new standards for truth and knowledge. These changes are all reflected in our discussion of verbal symbols. Specifically, we look at five aspects of language use by persuaders in the media age. First, persuaders use language strategically; second, persuaders work within a culture in which the meaning of verbal symbols is contested; third, language is a powerful way of creating social reality; fourth, persuaders use electronic eloquence to form intimate relationships with audiences; and fifth, the relationship between language and power influences how persuaders and audiences identify with each other.

Using Language Strategically

The first section of this chapter explores the ways that persuaders use language strategically to identify with audiences. When we use the word *strategically*, we are referring to the stylistic and structural choices persuaders make when they consider how to use language in a persuasive message.

LANGUAGE INTENSITY

Language intensity refers to the degree of affect reflected in the persuader's language, ranging from mild to intense (Hamilton & Hunter, 1998). Consider this statement made by President Bush concerning Saddam Hussein: "As Americans, we want peace—we work and sacrifice for peace. But there can be no peace if our security depends on the will and **whims** of a **ruthless** and **aggressive dictator.** I'm not willing to stake one American life on trusting Saddam Hussein. Failure to act would embolden other **tyrants,** allow **terrorists** access to new weapons and new resources, and make **blackmail** a permanent feature of world events." Note Bush's use of intense words that appear in bold.

Researchers who measure language intensity measure the ratio of intense words to the total words in the text. This measure is called marker density. They also measure the strength of the intense words, which is called marker power. The excerpt from Bush's speech in the previous paragraph would likely have high marker density and high marker power.

Language intensity does not benefit all persuaders equally. Mark A. Hamilton and John E. Hunter (1998) argue that language intensity influences attitude change only for discrepant messages delivered by credible sources. Audience members who are not ego-involved in a topic, when hearing a message contrary to their beliefs, are influenced by language intensity when the source is credible. Bush's Iraq speech quoted previously would likely be persuasive because of its language intensity, but only for audience members who were undecided about the war but see Bush as credible.

POWERFUL LANGUAGE

Researchers have studied the link between persuasion and the powerfulness of the language used by persuaders. Powerless language is characterized by the following features:

- Empty adjectives, such as "cute," "sweet," and "divine" (Burrell and Koper, 1998).

- Question forms or the use of questions—such as "right?"—at the end of statements.

- Polite forms, such as the use of "please" and "thank you."

- Hedges, which modify the previous statement. Examples include "I guess," "I think," "kinda," and "you know."

Powerful language is marked by the absence of such features. In other words, powerful persuaders do not use empty adjectives, they make strong statements instead of using questions, they do not use polite forms, and they use hedges less frequently than do powerless persuaders.

Evaluate the language you use in conversation and in more formal settings. Do you use powerful or powerless language? Is your language intense? How effective do you think you are in persuading others? How might you change your language to be more effective?

The results of research into powerful/powerless language have been contradictory (Burrell & Koper, 1998). Some studies indicate that powerless language does not effect persuasiveness; others indicate that powerful language may inhibit a persuader's effectiveness. To better understand the link between powerful language and persuasion, Nancy A. Burrell and Randal J. Koper conducted a meta-analysis of previous studies. They found that powerful language is "not only more persuasive but also more credible than powerless language" (p. 212). They advise persuaders to "use powerless language with great discretion/caution!" (p. 214).

LANGUAGE AND IMAGERY

Persuaders can create powerful images for their audience through language. Given what we have said about the dominance of images in our media today, it is easy to see how using imagery in language can make use of the audience's predisposition to visual communication. Visual imagery penetrates our consciousness and reaches us at an emotional level (Jew & Peterson, 1995). Visual language makes use of vivid descriptions of events, objects, and people. It helps audience members to picture themselves as part of the scene being described.

Jew and Peterson (1995) suggest using a "visual strategy" when presenting a case to the jury. A visual strategy helps jurors "absorb the issues without filtering them through the judgments they inadvertently apply to your words" (p. 76). A four-step approach can be used to develop a visual strategy. First, the persuader identifies a powerful, visualized theme. Second, the persuader supports that theme with comparisons to other testimony and facts. Third, audiences use their own life experiences to analyze what they have heard. Jew and Peterson report that juries draw conclusions about an automobile accident based only on the make of the car involved. Finally, audiences make decisions based on this analysis. If the speaker's visual cues are strong enough, the audience will make decision in the persuader's favor, report Jew and Peterson. They maintain that one jury decided a case based on the associations jury members made between the defendant and the make of the care he drove (a Porsche), which was observable only in a photograph. By creating pictures for their audiences, persuaders can harness the power of images with their words.

RHETORICAL FIGURES

Since the ancient Greeks, theorists have identified particular ways of using language to maximize its persuasive effects. Persuaders take great care to choose the right words and arrange them carefully to have the maximum effect on the audience. Let's now consider several aspects of speaking style.

- *Parallelism* is the repeated use of similar words, phrases, or sentences in the same position in a grammatical construction. The repetition creates a sense of rhythm that invites the audience to listen and remember what is being heard or read. These two lines from Martin Luther King Jr.'s 1963 "I Have a Dream" speech use parallelism: "But we refuse to believe that the bank of justice is bankrupt. We refuse to believe that there are insufficient funds in the great vaults of opportunity of this nation." King's use of "we refuse to believe" is parallel in both sentences.

- *Alliteration* is using words that start with the same first letter in close proximity to each other. King used alliteration in this sentence, "We must forever conduct our struggle on the high plane of dignity and discipline," where he paired the terms *dignity* and *discipline*.

- *Antithesis* is the use of contrasting ideas in the same sentence. King used antithesis in this line from his 1963 speech, "Nineteen sixty-three is not an end, but a beginning."

- *Repetition* involves restating a key word or phrase to reinforce the point being made. Perhaps the most well-recognized characteristic of King's 1963 speech is his use of repetition:

I have a dream that one day this nation will rise up and live out the true meaning of its creed: "We hold these truths to be self-evident, that all men are created equal."

I have a dream that one day on the red hills of Georgia the sons of former slaves and the sons of former slave owners will be able to sit down together at the table of brotherhood.

I have a dream that one day even the state of Mississippi, a state sweltering with the heat of injustice, sweltering with the heat of oppression, will be transformed into an oasis of freedom and justice.

I have a dream that my four little children will one day live in a nation where they will not be judged by the color of their skin but by the content of their character.

I have a dream today.

METAPHOR

Persuaders often use metaphors to compare things that are apparently different yet have something in common. Metaphors are persuasive because they help the audience see the relationship between something new and something they already know. Metaphors helps us to escape our previous way of seeing by looking at something from a different angle. Metaphors are effective means of transferring an audience's positive feelings from one object to another. Metaphors that reflect a premise held by the audience can also serve as a form of proof for the speaker's message.

Martin Luther King Jr. used a metaphor in his famous "I Have a Dream" speech delivered in front of nearly 250,000 civil rights marchers in Washington D.C., in 1963. King claimed that the marchers were in Washington to "cash a check." He argued that when the nation was founded, it issued a promissory note to each of its citizens. Until that time, the government had "defaulted" on its promise, as far as African Americans were concerned. King urged that the "bank of justice is not bankrupt" and that the government should pay what it owes African Americans. King was not talking in strictly monetary terms. He was talking about the right to vote and be free of segregation and discrimination. King associated the concept of a promise with the civil rights movement, encouraging White Americans to make the association. The metaphor had powerful implications for how society would view King's efforts to achieve equality for African Americans. In essence, the metaphor made the argument that African Americans should be given the same rights as all Americans.

Sopory and Dillard (2002) conducted a meta-analysis of previous studies related to metaphors. Fundamentally, they found that metaphors lead to greater attitude change than literal language and that metaphor use enhances the credibility of the persuader. Let's examine their findings in a bit more detail.

Although their statistical analysis revealed a "high degree of confidence about metaphor's positive effect on attitude" (p. 9), the authors warn against using any metaphor in any condition. Metaphors should be carefully chosen and skillfully employed. For instance, persuaders should use a single metaphor, they should extend it throughout the persuasive presentation, and they should use it at the beginning of the presentation (Sopory & Dillard, 2002). Additionally, metaphors that are delivered through an auditory medium are more persuasive than those that are written.

Fitzgibbon and Seeger (2002) studied the metaphors used by the Daimler Chrysler company when it announced plans for a merger between the international automobile manufacturers. An effective metaphor, they explained, could frame how stakeholders would respond to the merger and facilitate a smooth postmerger environment. Consequently Daimler Chrysler used metaphors such as "a single global entity," "a good fit," and "a marriage of equals" to describe the merger for their employees, news media, and employees. Fitzgibbon and Seeger explained, the metaphors became ambiguous and confusing. The reality of the merger also failed to live up to the promise of the metaphor. As a result, employees were less motivated and a number left the company. Further, the metaphors that were chosen could not be adapted to changing situations. Ultimately, Fitzgibbon and Seeger argued that metaphors can be effective in facilitating global mergers, but that they must be chosen and used carefully.

Sopory and Dillard (2002) also examined the impact of metaphor use on the persuader's credibility. One aspect of credibility is the dynamism of the persuader, which refers to the assertiveness or energy of the persuader. Using a metaphor, Sopory and Dillard found, enhances the persuader's dynamism and, consequently, the persuader's credibility. We'll study credibility in greater detail in Chapter 9.

Identify an effective metaphor you have recently heard or used. Why was the metaphor persuasive? What are some other examples of metaphors used in advertising or political speeches? Evaluate their effectiveness.

Contested Meanings

Let's next examine how persuaders contest the meaning of words. In Chapter 1, we discussed how media foster the development of a variety of perspectives about truth and knowledge. In previous eras, however, individuals within a culture shared—to a greater extent than they do now—similar ideas about what symbols meant. Some powerful institution in the culture, such as the church or the monarch, determined what words meant. People today have different ideas about what is true and false, and media allow us to communicate our ideas to others quickly. Thus, we are exposed to a great variety of symbols and meanings associated with those symbols. Consequently, we contest, or challenge, the meanings symbols suggest. In fact, persuasion often involves a struggle between competing meanings for words and images.

Let's consider the controversy surrounding display of the Confederate flag on government buildings. During 1999 and 2000, lawmakers in South Carolina debated whether to continue to display the Confederate flag on the state's capitol. To many residents of the South, the Confederate flag represents pride in the region's heritage, which was marked by the Civil War (Figure 7.1). To others, the Confederate flag represents the nation's painful experience with slavery (Figure 7.2). The two sides could not agree on what the flag means because both have different ideas about the object referred to by the flag. Ogden and Richards (1923) offer to this discussion the notion that meanings are in people, not in words. In this case, the meaning for the Confederate flag

Identify a controversy in the news today in which meaning is contested. What are the various sides in the disputes? What is the public's reaction to the controversy? How do you think the matter will be resolved?

Figure 7.1 Semantic Triangle with Civil War

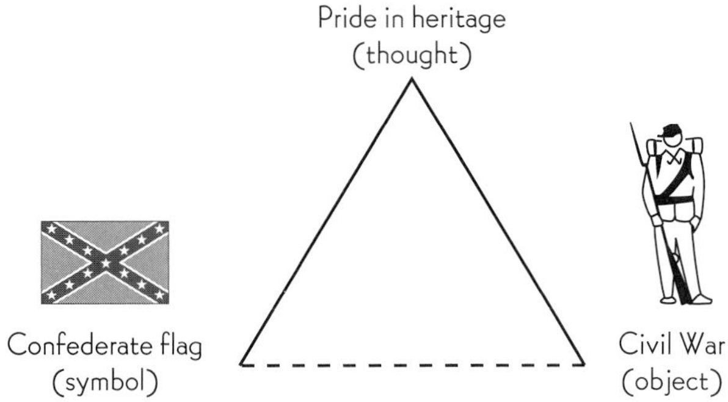

Pride in heritage
(thought)

Confederate flag
(symbol)

Civil War
(object)

Figure 7.2 Semantic Triangle with Slavery

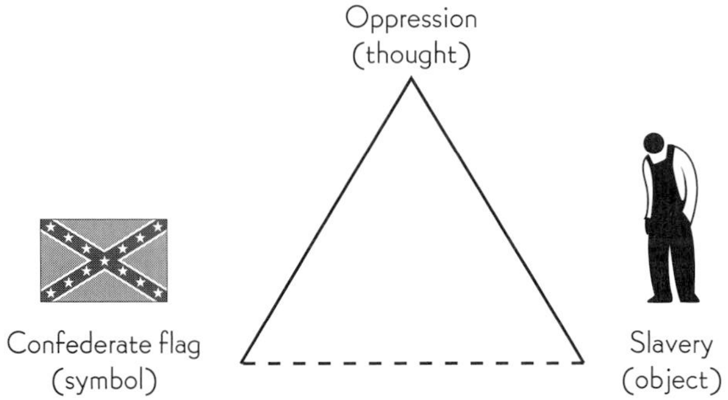

Oppression
(thought)

Confederate flag
(symbol)

Slavery
(object)

depends on the degree to which a person sympathizes with the South's efforts during the Civil War.

The Confederate flag is a visual image, but the same observations can be true of words in our culture. University and professional athletic teams with names related to Native American culture have been criticized in recent years for being disrespectful to Native Americans. Names such as the Redskins, Fighting Sioux, or Indians conjure different meanings in different people. For some, these names represent pride in our nation's Native American heritage. The names suggest courage, bravery, and honor. To others, however, the names mock Native Americans. In particular, the practices associated with the names, such as mascots, the "Tomahawk chop," and facepaint, all show disrespect to the practices and beliefs of Native Americans. Individuals who disagree with the generally accepted meanings our culture assigns these names contest their use. There are no easy solutions to this problem. Many schools have changed the names of their teams, but many more continue to use the potentially offensive monikers.

Persuaders enter the picture when they seek to exploit the meanings that we have for verbal symbols. Persuaders take advantage of the ambiguity in our language today and suggest meanings for words that work to their advantage. Kenneth Burke has called this "strategic ambiguity." A good example of strategic ambiguity is what William Lutz (1989) calls **doublespeak,** "language that pretends to communicate but really doesn't. It is language that makes the bad

doublespeak

language that pretends to communicate but really doesn't; language that uses ambiguity to hide its true message seem good, the negative appear positive, the unpleasant appear attractive or at least tolerable" (p. 1). Lutz argues that doublespeak is all around us. A tax increase is a "revenue enhancement." "Restructuring" or "downsizing" are convenient ways of telling workers that they are being fired. In the past, the words "lean" and "lite" suggested a variety of meanings to consumers, until the government regulated the meanings of those words.

Persuaders control debate over public issues when they can define for the public what terms mean. If you were to ask each person in your classroom what "affirmative action" or "political correctness" means, you would probably get a variety of definitions. By managing how the public defines issues such as these, persuaders can strengthen their own position and policies while undermining the positions of their opponents.

In some cases, symbols whose meanings are now contested were once seen as patriotic, religious, or spiritual. Postman (1992) calls this the "Great Symbol Drain." When advertisers, and other persuaders, freely and without reservation appropriate national icons such as George Washington and Abraham Lincoln, religious icons such as Jesus Christ, or cultural symbols such as the red AIDS ribbon, the value of these symbols is stripped away. Computer technology permits easy reproduction of symbols to meet advertisers' demands. The result, argues Postman, is a culture that has no moral center and one in which symbols represent very little. Thus, our first observation concerning verbal symbols and the media age is that persuaders exploit the ambiguities in our language in order to identify with us. On a deeper level, persuaders seek to create a reality for us through language.

Examine a recent edition of a newspaper or magazine to find some examples of doublespeak. Who benefits from the ambiguity of the doublespeak terms? Who is disadvantaged by how the words are used?

Creating Social Reality

If you accept the proposition that reality is constructed through our language, as we discussed in Chapter 2, then you can understand how important language is in the creation, maintenance, and transformation of social reality. We constantly use words to manage our reality and the reality of others. Politicians, advertisers, and activists all seek to create reality for their audience members, maintain current beliefs, or transform cultural beliefs to better serve their interests. To better understand this point, let's examine the theories of Kenneth Burke, one of the most influential communication theorists of the 20th century.

Symbol use is fundamental to our definition of persuasion, and Burke developed a comprehensive theory called **dramatism** to describe how humans use symbols. Burke theorizes that language is a way of acting: When we use words, we engage in action. We "do" things with language. For him, language is not a neutral technology, but one that has great power over those who engage in it. His theory of dramatism provides a complex account of how words operate to "induce" individuals to identify with each other. In this chapter, we examine some of the basic tenets of Burkean dramatism, including symbol use, the negative, hierarchy, perfection, guilt, and motives. Then we discuss three specific ways in which Burke suggests language accomplishes identification.

dramatism
a theory of human motivation that contends that language motivates individuals to act in certain ways

SYMBOL USE

First, Burke says, humans are symbol-using (and -misusing) animals. In Chapter 1, we saw that symbols stand for, or represent, some object or concept and that symbols lie at the core of our communication system. Burke provides a rich account of the power, both good and bad, of symbol use. Humans, he says, create symbols to name things, and these names contain an **attitude.** Burke's definition of an attitude is similar to what we studied in Chapter 5. Burke says an attitude is an introduction to an act; it is an "incipient act" (1969a, p. 476). It is our emotional state prior to acting. Language, he explains, reveals our attitudes. We cannot escape showing how we view ourselves, our world, and those around us when we use language. In his book *The Philosophy of Literary Form*, Burke writes that "language is the dancing of an attitude" (1973, p. 9). He says that when we use language, we are choosing from among "magics." Our symbol use is not always positive. We sometimes misuse symbols. Ultimately, says Burke, language shapes behavior and language is strategic. "These names shape our relations with our fellows. They prepare us for some functions and against others, for or against the persons representing these functions. The names go further, they suggest how you shall be for or against" (1984, p. 4). The symbols persuaders use and how they use those symbols are important determinants in how successful they will be.

In addition to language being strategic, language has within it several features that give it additional power. One of the features inherent to language is the **negative,** the linguistic act of saying that something is not something else. According to Burke, humans are the "inventors" of the negative. We make distinctions between different items in our world by using different words for those items. We say, "A cat is not a dog." The cat has no concept of the negative, nor do other items in nature. The items simply "are." Humans, because of our use of symbols, make these distinctions. Thus, the negative is inherent in our symbol use. The negative allows us to distinguish between elements of our world, and it also results in moral action. Because of language, we can say, "Thou shalt not kill," which implies a moral code of action. Those members of society who kill are deemed immoral. Burke's view is that we are invented by or moralized by the negative. As a consequence, we experience guilt that must be relieved.

Another implicit aspect of our language use is that we are "goaded by a spirit of hierarchy" (Burke, 1966, p. 16). When we use language to differentiate between people, places, or things, we inevitably create structures in which one word has a higher standing or place than others. Thus our language creates **hierarchies,** or social structures. Consider your class standing. You may be a freshman, sophomore, junior, or senior. Each of those words implies a kind of structure. In addition, we constantly try to move up the social structure. Most freshmen and sophomores wish to someday become juniors and seniors. If you were not making progress toward your degree, in fact, you could lose financial support or be put on academic probation. Because of symbol use, we feel constant pressure to do more or be more, to somehow move up the ladder of life. Competition results from this hierarchical feature of language use. The in-

attitude
a learned response to some person, object, or idea; an attitude has a positive or negative dimension; also, a way of seeing the world that is reflected in our language

negative
the linguistic act of saying that something is not something else

hierarchy
a symbolic structure, created by language use, that gives one person, place, or thing a higher standing than others in its group

evitable result of a symbolically created structure is, again, guilt. Those who do not rapidly ascend in the hierarchy feel guilt. Likewise, those who do achieve a higher social standing often experience guilt because of their success. Persuaders are quick to use our desire for success to sell us products that we think can help us achieve a higher status.

Another inherent aspect of our symbol use is the idea that we are "rotten with perfection" (Burke, 1966, p. 16). **Perfection** is our desire to take ideas or actions to their extreme. Symbol use causes us to constantly seek "the best." We are not content with being mediocre. We want to take things to the end of the line. When the United States built a bomb in World War II, we did not stop until we had created the ultimate bomb—the hydrogen bomb. When pro athletes negotiate their contracts, they do not agree to sign until they have gotten as much money as they can. Consider for a moment the appeals used in many advertisements: "best," "fastest," and "strongest." As consumers, we do not buy products that are simply "adequate." When we do not achieve our maximum potential, guilt again results from this "rotten with perfection" orientation.

perfection
the desire to take ideas or actions to the extreme

Guilt, a psychological feeling of discomfort that arises when order is violated, is an inevitable result of our language use. We have just discussed three sources of guilt: the negative, hierarchy, and perfection. All three produce guilt because of symbol use. The negative creates guilt because it specifies moral action. That is, our language specifies what we should and should not do. When we do what our language says is wrong, we experience guilt. We also experience guilt because of our place in the hierarchy. If we do not achieve success or if we somehow violate the rules of the hierarchy, we experience guilt. Guilt also arises when we do not achieve perfection—and sometimes, when we do. When we take something to its extreme, we may feel guilt because we have injured someone along the way.

guilt
a psychological feeling of discomfort that arises when order is violated

Guilt can be felt on an individual level or on a societal level. You might experience guilt when you do something that you know is wrong—when you are moralized by the negative. You feel guilt when you do not receive as high a grade as you know you should have on a test. You might also feel guilt if you score well on a test but your friend does not, when you know that your friend spent a great deal of time studying for the test and you didn't. On a societal level, we feel guilt when someone does something to harm our larger community. When young people commit crimes, for example, many in the community feel guilt. Some people feel that society at large is to blame; others blame the accused. In any case, the result is guilt, which must somehow be managed. Because guilt is created through language, Burke argues, we can use language to manage guilt.

For Burke, the primary function of symbolic acts is to produce identification, which we discussed in Chapter 1. **Identification** occurs when we share a similar way of viewing the world with someone else. Consider an advertisement for a fitness club. Advertisements for exercise clubs often use guilt to induce audience members to join the club and achieve their fitness goals. According to Burkean theory, an effective ad would argue that if you do not exercise you are not living up to your potential, you may develop health problems, and you are not enjoying life as much as you might. The use of the nega-

identification
a state of alignment that exists with another when we share a similar way of viewing the world

tive in this ad, as well as its appeal to perfection, would make you feel guilt about not being a member of this club. Toward the end of the ad, the club would likely provide information about how to join. You would then identify with the club and its way of seeing the world. You would share motives with the fitness club and would join the club to rid yourself of the guilt caused by not being a member.

Through the negative, symbols create hierarchy and a quest for perfection, which results in guilt. Because we experience guilt, we must use language to cleanse our society and ourselves. Burke's account of how language moves people to view their world should provide much insight for us as we continue our discussion of persuasion in subsequent chapters.

NAMING

Burke argued that language is magical. He also emphasized the idea of attitude—that the words we use contain attitudes toward the objects, ideas, or people we describe. Those attitudes suggest responses on the part of audience members. When persuaders name people, objects, or ideas, they are using the power of language. Let's discuss two examples of the power of **naming,** the first from Burke's own work and the second from contemporary politics.

In an article published before World War II erupted, Burke examined the language strategies used by the German leader Adolf Hitler. Burke's article, "The Rhetoric of Hitler's Battle," identified the language strategies used by Hitler in his book *Mein Kampf.* Burke found that Hitler transformed the word *Jew* into a negative label to allow him to mobilize the German people against the Jews. Specifically, Hitler elevated the meaning of the word *Aryan* so that people of Aryan descent were superior to those who were Jews. Hitler also labeled the Jewish people as being responsible for Germany's economic troubles, allowing the German people to scapegoat the Jews for their financial difficulties. Finally, Hitler used words to give Germans the sense that their lives could return to normal if they removed the Jews from Germany. Hitler used words to empower Aryans while at the same time disempowering Jews. The extermination of 6 million Jews in the Holocaust is proof that Hitler's naming strategy was effective. As this example demonstrates, the power of language presents us with challenging ethical concerns.

A second example of the power of naming comes from contemporary politics. The title of "frontrunner" has become an incredibly powerful way for the news media to shape our attitudes toward political candidates. The Republican "frontrunner" in the 2000 campaign was Texas Governor George W. Bush. Having received early public support, Bush was labeled the frontrunner by many in the news media. As a result, Bush was able to capture endorsements from important politicians and generate an enormous amount of money. Many Republican candidates dropped out of the race in 1999, nearly four months before the first primary was held and Bush easily won the GOP nomination. The name "frontrunner" contains an attitude and affords power to politicians who wear the title.

naming
use of labels that contain attitudes toward the object, ideas, or people they describe and that suggest audience responses

Consider a magazine advertisement for a product or service. How does the ad use Burke's idea of naming to create an attitude toward the product being sold? What name is used? What is the slogan? What do these words suggest about the product or service?

FRAMING

Symbols suggest a perspective from which we should look at something. Burke (1969a) writes that our language use reflects our motives. A motive is another word for a situation, explains Burke. The way we view the world depends on how we define the situation to which we are exposed. You might plan to meet a friend at the library at 2:00 P.M. to study for an upcoming test. If your friend fails to meet you at 2:00, you have several options for defining that situation. You might blame your friend and think that he or she is irresponsible for missing the appointment. Or you may assume that your friend has a perfectly sound reason for not being there. Your friend may have had car trouble, for instance. Burke would say that how you talk about this situation—your way of **framing** it—reveals something about how you view others and your world. He developed a pentad to help uncover the motives that cause us to look at our world in a certain way.

framing
a way of talking about a situation that reveals something about how the speaker views others and the world

The five parts to Burke's pentad are act, agent, agency, scene, and purpose. *Act* refers to what is done. It is the action that takes place in a statement or story. *Agent* refers to the person doing the action. *Agency* is the means by which an action occurs. *Scene* is the setting or background for the action. *Purpose* is the reason or rationale behind the action.

Sometimes two pentadic terms are correlated, such that one has a relationship with the other. In Burke's terminology, these terms form a *ratio*, where one controls, or determines, the other. The scene may give rise to the act, for example. In the example of your friend's failure to meet you, if you blame your friend's absence on him or her, you would be focusing on the ratio between agent and act. If you think that your friend's absence is due to car trouble or some other situation beyond his or her control, you would be emphasizing a scene-act ratio.

Knowing that audience members create ideas about their world based on one or more of the terms of the pentad, Burke theorizes that persuaders can use language to structure the world view of audience members. A persuader can focus on the terms of the pentad that would be favorable to his or her persuasive goals. David Ling (1970) illustrates the power of using the pentadic terms to achieve a persuasive goal. Ling studied the speech given by Senator Edward M. Kennedy following a car accident in which Kennedy was the driver and his assistant, Mary Jo Kopechne, died. Kennedy failed to report the fatal accident until the next day, causing some to question his sobriety at the time of the accident. Although the tragedy would have doomed the careers of many politicians, Kennedy's use of language allowed him to gain public redemption and remain in the U.S. Senate.

Kennedy, while claiming that he would take responsibility for his actions, subtly shifted the blame to the scene, absolving himself of responsibility for his actions. On the one hand, Kennedy said, "I do not seek to escape responsibility for my actions by placing blame either on the physical, emotional trauma brought on by the accident or on anyone else" and "this is a decision that I will have finally to make on my own" (quoted in Ling, 1970). However, in the speech, Kennedy argued that he (the agent) was the victim of the scene: the cold, turbulent, and murky water and the subsequent concussion he received from the accident. He also argued that if the people lacked confidence in him, he would quit, shifting responsibility for his future actions to the people. The people of Massachusetts continued to support Kennedy, thus illustrating the power of his language use to define the reality for his audience. The pentad, writes Ling, is a way of understanding "how the persuader has attempted to achieve the restructuring of the audience's view of reality" (Ling, 1970).

As the number of persuaders has increased in contemporary society, the number of perspectives to which we are exposed has increased as well. Persuaders continually seek to have their perspective become the dominant way in which their ideas are seen. This battle is sometimes called **spin control.** The job of persuaders today, including journalists, academics, and politicians, is to get the audience to accept a particular perspective for viewing a symbol or event. Political consultants, public relations professionals, and lawyers interpret, or **spin,** events, statements, and actions for audiences in ways that are favorable for their clients. In some cases, those who try to influence media sources do not reveal that they are doing so. Ethics, then, is a concern for those who practice spin control, as the discussion in Ethical Insights: Ethics and Spin Control makes clear.

Journalists often write stories from a particular angle that leads to a particular definition. In fact, a 1999 *PRWeek*/Business Wire poll found that 93.5 percent of the time journalists write their stories from an angle that is different from that of the press release issued by the newsmaker ("Who's Spinning Who?" 1999, p. 15). The pictures used in media also privilege certain meanings of symbols. Photographs always leave something out. They are incomplete interpretations of an event. Burke's idea of framing is important to consider as we attempt to understand the variety of perspectives to which we are exposed.

DRAMATISTIC REDEMPTION

Much of Burke's theory of language use deals with the concept of guilt. Guilt is a product of the negative and of hierarchy. Thus, guilt is an ever-present part of our language system. Burke has identified two strategies of purification—tragic and comic—by which we cleanse ourselves and our society of guilt. Persuaders will adopt one of these approaches to manage the guilt that results from our symbol use.

Tragic purification is also known as the **Terms for Order,** which is composed of four stages (Burke, 1970). First, Burke explains, there is *order.* The negative, our quest for perfection, or hierarchy, inevitably disrupts order, resulting in *guilt.* To manage the guilt, we use symbols to purify the situation. *Purification* is achieved when the individual responsible for the guilt accepts responsibility—mortification—or when that person scapegoats someone else—victimage—by placing blame on him or her. If the purification restores order, *redemption* is achieved. If redemption is not achieved, further purification is necessary.

An example from the television series *ER* demonstrates Burke's theory of Terms for Order. As we discuss this example, keep in mind that entertainment

---

spin control

the attempt by persuaders to establish their perspective as the dominant way in which their ideas are seen

spin

the interpretation of persuasive events by journalists, academics, and politicians

---

Read an editorial in a newspaper. How does the writer frame the situation being discussed? How are the five pentadic terms used in the writing? Which of the terms is most dominant? What meaning does the author's use of this term suggest for readers?

Terms for Order

a four-stage model of guilt purification, in which a persuader scapegoats someone else or takes the blame for some guilt

ETHICAL INSIGHTS

Ethics and Spin Control

When persuaders seek to control the meaning of a political event, they often use surrogates to contact members of the news media. In some cases, the surrogates' relationship to the persuader is not made evident. Such was the case in the 2000 New York Senate campaign. When Senatorial candidate Hillary Clinton was accused of having made an anti-Semitic slur in 1974, her supporters came to her defense by calling the local news media and telling reporters that Clinton would not have made the offensive remark. A campaign memo, addressed to Clinton's Jewish Advisory Group and written by Clinton aide Karen Adler, outlined the spin control strategy. Clinton's supporters were not supposed to reveal their connection to Clinton; they were to claim only that they were concerned citizens. The memo also highlighted a series of "talking points" callers should address.

Such spin control tactics raise questions of honesty and deception. In the media age, it is not difficult to obscure the identity and bias of sources, particularly when the news media often cite "unnamed sources" whom audience members cannot question. Two ethical codes can help us to sort through situations of deceptive spin. The Public Re-

lations Society of America (PRSA, 2000) charges its members to "be honest and accurate in all communications," to "reveal the sponsors for causes and interests represented," and to "avoid deceptive practices." The Clinton aide who directed supporters to appear independent or unbiased was violating this aspect of the PRSA code. Likewise, the National Communication Association (NCA, 1999) advocates that "truthfulness, accuracy, honesty, and reason are essential to the integrity of communication." Again, the Clinton campaign's use of biased supporters would harm the "integrity" of the journalism process.

As you think about deceptive spin, consider these questions:

1. To what extent should journalists check their sources before printing or broadcasting information they obtain through interviews?

2. Is it reasonable to suggest that supporters of a political candidate be objective when communicating to others about the candidate?

3. What action do you think should be taken against Clinton's aide Karen Adler for her use of deceptive spin practices?

programming often persuades us to accept certain beliefs, although this type of persuasion is often obscured. Theories such as Burke's allow us to understand how we are persuaded. In the 1998 season of *ER*, George Clooney's character, Dr. Doug Ross, left the show following several incidents in which he violated hospital policy. In one case, Dr. Ross helped a terminally ill child to die at the request of the child's mother, but contrary to hospital rules. In another case, Dr. Ross performed a risky procedure on an infant despite rules prohibiting such procedures. Dr. Ross performed the procedure knowing that he was violating hospital policy. As a result of his actions, the hospital faced legal action in both instances.

In Burkean terms, hospital policy represents the idea of the negative, in that it specifies which actions are moral and which are immoral. Dr. Ross performed the actions he did in order to help his patients; you might say he was driven by a quest for perfection. As a result, the hierarchy of the hospital was disrupted, resulting in guilt. The guilt had to be managed somehow. After several attempts by hospital administrators to control Dr. Ross's actions, he was finally forced out of the hospital. He was, in Burke's words, made a scapegoat for the hospital administration. Dr. Ross accepted the punishment—Burke's idea of mortification—and resigned his position. His action may have per-suaded the show's viewers that those who violate an organization's policy are forced to suffer the consequences. These episodes of *ER* represent Burke's idea of tragic purification.

Tragic purification requires that the guilty be punished or removed—or the tragic scapegoat metaphorically "killed." In comic purification, the scape-goat is simply laughed at and encouraged to change his or her ways. Comic purification recognizes that all people are at times mistaken. Like tragic purifi-cation, comic purification follows four stages, beginning with order. The nega-tive, perfection, and hierarchy inevitably disrupt order. Instead of labeling the disruption of order as guilt, persuaders who use language to achieve comic pu-rification call this disruption an *incongruity*. They say that "something is wrong" with the way things are. Next, persuaders focus on who is responsible for the incongruity, in the process *belittling* the fool. Belittling may take the form of humor, cartoons, or sarcasm. Like purification, belittling can be achieved by poking fun at oneself or at others. Finally, *enlightenment* results when the fool reaches a higher level of knowledge about the world. The fool is not banished, but is instead embraced by society.

Comedians typically use language to purify an incongruous situation, thus engaging in comic purification. David Letterman is an example of someone who regularly pokes fun at those in political office in order to bring public at-tention to scandals and political events. New York Senator Hillary Clinton is often a target of Letterman's humor. Clinton ran for the Senate in 2000 from New York, a state to which she had moved only a short time before announcing her candidacy. A nightly feature on Letterman's show is his Top Ten List, which has some kind of current events–related theme. A 1999 Letterman list focused on "Signs Hillary Clinton Doesn't Understand New York City," in reference to her campaign for the state's Senate seat. One item on the list was "Thinks the 'subway' is just one place Bill takes her for their anniversary dinner." Another list focused on Internet domain names that Hillary had supposedly registered. Included was "CarpetBagger99," in reference to her campaign in New York.

Letterman's humor seeks to convey that Clinton's campaign is indicative of some disorder, perhaps that New York could not find a Democrat of its own to run for Senate. He pokes fun at Clinton to get New Yorkers to talk about her campaign and its legitimacy. By belittling Clinton, Letterman seeks to scape-goat someone for this disorder and perceived problem. This discussion of the matter, however, enlightens us about how our political system works and how it might be improved. In fact, when Clinton appeared on the Letterman show on January 12, 2000, he asked her about her decision to run from a state in which she had not lived until recently. Letterman did not use language to tragically remove Clinton, but rather to prod her into answering questions about her cam-paign. His humor in this case is a good example of how persuaders can identify with audiences by using a comic style.

Find an advertisement in a magazine that uses dramatistic redemp-tion. Which strategy—tragedy or comedy—is used? Who is/are the scapegoat(s)?

Burke argues that symbols create an order to the world. Symbol use also disrupts this order from time to time, requiring that we use language to rid our-selves and our society of guilt. As we do so, we identify with others. Persuaders use symbols to name objects in their world, to frame their perspectives for oth-ers, and to manage relationships in society. We are not always aware of the power of language, though, and must watch for how it achieves identification. In the next section, we examine additional ways that language is used to identify with audiences.

Electronic Eloquence

Persuaders today make use of an intimate style of communication that takes advantage of the medium to form relationships with audience members (Jamieson, 1988; Nesbit, 1988). In this chapter, we discuss in greater depth how persuaders establish this intimate style through their word choice. **Electronic eloquence,** Jamieson (1988) explains, has five characteristics: It is personified, self-disclosive, conversational, synoptic, and visually dramatic.

Jamieson (1988) notes that the intimate communication style of today resembles a style of oratory traditionally used by females. She explains that men use language as an instrument to accomplish goals, whereas women see it as a means of establishing relationships by expressing internal states. Language used in this manner is primed to establish emotional connections with audience members. When persuaders communicate to audience members in the privacy of their living rooms, establishing relationships takes precedence over verbal sparring. Today's style of speaking and writing has as its primary emphasis establishing relationships with audience members. It enables identification with audience members. Let's look more closely at the ways persuaders can develop an intimate discourse with their audiences.

electronic eloquence
a theory of symbol use that contends that effective speakers today use an intimate style of language

PERSONIFICATION

Persuaders can build intimacy with an audience by using an individual to embody, or represent, the ideas of the persuader's message. When persuaders tell stories of individual courage, for instance, they are personifying the values of courage and bravery. They are also creating a relationship with the audience because the audience sees them as caring about the needs and values of the individuals they cite. President George W. Bush used personification in an April 11, 2000, campaign speech:

> First, we must change an oppressive tax system that punishes workers on the lowest rung of the economic ladder.
> Picture a single mother with two children, working full-time, juggling all the responsibilities of home and work, and making $22,000 a year. Now picture a young corporate lawyer making ten times that much—$220,000 a year. Under the current tax code, that single mom actually pays a higher marginal tax rate than the lawyer does. In other words, just as she moves up and starts making more money, the federal government takes away nearly half of every dollar she earns through overtime and pay raises.
> She is punished for working her hardest hours. This is unfair. It is unjust. And it must be ended.

Audience members may feel empathy for the woman's situation and transfer those feelings to the persuader seeking to help her. Bush's use of personification helped him to identify with his audience.

SELF-DISCLOSURE

Another way that persuaders achieve intimacy with their audience is through self-disclosure. Through self-disclosure, persuaders allow us to learn about the reasons behind their personal convictions and about the experiences that have shaped them. We come to know and like them. Self-disclosure in this sense refers to the personal, not the professional, experiences of the persuader. In other words, self-disclosure does not refer to the accomplishments or resume of the persuader (Jamieson, 1988). Talking about one's personal experiences also encourages dramatic narratives that audiences accept as proof for a persuader's claim.

Al Gore, in his acceptance speech for the vice presidential nomination at the 1996 Democratic National Convention, told the story of his sister, who had died of lung cancer due to smoking. Gore used self-disclosive narrative to illustrate the problems of real families, saying:

> Some of the most powerful forces that do the most harm are often hard to see and even harder to understand. When I was a child, my family was attacked by an invisible force that was then considered harmless. My sister Nancy was older than me. There were only two of us and I loved her more than life itself. She started smoking when she was 13 years old. The connection between smoking and lung cancer had not yet been established but years later the cigarettes had taken their toll.
>
> When she was 45, she had a lung removed. A year later, the disease had come back and she returned to the hospital. We all took turns staying with her. One day I was called to come quickly because things had taken a turn for the worse.
>
> All of us had tried to find whatever new treatment or new approach might help, but all I could do was to say back to her with all the gentleness in my heart, "I love you." And then I knelt by her bed and held her hand. And in a very short time her breathing became labored and then she breathed her last breath.
>
> Tomorrow morning another 13-year-old girl will start smoking. I love her, too.

The words Gore chose to tell his story created a powerful image and revealed a side of the candidate that many voters had not seen before. This story helped Gore to connect with voters, while also supporting his argument that tobacco use should be restricted.

CONVERSATIONAL STYLE

Self-disclosure is one way to forge an intimate relationship with an audience. A conversational style of speaking is another. A conversational style refers both to how the words in the speech are used as well as the way those words are presented to the audience. We will discuss delivery in Chapter 9. Here we will concern ourselves with how the persuader's words create a conversational—and intimate—style.

A conversational style of using language departs from many of the formal words and conventions we are used to. For instance, conversational speakers often use contractions, informal transitions such as "Well" and "Now," and incomplete sentences. Eloquent persuaders also use a casual vocabulary as well. Conversational persuaders use simple, rather than compound or complex, sentences. Conversational style also promotes dialogue. Conversational speakers allow the audience an opportunity to take part in the conversation. In short, a conversational style of delivery gives the impression that the persuader is "plain spoken." Jamieson (1988) contends that President Reagan epitomized the conversational approach to speaking. Even in the most formal situations, such as his inaugural addresses and State of the Union speeches, Reagan used a conversational style. Compare these two excerpts from inaugural addresses by two different U.S. presidents. Which one do you think was said by Reagan?

Excerpt 1

Well, with heart and hand, let us stand as one today: One people under God determined that our future shall be worthy of our past. As we do, we must not repeat the well-intentioned errors of our past. We must never again abuse the trust of working men and women, by sending their earnings on a futile chase after the spiraling demands of a bloated Federal Establishment.

Excerpt 2

It is believed that with the changes to be recommended American business can be assured of that measure of stability and certainty in respect to those things that may be done and those that are prohibited which is essential to the life and growth of all business. Such a plan must include the right of the people to avail themselves of those methods of combining capital and effort deemed necessary to reach the highest degree of economic efficiency, at the same time differentiating between combinations based upon legitimate economic reasons and those formed with the intent of creating monopolies and artificially controlling prices.

If you guessed the first passage is Reagan's, you are correct. Especially indicative of the conversational style is starting a sentence with the word "Well." Throughout the first passage, Reagan speaks directly and without the embellishment of fancy phrasings. The second passage comes from the inaugural address of William Howard Taft in 1909. Taft's speech was delivered before the advent of electronic media and is reminiscent of the dominant medium of his day, print.

The Internet provides additional opportunities for persuaders to have conversations with their audience members. Through chat or e-mail or streaming video, persuaders can forge personal relationships with Internet users. In fact, the Internet has taken conversational communication to a new level. E-mail messages are full of grammatical mistakes, spelling errors, and casual phrasing. Internet portals frequently host chat sessions with persuaders.

VERBAL DISTILLATION

If you look again at President Taft's statement, you'll see that it is complex and full of propositions and arguments. Today, persuaders do not use language to develop complex ideas, instead relying on short snippets of words to represent their ideas (Jamieson, 1988). In fact, as you'll see in Chapter 10, persuaders often encapsulate arguments in single words or short phrases, sometimes because media only provide persuaders with short amounts of time and space to express their ideas. Postman (1985) would add that audiences are incapable of appreciating statements such as Taft's today. This abbreviated style of speaking is often called **synecdoche,** the *representation* of large amounts of information in a short, memorable part of that body of information. Let's look more closely at synecdoche.

Jamieson (1988) contends that a mark of eloquence today is the ability to synopsize an issue in a clear, concise, and dramatic statement. She says that we make judgments about persuaders based on how skillfully they create synoptic phrases. In the media age, audience members receive fragments from persuaders that they fashion into meaningful texts (M. C. McGee, 1990). Synecdochic phrases are a prime example of how fragments are combined to create texts that are more complete. Jamieson identifies several functions that synecdoche fulfills for persuaders in a mediated world.

Initially, synoptic phrases *are more likely to be aired on news broadcasts.* As the time devoted to the words of persuaders continues to decrease on newscasts and in newspapers, succinctly stating a point is the best way for persuaders to ensure that they receive coverage. In fact, a synoptic phrase often becomes the next morning's headline. In the advertising realm, spot ads are continuing to decrease in length as well. Again, it becomes important that persuaders be able to say in a short statement what they want the audience to remember. Ultimately, argues Jamieson (1988), the reporter defines which part of the whole should serve to stand for the whole—for instance, by reducing a political debate to a few memorable statements. By providing the reporter with one or more representative short phrases, the persuaders ensure that their voices will be heard. For the rest of our discussion, consider the powerful filter of media in our perception of a persuader's words.

Besides reflecting the needs of the news media, synoptic phrases *reinforce the communal bond between audience members and the persuader.* The phrase "life, liberty, and the pursuit of happiness" makes certain guarantees about the equality of opportunity U.S. citizens have. "Innocent until proven guilty" assumes that our legal system has the burden of proving the guilt of suspected criminals. These phrases do more than bring us together; they become the "truths" upon which future discourse is based. Several years ago, a commercial for Wendy's asked, "Where's the beef?" The statement remains with us today and indicates that we should expect more from businesses. The name of the game show "Who Wants to Be a Millionaire?" serves as proof that everyday citizens can achieve great fortune in today's world.

Synecdochic phrases also *become the "capsule" by which audiences store persuasive events.* The phrase is remembered long after the moment has passed. In fact, Jamieson (1988) claims that a phrase can stand for an entire construction of reality. Consider Bormann's argument in Chapter 2: that a rhetorical vision can be built upon a few carefully crafted, memorable fantasy themes.

Synecdoche is perhaps best exemplified by slogans. **Slogans** are linguistic statements designed to produce an emotional connection between an audience member and a persuader. According to Caroline Marshall (1997), "The word *slogan* originally referred to the 'bloodcurdling Scots battle cry'" (p. 136). The

synecdoche

the representation of large amounts of information in a short, memorable part of that body of information

slogan

a short statement that represents a product or a person and that is memorable because it establishes an emotional connection between audience and persuader; also, a word, phrase, or expression that suggests a course of action

THINKING CRITICALLY

Memorable Slogans

Persuaders often use slogans to communicate with audiences in the media age. Slogans are powerful persuasive tools because they quickly express a memorable aspect of the persuader's message. The intent of a slogan is to create a favorable impression on the audience, which fosters an emotional tie to the source. Let's examine some of the linguistic strategies that help to make a slogan memorable for audience members.

- *Alliteration* is the technique of stringing together words that begin with the same consonant sound. Lexus uses alliteration in its slogan—"The relentless pursuit of perfection"—by repeating the "p" sound in *pursuit* and *perfection*.

- In some cases, sources use language incorrectly to create a memorable phrase. The National Fluid Milk Processor Promotion Board's famous slogan—got milk?—is grammatically incorrect. The full sentence on which the phrase is based would be "You got milk?" which is a poor way of asking if someone has milk.

- Slogans make use of metaphors to associate a product or brand with something familiar to the

audience. Olympus's slogan—"Focus on Life"—implies that Olympus cameras can capture the important moments of our lives. Chevy says that its cars and trucks are "Like a rock," implying strength and stability.

- Slogans also make use of the concept of framing, which we discussed earlier in this chapter. Hewlett-Packard's slogan—"Expanding Possibilities"—positions it as the agency, to use Burke's term, for an individual's or an organization's computing success. Microsoft's slogan—"Where do you want to go today?"—also implies that its products can help individuals or organizations achieve their goals.

As you reflect on the examples we've just provided, consider these questions:

1. What are some slogans you find easy to remember? What linguistic strategy does each slogan utilize?
2. To what extent do slogans sacrifice substance—knowledge of a persuader's message—for style?

primary goal of a slogan is to be remembered by the audience with little or no effort. You can probably recite or identify hundreds of slogans without having spent a minute studying those slogans. Coca-Cola's "It's the real thing," Ford's "Built Ford Tough," and Nike's "Just do it" are examples of slogans that have become popular in contemporary advertising. For information about the strategies persuaders use to create unforgettable slogans, see Thinking Critically: Memorable Slogans.

VISUAL DRAMATIZATION

Electronic eloquence is most effective when it combines words and images. Jamieson (1988) explains that combining words with images can create memorable vignettes for audiences. The synergy that occurs when language is combined with images creates a lasting visual impression in audiences. We'll examine two ways that persuaders can integrate words and images for their audiences: through the use of visual props and by staging pseudoevents.

Persuaders often surround themselves and their words with visual images that are captured on video or in photographs. Ronald Reagan, notes Jamieson,

**Figure 7.3
President Bush
Greets Troops on
the USS Lincoln fol-
lowing the Iraqi War.**
What do these props
suggest about Bush?

staged his first inaugural on the west front of the U.S. Capitol. This was the first time in history that this side of the Capitol had been used. The advantage for Reagan was that from this vantage point the television cameras could show the monuments of former Presidents whose names Reagan evoked in his inaugural address. For instance, Reagan recalled the image of President Washington: "Directly in front of me, the monument to a monumental man, George Washington, founder of our country. A man of humility who came to greatness reluctantly" (quoted in Jamieson, 1988, p. 120). Reagan used the visual image of the Washington Monument, which stood amidst the crowd of spectators, to reinforce his point. You'll also note from this passage that Reagan used a conversational tone, speaking in phrases rather than complete sentences.

Subsequent politicians have also used visual props to reinforce their point. Political candidates are sometimes photographed with police officers, victims of crime, and family members. Figure 7.3 shows President George W. Bush on the deck of a U.S. aircraft carrier following major combat operations of the Iraqi war. The image reinforces the point that Bush was commander in chief of the armed forces during the Iraqi War. The image implies that Bush is the strong leader of the world's most powerful nation. The image also substitutes for words, giving extra credibility to what Bush does say.

Pseudoevents are staged events that make use of visual images to punctuate a persuader's verbal message. Pseudoevents, according to Daniel Boorstin (1975), are "false" events, staged simply to prompt news coverage of a person, place, or thing. An interview, a protest, and a ribbon-cutting ceremony at a new business are examples of pseudoevents. Jamieson (1988) contends that pseu-

pseudoevent
a "false" event, staged
simply to promote news
coverage of a person,
place, or thing

doevents "abound" in today's world. Our news is filled with pseudoevents. In fact, persuaders, who carefully manage pseudoevents, craft much of what we see and learn about the world. Pseudoevents make use of both linguistic and visual signs. Boorstin argues that pseudoevents are dramatic, repeatable, convenient, and commoditized.

Pseudoevents are *dramatic,* which makes them newsworthy. The news media, as we discussed in Chapter 2, seek stories that are dramatic, so that viewers and readers will tune in to their broadcasts or read what they have written. Thus, stories that depart from the norm are considered newsworthy. Pseudoevents make every effort to attract the news media's attention. Protests are good examples of dramatic pseudoevents. A group called the Economic Way of the Cross holds protests each Good Friday to call attention to the problem of Third World debt. In 1999, more than 120 protestors sang and prayed in front of the International Monetary Fund headquarters for nearly two hours before several members were arrested for unlawfully entering the building. The group used 75 white wooden crosses to identify 75 poor nations. The presence of the crosses, the fact that the protest was held on Good Friday, and the illegality of a few group members' actions made the event dramatic and worthy of news coverage. When celebrities are involved, protests are even more dramatic. Activist Jesse Jackson, actress Susan Sarandon, and politician Kweisi Mfume were all arrested in 1999 for protesting police brutality in New York. Dramatic pseudoevents are designed specifically to draw media coverage.

Boorstin (1975) notes that pseudoevents are also *repeatable.* They are not singular events staged by a persuader. Instead, they are held repeatedly to reinforce the persuader's message and receive continuing news coverage. It has become common for political candidates to draw out the announcement of their candidacy for public office. They may announce their candidacy several times, at different locations and at different times. Among the most prominent, Senator Hillary Clinton held a series of "listening sessions" during the exploratory stage of her U.S. Senate candidacy in New York. The listening sessions were 90-minute roundtable discussions of various issues, such as health care and education reform, held with Clinton, experts in various areas, and sample voters. Although the stated purpose of the listening sessions was to bore media and allow Clinton to carry on a normal campaign, the sessions received repeated media attention and let Clinton sharpen her image as she considered a run for the Senate seat. The listening sessions were the perfect pseudoevent because they were dramatic — the First Lady running for the U.S. Senate — and they were repeated time after time in New York state.

Pseudoevents are *convenient* as well. The time and place of pseudoevents often determine their success in receiving media attention. As we learned in Chapter 4, media are constrained by resources of time and money and often focus on events that they can cover cheaply and easily. Pseudoevents are typically held in places that target media can access easily and at times that are compatible with the media's schedule. Protests of police brutality in New York City in 1999 were carefully orchestrated pseudoevents. The protests were held at noon each day over a two-week period, allowing newspapers and television news ample time to cover the story and meet their deadlines. Lawyers for the protestors negotiated with the police to ensure that no violence would take

INTERNET ACTIVITY

Presidential Eloquence

We have just discussed Kathleen Jamieson's theory of electronic eloquence. In short, she claims that due to television, persuaders seek to use an intimate style of communication with us today. This style is characterized by personification, self-disclosure, conversation, synoptic communication, and visual dramatism. Go to the website for the president, located at http://www.whitehouse.gov. Locate a recent speech given by the president. You can look under links for "speeches" or "news." Identify how the president used each of the elements of electronic eloquence we have discussed. Overall, do you think the speech effectively used language?

place. The protestors also provided the names of those who would be protesting each day so that police could initiate background checks and be able to free protestors quickly once they were arrested. *New York Times* reporter Dan Barry (1999) observed that "the desire for a symbolic photo-op—essential to a protest's success—will be met one way or another" due to pre-protest negotiations (pp. 1, 4).

Finally, pseudoevents are *commoditized*, meaning that the content of pseudoevents has value for us. We value being "informed" about the latest pseudoevents. Being informed about pseudoevents is a status symbol in the public's view. The announcement of Academy Award nominations is a big event broadcast live to the nation each winter. The 10-minute production reveals the nominees for the Academy Awards, which are presented several months later. Despite the brevity of the show and the fact that it is held at 5:00 A.M. local time in Los Angeles, millions view this pseudoevent in their desire to know the latest news about which celebrities are Oscar nominees and which movies have been declared the year's best. As a pseudoevent, the show has value for its viewers.

Jamieson's ideas about electronic eloquence help us to envision a theory of the type of language that is common, and effective, in today's world. As audience members, we must keep a critical ear tuned to persuaders who try to create relationships with us. We should continue to use reasoned judgment to evaluate what they say, no matter the form in which their words appear. Complete the Internet Activity: Presidential Eloquence to explore more fully Jamieson's ideas.

Language and Power

A final aspect of language that we will consider is its relationship to power. Theorists contend that when we use language, we do more than communicate an idea. We also communicate a great deal about how we think of ourselves, others, and the world in which we live. In fact, theorists contend that the language we use both creates and maintains power. Thus, language itself is persuasive because it reinforces power relations in a culture. To better understand this idea, we examine two ideas: ideology and power. We then illustrate these concepts by examining a feminist perspective on power and language.

IDEOLOGY

M. C. McGee (1980) argues that humans think and behave differently when they are in a group than they do individually. We do so because myths, or ideologies, are present in the words we use to communicate. McGee explains that if a mass consciousness exists, it must be "present," or manifest, in language. This mass consciousness is called an **ideology,** which is "a political language, preserved in rhetorical documents, with the capacity to dictate decision and control public belief and behavior" (p. 5). Slogans, or ideographs, he argues, characterize political language, or ideology. **Ideographs** are words or phrases that are "pregnant" with ideological commitment. Some examples include "liberty," "rights of privacy," and "religion." Ideographs suggest to their audience a vast set of meanings about what is valuable or appropriate within a culture. These meanings control "power" and influence the shape and texture of each individual's reality. McGee explains that ideographs function as guides, warrants, reasons, or excuses for behavior. Ideographs are one-term sums of an orientation, and we do not question their fundamental logic. Thus, persuaders use ideographs as a way of referring to a culturally understood set of meanings and behaviors.

> **ideology**
> a set of beliefs, or mass consciousness, that is shared by a group of individuals and that dictates their attitudes and behaviors

> **ideograph**
> a word or phrase that refers to a culturally understood set of meanings and behaviors or that is "pregnant" with ideological commitment: examples include liberty, rights of privacy, and religion

Political candidates use ideographs to engage the beliefs, values, and behaviors of their audiences. In a speech he gave on April 11, 2000, President George W. Bush used ideographs in his text. See if you can pick out the ideograph in each passage:

- From the beginning of this campaign, I have said that prosperity must have a purpose. That our nation must close the gap of hope. Today, I want to expand on that agenda.

- We must have a "society of free work, of enterprise, of participation." Those are the words of Pope John Paul II. They are the substance of the American dream.

- We can help people to build other assets, starting literally with money in the bank. The fourth key to upward mobility.

In the first passage, the ideograph is the word *prosperity.* This word implies a set of meanings related to freedom, equality, and achievement that, as we will see in Chapter 8, are all values embraced by our culture. In the second passage, Bush uses three ideographs: *free work, enterprise,* and *participation.* Again, these words call upon the audience to reaffirm traditional values. In the final passage, Bush uses the phrase *upward mobility* as an ideograph. An ideograph is a powerful way for persuaders to gain the audience's commitment to share their values and beliefs.

POWER

In addition to its ideological implications, language has implications for how power is managed in society. The names we use for people and objects have tremendous power in defining how others respond to these people and objects. We have discussed this point earlier in the chapter. Recall our example of Hitler's use of naming strategies to disempower Jews and empower the Nazi regime. That example—and our discussion of naming—focuses on the explicit use of language to manage power. Power also lurks implicitly in our language use. To explore this point, we'll look at the theories of Michel Foucault.

Foucault was interested in how communication creates power relationships in society. He studied how power influences persuasion and the choices audience members make in identifying themselves with a persuader's message. To Foucault, language use is a product of the rules of a given time period, which dictate how individuals should speak and which type of communication is valued most highly.

Power is an ever-present part of society. We cannot escape being influenced by power, and we cannot escape using power to influence others. "Power," writes Foucault, "is everywhere; not because it embraces everything, but because it comes from everywhere" (1990, p. 93). We often think of power as a force that some people possess and that they use to influence others. This is not how Foucault sees power. Power is not something that someone possesses. Instead, Foucault sees power as being present in a network of relationships. Each person in the network influences others in the network through power. Power can come from below, or it can come from the top of a social structure. Where there is power, there is resistance. We constantly resist the powers of those who attempt to influence us. Finally, Foucault notes, power is sometimes unintelligible. We do not recognize its presence, but it is always there.

Recall our model of the persuasive process in Chapter 1. That model demonstrates Foucault's theory of power. Power is reflected in every aspect of the model. While the persuader exerts power on the audience, the audience also influences the persuader. In fact, the audience sometimes reverses the power relationship. The producer of the national nightly news has power, the owner of the local television station has power, the politician interviewed on the news has power, and the audience member has power as well. Each influences and resists the other at the same time.

POWER AND LANGUAGE: A FEMINIST PERSPECTIVE

Feminist theorists are interested in how the world has been shaped and influenced by men, and in how this shaping has silenced women and the expression of their interests. Some persuaders, typically men, have more persuasive power than others, typically women, do because the symbols we use reflect a view of the world from the male perspective. Feminists are interested in leveling the playing field on which persuasion occurs. The media age has had positive and negative implications for female persuaders. On the one hand, women have been able to use media to express their interests and concerns. On the other hand, the dominant media continue to be controlled by men and, feminists contend, to reflect the male view of the world. We briefly discuss some of the influences a patriarchal world has on persuasion.

Cheris Kramarae (1981) explains that a woman's presence as a persuasive source is not "always fully acceptable" (p. xiv) and that women face disadvantages when they communicate with men. Kramarae argues that to say women are a "muted group" means that the language of our culture does not serve women as well as it does men. Women cannot express themselves as easily as men because the words we use were formulated based on the male experience. Women, she argues, have different experiences and require different words than our language contains in order to express themselves. Because of language, women are forced to see the world through the experiences of men and to communicate using male words. Women are "muted" because they cannot easily express their perspective and experiences.

Kramarae (1981) identifies several hypotheses that result from women being muted by male language. First, "females are more likely to have difficulty expressing themselves fluently within dominant (public) modes of expression" (p. 4). Because females have different experiences than men, they are likely to have difficulty translating their experiences into words based on male experiences. Second, males have more difficulty understanding females than females do understanding males. Females are used to seeing the world through the eyes and language of men, but men are seldom forced outside of their own experience. This hypothesis directly relates to our idea of identification in the persuasive process. Kramarae's third hypothesis is that females seek ways to express themselves outside of the male experience. Women seek alternative forms of expression that do not always take the form of traditional ways of communicating.

Kramarae (1981) writes that women are more likely to state their dissatisfaction with dominant modes of public discourse. Because those modes do not fit with female experiences, women will call attention to the inadequacy of male language. Literature, notes Kramarae, is often used to voice this dissatisfaction. Fifth, Kramarae posits that women will seek to change "dominant public modes of expression" when those modes do not allow for female expression. The influence of new media technologies, such as the Internet, may allow women to create their own places for public persuasion. Kramarae's sixth hypothesis is that women are less likely than men to create words that become highly recognized and used by both men and women. Women are often excluded from the production of new words. Finally, Kramarae explains that women's sense of humor is different than men's because women have different experiences and ways of seeing the world. Does cyberspace provide an opportunity to create a world free of gendered language? Complete the Internet Activity: Gender, Power, and Cyberspace, to explore some possible answers to this question.

We said earlier that the media style of language use resembles that which has been used by women for years. It may seem odd to now say that language excludes women, if the media style is the style that women typically use. Jamieson (1988) explains that actually, the use of a feminine style in persuasion today creates a "double bind" for women. On the one hand, women have been told to reject their style and to adopt a "manly style," which is often considered more persuasive. When they do so, however, they fail to realize the benefits of using their womanly style in a media context. Yet, electronic eloquence requires that the persuader have a high level of credibility, a judgment we usually reserve for males in positions of power. In addition, credible men, such as Ronald Reagan, Al Gore, and George W. Bush, will have to solidify the place of electronic eloquence in our culture before it will be widely accepted by all, including women.

INTERNET ACTIVITY

Gender, Power, and Cyberspace

Cheris Kramarae and other feminist theorists contend that our language creates gendered views of the world. In other words, our ways of talking lead to certain ways of thinking that reinforce and create power relationships. Read Kramarae's article, "Technology Policy, Gender, and Cyberspace," at: http://www.law.duke.edu/journals/djglp/articles/gen4p149.htm. How do traditional power and ideology arrangements influence communication in cyberspace? How might these arrangements be altered?

As you watch your favorite television show, pay attention to how power is created by how the characters communicate. Specifically, what ideographs are used? What rules are suggested by the interaction patterns of the characters? That is, what type of character is allowed to make important judgments? What type of character is not allowed to say what he or she thinks? To what extent do your observations reflect the feminist perspective?

We have examined one theory of the influence of sex on language and power here. We will continue to focus on the feminist critique of persuasion and the power for abuse that is ever present when persuasion is viewed through the lens of power and influence. In Chapter 8, we discuss how our culture disempowers feminist beliefs, values, and practices.

Summary

Persuasion and language are linked on several levels. Persuaders use language strategically to identify with audiences. They use intense words, powerful words, imagery, rhetorical figures, and metaphors.

The meanings suggested by words today are often ambiguous and contested. This ambiguity presents an opportunity for persuaders to use doublespeak and to profane symbols in their attempt to identify with us.

Words also serve to create social reality. The world we live in, say theorists, is the product of how we talk about ideas, people, and objects. That is, our world is created through language. Burke's theory of dramatism explains that words name things in ways that contain attitudes toward them. We also use words to frame social reality. In addition, the words we use help us to manage guilt, which is caused by our symbol use. We can purify guilt through tragic or comic means.

Electronic eloquence refers to the intimate style of language used by persuaders today. Persuaders use personal stories and share information about themselves with audiences. They speak in a tone that is conversational, suited for our living rooms. Eloquent persuaders today communicate through synoptic phrases that carry with them statements about a culture's values and experiences. In addition, persuaders use visual images to complement what they say so that we will identify with them.

Language is also linked to power. M. C. McGee's discussion of the ideograph helps us to see how cultural values and beliefs are embedded in language. Foucault contends that power arrangements in a society determine what may be said. Feminists contend that language does not fully capture the female reality or perspective and that female persuaders must overcome this limitation.

Key Terms

Visit the book's website at http://www.mhhe.com/borchers2 for multiple-choice quizzes, Internet activities, and key terms flashcards.

WWW:

doublespeak 192	spin control 198
dramatism 193	spin 198
attitude 194	Terms for Order 198
negative 194	electronic eloquence 201
hierarchy 194	synecdoche 204
perfection 195	slogan 204
guilt 195	pseudoevent 206
identification 195	ideology 209
naming 196	ideograph 209
framing 197	

8

Persuasion and Culture

Learning Objectives

After reading this chapter, you should be able to:

1. Define culture.

2. Understand how cultural beliefs, values, and attitudes are created, maintained, and transformed through persuasion.

3. Define cultural trends and illustrate their relationship to persuasion.

4. Identify several cultural beliefs of American culture.

5. Identify several American cultural values.

6. Identify several cultural behaviors and forces.

7. Understand how consumer culture and multiculturalism affect persuasion.

The Marlboro Company's cigarette advertisements have been among the most successful of all time. On one level, the advertising campaign—featuring a rugged cowboy, beautiful scenery, and hard, physical work—created an image of the cigarette that made the company successful among smokers for many years. Smoking Marlboros is associated with the positive traits of being tough, strong, and rugged. On a deeper level, Marlboro advertisements have solidified the place of these values in American culture. Whether you smoke or not, enjoy the outdoors or not, or have ever ridden a horse, you can recognize the importance of these characteristics in our culture. The Marlboro campaign reinforces values that Americans have traditionally held dear. The persuasive efforts of the Marlboro Company have sold cigarettes, but they have also helped to maintain certain cultural values.

The culture in which we live—the United States, in this case—creates certain standards for what is important, what is true, and what is valuable. We make many decisions based on these standards. We choose what kind of car we drive, which career to pursue, or which style of jean to purchase based on what is communicated through culture. Culture and persuasion are linked on at least three levels. Persuaders constantly seek to understand culture and predict cultural trends to position themselves, their ideas, and their products in such a way that audience members will see their message as relevant. Culture, then, influences the kind of relationship that persuaders form with audience members. On a deeper level, persuaders seek to shape American culture in certain ways. Culture is not static; it is constantly transformed and re-created. As culture changes—as certain ideas become more acceptable than others—some individuals are empowered and some are disempowered. Thus, management of culture is a persuasion strategy because it allows persuaders to create value for their products, services, and ideas. Finally, M. C. McGee (1990) argues that culture permeates all communication. Culture is always lurking among the words and images that we use when we communicate. That is, persuaders cannot help but involve and shape culture when they communicate to audiences.

Words and images combine to create culture, and culture plays an important role in the discussions of the next three chapters. Our ideas about credibility (Chapter 9) stem from our cultural beliefs and values. Cultural beliefs and values also form the basis for our reasoning (Chapter 10). Our emotions and needs (Chapter 11) are often derived from culture as well. In this chapter we present a framework through which to view discussions that involve culture. We first define culture and then examine cultural trends, beliefs, values, and behaviors. We also address how persuasion maintains and transforms cultures.

Defining Culture

Culture refers to two different, but related, concepts. In one sense, it refers to the types of products produced by people in a particular society (R. Williams, 1977). These products include art, literature, television shows, films, and architecture. Culture also refers to the "whole ways of life" of a society (R. Williams, 1977). Culture is, in this case, the "active process of generating and circulating meanings and pleasures within a social system" (Fiske, 1989, p. 23). This sense of the word includes the beliefs, norms, and values developed by a group of people in response to the demands of their day-to-day existence. Laws, educational systems, and ways of believing operationalize these beliefs and values. Brummett (1994) combines these two meanings by claiming that cultures are complex organizations of beliefs, values, and practices. Cultures are made up of "food, clothing styles, ways of walking and sitting, architecture, forms of entertainment, sayings and expressions, moral and ethical norms, religious practices, and other artifacts" (p. 22). Raymond Williams (1977) says that cultures are "structures of feeling" (p. 132). As such, cultures encompass not only formally held and systematic beliefs, but also "meanings and values as they are

culture
a set of beliefs, values, and practices that sustains a particular people; also, the products those people produce

actively lived and felt" (p. 132). In short, culture refers to the process by which meanings are created in a society of people as well as the products of this process. We will use the term *culture* to refer to the meaning-creation "process" and *cultural products* to refer to the arts, television programming, architecture, clothing, and so forth, of society.

It is important to note that culture is socially created. We are born without a sense of culture. Instead, we must learn culture. The social aspect of culture means that it is constantly changing, depending on the communication of its members. Over time, a society's beliefs change to adapt to new circumstances. Persuaders play a key role in how cultures change. We'll explore this point more later in the chapter.

The social aspect of culture also means that we are often members of multiple cultures. We might think of our ethnic identity as a culture, our school as a culture, and our family as a culture. We are pulled in different directions by these various cultures. Some researchers refer to smaller cultural groupings as subcultures. Throughout this chapter, we focus mainly on what George Spindler and Louise Spindler (1990) call the "mainstream" culture of the United States. We also address the idea of mainstream and marginalized cultures.

Culture is expressed through the content of a culture's products, including its art, television programming, music, architecture, and so forth. Each type of content communicates the beliefs, values, and behaviors of a given culture. Of particular interest to researchers is the role of popular culture in creating, maintaining, and transforming culture. **Popular culture** is industrialized, notes John Fiske (1989). The products of popular culture are owned and produced by businesses for the purpose of making a profit. If you think about holidays such as Christmas, you can understand how businesses use religious holidays to make a profit. Without Christmas shopping, many businesses would not survive. Yet Fiske also observes that audiences play an active role in which of the products of popular culture they choose to use or reject. Popular culture, Fiske writes, is culture. It is not simply consumption. Popular culture is made by the people, not imposed upon them by the culture industry, Fiske argues.

popular culture

the products of a culture that are owned and produced by businesses for the purpose of making a profit

In Chapter 1, we discussed how each element of the persuasion model is itself a product of persuasion. This statement is especially true in our discussion of culture. Cultural beliefs and values are, in part, the product of persuasion. Joel Spring (1992) notes: "Particularly since the nineteenth century, the control of ideas is considered a source of power. What people know, what they believe in, and how they interpret the world have an important effect on their choices and consequently their actions" (p. 2). Persuaders play an influential role in determining what people know and believe and how they interpret the world. Let's now look at how culture is manifest in a people's beliefs, values, and behaviors.

BELIEFS, VALUES, AND BEHAVIORS

Cultures entail specific beliefs, values, and behaviors. In Chapter 5, we discussed Rokeach's ideas about belief systems. To recap: A belief is an idea we have about what is true and false. You might believe that the earth is round, for example, or that you are a good person. Many of our beliefs are derived from other sources, such as our parents, our teachers, and our culture. Because beliefs are, in part, created by culture and transmitted in a culture, we tend to have the same beliefs as other members of the culture. Many Americans believe that with hard work, they can achieve success. Cultural beliefs are, in part, developed to ensure survival of the culture and allow it to adapt to its environment. The belief in the value of hard work, for instance, may be related to our ancestors' need to work hard to overcome environmental forces such as weather. Since the belief in the value of hard work was necessary for survival, it became an important cultural belief.

Robin M. Williams (1979) defines a **value** as a criterion or standard of preference. Values guide our actions, help us to develop attitudes toward objects, and allow us to morally judge ourselves and others (Rokeach, 1968). In Chapter 11, we discuss individual values and how they guide audience members. In this chapter, we explore **cultural values,** defined as "a set of organized rules for making choices, reducing uncertainty, and reducing conflicts within a given society. They are usually derived from the larger philosophical issues inherent in a culture" (Porter & Samovar, 1998, p. 15). Values are derived, in part, from the belief systems of cultures and members of a culture. If we, as Americans, believe that hard work will lead to success, then we tend to value success and achievement. These become standards by which we evaluate other members of the culture and our own standing within the culture. In this chapter, we examine the development of U.S. cultural values. In Chapter 11, we discuss more specifically how these values are useful to individual audience members.

We learned in Chapter 5 that cognitive beliefs and affective information form attitudes that result in behavioral intentions, which may lead to actual behaviors. In this chapter, we discuss how cultural beliefs—a type of cognitive information—and values—a form of affective information—have led to certain behaviors in our culture. For instance, our belief in hard work has led us to value achievement, which has resulted in behaviors that create "new and improved" and "bigger and better" consumer goods.

MAINSTREAM CULTURAL BELIEFS, VALUES, AND BEHAVIORS

It is important to note that cultural beliefs, although widely accepted, are not held by every member of a society. In fact, some groups of people may have beliefs, attitudes, and values that are quite different from the majority. The point is that, as an aggregate, there are some factors that distinguish people living in the United States from other groups of people. American culture, for better or worse, has been influenced by the early European settlers. These factors are useful for persuaders, but only to the degree that other potential audience members are not ignored. Later in the chapter, we will discuss ways in which culture disempowers groups of people who do not fit with the "norm." For now, let us discuss what is meant by mainstream culture.

Spindler and Spindler (1990) explain that **mainstream culture** refers to the core beliefs, values, and behaviors that "have been part of the American dialogue since the beginning" and that have been "carried on within a

value
a criterion or a standard of preference

cultural values
sets of rules for making choices and reducing conflicts in a society

mainstream culture
the core beliefs, values, and behaviors that have been part of the American dialogue since the 1600s and that have been maintained and are accepted by a majority of Americans

mainstream construction of American culture" (p. 4). Included in U.S. mainstream culture is "anyone who acts like a member of the mainstream, dominant American population and has the income to support this lifestyle" (p. 22). The mainstream culture obviously excludes many members of our society. R. Williams (1977) explains that "no dominant culture ever in reality includes or exhausts all human practice, human energy and human intention" (p. 125). The dominant culture selects from all the available beliefs, values, and behaviors those that best serve its interests.

Europeans, African Americans, Hispanics, Asian Americans, and Native Americans may all be included in mainstream U.S. culture. Class differences, rather than racial differences, may be one way of distinguishing mainstream members of our culture from marginalized members. Despite its inability to capture the beliefs, values, and behaviors of all, mainstream culture tends to dominate what we believe, value, and do in our culture. Keep in mind that we are discussing mainstream U.S. culture.

referent class
a subgroup of the mainstream against which mainstream culture measures itself

Mainstream culture measures itself against a subgroup of the mainstream: the **referent class.** Spindler and Spindler (1990) say that in the narrowest sense, males and European Protestants dominate the referent class. In a broader sense, they explain, the referent class is "an urban professional and business population, college educated, and increasingly characterized in the younger age groups by double incomes" (p. 38). This class is driven by success and career and strives to achieve higher social status. The referent class expresses a certain style, characterized by particular forms of speech, humor, clothing, possessions, travel, television viewing, and self-presentation.

Examine your cultural assumptions. What magazines do you read, what television do you watch, and what songs do you listen to? What beliefs, values, and practices are inherent in these cultural elements?

Spindler and Spindler (1990) explain that the referent class has for a long time dominated positions of power in business and politics. In recent years, however, this group's power position has eroded. Positions of power are increasingly being filled by members of "every social class and every kind of ethnicity" (p. 35). In particular, women have made significant progress in obtaining positions of power once held by men. Yet despite the achievements of these "outsiders," Spindler and Spindler point out that the central positions in the most important contexts continue to be dominated in large numbers by members of the referent class.

CULTURE AND CONFLICT

Not everyone holds those beliefs expressed by members of the mainstream to be true. In fact, members of a culture often disagree about the appropriateness of particular cultural beliefs, values, and behaviors. Nick Trujillo and L. R. Ekdom (1985) explain that conflict is inevitable because our culture is built upon a set of dynamic individuals and groups. The dominant culture has, in ways we will discuss, suppressed the beliefs, values, and behaviors of those who are different. James Davison Hunter (1991) argues that in the past, cultural members have disagreed about how best to put into practice certain values that a majority agreed on. Today, however, our culture faces conflict over the fundamental nature of its values. In addition, media give "public discourse a life and logic of its own, a life and logic separated from the intentions of the speaker or the subtleties of the arguments they employ" (Hunter, 1991, p. 34). Later in this chapter, we look more closely at how some persuaders seek to maintain cultural practices, whereas others seek to transform those practices. For now, keep in mind that culture is not a set of principles that all agree on.

We have seen that culture is a particular "structure of feeling" that permeates a given group of people. Of all the beliefs, values, and behaviors that exist in a culture, those held by the mainstream culture tend to dominate the experiences of cultural members. An even smaller group—the referent class—sets the standard for how the mainstream culture sees itself. At the same time, cultures constantly change, and new beliefs, values, and behaviors emerge as acceptable in a culture. As we begin our discussion of what constitutes U.S. culture today, we first examine some of the short-term influences on how we experience our world and then discuss more enduring cultural beliefs, values, and behaviors. We follow this discussion with an examination of how cultures change.

Cultural Trends

Our culture is awash with short-term beliefs, values, and behaviors. If you have danced the Macarena, collected Beanie Babies, or watched *The Bachelor,* you have taken part in cultural trends. **Trends** are short-term preferences, not enduring ways of believing, feeling, and acting. Edward Rothstein (1996) explains that trends demand newness, not the test of time. Trends are widely accepted, require no proof, and attract followers, not leaders (Rothstein, 1996). Trends are popular because they provide us with "immediate bonds in a world without traditional ones" (p. 28). We follow trends because we have only a small amount of information with which to make choices. Faced with uncertainty because of our lack of information, we follow what others do. Persuaders seek to show us the way.

trend
a widespread short-term preference for something new

BUZZ

Persuaders focus the culture's attention on their messages to give them value and to make them a part of what the audience believes is important. Cultural trends become commodities that have value. One way persuaders assign value to cultural trends is by creating buzz for their products. **Buzz** is the labeling of some cultural phenomenon as something members of the culture must know about. Buzz is the fact that people are talking about some person, product, or idea. Buzz creates a need for people to learn about something, placing value on that information. Thus, the phenomenon becomes an important part of our culture. Politicians seek to create buzz about their candidacies. Every holiday season, there is one toy that children just have to have. Oprah Winfrey's discussions of current books instantly propel those books to the top of the bestseller lists. Learning about the politician, buying the most popular toy, or reading the book featured on Oprah are all responses based on the view that knowing about what's being discussed is valuable.

buzz
establishment of a person, or product, or idea as something members of a culture must know about—that is, as a cultural phenomenon

Sometimes, despite strategic marketing, buzz results from cultural events. In 2003, the most talked-about summer television show was closely related to other talked-about events of the culture. In the summer of 2003, United States Supreme Court struck down a Texas law outlawing sodomy, the Episcopelian Church confirmed an openly gay bishop, and Canada legalized same-sex unions. The news events created a wave of momentum for the hottest television show of that summer, *Queer Eye for the Straight Guy.* The show was the highest rated show in the history of the Bravo network, drawing 2.8 million viewers. The show, in which five gay men make over a straight man, was also part of the reality-TV genre, which was quite popular with viewers during 2003.

In other cases, buzz is the result of careful planning on the part of the persuader. Fundraising success by presidential candidates generates a considerable amount of buzz in the media and political circles. Candidates who can raise money and generate buzz are often effective at future fundraising and become seen as the frontrunner. (In the previous chapter, you'll recall, we discussed the importance of being called a political frontrunner.) In June 2003, Democratic presidential candidate Howard Dean shocked his Democratic rivals and political pundits by raising $7 million in the second quarter of 2003 (April–June). Dean's fundraising success, and resulting buzz, can be attributed to strategic persuasion. In Dean's case, this meant using the Internet to gather supporters. In fact, Dean's campaign was able to register more than 200,000 Internet users by July 2003. These supporters contributed more than $3 million in online contributions during the last week in June. Additionally, more than 30,000 people in 400 cities took part in Dean's virtual candidacy announcement speech. Finally, Dean was able to generate online support to win the Moveon.org "primary," winning 48 percent of the vote. By using the Internet in these ways, Dean's campaign was able to generate a lot of political buzz and place him in the top tier of Democratic candidates.

CULTURE SCANNING

culture scanning
the surveying of culture to understand current trends, beliefs, values, and practices

Persuaders must somehow monitor culture to maximize their persuasive appeals. Persuaders regularly engage in **culture scanning,** or the surveying of culture to understand current trends, beliefs, values, and practices. Culture scanning extends beyond public opinion polling, which we discussed in Chapter 5. In addition to polling, culture scanning also examines media sources and consumer trends. Advertisers, for example, must understand what makes Americans tick. They must survey current trends and behavioral practices to make sure that their products and persuasive strategies reflect the current lives of their audience members.

One method of culture scanning is that used by Faith Popcorn and her firm, BrainReserve. Popcorn's TrendBank is a culture scan compiled of consumer interviews, media analysis, and retail observations. To compile Trend-Bank, BrainReserve conducts 4,000 phone interviews a year with consumers, reads 350 magazines, and listens to popular music (Gustke, 1997). This method of culture scanning allows the firm to isolate such trends as cocooning and small indulgences. *Cocooning* is the need to protect oneself from the harsh,

INTERNET ACTIVITY

Culture Scanning

By scanning the latest trends in our culture, persuaders are able to create messages that appeal to audience members. You have read about one such culture scanner, Faith Popcorn. Read the descriptions of some of the trends she has identified, located on her Web page at http://www.faithpopcorn.com/trends/ trends.htm. Which of these trends is a cultural behavior today? Which have you practiced? How accurate is culture scanning? Which trends on this page do you think will endure? Can you think of any trends that aren't on this list?

unpredictable realities of the outside world. It is manifest in the popularity of Martha Stewart, gated communities, and home offices. Popcorn identified cocooning as a cultural trend in 1981 (Gustke, 1997). Popcorn also observed consumers' migration to *small indulgences*—affordable luxuries—as a way to reward themselves. Small indulgences include such purchases as expensive sunglasses, one-zip plastic storage bags, and premium shavers. Purchasing Popcorn's culture scanning research is not cheap. Firms such as RJR/Nabisco, American Express, and IBM pay as much as $1.5 million a year for her ideas (Gustke, 1997). In short, by understanding our current beliefs, values, and practices, Popcorn has her finger on the pulse of American culture. To learn more about culture scanning, complete the Internet Activity: Culture Scanning.

Cultural trends result in momentary beliefs, values, and behaviors. Although trends are transitory, persuaders harness their power to identify with audiences. We purchase products, engage in certain behaviors, and believe certain ideas because of their current position in our culture—their trendiness. Of greater importance to persuaders, however, are the enduring cultural beliefs, values, and behaviors of our culture.

Cultural Beliefs

Cultures are complex combinations of history and current practices. In many cases, our culture influences our perceptions of others and our world. To understand how we have come to believe certain ideas, we need to understand some of the historical forces that have shaped our culture. Although our culture is constantly changing, we can trace its origins by examining some of the historical forces that have created it. In the process, we explore the ways persuaders have used media to influence our conceptions of what it means to be American.

For now, let's discuss a set of cultural beliefs developed by John Harmon McElroy (1999), who takes a historical view of U.S. culture. In a wide-ranging study of cultural artifacts, such as pioneer diaries, American literature, and historical papers, McElroy identified seven sets of beliefs that Americans have held. These beliefs have formed the basis for our culture and distinguish Americans from other people, McElroy argues.

McElroy's seven types of cultural beliefs are

- Primary beliefs
- Immigrant beliefs
- Frontier beliefs
- Religious and moral beliefs
- Social beliefs
- Political beliefs
- Beliefs on human nature

PRIMARY BELIEFS

McElroy's first set of beliefs concerns work and was formed from the experiences of the initial European settlers. The three beliefs in this category include *Everyone Must Work, People Must Benefit from Their Work,* and *Manual Work Is Respectable.* One of the first occupations of the colonial settlers was farming: The settlers had to grow food to survive. Thus, manual labor achieved a respectable status in the early years of our country, whereas it did not enjoy such status in Europe. McElroy (1999) identifies the Homestead Act as one of the primary influences of our belief that we should benefit from our work. The Homestead Act awarded to farmers 160 acres of land for a small fee if the farmer's family lived on and worked the land. Not only did their work earn these families land, but the migration that resulted from the Homestead Act created labor supply problems in the East, which resulted in higher wages for workers there than they had been used to in Europe.

Our culture today still maintains its belief in work. Politicians promise jobs for all. Our system of education today is valued mostly for its ability to provide American businesses with skilled workers. Today, our play has almost become work. We take our hobbies almost as seriously as our jobs. Many Americans desire to start their own businesses so they can do a job they truly enjoy. The belief in hard work is not unchallenged, however. The success of technology stocks in the late 1990s allowed some investors to become millionaires with little physical effort. The long-term success of many of these investors, however, is tied to the future of the stock market and the nation's economy. The downturn in the stock market in 2001 reinforced the belief that hard work—not simply making a quick buck—is necessary for success.

IMMIGRANT BELIEFS

Fifty-five million immigrants have entered the United States in the past four centuries (McElroy, 1999). With them came beliefs, values, and practices from diverse cultures. Immigrants also found great success in the new country. McElroy (1999) isolates three American beliefs that stem from the immigrant experience: *Improvement Is Possible, Opportunities Must Be Imagined, and Freedom of Movement Is Needed for Success.* Many of these immigrants left their home country to improve their lives. In America, they were able to imagine success and to act on that belief. McElroy (1999) posits that more immigrants found success than failure in the new country. In America, it seemed as if anything was possible. McElroy (1999) notes that the self-selection process of immigrants and their common experiences with success and improvement helped them to foster new shared beliefs even though they had come from different homelands. Thus, a unique new culture emerged that was both a blend of other cultures yet different from them.

With their desire to improve, Americans sought to spread their influence throughout the country. They cleared fields of trees to plant crops. They built towns where there were none previously. They built roads and railroads. Movement and improvement became ways of measuring success. The ruts of the Oregon and Mormon Trails are testaments to the throngs of pioneers who braved blizzards, drought, and locust plagues to reach new parts of the country and achieve for themselves the same success as those who settled in the large eastern cities.

Our country today strives for equality of opportunity for success. Even today, Americans move up and down the social hierarchy and they physically move around the country in ways that are quite different from other cultures. A 1999 Gallup Poll found that 82 percent of all Americans still believe that if they work hard, they can achieve success. Our government has instituted loan programs that make it easier for lower-income individuals to purchase homes. Private organizations such as Habitat for Humanity also provide opportunities for home ownership to individuals. "The American Dream" of improvement and movement has become a significant belief for many Americans.

FRONTIER BELIEFS

The third set of beliefs identified by McElroy (1999) is derived from the experiences of the pioneer settlers of the central United States. Pioneer beliefs include *what has to be done will teach you how to do it; each person is responsible for his own well-being; helping others helps yourself;* and *progress requires organization* (McElroy, 1999). Together these beliefs emphasize the values of creativity, hands-on learning, self-sufficiency, and cooperation that were so necessary for survival in the Midwest wilderness. The success of the early pioneers depended on their ability to work independently. There were no social programs for those who fell through the cracks, so each person was responsible for his or her own welfare. At the same time, the pioneers recognized the enormity of the struggle they were facing and were quick to help others when needed. Often, pioneers formed organizations to accomplish as a group what individuals could not do by themselves. McElroy (1999) observes that many contemporary associations were started in the late 1800s or early 1900s. Pioneers often learned through the "school of hard knocks." That is, hands-on learning was valued as a way to pass down skills from generation to generation. People who were self-educated were more respected than those who were formally schooled (McElroy, 1999).

Today, pioneer beliefs still guide our actions and values. McElroy (1999) writes that the United States has the highest rate of volunteerism in the world.

Youth, in particular, are volunteering in record numbers (Moseley, 1999). In four years, the volunteer program AmeriCorps inducted 100,000 members. Politicians frequently promote programs that encourage self-sufficiency. At the same time, politicians preach the importance of helping others. In fact, these pioneer beliefs came together in George W. Bush's "Compassionate Conservatism" presidential campaign theme of 2000. The experiences of the early settlers on the plains provided a significant set of beliefs for American culture.

RELIGIOUS AND MORAL BELIEFS

Religion played an important role in the lives of early settlers and influences our cultural orientation today. McElroy (1999) identifies the following set of religious and moral beliefs: *God Created Nature and Human Beings, God Created a Law of Right and Wrong, Doing What Is Right Is Necessary for Happiness, God Gave Man the Same Birthrights,* and *America Is a Chosen Country.* McElroy argues that living so close to nature in the wilderness, early settlers experienced firsthand what they perceived to be a higher being. Belief in a higher being was the moral basis for laws in the new civilization. As an expanded version of the Ten Commandments, our nation's legal customs reflect early pioneer morality. "Laws of Nature and of Nature's God" were cited as a reason to declare independence from Britain. Writings of early colonial political leaders, such as Thomas Jefferson and Benjamin Franklin, contain additional traces of a religious morality as the basis for our government and law.

Religion and morality continue to play a role in the lives of Americans today. Nearly four in five believe that God played a role in creation, and 68 percent of Americans belong to a church, temple, mosque, or synagogue (McElroy, 1999). Although many of our moral and religious values are based on Christianity, a prevailing belief of our culture is that everyone should be entitled to practice the religion of his or her choosing. Since the earliest of times, the United States has been a culture that has embraced morality and religion.

SOCIAL BELIEFS

McElroy (1999) writes that Americans have worked hard as individuals to achieve success. As such, our social status is determined not by the family we are born into, but rather by what we become through individual effort. This orientation gives rise to three beliefs: *Society Is a Collection of Individuals, Every Person's Success Improves Society,* and *Achievement Determines Social Rank.* In European cultures, explains McElroy, class standing is largely determined by birth. In the United States, individuals can move into higher social classes by achievement and success. In the early days of the country, owning property and contributing to the development of the nation was respected. There was also the notion that many Americans aspired to "not be poor," even if they did not achieve fame and fortune. The ability to leave an inheritance for one's descendants has been another social belief. The fundamental belief behind these premises is that the culture will succeed only if each member contributes in some way. Thus, society meant something different to American pioneers than it had to their European ancestors.

The idea that society is a mix of the successes of its individual members is still with us today. Advertisers promise that certain products will make us appear successful. Politicians promise a chance for all to "get ahead" under their economic and social proposals. Educators urge their students to study hard so they will be successful professionals. The belief that society is constructed by the work of its members remains powerful today.

POLITICAL BELIEFS

American culture has been guided by these political beliefs: *The People Are Sovereign, The Least Government Possible Is Best, A Written Constitution Is Essential to Government, A Majority Decides,* and *Worship Is a Matter of Conscience* (McElroy, 1999). The United States is distinctive from other world governments. McElroy notes that in Great Britain, no written constitution exists, and there is no supreme court to rule on the legality of the nation's laws. The chief executive is a member of the legislature. The people have no specific constitutional rights. The Revolutionary War was fought to allow Americans the right to elect their leaders and form of government. Great care was taken in the framing of the Constitution to ensure that individuals—although not all individuals at that time—would have specific rights guaranteed in writing. There was also a sense that the people and their local governments should be free from the tyranny of a centralized, federal government. The early Americans also guaranteed that no one religion would be the national religion, as was the case in Britain.

In recent years, major candidates for president have moved to the center of the political spectrum. In so doing, they have reduced the size of the federal government and have given more power to state and local governments. The major contenders for the 2004 presidential election were centrist candidates. These political beliefs continue to play a role in American politics.

BELIEFS ON HUMAN NATURE

McElroy's (1999) final category of beliefs centers on human nature: *Almost All Human Beings Want to Do What Is Right* and *Human Beings Will Abuse Power When They Have It.* Two ideas run throughout McElroy's theory: that Americans come together to help each other when necessary and that America is a land of opportunity, not birthright. These ideas unite in the first of his beliefs about human nature. Virtue is not associated with birth, but rather is determined by what one accomplishes. In addition, Americans work hard to achieve success. What individuals do to achieve success generally benefits the community simply because their being successful is beneficial to the community.

On the other hand, Americans have always mistrusted those in power. The early Americans knew that their orientation toward self-interest had its limits. If people acted selfishly, they would move too far in the direction of self-interest and lose their sense of community. The tyranny of the English kings—who once ruled this country—led early Americans to write in the Constitution rules limiting the power of elected officials. Today's political scene is filled with candidates who are running for office on the grounds that those in office cannot be trusted. The Reform Party and the Green Party provided alternative choices for disgruntled American voters in 2000. Yet Americans also want to give the benefit of the doubt to individuals.

Cultural Values

A number of cultural values arise from the cultural beliefs we have just discussed. For instance, if we believe that the success of society depends on the success of each individual member, we will value personal achievement because it improves society as a whole. Numerous researchers have identified significant U.S. cultural values (Naylor, 1998; Rokeach, 1973; Spindler & Spindler, 1990; Steele & Redding, 1962; Trujillo & Ekdom, 1985; and others). By surveying the work of these researchers, we can develop the following list of cultural values. Persuaders appeal to these values in their messages so that we will see their product or idea as a means of achieving important cultural values.

- Achievement and success
- Efficiency and practicality
- Progress
- Freedom and equality
- Individualism
- Effort and optimism

The value of *achievement and success* refers to the criteria we use to evaluate individuals in our culture (Steele & Redding, 1962). Trujillo and Ekdom (1985) argue that winning is an overarching frame through which we view all other values. We award a higher place in the social order to those individuals who achieve professional, financial, or social success. We center our lives around the pursuit of success. Placing value in achievement motivates individuals. Many students take college courses so that they can earn gainful employment. Our culture looks down on individuals who are lazy and do not work hard.

An advertisement for IBM Lotus software links its product to the achievement and success of its users. The ad states, "Lynn's team chose IBM Netfinity servers running Lotus Notes and Domino. This has improved productivity, raised system reliability, and eased network administration." Thus, a software user can achieve success by using the right product.

The value of *efficiency and practicality* places importance in a reasoned, systematic approach to work (Steele & Redding, 1962). This value also reinforces the notion that Americans are practical people who have firsthand experiences with their environment. We value those people who are self-taught, for instance, and are skeptical of formal experts or authorities who tell us what we should do.

The current trend toward do-it-yourself home improvement is a reflection of the value we place on efficiency and practicality. A variety of influences make it easy for people to complete home improvement projects without using, and paying for, expert workers. Home improvement stores, for instance, provide access to products that are easy to use and inexpensive. The stores often have training sessions to teach consumers how to use their products. Home improvement television shows and networks show home owners succeeding at being efficient and practical and provide the know-how to complete complicated projects. The hit TV show *Trading Spaces,* for instance, demonstrates what is possible on a limited budget. The show clearly demonstrates being efficient and practical—home owners only have $1000 and 48 hours to complete their projects. With today's media and resources, the value of efficiency and practicality is easy to achieve for contemporary home owners.

We also value *progress,* which refers to advancement and improvement. We see change as necessary and good. We try to make the future better than the present, which is better than the past (Steele & Redding, 1962). We treat as unimportant those things that are "old-fashioned," "backward," or "obsolete." Our society's economic system is predicated on progress, and companies spend a great deal of time and energy researching ways to improve their business. In short, we see progress as a way of improving our lives.

Lucent Technologies, in an advertisement for "breakthrough" technology that will allow companies to have faster Internet connections, explains: "Lucent's Wave Star DataExpress is the first 10G optical networking system designed for Internet Service Providers (ISPs) to deliver high-speed data services. Now ISPs can build local data networks with 10 gigabit capacity (enough to transmit 2 million pages a second)—that's up to 4× the speed of competitive systems. With up to 60% savings on equipment." Lucent—perhaps using a bit of doublespeak—is attempting to sell the value of progress to its customers, on the premise that its customers believe progress is an important value in today's world.

Another fundamental value, *freedom and equality,* is based on a common moral value that all people are created equal (Steele & Redding, 1962). Our laws have been continually amended to guarantee rights to all people, including the right to vote, participate in government, and own property. Our equality is based upon certain freedoms, such as the right to express ourselves.

Political candidates often appeal to equality in their campaigns. Presidential candidate John Kerry called for equality in the country's health care system in a speech on May 16, 2003:

> Americans without health care coverage get treatment. But they get too little of it and get it too late. Too many emergency room visits and not enough preventive care. We all pay too much for that and too many of them end up paying the highest price of all: they get sick more often; they stay sick longer; they live shorter lives. And that is too high a price to bear.
>
> But we're not being honest if we limit this debate to one of coverage or if we let it be broken down into those without health insurance versus those with insurance. If we are going to be serious about tackling this problem, then we need to realize this is not just about covering the uninsured but about giving all Americans coverage they can afford.

Kerry called for support to improve the equality in the nation's health care system.

We also value *individualism,* placing the rights of individuals ahead of the rights of society. Although we may, at times, seek to limit individual freedom, individual rights and liberties serve as a cornerstone of our culture. We view people as being unique, autonomous, and possessing dignity (Steele & Redding,

1962). We celebrate the individual's right to choose who he or she wants to be and what he or she wants to do.

George W. Bush upholds the importance of personal success in this statement from an April 11, 2000, speech: "America has been successful because it offers a realistic shot at a better life. America has been successful because poverty has been a stage, not a fate. America has been successful because anyone can ascend the ladder and transcend their birth." Bush made this statement to support his point that our economic system should be designed to help individuals prosper. He was reaffirming the value of individualism.

Finally, the values of *effort and optimism* refer to our emphasis on work and action. Although contemporary culture may celebrate, to some degree, the "couch potato," we typically look down on those who do not try to succeed. We think that no problem is too big or complicated for us to overcome (Steele & Redding, 1962). We celebrate those individuals who take on big projects and even allow them to fail, as long as they maintain an optimistic attitude.

The Stuttering Foundation of America appeals to these values in an advertisement featuring ABC reporter John Stossel, whose stuttering "didn't silence his story." The ad continues, "*20/20*'s John Stossel knows news. He also knows what it's like to deal with a stuttering problem. John still struggles with stuttering yet has become one of the most successful reporters in broadcast journalism today." By using Stossel as a representative of all stutterers, the Stuttering Foundation persuades the audience that the people it helps share the same values of effort and optimism Stossel displays and are worthy of financial support.

Rank the values we discussed in this chapter in order of their importance to our society. Look through magazines and newspapers to find evidence to support your ranking. How does your hierarchy compare with those of other class members?

Cultural Behaviors

Like McElroy (1999) and Steele and Redding (1962), Joshua Hammond and James Morrison (1996) attempt to determine what makes us Americans. Drawing on the work of anthropologists, political scientists, historians, and market researchers, as well as their own survey and focus group research, Hammond and Morrison identify seven cultural forces that have shaped our culture. Cultural forces, they explain, are constant over time, consistently accepted, and emotionally driven. Essentially, the cultural forces they describe are behaviors that we engage in based on our beliefs and values. Hammond and Morrison's seven cultural forces are so much a part of our lives that you may not consider them new information. But that is the point of culture. It is like air. We do not always realize we are breathing it, but it constantly surrounds us. It is a part of us. These are the seven cultural forces Hammond and Morrison identify:

- Insistence on choice
- Pursuit of impossible dreams
- Obsession with big and more
- Impatience with time
- Acceptance of mistakes
- Urge to improvise
- Fixation with what's new

The American consumer is surrounded by choices. We can choose from a wide assortment of products, services, and ideas. Our *insistence on choice* stems from several historical factors. Many European Americans chose to come to the United States. The U.S. Constitution is a document that, with its amendments, guarantees choice to Americans. We also choose careers, where we live, and the homes we live in. We must keep in mind that not all Americans have had the luxury of choice in the past, and many do not today. Yet choice is something we strive for.

Today, persuaders continue to offer choices to us. We can get the same clothing in multiple colors and sizes and we can choose from several brands of laundry detergent. Insistence on choice is clearly an important part of our culture. An advertisement for Nokia cell phones boasts of the company's color choices: "You have the power to change things. Well, at least the power to change the color of your phone." The Nokia phone features snap-on covers in eight different colors.

Since the Europeans settled the United States, Americans have been *pursuing impossible dreams*. Immigrants continue to come to this country for the same possibilities of success imagined by the early Europeans. Dreaming is big business today. Corporations spend a great deal of time and energy crafting vision statements. From the proliferation of dreamlike theme parks around the country to the hundreds, if not thousands, of start-up Internet businesses, Americans continue to dream impossible dreams. Lotteries allow millions to dream the impossible dream of winning the jackpot. Hammond and Morrison (1996) write that technology and impossible dreams are inextricably tied together. In fact, they question which came first: the dream or the technology that makes dreaming possible.

Hammond and Morrison's (1996) third cultural force is *obsession with big and more*. Americans like things big, they argue. The bigger, the better. Being big is tied to being number one. As Americans we like to be the best at everything we do. Evidence of this is the trend toward superstores. From Home Depot to Barnes & Noble to Office Max, shoppers now turn to mammoth, warehouselike stores for their shopping instead of to the small "mom and pop" stores of the past. Placing this premium on bigness reinforces the first two cultural forces: choice and dreams. Big stores have more choices for consumers, and striving to be number one helps us achieve impossible dreams. Hammond and Morrison observe that big is not always better, though. Our obsession with "bigger is better" leads us to create some big problems as well. Yet striving to be the best is a truly American cultural behavior.

Americans are also *impatient with time*. We are driven by a "now imperative" (Hammond and Morrison, 1996, p. 28). Hammond and Morrison argue America is the most time-compartmentalized culture in the world. Our days are divided into 15-minute time blocks. We use such phrases as "Can I have a second?" Computer technology has created a culture that is based on miniscule units of time like the nanosecond, which is one billionth of a second. In this country we focus on the present and the future, not the past. We also use short time frames to set our goals. Hammond and Morrison (1996) explain that Japanese managers make 25-year strategic plans. In the United States, we often focus on 3-month or 6-month goals.

A fifth cultural force is *acceptance of mistakes.* We do not hold people accountable for their failures on their first try. Our culture is full of such phrases as "Try, try, try again." Hammond and Morrison (1996) identify *Rocky* as the quintessential American movie. Sylvester Stallone's character, Rocky, a championship boxer, takes on impossible dreams and through hard work—and failure—finally wins the title. We celebrate those who overcome overwhelming odds, such as Abraham Lincoln, who lost several political elections before winning the presidency. Hammond and Morrison argue that our acceptance of mistakes causes us to not do things right the first time. We know that we have another chance, and by improving, we keep moving forward.

The sixth cultural force identified by Hammond and Morrison (1996) is the *urge to improvise.* Our urge to invent new ways of doing things can probably be traced back to our ancestors, who, because they lacked tools and knowledge, were forced to learn for themselves. Trial and error was the method of invention for early Americans. Jazz music exemplifies how improvisation created a distinctly American art form. Comedy often relies on improvisation. Like the early Americans, we still value people who are self-educated and who learn by doing. Above all, we hate falling into a rut. We hate doing things the same way every time. We might take a different route home from work or school, we might combine flavors in a different way in the kitchen, or we might style our hair differently. As Americans, we like to improvise with doing new things.

Finally, we have a *fixation with what's new.* Hammond and Morrison (1996) write that our fixation with new things is a reflection of our desire to define our potential identity. We are never satisfied with who we are. We constantly seek to add new elements to our lives and personalities. The news media focus our attention on what's new. Each year, the new car models attract a barrage of media attention. In fact, car shows showcasing the new models are big events around the country. Americans truly are interested in what's new.

What similarities do you see among McElroy's list of cultural beliefs, the list of cultural values, and Hammond and Morrison's description of cultural forces? What differences do you see?

Throughout our nation's history, persuaders have mined culture for proof of their statements. Our previous discussion has examined some of the beliefs, values, and behaviors that have guided our nation. It is worth repeating, however, that culture is not static; it is always changing. Although culture is based on some enduring principles common to many of its members, it also changes due to the widespread availability of voices that interpret it through mediated channels. As the United States moves from being an industrial society to an information society, it is experiencing changes in cultural beliefs, attitudes, and norms. In addition, the sound of more diverse voices in our culture presents us with new ideas about how to live. Persuaders play a key role in both the maintenance and the transformation of cultures.

Maintaining Culture

Our previous discussion leaves open the possibility that minority viewpoints may at some point become dominant in a particular culture. This is possible because "new meanings and values, new practices, new relationships and kinds of relationships are continually being created" (R. Williams, 1977, p. 123). Cultural beliefs, values, and norms are created and transformed through a variety of channels, including media, formal institutions, art, and everyday conversations among members of a culture. That is, we come to learn about our culture through cultural content, and we use this content to change our culture. In some cases, culture is written down, as in the case of novels or diaries that tell us about previous generations. Media sources transmit culture as well. Movies such as *Gone with the Wind* reflect a particular aspect of American culture. In some cases, stories are repeated from one generation to the next, such as the stories told by grandparents to their children and grandchildren. Cultures also have a set of practices that their members regularly enact. Gathering with friends and relatives for the holidays or shooting off fireworks on the Fourth of July are examples of cultural practices that transmit beliefs and values to future generations.

As you have probably realized, our culture privileges certain ways of thinking and acting. For instance, we have talked about how Americans believe that "bigger is better." That is, the bigger the car you drive, the higher your social standing. A large house means you need somewhere to put your many possessions and family members. A large diamond ring signifies a higher level of commitment on the part of the groom to the bride. But what about those who cannot afford to have the biggest and the best or who choose not to. When "bigger is better" is a cultural belief, many are marginalized. The way those in power manage culture disempowers some people.

In the next few paragraphs, we examine two concepts—hegemony and patriarchy—that help explain how culture is maintained. The point to keep in mind is that we are often persuaded by culture, even though we may not easily see how.

HEGEMONY

Hegemony is the domination of culture by one particular cultural group, resulting in the empowerment of certain cultural beliefs, values, and practices over others. In the United States today, the beliefs, values, and behaviors of European Americans dominate an increasingly diverse population. Brummett (1994) explains that hegemony occurs when members of a subordinate cultural group accept the ideas of the dominant group, even if it means their disempowerment. Hegemony is the interpretation of persuasive messages in the way the persuader intends. We accept what is presented to us without questioning its validity or asking who the message empowers. Brummett (1994) writes, "Hegemony is a remarkable phenomenon; because of it, oppressed people not only accept but often participate in their own oppression" (p. 118). Hegemony, then, is a form of persuasion, but one that is usually hidden from us. Read Thinking Critically: Hegemony and Advertising to understand how advertising perpetuates hegemony.

Popular culture is the source of many hegemonic messages. An episode of the comedy *Friends* illustrates how popular culture influences our interpretation of cultural values. In the episode, Rachel purchases from the department store Pottery Barn an "apothecary cabinet" for the apartment that she shares with Phoebe. Rachel faces a dilemma, however, when she is told that Phoebe

hegemony
the domination of culture by one particular cultural group, resulting in the empowerment of certain cultural beliefs, values, and practices over others

THINKING CRITICALLY

Hegemony and Advertising

Advertising is often a source of hegemonic messages about cultural beliefs, values, and behaviors. We often read, hear, or see advertisements without realizing their underlying messages and how those messages perpetuate culture. Consider the advertisement for California Closets that appears in this box. What are some of the cultural beliefs, values, and behaviors that are expressed?

California Closets asserts that what we consume defines who we are, and we need space for all the "stuff" that makes up our lives. Thus consumption is an important cultural behavior based on the belief that it is important to display financial success. Also, the woman's closet is large, indicating that she has purchased a great deal of consumer goods, reflecting our culture's preoccupation with being bigger and best. The ad also extols the value of the individual, offering "custom solutions." While the message of this ad appears to offer a solution to a problem, it reinforces the notion that it is good to have things to store. It also argues that "stuff" is what we are about. A person's self-image, then, according to the advertisement, is dependent on what he or she consumes. This is a very reasonable assertion given contemporary culture, but it is a belief that privileges certain ways of life and makes other ideas about how we develop our self-image seem less valuable. The ad does not talk about other ways of defining who we are. It does not make conservation an important value. Thus, by looking at the ad, we are led to see only one idea about how we should form our self-concept.

As you react to this analysis and look at the advertisement, consider these questions:

1. To what extent do you agree or disagree with the preceding observations about the advertisement and its relationship to culture? What are some other hegemonic messages of this advertisement?

2. What are some messages in this advertisement that oppose cultural beliefs, values, and attitudes?

life   stuff   storage

Where do you put the stuff that you're about? All that you are? Tell us. We're listening. And this is how we start to create your custom solution.

Call us for your complimentary in-home consultation at 800.336.9206 in the US and Canada or visit us at www.calclosets.com.

CALIFORNIA CLOSETS

hates products from Pottery Barn because the store profits from producing reproductions of genuine pieces of furniture and household accessories. In other words, Pottery Barn produces fake goods and represents all that is wrong with the world, according to Phoebe. Rachel tells Phoebe the cabinet is instead a genuine antique that she purchased from a flea market. Phoebe goes along with the lie until she discovers that their friend Ross has a similar cabinet. Toward the end of the show, Rachel tells Phoebe about the lie. To this point, Phoebe's opposition to Pottery Barn represents a rejection of hegemony and a celebration of contradictory values. Yet before the show ends, Phoebe admits that she, in fact, likes Pottery Barn and wants to purchase a lamp from the store. In the

INTERNET ACTIVITY

Managing Power in *The Simpsons*

We have discussed how popular culture is a battle-ground of persuasive messages that attempt to manage power in a culture. The concept of hegemony helps us to understand how those in power maintain influence over the marginalized. Not only can the texts of popular culture oppress, but they can liber-ate. Read Sam Tingleff's paper "*The Simpsons* as a Critique of Consumer Culture" at http://www.snpp .com/other/papers/st.paper.html. Do you agree with the author's argument? What are some other examples of popular television shows that resist the hegemonic messages of consumer culture?

end, then, the episode embraces the dominant view of culture: that purchasing goods makes us happy and fulfilled. The show and its characters function as persuaders, perpetuating hegemonic values. Even *The Simpsons* television show shapes our views of cultural values. Complete the Internet Activity: Managing Power in *The Simpsons* to learn more.

Trujillo (1991) examines media representations of former baseball pitcher Nolan Ryan to illustrate how images of male athletes are reproduced in American culture. Specifically, Trujillo isolates five aspects of masculinity highlighted by media depictions of Ryan: physical force and control, occupational achievement, familial patriarchy, frontiersmanship, and heterosexuality. In terms of physical force and control, Ryan was portrayed throughout his career as a fastball, power pitcher with precise control over his pitches. He held records for strike-outs and pitched several no-hit games, marks indicative of a pitcher's strength and control. His career statistics and strong work ethic also contributed to images of Ryan's occupational achievement. In addition, media portrayals of Ryan focused on his role as a family man. He married his high school sweetheart and was constantly photographed with his family. Ryan also fit the description of a frontiersman. He owned a ranch and was described as being wholesome and unassuming, characteristics we often associate with the rugged prairie pioneers. Finally, Ryan was depicted as the perfect heterosexual sex symbol. As a result of its view of masculinity, popular culture was transmitting the defining characteristics men should possess. This view of masculinity can be considered hegemonic because audience members fail to appreciate its power in defining who we are.

PATRIARCHY

Although we are born male or female, we are not necessarily born with masculine or feminine traits, argue some feminists. Being masculine and feminine refers to gender, which is something we learn from an early age through a process known as socialization. Julia Wood (1998) explains that from the pink and blue blankets of the nursery to the games parents play with their children, boys and girls are socialized to become men and women. Media organizations are powerful sources of these socialization messages. In fact, we often do not recognize the gender messages in much of what we see in media. Susan Douglas (1995) argues: "We must reject the notion that popular culture for girls and women didn't matter, or that it consisted only of retrograde images. American women today are a bundle of contradictions because much of media imagery we grew up with was itself filled with mixed messages about what women should and should not do, what women could and could not be" (p. 9).

patriarchy

the oppressive structure in society that privileges the beliefs, values, and practices of men

The feminist equivalent of hegemony is patriarchy. To feminists, the **patriarchy** is the oppressive structure in society that privileges the beliefs, values, and practices of men. The patriarchy determines the roles women should play and what value should be attached to those roles. The idea that women should stay at home and raise the family is patriarchal. The idea that a woman is too irrational to be president is patriarchal. Feminism is interested in reducing the power of patriarchy through several methods. Liberal feminists are concerned with achieving political equality by outlawing such practices as sexual harassment and employment discrimination through changes in law or legal precedent. Radical feminists are interested in changing societal structures that oppress women, such as marriage.

The patriarchy is perpetuated in several ways. First, media create expectations about a woman's body image, which lead to problems of self-esteem and health (Telford, 1997). Research indicates that women come away from fashion magazines, for example, with conflicting messages from the images they see. Anne Telford (1997) found that 1 out of 11 advertisements we see have to do with beauty. She calls these ads "misogynistic, sexist, and demeaning" (p. 84). Jennifer A. Schlenker (1998) examined 50 years of *Seventeen* magazine to identify how its content created cultural norms for its readers, mostly teenage girls. Assuming that female adolescence is a period in which girls face questions of identity and self-worth, she set out to determine how *Seventeen* helped or hindered girls in the process of negotiating themselves. She found that in all the issues she examined, the largest percentage of content was devoted to articles about appearance. Schlenker (1998) argues that although women today have a greater variety of opportunities available to them, teen magazines do not make these opportunities known to their young female readers. In fact, *Seventeen* continued to market a girl's beauty as the way to win the boy of her dreams (Schlenker, 1998). Attractiveness, rather than the development of personal and academic interests, is desirable.

The patriarchy is supported by the "feminist backlash." Author Susan Faludi (1991) explains that because many individuals felt threatened by the advances in the women's movement, men—and women—have actively resisted the ideas of feminism. Charlotte Templin (1999) argues that cartoon images portraying Senator Hillary Rodham Clinton as a "failed woman" reflect this idea of backlash. These depictions show Clinton as not fulfilling the role of a typical wife and mother. In them, she is used to scapegoat many of the perceived ills of today's world. Media portrayals such as these confirm the patriarchy and disempower women's voices.

Victoria's Secret implicitly shapes cultural values as well through its product lines and use of visual signs. At the heart of Victoria's Secret's success is its lingerie, which Nancy V. Workman (1996) identifies as patterned after the corset and bodysuit of the Victorian period. The corset of the Victorian period was designed to cage women's bodies and reduce the size of their waists, re-

ETHICAL INSIGHTS

Protecting the Interests of Minorities

Aish Ha Torah—an apolitical, international network of Jewish educational centers—sponsored a petition drive in 2000 to force Amazon.com and Barnesand-Noble.com to remove the book *The Protocols of the Elders of Zion* from their listings. The book is alleged to be a fabricated discussion among Jewish leaders plotting to take over the world and reduce non-Jews to slavery. Aish Ha Torah claimed the book was anti-Semitic and contained dangerous information that perpetuated stereotypes against Jews. Not everyone supported the organization's petition, however. Those who opposed it argued that independent booksellers have the right to sell what they wish and authors, the freedom to express their ideas.

Our culture is often marked by struggles between the interests of the dominant culture and the rights and needs of a minority culture. We spend a great deal of time determining how these interests can be balanced. Our legal and political systems are designed to achieve some balance between competing interests. The National Communication Association

Credo for Ethical Communication (1999) discusses both sides of this issue with its statement: "We endorse freedom of expression, diversity of perspective, and tolerance of dissent to achieve the informed and responsible decision making fundamental to a civil society." In addition, the NCA states, "We condemn communication that degrades individuals and humanity through distortion, intolerance, intimidation, coercion, hatred, and violence." It would seem there are no easy solutions to the problem identified in this chapter. Think about what you have read as you answer these questions:

1. Would you have signed the petition to ask the booksellers to stop selling the book in question? Why or why not?

2. If you owned a bookstore that was selling the book and you received a petition similar to this, would you have stopped selling the book? Why or why not?

sulting in weakened muscles and restricted airflow. The corset also had moral implications: It promoted modesty, but at the same time drew attention to the curves of the woman's body. The corset, argues Workman, is recalled in the tone and ambience of today's Victoria's Secret stores. The scents, colors, and bedroom-type setting of the stores contribute to a focus on sexuality. Ultimately, Workman argues, the commercialization of Victorian-era lingerie reinforces the cultural belief that women are sex objects and inferior to men. Through its persuasive marketing strategy, Victoria's Secret contributes to cultural values concerning male and female equality. Feminists carefully examine our cultural beliefs, values, and practices to determine the degree to which they confirm or transform the patriarchy.

Hegemony and patriarchy are powerful forces that maintain particular cultural beliefs, values, and practices. Persuaders who benefit from the status quo use these tools to maintain the culture that supports them. Opposing these forces are persuaders who seek to change culture. In some cases, cultural change entails a struggle between those who have power and those who do not. Our legal system has developed laws to ensure that minority views can be heard and represented, but balancing the views of the majority and those of the minority continues to raise ethical questions for persuaders. In Ethical Insights: Protecting the Interests of Minorities, you will read about how one persuasive organization attempted to protect the interests of its members.

Consider an advertisement in a magazine. What evidence do you see of hegemony in the ad? What evidence do you see of patriarchy in the ad? In what ways do you resist cultural hegemony? How do you resist patriarchy?

Transforming Culture

Cultures are transformed when persuaders, responding to economic or demographic forces, seek to change cultural values, beliefs, and behaviors. Technology and widespread media use have made it possible for persuaders to more easily manage culture because these channels offer enhanced means of direct access to audiences. Traditional gatekeepers are less powerful because producing mediated messages is less costly than it once was. Persuaders transform culture in a variety of ways.

In the popular press, several magazines challenge the hegemonic power of mythmaking by persuasive sources. *Adbusters* is one such publication. *Adbusters* offers commentary about culture as well as fictional ads that resist the messages of traditional advertising. Review the ad from *Adbusters* in Figure 8.1. How does the ad communicate the idea of hegemony? Does the ad imply a way to resist hegemony?

Persuasive movements, which we discuss in detail in Chapter 13, have shaped our culture in numerous ways as well. The feminist movement resulted in changes in how women are treated in the workforce, for example. The civil rights movement prompted federal legislation protecting the right of African Americans to vote. The White supremacy movement seeks to return the United States to a time of racial segregation. In each case, persuasive movements attempt to change what society believes and values and how it behaves.

Individual persuaders also seek to influence how we view culture. Throughout the 1980s, the Republican Party successfully defined "family values"—prohibiting abortion, permitting school prayer, and limiting gay rights—for the American public. In 1996, however, Democratic President Bill Clinton began to reshape how we think about family values. Clinton broadened the definition of family values by focusing on issues such as using V-chip technology to block violent television programming, requiring students to wear uniforms to school, and reducing teen pregnancy and smoking (Sandel, 1996). Clinton argued that our cultural values should include keeping children safe from violence, crime, and illness. Whether Clinton effectively changed the way we think about family values or whether his redefinition was simply an effort to win reelection remains to be seen. What is clear from this example is that politicians can affect the way Americans talk about the ideas most important to them.

The movie *It's Elementary: Talking about Gay Issues in School* is another recent attempt to redefine American cultural values. The goal of the movie, which discusses whether and how gay and lesbian issues should be discussed in the classroom, is to encourage teachers and parents to talk about these issues with their children. The film discusses the prejudice homosexuals face and encourages parents, teachers, and students to create an environment of respect (Schenden, 1999). The decision to air the film in 1999 on the Public Broadcasting System (PBS) was controversial. Several PBS affiliates declined to show the film, and many more received letters from angry viewers. This controversy reveals the struggle in society over defining cultural values. In the next two sections, we explore two ways in which our culture is being fundamentally transformed: consumer culture and multiculturalism.

Tommy

TOMMY

HILFINGER

follow the flock

Figure 8.1
Adbusters **Fictional Advertisement**

CONSUMER CULTURE

On a more fundamental level, persuaders and the forces of marketing and economics are transforming culture. We are becoming a **consumer culture,** argue many theorists. T. J. Jackson Lears (1983) explains that around the turn of the 20th century, a change in morality, coupled with marketing and advertising, established "self-realization" as a dominant cultural belief. Advertisers, Lears explains, began preaching the culture of consumption to eager listeners. Advertisers promised their products "would contribute to the buyer's physical, psychic, or social well-being" (p. 19). Consumers began to associate products with imaginary states of being. Advertisers promoted *feeling* rather than *information*. Advertisers sold the idea of speed, instead of a particular brand of car. They sold style, as opposed to particular clothing. Baudrillard (1998) considers this "magical thinking." Participating in consumer culture means that we continually invent ourselves through the clothes we wear, the car we drive, and the house in which we live. Consumer culture is persuasive when it makes us want to acquire objects that have a high value.

Likewise, consumer culture is itself a product of persuasion. Persuaders seek to assign value to their objects. Clothing from the Gap has more value than clothing from Kmart, for instance. It means more to purchase and wear

consumer culture
a culture in which "self-realization" through the purchase of consumer goods is a dominant cultural belief

clothing that has the Gap logo attached to it. Thus, Gap spends a great deal of persuasive effort instilling value in its logo. Its advertising seeks to elevate the meaning of the Gap logo above the logos of other manufacturers. Consumers, then, think that when they purchase something from the Gap, they are purchasing the values associated with the Gap: being cool, hip, and trendy.

Consumer culture, critics argue, fosters a sense of alienation among those who participate. We think this lifestyle will bring us happiness and joy. We equate consumption with feeling good. We often consume for the mere sake of consuming. We seek to fill emotional desires with physical objects. When those objects do not fulfill our desires, we become alienated. We discard the objects and purchase new products, hoping that they will fulfill our needs and bring us magic. This cycle of production-consumption-disposal leads to a host of problems, including environmental decay and personal debt. Yet we cannot escape the cycle of consumerism and keep trying to achieve self-realization.

An orientation toward consumption extends beyond advertising and marketing. Persuaders from a variety of contexts seek to assign value to their messages and ideas. Broadcasters create value for their programs. Action figures of Minnesota Governor Jesse Ventura were hot commodities during his 1998 campaign. Creating value for cultural objects is a significant persuasive strategy today.

The transformation of culture to consumerist beliefs, values, and practices has ethical implications. The movie *The Ad and the Ego* (Boihem & Emmanouilides, 1996) identifies three ethical dilemmas facing Americans in the advent of consumer culture: premeditated waste, objectification, and violence. The idea of premeditated waste centers on the notion that much of what we consume creates waste, in the form of packaging materials or natural resources. We consume products and throw away their remains without regard for where our waste goes. Americans consume much of the world's resources, although we are but a small part of the world's 6 billion people. The latest fascination with sport-utility vehicles is but one example of our lack of concern with resource consumption. *The Ad and the Ego* questions the extent to which Americans will go to protect our culture, preserve our way of life, and defend the luxuries we enjoy. *The Ad and the Ego* argues that the Persian Gulf War of 1991 was the result of our demand for cheap oil. Protestors in Seattle in 1999 and in Washington, D.C., in 2000 made the point that the pursuit of consumer culture on a global level disempowers those who are paid low wages to create goods that we in the United States consume. In particular, protestors attacked storefronts bearing famous brand names, such as Starbuck's Coffee. These protestors also argued that consumer culture creates environmental problems that the "consumers" must not ignore.

Culture is transformed through a variety of forces. In many cases, attempts to change culture are only temporary. The protests in Seattle, for instance, died away as soon as the World Trade Organization concluded its meetings there. In other cases, cultural transformation is more enduring, as has been the case with consumer culture. In any case, culture is not fixed or permanent, but is constantly undergoing change and adaptation in response to the needs and values of its members. Persuaders play an important role in shaping how cultures maintain and transform their beliefs, values, and practices.

MULTICULTURALISM

American cultural beliefs, values, and behaviors have been heavily influenced by a particular perspective: that of Caucasian males who belong to the middle and upper classes of our society. We have called this perspective the mainstream culture. Yet American culture is increasingly influenced by the beliefs, values, and behaviors of people from other racial and ethnic backgrounds. As we noted in Chapter 5, the numbers of minorities in our culture are increasing. Within 50 years, Hispanics, for instance, will comprise nearly 25 percent of the U.S. population. Currently, people of Hispanic descent account for 11 percent. The populations of other ethnic groups are increasing as well. Implicit in our discussion of **multiculturalism** is that people from non-U.S. cultural backgrounds may have different beliefs, values, and behaviors than those of the mainstream culture. As a result, persuaders must seek to understand how these differences will influence the kinds of relationships they form with audience members. The nature of a multicultural society and how best to accommodate its competing cultural beliefs, values, and behaviors are themselves the subjects of persuasive debate. For now, we will draw on the work of Geert Hofstede (1980), who argues that four dimensions characterize cultures and differentiate them from one another:

multiculturalism
existence of diverse, and often competing or conflicting, cultural beliefs, values, and behaviors in one culture

1. Power distance
2. Uncertainty avoidance
3. Individualism
4. Masculinity

The first of Hofstede's (1980) dimensions is *power distance,* which refers to how cultures deal with inequality and status. Cultures that are low in power distance seek to minimize inequality, judge the use of power as legitimate or illegitimate, and seek to change the power system by redistributing power. Cultures that are high in power distance see powerholders as having special privilege, blame those who have less power, and stress coercive power. Malaysia, Guatemala, and Panama have high power distance; Austria, Israel, and Denmark have low power distance. The United States has a relatively low power distance. Hofstede argues that a variety of conditions lead to a culture's power distance. In cultures where survival and population growth depend on intervening with nature (such as we have seen in the United States' history), people develop a low power distance. In cultures where there is a centralization of political power, people develop a high power distance.

The second of Hofstede's (1980) cultural dimensions is *uncertainty avoidance.* Some cultures avoid uncertainty at all costs; others embrace uncertainty. Cultures develop customs, rituals, and traditions to deal with uncertainty. Countries that seek to avoid uncertainty include Greece, Portugal, and Guatemala. Members of these cultures worry about the future, fear failure, and prefer clear rules and instructions. Countries that do not avoid uncertainty include Denmark, Jamaica, and Singapore. The United States is relatively tolerant of uncertainty. Uncertainty-tolerant cultures have lower job stress, stronger achievement and motivation, and more risk taking than do uncertainty-avoidant cultures.

Hofstede (1980) also explains that cultures vary in how they view the relationship between the individual and the greater society. He calls this the *individualism* dimension. In some cultures, people are content to subordinate themselves to the family, the organization, or the government. In other cultures, the individual's rights are paramount. As you may have guessed from our earlier discussion of beliefs, values, and practices, the United States is high in individualism, followed by Australia and Great Britain. Panama, Ecuador, and Guatemala are low on the individualism dimension. Highly individualistic cultures place importance in an individual's personal time, emphasize each individual's responsibility to care for him- or herself, and believe in individual decisions. Cultures that are low in individualism believe in group decisions, place value in family time, and emphasize belonging to an organization.

The final cultural dimension identified by Hofstede (1980) is *masculinity*. This dimension deals with how sex roles are distributed among cultural members and how members of the sexes are socialized to think, act, and feel. Countries that are high in masculinity include Japan, Austria, and Switzerland. Those that are low in masculinity (high in femininity) include Sweden, Norway, and the Netherlands. The United States is relatively high in masculinity. Cultures that are high in masculinity value achievement, independence, and decisiveness. Cultures that are low in masculinity stress service, interdependence, and intuition.

Hofstede provides us with one way of discussing how cultures differ. What these differences mean for the transformation of American culture is still subject to persuasive debate. In many ways, Americans are using persuasion to influence how we conceive of ourselves and what we should believe and value. The debate over school curricula is one area in which persuasion plays a role in determining our culture. Some persuaders claim that our schools should teach about multiculturalism by having students read works written by minority authors, such as Maya Angelou. Opponents of such teaching practices argue that the "great books" of history, such as Shakespeare and Chaucer, should be taught instead. Persuaders also debate the merits of affirmative action and sexual harassment laws. The outcomes of such debates like these will influence how we think about diversity and the beliefs, values, and behaviors of minority cultures.

Identify an issue of cultural conflict and the persuaders who are involved. What beliefs, attitudes, and values are in conflict? What do you think will be the lasting impact of the conflict's resolution?

Summary

Culture is a set of beliefs, values, and behaviors that sustains a group of people. Culture and persuasion intersect in three ways. First, persuaders use cultural beliefs, values, and behaviors to identify with their audience members, who may share the same beliefs, values, and behaviors. In particular, persuaders appeal to mainstream culture, which can be described by McElroy's research, our discussion of cultural values, and Hammond and Morrison's cultural forces. It is important to note that not all members of our culture share these ideas.

Persuaders also seek to shape culture by maintenance and transformation. Maintenance occurs through hegemony and patriarchy, where the values and beliefs of the dominant group are perpetuated through cultural practices and media. Transformation occurs on many levels and is often short lived.

Key Terms

Visit the book's website at http://www.mhhe.com/borchers2 for multiple-choice quizzes, Internet activities, and key terms flashcards.

WWW:

culture 215	buzz 219
popular culture 216	culture scanning 220
value 217	hegemony 231
cultural values 217	patriarchy 234
mainstream culture 217	consumer culture 237
referent class 218	multiculturalism 239
trend 219	

9

The Persuasiveness of the Source

Learning Objectives

After reading this chapter, you should be able to:

1. Understand the influence of media on how audience members perceive persuasive sources.

2. Define credibility, using rhetorical and social science perspectives.

3. Describe what is meant by image, explain how images are created, understand the effect images have on audiences, and evaluate images of persuaders.

4. Explain aspects of institutional sources, such as organizational image and the use of spokespersons.

5. Identify the key components of an individual's credibility, including nonverbal and verbal communication and impression management.

6. Describe ways that images are repaired through persuasion.

7. Understand propaganda and how it is used today by persuaders.

The February 18, 2001, death of race car driver Dale Earnhardt evoked national grief. His fans flocked to the headquarters of his racing team, leaving flowers, balloons, and other memorials. Newspapers published special issues devoted to the stock car legend. Funeral homes across the nation offered condolence books for fans to sign. Thousands watched his memorial service on national television. To many Americans, Earnhardt was a hero, a role model, and someone with whom they had a personal connection. Despite the fact that they had never met him, many Americans felt a profound sense of loss at Earnhardt's death. The connection racing car fans had with Earnhardt is not unlike our relationship with other celebrities who have passed away in recent years, such as John F. Kennedy Jr. and Princess Diana. The power of the media to foster relationships between audience members and celebrities is remarkable.

We have said that media create pictures that appear very real to us. We act toward people and organizations based on the idea we have of them. We do not actually know the individuals or organizations that persuade us; we only think we do. The Earnhardt example illustrates the strength of the relationships we form with individuals we do not even know. The media age forces us to look at the source of persuasive messages differently. In the past, audiences knew and related to persuaders on a personal basis; today, our relationships with persuaders are formed by mediated images of them.

We are confronted daily with questions of a persuader's credibility. From allegations against our president to deciding where to purchase an automobile or other consumer item, we are forced to judge whether the institutions and individuals who are persuading us are truthful and competent. Aristotle theorized that the *source* of a persuasive message could cause audience members to be persuaded. He called this type of persuasive proof ethos. We identify with effective persuaders and thus accept their ideas. In the media age, we often form relationships with persuaders because of the *image* they present. Audience perceptions of a persuader's credibility, however, are shaped by other persuaders and media images.

In this chapter, we discuss persuaders as individuals and as organizations. In Chapters 10 and 11, we examine how persuaders use reasoning to support their persuasive claims and how they create emotional involvement with their audiences. Here, we examine how persuasive sources use language and visual images, along with cultural beliefs, values, and behaviors, to form intimate relationships with an audience.

This chapter begins with a look at the persuasive source in the media age. We then explore different concepts of credibility. From that discussion, we move to a new concept of source, that of image, or the mental picture audience members have of a persuasive source. We then study institutional sources (organizations such as Sears) and individual sources (such as politicians) and how each may repair a tarnished image. Because today we often do not know the identity of the individuals behind the messages we encounter, we also consider anonymous sources and how to guard against their persuasive appeal.

The Source in the Media Age

Recalling our persuasion model, let's focus on the role of the persuader. We have said that a persuader selects, organizes, and uses language and visual images in order to identify with audience members. The fact that persuaders convey their messages through media has four profound effects on how we view persuaders:

1. Media allow us to see, hear, and be close to persuaders.
2. Media distill information about them into images.
3. Media give meaning to the images of persuaders.
4. Media privilege certain kinds of information about persuaders.

First, media make it possible for us to *see, hear, and be close to* persuaders. We are able to have virtual interactions with the sources of persuasive messages. In some cases, we can chat online with movie actors, politicians, recording artists, or organizational spokespersons. We read about them in the morning newspaper, listen to them on the noon call-in show, or see them on the evening news. As a result, we are able to form images about the people, institutions, and companies that target us with their communication.

However, the ideas we form of persuaders are based on only a small amount of information about them. Media *distill* the enormous amount of information available about individuals into easily understood images of them. It is impossible to fully grasp the various components of a person's ethos, or source credibility. This is true not only of sources we come to know through media, but also of sources we encounter in face-to-face communication. We form a mental picture of a person or an organization from the distilled information we receive.

Media also *give meaning* to persuaders. Persuaders today do not completely control how they present themselves to the public (Nesbit, 1988). Not only must persuaders conform to the limitations of media that we have discussed, but news coverage often interprets people and organizations in particular ways. Presidential candidates are "smart" or "prone to angry outbursts" or "personable." We learn about sources, but we do so through a photographer's lens or a journalist's keystrokes. When the news media say that a politician has a problem with anger, that influences our interpretation of who the politician is. When we see an interview with an actor, we see his or her response only to the questions that are asked. We think we know the whole story about a celebrity, but what we know is only a fraction of the information available. In essence, we have in our heads a picture of a source, not an idea of who that source is as a person.

Finally, media *privilege certain types of information* about sources. Recall from Postman's discussion of truth and knowledge in Chapter 1 that the media age characterizes some types of information as more important than others. The same observation holds true for our discussion of credibility. Ann Geracimos (1998) explains that persuaders must "be able to tell a story (preferably on television), attach [themselves] to a celebrity (fame is in), refrain from bragging (flamboyance is out) and control the content of the media message whenever and however possible" (p. 40). A source must be a good storyteller, capable of massaging media with images and words.

Defining Credibility

There has been a great deal of discussion among researchers about what constitutes a persuader's credibility. In this section, we survey some of this research.

Two ideas about credibility are apparent in a great deal of the research: credibility is the audience's perception of the persuader, and it is dynamic. Credibility is a judgment the audience makes about the persuader (Berlo, Lemert, & Mertz, 1969). Ideas about credibility vary with each audience member. One group of voters might see a particular political candidate as competent, while another group sees the same candidate as incompetent. There is no easy way to determine a persuader's credibility. Credibility is not worn like a shirt or created easily. Credibility is a social construct, something that is created, maintained, and changed through communication. Our ideas about credibility are subject to persuasive influence. Persuaders can affect what we perceive to be credible.

Credibility is also dynamic (Berlo, Lemmert, & Mertz, 1969). Because credibility is a social construct, ideas about what is credible vary from time to time and culture to culture. An audience might judge a persuader's credibility as high one day and low the next. In October 1999, Minnesota Governor Jesse Ventura made some provocative statements, including the assertion that religion was a crutch for "weak-minded" individuals, in a *Playboy* magazine interview. A public opinion poll of his constituents that was conducted shortly after the interview appeared showed that his approval rating had fallen by almost 20 points. A few months later, when public discussion of the interview had subsided, Ventura's approval rating had rebounded almost to its preinterview level (Whereatt, 2000). Ventura's falling and rising credibility, as measured by public opinion polls, is a good example of the dynamic nature of credibility. Let's now discuss several constitutive factors of credibility.

ETHOS

Aristotle and the ancient rhetorical theorists studied the persuader using the concept of ethos. In Aristotle's day, speakers often used persuasion to defend themselves in court. Aristotle believed that the character of the speaker was "almost" the most important type of persuasive proof (Aristotle, trans. 1991). Aristotle identified three reasons why some speakers were believed more readily than others: practical wisdom, virtue, and goodwill. The basis for judging practical wisdom was the correctness of the speaker's ideas and the speaker's ability to express those opinions (Aristotle, trans. 1991). Wisdom concerned the ability of the speaker to form valid judgments. Virtue was an "ability for doing good" and included the characteristics of justice, courage, and self-control (Aristotle, trans. 1991). Goodwill was seen as the speaker's having the best interests of the audience in mind. The speaker should not serve only personal interests (Aristotle, trans. 1991).

The classical theorists—Plato, Aristotle, Quintilian, and Cicero—taught that knowledge was an important part of a persuader's ethos. They stressed the importance of knowing a great deal of information about many subjects. In fact, our liberal arts education tradition stems from this ancient notion that a persuader should be well versed in a variety of subjects. Plato, in particular, criticized the Sophists of ancient Greece because many of the Sophists taught their students only the "tricks of the trade" and did not require the extensive education that Plato and other teachers demanded. Another component of the classical theory of ethos is that the persuader sincerely believe the cause he or she is addressing. Quintilian believed that a persuader could not convince an audience unless he or she believed in the message.

Cal M. Logue and Eugene F. Miller (1995) explain that ethos may more appropriately be seen as a persuader's response to a given situation. Different situations call for different responses from persuaders. How a persuader communicates in a given situation affects his or her rhetorical status, or the perception of the persuader by the audience member. Logue and Miller contend that sometimes people of lower social status may communicate in ways that resemble those individuals of higher social status—and consequently be seen as having a higher rhetorical status.

Secretary of State Colin Powell (Figure 9.1) is a persuader who exemplifies ethos. Powell's presence in George W. Bush's administration is widely regarded by Americans, Republicans and Democrats alike. Powell, a retired army general, displayed wisdom as Chair of the Joint Chiefs of Staff under Presidents Bush and Clinton. As director of America's Promise, an umbrella organization that is committed to helping America's youth, Powell has organized efforts to provide mentoring to 10.3 million children and has raised more than $295.5 million in donations (Carlson, 1999). To do so, writes Margaret Carlson, Powell has had to make careful decisions about which organizations to include under the umbrella and how to motivate others. Powell also displays elements of virtue, including donating his time to promoting volunteerism. Powell has also shown that he has the interests of others in mind. In 1996, he announced he would not run for president so as not to jeopardize the privacy of his family. Keep in mind that any discussion of credible persuaders must be tempered by the observation that all we know about them is what we see of them in media. If you knew Colin Powell personally, he might not be anything like his public persona. As you consider the question of ethos, what examples other than Colin Powell come to mind?

SOURCE CREDIBILITY

Scholars today use the construct of ethos to understand a persuader's credibility, but they have complemented the rhetorical approach with social scientific methods. Social science researchers use the term **source credibility** to refer to their idea of credibility. Researchers David K. Berlo, James B. Lemert, and Robert J. Mertz (1969) discuss three factors that they believe define credibility: safety, qualification, and dynamism. These characteristics have received a high level of support among researchers, so let's consider them further.

source credibility
a persuader's degree of safety, qualification, and dynamism

Safety refers to the degree to which we trust the source. Berlo, Lemert, and Mertz (1969) explain that several traits contribute to the sense that a source is safe. A source should have a sense of justice as well as a high level of honesty. The researchers argue that *safety* is more general than a term such as *trustworthiness* because safety also describes the "affiliative relationship" between source and receiver. Credible sources are seen by others as calm, safe, friendly, and kind.

Figure 9.1 Colin Powell is a speaker who displays the attributes of ethos. How does Powell communicate honesty? Trustworthiness? Wisdom?

Despite the fact that their study is more than 30 years old, Berlo, Lemert, and Mertz's discussion of safety provides a way for us to view persuaders in the media age. We must keep in mind, however, that these researchers focused on face-to-face speaking situations, whereas today, media come between us and persuaders. What we perceive as safe today is somewhat different than it was in the past. Media are especially effective at developing affective relationships between audience members and persuaders. When political candidates make personal appearances, they often show us their personal side. Candidates are generally seen shaking hands, kissing babies, or talking with senior citizens. As they do so, they provide us with a glimpse of who they are. Of course, the image they project of safety is often manufactured by their consultants. We discuss this concept—called impression management—in greater depth later in the chapter.

Qualification, a second characteristic of source credibility, refers to the expertise of the source. Qualification traits include training, experience, and intelligence. Berlo, Lemert, and Mertz (1969) conclude that qualification refers both to the specific persuasive situation as well as to general traits about the persuader. Thus, source credibility includes a judgment about how much a persuader knows in a specific situation as well as how intelligent the persuader is perceived to be overall.

Today, qualification is often established through media channels. Once again, media coverage often distills the qualifications of a persuader to only a few ideas. Former Vice President Dan Quayle had the reputation of being unintelligent because of how he was portrayed in the media. On numerous occasions, unflattering comments made by Quayle were repeated in the media. The most famous of these was his incorrect spelling of the word *potato*. This type of coverage portrayed Quayle as lacking the qualifications to be vice president, despite what many others had said about his intelligence and grasp of politics. Quayle's public image jeopardized his run for president in 2000, and he dropped out of the campaign early.

Dynamism is the third component of ethos. It includes aggressiveness, boldness, and energy. Berlo, Lemert, and Mertz (1969) explain that dynamism is used to emphasize, augment, and implement the persuader's ideas. Dynamism functions primarily to intensify the audience's judgment about a persuader's safety and qualifications. A highly dynamic source that is perceived to be safe and qualified would be more credible than a source that is safe and qualified, but has low dynamism.

In the media age, dynamism plays an important role in a persuader's credibility. Recalling Postman's ideas from Chapter 1, audiences today like to be entertained. We are not content to listen to the lengthy policy statements of dispassionate persuaders. Dynamic sources breathe life into their audience's response. When companies seek spokespeople, they tend to look for dynamic individuals who can intensify the audience's perceptions of the organization and its products.

Name a persuader today who is dynamic. What qualities about that person lead you to believe he or she is dynamic?

Credibility can be partially understood by looking at two research constructs: ethos and source credibility. The concept of ethos directs us to examine the wisdom, virtue, and goodwill of the persuader; source credibility includes the persuader's safety, qualification, and dynamism. In addition, credibility is determined by the audience's perceptions of the persuader, and it is dynamic. In the next section, we look more closely at how media channels affect an audience's perception of the persuader. But first, complete the Internet Activity: Judging Credibility.

The Image of the Source

As we have discussed scholarly approaches to understanding a persuader's credibility, we have made note of media's involvement in our perception of the persuader. Quite often, the beliefs we have about a persuader are not formed through direct interaction with the persuader or careful research of the persuader's qualifications. We instead form a belief about a persuader through our interaction with media and based on mediated information. This belief is often called an **image,** a conception or mental picture of a person, an institution, or a nation. Kenneth Boulding (1956) explains that an image is another word for knowledge. Boulding adds that images are formed by subjective knowledge, or

image
a conception that we have of people, institutions, or nations; a mental picture we have of something that is not physically present

Judging Credibility

We have discussed various ways of describing credibility. Not only does the way someone communicates contribute to their credibility, but their knowledge and background can be persuasive to audiences as well. Locate the website for someone our culture thinks is credible. Read about this person. Why does culture think this person is credible? Do you agree with society's assessment?

knowledge that we believe to be true. An image is a mental picture we have of something that is not physically present. We use all kinds of information about a persuader when we construct an image. We might consider the appearance of an individual persuader or a recent scandal involving an organization. When you think of Bill Gates, for instance, you may have an image of someone who is smart, generous, and a shrewd businessperson. When you think of McDonald's, you might think of Ronald McDonald and the golden arches. You might also think that McDonald's is a fun place to eat.

Although image has much in common with the ancient idea of ethos, it is important to note that Aristotle's definition of ethos is much different than today's understanding of image. Aristotle believed that persuaders could not "fake" ethos (Rein, 1994). A persuader who had credibility and trust projected an image of credibility. A persuader who lacked ethos was not believed by audiences. In the media age, however, persuaders are highly adept at portraying themselves as credible and trustworthy when, in fact, they may lack these characteristics. By using visual images or electronic eloquence, for instance, persuaders can appear credible. It is particularly difficult, then, for audiences, to determine whether they can trust a persuader in the media age.

Persuaders spend a great deal of time and resources creating images for audience members. Many companies, for instance, create their image through extensive advertising. A product's packaging may also contribute to the image audience members have of the product. Individuals also create images of themselves for audiences. Political candidates, for instance, have used video montages at recent political conventions to show the public what they are like as people. The Beetle Bailey cartoon in Figure 9.2 pokes fun at image creation. Are the images persuaders create always valid?

CHARACTERISTICS OF IMAGES

Daniel Boorstin (1975) identifies five characteristics of images:

1. Synthetic
2. Believable
3. Vivid and concrete
4. Simplified
5. Ambiguous

**Figure 9.2
Beetle Bailey Creates
an Image for Himself**
Why might images fail
to persuade audiences?
Is there some way to
evaluate an image?
Reprinted with permission
of King Features Syndicate.

BEETLE BAILEY

First, images are *synthetic,* or planned by persuaders. Images are rhetorically
constructed to serve a purpose: electing someone to office or selling a product.
Boorstin explains that images are crafted by specialists and are peculiar products of the media age. He likens an image to an individual's personality: An
image is an outward expression of how a person or an organization wants to be
seen by others. Politicians discuss with their consultants what color of clothing
to wear or how to style their hair. Persuaders from many different fields now
use publicists to help them create media images. Even Darva Conger, a woman
who was married in 2000 on live television to a multimillionaire, used a publi-
cist to help her manage her public image following the controversial show.

Recently, persuaders have engaged in meta-imaging, which Shawn J.
Parry-Giles and Trevor Parry-Giles (1999) explain is "the communicative act
in which political campaigns and their chroniclers publicly display and fore-
ground the art and practice of political image construction" (p. 29). That is,
political campaigns, or other organizations, give access to reporters, who tell
the public about the "real" person behind the image. Of course, this public display is no more than a contrived image-building event itself. In the documentary movie *The War Room,* for example, viewers are able to see the "real" life
action of the 1992 Clinton campaign. Since the documentary is "real," we think
we know the characters involved. The popular television show *Entertainment
Tonight* works on the same premise. Its interviews with celebrities convey the
idea that celebrities are "real" people whom we should like. By giving us a
glimpse of the workings of the persuasive process, persuaders are implying that
what we see is real, not manufactured.

Second, images are *believable.* Despite their intangible nature—you can't
hear, feel, or smell an image—images are powerful mental pictures that shape
how we think, feel, and act. They are very believable. Boorstin (1975) argues
that images cannot violate rules of common sense. To use Walter Fisher's (1987)
terminology, an image must have "narrative fidelity." It must appear to be true
to the audience. Boorstin observes that when there is room for error, an image
is more believable. He uses the example of Ivory soap, which claims to be 99.44
percent pure. Acknowledging a few impurities makes the soap's claim stronger.

Third, images are *vivid and concrete*. Although they are mental pictures, images can seem quite real. Boorstin (1975) explains that images should include vivid qualities. The attributes about a person or an organization that an image focuses on should be touchable, colorful, or striking in some way. Claritin allergy medication uses the slogan "Nothing but blue skies from now on" to illustrate the relief offered by its formula. AT&T uses the slogan "It's all within your reach." Sears promises, "The good life at a great price. Guaranteed."

Images are also *simplified*. That is, images provide us with only a small amount of the total knowledge available about an individual or a company. They are shorthand ways of thinking about concepts and people. Boorstin (1975) writes that this is especially true of logos that cannot be reduced to words. Reducing an image to words, explains Boorstin, causes it to lose some of its magic. The initials IBM, for instance, stand for much more than words can represent. Likewise, the script words Coca-Cola have powerful meaning, as do the golden arches of McDonald's. The power of these images lies not in the type script alone or the color of the arches. The power lies in the meaning that persuaders have created for those images. Through time and repeated exposure, the logos have come to represent a powerful set of meanings. The reduction of these meanings to a simple logo allows audience members to conceive of the entire set of meanings quickly and powerfully.

Finally, images are *ambiguous*. They must serve multiple and unforeseen purposes. Images have to be open for interpretation so that many audience members can perceive their meaning. At the same time, the connection between source and image must be clear, or the image will fail to accomplish its persuasive goal. The image of Lucent Technologies is somewhat ambiguous. Its logo uses a red circle that appears to have been drawn with a crayon. The words "Lucent Technologies: Bell Labs Innovations" appear in the company's logo as well. The slogan "We make the things that make communications work" sums up the services offered by the company. Although the logo makes it clear that Lucent Technologies is somehow involved in cellular telephones, the Internet, and voice mail, it is unclear exactly how Lucent is involved in these products and activities. Because the company's image (logo) is flexible, the company's image can change as the company's products, services, and mission change. Use these characteristics of images to complete the Internet Activity: Describing Images.

EFFECTS OF IMAGES ON AUDIENCES

Images have cognitive, emotional, and behavioral effects on audiences. Thus, images contribute to the audience's attitudes toward the persuader and the persuader's message. Our image of a persuader affects how we cognitively evaluate messages about or from that persuader. Cognitive dissonance helps to explain how images relate to our attitudes toward the persuader. If we like someone and hear something positive about that person, it confirms the image we have. If we experience negative information about a persuader we regard positively, we are forced to reduce the dissonance this causes. Once a prospective voter forms an image of a political candidate, for instance, the way that

Describing Images

An effective image, we have learned, is concrete enough to form a clear image for the audience, but also flexible enough to serve many uses. In particular, images are created to have an emotional connection with their audience. Use Yahoo! (http://www.yahoo.com) to search for the website of your favorite brand of car, soft drink, or fast-food restaurant. Using what we have discussed about image, describe the image of the company. Does the online image of the company agree with your previous image of the company?

voter perceives messages about that candidate will be related to the image the voter has of the candidate. Many feminists saw former President Clinton as an effective advocate for women's issues. Messages to the contrary had little impact on them until Clinton admitted to an inappropriate affair with an intern. This changed the image many had of him, and feminists were consequently more likely to accept allegations against him. Images thus serve as filters by which we evaluate information about a person or an organization (Boulding, 1956).

If the image of a source is realistic, we form emotional connections to him or her. We come to identify with the source as if we know that person. We feel his or her pain and we share in his or her happiness. Recent national tragedies illustrate the degree of emotional involvement we have with sources. It is quite common for people to create large memorials for celebrities who have died. The death of John F. Kennedy Jr. and his wife prompted thousands to leave flowers, cards, and other items in front of their New York apartment. Ellis Cose (1999) writes that Kennedy was part of our lives from the moment we saw the adorable images of him as a small boy. His appearance on magazine covers and television shows over his short lifetime prompted the outpouring of grief for him. Because of the image they form of someone like Kennedy, audience members feel connected to him on an emotional level.

We often base our actions on how we think and feel about persuasive sources. Thus, the image we have of a persuasive source has behavioral effects as well. A former pro wrestler and movie actor, Minnesota gubernatorial candidate Jesse Ventura projected an image to voters that was charismatic and colorful. He cultivated the idea that he was just like the voters by wearing jeans, sneakers, and T-shirts on the campaign trail and by continuing to coach his high school football team throughout the campaign (Bai & Brauer, 1998). In fact, "Jesse Ventura" is the governor's stage name. His real name is James Janos. When a debate moderator prefaced a question by stating that to be governor of Minnesota, one had to know something about agriculture, Ventura quickly rejected the assertion, responding that he did not have to know about the subject (Beiler, 2000). Although Ventura promoted many policies that resonated with voters, the image he created for himself was, perhaps, a more compelling reason that Minnesotans voted for him.

CREATING AN IMAGE

Given the persuasive appeal of images, persuaders use strategy to create images that will help them sell their products or ideas. Bennett (1996) identifies three aspects of image creation: message composition, message salience, and message credibility. All three work together to create an idea about a source in the mind of the audience. As critical audience members, we must be aware of image-creation strategies and how they affect our beliefs and feelings toward a persuader.

Message composition involves composing a single theme or message for the audience to consider. The Girl Scouts of the USA recently modified its image. Based on public opinion polling, the organization learned that people thought the Girl Scouts was a good organization, but not vital in today's world (Flass, 1999, p. 2). The Girl Scouts organization was seen as being about camping and crafts and as dominated by Caucasian members ("Girl Scouts," 1999). As a result, the Girl Scouts created a new message that focused on the importance of the organization in developing future female leaders. The new image sought to create the idea that Girl Scouts was also about math, sports, and computing ("Girl Scouts," 1999). Its new slogan—"Girl Scouts. Where Girls Grow Strong"— better captures the mission and role of the organization, its leaders believe.

The second aspect of image building—saturating the communications channels with the message so that it receives attention and is perceived as important—is called *message salience*. The Girl Scouts disseminated its new message with a variety of communication devices. The new logo is seen on its cookie boxes, letterhead, internal magazine, and handbooks (Flass, 1999, p. 2). Girl Scouts also wear new uniforms that reflect the new image.

The final step in building an image is convincing the audience that the message is credible by surrounding it with the "trappings of credibility" (Bennett, 1996, p. 82). Bennett calls this *message credibility*. Persuaders portray their messages in the company of other symbols that the audience believes to be credible. The Girl Scouts recently used popular female celebrities to give its campaign credibility. A series of public service announcements telling about Girl Scouts featured well-known former scouts, including columnist Ann Landers and basketball star Rebecca Lobo. All of the women are viewed by at least some segment of society as being worthy role models for young women. They are independent women, leaders in their field, and morally upright. Thus, they are effective in building credibility for the new image of the Girl Scouts.

Although the Girl Scouts may have effectively overhauled its image for the public, Republican politician Dan Quayle was not so successful in his bid to run for president in 2000. Quayle had initial credibility, having served as George Bush's vice president. He also had a base of support among conservative Republicans. Quayle tried to surround himself with the "trappings of credibility," including then–U.S. Senator Spencer Abraham (Borger, 1997). Despite appearances, Quayle lacked a message and a theme. His message composition failed to garner the support necessary to keep him in the race for the GOP nomination. Gloria Borger reports that Quayle supporters claimed his main selling point was "that he is the most recent former Republican vice president"

(p. 40). As this example indicates, in addition to name recognition and other aspects of image creation, persuaders must have a strong message if their image is to take hold. In addition, persuaders must be able to sell their image to the news media in order to gain public approval. Quayle failed to sell his image to those covering his campaign.

MEDIA AND IMAGES

Persuaders do not create images of themselves and their products independent of the news media. Parry-Giles (2000) identifies several effects media have on image making. On one level, news media coverage of persuaders often makes use of stereotypes. Parry-Giles's analysis of Hillary Rodham Clinton found that members of the news media portrayed Clinton as a "hard-edged" feminist and the "embodiment of all that was wrong with the sixties" (p. 206). Even after Clinton modified her image to that of a more traditional First Lady, she faced media criticism. One commentator noted that the Clintons' marriage was a political arrangement, instead of a personal relationship. Stereotyping persuaders is one way the news media influence our perception of them.

The images the news media select for their coverage of persuaders also influence how the audience perceives persuaders. We often forget that we see in media only those images members of media want us to see. Reporters and editors choose from among many possible images and meanings and provide us with the ones that fit the nature of the story they are producing. Parry-Giles (2000) argues that positive images of Hillary Rodham Clinton were often absent from media coverage of her, which focused mainly on negative images of her. In one black-and-white image of the Clintons, Hillary is shown speaking to her husband while he looks away. The image underlines the written text of the story, which argues that Hillary Clinton had too much power in the White House.

Images are also manipulated by the news media, and this influences how we think about persuaders. It is common for news organizations to use stock images in their coverage. For instance, a picture of someone at a funeral may be used in a wide variety of other settings. Just such a use occurred with an image of Hillary Clinton, argues Parry-Giles (2000). A broadcast concerning Bill Clinton's affair with Monica Lewinsky contained an image of Hillary in which she appeared to be crying or as if she had just cried. The viewers, no doubt, associated the image of Hillary with the personal turmoil caused by her husband's affair. Yet the image was taken while Hillary was attending a memorial service for the Americans killed in embassy bombings in Africa.

Finally, the news media repeat, retell, and recycle stories so that audience members see the same image of a persuader over and over again. Hillary Rodham Clinton's interview with NBC's *Today* show host Matt Lauer—in which she identified a "right wing conspiracy" as responsible for accusations against her husband—is one example of an image that has been shown over and over again. In all, as a result of media, audiences have an image of persuaders that is not real, but that is believable.

CHOOSING MEANINGS FOR AN IMAGE

Audience members must often choose between competing meanings for an image. We experience cognitive dissonance over which image of a source to believe. Bennett (1996) outlines three situations in which audience members must select a meaning for an image. First, he explains that in times of uncertainty we cling to our old images, especially if they continue to provide meaning for the situation. Bennett argues that we rarely replace old images with no image. A new, easy-to-grasp image must come along for us to give up our previous image.

Second, if the truth is ambiguous because the audience does not know who to trust, the audience will hold on to the old image. The bombing of Serbia by NATO forces in 1999 exemplifies the public's struggle over ambiguous images. U.S. leaders and NATO officials successfully convinced the American public to support the bombing campaign. Throughout the military action, however, the credibility of this appeal was repeatedly questioned as potentially damaging information emerged. Americans saw images of civilians being killed by NATO bombs, yet they were told that these images were not true. In addition, claims of damage to Serbian armed forces were often exaggerated. Yet, the importance of the campaign was continually stressed to the public, creating uncertainty about which side to believe: NATO's or Serbia's. In the end, many Americans continued to support our nation's leaders.

Third, we hold on to old images when they remain more salient for us than the contradictory information. Bennett (1996) explains that images are often formed based on large-scale pseudoevents that capture the media's and the audience's attention. John McCain's 2000 presidential campaign was in many ways a large-scale pseudoevent that captured the hearts of reporters and voters. Using a bus tour called the Straight Talk Express, McCain invited reporters to ride with him around the country, answering their questions and being truthful with them. As a result of this easy access to the candidate, the news media gave McCain a great deal of attention. In fact, when minor questions about his truthfulness and image emerged, media downplayed them, and they did not become as salient to voters as the dominant image.

EVALUATING IMAGES

Because a persuader's image is contrived and is filtered by media, audience members should see it as a highly suspect form of proof. Jamieson (1988) notes that ethos is less reliable today than in the past. Yet we often take images at face value, identifying with a persuader's message because of how we feel and think about the persuader. The problems with images are that persuaders can easily manipulate them and that images fail to provide us with accurate information about a source. First, images can be easily manipulated. Politicians can say the right thing to convince us to vote for them. Organizational spokespeople can create images for their companies based not on accurate data, but on hollow ideals. When images are manipulated, we have no reference for what the symbols mean.

Second, images deny us important information with which to make decisions. When politicians present themselves in a way designed to attract votes, rather than in one that will produce support for their ideas, we lose our power as voters. When persuaders create brands that encourage a knee-jerk response from consumers, we quickly purchase products that may, in fact, endanger our planet and ourselves. Recall what we said about consumer culture in Chapter 8. It is important that we base all our decisions—political, shopping, and interpersonal—on accurate, reliable information.

Here are some ways to avoid being easily influenced by images. First, avoid prejudging a persuasive source until you know the persuader's position on an issue. Listen to persuaders you would not normally support in order to form a firsthand impression of them. When someone with whom you do not agree speaks on your campus, go to the speech anyway. Learn about the person, and then determine if your previous judgment should stand.

Second, understand the influence of media in creating images of persuaders. By understanding how media operate, you can understand attempts by individuals to influence your impression of them. By understanding how sound bites contribute to image politics, you can look past the sound bite and uncover substantive information about the candidate. By comprehending the power of brands to influence your perception of products, you can evaluate products on the basis of what they do for you, as opposed to what a source would have you believe.

Third, seek information about sources from a variety of media. Do not rely on the same media for all of your knowledge. Broaden your horizons by watching different television channels, reading different newspapers, and looking through different magazines. The website for this book contains a long list of links to news sites that you may not know about. Diverse information helps us fill out the images formed by persuaders and develop a more complete view of their ideas.

What image do you have of your state's governor? How did you develop that image? Does the image you have make you feel favorable or unfavorable toward the governor?

A persuader's image is our belief about that person's or institution's qualifications, safety, and dynamism that we form through our interactions—mediated or interpersonal—with that entity. Our image of a persuader is based on our judgments—beliefs—about that source. Images are created, simplistic, ambiguous, and vivid for their audiences. Images arise because of careful planning and promotion by image consultants. Images cause us to respond to the persuader in particular ways. Martha Stewart is a persuader who today enjoys a powerful image, as Thinking Critically: Martha Stewart's Image explains.

We've looked at the components of credibility. Let's now turn to exploring various types of sources: institutional, individual, and anonymous sources.

Institutional Sources

Not only do we form images of people, but we form images of large organizations and institutions. Large organizations spend considerable amounts of money to create a compelling image for their publics and for their own mem-

THINKING CRITICALLY

Martha Stewart's Image

From our study of the source in this chapter, you can begin to see how persuaders use the tools that we have discussed in previous chapters to create images that evoke an audience response. Keep in mind, though, that images and credibility are dynamic—they are constantly changing. Martha Stewart provides an interesting case study in how images are created, challenged, and repaired.

Stewart has enjoyed success as an author, television show host, and a businessperson. Her image is based on many factors, including media use, visual images, language strategies, and cultural values. Stewart's success has been due, in part, to her presence in print, broadcast, and Internet media. Through these media channels, Stewart came into the homes of millions of viewers. Her image is built on the word *living*. She refuses to use the word *housewife* in her magazine and books, television show, and website, preferring instead the term *housekeeper*. Visually, audience members seek beautiful pictures of people "living" the good life, and her television show provides visual proof that audience members themselves can cook and clean as effectively as Stewart. At the core of Stewart's success are the cultural values, beliefs, and behaviors that are conducive to her message. We want to live graciously as a culture, and Stewart provides a means to that end.

Stewart also shows how fragile images can be. Stewart built the success of her company, Martha Stewart Living Omnimedia, Inc., around her image as a successful housekeeper and caterer. When she was charged in 2003 with insider trading, her image and the image of her company suffered. The price of her company's shares fell, and Stewart herself faced a barrage of media criticism and comedian jokes. She even faced the threat of a lawsuit from shareholders who claimed that by damaging her personal image, Stewart damaged her company image as well. As a result of the insider trading charges, Stewart began a campaign to repair her image and that of her company. It remains to be seen how effective Stewart can be in fixing the damage done to her image and that of her company.

As you think about Martha Stewart's image, consider these questions:

1. How did you respond to Stewart's image before her legal problems? How do you respond to her image now?

2. How have other persuaders used media, images, language, and culture to create images of themselves?

3. How effective has Stewart been in repairing her image? How effective do you think she can be?

bers (Treadwell & Harrison, 1994). Like the image of a political candidate, images of organizations are perceptions others hold about the organization. Images are more temporary than a related concept: identity. An organization develops its identity through a great deal of thought and research. An organization's image is more transient than its identity and is only somewhat controlled by the organization. Events beyond the control of the organization can influence the organization's image. Yet organizations are concerned with their image and strategically manage the meaning of their image.

An organization's image is different from a brand image. A brand image applies to a particular product or service of the organization. For example, the Chrysler Corporation has an organizational image for its employees, its distributors, and potential car buyers. In addition to promoting its organizational image, Chrysler also promotes the brand images of its car models: Neon, Intrepid, and Dodge Ram pickups. You can think about Neon apart from Chrysler. You can also think of Chrysler apart from Neon.

To better understand how organizations build images, we first examine the idea of organizational image. We then explore how organizations use spokespeople.

ORGANIZATIONAL IMAGE

D. F. Treadwell and Teresa M. Harrison (1994) identify two functions of organizational images. First, images are related to how members and nonmembers think and feel about the organization, as well as to how they respond to the organization. Images influence our perceptions of the organization's character, build loyalty for the organization, and encourage support for the organization's products and services (Treadwell & Harrison, 1994). Images are vital to the financial success of the organization.

Second, images help the organization function on a day-to-day basis because they communicate the organization's knowledge, values, and beliefs. My university promotes the image that it is friendly, small, and familiar. Not only does this image give my university a unique position in its regional market, it instructs its members—faculty, staff, and students—as to what is important on campus and what is not. Respect, caring, and community are all ideas that spring from this image.

Organizations create images formally and informally. Mission statements, training procedures, newsletters, and advertising campaigns are formal methods used to create or modify an image. Organizations also use informal opportunities, such as holiday parties, storytelling, and interpersonal interactions, to foster their image.

When the computer company Dell launched a campaign to improve its image, the campaign had as its goals: to establish Dell as the leading direct distributor of personal computers and to foster relationships with potential customers. Using print, television, and Internet media, Dell used the slogan "Be Direct" to reflect its ability to cut through chains of suppliers to provide computers to its customers. Television ads portrayed a mouse frustrated in its attempt to get to the cheese at the end of a maze. The mouse ignited a bomb that cleared the way to the cheese. A voiceover asked, "What's the best way to deal with obstacles? Eliminate 'em." Print ads—aimed at decision makers responsible for purchasing computers—were used to reinforce this message. The company's website featured the "Be Direct" slogan and logo. The $70 million campaign hoped to make the audience see Dell as effective in cutting through product distribution clutter.

Organizations must be careful to create images that are consistent with their policies and practices. Tobacco companies, for instance, have recently tried to create new images of themselves. Not only has the public failed to accept these new images, but some audience members have argued that the new images are unethical. Think about the ethics of organizational images as you read Ethical Insights: Ethics and Organizational Image.

SPOKESPEOPLE

Institutions are often personified in a spokesperson, who is either a celebrity or an institutional member. Spokespeople are used to generate interest in a new

ETHICAL INSIGHTS

Ethics and Organizational Image

For years, tobacco companies and their spokespeople publicly declared that cigarette smoking was not addictive. They did so to maintain a positive image with lawmakers and the public. The persuasive efforts of the industry to support this claim are ethically questionable. The American Association of Advertising Agencies (1990) charges its members not to create advertising that features "claims insufficiently supported or that distort the true meaning or practicable application of statements made by professional or scientific authority." Likewise the Public Relations Society of America (2000) charges its members to "adhere to the highest standards of accuracy and truth in advancing the interests of those we represent and in communicating with the public." These statements help us to understand the possible ethical lapses of previous smoking advertising campaigns.

In recent years, the tobacco industry—and the persuaders associated with it—have been challenged for this ethical lapse. Numerous lawsuits and a national settlement have caused industry executives to now admit that tobacco is addictive and that their products kill those who smoke them. In fact, the Philip Morris Company has created a website that admits smoking's role in lung cancer, heart disease, emphysema, and other health problems. Philip Morris has also been promoting its support for domestic violence and homeless programs as well as its opposition to youth smoking. The company is attempting to create a new public image for itself.

Yet the new Philip Morris image is just as troublesome for antismoking advocates as is the company's old image. The new image, some critics say, attempts to legitimize the company by presenting it as being concerned with health issues. At the same time, however, the company continues to produce, market, and sell deadly cigarettes. Thus, critics challenge the new image of Philip Morris as being unethical. The National Communication Association (1999) offers this statement to help us think about the ethics of the new Philip Morris campaign: "We accept responsibility for the short- and long-term consequences for our own communication and expect the same of others." The Philip Morris company does not seem to accept the long-term consequences of its persuasive messages; instead, it appears to be concerned only with its image in the short term.

Consider these questions to help you think more about the persuasive efforts of tobacco companies:

1. Do you find Philip Morris's new image ethical or unethical? If so, what guidelines that we have discussed lead you to this conclusion?
2. How can Philip Morris create an ethical public image in light of the products it sells?
3. What role does the persuader's motive play in how we make ethical judgments?

product or to regenerate interest in an established product (Durham, 1997). Spokespeople are also used to appeal to a particular market segment, support an ad campaign, or connect the organization's product or service with a designated "national month" (Durham, 1997). Organizations often use celebrities to speak for their products or services. Celebrities function as persuaders in any number of ways. Deborah Durham (1997) explains that celebrities can be used to draw a large crowd to an event. Celebrities are often media savvy and can represent the organization effectively.

Katie Couric, anchor of NBC's *Today* show, has used her celebrity status to promote public awareness of colon cancer (Figure 9.3). Following her husband's death from the disease, Couric has testified before Congress, spoken about the cancer, and even broadcast footage from her own colonoscopy during a special series on the morning news program. Couric is lending her name to fundraising efforts for a public information and research campaign for colon

Figure 9.3 News Anchor Katie Couric Testifying before Congress about Colon Cancer   What persuasive power do celebrities have for causes such as cancer? What are some limitations facing celebrities who champion such causes?

What advantages do celebrity spokespeople have as a persuasive source? What are some drawbacks to a company's hiring celebrities to sell its product?

cancer. Couric's celebrity status has resulted in a great deal of public attention to the disease and has prompted members of the public to be tested (Jackson, Park, & Thompson, 2000). Celebrities often have a multiplier effect for fundraising efforts for special interests. Couric has joined forces with Lisa Paulsen, CEO of the nonprofit Entertainment Industry Foundation (EIF), to raise money for colon cancer. Paulsen's organization has raised more than $140 million for various charities by organizing the efforts of other celebrities (Jackson et al., 2000). Celebrities who are interested in colon cancer also include actor Dennis Franz, baseball star Eric Davis, and Judge Judy, of television fame.

Audiences often equate an organization with the person who talks to media sources or makes public statements on its behalf. Those who manage the relationship between an organization and its public often must negotiate competing needs and interests. The organization tries to preserve its image, and the news media try to get at the "facts" of the situation, whatever those may be. The news media and press spokespeople often play by a set of unwritten ground rules concerning what can be published or broadcast and what is off limits. When a spokesperson says that a comment is "on the record," for instance, reporters are free to use the comment and attribute it to the source. When a comment is "on background," the reporter must find another source who says the same thing. If a comment is made "off the record," the reporter cannot use it in any way. News leaks—anonymous "tips" given by insiders to news media—both undermine and enhance the spokesperson's role. We'll discuss leaks later in this chapter when we look at anonymous sources.

During much of Clinton's second term, the administration's image was conveyed by its spokesperson Mike McCurry. During his stint as White House spokesperson, McCurry handled the media frenzy surrounding Clinton's impeachment. McCurry's job during this time was difficult because he was often asked questions to which he did not know the answers (Tumulty, 1998). His communication with media sources was often undermined by other White House officials and by Clinton's legal defense team, who wanted to have their voices heard.

Spokespeople such as Couric and McCurry represent an organization, institution, or cause other than themselves. In the next section, we look at how individual persuaders represent themselves to the public.

Individual Persuaders

We see and hear political candidates, and we exchange communication with the salesperson trying to sell us a new car. Our exposure to some individual persuaders is mediated; we communicate with others face-to-face. This section examines the tools individual persuaders use, as well as how audience members can critically evaluate individual persuaders. We first examine a persuader's use of nonverbal communication and then explore the concept of impression management.

NONVERBALS

A key ingredient in a persuader's image is his or her ability to use **nonverbal communication**—eye movement, facial expression, body language. We are constantly exposed to the nonverbal messages of politicians who appear on our televisions, celebrities who appear in print and broadcast advertisements, and colleagues with whom we meet at work. Media give us the opportunity to assess the nonverbal communication of persuaders. The literature on nonverbal communication is extensive. We focus here on those aspects that directly contribute to persuasion.

nonverbal communication conveying information without words—through such methods as eye movement, facial expression, and body language

Researchers have studied *eye movements* for their meanings and persuasive effects. Dale G. Leathers (1997) identifies six persuasive functions of eye movements: attention, persuasion, regulatory, affective, power, and impression management. The attention function describes the ability of eye movement to signal the readiness to communicate and "degree of mutual interest" the two parties in the communication exhibit (p. 54). Length of gaze, direction of gaze, kind of gaze, and pupil size are the key variables that contribute to understanding the attention function. Researchers found that enlarged pupil size indicates that the individual is interested in a stimulus and that he or she is emotionally aroused.

The persuasive function of eye movement relates to the credibility of a source, as determined by his or her eye contact. Looking down, rapidly moving one's eyes, and blinking frequently are indications that the source is not being honest. Direct eye contact, on the other hand, is indicative of honesty and trustworthiness.

The regulatory function of eye movement lets you know when it is your turn to talk in a conversation. The person with whom you are speaking is likely to look away from you when beginning to speak to you and while speaking to you, but to signal that it is your turn to speak, he or she will look at you.

The eyes also display emotions, known as the affective function. Our eyes display our moods and feelings, as well as the intensity of those feelings. In particular, the pupils enlarge as we experience positive emotions.

The eyes also communicate power, status, and personal dominance. This is labeled the power function. Leathers (1997) explains, "The license to stare at others for the purpose of domination is the exclusive prerogative of powerful people" (p. 59). By contrast, individuals who view themselves as weak avert their eye contact from others and often look downward.

Finally, eye contact serves an impression management function. Eye contact is one nonverbal behavior that can be controlled to a certain degree. Effective sources of persuasion monitor their eye behavior to display assertiveness, self-esteem, and communicativeness. Leathers argues that powerful leaders have a "look" that is created, in part, by their eye movements.

Culture affects how we perceive others' nonverbal communication. Shawn Rosenberg, Shulamit Kahn, and Thuy Tran (1991) note, "The guiding theoretical view here is that the rules for the direction and interpretation of nonverbal cues are socially defined" (p. 347). Rosenberg, Kahn, and Tran cite the example of how inner-city African Americans and middle-class Caucasians use eye contact when in conversation. These cultural groups follow certain rules when conversing. African American persuaders look continually at the listener, and African American listeners tend to look away from the persuader most of the time. The opposite is true for Caucasians. Caucasian persuaders look occasionally at the listener, and listeners look continuously at the persuader. Because members of these two cultures have different expectations for nonverbal communication, the two may draw incorrect inferences about the degree of interest the other has in the conversation when they communicate.

The *body* also expresses meaning and contributes to the overall image presented by a persuader. Leathers (1997) examines three dichotomies presented by bodily communication: liking versus nonliking, assertiveness versus nonassertiveness, and power versus powerlessness. He stresses that persuaders usually can control their body movements and should engage in certain behaviors in order to communicate certain ideas. Thus, body movement is one element of nonverbal communication that individuals can monitor.

Just as persuaders can foster emotional connections with their audience through their eyes, they can do so through bodily communication. Leathers (1997) explains that *positive nonverbal indicators of liking* express interest in another person. These indicators include a forward-leaning posture, body and head orientations that directly face the other person, open-body positions, affirmative head nods, close interpersonal distances, smiling, and assuming a posture that is similar to the other person's. Leathers (1997) warns, however, that overuse of positive indicators of liking may actually promote dislike. On the other hand, *nonverbal indicators of disliking* include a relative absence of gestures, bodily rigidity, closed body posture, assuming postures different than the other person's, and bodily tension (Leathers, 1997).

Audiences can also detect a persuader's degree of assertiveness. We have previously discussed that credibility requires assertiveness. Thus, assertiveness is a characteristic that contributes to a source's persuasiveness. Leathers (1997) reports that *positive nonverbal indicators of assertiveness* include consistency in verbal and nonverbal messages, relaxed gestures and postures, emphasizing key words and phrases with vocal inflection and illustrator gestures, and touching, if appropriate. *Nonverbal indicators of nonassertiveness* include hand wringing and lip licking, hunching the shoulders, covering the mouth with the hand, frequent throat clearing, and rigid body posture.

Power cues refer to the use of the body to indicate power, status, or dominance. *Positive nonverbal indicators of perceived power* include relaxed posture, erect rather than slumped posture, dynamic and purposeful gestures, and the option to approach another person closely (Leathers, 1997). *Nonverbal indicators of powerlessness* include body tension, arriving early for parties, sitting in the 11 o'clock position at a conference table, not exposing the soles of your shoes, and assuming closed postures (Leathers, 1997).

Personal appearance communicates a great deal to others. In the media age, when we see only brief glimpses of persuasive sources, we quickly make judgments about the credibility of persuaders based on their appearance. Our society, claims Leathers (1997), buys into a stereotype that says attractiveness implies goodness, talent, and success. Rosenberg, Kahn, and Tran (1991) explain that we generalize about a person's personality based on his or her physical appearance. We unconsciously associate certain behaviors with certain physical attributes. For example, we think that babies are weak and defenseless. Rosenberg, Kahn, and Tran argue that when adults possess a baby-faced appearance, we see them as honest, trustworthy, and sincere. Leathers explains that in addition to cultural stereotypes about beauty, how we feel about ourselves contributes to our self-image, which influences much of how we communicate. We often inflate our image of ourselves so as to approximate the cultural ideal and prevent crises in self-image.

Leathers (1997) outlines several aspects of physical appearance that relate to these intricate interactions between attractiveness, self-image, and the image others have of us. First, facial attractiveness has been the subject of numerous medical and sociologial studies. Leathers explains that plastic surgeons have adopted a standard for facial beauty that closely reflects the standard society uses to judge attractiveness. The surgeons' standard defines a proportional relationship of the forehead, nose, lips, and chin.

Persuaders can use several methods to modify their personal appearance. Most significantly, a person can have plastic surgery performed to change his or her appearance. Our popular culture is filled with examples of movie stars and other celebrities who elect to modify their attractiveness through plastic surgery. Less drastic measures are also available. Leathers (1997) explains that individuals can use various artifacts to change their appearance, such as clothing, hairstyle, contact lenses, or jewelry. Clothing can be used to make an individual more powerful or less intimidating, depending on the situation. People also change their hairstyle to emphasize or hide some part of their physical appearance. Wearing jewelry or contact lenses can make individuals appear more attractive to others.

Rosenberg, Kahn, and Tran (1991) were interested in what specific features of a female politician's physical appearance contributed to a higher degree of credibility. Their study isolated several such characteristics. Voters see faces that have these attributes as more credible: almond-shaped eyes or eyes that have a greater curvature at the top than at the bottom; a hairline that comes to a sharp widow's peak; hair that is combed back or that has a side part; short hair; and a face that is broad or normal. Older women, such as former Texas governor Ann Richards or Senator Elizabeth Dole, were seen as being more politically appealing than younger women. Formal, conservative dress was important. Necklaces and earrings created a more positive impression than no jewelry at all. The background of the image was also important. Studio shots were seen as more persuasive than those in an indoor setting such as an office or a library. A second study by these researchers found that a woman's image can be manipulated to her advantage in political campaigns.

DELIVERY

In Chapter 7, we discussed how television and electronic media have brought persuasion to the living rooms of audience members. Besides influencing the discursive style of the persuader—the words the persuader uses—the intimate setting of mediated persuasion calls for a different style of delivery as well. Eloquent persuaders today use a conversational style of communicating to their audience (Jamieson, 1988). Robert James Branham and W. Barnett Pearce (1996) define the conversational style by saying it is a strategic choice made by the persuader to (re)construct an apparent relationship with an audience. Conversational speakers often go without a scripted speech, instead using an outline as the basis for their speech. An outline allows the speaker to react to the audience and modify the wording as needed to fit the moment. Conversational speakers also vary the tone, rate, and pitch of their delivery. With amplification technology, speakers do not have to project their voice in an unnatural manner, sounding forceful, as they did in the past (Jamieson, 1988). Which qualities of conversational delivery did President Bush display when he spoke at Ground Zero in September 2001? See Figure 9.4.

IMPRESSION MANAGEMENT

impression management

our conscious attempt to control how others perceive us

The study of such concepts as nonverbals, delivery, and characteristics of language is often called impression management. Leathers (1997) defines **impression management** as "an individual's conscious attempt to exercise conscious control over selected communicative behaviors and cues—particularly nonverbal cues—for purposes of making a desired impression" (p. 193). Erving Goffman (1959) explains that individuals seek to define situations in ways that benefit them and that they consciously seek to manipulate those situations by altering their manners of interaction. Impression management is predicated on the assumption that individuals can monitor certain verbal and nonverbal behaviors and consciously enact those behaviors that will form the best image of them in another's mind. In other words, we are aware of the effect that our behavior has on other people (Bromley, 1993). The dominance of media in bringing pictures of persuaders to us makes it important that we study

Figure 9.4 President Bush Speaks at Ground Zero How was Bush's speech interactive? What was the impact of speaking without notes on this occasion?

how individual persuaders use impression management to manipulate how we respond to them.

Goffman (1959) explains that persuaders often put up a front, which is "all the activity of an individual which occurs during a period marked by his continuous presence before a particular set of observers and which has some influence on the observers" (p. 22). Persuaders reveal cues about their social status to the audience as well as suggest how the audience should react to them. We might also think of impression management as a role that the persuader plays, much like the role that an actor or actress plays in the theater. Goffman explains that the impressions formed by persuaders are very fragile and that they can be "shattered by very minor mishaps" (p. 56). Persuaders thus seek to manipulate their front by faithfully fulfilling the obligations of some role. When persuaders act faithfully, we afford them credibility and identify with them.

In the media age, we can also make use of Goffman's concept of *backstage*, which is usually hidden from the audience's view. Frontstage is the conscious activity of an individual when attempting to influence others. Backstage is what we often do not see; it is the natural state of the individual. However, media bring the backstage of public figures to us. We see our presidents eating at fast-food restaurants, jogging, or interacting with their families. Today, then, persuaders must also control those elements of their activity that in the past were considered private. The blurring of the line between frontstage and backstage, public and private, has sparked a great deal of discussion today.

To faithfully negotiate the demands of impression management, persuaders make use of image consultants, who help them understand the role they are to play as well as adapt to that role. Image consultants work with persuaders to help them create a favorable image. Although image consultants are sometimes effective in shaping how audiences respond to persuaders, impression management can have contrary effects if the audience perceives the image as insincere (Bromley, 1993).

D. B. Bromley (1993) warns that impression management raises ethical issues. In particular, he is concerned with how individuals can manipulate their image for immoral purposes, such as lying. Because we do not interact directly with persuaders, we have no way to test whether they are sincere or are merely creating a favorable front. The media have hindered our ability to accurately judge a persuader's persona.

Image Repair

There are times when a person or a company must repair its image. For example, President Clinton was forced to repair his image on numerous occasions, following allegations of extramarital affairs, illegal fund-raising, and controversial pardons. Companies, too, must often repair their image. We look at two examples of image repair in this section. The first case involves the fruit juice company Odwalla. In 1996, its company's product was linked to the death of a 16-month-old Colorado infant and to the illness of more than 60 people in several states. The cause of this food poisoning outbreak was that Odwalla does not use heat to pasteurize its products; thus, it does not kill any *E. coli* bacteria that might contaminate its products. We also look at how Queen Elizabeth II of Great Britain used image repair strategies to bolster her public image following the death of Princess Diana.

William Benoit (1995) outlines three image repair strategies that people or companies can use to defend themselves against persuasive attacks. Two strategies can be used to *deflect* charges of responsibility: denial and evasion of responsibility. Two strategies can be used to *minimize* the attack: reduction of the offensiveness of the act and corrective action. The accused may also engage in *mortification*, which acknowledges "the wrongful act and asks for forgiveness" (p. 90). Table 9.1 summarizes these strategies.

Denial can be accomplished through simple denial or by shifting blame. Simple denial involves denying that the act occurred, denying that one was responsible for it, or denying that the act was harmful. A second strategy places the blame for the act on someone else. Refer to our discussion of Kenneth Burke's theory of tragic redemption (Chapter 7) for more information on using blame shifting.

Evasion of responsibility occurs through one of four methods. First, the accused can use the provocation defense, arguing that the offense was simply a response to "some provocation" and that the accused is therefore not responsi-

Table 9.1 Benoit's Image Repair Strategies

Deflect charges	Minimize the attack	Mortification
Denial	*Reduce offensiveness*	Mortification
Simple denial	Bolstering	
Blame shifting	Minimization	
Evasion	Differentiation	
Provocation	Transcendence	
Defeasibility	Counterattack	
Accident	Compensation	
Something good	*Corrective action*	

From Benoit (1995, pp. 90-92).

ble for the act. The accused might evade responsibility by citing defeasibility—claiming to "have lacked information about or control over important elements in the situation that caused the offensive act." Third, the accused can claim the offensive act was an accident, something he or she had no control over. Fourth, the accused can claim that the offensive act occurred while he or she was trying to do something good. Thus, the consequences were "unforeseen and unintended" (Benoit, 1995, p. 91).

Reduction of offensiveness strategies are used to argue that the action was not as bad as the accuser suggests. Six strategies can be used. First, bolstering attempts to "strengthen the audience's positive affect for the accused, thereby offsetting the negative feelings resulting from the wrongful act" (Benoit, 1995, p. 91). Second, minimization seeks to reduce the audience's negative impression of the offensive act. In essence, the accused argues that the act was not as bad as it is being made out to be. Third, differentiation can be used to show that the action was not as bad as other similar actions. Fourth, the accused can attempt transcendence, recontextualizing the act to show that higher values were at stake. Fifth, counterattack can be used to "assault the credibility of the accuser" (p. 91). Sixth, the accused can compensate the victim for monetary or other damages. *Corrective action* involves promising "either to repair the damage caused by an offensive act or to prevent recurrence of the offensive act or both" (Benoit, 1995, p. 92).

Mortification requires accepting responsibility for the action and asking for forgiveness. Benoit writes that if the public believes the apology is sincere, they may forgive the wrongdoing and seek no penalty.

Using these strategies successfully requires several elements. The accused company or individual can use a highly visible spokesperson to help the public identify with it. Audience members often refuse to accept dissonant information if they connect with the source that is refuting the information. It is also important for the accused to substantiate its denial with evidence. Denial can be a powerful persuasive strategy when those who are accused can document that they are not at fault. Publicizing plans to keep the problem from recurring is critical. However, using multiple repair strategies that are at odds with one another can be counterproductive.

In light of Benoit's theory, we can now see how the Odwalla Fruit Juice Company effectively repaired its image following instances of *E. coli* poisoning. Steven R. Thomsen and Bret Rawson (1998) explain that Odwalla initially used *quick corrective action* by recalling its products from 4,600 retail outlets. The recall helped consumers perceive Odwalla as a company concerned with health, not profits.

Odwalla next used *evasion of responsibility* arguments to show that its products and procedures met government standards for safety and were made using state-of-the-art production technology (Thomsen & Rawson, 1998). Through news conferences and an Internet website, Odwalla communicated to its customers. The company also used *bolstering* to spread the blame to apple growers, who may have been responsible for the *E. coli* contamination. When investigators uncovered that both the growers and Odwalla were to blame for the outbreak, Odwalla returned to its *corrective action* strategy. It developed a new method of treating apple juice—flash pasteurizing—that removes bacteria, but maintains nutrients. The use of image repair strategies saved Odwalla (Thomsen & Rawson, 1998). Check the website for this book for a link to Odwalla to learn more about its image creation strategies.

Benoit and Susan L. Brinson (1999) used Benoit's image restoration framework to study the response to Britain's Queen Elizabeth II's attempt to restore her good name following complaints that she was indifferent to the people who mourned British Princess Diana's death in 1997. Benoit and Brinson argue that the Queen used four image restoration strategies in a speech to the British people: denial, bolstering, defeasibility, and transcendence. Simply by giving the speech, the Queen *denied* that she did not care about Diana's death. Because the speech was unprecedented, the very act of speaking was itself a powerful persuasive strategy. Throughout the speech, the Queen asserted in forceful terms that the royal family was saddened by the death of an "exceptional and gifted human being."

Analyze a recent organizational crisis or political scandal. How did the source engage in image repair? Which of Benoit's strategies were used? Did the source effectively use image repair strategies? Why or why not?

The Queen also used *bolstering* to strengthen her image with her subjects. She appealed to them as a "Queen and as a grandmother." She spoke "from her heart." She also thanked the British people for their support during the weekend of the automobile accident. The Queen explained her initial lack of response by using the strategy of *defeasibility*. She explained that it was not easy to express the feelings of the royal family when they learned about Diana's death. The Queen also used *transcendence* by arguing that the tragedy was allowing the British people to show the world a united nation. By using this strategy, the Queen was attempting to persuade her audience to band together and end their criticism of the royal family. By using a carefully crafted strategy, based on the elements identified by Benoit, persuaders as diverse as the Queen of England and the Odwalla Fruit Juice Company can restore their credibility.

Covert Persuasion: Propaganda

Our discussion to this point has been predicated on the fact that we know, institutionally or interpersonally, who is persuading us. However, we often do *not*

know the source of a persuasive message. For some reason, the source wishes
to remain hidden or disappears into the web of influence that surrounds us.
Researchers contend that the presence of anonymous sources is one indicator
of propaganda. **Propaganda** is defined as an attempt to persuade without
seeming to do so (Sproule, 1994). Propaganda is usually seen as a type of persuasion that has negative consequences for society. J. Michael Sproule explains
that propaganda is a covert, massive attempt to use "tricky symbols" to pursue
special interests that may be contrary to the wider public good. We focus here
on the "covert" aspect of Sproule's definition of propaganda. Let's examine
how persuaders remain hidden while exerting a powerful influence on society.

propaganda
an attempt to persuade
without seeming to
do so

ENTERTAINMENT MEDIA

Persuasion is commonly carried out by anonymous sources in the entertainment media. Entertainment programming often hides the identities of those
who are behind the messages that are presented. The Clinton administration
used entertainment programming as a vehicle for antidrug messages ("Networks Given," 2000). In an agreement between the Office of National Drug
Control Policy and the television networks, the networks were offered financial
incentives to incorporate antidrug messages in their programs. Although the
Drug Control Policy office did not actually write scripts, it reviewed scripts for
shows such as *ER, Beverly Hills 90210,* and *Chicago Hope* and suggested
changes. The networks insisted that the Drug Control Policy office was not exerting creative control over programs, but media experts question the appearance of such a policy. From a persuasion perspective, the policy raises questions
about anonymous sources and propaganda.

Producers of the movie *Password* used covert sources to promote their film.
The independent movie, directed by Ogi Ogas, is the story of a graduate student obsessed with "password theory." The theory states that beings on another planet have technological skills superior to those of humans and are
waiting for humans to achieve some kind of significant event, such as world
peace, before making contact with us. Password theory, however, is pure fiction. There is no such theory. Yet, to promote the movie, its producers created
Web pages for fake scientists throughout the world, listing "password theory"
as a research interest in order to make the theory appear to be true. These fake
Web pages were posted on actual university sites to make them appear genuine. The point is that the movie's producers masked their identity in a marketing effort for the movie. The independent movie appears to be based on a real
concept, and its audiences have forgotten, or won't know, who started the idea
that the theory is true.

NEWS MEDIA

Persuaders also take the form of anonymous news sources and news leaks.
Quite often, journalists interview persuaders who wish to remain anonymous.
Most often, the journalist corroborates the persuader's information with other
sources, who may also wish to remain anonymous. The result is a story that

cites "anonymous sources" instead of named sources. Editors claim that protecting the identity of sources is the only way to acquire publishable information about important events (Childs, 1998). However, even after multiple checks of information, reporters can get the story wrong (Cranberg, 1999).

leak

a statement made by a persuader to attract the attention of the media

Leaks are statements made by persuaders to attract the attention of media. Leaks are used for a variety of reasons. In some cases, persuaders use leaks to test certain ideas with the public. In this situation, a persuader tells a reporter some information, and the reporter prints or broadcasts the idea. The persuader monitors the reaction the information receives and decides whether to acknowledge that the information is true or to denounce it as false. Leaks can also be used to undermine one's opponents. By providing negative information to journalists about an opponent, a persuader can damage the opponent's credibility. Leaks are also used to give one media outlet an advantage over its competitors. Because reporter and source depend on each other for information, sources may, at times, provide information to reporters to win favor with them. As in the case of anonymous sources, it is difficult for audience members to determine the validity of a leaked statement because it is not attributed to a source. As you read the newspaper or watch the news, look for anonymous sources and view what they say with some healthy skepticism.

What examples of covert persuasion have you observed recently? Who was the source? How was the source obscured? How was the nature of the message obscured?

Summary

Aristotle believed that who the persuader is can cause audiences to be persuaded. He called this element of persuasion ethos, which is comprised of wisdom, virtue, and goodwill. A related concept is source credibility, which includes attributes of safety, qualification, and dynamism. In the media age, we often do not have exact information about the source to consider, so we form an image of the source.

Boulding writes that *image* is another word for *knowledge* (1956, p. 6). An image is comprised of the verbal and visual symbols used by people or organizations. Images are synthetic, or planned. Given the persuasive appeal of images, persuaders use careful strategies to create images that will help them sell their products or ideas. Bennett identifies three aspects of creating an image: message composition, message salience, and message credibility. Images are also believable, vivid and concrete, simplified, and ambiguous. At the same, the connection between source and image must be clear or the image will fail to accomplish its persuasive goal. Images have cognitive, emotional, and behavioral effects on audiences.

We form images of organizations—often through celebrities—and of people, such as political candidates. When the images of organizations and individuals are damaged, persuaders use repair tactics to restore their name. In some cases, we do not know the source of a persuasive message. In the entertainment and news media, persuaders often obscure their identity when they communicate with us.

Key Terms

Visit the book's website at http://www.mhhe.com/borchers2 for multiple-choice quizzes, Internet activities, and key terms flashcards.

WWW:

source credibility 246

image 248

nonverbal communication 261

impression management 264

propaganda 269

leak 270

10

The Reasoning Process

Learning Objectives

After reading this chapter, you should be able to:

1. Identify characteristics of reasoning in the media age.

2. Describe the components of Toulmin's model of reasoning and apply them to contemporary arguments.

3. Understand the concept of narratives and how to evaluate narratives as reasoning.

4. Identify tests of reasoning and use them to evaluate arguments.

A number of media images captured the recent war with Iraq. The nation was captivated by live television images of U.S. troops storming through the Iraqi desert on their way to Baghdad. Images of POW Jessica Lynch's rescue inspired Americans and transformed Lynch into a hero. Photographs of Saddam Hussein's statue being toppled in several Iraqi cities (Figure 10.1) seemed to prove that Hussein's regime was finished. The Iraqi war will no doubt be remembered through the lens of the cameras that captured many of its events.

In the media age, photographs and other visual images are powerful ways of making arguments. For some audience members, images of Hussein's statues falling amidst throngs of celebrating Iraqis seemed to prove that the war was justified and that Iraq would be a better country without its previous leader. However, not all were persuaded by the images. In fact, pictures of Saddam's fall told only part of the story. While it appeared from media coverage that thousands of people witnessed or helped with the statue's demise in Baghdad, only a few hundred were actually on the scene. Additionally, it was difficult to

**Figure 10.1
Saddam Hussein's
Statue Falls in Iraq
in April 2003**
What arguments does
this image present?
What arguments does
it not present?

tell from the pictures who instigated the statue's fall: U.S. troops or Iraqi citizens. Despite the limitations of visual images as arguments, we are often persuaded by what we see.

An attitude, you'll remember, is comprised of cognitive, affective, and behavioral information. In this chapter, we examine the ways persuaders present cognitive information to audiences. Cognitive information often takes the form of a belief, which is an idea we have about what is true and false. We base our beliefs on evidence and **reasoning,** which makes a rational link between the evidence and the conclusion, or belief (Warnick & Inch, 1994). Reasoning is one way that persuaders give value to their products, services, or ideas. To better explore how persuaders reason with audiences, we discuss reasoning in the media age, two models of reasoning, and ways to evaluate reasoning.

reasoning
a systematic procedure
used to generalize from
specific data; the link
between evidence and
claim

Reasoning in the Media Age

Reasoning in the media age bears little resemblance to the reasoning of years past. Jamieson (1988) argues that in political discourse, traditional reasoning has been "replaced" by staged dramatization of images. We'll find her observation to be true in a variety of other contexts as well. Let's examine two aspects of reasoning today. First, persuaders today typically make assertions, rather than present research to support their claim. Roger Aden (1994) argues that persuaders today rely on the audience to possess a great deal of information about their topic because they typically do not present evidence. Think about a symbol such as the Nike swoosh logo that we discussed in Chapter 6. The logo makes a wide range of assertions: "Nike is cool," "Nike is worn by successful athletes," and "Nike can make you successful." Each of these claims exists without evidence to support it, yet we accept the claims made by the symbol as reasons to purchase Nike products. Jamieson (1988) notes that political candidates, too, seldom present evidence, instead relying on assertions to support their point. We discuss the implication of this reliance on assertion further in the next section.

When persuaders do offer proof, they tend to use dramatic and visual examples. Proof may take the form of an image, which we discussed in Chapter 6. In addition, many of the visual images used as evidence are staged to be dramatic. Persuaders also use synecdoche—which we discussed in Chapter 7—to represent their arguments and fail to provide audiences with complete argumentative proofs. Also, recall our discussion of pseudoevents, which only pretend to be real but which we are encouraged to accept as true and valid. Keep each of these substitutes in mind as we examine reasoning in the media age.

Toulmin's Model of Reasoning

Traditionally, reasoning has been examined from a formal argumentation perspective. Although arguments today do not necessarily follow a prescriptive model, knowledge of that ideal will help us better understand reasoning in the media age. Knowing what is missing from a persuader's argument will also help us to better evaluate a persuader's reasoning. In this section, we study a model of reasoning developed by Stephen Toulmin. As we discuss Toulmin's model, we also examine how media influence the various components of his model. Toulmin's model is outlined in Figure 10.2. Refer to this model as we discuss Toulmin's theory of argument. The components of Toulmin's model include:

1. Data
2. Warrant
3. Claim
4. Backing
5. Qualifiers
6. Rebuttal

CLAIMS

claim
a statement that communicates a persuader's message to an audience

Reasoning is concerned with making claims. A **claim** is a statement that communicates a persuader's message to an audience. In the media age, persuaders usually, but not always, state the claim. A politician's assertion that his or her economic policy will work because it expands markets abroad is an example of a stated claim. An advertiser who says its products garner high customer loyalty ratings is also stating a claim. In some instances, however, persuaders do not explicitly state their claim; instead, the persuader's message simply implies it. The Nike swoosh, for example, makes many unstated claims. A television

Figure 10.2 Toulmin's Model of Reasoning

Adapted from Toulmin, "Uses of Reasoning," (1958, p. 105)

program like *ER* presents ideas that audience members accept as true—such as that drug abuse harms families—without explicitly stating them. No matter if they are stated or implied, claims involve two related concepts: content and form. A claim has persuasive force because of the content (the data) that supports it as well as the form that makes it possible to move from the data to the claim. Toulmin calls the form of an argument its warrant.

Music videos are a vibrant source of argumentative claims, assert Gregg B. Walker and Melinda A. Bender (1994). Music videos contain salient social and political messages, and viewers see music videos as attempts by persuaders to gain their adherence to a particular point of view. Claims—although not explicitly stated—are expressed through the visual and lyrical cues of music videos. Walker and Bender found that rap music videos were among the most persuasive. Rap music communicates sociopolitical messages to its audience. Walker and Bender even contend that viewers act based on the messages contained in music videos. Michael Jackson's "Man in the Mirror" video reportedly moved its viewers to donate to charity, be less complacent, and express more concern for the homeless (Walker & Bender, 1994). Walker and Bender's study provides evidence that for some videos, viewers are engaged decision makers evaluating the persuasive reasons offered by musicians.

Claims can be absurd or ironic. Consider as an example a series of commercials for Petsmart.com. The claim at the end of the commercial states, "Petsmart.com. Because pets can't drive." The stated claim is absurd because although pets can't drive, they can't order from the Internet either. Yet this is the only claim that is stated in the commercial. An E★Trade.com commercial, with the dancing monkey and two men sitting in a garage, cost nearly $2 million to air because it was shown during the 2000 Super Bowl. The commercial made no attempt to show how the company could help investors achieve higher returns on their investments. Instead, the claim stated at the end was "We just wasted $2 million. What are you doing with your money today?" Normally, one would not invest with a company that openly admitted "wasting" money. Yet many viewers declared the commercial to be the best of those aired during the 2000 Super Bowl.

Michael G. Cruz (1998) found that when persuaders state their claims explicitly, audience members better comprehend their message. When they understand the message, audience members believe the persuader holds a more extreme position on the subject, which, Cruz argues, leads to more attitude change. Thus, the more explicit the persuader's claim, the greater the attitude change. Cruz explains that when the source's position is clear, as it often is in advertising, implicit messages may also produce attitude change. We might conclude, then, that the implicit claims so often offered by persuaders in the media age may lead to uncertainty about the nature of the message. On the other hand, because we have such a readily available supply of cultural knowledge and are familiar with advertising, political campaign speeches, and the like, implicit claims may suffice to produce attitude change today.

DATA

data
the "facts" from which persuaders make claims

There must be some basis, or **data,** for persuasive reasoning. Data serve as the "facts" from which persuaders make claims. Some data are obtained by observing our culture's beliefs, knowledge, and values, as we discussed in Chapter 8. Other types of data are obtained through systematic research and study. George Ziegelmueller and Jack Kay (1997) distinguish between the two types of data available to persuaders: premises and evidence. Audiences accept premises without external support, whereas evidence requires the support of some external source.

premise
a belief one has about one's world

Premises   Beliefs that audience members have about their world are expressed as **premises.** The statement "The earth is a sphere" is an example of a premise. Likewise, "People are inherently good" is a premise. Premises are statements that reflect what Rokeach termed beliefs. Whether they reflect primitive beliefs or derived beliefs, premises are statements that an individual believes to be true. Discussion of premises thus becomes as much a discussion about audience analysis (see Chapter 5) as one about reasoning.

You may not think that an assumption held by an individual audience member is a good basis for persuasion. After all, people can be mistaken, and many premises cannot be verified. For example, the premise "People are inherently good" cannot be proved with any degree of certainty. Aden (1994) explains that in the media age, audience members have knowledge of a great number of premises, and we use these premises to form judgments about persuaders and their statements. Recall from Chapter 8 that our culture is an important source of shared beliefs, values, and behaviors that form the basis for our reasoning. Persuaders, as we discussed in Chapter 5, seek to understand their audience's beliefs and values, which include their premises. As audience members, understanding the idea of premises can help us more critically evaluate the reasoning process.

Discuss with your classmates some premises they believe by addressing these questions: What are some perceptual premises about your campus? What are some value premises shared on your campus? Do members of your class have any beliefs in common?

Ziegelmueller and Kay (1997) describe two types of premises: perceptual premises and value premises. *Perceptual premises* are statements about the nature of the world and objects in the world. They include such statements as "The earth is a sphere" or "Water coming from a faucet labeled 'H' is hot." Perceptual premises usually stem from authority or derived beliefs, according to Rokeach's classification. We learn perceptual premises based on our experiences with objects, people, and events in the world. *Value premises* concern the worth of something. This statement expresses a value premise: "The quality of life is more important than the length of life." Value premises are usually reflections of Rokeach's primitive beliefs. We learn value premises at an early age, and they are central to our belief system. Value premises are not easily changed and have great force in how we respond to persuasive messages.

Evidence   The second category of data involved in reasoning is evidence. Whereas premises are beliefs held by an audience, **evidence** is data gathered from sources external to the audience and offered in support of a claim. Discovering evidence differs from identifying premises which reflect the beliefs of audience members. Persuaders who seek to discover evidence focus on actual events or scientific studies to support their claims. Persuaders who are speaking to an audience that does not agree with them often use evidence to counter the premises held by the audience. Evidence can also be used to validate the audience's premise.

> **evidence**
> data gathered from sources external to the audience and offered in support of a claim; there are three types: examples, statistics, and testimony

Keep in mind that in the media age, evidence is often suppressed. Jamieson (1988) argues that because the medium of television—which we have argued is the dominant medium today—reduces the persuader's message to an "abstract clip," persuaders do not bother to present carefully developed arguments that use evidence. When advertisers have only 30 seconds to get the audience's attention and offer a claim, they do not have time to provide a great deal of evidence in support of that claim. Recall Postman's assertion that we do not value the use of evidence; we are persuaded by flashy theatrics instead. For these reasons, persuaders forgo the use of evidence, substituting a short, visual, affective claim. It is important for us to examine what is being discussed so that we can be more critical consumers of persuasion.

We will discuss three types of evidence: examples, statistics, and testimony. Examples and statistics are called factual evidence because they are potentially verifiable. The third type of evidence—testimony—uses expert insight to interpret examples and statistics.

Examples   Descriptions of actual or hypothetical cases, events, or situations are called **examples.** Persuaders use examples to put a human face on a situation, to dramatize a situation, or to reduce a complex situation to an easily understood image. In these ways, examples allow persuaders to personalize ideas.

> **example**
> a description of an actual or hypothetical case, event, or situation

In his February 27, 2001, address to Congress, President Bush used the example of a family from Pennsylvania who would benefit from his tax cut plan. He said:

> With us tonight representing many American families are Steven and Josefina Ramos. They are from Pennsylvania. But they could be from any one of your districts. Steven is the network administrator for a school district. Josefina is a Spanish teacher at a charter school. And they have a two-year-old daughter. Steven and Josefina tell me they pay almost $8,000 a year in federal income taxes. My plan will save them more than $2,000. Let me tell you what Steven says: "Two thousand dollars a year means a lot to my family. If we had this money, it would help us reach our goal of paying off our personal debt in two years' time." After that, Steven and Josefina want to start saving for Lianna's college education.

Bush's use of the Ramos family's experience put a human face on the issue of tax cuts and budgets. Persuaders typically use examples to create similar effects. As you evaluate a persuader's use of examples, keep in mind that they should be typical of the situation that they represent and they should not be taken out of context. Images—in particular, photographs—often serve as persuasive examples. As we have discussed, a photograph is proof that something happened, although it does not tell the whole story.

statistics
calculated values that represent some characteristic of data; also, the techniques and theories of data analysis

Statistics   Another form of factual evidence is statistics. **Statistics** is a field of science concerned with theories and techniques of data analysis. We typically use the word *statistic* to refer to the calculated value that represents some characteristics of data (Frey et al., 1991). We will discuss two types of statistics: descriptive and inferential. *Descriptive statistics* organize and summarize "information about a collection of actual observations" (Witte, 1993, p. 4). *Inferential statistics* generalize "beyond actual observations" (Witte, 1993, p. 5). Most statistics are based on a small sample of subjects from a larger population. When a persuader conducts a survey to test public attitudes toward a product, the polling company does not ask the opinion of everyone in the population. Instead, a small sample is questioned, and from their answers, inferences are made for the entire population. There are a variety of statistics; we will limit our discussion to the types most commonly used in persuasion. Each of these statistics can be expressed with words or as images, such as charts or graphs, in a multimedia presentation.

We will discuss three descriptive statistics: frequency distributions, measures of central tendency, and correlations. One of the most basic descriptive statistics, a *frequency distribution,* sorts observations into classes by showing their frequency of occurrence within each class (Witte, 1993). In Table 10.1, you'll see a frequency distribution that expresses the voting preferences of members of several political parties for a particular candidate. A *relative frequency distribution* expresses the responses in each class as a proportion of the total frequency, or sample. A relative frequency distribution is usually expressed as a percentage. From Table 10.1, the percentage of Republicans in the sample favoring Candidate Smith is 50.4 percent; Reform, 24.3 percent; Democrats, 20.8 percent; and Green, 4.5 percent. You'll note that this sample contained only 601 voters: use of a small sample is common in voter polls. From this sample, conclusions about the general population are reached.

A second group of statistics is *measures of central tendency,* which refers to mean, median, and mode. You may have heard all of these terms referred to as an "average." The word *average* is a tricky word that doesn't tell an audience member much, unless the specific type of average is stated (Huff, 1954). Suppose the life span of seven sample refrigerators made by the same company is 1, 2, 2, 3, 5, 8, and 9 years. Each of the measures of central tendency could be used to provide information about the "average" life span of this brand of refrigerator. The *mean* is calculated by adding together all the values in the data set and dividing by the number of values. In this case, the mean would be 4.28 years. The *median* is the score that appears at the midpoint of a list of numbers arranged in order. In this case, 3 years is the median. The *mode* is the number that occurs most often; in this case, the mode is 2 years. Which figure would the company claim is the "average" life span of this refrigerator? Chances are the company would claim the average life span is 4.28 years, the arithmetic mean. Yet each of the other measures is also considered an average.

Another type of statistic, a *correlation,* measures the relationship between two variables. If two variables are found—through statistical analysis—to co-

Table 10.1 Public Opinion Poll: Frequency and Relative Frequency Distributions of Voter Preferences for Candidate Smith

Party	Frequency	Relative frequency (%)
Republican	303	50.4
Reform	146	24.3
Democratic	125	20.8
Green	27	4.5

incide with each other, either positively or negatively, the presence of one allows us to predict with some degree of certainty that the other will or will not soon follow. In other words, correlations help us to predict, but they do *not* specify a cause-effect relationship between two variables. Medical studies often make use of correlations. A 2000 study in the medical journal *Neurology,* for example, found that both moderate head injury and severe head injury were correlated with an increased risk of Alzheimer's disease (Plassman et al., 2000). The study cannot say, however, that head injuries cause Alzheimer's.

Finally, we discuss a group of inferential statistics designed to *test hypotheses.* These tests determine if differences between two samples are due to chance or some other factor. Hypothesis tests include *t* tests, ANOVAs, and MANOVAs. All of these tests compare test groups with control groups to determine if a variable administered to the test group produces significantly different results from those for the control group. Many health studies use these tests to determine if a drug is achieving its anticipated results. By using an experimental group, which takes the drug, and a control group, which is usually given a placebo, researchers can determine if differences in the outcomes between the two groups are due to chance or to the drug in question. The pharmaceutical company can then use this statistic to persuade the government and consumers that the drug is worth their money. Although we put our trust in statistics as a form of proof, persuaders often use statistics to mislead us or to obscure more important ideas.

Boster et al. (2000) found that the use of statistics "has a direct impact on judgments, and an indirect effect on attitudes" (p. 303). When statistics are used along with examples and they are consistent with each other, the persuasive effect is greater than when examples are used alone. When examples and statistics contradict each other, audience members are more likely to believe the statistical information than the examples (Boster et al., 2000). However, Boster points out that the audience's preconceived ideas about a topic may be more influential than either statistical or example evidence, or both used together. He observes, "Although these messages were effective, and although the evidence induction produced the anticipated results, participants were not *completely* convinced either by the statistics, the exemplars, or both" (p. 303). However, statistics have stronger persuasive effect than examples in situations where the audience is either positive, negative, or neutral toward the topic. Boster's study confirms that statistics have a strong persuasive pull on audience members in our culture.

testimony
a statement about a given topic; can be factual or expert

Testimony   A statement about a given topic is called **testimony.** There are two types of testimony: factual and expert. A statement given by a witness in a court of law is *factual testimony* if it simply provides information about the case. A witness to a car accident, for instance, can provide information about the cars involved and the directions in which they were traveling. A photographer present at a crime scene can relate what he or she observed.

Expert testimony interprets examples or statistics, providing meaning for them. It is important to make the distinction between lay and expert testimony. The witness in the previous paragraph usually cannot interpret the facts of the accident unless he or she is specially trained. The witness can describe the cars, for instance, but cannot indicate the cause of the accident. A police officer may be an expert if he or she has the training to interpret the skid marks, for instance, or to estimate how fast the vehicles were traveling. Thus, testimony is valid as interpretation if it comes from an expert.

Find an advertisement in a magazine. What premises does the ad assume that its readers believe? What evidence does the ad present? From your experience, are advertisements more likely to draw upon premises the audience believes, or do advertisements present the audience with evidence from which to reason?

Forensic pathologist Dr. Joseph Cohen's testimony in the 2000 murder trial of the four New York police officers accused of killing Amadou Diallo is a good example of expert testimony. Cohen told jurors that Diallo was either falling or already down when officers continued to shoot him. Cohen explained that Diallo's wounds revealed that the officers' bullets traveled with an upward trajectory. Because Cohen is a forensic pathologist and has viewed Diallo's autopsy results, we have reason to believe that he is in a position to know something about the cause of death in the case. Of course, legal proceedings are not the only places where expert testimony is used. Experts "testify" in political campaigns, in advertisements, and in organizational sales meetings.

WARRANT, OR THE REASONING PROCESS

warrant
the rationale for moving from data to a claim

The third element of Toulmin's model is the **warrant,** the rationale for moving from data to a claim. The content of our reasons must somehow relate to the claim that they support. That is, there must be some "reasoning process" involved in making the claim (Ziegelmueller & Kay, 1997). You might think of the warrant as a bridge from the data to the claim. One way that data are related to claims is through formal reasoning. Jamieson (1988) notes that in a mediated environment, it is "impossible to adequately warrant claims in sixty, thirty, twenty, or fourteen seconds" (p. 14). She says that we too readily accept the connection between smiling celebrities and the products they endorse.

To better understand the relationship between data and claim, let's spend some time discussing the warrant, or reasoning process. Specifically, there are two types of warrants: inductive and deductive.

inductive reasoning
the synthetic process used to reason from particulars to probable conclusions

Inductive Reasoning   Ziegelmueller and Kay explain that **inductive reasoning** "may be thought of as the synthetic process used in moving from particulars to probable conclusions" (1997, p. 42). That is, reasoning that uses induction brings together, or synthesizes, a series of particular events, ideas, or objects and draws probable conclusions from those data. Results of induction are only probable because persuaders must make a leap beyond the evidence at hand to come to their conclusion. Let's examine the three types of inductive

Table 10.2 Reasoning Types

Inductive	Deductive
Argument by example	Argument by causal generalization
Argument by analogy	Argument by sign
Argument by causal correlation	

reasoning: argument by example, argument by analogy, and argument by causal correlation (Table 10.2).

Argument by example "examines several specific cases in a given class and assumes that if the known cases are alike with regard to a specific characteristic, then other unknown cases in the same class will exhibit the same characteristic" (Ziegelmueller & Kay, 1997, p. 102). This type of reasoning makes a generalization about a larger group of objects based on a sample of that group. Advertisements for online investing make use of argument by example. The assumption is that if some regular, everyday people can make money investing in the stock market via the Internet, then all other regular, everyday people can also make money investing via the Internet. What's true of some members of the group of investors is true for all other members of that group.

Addressing three questions can test argument by example. First, are the examples *typical?* Does the sample observed truly represent the whole class for which it stands? That is, do the investors considered by the advertising have any special training that would make them more likely than other investors to make money in the stock market? Or are the successful investors people with no previous stock trading experience? Second, are *negative instances* considered? Is the persuader ignoring any contradictory evidence? Consider our online trading example: Are there any instances where people have lost a great deal of money trading online? Has the advertising considered those contradictory examples? Finally, audiences should ask if a *sufficient number of examples* have been examined. How many online traders have the online trading companies included in their sample, or are they basing their arguments on the success of a few? Argument by example is used quite often in persuasion, and these tests can help you to determine whether you should accept what is said. If the argument fails these tests, the persuader is maybe using faulty reasoning.

A second type of inductive reasoning, *argument by analogy*, examines two similar cases to understand which qualities they share. If the two cases are alike in every way that is known, it is assumed they will be alike with regard to a characteristic known in one case, but not in the other (Ziegelmueller & Kay, 1997). A member of Congress who is arguing for handgun control may use the analogy of Canada. Because the United States and Canada are alike in many ways—geographic location, economic system, and democratic government—then one could argue that proposed handgun legislation in the United States will have the same effects as existing, and successful, legislation in Canada. Argument by analogy is a common form of argument.

To evaluate a persuader's use of argument by analogy, Ziegelmueller and Kay (1997) suggest two tests. First, are the compared cases *essentially alike?* There must be no fundamental difference between the two cases that are used for the analogy. In the comparison between the United States and Canada, one could argue that there are fundamental differences between the two countries. The United States has a much larger population than does Canada, and the United States has a more widespread popular culture industry. These two differences make the United States and Canada fundamentally different. The differences between the two countries might explain why Canadian handgun legislation would not work in the United States. Second, you should ask, are the *compared characteristics accurate?* We must be certain that the handgun legislation under question is similar in both the United States and Canada. If Canadian law bans the purchase of handguns by any citizen and the U.S. law simply seeks to impose a waiting period on handgun purchases, the two laws are not alike. Thus, predicting the impact of the law in the United States based on the Canadian experience is difficult because the two laws differ.

A final type of inductive reasoning is *argument by causal correlation*. In this type of reasoning, two cases are examined to identify a functional correlation between them. There must be some pattern in the relationship between two cases. A seesaw is a good example. As one side of the seesaw goes up, the other side goes down. You can safely say that lowering one side of a seesaw *causes* the other side to rise. Causal correlation seeks to identify a causal relationship between two variables. There are three types of relationships that can form. *Concomitant variation* describes a relationship in which changes in one variable predictably lead to changes in the other variable. The seesaw example illustrates concomitant variation. Or consider the argument that passengers in motor vehicles should wear seatbelts. A persuader could show a correlation between use of seatbelts and traffic deaths, arguing that as seatbelt use increases, the number of traffic deaths decreases.

A second type of relationship is found by using the *method of agreement*. This method states that if two or more cases have something in common and then we find something else in common between the two cases, then we can argue that the second element is the cause or the effect of the first common feature. A great deal of scientific research makes use of this reasoning pattern. In a sample of breast cancer patients, for instance, researchers could locate one other feature this group had in common. Perhaps they ate a particular kind of food or did not have children. Using statistical tools, researchers could determine if this common feature was, potentially, a significant cause of breast cancer. As you read Ethical Insights: Ethics and Reasoning, consider how persuaders can easily misuse causal correlation.

The third type of relationship is found by using the *method of differences*. If we examine two or more cases that have something in common and then we can identify another feature in one of the cases, but not the other, we may reason that the other feature we have identified is the cause or the effect of the first (common) feature. Community leaders might argue for a new convention center by using this reasoning pattern. By comparing the community to another community of equal size, leaders might argue that both have similar pop-

ETHICAL INSIGHTS

Ethics and Reasoning

A recent Dannon yogurt advertising campaign makes use of argument by causal correlation. The ads feature two pictures of a celebrity athlete, volleyball player Gabrielle Reece or tennis star Pete Sampras. One picture shows the athlete as he or she now looks. The second photo shows the athlete as a child holding a cup of Dannon yogurt. The advertisement's headline asks the question, "Coincidence or Dannon?" to argue that because these athletes ate Dannon yogurt as children, they have become superstars in their sport. The pictures and the headline create an argument by causal correlation.

The ad campaign is ethically questionable on several grounds. First, the photographs of the stars holding Dannon yogurt are manipulated, and thus false. The American Association of Advertising Agencies (1990) charges its members to avoid "false or misleading statements or exaggerations, visual or verbal." Dannon thinks it has avoided making a false claim because the photographs are not to be taken seriously. According to company officials, consumers are meant to recognize that the photographs have been manipulated. Thus, consumers are expected to

see the humor in the supposed correlation and not be misled by the advertisement.

Even without the photographs, however, the advertisements are potentially misleading to consumers because they imply a causal relationship between eating Dannon yogurt and being a sports superstar. The statement by itself may be enough to mislead consumers into accepting Dannon's faulty reasoning. The National Communication Association (1999) recognizes the importance of solid reasoning in ethical communication: "We believe that truthfulness, accuracy, honesty, and reason are essential to the integrity of communication."

Think about the AAAA and NCA statements as you consider these questions:

1. What is a reasonable standard for determining whether consumers can recognize if a photograph has been manipulated?

2. How can consumers know that an advertisement should not be taken seriously?

3. To what extent should advertising be exempt from the rules of reasoning we discuss in this chapter?

ulation bases and economic structures. Yet the other town is more effective at attracting large conventions than the leaders' town. The difference, and therefore the cause, could be that the other town has a convention center. Building a convention center might eliminate this difference.

Asking four questions can test the reasoning produced by these three methods of analysis. First, is there a *consistent association* between cause and effect? In other words, the seesaw must move in the same pattern each time. Second, is the *association* between cause and effect *strong*? The persuader must somehow demonstrate or describe why the association occurs. It is easy to show why a seesaw totters as it does. Third, do cause and effect occur in a *regular time sequence*? Does one side of the seesaw rise before the other side falls? Or do the sides rise and fall at the same time? Fourth, is the cause-effect relationship *coherent*? Do all seesaws operate in the same way, or is the one we are observing different? There must be some external support for the cause-effect relationship.

Deductive Reasoning   The analytic process used to move from generalities to structurally certain conclusions is called **deductive reasoning** (Ziegelmueller & Kay, 1997). The process is analytic because it does not create new

deductive reasoning
the analytic process used to move from generalizations to structurally certain conclusions

syllogism

a series of three statements used to form a new relationship between two ideas; used in deductive reasoning

information; it simply combines existing information to come up with new associations. A deductive argument can be stated as a **syllogism,** which consists of three statements and three terms. Each statement contains two of the terms. When the three statements are combined in the prescribed order, they reveal a new relationship between previously unrelated terms. The three statements in a syllogism are called the major premise, the minor premise, and the conclusion. The major premise contains a generalization. The minor premise relates a specific case to the generalization. The conclusion is the structurally certain result of applying the specific case to the generalization. Let's look at an example:

> *Major premise:* All people are mortal.
>
> *Minor premise:* Socrates is a person.
>
> *Conclusion:* Socrates is mortal.

Two types of reasoning use the syllogism: argument by causal generalization and argument by sign (see Table 10.2).

Argument by causal generalization applies an assumed causal relationship to specific cases. If the specific case is included in the general cause, then the causal association is true for the specific case as well. An advertisement for Compaq computers exemplifies the use of argument by causal generalization. The ad read, in part: "It's the electronic highway—E-business—where companies that drive the most traffic win. No one understands all of this better than Compaq." The ad establishes a causal relationship between driving the most e-traffic and winning. That is, winning is caused by driving the most traffic. Compaq included itself as a specific case in the general cause of driving the most traffic. Compaq, in other words, can help you drive the most traffic. The conclusion is that an e-business should purchase Compaq computers in order to win. Let's put the argument into syllogistic form:

> *Major premise:* Driving a lot of traffic causes winning.
>
> *Minor premise:* Compaq drives a lot of traffic.
>
> *Conclusion:* With Compaq you win.

Thus, the association between Compaq and a company's success at using e-commerce is made.

There are three tests of argument by causal generalization. First, are there *intervening factors* that would inhibit the expected cause? The cause must lead directly to the effect, without being hindered by some other variable. If, for example, a company that desires to use e-commerce is not selling a product customers want, no computer system will help. Second, is the cause *sufficient* to bring about the effect? There must be a strength of association between cause and effect. As a potential Compaq purchaser, you would want to examine the features of the Compaq computer that would help your business establish an e-commerce presence. Finally, are there *unspecified effects* that may occur? There should not be any significant disadvantages from the cause-effect relationship. If your company goes broke purchasing Compaq computers, it won't be able to sell anything online.

Argument by sign says that every object or idea has certain distinguishing characteristics and that the presence, or absence, of those characteristics indicates the presence, or absence, of the object or idea. Much fashion advertising makes use of argument-by-sign reasoning. By showing potential consumers the necessary components of a fashionable wardrobe, fashion advertising entices audience members to purchase those items in order to be fashionable. Advertising seeks to create an association between items it deems fashionable and the audience member's self-image of who he or she is. In syllogistic form, we might say:

Major premise: Fashion consists of this clothing.

Minor premise: I want to be fashionable.

Conclusion: I will wear this clothing.

Argument by sign is quite common in society today, although it often operates at an implicit level, where the premises are not always stated. For example, fashion designers rarely state that their clothing is fashionable. Instead, we learn what is fashionable by reading magazines or watching commercials.

Asking three questions can test argument by sign. First, are the characteristics of an object or idea *invariably linked?* That is, is there a consistent relationship between an object and its characteristics? Fashion may not always be related to a particular type of clothing. In fact, the clothing may go out of style. It is important that the relationship be consistent and predictable. Second, are a *sufficient amount of signs* presented? Being fashionable may entail more than simply wearing a particular outfit. You might need the proper accessories as well. Or fashion may consist of items not identified as clothing. Third, have *contradictory signs* been considered? Different types of clothing may also be considered fashionable in some instances. Thus you would not have to wear just what is pictured in the advertisement to be fashionable.

Examine an advertisement and determine whether it uses inductive or deductive reasoning. What type of reasoning is used? Apply the appropriate tests of reasoning. Do you detect any errors in the persuader's use of reasoning?

ADDITIONAL COMPONENTS OF THE TOULMIN MODEL

We have discussed the main components of the Toulmin model of argument: data, warrant, and claim. However, because Toulmin was interested in how people argue, as opposed to more formal logic, he included additional elements in his model: qualifiers, rebuttal, and backing. A *qualifier* is a statement that we make about the strength of the argument. When you use the words *probably* or *certainly* in an argument, you are using a qualifier. A *rebuttal* expresses some kind of exception that would negate the argument being made. Consider this statement: "Unless our football team has a lot of injuries this year, they probably will win the conference championship." The rebuttal in this case is the phrase, "unless our football team has a lot of injuries this year." Of course, there are many more exceptions: the other teams in the conference could be better, the team could be unlucky this year, a new coach may hurt the team's chances, and so on. The qualifier, to accommodate this uncertainty, is the word *probably*. The claim (to review) is the statement that the team will win the conference championship.

**Figure 10.3
Toulmin's Model of
Reasoning with Argument Statements**

Data:
Our football
team won the
conference
championship
last year. So,

Warrant:
Since they only lost
a few players from
last year's team. . .

Backing:
Studies have shown
that college football
teams are similar from
year to year, unless
they lose a lot of
players to graduation

Qualifier:
probably,

Rebuttal:
Unless our
football team
has a lot of
injuries,

Claim:
they will win
the conference
championship
again this year.

The final element of Toulmin's model is the *backing*, which is the "categorical statements of fact" that support the warrant. The backing is the reason the warrant is valid. The backing is often a scientific study or a law or some other form of proof for the warrant. The backing should not be confused with the data, which is the initial observation or support for the claim. Let's consider the football example again. In its entirety, the argument about the football team winning the conference championship would look like that shown in Figure 10.3. The argument, when stated, would be, "Since our football team won the conference championship last year, they will probably win the conference championship again this year unless they have a lot of injuries." Often, the warrant and backing are not stated in an argument. As we'll see in the next section, though, other components of an argument are often left out of mediated arguments as well.

To review, you may have observed that the warrant in this case is deductive. The specific form is causal generalization and could be expressed as a syllogism:

Major premise: College football teams are similar from year to year unless they lose a lot of players to graduation.

Minor premise: Our football team did not lose a lot of players.

Conclusion: Our football team will be similar to last year's (which won the conference championship).

With this knowledge of Toulmin's model, complete the Internet Activity: Reasoning in Everyday Life to understand how the model reflects your style of reasoning.

TOULMIN'S MODEL IN THE MEDIA AGE

Aden (1994) suggests that, in the media age, audience members use a type of deductive reasoning, but one that does not explicitly state each premise. Rea-

INTERNET ACTIVITY

Reasoning in Everyday Life

We have just discussed Toulmin's model of reasoning. To what degree, do you think, you reason according to this model? To help you understand more about how you employ reasoning skills, read the article "Reasoning" by Rick Garlikov at http://www.akat .com/reasoning.htm. What is the author's central argument? Do you agree or disagree? How do you reason? To what extent do you discuss reasoning in your classes?

soning today, he writes, resembles what Aristotle called the enthymeme. An **enthymeme** is a syllogism that is missing one of its premises. Recall our earlier syllogism:

> All people are mortal.
>
> Socrates is a person.
>
> Socrates is mortal.

enthymeme
a syllogism that is missing one of its premises

As you examine these three statements, you realize that the first two do not need to be said. We all know that people are mortal, and by looking at someone named Socrates, we can tell that he is a human. Thus, it only needs to be said that Socrates is mortal. Aden explains that this is what we do in a mediated society. Because of television and other forms of media, our culture is a constant swirl of premises. When a persuader uses reasoning, he or she often leaves out a premise that the audience already understands because it has been established in our culture. We communicate in a sort of code, in which much is never really said. Visual images, as we discussed in Chapter 6, are good ways to communicate premises without explicitly stating them.

Aden (1994) examines the public interviews of the White supremacist politician David Duke, a former member of the Ku Klux Klan who ran for political office in the early 1990s. We might think that, as a former Klan member, Duke would have been at a disadvantage in trying to win public office. Aden argues that Duke communicated by using the enthymeme and thus was able to shed his earlier image as a White supremacist. Duke had to communicate only one premise of the syllogism for his supporters to see his complete argument. In essence, Duke used this syllogism:

Major premise: Government actions, especially welfare and affirmative action, hurt Whites economically and socially.

Minor premise: Minorities are the cause and recipients of government programs.

Conclusion: Minorities are the cause of the social and economic problems suffered by Whites.

Because the audience was able to fill in the minor premise and thus arrive at the conclusion, Duke needed to prove only the major premise. Aden explains that Duke's use of the enthymeme had several persuasive advantages. First,

Duke outwardly scapegoated the government for the failure of its policies while at the same time appealing to the prejudice of voters. In addition, Duke had to prove only that government programs hurt Whites. He did not have to prove the more difficult, and racist, minor premise and conclusion.

David Duke is an extreme example of someone who uses cultural premises to argue with the enthymematic form. Consider an advertisement for almost any brand of clothing. The full syllogism would look like this:

Major premise: It's important to look good.

Minor premise: People who shop at Brand X look good.

Conclusion: I should shop at Brand X.

Advertising for Brand X would not have to state the minor premise or the conclusion. All that is necessary is to show good-looking people wearing Brand X clothing. From this image, consumers fill in the missing premise and conclusion. The minor premise, in particular, is supplied by our exposure to popular culture. Because we the audience are constantly surrounded by cultural premises—both perceptual and value—we do not always process arguments in a rational manner. We sometimes neglect to use the formal rules of logic previously discussed and instead supply the missing premises in a persuader's argument on our own. The enthymeme is a good way to understand how persuaders use visuals to make arguments and to build relationships with audience members.

In Chapter 6, we discussed how visual images often substitute for words in a persuader's message. By understanding the enthymeme, we can better understand how images replace words. The photograph of George W. Bush holding a lobster while surrounded by supporters (Figure 10.4) implies two enthymemes, the premises and conclusions of which are all unstated. Only the minor premise of the first enthymeme is shown in the image:

Major premise (unstated): Candidates who have their pictures taken with ordinary citizens are friendly.

Minor premise (unstated, but depicted): I am having my picture taken with ordinary citizens.

Conclusion (unstated): I am friendly.

and

Major premise (unstated): If I am friendly, you will vote for me.

Minor premise (understood from the previous syllogism): I am friendly.

Conclusion (unstated): You will vote for me.

In this photograph, Bush uses two enthymemes to garner support from voters. The photograph replaces the minor premise in the first enthymeme. The conclusion of the first enthymeme is also the minor premise of the second enthymeme, the major premise and conclusion of which are understood.

Persuaders in the media age seek to build relationships with audience members. We tend to take these relationships for granted, but an understanding of

Figure 10.4
How is George W. Bush making an argument with this photo opportunity?

the enthymeme can reveal the complex interchange that occurs between persuader and audience member.

Narratives

As we have said, the reasoning used by persuaders today does not necessarily reflect the model proposed by Toulmin. Instead, dramatic **narratives**—stories—are used as both the content and form of reasoning. Walter Fisher (1987) proposes a model of persuasion in which "stories" take on the role of arguments. He claims that all people are essentially storytellers and that we constantly evaluate and choose from the stories we hear. Thus, closing arguments in a trial can be viewed as stories told to jurors, for example. This is not to say that these stories lack substance or that they are "mere rhetoric." In fact, the contrary is true. Fisher argues that our world is created through symbols and that by using symbolic structures—stories—we can induce others to see the world through our eyes. Stories, according to Fisher, have substance and weight because they reflect how we see our world.

Fisher's narrative approach is particularly well suited for the media age, in which we are constantly exposed to the narrative form on television and in movies. Jamieson (1988) contends that television invites the use of private narratives about persuaders. As we discussed in Chapter 7, the preferred style of language today is one of intimacy. Narratives, as ways of expressing reasons, work hand in hand with this intimate style of using language. Narratives also function as synecdoche because they allow persuaders to reduce complex ideas into short, easily understood arguments. Jamieson argues that the power of narratives lies in their ability "to create identity for an audience, to involve the

narrative
a story that serves as an argument

audience, and to bond that audience" to the persuader (p. 137). Because narratives are effective ways to express arguments in the media age, let's look more closely at Fisher's theory.

First, Fisher says, humans are "essentially storytellers" (1987, p. 64). That is, our communication can be considered a story, with a plot, characters, and other attributes of good fiction. Second, instead of using strict rules of logic, such as inductive and deductive reasoning, Fisher writes that we use "good reasons" when making decisions and persuading others. Good reasons include traditional ideas about logic, which we have previously discussed, along with ideas about the values the storyteller shares with his or her audience. What "good reasons" means varies—to some degree—among situations, genres, and media of communication (W. R. Fisher, 1987). Finally, "the world as we know it is a set of stories that must be chosen among" (p. 65). Viewing communication as a narrative is meaningful for people in a wide variety of cultures and communities because "we all live out narratives in our lives and because we understand our own lives in terms of narratives" (p. 66).

EVALUATING NARRATIVES

Humans employ narrative rationality when evaluating the stories they hear. Narrative rationality is comprised of two standards: narrative probability and narrative fidelity. *Narrative probability* asks whether the story is consistent with itself. *Narrative fidelity* evaluates the degree to which the story "rings true" with the audience. Narrative rationality depends, not entirely on hard-and-fast rules of logic, but also on the values that are a part of decision making. This is an important part of Fisher's (1987) theory. Let's consider these two standards in greater detail.

Narrative Probability   Narrative probability concerns the degree to which a story "hangs together." Fisher (1987) argues that stories must have structural coherence, material coherence, and characterological coherence. *Structural coherence* refers to whether the story contradicts itself. A witness who testifies in court and says something different than he or she said previously tells a story that lacks structural coherence. The witness's story does not "hang together." *Material coherence* refers to how well the story accounts for what the audience knows to be true. A witness who testifies that the car in the accident was green when all the other witnesses claim it was red would not have material coherence. *Characterological coherence* questions the reliability of the characters in the story. A witness accused of murder but who is claiming innocence would be difficult to believe if he or she did not display some emotion about being wrongly accused.

Narrative Fidelity   The second standard of Fisher's (1987) narrative paradigm is fidelity. Whereas coherence (probability) refers to the integrity of a whole story, fidelity refers to the story's individual components. Fisher explains that fidelity questions whether the components "represent accurate assertions about social reality" (p. 105). Fidelity, then, looks at the individual arguments, or stories, within the complete narrative. Each component is assessed according to five general types of questions, which all isolate five interdependent components of narratives. As we consider each criterion, we will apply it to a speech given by George W. Bush on April 11, 2000, at the New Prosperity Initiative in Cleveland, Ohio.

- The question of *fact* explores the values that are embedded in a story. For Fisher, all meaningful discourse concerns values. Thus, the question of fact, in actuality, addresses the story's values. In his speech, Bush shared with his audience a vision of "opportunity." Thus, Bush's narrative centered on the value of opportunity.

- The question of *relevance* concerns the appropriateness of the values to the nature of the decision. Bush explained that the value of prosperity is appropriate because "there are those living in prosperity's shadow." He was saying that it is appropriate to judge the stories of his campaign on the basis of prosperity.

- The question of *consequence* examines the effects of adhering to a particular value set when making a decision. As a consequence of focusing on prosperity, Bush claimed, we will achieve "the advancement of all Americans, including those who struggle."

- The question of *consistency* asks if the values of the story confirm one's personal experience. To underprivileged voters listening to Bush's message, the lack of prosperity in our culture today helped them to explain why they were not enjoying the same benefits as those who are more fortunate. His message rang true to this audience. To the affluent, however, Bush's message on that particular day might not have been consistent with their experience.

- The question of *transcendent issue* asks if the values in question "constitute the ideal basis for human conduct" (W. R. Fisher, 1987, p. 109). Bush argued that prosperity is an ideal value for conducting our lives and making our decisions. He explained, "It will be said of our times that we were prosperous. But let it also be said of us that we used our wealth wisely. We invested our property with purpose. We opened the gates of opportunity. And all were welcomed into the full promise of American life."

This analysis of Bush's speech from a narrative perspective suggests that on this day, Bush achieved narrative fidelity. His speech reaffirmed values that are held by Americans and supported the idea that these are values upon which our culture should rest. Political speakers often use narratives for these reasons. Narratives are used in other contexts as well.

USING NARRATIVES

Jack Kay (1994) argues that former Chrysler chair Lee Iacocca successfully used narratives throughout his speaking career. Iacocca gave many speeches to many audiences. He persuaded the government to make a controversial loan to Chrysler. He persuaded members of Congress to support tough trade legislation. He persuaded his employees to accept company policy proposals. Kay notes that Iacocca's speeches contained a series of coherent stories that rang true for the audience. Iacocca spoke of the American Dream, independence, and freedom. When addressing problems in the automobile industry, he argued that American business was being threatened by foreign competitors. Instead of using logical details and statistics about how his business was affected, he appealed to his audience's sense of American pride and independence. Chrysler was being victimized, he said, and Americans everywhere should support methods of saving the company. His narrative appeals were easy to accept when put into the larger framework of U.S. economic competitiveness. Fisher's narrative approach to argument provides us with a different way to view the form in which arguments are presented.

Jamieson (1988) contends that President Ronald Reagan masterfully used narratives to build support for his policies. He did so by personifying the evidence of his arguments, thereby creating compelling narratives. In his 1982 State of the Union address, Reagan told the story of Sergeant Stephen Trujillo, an army Ranger, who had participated in that year's military action in Grenada. Reagan applauded Trujillo's actions to save his fellow soldiers. By recognizing Trujillo, Reagan prompted applause from Republicans and Democrats seated in the Congress. Reagan then turned the applause into support for his Grenada mission, which many Democrats had opposed. By personalizing the Grenada mission in Trujillo's action, Reagan created a compelling narrative that recast the nature of the military mission.

Locate a transcript of a speech by a politician or an organizational spokesperson. How does the narrative express the speaker's arguments? Does the narrative have probability and fidelity?

Evaluating a Persuader's Reasoning

With a better understanding of how arguments are presented in the media age, we can move on to ways of evaluating a persuader's reasoning. It may be difficult to do so in the media age because so much of a persuader's argument is missing. However, to be critical audience members, we must look closely at persuaders' arguments and determine their validity. We have already discussed various ways of testing formal arguments. We now look at tests of evidence, argument fields, and fallacies as additional methods of evaluating reasoning.

TESTS OF EVIDENCE

A series of questions can be asked about evidence to test its validity. We divide our discussion of tests of evidence into several categories: general tests of data, tests of premises, tests of evidence, and special tests of statistical evidence.

General Tests of Data   Numerous scholars (McBurney & Mills, 1964; Mills, 1964; Ziegelmueller & Kay, 1997) have identified three general tests of data, which can be used to evaluate premises or evidence. The first general test is *internal consistency,* which asks if the data are consistent with other information from the same source. In legal persuasion, attorneys frequently seek to impeach witnesses who contradict themselves. To be believable, witnesses must give the same version of events throughout their testimony. If they do not, their testimony must be questioned. Likewise, reporters seek to identify what positions a politician holds on specific issues and then require that the politician maintain those positions. President Clinton was frequently accused of flip-flopping on issues. Because he changed his mind about particular policies, the news media questioned his internal consistency.

The second general test of data is *external consistency.* This test asks if the data are consistent with information from other sources. Persuaders should usually use data that are reliable. Of course, scientists often make discoveries that run counter to what is commonly believed, such as when Copernicus determined that the Earth revolved around the Sun. However, great care must be taken by scientists, and by persuaders who use scientific evidence, to make sure that established procedure is followed as new evidence is developed. A few years ago, scientists claimed to have discovered cold fusion, which would dramatically change much of how we think about physics. Since then, however, other scientists have been unable to duplicate the original work, casting doubt on the findings. The test of external consistency extends beyond the realm of science. During the bombing of Yugoslavia by NATO forces in 1999, NATO representatives were often asked by members of the news media to explain dramatic video or photographic images. Their explanations often ran counter to what the film showed, casting doubt on the official explanations. Arguments that NATO forces were not bombing civilian targets, for example, often failed the test of external consistency.

The test of *relevancy* asks if the data actually support the claim they are asserted to support. Often, persuaders will use data that do not prove what they claim the data prove. Political candidates are frequently accused of failing the test of relevancy in a political debate because they offer data that do not support the question they are answering. When asked about foreign policy, for instance, a candidate may provide evidence that the economy is doing well and that we need not worry about the security of the country. The data on the economy do not support the candidate's position on foreign policy and are, therefore, irrelevant to the question at hand.

Tests of Premises   In addition to the general tests of data, we must be aware of two tests of premises. Persuaders make use of highly developed statistical data to infer the premises of their audiences, and several steps must be taken to ensure that persuaders draw correct inferences from their data. The first precaution persuaders must take concerns the *nature of their audience measurement methods.* Focus group interviews are a highly complex research method that requires trained facilitators. Survey questions must be written in a way that allows them to measure the appropriate audience attitudes. Audience analysis methods must also conform to established scientific methodologies. Careless use of these methods will result in assumptions about the audience that are not true. The 1998 Minnesota gubernatorial campaign is a good example. The campaigns of State Attorney General Hubert (Skip) Humphrey III, the Democrat, and St. Paul Mayor Norm Coleman, the Republican, did not correctly infer the beliefs of their audience: potential Minnesota voters. Each candidate believed that the voters were interested in traditional issues such as education, crime, and taxes. The two candidates also inferred that voters would not cast their ballots for the third-party longshot, former professional wrestler Jesse Ventura. In the end, the Reform Party candidate defeated the two favorites because he was able to draw correct inferences about the widespread contempt for established politicians in the state. Ventura's campaign surprised many in the state. We discussed his campaign in more detail in Chapter 1.

In the media age, it is also important for persuaders to *accurately gauge their audience* when making statements regarding values and beliefs. It is quite common that what a persuader says to one audience may be broadcast by news media to a very different audience. When Vice President Dan Quayle made disparaging comments about unwed mothers several years ago, he was speaking to a specific audience that held views similar to his own. What Quayle failed to consider was that his speech would be discussed by many other audiences that did not necessarily share his premises. Quayle's "Murphy Brown" speech—as it became known—is a good example of how mass media create new problems for persuaders concerning audience premises.

Tests of Evidence   Theorists (Ehninger & Brockriede, 1963; McBurney & Mills, 1964; Mills, 1964; Ziegelmueller & Kay, 1997) have identified numerous tests of evidence. We examine five typical tests: recency, source identification, source ability, source willingness, and context. The test of *recency* asks if the data are current enough to be considered valid. Events change the world; it is important that our observations of the world be current. When the White House spokesperson addresses media in times of war, he or she must have current information about troop movements, casualties, and objectives. Even data that are a few minutes old may harm the credibility of the persuader and cause the audience to reject the message. In other cases, relying on older data may be desirable. In our discussion of persuasion, we have examined several new theories, but we have also looked at theories that date back to ancient Greece. Persuaders and audiences must judge the degree to which information is reliable and relevant to the claim being supported.

The test of *source identification* asks if the source of the information is known. Many times, reporters interview subjects and promise to protect their identity in exchange for information about something. Ideally, the reporter corroborates the information with other sources, who may remain nameless in the final story. When the story is published, the sources are identified with statements such as "a high-ranking White House official indicates" or "sources near the president say." Audience members must be careful of relying too heavily on information from anonymous sources. We discussed some of the implications of anonymous sources in Chapter 9.

A third test of evidence is *source ability*. This test probes the accessibility the source has to the information being discussed, as well as his or her expertness. For instance, the source must be physically present to view an example, or the source must have knowledge of the instances that he or she interprets. A witness to a traffic accident must have been able to see the accident. Likewise, a medical researcher must be familiar with the results of a study to interpret them for a broader audience. Likewise, the source must have expertness in the subject matter being discussed. Especially if called on to interpret an event, the source must have some basis for stating his or her opinion.

The test of *source willingness* examines bias. Sources must not gain some advantage by providing or interpreting information. Advocacy groups sometimes conduct surveys and release results that are compatible with their way of thinking. These results are sometimes based on faulty statistical measurement. When interested groups make their results known to the public, the audience must question the nature of their surveys to determine their scientific validity. Individuals who offer expert testimony should also have their biases revealed. The magazine *Brill's Content* regularly features profiles of "experts" interviewed by news media sources, to expose their biases. To learn how these standards can be used to determine if information you find online is credible, read Thinking Critically: Evaluating Web Pages.

Finally, the test of *context* examines the evidence and its relationship to the original source. Audience members who employ this test question whether the evidence is consistent with the meaning and intent of the original source. Politicians often accuse the news media of taking their statements out of context— that is, of extracting only part of their meaning. A 1999 interview with Minnesota Governor Jesse Ventura by *Playboy* magazine received a great deal of media attention. When it was revealed that Ventura had made disparaging comments about women, people who are overweight, and religion, the governor claimed that his statements had been "taken out of context" and that within the scope of the interview, the selected statements had meant something other than they were being portrayed to mean. The reporter refuted Ventura's claim.

Special Tests of Statistical Evidence   Numerous scholars have identified tests for statistics. We refer to four special tests of statistical evidence: adequate sampling, appropriate statistical unit, appropriate time period, and comparable units. The test of *adequate sampling* questions the scientific process by which statisticians select their sample. As we discussed, statistics are usually based on inferences made from a small sample of the entire population. For the inferences made about the population to be accurate, the sample must be large enough and it must be representative of the population. Persuaders should employ trained researchers to make these judgments. Recall our earlier discussion of the Nielsen ratings: inferences about the entire nation's television viewing habits based on the response of a small sample of viewers. In New York State, the Nielson sample was tainted by inclusion of family members of an employee of a local television station. That station received higher-than-average ratings because the Nielsen sample was not representative of the town. It included viewers who had close ties to a station and not everyone in town had those ties. Nielsen ratings are usually based on large, representative samples.

The second statistical test is *appropriate statistical unit*. Statistics is a complicated science that requires knowledge of which statistical measure to use when trying to obtain data. Use of the wrong statistical measurement results in data that are not valid. A recent medical study received a great deal of media attention. The study argued that women and African Americans were less likely

THINKING CRITICALLY

Evaluating Web Pages

The World Wide Web has emerged as a popular and significant form of information. Audience members must take great care to evaluate the information they obtain from the Web, however. The tests of evidence discussed in the text can help us to evaluate websites. The test of recency asks us to evaluate whether the information is timely enough to support a claim. You can often find the date a Web page was last updated at the bottom of the page. Many news sources provide a "Web posted" date for their articles. If you cannot find the date, choose Page Info from the View menu of Netscape Navigator or Get Info from the File menu of Internet Explorer.

It is also important to evaluate the author's ability, identification, and willingness. Ideally this information is included on the page you are viewing. Often, however, pages lack the names, qualifications, and biases of their authors. To assess these characteristics, you will have to do some work to uncover who authored the page you are viewing. You can begin by removing information from the page address, or uniform resource locator (URL). For example, you may be viewing the Web page that has the URL http://www.harvard.edu/smith/politics/politicaldebates.htm. The page provides an interesting article about political debates. However, you cannot find who wrote the article or anything about his

or her qualifications and biases. If you were to remove the words "politics/politicaldebates.htm" from the URL, you would probably arrive at a Web page for someone named Smith, who is affiliated somehow with Harvard University. If Smith is a faculty member, you may be able to view his or her vita and assess credibility. If Smith is a student, you will have a more difficult time assessing credibility.

In other cases, you might have to conduct more research to learn about the biases of a source. The URL http://www.cato.org/politicaldebates.htm might contain interesting information. By surveying the Cato Institute's Web page or by learning more about the Cato Institute, you would discover that the organization is a conservative think tank. That knowledge should provide a basis for viewing ideas on the Web page.

As you use the Internet to gain information, consider carefully the tests of evidence we have discussed. Please think about these questions:

1. To what extent does the Internet hide the identity of persuaders?

2. How reliable do you consider information you read on the Internet? What are some of the online sources you use for information? What do you know about these people or organizations?

to be referred for a potentially life-saving test for their hearts than were Caucasian males (Greenstein, 1999). The study made use of the wrong statistical measure in reporting its claim. The study used the "odds ratio" statistical test, which involves multiple calculations of a ratio between two sets of odds. The test is confusing for many people, including doctors (Greenstein, 1999). Instead, as an editorial in a later edition of the *New England Journal of Medicine* explained, the study should have used the "risk ratio" test, which is more commonly understood. The results of the study were quite shocking when they were first reported, but on later review the use of the inappropriate statistical unit was discovered.

The test of *appropriate time period* asks if the time period a reported statistic represents is appropriate. When comparing statistics from two time periods, for example, persuaders should make sure the two time periods are similar. A report that crime is at its lowest level in three decades (Bureau of Justice Statistics, 2000) serves to illustrate this test. Although a reduction in crime is good news, one must examine the past two decades to see if specific societal forces might have led this decrease in crime. Economically, the country was in bad shape in the 1970s; crime sometimes is prevalent during an economic recession. In the 1980s, the country faced a wave of drug use, which also may lead to crime. Thus, any comparison of crime rates over the decades of the 1970s, 1980s, and 1990s should consider all factors that contribute to a decrease in crime.

Finally, the test of *comparable units* asks if the data sets that are measured are similar. A governor running for president of the United States may argue that the welfare rolls in his or her state are lower than the national average and that the nation's welfare level will be reduced if he or she is elected. It is important to ask if the state and federal definitions of welfare are the same. Often, different governments use different standards to determine who qualifies for welfare. The candidate's state may have a more restrictive set of welfare regulations than the federal government, meaning that the number of people on welfare in that state would necessarily be lower than the number that would qualify based on federal guidelines. The candidate's opponents and audience members would be wise to examine this difference. By using general tests of data, tests of premises, tests of evidence, and special tests of statistics, persuaders and audience members can be sure that their good reasons are sound.

Find a statistic that is used persuasively in an advertisement, an editorial, or a political speech. Apply an appropriate test of statistical evidence to it. Is the statistic valid?

ARGUMENT FIELDS

When a persuader presents good reasons to an audience, there is a likelihood that the two parties will share common ways of seeing and understanding the world. These shared standards can be used to evaluate the persuader's reasoning. In Chapter 5, we noted that in the media age, the primary audience for a persuasive message is not always the only audience that hears the message. Secondary audiences may see, hear, and respond to the message as well. This raises the question of how to create and evaluate arguments that cut across audiences. When the speaker and the audience do not share assumptions about what should be accepted as reasonable truth, it is more difficult to create and evaluate arguments.

The concept of argument fields is very useful in helping us to understand how various audiences evaluate arguments. The idea was first suggested by Stephen Toulmin, who suggested that if we can understand an audience's core beliefs and values, we can better understand how members of the audience will evaluate a persuader's message. Following Toulmin, scholars have debated the nature of argument fields and their applicability to evaluating argument (Rowland, 1992). Ziegelmueller and Kay use the term *community* in their definition of an argument field. A community is composed of people who hold similar views about the evaluation of an argument. Thus, Republican senators may be a community because they hold certain ideas about what constitutes a good argument. Or a community may be you and your colleagues in this class. Good reasons to you might be those that will help you get a job or land a spot in graduate school some day. A community, then, shares fundamental values, perspectives, and commitments to ways of knowing (Ziegelmueller & Kay, 1997).

These components of a community—basic values, perceptual premises, and commitments to particular ways of knowing—determine what standards the community will use to evaluate arguments.

Let's consider for a moment an advertising campaign staged by Dodge in 1999. The campaign associated the word "Different" with "Dodge." Through a series of television commercials, print ads, and website images, Dodge implied that its cars were somehow different than others' cars and that this was good. Using the argument-field perspective, how might different audiences, or communities, evaluate this ad campaign? In Chapter 5, we discussed the VALS profile. We might think of that classification scheme as a way of dividing consumers into argument communities. We might conclude that Actualizers, Achievers, and Experiencers would evaluate the Dodge campaign positively. These communities share similar values, perceptual premises, and commitments to ways of knowing. In short, these groups value new things, see change as an important part of life, and seek to make their own decisions about taste and preference. They are willing to try new things.

Believers and Makers might respond positively to the campaign if they had previously owned Dodge or Chrysler cars and feel a sense of loyalty to the brand. These communities value tradition and are skeptical of change. Strivers and Strugglers might feel alienated by the Dodge ads because they cannot afford to be "different." These communities might see the Dodge campaign as disempowering because it values material wealth, in the form of new, expensive cars and trucks. This example shows the usefulness of the argument-field concept for evaluating arguments that are broadcast to a wide variety of audiences.

FALLACIES

fallacy

an error in reasoning or evidence

The form of an argument can also contain certain **fallacies,** or errors in reasoning. Fallacies can occur in our use of visual images or words. We focus on seven fallacies that are common in the media age: begging the question, non sequitur, ad hominem, ad verecundiam, straw argument, slippery slope, and ad populum.

The *begging the question* fallacy describes instances in which facts that have not yet been proved are assumed to be so. Begging the question can take one of three forms: persuasive prefaces, emotional language, or circular reasoning (Ehninger & Brockriede, 1963). *Persuasive prefaces* use such wordings as "Obviously," "It should go without saying," or "Everyone knows that . . ." In many cases, what comes after these words is *not* obvious, *should* be explicitly said, and is *not* known by all. Audience members who hear these words should carefully examine the external consistency of the statement in question. *Emotional language* inaccurately characterizes something by attaching emotional adjectives to it. Calling a policy proposal "radical" or "liberal" assumes certain facts about the proposal that may not have been established. *Circular reasoning* uses the claim of an argument as one of its premises. That is, it uses the conclusion of the argument to prove the conclusion of the argument. A politician who argues that a tax increase is bad because it means people will have to pay more money, which is bad, is using circular reasoning.

The *non sequitur* fallacy makes an unwarranted leap from one premise to another in an argument. There is no direct relationship between the premise and the conclusion in a non sequitur. The statement, "Feel young again. Drink Pepsi!" is an example of a non sequitur fallacy. There is no proved connection between drinking Pepsi and feeling young, no scientific evidence linking Pepsi consumption with youthfulness. The catchy slogan simply implies a connection.

Ad hominem arguments attack the source of a persuasive statement without addressing the reasoning on which the statement is based. Ad hominem arguments often take the form of name calling. Often, all we hear from political speeches are sound bites containing the speaker's most provocative statements. In some cases, those statements attack the character or reputation of another person. These kinds of attacks divert audience members from focusing on the issue at hand, instead riveting their attention on the name calling that is repeated in the media. President Clinton's opponents often accused him of being a "draft dodger" or a "pot smoker." Although these labels may have spoken to his character, they did not provide reasons for opposing his policy proposals, such as tax cuts or increased spending for education. Ziegelmueller and Kay (1997) point out that in some cases, character questions are relevant arguments. We should question the ethics of political candidates, but these charges should be factual and they should relate to the personal integrity or ethics of the person in question. Name calling should not be used to divert discussion from an issue or as the basis for attacking an argument not related to character.

The *ad verecundiam* fallacy uses an appeal to a higher authority or tradition. In Chapter 7, we discussed how some words in our language have greater standing than others. Often the connection is made simply on the basis of our reverence for the term and not on any valid relationship between the claim and the authority figure. When a parent offers a child the reason "Because I'm your parent," the parent is committing the ad verecundiam fallacy. Instead, the parent should offer reasoning based on his or her status as an "expert in life." Ziegelmueller and Kay (1997) distinguish between unwarranted appeals to authority figures and the use of expert testimony, which is a legitimate method of interpreting examples and statistics. We might also be careful of how persuaders use the ideograph, a concept we discussed in Chapter 7. Persuaders use ideographs to communicate a great amount of information in a word or phrase, and we often do not question these statements.

Given the tendency of media to metonymize, or reduce, ideas to more simple terms or images, mediated argument is especially susceptible to the *straw argument* fallacy. The straw argument fallacy uses a weak argument to represent the other side's case. Then, when the weak argument is easily defeated, the other side's entire case seems to fall. Audience members should be sure that what a persuader is representing as the other side's case is indeed an accurate portrayal of that side's arguments. The National Rifle Association (NRA) generally opposes restrictions on the use of guns and teaches its members how to use guns responsibly. A few years ago, the NRA opposed a measure to ban armor-piercing bullets, often called "cop killer bullets." In subsequent legislative battles, opponents of the NRA used the example of the NRA's support for "cop killer bullets" as indicative of the NRA's stance on gun control, despite

INTERNET ACTIVITY

Identifying Fallacies

When people make arguments, they do so in a variety of forums. For instance, we use reasoning in our everyday conversation, politicians use reasoning, and people who write letters to the editor often use reasoning. In each of these cases, though, we often use reasoning improperly. Visit Opinion Pages at http:// www.opinion-pages.org. Read a few letters to the editor or editorials on topics of your choosing. Can you identify any fallacies in the reasoning used by the authors of these articles? Which ones? Evaluate the evidence used in the articles.

Find examples of the seven fallacies discussed in this chapter in a magazine's advertisements. Are fallacies difficult to detect? Why or why not?

the fact that the NRA's stance on the issue of gun control is more involved than this one issue. "Cop killer bullets" is a straw argument used to argue against the NRA.

The *slippery slope* fallacy assumes that once a course of action is started, it will continue to its final conclusion. In other words, it assumes that once a set of actions is started, they cannot be stopped. It is a fallacy to assume this, however, because many actions can be stopped midstream. Members of the aforementioned National Rifle Association commit the slippery slope fallacy when they argue that banning a particular type of weapon will lead to a ban on all guns. In fact, many gun control opponents used this argument in the congressional debate on a bill concerning automatic weapons. Persuaders who commit the slippery slope fallacy see decisions as all or nothing: No weapons should be banned because then all weapons will be banned. It is possible, however, for gun control advocates to desire limitations on only certain types of weapons.

Finally, the *ad populum* fallacy assumes that because many people are doing something, the action is reasonable. Audience members who fall prey to this fallacy fail to see the reasons people engage in their behavior. Advertisements for online investing use the appeal that because a great number of people are investing online, it is a good idea. For some investors, however, online investing may not be a wise idea. An investor who chooses to trade stocks online simply because other people are doing it is committing the ad populum fallacy. With this knowledge of fallacies, complete the Internet Activity: Identifying Fallacies.

Summary

The reasoning process communicates data in some form to an audience to support a claim. In the media age, this process is often hidden, at least partially, from audience members. A model proposed by Toulmin can help us to understand whether elements of the reasoning process are hidden. His model includes a claim, data, warrant, rebuttal, qualifier, and backing.

There are two types of data: premises and evidence. Premises are widely held beliefs, values, or practices the audience accepts without external support.

Much of what we discussed about culture in Chapter 8 is useful to our understanding of a premise. Premises are of two types: perceptual and value.

Evidence is the second type of data. It is discovered through research and is of three types: examples, statistics, and testimony. Evidence must be tested to ensure that it accurately represents what it says it does. Inductive reasoning includes argument by example, analogy, and causal correlation. Deductive reasoning includes argument by causal generalization and sign. Deductive arguments are expressed in syllogistic or enthymematic form. Aden argues that much mediated argument takes the form of the enthymeme.

In the media age, a more useful way of viewing reasoning may be through the perspective of the narrative, as proposed by Walter Fisher. The narrative paradigm maintains that all humans are storytellers and that we constantly judge stories we hear according to the standards of narrative probability and narrative fidelity.

Reasoning may be evaluated by examining the argument itself or the data used to support the argument. Recognizing common fallacies helps audience members to identify erroneous arguments as well.

Key Terms

Visit the book's website at http://www.mhhe.com/borchers2 for multiple choice quizzes, Internet activities, and key terms flashcards.

WWW:

reasoning 273	warrant 280
claim 274	inductive reasoning 280
data 276	deductive reasoning 283
premise 276	syllogism 284
evidence 277	enthymeme 287
example 277	narrative 289
statistics 278	fallacy 298
testimony 280	

11
Motivational Appeals

Learning Objectives

After reading this chapter, you should be able to:

1. Understand the role of motivational appeals in persuasion.

2. Identify particular emotions and how persuaders use them.

3. Describe Maslow's hierarchy of needs and how they apply to persuasion.

4. Define values and ways persuaders use values to persuade audience members.

Think for a moment about your decision to attend your college or university. Given today's heavy competition to increase enrollments in higher education, you were probably recruited heavily by admissions counselors. These recruiters likely used a variety of techniques and arguments to get you to attend their school. Perhaps they told you about their excellent facilities for science, art, and athletics. They may have introduced you to the professors with whom you are now studying. Given all these pressures, how did you finally make your decision?

Research at my school indicates that quite often students decide to attend a particular institution not because of cold, hard facts about the school or the quality of its facilities. Instead, my admissions counselors tell me, students choose to attend a school based on various emotional factors. Perhaps your best friend or significant other had already decided to attend a certain school. You may have decided to attend the same school for that reason. Perhaps the school is close to your hometown, and being close to your family and friends is important. Maybe the cost of the school was the deciding factor. In families with limited resources, the degree of financial sacrifice is an important decision-making criterion. In any case, there is a good chance that your feelings influenced your decision to attend the school you do. There is nothing wrong with this. We use our feelings to make decisions all the time.

When we evaluate a persuader's message, we cannot help but be influenced by our feelings. Our emotions, needs, and values all play a role in how we identify with a persuader's ideas. Persuaders know that our feelings help us to make decisions, so they create messages designed to maximize this appeal. Aristotle called this type of persuasive strategy pathos: the type of proof in which the audience is led to feel emotion by the speech (Aristotle, trans. 1991). Aristotle said audiences do not make the same judgment about an idea when they feel happy as when they feel sad. Thus, a persuader can influence an audience's attitude toward a topic by calling upon audience members' emotional state (Jorgenson, 1998). The study of emotion today includes a variety of feelings-based, or affective, concepts, including psychological needs and values, as well as emotion. Researchers call these concepts **motivational appeals.**

Persuaders use motivational appeals in a number of ways today. As persuaders seek to build relationships with audience members, they appeal to the feelings of the audience. Political candidates attempt to show audiences that they can be trusted. Advertisers use brand names, such as Coca-Cola, to create positive feelings toward their products. Organizations provide ways for members to interact with other organizational members so that they become more comfortable with the organization's values and mission. Persuaders also use the informal style of electronic eloquence to foster intimate connections with us. On a deeper level, persuaders seek to create our emotions, needs, and values as well. They define for us what is important or beautiful, we internalize those feelings, and then we behave in ways that benefit the persuader. For instance, persuaders have influenced us to believe that it is important to have a beautiful home and garden. When we think this is true, we are likely to purchase *Better Homes and Gardens* magazine, shop at expensive stores like Pottery Barn, and pollute the atmosphere using fossil fuel–powered lawn mowers and edgers. Thus, our feelings are part of a great web of influences and pressures that we often take for granted.

In this chapter, we explore motivational appeals in the persuasion process. Recall from our model of persuasion that audience members bring emotions, needs, and values to the persuasion process. These feelings help them make sense of the persuader's language strategies and visual images. After first addressing the power of motivational appeals, we look individually at emotions, needs, and values. Then we examine how persuaders construct motivational appeals using visual images, language, and media. Finally, we discuss the degree to which our emotions, needs, and values are socially constructed.

Motivational appeals are effective ways for persuaders to create intimate relationships with audience members. Motivational appeals also help persuaders convince audience members of the value of their product, service, or idea.

> **motivational appeal**
> a feelings-based, or affective, approach by a persuader that targets the audience's emotions, needs, and values

The Power of Motivational Appeals

We often think that when feelings are involved in decision making, we make faulty decisions. For example, you might think that purchasing a car based on how it makes you feel is foolish. The best decisions, we think, are those based on credible evidence and valid reasoning. Thus, buying a car for how it makes us feel is often thought to be inferior to buying a car because of its gas mileage or resale value. Yet motivational appeals are important in the persuasive process. The most effective—and valid—persuasion uses credibility, logic, *and* motivational appeals. To better understand why this is so, let's examine two of the reasons feelings are important in persuasion. Motivational appeals motivate us, the audience, to act on the persuader's message, and they help us make moral decisions.

First, feelings are necessary to spark conviction on the part of the audience. That is why we refer to these appeals as motivational: They move, or *motivate*, the audience to take action. Usually the aim of the persuader's message is to get the audience member to do something. The audience member may be asked to believe something or to take action based on what is communicated. A logical appeal alone may lack the power to do this. Audience members may agree with the persuader, but without conviction, they will not act on their belief. Audience members must have passion for what the persuader says to be moved to action (Campbell, 1963). Persuaders are more likely to achieve their goal if they motivate their audience. Two examples will help us to better understand this point.

An advertisement for a fitness center might include information about price, available equipment, and staff experience. If this were all the advertisement included, it probably would not motivate many audience members to join the facility, let alone start a new exercise program. Instead, a motivational advertisement would be more effective. Such an ad might stimulate the audience's sense of pride and accomplishment in completing a tough workout. Or the ad might show healthy, active parents playing with their children. In either case, the persuader provides for the audience symbols that touch the audience's feelings.

For another example, let's look to politics. In the final days before an election, the candidate's primary goal is to get supporters to the polls to vote. Supporters often favor a candidate but do not feel the compulsion to spend their time and energy actually voting. As Election Day approaches, the campaign uses a Get Out the Vote (GOTV) strategy. Candidates must create an emotional connection with their supporters to ensure that the supporters act on their convictions. Voting requires action, and action necessitates motivational appeals.

In addition, the moral quality of motivational appeals can help audience members make ethical decisions. Craig Waddell (1990) explains that when we use reason alone we may draw faulty conclusions. Sidney Callahan (1988) writes, "Persons may have high I.Q. and be able to articulate verbally the culture's moral rules, but if they cannot feel the emotional force of inner obligation, they can disregard all moral rules or arguments without a qualm" (p. 10). Emotions allow individuals to make qualitative judgments about moral decisions. Our affective involvement in a moral issue also causes us to pursue its ethical solution (Callahan, 1988). When we are angry, for instance, we become invested in the persuasive process. We argue with a persuader to reach an acceptable decision about the persuasive message.

At times, however, our feelings can adversely affect the decisions we make. Douglas N. Walton (1992) explains that bias, such as prejudice, racism, or dogmatism, prevents decision making from functioning smoothly. Bias may prevent us from exploring and appreciating other experiences and perspectives. In our legal system, for instance, jurors who are shown to be biased are excused from serving. There may also be times, says Walton, when we must suspend our critical disbelief to understand the other side's arguments and positions.

Persuaders use motivational appeals to move their audiences to take action, and audiences use their feelings to help them make good decisions. In the next few pages, we look at three broad categories of motivational appeals: emotion, needs, and values. We examine each and then describe how persuaders use motivational appeals and how emotions, needs, and values are socially constructed.

Consider a decision you recently made. What role did emotions play in your making that decision? Did emotions help or hinder your decision-making process?

Emotion

The first type of motivational appeal draws on the audience's emotions. The study of emotion is currently enjoying a great deal of attention from a variety of scholars (Cacioppo & Gardner, 1999; B. R. McGee, 1998; C. R. Smith & Hyde, 1991; Warnick, 1989). One school of thought says emotions are comprised of two elements: a state of physiological arousal and cognition appropriate to this state (Schachter, 1971). Physiological arousal may be experienced as that "rush," or "high," you experience when faced with something exciting or dangerous or pleasurable. The cognitive aspect of emotion refers to how you perceive or describe the physiological arousal. Think about how you respond to the emotion you feel when seeing a loved one after an absence. You might experience that rush we have described and then feel you have to act in a certain way. For some people, hugging the loved one or kissing him or her would be appropriate. In my family, however, a simple handshake for a parent or grandparent is usually the preferred response. We learn how to respond to the rush we experience. Because the cognitive aspect of emotion is most applicable to our understanding of how persuaders use emotion, we will discuss that aspect of the definition more closely.

DEFINING EMOTION

Porter and Samovar (1998) explain that when we are born, we do not have an awareness of emotions, such as shame, pride, or remorse. Instead, emotions are something we learn. **Emotions** are belief systems, or schemas, that guide how we understand our feelings and how we organize our responses to those feelings (Averill, 1986). In other words, emotions are social constructions (Averill, 1980b). Michael J. Hyde (1984) puts it another way: Before we are aware of an emotion, we must be conscious of the emotion, and this consciousness emerges through our interaction with the world.

Our belief systems, or schemas, about emotions are based on beliefs we learn. These belief systems help us to identify when we are experiencing a certain emotion. Thus, they allow us to actively interpret emotional situations in

emotions
belief systems, or schemas, that guide how we understand our feelings and how we organize our responses to those feelings

which we find ourselves. So, despite the popularity of such clichés, we do not "fall in love" or "become paralyzed by fear." Instead, love and fear are emotions that we learn about. Averill (1980b) argues that we also learn to respond to emotions based upon our interactions with others in our culture. We learn from our parents, siblings, or television characters what it means to fall in love with someone. We come to an understanding of what happiness means. We learn appropriate and inappropriate responses to our feelings of anger. Finally, we express emotions in ways that are acceptable to members of our culture. In some cultures, emotion is expressed outwardly through hugs and kisses. In other cultures, emotions are not expressed publicly.

Averill (1980a) introduces two additional terms to help us more fully understand emotions: syndromes and social roles. Averill views emotions as *syndromes.* That is, an emotion does not have an "essence" or a single underlying force. Instead, emotions are sets of behaviors that we learn in response to some feeling we may have. When we are angry, for instance, we use a range of behaviors to express our anger: we might be physiologically aroused, we might be withdrawn, and we might quickly lash out at someone. To understand an individual's anger, we would look at all of these actions. In addition, each emotion is different or somehow unique from other emotions. An individual's sense of anger is different in each situation. It depends on the object of the anger and the reason for the anger.

Averill also explains that emotions are the enactment of transitory *social roles.* A role, he explains, is a socially prescribed set of responses followed by an individual in a given situation. We constantly interpret our situation and choose from among the emotions we have learned to enact. At a funeral, we play the role of a grieving person; at a wedding, we enact those behaviors associated with happiness. We learn about emotions from others, and this forms the basis for how we express emotions.

Emotions are experienced along a continuum (Smith & Hyde, 1991). At the center of the continuum is a restful state, where the individual does not feel the presence of the emotion. At either end of the continuum is an intense feeling of the emotion—so intense, say Smith and Hyde, that the individual may not be able to act reasonably. Thus, we experience emotions at varying degrees of intensity. Smith and Hyde explain that the intensity is related to the proximity of the emotion's referent. As the referent of the emotion comes nearer, we experience the emotion more intensely. As the big test in one of your classes approaches, you feel more strongly the emotions attached to the test, for example.

We also learn to identify emotions in others. We have learned throughout our lives what different syndromes of emotions look like. However, these syndromes do not always include the same behaviors. Each person expresses emotion a bit differently. When you came to college, you no doubt met a variety of new people. Chances are it took you a while to learn to identify their emotional states. You probably relied on cues that you had previously learned were associated with emotional states. A classmate might sit, arms crossed, in class, frowning and saying nothing. You would probably conclude that the classmate was angry or sad. If your new acquaintances were from another culture, you may have had a particularly difficult time identifying their emotional state. Porter and Samovar (1998) explain that there are cultural differences in how people express emotions. This is especially true when emotion is publicly displayed (Porter & Samovar, 1998).

As we learn about emotions from others, we learn about ourselves as well. We learn what kind of person we think we should be. Gerard A. Hauser (1986) explains that emotions involve our self-esteem, or our sense of who we are or ought to be. This is because we learn what our culture thinks are the appropriate emotional responses and behaviors in given situations. When we learn about emotions, we learn what is acceptable or what is normal for our culture. We measure ourselves against this norm to see how we compare. If we experience the same emotions as others, we feel good about ourselves. If we do not, we feel bad about ourselves. Our image of what kind of person we should be is inherently tied to what others say we should be.

A minivan advertisement, for instance, depicts parents talking about their desire to keep their children safe. The parents learn they should do all they can to protect their children. They take pride in the protection they offer their family. The emotional state that not protecting one's children produces is shame. Purchasing a vehicle that is not safe puts parents at risk of being shamed should anything happen to their family. The parents who see the advertisement develop a sense of what they should feel and how they should behave to obtain a certain emotion (pride) while avoiding another (shame). Ethical Insights: Ethics, Advertising, and Self-Esteem explores the idea of self-esteem and emotion further.

Not only do emotions influence how we perceive ourselves, Hyde (1984) argues that emotions structure and order our experiences. Emotions affect how we see our world and give meaning to the world in which we live. C. R. Smith and Hyde (1991) explain that emotions help us to see, interpret, and become involved with our world in meaningful ways. We determine what is important to think about, believe, and become involved with because of how emotions are created. Think back to our discussion of Bormann's symbolic convergence theory. Emotions are a type of fantasy in which members of society participate in the chaining out of the fantasy. Our culture takes on a collective emotional state in which members interpret events, determine an appropriate emotional response, and then act according to that response.

Being oriented toward the world by emotions has ideological implications. Much advertising today focuses on how we experience happiness. Whether it be owning a new house, driving a particular make of car, or wearing clothes from a particular store, persuaders often seek to shape our belief system about what it takes to experience happiness. We learn that to express happiness, we need to engage in certain behaviors. We experience feelings of happiness because of where we live, what we drive, or what we wear. Happiness is connected to our consumption of products and services. The chaining out of the happiness emotion clearly benefits some members of society. On the other hand, those who cannot afford to purchase products or services that are thought to bring happiness experience shame, guilt, or anger.

Consider a recent movie you've seen, and think about how emotions are socially constructed. What does it mean to "fall in love"? What does it mean to be angry? Sad? Mournful? Happy? Do these social constructions fit with what you already know about the various emotional states?

ETHICAL INSIGHTS

Ethics, Advertising, and Self-Esteem

A great deal of research suggests that exposure to media makes viewers believe that they are unattractive or overweight (see, for example, Posavek, Posavac, & Posavac, 1998; Harrison & Cantor, 1997). Viewers have an affective response to the images they consume. Viewers have emotional responses to the models they see and read about. Researchers suggest that viewers compare themselves with the standard of thinness promoted in advertising or entertainment media. For example, watching episodes of television shows that feature slim actors or actresses or paging through magazines picturing hundreds of thin supermodels results in feelings of inadequacy on the part of viewers. Some researchers even suggest that consumption of these images is linked to symptoms of eating disorders (Harrison & Cantor, 1997). Given the potential seriousness of this phenomenon, it is important for us to address its ethical considerations.

The National Communication Association Credo for Ethical Communication (NCA, 1999) states, "We promote communication climates of caring and mutual understanding that respect the unique needs and characteristics of individual communicators." No matter the intent of advertisers and programming executives, the choices they make concerning models and actors play a role in how individual communicators perceive of themselves. Think about these questions:

1. Is it ethical for advertisers to feature thin models in their advertising?
2. How might viewers be reassured that it is not necessary to look like the supermodels they see pictured?
3. What persuasive strategies could be used to counteract the images of thin supermodels used in advertising?

FEAR

One of the first researchers to study emotions was Aristotle, who identified several different emotional states (Table 11.1). Of the emotions, fear has been the one most studied. When an attorney tells a jury that the defendant is a violent criminal who threatens every member of the community, the attorney is using a fear appeal. A manager who argues that the company will go bankrupt if employees are not more efficient is using a fear appeal as well.

A fear appeal involves three dimensions (Mongeau, 1998). A fear appeal describes a threat, indicates that audience members are likely to experience the threat, and indicates that one way audience members can avoid the threat is by adopting the message of the persuader (Mongeau, 1998). An automobile mechanic may use a fear appeal to persuade you to have some work done on your car. The mechanic may tell you that continuing to drive your car in the state it is in will result in your being stranded on the side of the road. When you ask how likely this is, the mechanic may reply that it is "only a matter of time." Thus, to avoid having your car break down, you have the mechanic fix the problem. Let's examine more closely the implications of using fear as a persuasive strategy.

The research on fear appeals is confusing and contradictory. Early research suggests that fear has only limited impact on a persuader's message and that, in some situations, fear appeals may actually inhibit persuasion (Goldstein, 1959; Janis & Feshbach, 1953). Other researchers dispute these claims (Hewgill &

Table 11.1 Aristotle's Emotional Appeals

Emotion	Definition	Appeal
Anger	Desire for retaliation because of a slight directed, without justification, against oneself or others	"We cannot let terrorists inflict their will upon innocent victims around the world."
Calmness	A settling down and quieting of anger	"Now is not the time to harbor feelings of anger against each other; now is the time to come together as a united party to win the general election."
Fear	A sort of agitation derived from the imagination of a future destructive or painful evil	"Purchasing a cellular telephone is good insurance against being stranded in your car in a winter snowstorm."
Shame	A class of evils that brings a person into disrespect	"Your children deserve the best. Don't settle for anything less than the nutrition of Gerber foods."
Pity	A pain that happens to one who does not deserve it	"Help the less fortunate in our city by donating to the local food bank."
Envy	Distress at apparent success on the part of one's peers	"Nothing says style and success like a Lincoln Navigator."

Miller, 1966), and others find no relationship (Kohn et al., 1982). To sort through these conflicting claims, Paul A. Mongeau (1998) performed a meta-analysis of previous studies. He found that adding additional fear appeals to a persuasive message is likely to make the message more persuasive. He writes, "Specifically, no evidence exists that generating extremely strong levels of fear produces defensive avoidance processes and a corresponding decrease in persuasion" (p. 64). For nearly all audiences, the impact of a fear appeal is likely to be linear and positive (Mongeau, 1998). The extent of change that occurs as a result of the fear appeal depends on the audience, however. Fear appeals exert a stronger influence on low-anxiety audience members than on high-anxiety audience members. Mongeau (1998) explains that this is due to high-anxiety audience members' inability to cognitively process the solutions recommended by the fear appeal. In addition, fear has a stronger persuasive appeal on older audiences than on younger audiences. Mongeau explains that this may be because many fear appeals, such as those concerning health issues, are more relevant to older audiences.

Mongeau (1998) reaffirms support for the four critical components of a fear appeal: severity of threat, probability of occurrence, efficacy of coping response, and ability to enact solution. As we discuss these four components, refer to the State Farm advertisement in Figure 11.1.

First, the fear appeal must develop the noxiousness or severity of the threat. The audience member must feel that the threat, if it occurred, would be harmful. The State Farm ad states, "It's a sad day indeed when you learn that your landlord's coverage doesn't include your things." The severity of the threat is

Figure 11.1 State Farm Advertisement for Renter's Insurance Using a Fear Appeal   The ad makes the claim that without insurance, you could lose a considerable amount of money replacing your possessions. To what extent does the ad make you think differently about renter's insurance? Why or why not?

equated with an uninvited visit from mom, having a neighbor who plays the bongos, and getting caught with too much laundry and not enough change. For some renters, these may indeed be fearful events. The severity of the threat, however, may be limited to readers who do not fear the listed "nightmares." In fact, the humorous tone of the ad may belie the seriousness of not having renter's insurance.

Second, the appeal must prove the probability of the threat's occurring. By again equating needing renter's insurance to the other nightmares it lists, renters are invited to see how likely it is that they will need renter's insurance. After all, who hasn't run out of quarters while doing laundry? The ad also makes clear that renters' possessions are not automatically covered by their landlords' insurance policies, something that many renters may assume to be true. State Farm could strengthen this element of its fear appeal by providing evidence of apartment dwellers who have lost their possessions.

Third, the appeal must show the efficacy of the recommended coping response and that the audience member can enact a solution. The State Farm ad

shows that readers have the ability to obtain insurance and the protection it offers. The ad states, "State Farm renters insurance is really affordable too—
about the price of a couple of pizzas a month—even less if your car's insured
with us." By translating the cost of insurance to the cost of pizza, State Farm
shows that renter's insurance can easily fit into the budgets of most renters,
even those who are college students. To prove effectiveness, the ad proclaims
that State Farm is a company "millions trust to cover their stuff." By stating
that the coverage is inexpensive, as well as by stating that millions of others are
covered by State Farm, the persuader assures the reader that for a small amount
of money, the reader can avoid the dangers suggested earlier in the ad.

Fear is just one of many emotions studied by researchers. Emotions involve both physiological characteristics and cognitions. We learn to recognize
and express emotions based on the interactions we have with others. Emotions
are unique, involve sets of behaviors, and help us to play social roles. Emotions
are also linked to our ideas of self-esteem, and they orient us toward our world
in both positive and negative ways. Another type of motivational appeal is psychological needs.

Needs

Researchers contend that individuals have certain needs and that we strive to
fulfill those needs by believing something or doing something. Persuaders often
suggest that their ideas, products, or services can help us fulfill needs such as
love, safety, and self-fulfillment. Thus, we accept what the persuader has to
offer. Abraham Maslow's theory of needs has served to guide persuaders for
years. Maslow (1943) arranged his theory of needs with the idea of hierarchy
in mind. We cannot achieve higher-level needs until we have achieved lower-
level needs. Thus, we cannot experience love until our physiological needs are
met. Maslow points out that not all individuals follow this exact hierarchy, but
many of us do. Let's look more closely at Maslow's theory of needs, which include:

- Physiological needs
- Safety needs
- Love needs
- Esteem needs
- Self-actualization needs

The most basic category of needs is *physiological needs,* which include food,
drink, sleep, and sex. Maslow (1943) explains that if these needs are not met,
other needs become nonexistent or are pushed into the background. Maslow
says that people who are hungry, and perhaps those who live in poverty, put
aside their need to write poetry or to experience love in exchange for satisfying
their basic survival needs.

If you are paying your way through school, you probably do not have a lot
of free time. Perhaps you have even put off having a relationship with someone

INTERNET ACTIVITY

Fulfilling Safety Needs

Maslow's hierarchy of needs identifies five needs that humans typically experience. One such need is to be safe. Health websites often appeal to the safety needs of their users. One such site is http://www.drkoop.com. What information does the site offer its users? Do you think this information fulfills the viewers' safety needs? How might the site be more effective? Do you think there is any danger in relying on Internet sites for health information? Why or why not?

because you don't have time. Persuaders who are trying to sell "romantic getaways" would probably not be successful with you because you are struggling to fulfill your basic needs, such as paying rent, buying groceries, and making tuition payments.

Once physiological needs are met, individuals seek to fulfill higher needs, the most basic of which are *safety needs*. Safety needs, says Maslow (1943), include protection from wild animals, temperature extremes, and criminals. Maslow explains that individuals often use religion to fulfill their need for safety and security. If a person's safety needs are not met, the individual will be consumed by them in the same manner as physiological needs. In times of emergency, such as war, fire, or flooding, a community may become preoccupied with fulfilling its safety needs and its members may forgo higher needs.

An advertisement for an Internet health site appeals to the reader's safety needs. Individuals who have many medical questions and want fast answers to them can log on to thehealthchannel.com website to get the information they need to again feel safe and secure. In order to reassure Americans that the country would be safe from terrorists, President Bush created the Department of Homeland Security. As he announced the department's creation on November 25, 2002, he said these words to reinforce the idea that the department would keep Americans safe: "Today, we are taking historic action to defend the United States and protect our citizens against the dangers of a new era. With my signature, this act of Congress will create a new Department of Homeland Security, ensuring that our efforts to defend this country are comprehensive and united." Persuaders frequently try to convince their audiences that they can offer them safety and security. To see how health websites appeal to the safety need, complete the Internet Activity: Fulfilling Safety Needs.

At the third level of Maslow's hierarchy are *love needs*, which include love, affection, and belongingness. Maslow (1943) says we hunger for affectionate relationships with people. We seek to find our place in the group. We strive to obtain love from other people. Malsow points out that we seek, not only to receive love and affection, but to show love and affection to others. Here's where persuaders enter the picture. They convince us that to show love to others, we have to buy them diamond rings, or new cars, or a dozen roses on Valentine's Day.

At the next level are *esteem needs*, the desire for a stable, firmly based, high evaluation of ourselves (Maslow, 1943). We need to be respected and valued. There are two kinds of esteem needs: esteem we get from others and esteem we give to ourselves (Rowan, 1998). We receive esteem from others when we perform our social roles well. John Rowan says we want to be respected by those we respect. Receiving esteem from others provides us with a sense of self-confidence, worth, strength, capability, and adequacy (Rowan, 1998). Simply, these are ego needs that are satisfied or denied by what others say to us and how they behave toward us. We're surrounded by persuaders telling us we're important so that we will identify with them and their ideas. Persuaders seek to become our trusting friend, who builds our self-esteem. An advertisement for Edward Jones Investments uses an appeal to this type of esteem need. The ad asks if the reader is underpaid and promises that by coming to work for Edward Jones, the reader can make what he or she is worth. Edward Jones is attempting to show that it respects the employee's need for esteem.

At the same time, persuaders try to disrupt our sense of self-esteem. They tell us that we can be prettier, or smarter, or more respected. Hair care product commercials, for example, try to convince us that we can have prettier hair. Investment companies promise us that we can make more money by investing with them. Car companies attempt to convince us that we need to drive the latest, largest vehicle to adequately protect our family and show others how important we are. For instance, the Ford Excursion capitalizes on our desire to drive the biggest and best vehicle we can. Persuaders then use the esteem appeal in two ways: to tell us we're important as a way to identify with us, but also to tell us that we can become better by using their products. Think again about the discussion in the Ethical Insights box for this chapter, which examined how persuaders profit when individuals do not feel good about themselves. In short, the first type of esteem need—the need for esteem from others—concerns our self-image. Rowan (1998) contends that we must be comfortable with our self-image before we can move on to the second type of esteem need—esteem we give to ourselves.

Rowan (1998) says that esteem we give ourselves comes naturally from our inner nature and from our sense of "real" self. We no longer are playing a role that is rewarded by others, but rather, we are characters in our own stories. Persuaders encourage us to reward ourselves and recognize our own sense of self-esteem.

At the top of Maslow's hierarchy of needs is *self-actualization*. Maslow (1943) defines self-actualization as the need to achieve what we can. We must realize our potential. Maslow writes, "This tendency might be phrased as the desire to become more and more what one is, to become everything that one is capable of becoming" (1943, p. 163). This desire varies with the individual. Maslow says some women may wish to be the perfect mother, while others want to be the perfect businessperson. Others strive to reach their peak level of physical fitness. Some individuals, Maslow explains, may express themselves artistically.

Although there are still members of society who reach their potential through self-actualization, advertisers offer us another option. We can achieve our potential through consumer goods as well. A recent advertisement equates driving a Mercury Sable with historic forms of self-actualization, including yoga and meditation. Another commercial shows yoga practitioners imagining themselves trading stocks online. Again, the persuaders say, self-actualization is not achieved through a personal connection with self or God or nature, but rather through consuming goods and services.

Although Maslow (1943) argues that individuals achieve their needs in the order discussed, he points out that this structure may not be true for all individuals. Some people, for instance, see self-esteem as more important than love. Others abandon the attempt to satisfy higher-level needs due to continued problems satisfying basic needs. Some individuals lose the ability to give and receive love. When someone has had a need satisfied for a long period of time, such as the need for food, he or she may come to devalue the importance of the need.

Maslow's hierarchy of needs has guided persuaders for years because of its value in explaining how humans seek to fulfill their needs. A third type of motivational appeal concerns values. Like emotions and needs, values predispose audience members to accept certain persuasive messages and to ignore others.

What needs do you experience most commonly? How do persuaders fulfill those needs? Have you ever purchased something you did not need? Why? Are there any needs that you could add to Maslow's list?

Values

value

a criterion or standard of preference

Robin Williams (1979) defines a **value** as a criterion or standard of preference. Values guide our actions, help us to develop attitudes toward objects, and allow us to morally judge ourselves and others (Rokeach, 1968). Values can be openly admitted, advocated, exhorted, and defended by individuals (Rokeach, 1979a). Williams explains that we use values to continually judge our world and the people and events that comprise it. We make judgments about good and bad, right and wrong, beautiful or ugly, and appropriate or inappropriate based on our values. Rokeach explains, "We employ values as standards to guide the process of conscious and unconscious justification and rationalization of action, thought, and judgment (1979a, p. 48). Williams says that we cannot help but use values as we go about our daily lives. Thus, persuaders consider the values of their audiences.

Like emotions, values are learned. We develop them through our experiences with others. We value those things that give us pleasure, that cause us to be accepted by others, and that make us experience emotions such as love. It is important for us to make a slight distinction between *cultural* values and *individual* values. In Chapter 8, we discussed how cultural values are created, maintained, and transformed. As members of a culture share their experiences, they create value structures that guide what becomes widely accepted. As more people experience freedom, for instance, it becomes an important cultural value. Values are then taught to new members of the society. Your early educational experience, for instance, helped you to understand the values of honesty, politeness, and responsibility. Cultural values are maintained through practices of hegemony and patriarchy, and they are transformed by a variety of forces, including economic and demographic, as well as through the communication of persuaders. In Chapter 8, we discussed values that characterize the mainstream culture of the United States. Keep in mind that we said not all members of a culture share the values of the mainstream group. Thus, it is necessary that we consider how individuals create value hierarchies and how they use values to make decisions. In this chapter, we focus on the individual, rather than the cultural, value structure.

It is virtually impossible to ignore the force of cultural values on how we, as individuals, develop our own value structures. The presence of media, for instance, creates ideas about what is important and not important, what is pleasurable and not pleasurable, and what is beautiful and not beautiful. However, our individual value structures are not created entirely by media. Our parents, siblings, and peers, along with the institutions with which we are involved, also influence our values. Think for a moment about the value you place in hard work. Where did you learn your ideas about the value of manual work? What examples from your life have reinforced your ideas about the value of manual work? Do your ideas about work reflect our cultural value of work, as discussed in Chapter 8? If your idea about work is different from the mainstream's, why do you think this is so? Have your ideas about work changed? Why or why not? By exploring these questions, you can start to understand how values are created, maintained, and transformed.

Rokeach (1968) identifies two types of individual values: instrumental and terminal. **Instrumental values** guide the means by which we live, and **terminal values** are goals we have for our lives. "I believe that honesty is the best policy" is an instrumental goal. "I believe that everyone should be happy" is a terminal goal. Under these two broad categories, Rokeach identifies 36 values (Table 11.2). For example, your decision to pursue higher education reflects the terminal values of a sense of accomplishment, wisdom, and perhaps, family security because your degree should enable you to get a job and support a family someday. To achieve these terminal values, you might use the instrumental values of ambition, honesty, and intelligence. Rokeach (1979a) explains that these values are relatively universal. That is, these values are considered by almost everyone.

> **instrumental values**
> values that guide the means by which we live
>
> **terminal values**
> goals we have for our lives

What accounts for differences in value orientations, says Rokeach, is the way individuals put these values into hierarchies. We prioritize them differently, he maintains. The values Rokeach identifies can be ordered in countless ways. I might place family security at the top of my value hierarchy, whereas you might place an exciting life at the top of yours. As we have discussed, the priority we give to particular values is influenced by a variety of sources. The institutions of our society help to arrange and articulate certain values. Religion, for instance, transmits values of inner harmony and salvation; schools articulate the value of wisdom. Your parents influence how you prioritize your values, as do your siblings and peers.

Persuaders enter the picture in two ways. First, persuaders use value appeals to show us that they are like us. We identify with persuaders who appear to share our values. Because values are linked to attitudes and behavior, they help us to select actions in particular situations. When you choose a political candidate, for example, your values guide your attitudes toward the candidates. When you choose a particular brand of clothing, you use a value judgment. R. M. Williams (1979) explains that as we get older, our value structures become more tightly organized and our values serve to influence our behavior

Table 11.2 Rokeach's Individual Values

Terminal values	Instrumental values
A comfortable life	Ambitious
An exciting life	Broad-minded
A sense of accomplishment	Capable
A world at peace	Cheerful
A world of beauty	Clean
Equality	Courageous
Family security	Forgiving
Freedom	Helpful
Happiness	Honest
Inner harmony	Imaginative
Mature love	Independent
National security	Intellectual
Pleasure	Logical
Salvation	Loving
Self-respect	Obedient
Social recognition	Polite
True friendship	Responsible
Wisdom	Self-controlled

even more. Values also serve to anchor our perceptions. We filter the persuasion we encounter through our value hierarchies.

The company ShopForChange.com attempts to use values to identify with customers, which may result in those customers' using the company's website. An ad stated: "Clean water. Fresh air. Tough gun laws. Affordable housing. Quality education. Healthy food. Human rights. Reproductive freedom. Open minds. Next time you shop online, make your first click to ShopForChange.com. Because when you buy something from one of the popular merchants located on our new shopping site, Working Assets will donate 5% of every purchase to progressive causes." If your values are reflected in the list, you might be likely to shop at the site so that a part of your purchases would go to support the causes that you also support. By using a value appeal, the company hopes that you will identify with it. For more insight into this subject, read Thinking Critically: Values and Business Presentations.

Rank your top five values. Then, page through a magazine to see what values its advertising displays. Is there a correspondence between your values and those in the advertisements?

Persuaders also influence how individuals structure their values. The efforts of persuaders are perhaps most visible on the cultural level. In Chapter 8 you read about cultural values and how they are created, maintained, and transformed. In Chapter 13 you will read about persuasive movements that are concerned with reshaping a culture's value system. In addition to the cultural influence of persuaders on our values, persuaders communicate with us in more hidden ways about what we should value. In a later section in this chapter, we consider how the idea of love is socially constructed by media and peer

THINKING CRITICALLY

Values and Business Presentations

Business leaders typically use values when they market their products or services to audiences. Microsoft CEO Bill Gates, speaking at a small-business conference in Sydney, Australia, on September 11, 2000, appealed to his audience's values to win their business and support. In particular, Gates focused on how his products would achieve the values of efficiency and equality.

To explain to the small-business leaders how his company's products could make them more efficient, Gates said: "In some ways, it [technology] will eliminate a lot of the paperwork that we have right now. In some ways, it will eliminate a lot of the uncertainty we have about what our customers want and what's happening in the supply chain." An efficient workplace, argued Gates, would result in economic gain as well as satisfied customers and employees.

Gates also spoke to the value of equality and how computer technology is available to many people: "Today there are over 100 million personal comput-

ers sold. The price of those machines has come down pretty dramatically. For about US $1,000 you can buy a pretty powerful machine that gives you access to all the latest creativity software and also enables you to get connected to the Internet." The rate at which computer prices have fallen has surprised even Gates.

Gates also spoke about opportunities that Microsoft would create for business, and he spoke about the commitment Microsoft would make to customers using its products. As you think about Gates's speech, answer these questions:

1. To what extent are audiences persuaded by a speaker's use of values? Are values more persuasive than evidence in a speech?

2. How can speakers such as Gates discover the values held by their audience?

3. How can audiences tell if persuaders are sincere in their use of values?

groups. To evaluate how values influence your shopping decisions, complete the Internet Activity: Appealing to Values.

The Nature of Motivational Appeals

We now turn our attention to how persuaders construct motivational appeals. Jorgenson (1998) explains that persuaders use motivational appeals to produce some change in the values, beliefs, opinions, attitudes, and behaviors of audience members. A motivational appeal can also be viewed as the element of the message that signifies intensity, concern, or need (Jorgenson, 1998). Motivational appeals, then, are designed to elicit some feeling in the audience, which will result in some kind of socially constructed response from the audience. Knowledge of how society constructs responses to feelings can help persuaders predict, to some degree, which motivational appeals will result in acceptance of the persuader's message.

C. R. Smith and Hyde (1991) say that motivational appeals are linked to the experience of time. Persuaders who call upon the audience's emotions create images of a different time and place. As the persuader focuses on the audience's anger, for instance, the audience thinks about the future and how the anger will be avenged. Or the persuader may cause the audience to think about

Appealing to Values

One way that persuaders use motivational appeals is to show that they share similar values with the audience member. This technique is used to foster identification. Use Yahoo! at http://www.yahoo.com to find the website for a company of your choosing.

What values does the site appeal to? How? Do you think the site would be effective for audience members who hold these same values? Why or why not? Does the site appeal to values that audience members might not believe in?

the past and some event in the past that caused the audience to be angry. Alternatively, the persuader may want to bring the audience to a calm state by focusing on the present and minimizing the past experience or the future vengeful act. Thus, time plays a crucial role in developing the audience's emotional state.

In addition, persuaders use personal relationships to call upon the audience's emotions. Smith and Hyde (1991) explain that emotions are intensified when we experience them in relation to certain people. For instance, the feeling of shame is more intense when one is shamed in front of close friends. We feel less shame when we are shamed in front of people we do not know. Smith and Hyde (1991) also explain that the relationship between different emotions is related to the intensity of an audience's emotional state. When a person is fearful, he or she may likely be angry with the cause of the fear. Emotions are linked to one of our touchstones: relationship building. Through motivational appeals, audiences form relationships with persuaders and identify with them. Motivational appeals can be linguistic or visual, and the medium of the message often enhances the intensity of the emotional appeal.

NARRATIVE FORM

Verbal communication that uses narratives is effective at influencing an audience's motivation to identify with the persuader. Narratives evoke images of time and place and help audience members to feel emotions associated with the story. Narratives bring the emotion closer to the audience in time and space and evoke greater emotional response from the audience. Narratives also help the persuader to move the audience from one emotion at the beginning of the speech to another emotion at the end of the speech. For instance, the persuader may start with fear and build to joy (C. R. Smith & Hyde, 1991).

It has become popular for political candidates to use video documentaries of their life history to connect with voters. These videos use a narrative format and show the candidate's early life, developmental events in the candidate's life, and how the candidate entered politics. Usually, close friends, family members, and supporters of the candidate appear in these narrative films. Audiences form an emotional connection with the candidate because of the story told. Narratives are ways of providing cognitive as well as affective information to an audience. Narratives appeal to the consciousness of an electronic culture.

HUMOR

Persuaders can use humor to effectively create motivational appeals. A variety of emotions can be brought about by humor, such as happiness, contentment, and pride. If used skillfully, humor can excite fear and anger as well. Persuaders can also use humor to develop several of Maslow's needs, such as esteem, love, safety, and self-actualization. Some people argue that we all have a basic physiological need to laugh. Finally, persuaders can use humor to get us to think about our values and the values for which we strive. Humor is also a useful way for a persuader to enhance his or her credibility. Let's examine some of the basic ways of creating humor and how these techniques are useful for persuasion.

- *Puns* use a play on words as their source of humor. The speaker may use a word that has two different meanings or may use two words that sound the same but have different meanings. Or, the speaker may exploit the ambiguities in what words mean for humorous effect. The got milk? advertising campaign often relies on puns. An ad featuring tennis stars Venus and Serena Williams states, "Make ours doubles," in reference to their success in tennis doubles, but also to the larger size of a double shot of milk.

- *Satire* is a disparaging comment made about someone or something in order to bring about changes in that person or topic. Democratic presidential candidate Howard Dean was noted for saying that he "represents the Democratic wing of the Democratic party." His satirical statement was a reference to what he saw as similarity between the other Democrats running for president and the current president, Republican George W. Bush.

- *Farce* uses exaggerated characters and situations to produce humor. The characters on *Saturday Night Live* often use farce to make fun of politicians. Throughout the 2000 presidential campaign, *SNL* cast members portrayed George W. Bush and Al Gore in outlandish, but humorous, situations. Their use of farce identified areas in our political system that also seemed a bit outlandish.

VISUAL COMMUNICATION

Because of its resemblance to reality, visual communication is capable of creating physiological arousal in an audience. Persuaders who use emotional appeals can enhance their persuasive efforts by using the appropriate nonverbal communication behaviors (Caudle, 1990). Our facial expressions communicate a great deal of emotion. Viewers can easily identify facial expressions in advertisements, argues Fairfid M. Caudle. These facial expressions suggest ways that we should react to the person pictured in the ad. Caudle also explains that viewers can detect nongenuine emotional expressions. Robin L. Nabi (1998) found that disgusting photographs have a negative relationship to attitude change. That is, audience members are likely to turn against a persuader who uses disgusting photographs.

MEDIA

Emotions and media are inextricably linked. Media influence not only the physiological component of emotions, but how we socially construct emotions as well. Media provide persuaders with additional resources to reach the audience's emotions. If you have watched a horror film, you know that media used to transmit the message can create strong emotional reactions. From motion pictures to still images to music, media technologies influence how we feel. Because emotional appeals reach us on an affective level, media are an ideal tool for reaching an audience's emotions. As audience members in the media age, we must be conscious of how our culture's responses to emotions are being shaped.

Benjamin H. Detenber and Byron Reeves (1996) found that image size affects the viewer's physiological state of arousal. One explanation they suggest for this is that as the image becomes more lifelike, it more strongly resembles its "real-world" counterpart and thus becomes more of a threat to the viewer. When we see images, we respond automatically to them. We view them as a natural experience and respond accordingly (Detenber & Reeves, 1996). Thinking about the experience of watching a movie on a large theater screen as opposed to viewing it on a small television can help you appreciate the results of Detenber and Reeves's study. As high-definition television technology develops and individuals purchase larger television screens for their homes, we will experience even more emotional involvement with the images we see.

If you enjoy doing so, watch a frightening film. What elements of the film make it scary? The plot? The language? The special effects?

Detenber, Robert F. Simons, and Gary G. Bennett Jr. (1998) found that moving pictures increase the arousal level of audience members exposed to the images. That is, audience members exposed to moving images recorded a higher state of excitement, energy, and alertness than did audience members exposed to still images. Detenber, Simons, and Bennett also found that moving images amplify an audience member's positive or negative feelings toward the image compared with a still image. In addition, moving images keep an audience member's attention more so than do still images.

The Social Construction of Affect

We have previously discussed the social construction of emotions, needs, and values. Persuaders today are in the business of creating audience emotions, and media give persuaders a powerful means of shaping society's beliefs about its members' feelings. In this section, we discuss how feelings are socially constructed.

By the age of five, most children can look at facial expressions and correctly identify emotions of happiness, sadness, anger, and fear (Wilson & Smith, 1998). Young children can also match emotions to situations that cause them (Wilson & Smith, 1998). When they watch television, preschoolers can identify emotions experienced by the characters on the screen (Wilson & Smith, 1998). As they grow older and develop more complicated cognitive systems, children become more able to distinguish between similar emotional syndromes, such as happiness and pride. Television characters model certain attitudes and behaviors for children. The widespread adoption of television has given children more and varied models on which to base their ideas about emotions (Bandura, 1994). Children learn stereotyped attitudes about others, aggressive behaviors, and cooperation from watching television (Wilson & Smith, 1998).

Robin W. Simon, Donna Eder, and Cathy Evans (1992) argue that love is a social sentiment that has a label and a prescribed set of beliefs about feelings and behaviors. In a three-year study of sixth-, seventh-, and eighth-grade girls, the authors found that by the time girls reach the seventh grade, they begin to develop a set of norms about romantic love. The researchers discovered five beliefs in their study of middle school girls:

- *Norm 1:* Romantic relationships should be important, but not everything in life.
- *Norm 2:* One should have romantic feelings only for someone of the opposite sex.
- *Norm 3:* One should not have romantic feelings for a boy who is already attached.
- *Norm 4:* One should have romantic feelings for only one boy at a time.
- *Norm 5:* One should always be in love.

Simon, Eder, and Evans (1992) argue that emotions are in part socially constructed and that our emotions are subject to the norms of our social groups.

As we become adults, we continue to develop socially constructed beliefs about emotions, needs, and values. A particular challenge for persuaders today is the overabundance of choices that consumers can make. The constant barrage of new products, services, and ideas provides us with many ways to satisfy our needs. But because those needs are based on the consumption of goods, they are easily satisfied. Once the need is met, ideas, products, and services have little value. Thus, producers are forced to create new products and services to fulfill new needs, which must be created by persuaders. As we continue to consume, our ideas about what we feel, need, and value will continue to change as well.

Summary

Motivational appeals call upon the emotions, needs, and values of audience members. As audience members, we constantly view the persuasion in our world through these filters. In many cases, motivational appeals are necessary to motivate the audience to take action on the persuader's words or to use their ethical judgments to critically assess persuasion. At times, emotions, needs, and values can interfere with the persuasion process.

One type of motivational appeal is focused on the audience's emotions. Emotions involve both a physiological state of arousal and a set of beliefs about that feeling. We learn how to respond to certain feelings based on our interactions with others. A particular type of emotion is fear. Researchers have studied fear to determine when persuaders should use it. In analyzing prior studies, Mongeau (1998) argues that heightened fear in a persuader's message results in increased attitude change.

Persuaders also appeal to their audience's needs. Maslow has identified five needs: physiological, safety, love, esteem, and self-actualization. As audience members seek to fulfill these needs, persuaders demonstrate how their product meets particular needs. Persuaders also try to identify or create audience needs.

Values are criteria we use to judge thoughts, ideas, and actions. Values are arranged hierarchically and help us to determine how we should act in given situations. We filter a persuader's message through our value structures.

Motivational appeals can be developed through verbal and visual symbols. Media often enhance a persuader's use of motivational appeals. Media also contribute to the process of constructing emotions, needs, and values.

Key Terms

WWW: Visit the book's website at http://www.mhhe.com/borchers2 for multiple-choice quizzes, Internet activities, and key terms flashcards.

motivational appeal 303	instrumental values 315
emotions 305	terminal values 315
value 314	

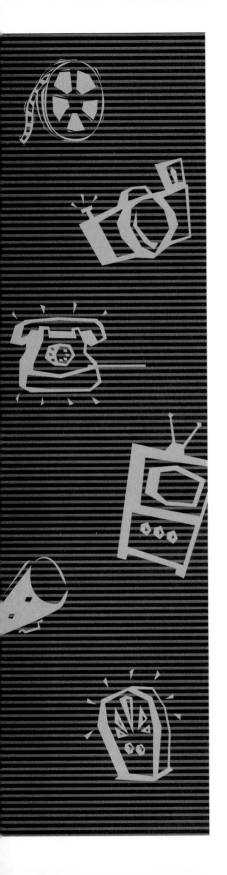

PART III
Contexts and Applications of Persuasion

In Chapters 12–15, you will see how persuaders in specific persuasion contexts use the variables of persuasion that we discussed in Part II. It is important to remember that although not all of these contexts are mediated, the impact of the media in our culture nonetheless bears upon the nature of persuasion that occurs within each context. In previous chapters, we isolated the variables of the persuasive process and discussed them separately. Although it is useful for our study of these elements, this approach does not always help us to understand how persuasion operates in the media age. Each context provides different ways of combining the variables to produce persuasive effects.

Chapter 12 focuses on political persuasion and persuasive movements and how the variables of persuasion come together in these events. Chapter 13 looks at advertising and how persuaders use the variables we have discussed to build relationships with consumers. Chapter 14 focuses on one-to-one communication and how persuaders adapt the variables to achieve interpersonal goals. Chapter 15 surveys how individuals use the persuasion variables to create effective presentations or texts.

12

Persuasive Campaigns
and Movements

Learning Objectives

After reading this chapter, you should be able to:

1. Define persuasive campaigns and movements.

2. Identify the relationship between media and campaigns and movements.

3. Discuss ways of using verbal and visual symbols in campaigns and movements.

4. Understand how political candidates manage the meaning of their message for voters through various media.

5. Describe the various types of movements and how they use persuasion to identify with the public.

On March 26, 2003, a movement led by the California organization People's Advocate began circulating petitions to recall the state's governor, Gray Davis. Reelected by a slim margin in November 2002, Davis faced much criticism for the poor California economy and his handling of power shortages during the previous summer. The recall movement had to gather nearly 1 million signatures to place the question of recalling the governor on a ballot for the voters. On July 23, 2003, the movement achieved its goal when the secretary of state certified that enough voters were in favor of the recall. The recall election was set for October 7.

Upon certification, those interested in being the California governor began announcing that they would run for the office. By paying $3500 and gathering a few signatures, anyone in the state could have their name on the ballot. Nearly

245 people came forward, including several prominent Californians: actors Arnold Schwarzenegger and Gary Coleman, millionaires such as Peter Ueberoth and Arianna Huffington, and current politicians such as Lieutenant Governor Cruz Bustamante and Davis's 2002 opponent, Republican Bill Simon. Within weeks of the deadline for declaring a candidacy, California was in full political campaign mode. Debates were held, candidates stumped for votes, and voters were inundated with political advertising. Eventually, voters went to the polls, voted to recall Davis, and then voted for his replacement, the actor Arnold Schwarzenegger.

California voters experienced two unique persuasive events in 2003: the movement to recall the governor and the political campaign that resulted from the movement's success. In this chapter, we'll explore these two related persuasive phenomena. Although campaigns and movements share many similarities, they also differ in several ways. A **campaign** is an organized and coordinated series of persuasive messages designed to achieve public acceptance of a person, idea, or product. We'll discuss product campaigns in the next chapter when we discuss advertising. **Persuasive movements** are "struggles on behalf of a cause by groups whose core organizations, modes of action, and/or guiding ideas are not fully legitimated by the larger society" (Simons, 1991, p. 100). The key differences between campaigns and movements are summarized below:

campaign
an organized and coordinated series of persuasive messages designed to achieve public acceptance of a person, idea, or product

persuasive movements
struggles on behalf of a cause by groups whose core organizations, modes of action, and/or guiding ideas are not fully legitimated by the larger society

- Campaigns exist for a period of time and then are finished. A persuasive movement exists until it achieves its goal or is terminated.
- Campaigns use generally accepted modes of persuasion while persuasive movements use modes of persuasion that are not always accepted by the larger society.
- Campaigns center on a specific person, idea, or product while persuasive movements exist for a cause, such as the right to vote.

In this chapter, we'll address both campaigns and persuasive movements. We'll begin our study by understanding how media affect these phenomena and some of the similarities in the persuasion used by campaigns and movements. Then, we'll study campaigns in greater detail, focusing on political campaigns and public health campaigns. Finally, we'll address persuasive movements and their unique use of persuasion to accomplish some kind of cause. Persuasive movements sometimes border on what may be considered unethical persuasion. As you begin to think about persuasion in this context, consider the Ethical Insights: Ethics and the Boundaries of Persuasion activity.

Media and Persuasive Campaigns and Movements

Persuasive campaigns and movements occur today within a highly mediated, public setting. The only way for either campaigns or movements to achieve their goals is by capturing media attention. The relationship between persuasive movements and media has five implications for our study. First, news media make us *aware* of persuasive campaigns and movements. Both cam-

ETHICAL INSIGHTS

Ethics and the Boundaries of Persuasion

The environmental protection group Greenpeace is known for staging newsworthy demonstrations of actions it considers detrimental to the environment. These events often include chaining themselves to trees destined to be cut down, occupying offseas oil rigs, or using boats to interfere with fishing and hunting expeditions. In some cases, court orders are necessary to remove the Greenpeace activists who are often arrested because of their actions. Consequently, the persuasive strategy used by Greenpeace is ethically questionable.

The National Communication Association (NCA) Credo for Ethical Communication calls for "the courageous expression of personal convictions in pursuit of fairness and justice." Certainly, protecting the environment would appear to be welcomed by the NCA credo. NCA also endorses "freedom of expression, diversity of perspective, and tolerance of dissent." Greenpeace would seem to be expressing diversity and dissent as well. Yet it could be argued that Greenpeace must also recognize the presence of corporate interests and the right of corporations to legally conduct their business. In fact, there may be times when expressing diversity and dissent endanger the good of the general public. A discussion of ethics and persuasive movements is especially difficult because many persuasive movements operate outside the bounds of traditional ethical codes. Consider the ethical guidelines we have discussed as you think about these questions:

1. To what extent is there a limit to the expression of personal convictions?
2. How should society determine that limit?
3. To what extent did the ends of Greenpeace's actions—environmental protection—justify the means used to achieve those ends?

paigns and movements must attract large-scale attention to be effective. In Chapter 2, we discussed agenda-setting theory, which says that media may not be able to tell the public what to think, but the media do tell the public what to think about. When news media show protests or interview movement leaders, the general public is made aware of the group's actions and ideologies. Likewise, political campaigns depend on media coverage to gain momentum and supporters. Howard Dean's 2004 Democratic campaign for the presidency was initially helped by media who made voters aware of his ideas.

Second, media allow persuaders to *take their messages directly* to the population. Media allow political candidates to take their message directly to the voter (Gronbeck, 1995). Candidates communicate with us through their Internet site and advertising, for instance. As a result, we learn more about the candidates today than we did in the pretelevision era, including a great deal about their personal lives. Electronic media emphasize personal traits not normally considered relevant to politics. Additionally, electronic media allow candidates to reach us in the comfort of our homes, through our televisions and computer screens. At the same time, the information we receive from candidates is filtered by media sources.

New media technology also enables persuasive movements to spread their message without the filter of the traditional news media. Specifically, the Internet has been an indispensable tool for the various persuasive movements. Militia organizations, for instance, use thousands of Web pages to spread their messages to audience members. There is a vast underground of Internet sites that offer inexpensive, interactive, and persuasive messages to potential supporters. Public access television is another way persuasive movement leaders spread their message to potential members.

Third, *public deliberation is expanded* when media allow an increasing number of persuasive campaigns and movements to emerge and influence the public's agenda. There is more potential for the fragmented public to engage in discussion about issues that concern them. Using technology such as Internet-based discussion groups, individuals can communicate with others about a variety of social issues and concerns. Usenet groups such as alt.politics.homosexual, alt.politics.radical-left, and alt.politics.nationalism.black provide spaces for persuasive movements to spread their word and discuss important issues with others. The use of blogging in the 2004 presidential campaign is another example of how the public can use new media to communicate with each other about political issues. However, the discussions in these and other mediated forums, including traditional news media, may not always be conducive to the development of Habermas's public sphere when persuaders exchange assertions without providing reasons for their claims. In any case, the availability of public discussion forums influences how persuasive campaigns and movements spread their message and respond to society.

Fourth, media *frame our perceptions* of persuasive campaigns and movements (Adams, 1991; McCarthy, 1994). Not only are we made aware of the presence of persuasive movements, but we understand a persuasive campaign or movement through the filter of media. Framing refers to the perspective adopted by the audience from the media's focus on an event, person, or idea. As we have discussed throughout this book, our mediated view of the world is only partial. We cannot completely understand the people or issues involved in a persuasive campaign or movement. We are dependent on media coverage to learn about our world. Yet media do more than educate us; they dramatize the campaign or movement (Gronbeck, 1995; Gusfield, 1994). Based on how the campaign or movement is framed we identify with some movements, while others will seem contrary to what we believe.

Finally, media *create cultures* that foster campaigns and movements. Recall our discussion from the first chapter that media create cultures. Persuasive events such as those we are discussing emerge from cultures and thus reflect the media of the movement's culture. A good example of this is rock and roll music that emerged in the United States in the 1950s and 1960s. Rock and roll provided a voice for marginalized youth and spurred their desires to reject the lifestyles of their parents. Rock and roll splintered our society and provided a new way of thinking and acting. From this culture emerged the youth movement, the antiwar movement, the civil rights movement, the feminist movement, and the gay rights movement. An example from political campaigns is that of Jesse Ventura's election as Minnesota governor in 1998. We have discussed his surprising election previously. If you'll recall, the culture of the time—suspicion of politicians, anger at higher taxes, and fascination with professional wrestling—all fueled Ventura's campaign.

Of which persuasive campaigns or movements are you aware? How did you learn about them? To what degree do you use media to participate with them?

Persuasive campaigns and movements use media to persuade audiences to identify with a person, issue, product, or cause. As such, media and persuasive campaigns and movements are closely connected. In the next section of this chapter, we will examine more closely the general persuasive techniques used by both campaigns and movements.

Verbal Symbols

By now you should realize that symbol use is an inherent part of the persuasive process. Persuasive campaigns and movements strategically use symbols in order to communicate their ideas to their public audiences. In this section, we will explore how language is used to influence public perception of issues, people, and causes. In short, effective campaigns and movements make use of the media style we discussed in Chapter 7. That is, persuaders seek to create intimacy with their audience through the use of synoptic phrases and visual imagery.

SLOGANS

Slogans are terms, phrases, or expressions that suggest a course of action to individuals. Stewart, Smith, and Denton (1994) claim that for centuries, protestors have chanted, shouted, and sung slogans, printed them on pamphlets, or worn them on clothing and buttons. Slogans have become especially common in today's media society. Stewart, Smith, and Denton say that slogans are powerful because they can crystallize in a few words the ideas or themes one wants to associate with a candidate, issue, or cause. Slogans also have an emotional component that elicits reactions from audience members (Bowers, Ochs, & Jensen, 1993). Slogans promote acceptance of the candidate or movement and identify those issues that are important to the persuaders (Bowers, Ochs, & Jensen, 1993). Let's look more closely at how slogans are used.

slogan
term, phrase, or expression that suggests a course of action to individuals

Political slogans have been a mainstay of campaigns for many years. Usually appearing on buttons or signs, campaign slogans sum up the candidate's views and reasons for running for office. Dwight D. Eisenhower's "Peace, Prosperity, Progress" reflected the important issues of the 1950s. Jimmy Carter's slogan, "A Leader, for a Change," was a direct reference to the corruption of his predecessor, Richard Nixon. George W. Bush's "Compassionate Conservatism" was designed to appeal to conservative voters, but also to those looking for sensible, practical government solutions.

Identify a current political campaign's slogans. What does the slogan mean? How powerful do you think the slogan will be for voters?

The slogans used by persuasive movements are often short, rhythmic chants that are easy for large groups to repeat and chant in unison (Stewart, Smith, & Denton, 1994). World Bank protestors chanted "More world, less bank" in April 2000 protests in Washington, D.C. Vietnam War protestors chanted "Hey, hey LBJ [President Lyndon Banes Johnson], how many kids did you kill today?" or "ROTC has to go." Some slogans are officially sanctioned by the persuasive movement organization. Stewart, Smith, and Denton refer to these as sanctioned slogans. The youth movement's slogan—"Don't Trust Anyone over 30"—is an example of a sanctioned slogan. Advertising slogans are the easily marketed names given to a persuasive movement or an organization

Figure 12.1   These slogans of the antiwar movement of the 1960s mobilized viewers to action by showing defiance for the establishment and proclaiming the power of the movement. What argumentative claims do they support?

(Stewart, Smith, & Denton, 1994). An example would be the antiabortion movement's use of the slogan, "Right to Life" or the antinuclear weapon movement's phrase, "No Nukes." Effective slogans are remembered for years and summarize the movement's ideology. Figure 12.1 depicts some of the dominant slogans from the peace movement of the 60s. These slogans have become part of popular culture because of their effectiveness.

SONGS

Another popular form of verbal persuasion is music. The songs of persuasive movements often serve as alternatives to formal argument and speech making. Knupp (1981) argues that songs used by persuasive movements create new visions of reality through their messages of discontent. Songs are *meant to be remembered* and repeated and are thus more useful to persuasive movements than are speeches or editorials (Stewart, 1991). Like slogans, songs reflect what we have discussed previously as a media style.

Songs communicate to the larger audience the *discontent* perceived by the persuasive movement. They are reactive in this sense. Knupp (1981) explains that songs often communicate more about the adversary and the oppressive societal situation than they do about those in the movement. Songs of the 1960s had titles such as "Eve of Destruction," "The Times They Are a Changin'," and "The Cruel War Is Ragin'." These titles suggest discontent with the world and a desire to change the world.

Persuasive movement songs also rely on a *simplistic vision* of the world to achieve a persuasive advantage. Knupp (1981) explains that songs thrive on ambiguities, sweeping assertions, and panoramic criticisms instead of on issues, policies, or specific arguments. Protest songs ignore historical references and remain focused on the present, which allows the musician to avoid complex interpretations of society that come from historical analyses. History also bores the audience, says Knupp. By being simplistic, Knupp argues, the protest song orients the audience toward action. It is not concerned with thinking as much as it is with taking action.

A popular component of movements for many years, songs are also becoming significant in political campaigns as well. In 1992, Bill Clinton used the Fleetwood Mac song, "Don't Stop Thinking about Tomorrow" at his campaign rallies on the 1992 Democratic National Convention. The song reflected his campaign theme and it also created the image of Clinton as a candidate in touch with the popular culture. In the 2004 campaign, Howard Dean's rallies featured the recording artist Joanna and her song, "We Can." Dean's theme is to return the political process to people and the words from this song reinforce the message of Dean's speeches. Both songs and slogans are verbal forms of communication used by persuasive movements. Of course, movements also make use of a variety of other verbal forms of communication, including speeches, advertising, editorials, and pamphlets. In the next section, we will focus on how persuasive movements use visual symbols to communicate their ideology.

Visual Images

The use of visual symbols is an important aspect of the persuasive strategy of a campaign or movement. The study of persuasion is replete with examples of how movements and campaigns have used visual forms of communication to persuade audience members. We will examine how persuaders use both images, such as photographs or symbols, as well as image events to alter audience attitudes.

IMAGES

Using Messaris's typology of visual symbols that we discussed in Chapter 6, we can understand how photographs and symbols persuade audiences. If you recall, images can be used to represent reality by attracting attention or eliciting an emotional response from the viewer. The antiabortion organization Operation Rescue has used white crosses at their rallies to symbolize fetuses that have been aborted. The white crosses both attract attention to the cause of the organization as well as elicit an emotional response from viewers. The AIDS quilt, which brings together the lives of those who have died of AIDS, is another example of an image that represents reality. The names stitched in the design of the quilt symbolize that those who died of AIDS were brothers, sisters, sons, daughters, mothers, fathers, friends, and lovers. Verbal forms of argument cannot fully express the emotional power of the quilt.

Images are also used as proof for the claim of the persuasive movement. The animal rights movement has made extensive use of photographs in their persuasive message. Images of clubbed baby seals, for example, offer photographic proof that the animals need to be protected. Images of animals that have been used in eye makeup tests are also used as proof of the harmful effects of testing cosmetics on animals.

Images are also used to say what words cannot. Images often convey argumentative propositions when words cannot. Look again at the 60s symbols in Figure 12.1. What propositions can been identified from these symbols? You might decide that the flowery script communicates that the protestors are peaceful. The childish informality of the script communicates distance from the more rigid script that might have been used by someone in the establishment. What other propositions do you see in these symbols?

In a political campaign, images of the candidate with voters and family members and in other positive situations can be very persuasive to voters. Candidates use photo opportunities to draw attention to their campaign and their message. These photo opportunities may include parades, store openings, or charity benefits. Iowa Governor Tom Vilsack was very successful using "Main Street Walks" in his 1998 campaign. Vilsack and his running mate, Sally Pederson, conducted more than one hundred walks along Iowa's Main Streets in an effort to show that they were in touch with the values and concerns of Iowans (Kupper, 1999). The appearances received positive local press coverage and helped Vilsack defeat his heavily favored opponent. The walks helped Vilsack create relationships with voters.

A popular part of the nominating convention for presidential candidates is a video that is played shortly before the candidate's acceptance speech. The video uses pictures to tell the story of the candidate's life. Voters have seen pictures of the candidate with his family, in life-altering situations (such as fighting in war), and in previous political positions. In 2000, Democratic nominee Al Gore's wife, Tipper, narrated a video about his life and used pictures she had taken throughout their life together to illustrate the idea that he would be a good president. In this case, Gore's use of video "proved" that he was a good person and suggested that he would be a good president.

IMAGE EVENTS

Besides the use of single photographs or symbols, persuasive campaigns and movements combine visual signs to create what DeLuca (1999) has called **image events.** Image events are visual in nature and communicate identity, ideology, and consciousness (DeLuca, 1999).

For persuasive movements, image events serve to question the prevailing ideology of a culture. Because of television, image events can powerfully communicate a movement's message to the larger public. DeLuca argues that

image event

a staged occurrence that is visual in nature; communicates identity, ideology, and consciousness

Figure 12.2
PETA activists stage image events to communicate their ideology. In the media age, image events can be powerful forms of communication. What message does this image send to you?

Greenpeace is the first organization to use image events as its primary means of persuasive activity. Greenpeace boats often block the efforts of much larger whaling ships attempting to hunt whales. DeLuca argued that this confrontation questions the commonly accepted hierarchy that places humans at the top of the animal kingdom. By risking their lives for the whales, Greenpeace protestors show that the whales are more than just economic resources. The image events communicate that whales have value and rights (DeLuca, 1999). Greenpeace's image events also receive media attention. Another group that has effectively used images is People for the Ethical Treatment of Animals (PETA). Figure 12.2 illustrates how PETA uses images to persuade audiences.

Political campaigns abound with image events. Review, for example, the image in Chapter 7 of President Bush on the USS *Lincoln* following the Iraq War. Campaigns often seem to be a series of image events designed to support the candidate. One of the first appearances candidates make is when they announce that they will be running for office. The *announcement speech* occurs during the first phase of the campaign and is largely ritualistic. In fact, candidates may sometimes make several announcement speeches at different times and in different locations. The location of the announcement speech is carefully chosen. Prior to the 2000 campaign, George W. Bush announced from his home state of Texas that he would seek the presidency. The announcement speech features the family of the candidate, several influential supporters, and all the trappings of a political rally.

Another type of image event is the town hall meeting. Candidates use town hall meetings to communicate directly to the public. A town hall meeting is a pseudoevent in which a single candidate meets a group of voters who ask questions of the candidate. Muir (1994) explains that town hall meetings allow candidates a way to get their message out to as many audiences as possible in a format that at least appears to be participatory. Republican John McCain held

Figure 12.3 John McCain Conducting One of More Than 100 Town Hall Meetings in New Hampshire during the 2000 Republican Presidential Primary Campaign   What advantages do town hall meetings have for the candidate? For the voter?

more than 100 town hall meetings in New Hampshire in the months prior to its February 2000 primary, which he won (see Figure 12.3).

Candidates who effectively use the town hall meeting format identify with their audience and recognize the public's desire to participate in the electoral process. Muir (1994) notes that in 1992, Clinton used language that helped him identify with his audience. He used personal narratives to underscore the similarities between himself and the voters, he used inclusive language such as the word *we*, and he identified the groups and individuals that he opposed. Clinton also interacted with audience members on an individual basis, calling them by name or asking for their input on questions (Muir, 1994).

Despite Clinton's effective use of the town hall meeting, Muir (1994) questions the degree to which these meetings add to the electoral process. In 1992, Clinton was able to avoid the tough questions asked by journalists. Candidates are also able to avoid follow-up questions asked by the audience. Despite appearances to the opposite, town hall meetings do not allow for much interaction between candidate and audience, aside from the questioning. The public is involved, but only on a shallow level (Muir, 1994). In the future, Muir notes that electronic technology could allow for more interaction between candidate and voter, including having votes at the end of the meeting to determine the audience's stand on the issues discussed. In 2000, however, the town hall meeting remained a symbolic gesture on the part of the candidate to express his views to the voting public.

Political Campaigns

Having looked at some general characteristics of persuasive campaigns and movements, we'll turn our attention now to the specific forms of these phenomena. First, we'll examine political campaigns. The past 20 years have seen dramatic changes in the nature of political persuasion in the United States. In addition to technological innovations in the media industry and widespread use of public opinion polling by persuaders, the rules governing the election of our political leaders have also changed. Political party leaders used to decide the party's candidates, its issue positions, and electoral strategies without the direct input of the public. Gradually, the party has played less of a role and the general public has played a greater role in the electoral process. In 1968, the public chose only 40 percent of the delegates to the national political conventions. By 1978, the number of delegates elected by the public had increased to 78 percent. Although it still takes many voting cues from the party, the public is much more likely to split its voting ticket today, voting for candidates from either major party or from a number of smaller parties represented on the ballot. In short, candidates today take their messages and ideas directly to the public and they do so primarily through media. At the same time, some researchers fear the mediated nature of politics alienates voters (Bennett, 1992). Political campaigns are productions staged by political consultants and portrayed to the world via the mass media.

This section explores how political persuaders use relationship-building strategies, repetition, electronic eloquence, and commoditization to shape voter attitudes. Underlying this discussion is the assumption that voting is a "comparative act" in which voters must choose which candidate in the election appears most preferable to them (Benoit, Blaney & Pier, 1998). While in the past voters made many decisions based on their party affiliation, today voters are less likely to use party identification as the sole determinant of their vote (Benoit, Blaney & Pier, 1998). Keep in mind as well that in each two-candidate campaign there are three groups of voters: those in favor of candidate A, those in favor of candidate B, and those who are undecided. Candidates aim to win the votes of those who are undecided, ignoring the partisans who support the other candidate. Research suggests that 20 to 40 percent of voters today are undecided in a typical race. With this in mind, let's discuss how candidates build relationships with audiences through the media.

HOW THE NEWS MEDIA COVER POLITICS

Earlier in this chapter, we looked at the influence of media on persuasive campaigns and movements. Here, we focus more specifically on political campaigns. In Chapter 4, we discussed the constraints on the news media and the effect those constraints have on the way news is covered. Recall that the media industry has as its goal making money. Therefore, it must keep its costs associated with producing news stories low while keeping audience interest high. In this chapter, we examine the specific effect the news media have on politics.

News as Melodrama   Researchers have asserted that mediated politics is a melodrama. Nimmo and Combs assert, "The popularity of the melodrama is undiminished" (1990, p. 16). They explain, "Moral justice is at the heart of most melodrama—trials of the virtuous, calumny of the villainous, good rewarded, evil punished" (1990, p. 16). Hovind (1999) identifies four aspects of television news that make it similar to melodrama: dramatic conflict, simple and familiar plots, simple and predictable character development, and eye-catching visuals. Hovind observed these variables in television news during the 1996 presidential campaign and compared news to the soap opera *Days of Our Lives* and the talk show *Oprah*. He found that the news—*ABC World News Tonight with Peter Jennings* and CNN's *Inside Politics*—exhibited more elements of melodrama than did the soap opera or talk show. Hovind (1999) concludes that the "melodramatic imperative" results in political news that is conflict oriented and visual in nature. He also asserts that to change the melodramatic nature of television news is impossible, given the profit orientation of the media industry.

Campaign as Horse Race   In addition to observing that media often set the public's agenda and that the news media cover politics as melodrama, media focus on the "horse race" aspect of the campaign, using the results of their polling as evidence for who is winning and losing. Reporters and anchors discuss the strategies used by the leading candidate and how the candidate can maintain his or her lead. Media pundits also focus on the problems of the losing candidate and what he or she may do to take the lead. In the 1988 and 1992 campaigns, "horse race" stories accounted for 58 percent of all campaign stories; in 1996, "horse race" stories comprised 48 percent of all stories (Lichter, Noyes, & Kaid, 1999).

Media coverage that focuses on who is winning and who is losing prevents the public from learning about the candidates' policy stands. This type of coverage also requires speculation on the part of so-called political experts. Patterson (1994) is highly critical of this type of coverage. He argues that media sources are highly cynical of politicians and, in particular, campaign promises. As a result, the public holds a cynical view toward politics. Yet Patterson contends that most politicians keep their promises once they are elected, a fact that media sources ignore. The horserace aspect of media coverage has caused many critics to question whether our campaign system works to elect the best candidates for political office. Explore some alternative voting systems in Thinking Critically: Alternative Voting Methods.

News as Interpretation   A final observation about media coverage of politics is that the "news media no longer simply report; they interpret" (Kaid & Bystrom, 1999, p. 363). That is, journalists and political pundits, including consultants

THINKING CRITICALLY

Alternative Voting Methods

Most elections in the United States use a "winner take all" format in which each voter casts one vote for one candidate. The winner of the election is the candidate who wins a simple majority of the ballots. In recent presidential elections—where there were at least three major candidates receiving votes—the winner did not receive more than 50 percent of the vote. Critics say that such a method of voting denies opportunity to third party candidates, many of whom express minority viewpoints. Our system of voting, then, privileges the dominant way of thinking. In order to provide more opportunity for alternative voices to be heard, some political experts favor changing the way we vote in this country.

Cumulative voting, for instance, allows voters to cast more than one vote for a candidate. For example, in a city council election featuring three open seats, voters could cast three votes. A voter might cast all three votes for one candidate or the voter might spread the three votes among all candidates. In pro-

portional representation—which is used by most of the world's democracies—a political party wins seats in a legislative body in proportion to the number of votes they win the election. Thus, voters do not vote for candidates, but for parties. If the Republicans win 30 percent of the vote, Democrats 40 percent of the vote, and the Green Party 30 percent, then the legislature is made up members from each party, with the Democrats having the majority. Advocates of proportional voting argue that it would increase voter turnout and allow for the expression of minority viewpoints. The proportional voting method could not be used for the presidency. Consider these alternatives as you answer these questions:

1. To what degree is low voter turnout a problem in U.S. elections?

2. What are some other alternative voting methods?

3. What are some additional advantages and disadvantages of the ideas presented here?

and professors, put their own spin on the events that take place instead of allowing the events to speak for themselves. Journalists play a prominent role in political discussions, becoming celebrities. Lichter, Noyes, and Kaid (1999) observe, "Journalists at the national networks and other media outlets elevated their own comments above those of the candidates" (p. 4). Because more time is taken by media sources, there is less time to hear the voices of the candidates. What we do hear is a "soundbite," a short excerpt of what the candidate has said. The average soundbite in the 1996 presidential election was only 8.2 seconds (Lichter, Noyes, & Kaid, 1999, p. 11). In addition, Lichter, Noyes, and Kaid contend that the narratives of the journalists are increasingly negative. Journalists focus on the mistakes made by candidates or on candidate strategy. The result of this so-called media narcissism is that the public becomes even more alienated from the political system because media make us feel good about feeling bad (Hart, 1999).

POLITICAL CONSULTANTS

Given the demands placed on political candidates to be media savvy and audience sensitive, a new field of political experts has emerged: political consultants. Friedenberg (1997) identifies the importance of political consultants by calling them "perhaps America's most sophisticated communicators" (p. 26). Public relations personnel are influential at not just selecting strategies, but at setting policy. Pollsters are now indispensable. Media experts are hired to market the candidate to the viewing public. People such as Karl Rove, James Carville, and Mary Matalin have become fixtures in the campaign process. Even candidates in local elections seek out consultants to help them make decisions about how to appeal to the voters. Politicians frequently use consultants after they have been elected as well.

THE MESSAGE

At the heart of the campaign is the message of the candidate. We can divide message into two types of communication: image and issues. Both use verbal and visual symbols and both rely on cognitive and affective information. The line between image and issue is sometimes blurred, as we will soon discover.

Images   The image is the overall perception that voters have of the candidate. The candidate's image is created from a variety of factors: manner of speaking, appearance, and character. Recall what we have discussed in Chapter 7 concerning media style and in Chapter 9 concerning the image of the persuader. The image projected by a candidate is increasingly important in political campaigns. When you consider some of our recent political leaders, such as John F. Kennedy, Ronald Reagan, and Bill Clinton, this statement should come as no surprise. You may be interested to learn that image politics actually began in 1840, when the Whigs, desperate for a candidate, "created" William Henry Harrison. Harrison was a retired military officer, who did not have a distinguished military or political record. In fact, his military heroics were limited to a one-day battle with the Shawnee at Tippecanoe on the Wabash River. The Whigs portrayed Harrison as a common man and reinforced this perception with log cabin images and cider barrels. He was given the nickname "Old Tippecanoe" and songs were written about him that celebrated his image as a common man. Harrison won the White House and forever changed politics.

Images are created through the careful planning of the campaign staff. Advertising strategy plays a key role in developing an image for the public. Some observers say former President Clinton won the 1996 election before it even started because advertising re-created his image for the public long before we even knew Bob Dole was running for president. The appearances of the candidates also help create an image of the candidate. For instance, Al Gore has used President Clinton's former advisor Michael Sheehan for speech coaching (Simon, 1999). Events such as political conventions also allow candidates to modify how the public sees them. We will discuss the various strategies used by political candidates later in this chapter.

Our reliance on images in political communication raises troubling questions for our democracy. First, there is no check on the truthfulness of the image. Jamieson (1992) argues that the 1988 presidential campaign, in particular, revealed weaknesses in defense systems against political advertising. The debates and news broadcasts were ineffective in protecting the public from the misrepresentations of the campaign's advertising. Second, the public has difficulty discerning the credibility of the images with which we are confronted.

Bennett (1988) notes, "There is, therefore, a profound irony in newsmaking. The credibility of a political image lies not in some independent check on its accuracy but in its past success as a news formula" (p. 72).

Issues   Not only do candidates talk about their image and the image of their opponent, but candidates also talk about their position on various policy issues. In fact, research suggests that winning candidates speak more often about policy issues than their opponents, who spend more time talking about character, or image (Benoit, 2000). Despite this research finding, the news media create an expectation that candidates should instead talk about their image and attack the image of their opponent. *Newsweek* columnist Jonathan Alter (2000) explains that in the 2000 campaign, Al Gore was effective talking about issues despite what members of the news media claimed would be effective. Alter writes, "Yet by energetically working his way through 'the issues' so maligned by world-weary journalists, Gore connected with the kitchen-table concerns of ordinary Americans and at long last developed his own political profile" (p. 26).

Often politicians will focus on issues that will help them create an audience that has enough votes to elect them. By studying the large block of undecided voters, candidates can choose issues that will appeal to those voters. Consider again the example of Clinton's 1992 campaign, in which his polling found two groups of undecided voters. By talking about issues that appealed to members of those swing groups, Clinton was able to win the campaign. The 2000 campaign was fought over issues that appealed to working class voters, including Social Security, prescription drug prices, and targeted tax cuts.

The most successful candidates are able to integrate their issue stands and articulate a theme throughout their campaign. A theme has the advantage of creating a rhetorical vision for voters. For Clinton in 1996, "Building a Bridge to the 21st Century" was an effective theme. It brought together many of his issue positions, characterized him as a forward-thinking candidate, and provided a rhetorical vision that encouraged the country to think toward the future. Clinton developed this theme throughout his campaign communication: in his advertising, debate appearances, and the Democratic National Convention.

Motivating Voters   No matter the issues discussed or the image of the candidate, politicians must generate support for their cause. They must motivate voters to go to the polls to vote. Whether they have their picture taken holding an infant or they appeal to their audience's desire to achieve a prosperous lifestyle, emotion is a part of every political campaign. Bruce Gronbeck (1999) argues that politics today is too complicated for rational discussion. Instead, politicians appeal to their audience's emotions as a way to cut through the clutter of the media age and form relationships with voters. He labels this phenomenon "Feelingstalk."

Politicians take action to make the campaign relevant to potential voters. Gronbeck (1999) says that in particular, patriotic displays are used to impress upon voters the importance of political action. Rallies use red, white, and blue bunting, we see flags, and we hear patriotic music. Gronbeck also says political persuaders personalize their persuasion in order to tap feelings of obligation on the part of the audience member. When President Clinton appeared on MTV during his campaigns, he was attempting to reach out to the younger voter and make them feel a part of the campaign. Vice President Al Gore, at the 1996 Democratic national convention, delivered a very personal speech in which he described how his sister died of lung cancer because of smoking. The very personal appeal was designed to mobilize support against the tobacco industry. One hallmark of the 2000 campaign was the autobiographies that were published for each candidate. The books made the candidates seem more personal so that voters would have a direct connection to them.

Gronbeck (1999) sees dangers in sentimental politics, however. When audience members act based on feelings, they may be more likely to engage in extreme actions, such as those taken by militia or patriot movements. In addition, we may vote for a candidate that does not represent our interests or beliefs. Yet Gronbeck (1999) sees sentimentalization of politics as an important way to foster involvement in politics in a day when we have become politically lethargic.

Whether the candidate is building an image, discussing issues, or motivating voters, the political process does not occur without media. Politicians must manage how the audience creates meaning from the candidate's use of words and images. In the next section, we discuss the various channels used by political persuaders.

MANAGING THE MEANING OF THE MESSAGE

Jamieson (1992) explains that the effective candidate's message, carried through all media, is coherent and consistent. In the next several pages, we look specifically at how political candidates communicate their message to the public through various campaign channels. Thus, for each type of message, we consider the impact of media on how the message is created, how it is disseminated, and how the public receives the message. In each case, the candidate both uses and is used by media as they use language and visual images to create relationships with audiences. Our discussion is organized along a continuum based on how much control the candidate has on the message. We'll examine these channels in order of most candidate control to least candidate control. The channels we will discuss are methods of the Internet, advertising, personal appearances, and debates.

Internet   The Internet is quickly emerging as an effective way to get a politician's message to the people. Since the Internet is not owned or controlled by anyone, the candidate can freely express his or her ideas to the public. The public has access to all the information provided on a candidate's site. Media can influence what the site means to viewers or can inform the public of the site's popularity, but media cannot change the content of the site. Observers have speculated that 2004 Democratic presidential candidate Howard Dean would not have had his early support without the Internet. The Internet presents new opportunities to candidates, but also poses new challenges for audience members who face an abundance of unfiltered information about the candidates.

First, Internet sites are an inexpensive way to reach a large audience of potential voters. For $8,000, 1996 Republican presidential candidate Phil Gramm was able to reach nearly 200,000 Internet viewers with his site (Whillock, 1998). A direct mail campaign for the same expense would have only reached 25,000 potential voters (Whillock, 1998).

Second, Internet sites are capable of presenting large quantities of information to their viewers. Potential voters can go directly to the source to learn more about the candidates. Campaign Internet sites feature unedited news releases, transcripts of speeches and position papers, video, candidate schedules, and even personal Web logs from the candidate and his or her staff. Usually the sites contain some kind of campaign material, such as computer wallpaper, that the users can download and configure to appear on the computer desktop. John C. Tedesco, Jerry L. Miller, and Julia A. Spiker, (1999) after studying candidate sites in the 1996 presidential election, note, "It appears that the biggest advantage of the Internet for campaigning is that it feeds the public's desire for information. Regardless of who is accessing the Web for information, there is an abundance of material provided by candidates" (p. 63). This was particularly true in 2004, when voters turned to websites for blogs (diaries posted to Web pages), digital photos uploaded from rallies from across the nation, and live Web broadcasts of political events.

Third, Internet sites can also help mobilize potential volunteers and raise campaign funds. Dean had more than 500,000 interested supporters register for his website by November 2003. More than 140,000 of these supporters had also registered at a commercial site, Meetup.org, so that they could be informed of local meetings and rallies for Dean. Dean also used his website to generate millions of dollars prior to the campaign. Monthly e-mails to his supporters were able to stimulate donations. In the first three-quarters, Dean was the leading Democratic fundraiser, with much of his money coming from the Internet. Figure 12.4 humorously illustrates Dean's effectiveness at using the Internet to mobilize enthusiastic supporters.

Fourth, and perhaps most significantly, Internet sites allow the candidate to control campaign information. The information that is presented does not carry with it media spin. Users can read and evaluate the information for themselves without relying on journalists or other "experts" to interpret the information. Tedesco, Miller, and Spiker (1999) argue, "For skeptics of the media, this is good" (p. 63). Yet for others, who are "reliant on the media to help provide a context for the information and place the meaning into the bigger picture, the Internet may prove less helpful" (p. 63). Another potential drawback of campaign Internet sites is that there is no check on the accuracy of the information provided. Tedesco, Miller, and Spiker explain, "To question the statements disseminated from one campaign, it would be necessary to locate the other candidate's page to check for consistency or turn to an online media outlet for critique" (p. 62).

Advertising   Candidates exert a great deal of control over their advertisements. There are some legal restrictions, and media sources have the power to

Figure 12.4

A flash mob is an impromptu gathering organized by e-mail in which people perform some kind of brief activity and then disperse. Although Howard Dean didn't use flash mobs, his use of the Internet helped him become one of the Democratic front-runners for the 2004 presidential election. DOONESBURY © 2003 G. B. Trudeau. Reprinted with permission of UNIVERSAL PRESS SYNDICATE. All rights reserved.

interpret ads for voters, but the candidate scripts the ads, chooses appropriate electronic music and images, and decides where and when to air the ads. Jamieson (1992) explains that ads "enable candidates to build name recognition, frame the questions they view as central to the election, and expose their temperaments, talents, and agendas for the future in a favorable light" (p. 485). Jamieson contends that more voters attend to advertising than to the network news. Let's now consider the types, strategies, and effects of advertising.

Jamieson (2000) contends there are three types of political advertisements: advocacy, attack, and contrast. Let's discuss these three types. *Advocacy* ads focus on the candidates qualifications and his or her image. Jamieson's research concludes that advocacy ads do not contain as much policy discussion as do attack ads. Instead, advocacy ads seek to promote the image of the candidate. A great deal of advertising in the 2000 presidential campaign was advocacy in nature. One ad for Vice President Al Gore showed images of his life's story, including the Vietnam War, his family, and his career in Congress.

Another type of advertisement is the *attack* ad. Jamieson contends that attack ads are often policy oriented and they usually focus on the opponent's failings. Some of the most effective, and controversial, attack ads were run in 1988 by President George Bush. In a series of ads, he attacked his opponent, Massachusetts Governor Michael Dukakis, for his environmental and crime records. The infamous ads featured a convicted murderer, Willie Horton, who Bush claimed received a furlough from jail and committed murder while on the furlough.

It is important to respond to attack ads immediately. The 1988 Dukakis campaign went for weeks without responding to the Horton ad and other attack ads run by the Bush campaign. The Clinton staff learned from this blunder and was quick to respond to negative ads aired by Bush in 1992. In fact, the Clinton team created "the War Room," a room in the Little Rock campaign headquarters that monitored media coverage and Bush advertising and launched quick responses to attacks. James Carville (1994) explains, "The War Room was up all night. Nocturnal information coordinator Ken Segal and his assistant, Matt Smith, would come in at ten P.M. and tape *Nightline*, the news, and anything else that was on. The big function of the War Room was to be the nerve center and instantly assess news as it came up" (Matalin & Carville,

1994, pp. 244-245). The nightly developments were reported to the campaign staff at seven A.M. each morning. The War Room enabled the campaign to monitor attack advertising by Bush and respond quickly.

Some advertising includes both positive and negative image and issue components. Jamieson (2000) calls these *contrast ads*. These ads are more than 30 percent, but less than 70 percent, attack. They often discuss differences in the policies of those running for office. A good example of a contrast ad from the 2000 campaign is one run by President George W. Bush that featured a notebook with a column describing his prescription drug plan and a column describing Al Gore's. The ad discussed the two policies, outlining the differences between them. Jamieson contends that contrast ads are the most effective type of advertising because they show both sides and discuss policy.

Jamieson (2000) notes two important variables in political advertising that warrant further attention. Jamieson argues that all three types of advertising can discuss policy or nonpolicy issues. She argues that policy discussions are superior to nonpolicy issues because they help voters make up their minds. Thus, it is important to watch ads to assess the extent to which they discuss policy matters. In addition, Jamieson claims some attack advertising is good for the campaign and helps voters make up their minds. Frequently, we refer to all attack advertising as "negative" advertising. Jamieson says that what is important to note about attack advertising is if the attacks are fair. Thus, negative advertising unfairly attacks some policy position or character trait of an opponent. Attack advertising, however, can be positive for the voters if it discusses policy matters.

Although voters tend to view advertising with skepticism and think they are immune to political ads, research and anecdotal evidence suggests otherwise. Morris (1997) argues, "The effect was devastating. In swing states like Michigan and Wisconsin, where our ads had run, Clinton's lead over Dole was actually larger than in core Democratic states, like Rhode Island and New York" (p. 153). Scholarly research bears out the truth of Morris's claim. Even negative advertising appears to be effective, as was the case in 1988 (Jamieson, 1992). While you might think negative ads turn off voters or cause them to favor the opposition, research indicates that the overwhelming effect of negative ads is positive for the candidate running them.

Conventions   Conventions are scripted media events designed to showcase party unity and launch the nominee's general election campaign. As such, the candidate has a good deal of control over what happens at the convention. However, media control how much of the convention we see and interpret for us what the convention means.

Smith (1994) argues that conventions achieve three goals for the candidate: They identify the combatants, they establish party values, and they generate story lines, or narratives, that shape voter attitudes. Through numerous speeches and video productions, images of the party's own candidate and the opposition's candidate are created. By voting on the party's platform, the party's values are communicated to the public. Smith explains that the narrative of the 1992 Democratic convention—"The New Covenant"—argued for a need to change the direction of the nation by returning to an old philosophy.

The key to the success of the 1992 convention, explains Smith, was the continuity of message from speaker to speaker. Each speaker built upon the themes established by previous speakers and created a compelling narrative in support of Bill Clinton.

In the media age, conventions have presented campaigns with somewhat of a paradox. On the one hand, party officials hope that conventions will be free of controversy and conflict. Since party unity is one of the functions of the convention, it is important the party members not engage in bitter arguments about platform issues. At the same time, media requires excitement from the convention. The 2000 national conventions were tightly scripted events and were well run by the two major parties. The news media, however, provided only one to two hours of prime time programming each night for the conventions because they have become rather predictable. In the future, conventions may only receive air time during news programs; live broadcasts may occur only on the Internet. In 2000, much of the live coverage took place on cable stations instead of the broadcast networks.

An important part of the convention is the *acceptance speech*. The acceptance speech is an important speech for the candidate because the audience is usually quite large, both in person and on television, and for many voters, the acceptance speech is one of the first times they have devoted a large amount of time to the candidate. The acceptance speech can be thought of as the first speech of the general election and sets the tone for the upcoming campaign. The image presented by the acceptance speech is important. Flags, bunting, family members, and influential supporters are commonly a part of the spectacle of the acceptance speech. Smith (1994) explains that Clinton's acceptance in 1992 reinforced the narrative of the convention, crystallized Clinton's primary campaign messages, and provided Clinton with a way to attack George Bush in the general election.

Stump Speaking   A stump speech is a speech given to an audience on the campaign trail. Llewellyn (1994) calls the stump speech the "single clearest presentation of the candidate's world view" (p. 52). Stump speech audiences are carefully chosen. Stump speeches usually take place in a swing state or region. For example, candidates will make frequent appearances in states like Michigan, Ohio, or Illinois in order to swing the undecided vote in those states. In some states, the undecided region can be even more closely targeted. Macomb County, Michigan, is a county that is composed of many "Reagan Democrats," Democrats who voted for the conservative Ronald Reagan in 1980 and 1984. Because these voters are politically ambivalent and because Macomb County would swing the state of Michigan, candidates made frequent appearances there during the 1992 and 1996 campaign. It is not uncommon for presidential candidates to ignore states such as North Dakota or Nebraska, small states that have few electoral votes. Candidates will also choose audiences that are unique in order to receive free media attention. Candidates will talk to senior citizens, for example, or to students in the hope of gaining press coverage.

Stump speeches usually reflect the overall theme of the campaign, although the speech may be tailored to the specific audience. Candidates will typically use a module approach to the speech, using the same introduction and conclusion, but with audience-specific modules inserted in the body of the speech (Muir, 1994). It is vitally important that candidates provide a maximum number of quick soundbites for media sources to play on the evening news or quote in a print article. The media often do not have the time or space resources to cover long, complex ideas. Thus, candidates must provide clips that can be played in a short amount of time, sometimes as short as 10 to 15 seconds. Stump speeches are carefully choreographed. The audience is crowded into a small area directly between the media cameras and the candidates. Bands and cheerleaders are often used. Local dignitaries often stand behind the candidate on the dais. Campaigns make it look like the candidate is being well received by a large, enthusiastic audience.

Debates   Candidates exert control over many aspects of the debating process, including time, place, and format. Candidates can also predict the type of questions they will be asked and how those questions should be answered. Yet, members of the media or public ask unscripted questions that sometimes spark unpredictable discussion among the candidates. In addition, media have enormous power to determine who won or lost the debate. Debates are popular with voters, typically attracting 60 to 100 million viewers, which make them more popular than most televised events, including the Super Bowl.

You might think that a political debate would be a great way for voters to learn about the stands of the candidates on various issues. There are several factors that mitigate against such optimism. Jamieson and Birdsell (1988) contend that debates often lack confrontation because the candidates do not confront each other directly, instead responding to a questioner, often a reporter. Additionally, slogans used by candidates often displace argument in political debates, thus diminishing the usefulness of the interaction. We have previously discussed factors that have led to shortened arguments. These factors are just as present in political debates. Debates also lack focus as the topics shift by the minute. As a result, argue Jamieson and Birdsell, ideas are not competitive with each other and are not used to prove a particular point. Instead, the ideas that are presented help to "prove" the candidate's image. Given these limitations, candidates adapt in several ways to the political debating process.

Media attention on debates typically focuses on who won or lost the debate. Herbeck (1994) argues in the 1992 presidential campaign, media declared a winner in the debates "almost immediately after each of the contests" (p. 265). In many cases, the process of determining a winner results from the communication strategies used by the candidates and the campaign staffs for each candidate.

In addition to public response, media response, and campaign spin, misstatements, errors, and witty one-liners by the candidates during the debate are used to determine who wins. A great deal of media attention centers on the positive or negative statements made by the candidates. In 1980, Ronald Reagan—on several occasions—quipped, "There you go again," as a putdown for his opponent, President Jimmy Carter. Vice Presidential candidate Lloyd Bentsen launched a memorable attack against Vice President Dan Quayle in

1992 when Quayle attempted to compare himself to John F. Kennedy. Bentsen said, "I knew Jack Kennedy and you, sir, are no Jack Kennedy." If you'll remember our discussion in Chapter 7, Jamieson (1988) argues that these short one-liners or misstatements stand for the whole debate. A debater who can pull off the memorable phrase is more likely to be seen as eloquent by today's standards. Candidates will create and practice these statements so they achieve maximum effect.

How do you think debates help voters determine which candidate to select? Since candidates are not currently required to debate, do you think a law should be passed that mandates debate participation? What cues do you use to determine who wins and loses a political debate?

Likewise, a persuader who unwittingly offers media sources an unfavorable statement or action is at the mercy of the media. In 1992, President Bush glanced at his watch during the town hall debate. While he claimed to be checking the speaking time of his opponent, many thought the nonverbal signal communicated that he wanted the ordeal of the campaign and his presidency to be over. In 1976, President Gerald Ford said that several eastern European countries were not under the control of the Soviet Union, when in fact, they were. Ford continued this line of argument the next day in interviews. Bush and Ford hurt themselves by offering members of the media a convenient way of viewing the entire debate.

Despite the difficulties posed by media interpretation of a debate, there are several important effects from political debates that are good for the political campaign. Initially, debates change the minds of only a limited number of undecided voters. More often, debates reinforce the views of a candidate's supporters (Mayer & Carlin, 1994). In fact, public opinion polls asking who won or lost a debate usually reflect the standings of the candidates in the polls at that time. Nonetheless, debates are an important form of political persuasion.

However, voters do gain information from political debates. Despite what might be said about the apparent lack of confrontation in political debates, studies show that voters do learn about the candidates and their stands on the issues. Mayer and Carlin (1994) posit, "Thus, even with their limitations, political debates undoubtedly play a major role in educating voters who are both conversant about the issues and those who are not" (p. 133). Debates are also a good way for voters to learn about the candidate's competence, performance, and personality. Voters believe that debates showcase how a candidate will respond to the pressure of elected office (Mayer & Carlin, 1994).

A second effect of debates is that they serve an agenda-setting function by suggesting which issues are important for the public to think about. Benoit, McKinney, and Holbert (2001) found that debates magnify the importance of having a policy stance and being an effective leader. In other words, audience members who watch debates believed that policy positions were important for candidates and that leadership was an important factor in making the voting decisions. On a micro level, they observed, specific policy positions on economic, foreign policy, civil liberties, and social policy were seen as important components of the decision for whom to vote. In 2000, Gore was able to convince voters that his policy stands were closer to their positions than were Bush's. Bush, on the other hand, was able to improve perceptions of his character while Gore was not. Thus, the 2000 debates had different effects for the two candidates, Gore and Bush.

Finally, debates energize the public for the campaign and the democratic process. Given the large number of viewers, it is easy to see that debates are

INTERNET ACTIVITY

Watching Debates

Debates can be a vital source of information for voters. However, some critics contend the news media may reduce the usefulness of debates by focusing on strategies, techniques, and who won or lost. Read the Viewer's Guide to Watching Debates at http://www.debates.org/pages/vguide.html. Use this advice when you watch a political debate. What additional advice would you offer? Do you think most viewers are able to put aside their partisan views as they watch a debate? Do you think debates are useful to voters?

popular. Debates have become an expectation of the voters. They enable us to feel good about democracy and the process of choosing our leaders. In this sense, debates are largely symbolic rituals designed to strengthen our democratic form of government. To learn more about how to use debates as an effective education tool, complete the Internet Activity: Watching Debates.

Persuasive Movements

Persuasive campaigns, as we discussed earlier, have a shorter time span and are more focused on a person than are persuasive movements. Persuasive movements are often seen as ways of fulfilling the American Dream for some group that has been excluded from mainstream society. The civil rights movement, for example, sought to improve the economic and political status of black Americans. To some, the American Dream is narrow and exclusive, used not to include additional members, but to exclude them. Members of the white supremacy movement, for example, subscribe to a view of America that offers equality and prosperity only to those of the Aryan race. In either case, the American Dream is a powerful force for members of persuasive movements.

Persuasion plays an important role in these and other movements. Persuasive movements develop when a group of individuals becomes dissatisfied with something in society. The group dissociates from the status quo, rejects the reigning symbols of the dominant culture, and verbalizes its dissatisfaction to others who are persuaded to support the movement. Persuasion allows group members to identify who is with the group and who opposes the group and prescribe courses of action. Some scholars argue that persuasion actually comprises the movement (McGee, 1983; DeLuca, 1999). To them, a movement is not a body of individuals and structures, but rather the meanings that individuals hold about the movement. Both views of how persuasion operates will be useful for us in the next few pages.

When persuaders identify with enough audience members, social movements form and influence public policy, our perceptions of our society, and our perceptions of ourselves. Next, we will explore several types of persuasive movements, and examine how movements develop and form. We will also explore the influence of media and culture on the persuasive efforts of social persuaders.

TYPES OF PERSUASIVE MOVEMENTS

One way we can analyze persuasive movements is by the nature of their cause. Blumer (1969a) identifies three types of persuasive movements: reform, revolutionary, and expressive. To Blumer's list, we will add a fourth type: countermovements. The first type of movement is a *reform* movement, which attempts to change some policy or law in the current system. The movement may attempt to gain voting rights, equal pay, and/or other legal protections. The civil rights and women's movements are examples of reform movements. Reform movements accomplish their goals by petitioning the current power structure, protesting its policies, and gaining strength through membership. The civil rights movement, for instance, petitioned the government to allow blacks the right to vote.

A *revolutionary* movement seeks to change the entire social structure. Revolutionary movements desire to overturn institutions and entire ways of life. The antislavery movement of the 1850s is an example of a revolutionary movement. It sought to change the political, legal, economic, and social structure of the country by abolishing slavery. Today, the antiglobalization movement seeks to change the nature of international business and trade. Its efforts have been highlighted recently in Seattle, Washington, and Venice. Revolutionary movements reject the societal structure and seek to change the structure by destroying it.

An *expressive* movement seeks to relieve personal tension in society or create identity for societal members. Members of expressive movements struggle to find some meaning for their lives. The New Age movement or the Christian men's movement are examples of expressive movements. Rituals and religious strategies are used to give meaning to the lives of supporters. The Promisekeepers, for example, hold large religious rallies in which the men who attend pledge to be better husbands and fathers.

A *countermovement* develops in response to the success of a reform, revolutionary, or expressive movement. The movement seeks to block the reforms demanded by other persuasive movements. The white supremacy movement is a good example of a countermovement. Meyer and Staggenborg (1996) argue that three conditions give rise to countermovements. First, the original movement shows signs of success. Second, some group is threatened by this success. Third, political allies are available to give support to the countermovement. The White supremacy movement arose in response to the emancipation of the slaves following the Civil War. The movement gained strength in the 1960s, when blacks were given even more rights. The civil rights movement threatened the prosperity of Whites, who until then, enjoyed a dominant position in society. The White supremacy movement has also used the support of political allies.

MEDIA FRAMING AND PERSUASIVE MOVEMENTS

In this chapter, we have examined the major intersections between media and persuasive campaigns and movements. Here, we'll look at how media uniquely frame persuasive movements for the larger society. In some ways, movements are framed by media in different ways than are political campaigns. McCarthy

(1994) argued that media create frames for the audience's perception of persuasive movements. As we have seen in Chapter 7, frames are perspectives by which we view the world. The public comes to understand movements through one of several frames circulated through media. The movement itself, as well as any countermovements, seeks to create frames for their ideas. These frames often compete with one another for audience acceptance. McCarthy explains that a frame involves four elements. First, the frame defines the root of the problem. The frame identifies what is wrong in the current system, why the problem exists, and what solutions should be enacted. Second, the frame defines the antagonists. The frame identifies those individuals who are on one side of the cause and those who oppose them. Third, the frame defines an injustice that can be corrected. That is, there is a moral tone to the frame. Finally, the frame resonates with the experience of some collectivity. To use Fisher's terminology, the frame has fidelity—it rings true with a group's experiences. As media circulate the frames of persuasive movements, one frame usually becomes dominant in public discourse. To understand how this occurs, we will examine how the anti–drunk driving movement was framed in media coverage.

How do the news media cover the various movements you identified? Do you have a positive or negative image of the movement? Which frame is most widely accepted for each movement?

McCarthy (1994) identifies two frames that were used to explain automobile accidents in this country during the 1960s and 70s. In the 1970s, public advocates such as Ralph Nader began to argue that automobile design changes could save lives and prevent accidents. Items such as seatbelts and safety glass, for example, could make driving safer. By the late 1960s, based on research that indicated that 25,000 deaths each year resulted from drunk driving accidents, the drunk driving frame gained acceptance as well. The drunk driver frame advanced an alternative cause and solution to the frame advanced by auto safety experts. The optimal solution advanced from this perspective was not the improved design of automobiles, but stricter law enforcement standards for drunk drivers.

At first, the auto safety frame dominated media coverage of traffic accidents (McCarthy, 1994). Beginning in the late 1970s, however, Mothers Against Drunk Driving (MADD) and Remove Intoxicated Drivers—USA (RID) were organized in order to give a stronger voice to the drunk driving frame. The anti–drunk driving movement was organized around these national organizations, their local chapters, and several nonaffiliated local groups. The groups organized candlelight vigils to honor the victims of drunk driving, pursued legislative efforts to curb drunk driving, and organized nonalcoholic "proms" at local high schools.

The various drunk driving activist groups had a profound influence on both the type and amount of media coverage given to the movement. The very presence of a local group increased local media coverage of the drunk driving issue in a community (McCarthy, 1994). In addition the activists were able to create an "issue culture" that shaped media coverage. McCarthy argues that the activists shaped public debate about the issue, resulting in the passage of numerous drunk driving enforcement laws. For the past 30 years, the drunk driving frame has dominated public discussion about automobile safety. To understand how the drunk driving movement attempts to influence the media's frame of them, complete the Internet Activity: Understanding Media Frames.

Understanding Media Frames

You have just read about how the media frame persuasive movements. One movement that has recently captured media attention is the anti–drunk driving movement. Read several press releases from Mothers against Drunk Driving, available at http://www.madd.org/news. How does MADD frame the drunk driving issue for the public? How does MADD frame the problem of drunk driving? Its solutions? Who is at fault? Who is the victim? Why do you think the organization has been successful framing the issue in this way?

McCarthy (1994) explains that how a persuasive movement is seen through the lens and pens of the news media is significant for how members of the public respond to the movement. We'll see how media frames, public perception, and the movement itself collide in the next section, when we examine the peace movement of the 1960s through the lens of one of the leading theories of persuasive movements.

UNDERSTANDING THE PERSUASION OF MOVEMENTS

John W. Bowers, Donovan J. Ochs, and Richard J. Jensen have developed a model which describes how persuasive movements make demands of the establishment and how the establishment responds. Their model, called the Rhetoric of Agitation and Control, integrates many of the concepts we have previously discussed: media, language, images, and source. We will examine the model and then apply it to student protests at the 1968 Democratic Convention in Chicago. First, let's take a quick look at the context of the 1960s to learn more about the student movement.

Todd Gitlin, writing in his definitive book, *The Sixties,* argues that the persuasive movements of the 60s were born in the 50s, a decade of affluence in America. The generation of the 60s, he writes, "was formed in the jaws of an extreme and wrenching tension between the assumption of affluence and its opposite, a terror of loss, destruction, and failure" (1987, p. 12). The 50s, by most accounts, were a period of affluence. Inflation was negligible, the depression was over, and so were the deprivations of World War II (Gitlin, 1987, p.13). Americans had babies, bought larger houses, and moved to the suburbs. Americans enjoyed new consumer items and cultural events. And many Americans went to college.

The affluence of the 50s was troubling, though. Gitlin (1987) writes, "Conformity was supposed to buy contentment, cornucopia promised both private and public utopia, but satisfaction keep slipping out of reach" (p. 21). A sense of fear gripped many in the nation, a fear of the "uncontrollable," writes Gitlin. National security also became a concern as the United States and Soviet Union both tested atomic weapons. Senator Joseph McCarthy's pursuit of American Communists added to the tension felt by all in society. Young schoolchildren experienced bomb drills. Americans feared not just war; they feared the end of time. Economically, too, America became divided between rich and poor.

The cinderbox of economic and sociopolitical conditions only needed to be ignited. A small minority of college students would light the flames. Members of this minority, often called the New Left, were more morally conscious than others in their generation. Soon they had developed a unique culture and style; a "counterculture" emerged, complete with its own literature and music: the longhaired Beatles, James Dean's t-shirt-clad hero in *Rebel Without a Cause*, and novelist J. D. Salinger's rebellious main character Holden Caufield.

As the 60s began, President Dwight Eisenhower's presidency was in its last year. The youthful John F. Kennedy would soon become the nation's leader. A new feeling was in the air. Gitlin writes that it was as if "all over the country, young people had been waiting for these signals" (1987, p. 81). Student groups sprang up around the country: the Youth Council of the National Association for the Advancement of Colored People, the Student Nonviolent Coordinating Committee (SNCC), and Students for a Democratic Society (SDS), to name a few. Teach-ins and sit-ins began to spread the word that a segment of society was unsatisfied with the way things were. With an idea of what sparked the 60s movements, let us return to Bowers, Ochs, and Jensen's framework.

Bowers, Ochs, and Jensen's (1993) model begins by examining the strategies of the **agitation.** Agitators are those individuals who are outside the decision-making establishment who desire significant social change and meet resistance from the establishment. In the 1960s, agitators were the students who were upset with society and wanted to change society. Bowers, Ochs, and Jensen explain that agitators seek significant social change. Agitators also encounter resistance from the establishment that requires more than normal means of persuasion.

agitation
a group operating outside the decision-making establishment who desires significant social change but meets resistance from the establishment

The first strategy when seeking social change is *petition*, where the movement works through the established channels of society to request change. If that effort fails, the group engages in *promulgation*. In this stage, the movement seeks legitimizers, or credible spokespersons who will support the movement. The movement also stages newsworthy events designed to persuade the larger society to accept the arguments presented by the movement. The third stage is *solidification*. In this stage, the movement creates slogans and gains members who solidly support the cause. The next step is *polarization*. During this phase, the movement isolates flag individuals and issues. Flag individuals and issues are targets of the group. For many Vietnam War protestors, President Johnson was a flag individual. The chant "Hey, Hey LBJ. How many kids did you kill today?" isolated him as being the cause of the war. The mere mention of his name, or of an issue like Agent Orange, became a rallying cry for the antiwar movement.

The movement next engages in *nonviolent resistance*, where peaceful means are used to publicize the group's ideology. Occupying public buildings, staging protests, and sponsoring discussion forums are good examples of nonviolent resistance. Often, the movement will escalate and engage in *confrontation* with the establishment. This escalation usually causes the movement to split into the *Gandhi*, or peaceful, faction, and the *guerrilla*, or violent, faction.

control

the group in power that blocks the persuasive efforts of the agitation

As the agitation engages in its persuasive campaign, the establishment engages in a persuasive campaign as well. Bowers, Ochs, and Jensen (1993) call this the **control.** The first control strategy is *avoidance.* The establishment may engage in counterpersuasion to block the persuasive efforts of the movement or it may engage in evasion, where it ignores the movement and its demands. The next control strategy is *suppression,* where the establishment seeks to put down the movement. The establishment engages in purgation or banishment in this phase. The establishment may engage in arrests or other means to stop the movement. The fourth stage is *adjustment,* where the establishment sacrifices personnel, meets some of the demands of the movement, or incorporates the movement's personnel or ideology into the mainstream. The final control strategy is *capitulation,* where the establishment grants all of the movement's demands. Usually this does not happen.

OUTCOMES

Bowers, Ochs, and Jensen examine several specific movements in order to make theoretical generalizations about the outcomes of persuasive movements. The generalizations are the result of measuring certain variables on the side of the agitation and control. For the agitation, the variables are actual membership, potential membership, and rhetorical sophistication. For the control, the variables are power, strength of ideology, and rhetorical sophistication. You might think of rhetorical sophistication as the persuasive ability of either side. Some of the 64 resulting generalizations include:

- "An establishment high in rhetorical sophistication adjusts as soon as it perceives that the agitative group is high in potential membership, especially—but not only—when the agitative group's potential is buttressed by rhetorical sophistication" (Bowers, Ochs, and Jensen, 1993, pp. 145–146). If the agitators gain power through membership and persuasive skill, the establishment responds quickly.
- "When the agitative group is low in actual membership, low in potential membership, and high in rhetorical sophistication control always successfully uses the strategy of avoidance" (Bowers, Ochs, and Jensen, 1993, p. 147). In other words, by ignoring a small, but rhetorically gifted group, the establishment can maintain control of the public's perception of the movement.

AN EXAMPLE

On August 25 through August 29, 1968, the Democratic Party held its nominating convention in Chicago. Amidst the turmoil of that year, the 1968 campaign had seen the assassination of one candidate, Robert F. Kennedy. Another candidate, Eugene McCarthy, who opposed the ongoing Vietnam War, had gained the support of many student protestors, but it was unlikely he would win the nomination at the convention. The agitation in Chicago consisted of several student groups who objected to the Vietnam War, the Democratic Party, and its eventual nominee, Vice President Hubert Humphrey (Bowers, Ochs, & Jensen, 1993). The control was comprised of the City of Chicago, Democratic

Party officials, and President Lyndon Johnson (Bowers, Ochs, & Jensen, 1993). This brief glimpse of the student protests of the 1960s will provide a snapshot into how student agitators persuaded the establishment and the larger American culture to change its attitudes toward youth, the Vietnam War, minorities, and women.

In the months and days leading up to the convention, the agitators *petitioned* the City of Chicago to allow sleeping in the city parks and to allow the students to parade. Most of the requests were denied, indicative of the control's *avoidance* strategy. Soon, however, thousands of youth would be arriving to protest at the convention. The control responded with *suppression* by enforcing the city's 11 P.M. curfew in city parks, which forced the students to the streets. Police also strictly enforced city laws regarding rallies and defacing public property. In addition, because there were restrictions placed on live television coverage in the city, some police actions took place without much media coverage.

The situation then escalated as deep lines were drawn between agitation and control. The students solidified their position by *polarizing* themselves against the control. Gitlin (1987) notes that chants from the students shifted from "Hell no, we won't go," when asked to leave the parks, to "Pigs are whores," in reference to the Chicago police. When the students nominated a pig for president, the police quickly arrested the pig on the grounds that livestock was prohibited in the city. The students sang, shouted slogans, and practiced self-defense tactics. In short, the agitators used "a combination of tactics that would lead to public, direct, and violent suppression by the city" (Bowers, Ochs, & Jensen, 1993, p. 71).

On Wednesday of convention week, a split developed between two leaders of the students. Antiwar activist Dave Dellinger advocated a nonviolent march, which was quickly blocked by police (Gitlin, 1987). Meanwhile, Tom Hayden, leader of Students for a Democratic Society, advocated that "if blood flows, it flows all over the city" (qtd. in Gitlin, 1987, p. 332). The violent agitators sought to make their point by goading the police into using brutality to enforce the laws (Bowers, Ochs, & Jensen, 1993). The students met with violent suppression by the establishment. Gitlin (1987) recalls, "On Wednesday a great deal of blood flowed for the networks' conveniently positioned cameras, and 'the whole world' (America, anyway) proverbially watched" (p. 327). In the end, student use of obscenity probably prompted police to take the violent action that they did (Bowers, Ochs, and Jensen, 1993). In fact, Gitlin notes: "At last. We've shown they can only rule at gunpoint. The world is going to see" (p. 331).

In the end, Gitlin notes, the movement met with mixed success. It did not achieve complete capitulation from the control, but it was not quickly terminated either. Gitlin writes, "As an impossible revolution it had failed—how could it have succeeded?—but as an amalgam of reform efforts, especially for civil rights (ultimately for Hispanics, Native Americans, and other minorities as well as blacks) and women's rights and the environment and against the war, it had been a formidable success" (p. 433).

From this example, we can see how the Bowers, Ochs, and Jensen model helps to explain the strategies used by persuasive movements. The student movement of the 1960s represents what is often called a historical social movement. It sought to change the ideology and policies of society. In the next section, we will examine more closely a different type of persuasive movement.

EXPRESSIVE PERSUASIVE MOVEMENTS

Our study thus far has focused mostly on reform or revolutionary movements and their countermovements. In this section, we will explore another type of movement: the expressive movement. To do so, we will have to slightly modify our approach to studying persuasive movements. Some scholars contend that the theories we have previously discussed are not as useful for studying emerging types of persuasive movements because the previous theories focus on movements aimed at societal change. A new body of theory, called new social movement theory, is being developed to better understand new forms of movements that desire instead to change the identities of individual members. While this new theory is not unified in the work of one individual, article, or book, some general statements can be made about how scholars are studying persuasive movements. Sociologist Nelson A. Pichardo (1997) outlines some of the basic ideas behind new social movement (NSM) theories. As we examine NSM theory, we will consider the example of the New Age movement.

First, the *ideology and goals* of NSMs focus on quality of life and lifestyle concerns (Pichardo, 1997). NSMs question the goals of the current society. They seek to allow individuals to create their own identity and to give the individual autonomy to make decisions concerning identity. NSMs also question the organization, strategies, and tactics taken by the group's leaders and its members. In fact, many NSMs are decentralized, meaning they have no centralized power structure, but instead operate without a clearly defined power structure.

The New Age movement is a leaderless but powerful network of people hoping to bring radical change to the United States. The contemporary movement traces its roots to a variety of historical influences. Eastern religions such as Hinduism, Buddhism, Taoism, and Nosticism have influenced the movement. So too has Christian Science. A central premise of these religions is that humans can be enlightened and have a greater sense of themselves and their role in the world. The ideology of the movement focuses on self-identity and self-awareness in order to improve the quality of life of its participants.

Second, the *tactics* used by NSMs are anti-institutional in nature (Pichardo, 1997). They use disruptive tactics and highly dramatic and preplanned forms of demonstrations. The New Age movement believes that change comes from within. In the religious realm, religion should be a connection to a higher being, instead of obedience to that being. Reality, they say, is spiritual and anti-scientific. This ideology is reflected in the ideas of astrology, ecology, and feminism. Essentially, the New Age Movement seeks to unify humanity, eliminating barriers and boundaries between people and nations. Channeling is used to communicate information to or through a physically embodied human from a source that exists on some other level of reality. Massage, use of herbs and crystals, and channeling are rituals associated with the New Age. Thus, the tactics of the New Age movement are anti-institutional in nature.

The *structure* of the NSMs reflects the ideology of the movement. In many cases, says Pichardo (1997), NSMs seek to operate under the same type of structure they would like to see implemented in society at large. Rotating leadership, ad hoc organizational structures, and widespread use of voting are all components of a NSM's structure. The structure of the New Age movement is very loose, with thousands of individual organizations. Occasionally, large events, such as the Harmonic Convergence, occur, which bring together the disparate organizations and members. Some leaders include Elizabeth Claire Profit, Marylin Ferguson, and Shirley MacLaine.

Finally, in terms of *participants* in NSMs, Pichardo (1997) says there are two schools of thought among NSM scholars. One theory says that NSM participants come from the middle class and represent occupations such as academia, the arts, and human service agencies. Another theory says that NSM participants come together because of their concern over social issues, such as the environment. Pichardo (1997) explains that current research has not been sufficient to determine exactly who participates in NSMs.

Members of the New Age movement are likely to be single, young, affluent, urban, and white. For many in the movement, traditional religion has failed, so they gravitate to natural religion. The New Age movement does not get rid of religion; it simply replaces traditional religions with one that is more individualized and spiritual. Again, connection, not obedience, is emphasized. Followers to the movement argue that it is a way to provide people with the tools they need for personal transformation. They argue that the movement will promote widespread changes in society. Opponents to the movement argue that it reduces personal responsibility. Moral and ethical standards are dissolved, it is argued, and people are responsible only to themselves.

The New Age movement is but one example of what some theorists have called new social movements. Other movements such as the Black men's movement—exemplified by the Million Man March—or the Christian men's movement reflect some of the same principles. The most significant commonality of these groups is their desire to change individuals rather than society. As individuals struggle to deal with the world that has been forever changed by media, they question their identity and their role in society. The New Age movement and other expressive movements seek to help individuals create meaning for their lives in a mediated world.

Summary

Persuasive campaigns and movements are important phenomena in our culture. Not only do we select the person whom many see as the most powerful person in the world, but we select through the political process those people who make decisions at our local schools, in our city government, and in our state legislatures. We also identify with movements that we think can help us and others achieve the American Dream.

Media filter how we think about campaigns and movements while at the same time allowing members of the public to become engaged with these events and discuss them with other people.

Verbal symbols, such as slogans and songs, are powerful means through which voters and citizens identify with persuaders. Likewise, the use of images and image events are effective methods of persuasion in the media age.

Political campaigns are covered by news media as horse races and melodrama and reporters often offer their interpretation of the campaign. Candidates communicate about their image and issue positions and must convince voters to cast ballots for them. Candidates manage the meaning voters have of them through the Internet, advertising, conventions, stump speeches, and debates.

There are several types of persuasive movements, all of which are framed by media for the public. Movements tend to a follow a typical life cycle and fade away as they lose support or have their issues implemented in the system. A variety of strategies are used by movements and the establishment. Some movements are expressive movements, and are designed to change individuals in society.

Key Terms

WWW: Visit the book's website at http://www.mhhe.com/borchers2 for multiple-choice quizzes, Internet activities, and key terms flashcards.

campaign 326	image event 332
persuasive movement 326	agitation 351
slogan 329	control 352

13
Advertising

Learning Objectives

After reading this chapter, you should be able to:

1. Name some of the key characteristics of advertising in the media age.

2. Understand how advertising audiences are researched and targeted.

3. Identify the main types of media used for advertising and their advantages to persuaders.

4. List the key challenges to advertisers in the media age and ways advertisers overcome these challenges.

5. Discuss various perspectives on advertising's effects.

Perhaps you engage in the same ritual as millions of other Americans each winter when you gather with your friends to watch the Super Bowl. Each year, the Super Bowl is usually the most watched event on television. It is probably safe to assume that millions of those watching the football game do not care who wins the game. Instead, they are interested in which company develops the most creative and memorable advertisement. The Super Bowl has become known as much for its advertising as for its athleticism. Companies pay millions of dollars to have their name and products put in front of millions of television viewers.

In 2000, one company, Computer.com, a start-up computer assistance company, invested $3 million—more than half of its initial financing—in three Super Bowl ads. Computer.com's owners knew that getting their message to a large audience would require buying time on the biggest television event of the year. The ads, which featured the company's owners begging consumers to give them business, also had to be memorable to compete against the other ads of the day. Advertising on the Super Bowl is a symbolic event that means a company is serious about its business and about forming relationships with audiences, including consumers and investors.

Perhaps the most frequent encounter we have with mediated persuasion is through advertising. Researchers estimate that the typical American is exposed to some 3,000 advertisements a day (Twitchell, 1996). Advertising reaches us as we listen to the radio, watch television, read our favorite magazine, sit at a bus stop, or drive past billboards. Advertising also reaches us in less conspicuous ways. When we tune in to the latest episode of our favorite television show, we might see our favorite sitcom star use a Macintosh laptop. When we watch our favorite college football team, we see the logo of an athletic shoe company emblazoned on the uniforms. As we surf the Internet, we see a constant barrage of advertising messages all wanting us to click on some site. Indeed, we are surrounded by the messages of companies that desire to attract our eyeballs and change our attitudes.

The mediated environment of the 21st century places new demands on advertisers. They must try to make their product or service stand apart from other similar products or services. They must cut through the clutter of our mediated world, keep audience members' attention, and find ways of forming relationships with audience members. Because advertising is increasingly sophisticated, we as consumers must understand how advertising influences our decisions and lifestyles. After all, we often make spending decisions based on advertising. At a deeper level, we form emotional attachments to certain brands of products. Advertising also has a profound influence on what we value.

The central discussion in this chapter revolves around the ways advertisers use relationship-building strategies, repetition, electronic eloquence, and commoditization to respond to the challenges posed by the media age. Before examining strategies, however, we discuss several topics to help us better understand advertising and the challenges of the media age. We conclude the chapter by assessing the effects of advertising.

Advertising in the Media Age

Let's again examine the model of persuasion to see how it explains advertising in the media age. The advertising process begins when *clients* approach an *advertising agency* in order to create a message that can be transmitted to potential customers via the *media*. The advertising agency researches the potential audience, creates a message, chooses media to transmit the message to the audience, and evaluates the results of the advertising. Often, the advertising agency works with other organizations, such as research companies or media-buying agencies, to complete its tasks. Media create vehicles, such as a magazine or television show, that attract audiences. The audiences are then sold to the advertising agency, which buys time or space for the advertisement.

Advertising provides a constant stream of persuasive messages that are transmitted through media to audience members. Advertisers make use of language and visual images to induce us to identify with their message. Our acceptance of their message is tied to our emotional state and our perception of what we need and value. Identification takes the form of purchasing the advertiser's product or feeling some kind of connection to the advertiser's brand. Throughout this process, we as audience members provide information to the advertiser that can be used in audience analysis. Our interests, preferences, and demographic information all influence how advertisers shape their messages for us. A great deal of our discussion in this chapter concerns the most prevalent type of advertising we face—that for consumer goods. We'll also consider advertising for nonprofit organizations and public service announcements. Keep in mind that we have already discussed political advertising in Chapter 12.

James B. Twitchell (1996) describes several qualities of advertising in today's culture. Advertising, he writes, is ubiquitous, symbiotic, profane, and magical. Advertising is *ubiquitous;* it is all around us. Twitchell (1996) writes that advertising cannot not be found. It is in magazines, newspapers, and on television. It surrounds us on the Internet. Products are featured in movies and television shows. Babies' diapers contain images of Warner Brothers' cartoon characters. The Olympics are sponsored by companies. Athletic venues feature the names of beer companies, technology companies, and banks. We cannot escape advertising's reach. Our model clearly depicts the presence of multiple persuaders in our lives.

Advertising is *symbiotic*. It lives on other cultural organisms. It thrives on the success of cultural icons and events. A good example is advertising's association of sports stars with companies. Tiger Woods and Nike have been synonymous in recent years. As the golf star continues to win championships, his success is tied to Nike's. Nike uses a premise—Tiger Woods is a great golfer—and we fill in the rest of the enthymeme to draw the conclusion that Nike can somehow make us better athletes and people. The role of cultural knowledge is an important part of our model.

Advertising is also *profane*. It is of this world, it is shocking, and it is repetitious (Twitchell, 1996). Advertising sells goods and services to us for our use in this world. There is nothing supernatural about advertising. In addition, advertising is shocking. Whether it is sexual in nature, intense, or grotesque, advertising must seek to gain our attention. Advertisements burn themselves into our consciousness by repetition.

Finally, advertising is *magical*. Twitchell (1996) argues that the process by which "things" come to have meaning is magical. When we purchase some good, we expect magical results. We expect the product to work as advertised, and we expect to feel different having purchased the item. You might think, for instance, that driving a particular kind of car will make you feel like a different person.

When we purchase a product or service or adopt a particular kind of lifestyle, we identify with the persuader's message. Identification occurs because we bring to the persuader's message our ideas about cultural expectations and beliefs. As we continue our discussion, keep in mind these observations about advertising in the media age and how our model reflects Twitchell's observations.

Researching Audiences for Advertising

Advertising agencies must conduct research about their clients' product or service to determine an appropriate target audience for advertising. This process is usually hidden from consumers. We often don't consider how we have been carefully selected to hear, read, or see an advertisement. Advertisers constantly adapt their messages and strategies to the demands of the day. As media, audience measurement techniques, and consumers themselves have changed, so too have advertisers' attempts to reach consumers. A brief history of advertising reveals three major approaches to the advertising audience: mass marketing, segmentation, and mass customization (Lavidge, 1999). Advertisers today use all three approaches.

TARGETING AUDIENCES

In the 1940s and 50s, advertisers used media to target large audiences. With relatively few media, few products, and more homogenous customers, mass marketing worked well. Advertisers delivered information about products to large audiences via radio and television programs. Today the owner of a pizza delivery store near your campus may use mass marketing to reach local residents. By advertising in such media as a local newspaper or a popular local radio station, the owner can reach a large part of the target audience.

During the 1970s, advertising researchers realized that not every consumer wanted the same product or service (Lavidge, 1999). As a result, advertisers sought to segment audiences so that they could adapt both their message content and the media channel to reach the ideal target audience for their product or service. In Chapter 5, we discussed three popular methods of audience segmentation: demographics, psychographics, and geodemographics. Demographics refers to such audience characteristics as age, sex, race, and religion. Psychographics refers to the personality and lifestyle characteristics of consumers. Geodemographics shows advertisers where particular audiences live. Segmentation helps persuaders to understand who is likely to purchase their products and how to target those potential customers. It is important to note that although it is based on research, audience segmentation cannot perfectly predict the beliefs, attitudes, and values of each audience member.

A grocery store located in your city might use segmentation to sell products to you and your peers by targeting two student groups: on-campus residents and off-campus residents. The store would tailor its advertisements to focus on the products each group would be likely to purchase. In its advertising on the campus radio or television station, the store might advertise snack foods, beverages, and other items used by on-campus residents. Advertising on local broadcast radio stations would reach commuter students who drive to school. These students could be informed about specials on items necessary for survival in an off-campus apartment or house.

Since the 1970s, there has been a great increase in the number of products available to consumers, in the number and type of media channels available to reach consumers, and in the diversity of consumer interests. As a result, advertisers now see limitations with audience segmentation. Robert J. Lavidge (1999) argues that we see ourselves as individuals and prefer to be targeted as individuals. Thus, the term that marks current advertising approaches is *relationship marketing*, which we examine later in this chapter. Using database technology, advertisers are able to reach consumers on an individual basis.

Consider a grocery store in your city where you purchase a case of Pepsi. At the checkout, you show your "preferred customer card" to receive an additional discount. In a few weeks, you might receive a coupon in the mail for your next purchase of Pepsi. The grocery store is using relationship marketing to sell you a product. We discuss this concept further—including its ethical implications—later in the chapter.

MEASURING AUDIENCES

The two most common ways of measuring media audiences are reach and frequency. *Reach* refers to the number of targeted audience members who see a particular advertisement (Sharpe, 1999). *Frequency* is the number of exposures the target audience has to a particular advertisement. John D. Leckenby and Heejin Kim (1994) found that in 1993, 90.5 percent of the top 200 advertising agencies in the United States used reach and 87.3 percent used frequency as measures of media audiences. Advertisers seek to achieve both reach and frequency with their messages. An advertisement placed in your campus newspaper would probably reach a lot of the students on your campus. On my campus, the paper is published only once per week, however, meaning an advertisement would not achieve much frequency. An ad on the campus radio station would achieve greater frequency. There is some discussion in the academic literature concerning the use of these measures for the Internet. Initial studies (Leckenby & Hong, 1998; L. Wood, 1998) suggest that reach and frequency measures can also be applied to Internet advertising.

Media Selection

After they determine the target audience for a product or service, advertising agencies must select the appropriate medium or media for the advertisement. Media organizations promise audiences to advertising agencies, which buy time on a particular medium. After an audience has been gathered, its attention is "rented" to an advertiser (Twitchell, 1996). The audience is forced to watch the advertisement, but it is given something in return: entertainment. Viewing advertisements is the "work" that we do to receive cheap entertainment. We discuss here the major types of media used in advertising. We focus our attention on seven types of advertising: television, newspapers, radio, magazines, out-of-home, Internet, and direct mail. As you read this section, keep in mind the idea of ratings, discussed in Chapter 5. Ratings companies, such as Nielsen, Arbitron, and the American Bureau of Circulation, determine the viewership of a certain medium and thus help to set prices for advertising on that medium.

TELEVISION

Television is an attractive medium for advertising because it delivers mass audiences to advertisers. When you consider that nearly three out of four Americans have seen the game show *Who Wants to Be a Millionaire?* you can understand the power of television to communicate with a large audience. When advertisers create a brand, for example, they want to inundate consumers with the brand and its image. Television provides an ideal vehicle for this type of communication. Local television provides a medium for local businesses to target those consumers in the community likely to use their products or services. In many markets, syndication is the only way for national advertisers to reach audience members during the 4 P.M. to 8 P.M. time slot, when local stations cover news. Television is an expensive medium, however, and not all advertisers can afford to use it.

Television's influence on advertising is fourfold. First, narrowcasting means that television channels are seen by an increasingly narrow segment of the audience. The Golf Channel, for instance, is watched by people who play golf. Home and Garden Television is seen by those interested in household improvement projects. Thus, audiences are smaller and more homogenous than they have been in the past. Second, there is an increase in the number of television channels available to viewers, and thus, advertisers. This has also resulted in an increase in the sheer number of advertisements to which audiences are exposed. Third, digital recording devices allow audience members more control over which commercials they watch. Fourth, control over programming is being passed from the networks to local cable operators and satellite programmers.

NEWSPAPERS

After television, the medium attracting the next largest annual ad revenue is newspapers. Local advertising is increasing, as is advertising aimed at regional and national audiences. Newspapers are seen as the last mass medium, and this accounts for their popularity among advertisers. The *New York Times*, which reaches a national audience, accounts for $1 billion in ad revenue annually. It has increased its national circulation by 40 percent and is now available for home delivery in 168 cities (Hollie, 1999e). Locally, newspapers are the largest advertising medium.

Newspapers are a less expensive advertising venue than television and provide a way for advertisers to communicate a longer, more detailed message to their audience than they can through television. Given new production techniques, advertisements can be printed in newspapers in about 48 hours, meaning newspapers are also a quick way of getting the message out. Newspapers are often the most important form of news for a local community, and they develop a high degree of loyalty from local readers.

RADIO

Advertising on radio continues to grow. Hosts such as Howard Stern, Don Imus, and Rush Limbaugh attract large audiences. Radio is often used in conjunction with other media, such as outdoor billboards and the Internet, to reach even more customers than television. Advertisers are likely to use radio because it is a less expensive medium than television, which means advertisers can afford to repeat their ads often. Internet companies, such as Priceline.com, are also turning to radio advertising. Radio provides a way for advertisers to communicate with audience members at all times of the day. Consumers listen to radio on their way to school or work, at work, on the way home, and in the evening hours.

Two major changes—satellite and Internet radio—will force radio advertisers to adapt their methods. Both of these radio forms allow listeners to tune in stations that are more distant than the local stations they could receive in the past. As a result, radio will increasingly target specific niche audiences who live many miles apart.

MAGAZINES

Newsweeklies, women's titles, and business magazines have all seen increases in advertising because they attract an upscale demographic market (Hollie, 1999c). The prescription drug industry is one of the heaviest advertisers in magazines. Magazines are popular with advertisers because of the narrow market that they deliver. A broadcast medium such as network television attracts all types of audience members, but magazine audiences are more homogenous. If you read *Sports Illustrated*, for example, you have much in common with the magazine's other readers. Advertisers see magazines as an efficient way of reaching target audience members.

Advertisers using the print media—magazines and newspapers—will need to adapt to two main changes. First, the Internet will bring larger audiences to local newspapers. These audiences will be more heterogeneous and geographically dispersed than in the past. Second, advertisers will have to understand how to use an increasing number of magazines aimed at niche audiences. Although some magazines will maintain national audiences, a large number of niche magazines and e-zines will entertain narrower audiences.

OUT-OF-HOME ADVERTISING

Out-of-home advertising, also called place-based advertising, has become an increasingly effective way of reaching consumers, who are more active than ever before. Many consumers today do not sit at home and watch television. Using billboards, newsstands, and bus shelters for advertising is an effective way of reaching these on-the-go consumers. More consumers travel longer distances to and from work, which also makes out-of-home advertising effective. Technology has changed the nature of the billboard business, making it a more viable medium than in the past. Using digital printing, billboard companies can print a billboard in 2 hours, compared with 6 days previously. This allows advertisers more variety in the types of messages they create because they can change their messages more quickly.

INTERNET

As consumers become more comfortable with online shopping, advertisers will seek to reach this market. As consumers get more of their news and information from the Internet, the ability of television and radio to get the word out to consumers will decrease. The challenge to Internet advertisers is to create ads that audience members remember. We discuss the unique aspects of Internet advertising later in this chapter.

Internet advertising will play a more prominent role in organizations' advertising in the near future. Internet audiences tend to be quite homogenous, but small. Advertisers will have to adjust their methods to reach these audiences and will have to adapt their persuasive strategies to the online medium as well.

DIRECT MAIL

A final advertising medium that we will consider is direct mail, which uses mailings to consumers to communicate a client's message. Direct mail includes newsletters, postcards, and special promotions. For many businesses, direct mail is the most effective form of advertising. Direct mail is an effective way to build relationships with consumers.

Consider for a moment your exposure to the various media we have discussed thus far. With which medium do you spend most of your time?

Challenges to Advertisers in the Media Age

The past 20 years have brought about major changes in the advertising business. These challenges mean that advertisers are using and will continue to use ever more sophisticated methods of communicating with us. As a result, we must be aware of how advertisers attempt to identify with us, the consumers of advertising. Although each medium provides its own challenges, Matthew P. McAllister (1996) identifies three cumulative challenges facing advertisers in the media age: media-user behavior challenges, audience demographic challenges, and advertising environment challenges. To demonstrate these challenges, we consider the difficult time that an advertiser, such as Pizza Hut, has in reaching you and your fellow students.

MEDIA-USER BEHAVIOR CHALLENGES

The first challenge identified by McAllister (1996) concerns how audience members interact with media sources. Today, audience members have more control over the media to which they are exposed and over how they are exposed to these media. McAllister explains that if audience members do not see or pay attention to an ad, they cannot do what the advertisement intends them to do. The technology of today's media environment gives much more control to the audience member than in years past.

First, recording technology such as VCRs and personal digital recorders influences the time at which viewers watch programs, and thus, their commercials. Much advertising on Thursday evenings is aimed at educating consumers about purchasing decisions they will make the coming weekend, such as movie attendance and automobile shopping. When viewers watch Thursday evening shows on videotape on Sunday afternoons, the power of the commercials is lost (McAllister, 1996).

Pizza Hut might think that advertising during the evening hours would be a good time to convince you to order a pizza. Prime time television shows or evening radio broadcasts, for example, would be good ways to reach college students. Yet many college students work or study during the evening hours. You and your friends probably tape evening shows to watch later, often at times when you are not likely to order a pizza. Or you may not watch television at all. Pizza Hut loses valuable advertising exposure because your behavior disrupts the timing of its advertisements.

Second, viewers can bypass commercials today. With a remote control, the viewer can engage in zapping, or watching other channels while commercials air. Lex van Meurs (1998) found that in the Netherlands, the audience of a particular show dropped by 28.6 percent during a commercial break, although it also gained 7.1 percent from similar viewers who had left the program they had been watching. Zapping, in this study, was not related to the type of advertisement being aired, but was instead related to other factors (Meurs, 1998). Personal digital recorders and VCRs let the viewer fast-forward through previously recorded commercials. This practice is often called zipping. Grazing is the practice of aimlessly wandering through the television lineup without paying particular attention to any one program. Sports fans, in particular, graze from one sports event to another to keep up with the current scores (McAllister, 1996). Before remote control, these three practices were less common. Radio experiences similar problems due to the scan-and-seek functions that are common today. When our televisions are truly interactive with the Web, users will be able to chat with their friends during commercial breaks about the show they are watching.

Even if you are in the mood for pizza when you watch a tape of your favorite prime time television program, you might not see Pizza Hut's commercials because you always fast-forward through the commercials. Or if you are watching the show live at the ideal time for the advertiser, you might skip the commercials to see what is on a different network. With all the choices available, channel switching is very tempting for television viewers. Or if you have no favorite television show, you might graze through the lineup looking for something to watch, without paying particular attention to Pizza Hut's commercials.

AUDIENCE DEMOGRAPHIC CHALLENGES

A second challenge McAllister (1996) identifies is our "fragmented society." Society today is marked by diverse people with diverse interests, educations, and viewpoints. We have different hobbies, careers, and preferences, meaning that audience members are not congregated around a particular medium. In addition, media are highly diverse, reaching small audiences centered around narrow interests and tastes. As a result, the broadcast networks can no longer guarantee advertisers a mass audience. Audiences are split by their interests among a wide variety of media. McAllister identifies two problems associated with a segmented audience: finding the right media mix and reaching desirable audiences.

Finding the right media strategy is more complicated in today's mediated world. In the past, advertisers turned to network television to reach a large audience. In 1977, the networks reached 93 percent of the TV viewing audience. As the technology to allow more networks develops, audiences will be even more dispersed. For Pizza Hut, this presents a challenge when it chooses media for its advertising. While in the past, network advertising, such as on ABC, NBC, or CBS, would have been an effective media strategy, today's decisions are more complicated. Pizza Hut would be wise to supplement network television advertising with radio, newspaper, and billboard advertising as well. The nature of media audiences makes these decisions difficult for advertisers.

Finding the right audience is difficult as well (McAllister, 1996). With pay-per-view options, home video, and video games, the audience members an advertiser wants to reach may not even be exposed to commercial media. McAllister (1996) says that consumers "have more places to escape advertising and are often willing to spend the money to do so" (p. 23). Think of how you and your friends spend your time. If you watch home videos a lot, you miss the pizza restaurant advertising we just discussed. If you go to movies, you might miss that advertising as well. Some theaters, however, advertise in the time before the movies start, so you just might see an advertisement for our pizza restaurant at the theater. Pizza Hut, then, faces the challenge of determining how to best reach audience members who might not be exposed to traditional advertising.

ADVERTISEMENT ENVIRONMENT CHALLENGES

clutter
the amount of time devoted to nonprogram content (advertising, promotions, public service announcements) on a particular medium

The third challenge identified by McAllister (1996) addresses the relative attention the audience gives to one advertisement over another. For an advertisement to persuade its audience, it must somehow get and keep audience members' attention. The contemporary world of media is one in which many advertisers vie for our attention—resulting in what is popularly termed **clutter.** Researchers have defined the term in various ways. McAllister (1996) defines clutter as "the amount of time devoted to nonprogram content on television, including product commercials, program promotions and public service announcements" (p. 24).

Louisa Ha and Barry R. Litman (1997) identify three variables used to define clutter: quantity, competitiveness, and intrusiveness. *Quantity* refers to the amount of advertising space in a medium. Advertising makes up 24 percent of television programming, and it comprises 50 percent of the content in most magazines (Elliott & Speck, 1998). *Competitiveness* concerns the similarity and proximity of advertising. During the holiday shopping season, for instance, audience members are inundated with many commercials for online shopping companies. These ads often appear together during the same commercial break or in the same publication. The similarity and proximity of the ads contribute to a general sense of clutter in media. *Intrusiveness* is the degree to which advertisements disrupt message processing. Having fewer breaks each containing more commercials is less intrusive than having many breaks during a program.

McAllister (1996) identifies three reasons clutter has increased in recent years. First, there are more media outlets now than ever before. The number of television stations doubled during the 1980s and continues to increase due to satellite and cable technology. The number of print and online publications has also increased. Thus, our exposure to advertising has increased. As you experience advertising throughout your day, you probably become oblivious to it. We do not pay attention to a great deal of the advertising we see. It becomes difficult, then, for Pizza Hut to get you to pay attention to its ads among all the others you see.

Second, McAllister (1996) writes that media are carrying more advertisements than ever before. In 1983, nonprogram television content took up 10 minutes of every hour; by 1992, that amount had increased by 4 minutes, to 14 minutes. In 1994, Fox was the first station to have more than 15 minutes of nonprogram content for each hour of programming (McAllister, 1996). At the same time, the length of television commercials has decreased, so now we see shorter commercials, but more of them. In 1999, an episode of *Law and Order* aired a 5-minute, 20-second commercial break that featured 19 separate messages. Imagine that Pizza Hut's advertisement was one of the 19 you saw during that commercial break. You probably would not remember it unless you had an immediate taste for pizza. One Fox network affiliate in New York has used banner ads on the screen during the program itself, meaning that advertising on the station is constant and occurs between commercial breaks.

Third, McAllister (1996) explains that the audience's perception of clutter has increased because of how advertisements are grouped. During prime-time television, for example, advertisements for competitive products are grouped in the same commercial break. When you read your student newspaper, you probably see several ads for pizza restaurants. Perhaps they appear on the same page. It is difficult for you to distinguish between the advertisements, and you do not form a lasting impression of one pizza restaurant over another.

Clutter results in several communication problems:

- Advertising clutter *hinders* the audience's *search for information* (Elliott & Speck, 1998). Television advertising makes it difficult to find out about particular products or services. It is difficult for you to find Pizza Hut's specials when they are shown along with specials from every other company targeting college students.

- Advertising clutter *disrupts message processing* (Elliott & Speck, 1998). Commercial breaks in television programming, for instance, break up the flow of the program and the audience's identification with the show's message. When audience members do not identify with a program, they are less likely to stay tuned for commercial breaks. Even though you might be a regular viewer of a prime-time show, the commercial break disrupts your attention to the show, and you use your remote control to skip the advertisements.

• Clutter results in a more *negative attitude toward advertising* in general (Elliott & Speck, 1998). In other words, we become irritated with advertising when we think there is too much of it or when it disrupts our media use. You are skeptical of Pizza Hut's claim that it uses quality ingredients. You might even go as far so to avoid giving your business to companies that you feel advertise too much.

• Clutter may lead to *ad avoidance* by audience members (Elliott & Speck, 1998). We seek to control our exposure to ads when we feel threatened by them. The choice we make, then, is to ignore the advertising. Ha and Litman (1997) explain that when advertising clutter reached 50 percent in entertainment magazines, circulation decreased. You might not read the advertisements in your school newspaper because there are so many of them.

Michael T. Elliott and Paul Surgi Speck (1998) argue that people perceive television to have the greatest clutter, followed by direct mail, magazines, radio, newspaper, and yellow pages. Disruption is highest for television, followed by magazines, radio, newspapers, direct mail, and yellow pages. Television advertising hinders the user's search for information the most, followed by magazines, radio, direct mail, yellow pages, and newspapers. In terms of attitude toward advertising, direct mail is considered more negatively than are the other media. Ad avoidance is most likely for television, followed by yellow pages, newspapers, radio, and direct mail. Elliott and Speck (1998) explain that perceptions of ad clutter and attitudes toward advertising were not related to demographic variables.

As we have seen, advertisers face challenges related to media user behavior, audience demographics, and the advertising environment. Taken as a whole, these challenges suggest that advertisers can no longer rely on a broadcast medium such as television to convey their message to audiences. Audiences are diverse, active, and prone to using a variety of media. In addition, the very nature of media today creates a great deal of clutter that advertisers must overcome.

Responding to the Challenges

To compensate for the challenges posed by the media age, advertisers use an arsenal of tools to reach audiences—to foster relationships with them. As audience members, we must be aware of how advertisers seek to identify with us. In this section, we explore how advertisers use branding, cross-promotion, product placement, relationship marketing, and Internet advertising to overcome the challenges we have just described.

BRANDING

One of the primary ways advertisers overcome the challenges posed by media is through branding. **Brand** refers to a particular product, but also to the meaning and presence associated with the product because of the symbols and meanings embodied in it (Kohli & LaBahn, 1997). The brand defines the product for the customer and differentiates the product from its competitors (Padgett & Allen, 1997). **Branding** is the process through which objects obtain value. A brand name not only leads customers to purchase a particular product, but it conveys information about what it means to use the product. A brand is an image of a product and its company, in a way. The more potent the meaning of the brand, the more the brand is able to cut through the clutter of contemporary advertising. In the media age, this power is important. Coca-Cola's brand is estimated to be worth $36 billion, Budweiser's $9.7 billion, and Barbie's $1.7 billion (Kohli & LaBahn, 1997).

Brand names are chosen with several ideas in mind. Customers have preconceived ideas about what a brand name for a particular product should sound like. "Whumies" would work for breakfast cereal, but not for detergent (Peterson & Ross, 1972). Companies spend a great deal of time—an average of 64 hours—and money—an average of $7,600—simply naming the brand, according to one study (Kohli & LaBahn, 1997). Once the name is chosen, advertisers work to create meaning for the name. Researchers use two concepts to understand how brands influence consumers: brand salience and brand image. There is some question about which objective is the most important goal for advertisers to pursue. Stephen Miller and Lisette Berry (1998) argue that brand salience is more important.

Brand salience refers to the order in which brands come to mind. Brand salience concerns, not *what* consumers think about a brand, but *which* brands they think about (Miller & Berry, 1998). To test brand salience, researchers ask consumers to list brands for a particular product. The first one consumers list is said to have high brand salience. If I ask you to name five hamburger restaurants, for example, and you list McDonald's first, then that brand is said to have salience. Brand salience is achieved by developing advertising that is intrusive and/or entertaining and that repeatedly reinforces the brand and the meanings associated with it (Miller & Berry, 1998). Repeatedly exposing potential customers to advertisements that are amusing, unique, or provocative helps a brand achieve salience. Audiences found the online company E★Trade's Super Bowl commercial (which we have discussed previously) particularly amusing. Despite the silliness of the ad (or perhaps because of it), viewers remembered the tag line: "We just wasted 2 million dollars. What have you done with your money today?"

Brand image refers to the ideas consumers have about a particular brand. It includes attributes such as relevance, performance, and advantages (Miller & Berry, 1998). If you think that McDonald's hamburgers are tasty and inexpensive, then that is the image you have of the McDonald's brand. Miller and Berry identify three objectives advertisers have in their creation of brand image.

brand
a particular product and the meanings associated with it because of the symbols and meanings embodied in it

branding
the process through which objects obtain value

THINKING CRITICALLY

Creating the Krispy Kreme Brand

The hottest brand today, according to *Fortune* magazine's Andy Serwer (2003), is a small doughnut company named Krispy Kreme. The brand has such a following that customers will line up the day before a new store opens in anticipation of purchasing its products. Yet, Krispy Kreme has no budget for national advertising; instead, it relies on generous giveaways of its product and word-of-mouth buzz. Let's examine how Krispy Kreme has become a persuasive force.

Krispy Kreme generates buzz in local communities by providing free doughnuts to radio and television stations prior to the store's grand opening. One of its most significant giveaways was on live television during the *Today* show in 1996 prior to the New York opening of a Krispy Kreme restaurant. The practice has ensued in communities across the country. Prior to its opening in Fargo, North Dakota in 2002, the doughnut shop was the subject of several newspaper articles, including one in which local police officers rated the best doughnuts in town. When the store opened, local radio personalities broadcast from the event and new customers were lined up. Local police were needed to direct traffic in the area. The store's doughnuts have been featured on shows such

as *Will and Grace* and *The Sopranos* and movies such as *Bruce Almighty* and *How to Lose a Guy in Ten Days* (Serwer, 2003). The company also provides millions of cheap doughnuts to fund-raising groups, who resell the doughnuts for profit. Each of these activities helps Krispy Kreme achieve brand salience.

If you've ever driven past a Krispy Kreme shop, you know that when the "Hot Doughnuts Now" sign is lit, the doughnuts are hot and ready to eat. The sign is one of the hallmarks of the brand and often serves as one of the final enticements for customers to stop in for a doughnut. The sign and classic logo design create the brand image of Krispy Kreme and serve as powerful persuasive symbols.

As you consider how Krispy Kreme uses product placement and buzz to build its brand, think about other brands with which you are familiar and answer these questions:

1. What strategies are used to build brand image? Brand salience?

2. How does product placement contribute to brand development?

3. How powerful is buzz in brand development?

First, advertisers help consumers understand the brand's *equity,* the value or meaning of the brand to them. Some brands, such as Coca-Cola, have greater value than other brands. Elizabeth C. Hirschman, Linda Scott, and William B. Wells (1998) explain that brands get their meaning through their present and historical use in consumer culture and by the texts of popular culture, such as television, which "coat" the product with meaning. A product becomes a signifier, as we discussed in Chapter 2, when it takes on meaning. Read the discussion in Thinking Critically: Creating the Krispy Kreme Brand to learn how Krispy Kreme has created both brand image and brand salience for its doughnuts.

Second, advertisers develop a *position* for the brand that is appealing and unique. They work to distinguish the brand somehow from its competitors. Susan Fournier (1998) found that consumers form relationships with brands in ways that resemble relationship formation with real people. Using in-depth interviews with consumers, Fournier discovered that brands are linked to the identity of those who use them. Consumers purchase brands, not just because of their quality, but because brands give meaning to their lives, meanings that are both functional and emotional (Fournier, 1998). Here is where brand advertising makes use of motivational appeals to form relationships with the audience and to identify with them.

One interviewee in Fournier's (1998) study, a woman who values her traditional roles of homemaker, mother, and wife, has formed more than 40 strong relationships with foods and cleaning products. She is loyal to her brands and demands the highest quality in her own life and in the products she uses. Read as she describes making spaghetti sauce:

> When I make the sauce, it takes all day. I let it cook on the stove for 8 hours. I have a really big pot. Stainless steel from Revere Ware. 12 quarts. The best pot I ever had. I bought one for my daughter, too. The sauce doesn't burn and stick to the bottom like it used to with my old one. Anyway, like I told you, I blend the Pastene tomatoes in the blender. Whole tomatoes. "Kitchen Ready" it says on the can. Now I use three at least, maybe four cans usually. And I add a little can of the Hunt's special sauce. Not much, just the little can. Then I fry up the sausage in a frying pan with the Bertolli olive oil . . . (p. 350)

In this short description, the consumer mentions four brands with which she has formed a strong, loyal relationship. Fournier (1998) found similar patterns in other people she interviewed for the study.

Third, advertisers seek to communicate or *reinforce* the brand's *position*. We have previously discussed that in the media age, advertisers often seek to segment their audiences to more effectively target their messages. Ned Anschuetz (1997) argues that for branding purposes, however, targeting a broad audience works best. He found that brands should be as popular as possible to attract a wide range of customers. More popular brands are bought more frequently than less popular brands within specific target audiences. More popularity means greater equity (value or worth) for the brand. Anschuetz explains that advertisers integrate audiences, appeals, and media to reach the widest audience possible. Thus, in broadcast media, such as the television networks, brand advertisements will continue to be widespread because it is a good way to build brand consciousness among a wide audience.

Brands are a powerful way for advertisers to break through the clutter of the media age. Brand development involves careful choice of a brand name and the use of strategic communication aimed at establishing brand salience and brand image. Branding enables advertisers to set their products or services apart from those of others.

CROSS-PROMOTION

Advertisers also use the strategy of cross-promotion, also known as synergy, to respond to challenges of the media age. In **cross-promotion,** two or more companies that seek to reach the same audience pool their resources to develop a joint persuasive campaign to reach the intended audience (McAllister, 1996). Some recent examples include Levi's and *The Mod Squad* movie, Burger King and Pokemon, and McDonald's and *Toy Story 2*. McAllister explains that cross-promotion works because "big, flashy and pervasive campaigns may completely overwhelm the smaller efforts by the competition" (p. 137). Thus, repetition is the primary aim of cross-promotion.

cross-promotion
a joint persuasive campaign in which two or more companies seeking to reach the same audience pool their resources to make a stronger appeal than each could alone

McAllister (1996) identifies three functions of cross-promotion. The first, the *microcommercial function,* focuses on the concept of impressions. **Impressions** are the number of times consumers are exposed to a persuader's message (McAllister, 1996). An impression occurs when a viewer sees an organization's image. A television commercial, a poster at the local Taco Bell advertising a movie, or a cereal box promoting a new toy are all examples of impressions. Advertisers seek to create literally "billions" of impressions, and they see "anything" as capable of carrying an impression (McAllister, 1996).

The second function of cross-promotion is the *multilevel commercial function* (McAllister, 1996). The multilevel commercial function seeks to maximize the promotional advantage of commercials by using them to advertise several products at once. Advertisers share commercial space, in essence. When you see an advertisement that encourages you to buy a Happy Meal at McDonald's that is tied to a current movie, you are seeing the multilevel commercial function at work. Both McDonald's and the movie are receiving advertising benefits from the spot.

The *multiplaced commercial function* refers to the ability of cross-promotional advertising to reach a market through various channels, or places. Advertisers using cross-promotion place their message on television commercials, movie screens, and restaurant walls. Often, consumers will see an advertisement on television that directs them to another advertiser. In early 2000, Burger King and Pokemon used multiplaced cross-promotion to lure customers to Burger King as well as to get them to purchase Pokemon trading cards. In addition, the Pokemon movie reinforced Burger King's image and sent viewers to the restaurant to take part in the Pokemon trading card craze.

Audience members and professional watchdogs also voice concern about the audience's ability to identify the members of these cross-promotional ventures. Ethical Insights: Ethics and Cross-Promotion looks at one such venture.

McAllister (1996) warns that cross-promotion may reduce the amount of information in our society because we hear louder messages from fewer sources. He identifies four dangers posed by cross-promotion: amplified voices, impersonated voices, controlled voices, and nonstop voices. McAllister writes, "The danger here is that such characteristics may make it difficult to hear over commercial speech" (p. 169).

- *Amplified voices* refers to the magnification that occurs when advertisers team with other advertisers to deliver the same message. When McDonald's and an about-to-be-released movie team up for their advertising, a great deal of buzz is created about both the movie and the fast-food chain.

- *Impersonated voices* refers to commercials that do not appear to be commercials. When Martha Stewart promotes Kmart, for example, is she promoting the store or is she promoting her own line of household goods? Questions are raised by cross-promotional arrangements such as this.

- When promoters team up to produce persuasion, there is a danger that one of the partners will have its *voice controlled* by the other. The talk show host/comedian Rosie O'Donnell ended her promotion of Kmart because of the store's sale of guns, which O'Donnell opposes. O'Donnell ended her partnership in an effort to maintain control of her voice.

ETHICAL INSIGHTS

Ethics and Cross-Promotion

The online health information site drkoop.com looks like any other website devoted to helping patients understand their health. The site includes expert advice, messages boards, and other health-related information. Although the site took care to protect the ethical integrity of the information it provided, there were instances where it was difficult to distinguish advice from advertisement (Sherrid, 1999). For instance, on the site's homepage, there was a link to locate health services in the user's area. The hospitals were described as the most innovative and advanced institutions in the nation. The site did not mention that the hospitals listed had paid to have their names appear. Following criticism, drkoop.com has now listed the word *sponsor* next to advertisements that appear on its pages. The site has also joined with 90 leading health Internet services to develop a set of 14 ethical principles to govern their practices (Charatan, 2000). As the line between advice and advertisement is increasingly blurred in the media age, it is important to consider the ethics of websites such as drkoop.com and other advice and information sites.

The Public Relations Society of America discusses the core value of disclosure of information in its Member Code of Ethics 2000. PRSA (2000) guides its members to "be honest and accurate in all communications" and to "reveal the sponsors for causes and interests represented." When websites hide the identity of their sponsors, they fail to live up to the ethical guidelines established by PRSA. Likewise, the National Communication Association (1999) believes that "truthfulness, accuracy, honesty, and reason are essential to the integrity of communication."

Although drkoop.com has taken steps to ensure that it communicates ethically with its users, it is important for us to consider the accuracy, truthfulness, and honesty of other information and news sites on the World Wide Web. As you surf the Web for information, think about these questions.

1. To what extent should information sites mark the presence and identity of advertisers?

2. What are some possible dangers of sites, such as drkoop.com, that blend information with advertising?

3. What kind of controls should be used to prevent advertisers from exercising influence on editorial content?

4. How can consumers better protect themselves from hidden advertising on Internet information sites?

- *Nonstop voices* refers to the long-term agreements signed between cross-promotion partners. Expect to see more sequels of movies because of the advertising deals struck by the movie's producer and its sponsors.

Through cross-promotion, advertisers can have their messages heard by more audience members in more places more often. As such, cross-promotion is an effective way to overcome the challenges posed by the media age. Inherent to the cross-promotional strategy, however, are dangers related to the free expression of ideas in our society, such as the danger of one partner's controlling the voice of the other.

PRODUCT PLACEMENT

Yet another way for advertising to meet the challenges posed by the media age is through **product placement,** the featuring of branded products in entertainment media. When you watch your favorite television show and see a Macintosh computer sitting on the star's desk, Apple probably paid the television studio for its appearance. When the movie character James Bond races away

product placement
featuring branded products in entertainment media

from his nemesis in a shiny BMW, the car company no doubt has paid to have its car save the day. Realizing that viewers today skip advertisements, advertisers are using product placements to bring their messages to us at times other than during commercial breaks. Product placement is similar to cross-promotion, but the degree to which the product is featured differs. Product placements are designed to appear incidental.

The NBC reality series *The Restaurant* takes product placement to new levels. In fact, agreements with Mitsubishi, American Express, and Coors ensured that NBC would not have to pay to produce the show. Instead, production costs were paid by the three advertisers, whose products are tightly integrated into the show. The main character, Rocco DiSpirito, drives a Mitsubishi SUV, which is prominently shown throughout the series, and Coors is the brew of choice at the restaurant. The goal of the unique agreement is to reduce the risk for NBC while at the same time promoting products during the course of the program, so that if viewers skip the commercials, they will still be exposed to the sponsors' products. *The Restaurant* may usher in a new type of product placement agreement on network television.

Investing in product placement is risky because viewers cannot be reliably measured or guaranteed (Buss, 1998). Yet the benefits are numerous. Product placements function as a type of celebrity endorsement. Placements create buzz about a product or service. When Tom Cruise sipped Red Stripe beer in *The Firm*, sales of the product increased 50 percent.

Using computer technology, advertisers are able to place products in shows that previously featured generic products or no products at all. The products are "added" to the scene after the scene has been shot. This way, the show's producers and the advertiser ensure that the product fits with the show. Often, the program may air once before the products are placed. Such was the case with a rerun of the UPN show *Seven Days,* which featured computer-generated products including a can of Coca-Cola and a Kenneth Cole bag (Natale, 1999).

Televised athletic events use the same technology to sell advertising on virtual billboards. If you watch a San Diego Padres baseball game, you will notice that the advertisement on the billboard behind home plate changes throughout the game. The billboard is actually a computer graphic that uses blue-screen technology to create the illusion of a billboard for viewers. The billboard can transmit two different advertisements at the same time to different audiences. The San Diego audience sees one advertisement, while the audience in Houston, for example, may see an ad for a Houston business.

Video games also feature virtual product placements. Games feature the products and/or logos of major companies. *Madden NFL,* for example, has featured the Fox Sports logo on end-zone billboards (Mannes, 1995). *Andre Agassi Tennis* features the logos of Nike and Canon on the walls of the tennis court (Mannes, 1995). Persuaders use the ads to increase their exposure in certain markets. Game producers like the placements because they add to the realism of the game (Mannes, 1995).

Product placement is an effective way for advertisers to have audience members see their products between commercial breaks. Advertisers gain more than exposure, however, when the placement creates buzz for the product or service.

RELATIONSHIP MARKETING

Relationship marketing uses media and technology to communicate on a one-to-one basis with consumers. Often called one-to-one marketing, relationship marketing is based on the idea that it is easier and less expensive to keep a customer than it is to attract a new one. In fact, some advertising executives estimate that it may cost a toothpaste company $250 to persuade a new customer to use its brand. Eighty percent of all television advertising expenditures is spent on people who are in no way prospects for the product being advertised (Lobove, 1998). Relationship marketing tries to keep customers by recognizing that they exist, communicating with them, and responding to their needs (A. Mitchell, 1998). Relationship marketing is necessitated by the demands consumers and their technology place on advertisers; it is made possible by new technology that allows advertisers to understand and reach consumers. Gateway Computer and Dell Computer, for example, assemble computers to customer specifications. Custom Foot makes shoes to order, based on each customer's foot measurements. Relationship marketing is not possible for every company, but advertising researchers foresee the practice as a sign of things to come.

> **relationship marketing**
> a persuasive strategy aimed at keeping customers loyal by communicating with them one-to-one on a regular basis; also called one-to-one marketing

The media age has expanded the opportunities for relationship marketing. Messages directed at individual customers were once too costly, but with digital printing and e-mail, companies can now reach their customers inexpensively. Technology is also making it possible to customize products for individual customers. In addition to the computer companies just mentioned, Ford Motor Company is using technology to create custom products for customers. Communication and technology researchers have developed software systems capable of supporting relationship marketing activities. As barriers continue to disappear, relationship marketing will play an increased role in the advertising campaigns of today's companies.

Seth Lobove (1998) says it will be only a short time until cable companies can transmit commercials to our homes based on our interests and needs. You may see a different commercial than your neighbor while you both watch the same show. Market researchers have tested software that records the viewing habits of cable subscribers. The researchers measured the viewers' viewing habits as well, such as when they increased or decreased the volume of their sets. The data were combined with interview data about the people who lived in the homes. Eventually, cable operators will be able to insert commercials into shows and send them to specific viewers via their addressable cable box, which will continue to monitor their viewing habits.

The Internet may be the ideal medium for relationship marketing. iQVC.com e-mails customers about new products they may be interested in based on their response to several questions on the site. Internet portals such as Yahoo! feature My Yahoo! which allows users to customize their Internet homepage with scores of their favorite sports teams, prices of their stocks, or news from their preferred areas of interest. Many airline companies e-mail customers about special rates from their city. Amazon.com recommends books for shoppers based on their prior purchases (Geller, 1998).

Don Peppers and Martha Rogers (1993) outline four components of relationship marketing. The first is *identification* of individual customers. For some firms, this is simple; for others, it is more difficult. A coffee shop would have a difficult time tracking its customers. A car dealership, however, can easily keep track of who purchased cars from the company during a given period.

The second component is *distinguishing* between these customers based on the characteristics of need and value. A coffee shop owner, for instance, deals with customers who have varying needs and who are relatively equal in their value. Relationship marketing to these customers would be difficult. The automobile dealer would be able to determine which customers are repeat customers who come back every two or three years for a car and those who only occasionally purchase an automobile. Those customers who purchase or lease cars frequently would be good targets for relationship marketing.

Peppers and Rogers's (1993) third component is *interaction*. The company must communicate directly with its customers on a personal basis, reflecting their needs. This interaction not only communicates to the customer that he or she is valued, but it helps the company know what the customer will need in the future. To enable interaction, Alan Mitchell (1998) suggests companies need databases that track the customer's interactions with the company.

The final component of relationship marketing is *customization* of the service or product to reflect the needs of the customer (Peppers & Rogers, 1993). That is, the company must be built around the customer. For some industries, such as the airlines, this is not possible. Many of their services, such as flight times, must be standardized. An automobile dealership, however, can order vehicles with specifications matching customer needs. A flower shop can call or e-mail customers as annual events such as birthdays and anniversaries approach.

Advertisers use relationship marketing for several reasons. Relationship marketing helps them cut through the clutter of the media age. When consumers can quickly identify the source of an advertisement, they may pay more attention to the ad. We tend to listen to messages that are more personal to us. Relationship marketing helps develop that personal connection.

Relationship marketing also keeps customers loyal. Peppers and Rogers (1998) explain that making a decision today takes up valuable time and energy for consumers. Imagine that you are shopping for electronic equipment. You go to the first electronics store in town and learn all about speakers, receivers, home theater systems, and DVD players. You ask questions, jot down some prices, and go to the next store. At the next store, you spend a few minutes talking to a salesperson, who asks you to fill out a short survey about your budget, needs, wants, and current system. The salesperson makes a recommendation for a new television, for instance, based on the information you have provided. The price you are quoted seems reasonable, and so you purchase the television. A few weeks later, you receive a phone call from the salesperson asking about your television and informing you of a current sale. When you get ready to purchase a DVD player, you remember that the store where you purchased your television knows you. It knows your budget and your long-term home theater goals. You go back to the store simply because it is easy. It saves you time and energy. You purchase your DVD player there, and you begin to build a long-term relationship with the store.

Relationship marketing faces several limitations. Susan Fournier, Susan Dobscha, and David Glen Mick (1998) explain that customers are asked to be part of hundreds of one-to-one relationships, not only with companies, but with their coworkers, family, and friends. Customers find it easy to discard offers from companies seeking to form better relationships with them. Companies are not always friendly or loyal in their relationships with customers, either. In addition, many critics of relationship marketing contend that such methods are unwarranted invasions of consumer privacy.

Many advertisers think that relationship marketing will be the next major type of advertising. For some consumers, relationship marketing is a welcome convenience. It is also a good example of how persuaders identify with audience members based on audience analysis techniques. In the next section, we focus on a final way advertisers are overcoming the challenges of the media age.

INTERNET ADVERTISING

Web marketing and advertising is seen as a way for businesses to escape the constraints of physical space and offer their goods and services to consumers in virtual space (Palmer & Griffith, 1998). The Web promises to dramatically reshape how the advertising and marketing worlds form relationships with customers. To better understand Internet advertising, we examine its users and their motivations, Internet communities, and types of Internet advertising.

Who Uses the Internet and Why?   Basing their work on the uses and gratifications theory that we discussed in Chapter 2, Pradeep K. Korgaonkar and Lori D. Wolin (1999) identify seven needs and concerns audience members have for using the Web. These needs and concerns influence how individuals use the Web, as well as indicate the likelihood that they will make purchases on the Web. The seven needs and concerns are

- *Social escapism motivation:* We seek the pleasurable activities offered by the Web (Korgaonkar & Wolin, 1999). In other words, we enjoy using the Web and see it is a form of entertainment.

- *Transaction-based security and privacy concerns:* We are concerned about the security of using the Web for purchases (Korgaonkar & Wolin, 1999). We are reluctant to give out our credit card numbers to websites.

- *Information motivation:* We use the Web to research products, read the news, and learn about various aspects of our society. The Web is good at presenting information to us that we can use on our own time.

- *Interactive control motivation:* We can personalize our Web environment to control what information is presented to us, how that information is presented, and with whom we interact. Research indicates that audience members prefer sites with greater degrees of interactivity (Korgaonkar & Wolin, 1999).

Figure 13.1
The iVillage.com website creates a community for its viewers. To which online communities do you belong? What benefits do you receive from membership?

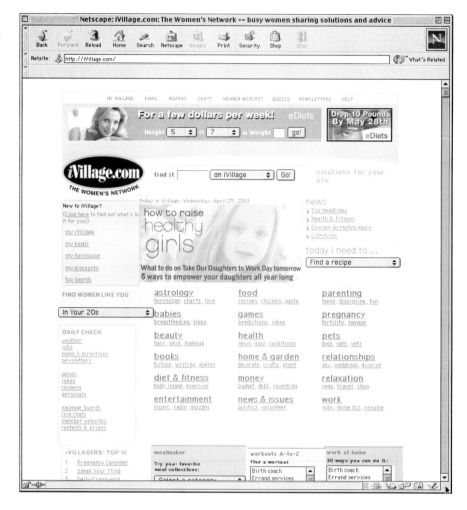

- *Socialization motivation:* We like to use the Web so that we can talk about it with our friends and acquaintances. We also use e-mail and chat rooms to communicate with others over the Internet.

- *Nontransactional privacy concerns:* We are concerned about privacy in general on the Internet. We dislike receiving "junk" e-mail and fear false advertising.

- *Economic motivation:* We have economic reasons for using the Internet, including collecting information, shopping, and selling. We think we can save money by shopping online or that we can make money by selling products or services online.

Although gender, education, income, and age can be used to predict how often and how long individuals use the Internet, the needs and motivations just described play a greater role in how individuals use the Web (Korgaonkar & Wolin, 1999). Korgaonkar and Wolin (1999) predict that in the future, these needs and motivations will play an even greater role in how the Web is used.

Internet Communities   In addition to traditional methods of segmenting audiences, Ashok Ranchhod (1998) suggests that **Internet communities** will emerge as effective ways to identify target audiences and reach them through advertising. Communities of Internet users who have similar interests, lifestyles, and beliefs are emerging. Users who are interested in certain products visit websites that satisfy their needs and provide a place for them to virtually communicate in chat rooms. Advertisers advertise on these websites to reach a very specific type of consumer who might be interested in the persuader's product. One such community is iVillage.com (Figure 13.1), a community designed to meet the needs of female Internet users. iVillage.com provides information, chat opportunities, and threaded discussion lists for users. It also includes several subcommunities, such as ParentSoup, which itself is divided into increasingly smaller communities. The growth of online communities will provide specific audience segments for advertisers. Learn more about these communities by completing the Internet Activity: Exploring Internet Communities.

Internet community
a virtual "place" where people with similar interests gather to obtain information or interact

Types of Internet Advertising   There are several ways for advertisers to use Web pages. The most common method is banner advertising, which often appears at the top of a Web page as a hyperlink. On a search engine, such as Yahoo! or Lycos, banner ads often provide advertising for a product or service related to what the user is searching for. The primary goal of these ads is for the viewer to click on the banner to reach the advertiser's website.

S. Shyam Sundar and colleagues (1998) found no difference between user recall of print and online advertisements that relied on text only. The authors recommend that advertisers incorporate features of the Internet—animation, video, and hyperlinks—to make online advertising more memorable. However, Rex Briggs and Nigel Hollis (1997) found that audience characteristics are the primary indicators of whether a viewer clicks through the ad or not. Audience members who have certain needs or emotions may be more likely to click through than those with different needs or emotions. Briggs and Hollis (1997) explain that banner advertisements are effective even if viewers do not click on the ad. Banner advertisements increase consumer loyalty and awareness (Briggs

INTERNET ACTIVITY

Exploring Internet Advertising

Internet search engines, such as Yahoo! or Google use advertising in ways that are sometimes difficult to detect. For instance, some search engines use "sponsored links" that appear to be returned with your search, but are paid for by the company and may not be the best site for you to use. Look at Google, at http://www.google.com, and answer the questions that follow. How does the site use advertising? Are the advertisements customized to the topic of the site? Did you click on any of the ads? Why or why not? How might the ads on this site have been more effective?

& Hollis, 1997). How do search engines advertise? Complete the Internet Activity: Exploring Internet Advertising to find out.

Internet advertising is yet another way for advertisers to respond to the challenges of the media age. Internet advertising appeals to certain types of users, and the Internet is seen by advertisers as a measurable medium for advertising. Let's use our previous discussion of advertising and its challenges to finally look at the impact of advertising on individual audience members and society.

Advertising's Effects

You may assume that advertising results in purchases by consumers of products or services they see advertised. Research indicates that this is only partially true. Twitchell (1996) argues that advertising today does not have a strong effect on what we buy, but it is effective in creating our culture. Advertising's most profound effect on consumers is in creating a culture that values the pursuit of certain lifestyles. Advertising's influence on the choices consumers make, then, is probably strongest on a secondary level.

A great deal of research suggests that advertising plays, at best, a minor role in the choices consumers make (see, for example, Ehrenberg, 1974; Tellis & Weiss, 1995). Twitchell (1996) explains that of the 3,000 ads we see each day, we notice only 80 and have some sort of reaction to only 12. He argues that if advertising worked, companies would purchase even more advertising. Companies spend billions of dollars a year on advertising, but if we consider how much of the value of each product advertised is spent to advertise it, the amount is far smaller. The cost of advertising Coca-Cola, for instance, adds only 0.006 cent per can, and the cost of advertising a new car is about 18 cents per $3,000 (Twitchell, 1996). Other researchers (for example, White, 1999) see advertising as playing a strong role in creating awareness of products and brands, providing information to consumers, helping to build brand images, and reminding audience members about products or brands.

The real impact of advertising, argues Twitchell (1996), is the value that it gives to our lives. We consume the advertising more than we do the goods advertised (Twitchell, 1996). Twitchell terms this feature of contemporary culture Adcult, which refers to the process by which culture is transmitted through advertising. Twitchell explains: "For what is carried in and with advertising is what we know, what we share, what we believe in. It is who we are. It is us" (p. 4). Advertising gives value to the things of our life (Twitchell, 1996). We are attracted to things: We call products "goods," not "bads," for example. Twitchell argues that the Berlin Wall fell and China opened its doors to the Western world because the people of these countries desired to consume goods that the countries could not provide under a closed system of government and production. Twitchell argues that we have to know what to gather. We crave the meanings of objects. Advertising performs a role that in the past has been filled by religion, education, or art (Twitchell, 1996). Advertisers are interested in what we want, as determined by what, and how, we purchase (Twitchell, 1996). Advertisers find our desires and exploit them. It is not the audience that is manipulated, it is the advertising, says Twitchell.

David Slayden (1999) offers a complementary view of advertising. He notes that in the past 20 years, advertising has changed from being about the product to being about the user of the product. How the product works is less important than what the product does for us symbolically. Advertising identifies the important myths, symbols, and stories of our culture and associates them with a product or service (Slayden, 1999). Thus, when we purchase the product or service, we place ourselves within this myth, symbol, or story. The benefit we receive from a product is social identity. Advertisers thus seek to understand how their products can fit into our lives. Whether or not you accept the perspectives offered by Twitchell and Slayden, it should be clear that advertising plays a more profound function in contemporary culture than simply identifying products and their benefits.

The view of persuasion we have presented may seem quite extreme. It may appear that advertisers must go to ever greater lengths to get their point across to us. What will the future hold for advertising? Two scholars offer their insights. Twitchell (1996) writes that irony will contribute to a deflation of the advertising culture. To get their point across, advertisements have recently presented themselves as advertisements. Advertisers are stepping out from behind the curtain and announcing that what we are seeing is only an ad. The mystery is gone from advertising. Recent Super Bowl ads illustrate this point. One ad proclaimed itself the worst ad ever. It featured no fancy graphics or images. Instead, the ad used simple text, with someone trying to play chopsticks on a piano in the background.

Twitchell (1996) writes that audiences today expect ads to be a joke that neither advertiser nor audience takes seriously. Slayden (1999) agrees, asking: "Have we all become too hip? Have we overdosed on irony within a heavily mediated environment where everything is experienced from an ironic because mediated distance? Is communication now more or less an entertainment, a presentation of a public self with any number of knowing asides to an imaginary, clued-in audience?" (p. 270). The result is that we do not take advertising seriously (Twitchell, 1996).

Summary

Advertising invades our every waking minute. Some researchers estimate that the typical American sees some 3,000 advertisements a day. Advertising constantly surrounds us and comes from anonymous sources. It exists in a symbiotic relationship with our culture. In addition, advertising is profane and magical at the same time.

Advertising involves clients who have some product or service or idea that they would like to sell to audience members. Audiences are created by media organizations and then sold to advertisers for their demographic or psychographic qualities.

Today's mediated environment creates three challenges for advertisers. Specific media pose their own challenges as well. Media users, who are consumers of the products advertised, have greater power to circumvent the voices of advertisers today. In addition, today's audiences are highly fragmented and have active lifestyles, making it difficult for advertisers to reach them. Finally, today's advertising environment is cluttered.

To overcome the challenges posed by the media age, advertisers turn to branding, which fosters emotional connections between a product and its audience. Cross-promotion and product placement effectively create advertising in the midst of entertainment. Relationship marketing uses technology to create a one-to-one relationship with consumers. Internet advertising is seen by many as an effective way, not only to target consumers, but to create communities of consumers for advertisers.

Key Terms

WWW: Visit the book's website at http://www.mhhe.com/borchers2 for multiple-choice quizzes, Internet activities, and key terms flashcards.

clutter 366	impression 372
brand 369	product placement 373
branding 369	relationship marketing 375
cross-promotion 371	Internet community 379

14

Interpersonal Persuasion

Learning Objectives

After reading this chapter, you should be able to:

1. Understand how variables of interpersonal communication affect the persuasive relationship between individuals in the media age.

2. Identify the techniques of compliance gaining and the variables that influence their effectiveness.

3. Describe two sequential request strategies used by persuaders.

4. Identify the steps of personal selling.

5. Describe several types of persuasive interviews and characteristics of interviews.

6. Understand the nature and causes of conflict and ways to overcome conflict.

7. Explain how to detect interpersonal deception.

Your old car is dying a slow death. Your maintenance and repair bills for the past month were more than the car is worth. You decide that it is time to purchase a new vehicle. As a smart consumer of persuasion, you decide to visit two dealerships to compare prices. At the first dealership, you test-drive three cars. You like one of the cars, so you sit down with the sales representative to find out its price. After talking with a manager, the sales rep gives you a price, which is much higher than you thought it would be. You make a counteroffer, but the price the dealership offers in response is still too high. You decide to go to the next dealership.

At the second dealership, you test-drive the same car model as at the first dealership. You also find out about this dealership's service department. The sales representative offers you a soda and some popcorn, and you gladly accept because it has been a long day. When the sales representative gives you the price of the car you like, it is much lower than the first dealership's.

How could the price for the same car model differ so much from one dealership to another? Is the second dealership offering a better deal? Should you purchase the car right away at the second dealership? Or is there room to negotiate with the first dealer? What is the best way to close the sale?

This chapter helps you explore the answers to those questions. As you read about interpersonal persuasion, you will begin to understand the persuasive strategies used by your friends, coworkers, family members, and others you deal with every day in one-on-one interactions. In interpersonal situations, in particular, persuaders seek to create intimate relationships with other individuals. We explore some of the key variables in interpersonal persuasion. We then examine two theories of interpersonal persuasion—compliance gaining and sequential-request strategies—before discussing three contexts of interpersonal persuasion—personal selling, conflict resolution, and interviewing. We conclude the chapter by discussing deception.

Interpersonal Persuasion in the Media Age

This chapter may seem out of place in this text at first because it focuses on interpersonal communication rather than on media. Yet the mediated world in which we live has important implications for how we communicate with others. Gary Gumpert and Robert Cathcart (1979) explain that how we communicate with others cannot help but be influenced by the media that surround us. Let's explore three implications here.

The first implication relates to the knowledge we have about our world. We are able to communicate about more topics with more knowledge than has ever before been possible. Consider an example from the television show *Saturday Night Live*. For several years, one of the characters, played by Chris Farley, would play a television talk show host interviewing famous guests. However, the interviews were always a bit strange. Instead of asking questions, Farley would simply recall movies or television shows in which the actor or actress had starred. Farley would say something like this: "Remember when you were in that one movie? With the burning building?" He would wait a minute and then say, "That was great." The audience and the guest would be able to fill in what was missing and to agree with Farley when he said, "That was great." Because we had all been exposed to the same information, we were able to follow the interview easily despite its oddness. Our everyday interpersonal communication follows the same model. We refer to bits of information that our friends understand. Media provide us with a great warehouse of information that we use when we communicate.

Second, the methods we use for interpersonal communication are increasingly mediated. We often send e-mail or chat on the Internet with our friends instead of talking to them face-to-face. Our choice of medium has important implications for the type of message we send and how we perceive that message. It is popular to use "emoticons" in e-mail or chat messages, for instance, to communicate our feelings because e-mail lacks the nonverbal cues for doing so. Emoticons use standard keyboard symbols to create faces, such as :) for smiling face or :(for a frowning face. In fact, the latest versions of Microsoft products automatically convert these symbols to their emotional counterparts—for instance, ☺. As we turn increasingly to videoconferencing and videophones, we will have more cues to send those with whom we converse.

Third, our values and attitudes are formed, in part, through our interactions with media. In Chapter 11, we saw how emotions, needs, and values are feelings that are developed through our interaction with others. Exposure to a great variety of feelings in media messages no doubt changes how we feel about ourselves and others. When we see couples fall in and out of love on soap operas, our ideas about love are influenced, at least to some degree. Thus, media serve to facilitate the development of emotions, needs, and values, which then play a role in how we communicate with and persuade others. With these general ideas in mind, let's now discuss some of the variables involved in interpersonal communication.

Interpersonal Persuasion Variables

The ability of individuals to identify with others rests in part on the relationship they have with those others. Researchers have identified four variables that influence how people communicate with each other: attraction, dominance, involvement, and situation (Andrews & Baird, 2000). These variables play a role in most theories of interpersonal persuasion, so let's look at them first.

ATTRACTION

Attraction refers to how individuals feel about each other. They may be attracted to the other person, in which case they would have positive feelings toward him or her, or they may not be attracted to the other person and we would say that they have negative feelings. Several variables influence the attraction between two individuals:

- *Physical proximity* allows us to get to know other people. Consider those with whom you live or work or your colleagues in this class. You have the opportunity to get to know these people and thus form relationships with them. Proximity does not necessarily mean that you will like someone, however. Whether the feelings it prompts are positive or negative, proximity fosters the development of attraction.

- Attraction may also result from *physical attractiveness*. We tend to spend more time with and enjoy the company of those individuals to whom we are physically attracted. Research indicates that those who are attractive have more friendships, whereas those who are unattractive have fewer personal relationships.

- We are also attracted to those individuals whom we perceive as *similar* to us. We prefer to associate with people who share similar attitudes, tastes, preferences, and backgrounds. If you think for a moment about your friends, you might realize that they are quite similar to you.
- *Status* influences the attraction we have to others. We are attracted to those who have higher status, and we are less attracted to those who have lower status.
- We are attracted to individuals who can provide us with *personal rewards*. We are attracted to individuals who offer us praise, and we are less attracted to individuals who criticize us.

DOMINANCE

The second variable that influences how we interact with others is dominance, which is defined as the ability to control or influence another individual. Dominance is determined by three variables: the person trying to influence, the person being influenced, and the strategies used to influence the other person. People are more influential if they are perceived to be expert in a particular area, if they are skillful at influencing others, and if they have higher status than the person being influenced (Andrews & Baird, 2000). On the other hand, you are likely to be influenced if you seek to receive a reward from another person, if you seek to avoid punishment from another person, if you are attracted to the other person, or if the other person can persuade you.

INVOLVEMENT

A third variable that will influence our discussion of interpersonal persuasion is involvement, which refers to the breadth and depth of our relationship with the other person (Andrews & Baird, 2000). Researchers suggest that as we get to know other people, we develop more intimate relationships with them. The concept of self-disclosure is useful to understanding involvement. Self-disclosure is telling another person information about yourself that is not visible otherwise. Self-disclosure is used strategically by individuals as they develop trust and intimacy with others. Self-disclosure leads to involvement, which influences the persuasive strategies used within the relationship.

SITUATION

Patricia Hayes Andrews and John E. Baird (2000) contend that a fourth variable, situation, influences interpersonal communication. We communicate differently with others when we are in different situations. The *physical environment,* for instance, influences how individuals communicate. It is popular today for offices to use cubicles to separate employees. Cubicles delineate one worker's space from another's, but they also facilitate interaction between workers. The *social environment* also influences interpersonal communication. When you go to a party, for instance, the people, the number of people, and the volume of their discussion influence your interactions with others. Finally, Andrews and Baird contend that the *tasks and purposes present* in an interaction influence communication. In other words, the goals of the interaction and the motivations of individuals involved influence how they will communicate.

With a better understanding of the nature of interpersonal communication, let's now discuss some specific theories of interpersonal persuasion. We first examine compliance gaining, which studies strategies used to persuade, and then we discuss sequential request strategies, which explore how persuasive messages are arranged.

Compliance Gaining

Compliance gaining, one of the most widely studied aspects of interpersonal persuasion, is the use of persuasive strategies to induce behavior in another person. You might threaten to quit your job if you do not receive a raise, or you might promise your roommate that you will clean the bathroom if he or she cleans the kitchen. In both situations, you are using compliance-gaining techniques. Compliance gaining forms the basis for much of the interpersonal persuasion research, so let's look more closely at the subject.

compliance gaining
the use of persuasive strategies to induce behavior in another

TECHNIQUES

Gerald Marwell and David R. Schmitt (1967) isolate 16 techniques that persuaders use to change the behavior of an audience member (Table 14.1). As you look at the list, think about which techniques you often use. Chances are, you have used quite a few of these techniques. Marwell and Schmitt then group this list of 16 techniques into five general strategies used by persuaders in compliance-gaining situations. These general strategies can help us better understand the goals and functions of persuaders who seek compliance. The five general strategies are rewarding activity, punishing activity, expertise, activation of internalized commitments, and activation of interpersonal commitments.

- *Rewarding activity* includes the techniques of pre-giving, liking, and promise. The persuader who uses a rewarding strategy attempts to manipulate the receiver's environment in a positive manner. The salesperson at the car dealership who offered you a soda was using the rewarding activity of pre-giving.
- In *punishing activity,* the persuader seeks to negatively alter the receiver's environment. Threat and aversive stimulation are punishing techniques. A parent who threatens a "timeout" for a child is using a punishing strategy.
- The positive and negative expertise techniques make up the *expertise* strategy. A parent who makes a child learn to play the piano because "it's good for you" is using expertise.
- The fourth strategy, *activation of internalized commitments,* includes the techniques of positive and negative self-feelings, positive altercasting, positive esteem, and moral appeal. These strategies are effective because they

Table 14.1 Marwell and Schmitt's Compliance-Gaining Techniques

General strategy	Technique	Explanation	Example
Rewarding	Promise	If you comply, I will reward you.	"If you go to the gym with me, I'll help you with your homework."
Rewarding	Liking	Being friendly to someone so that he or she complies.	"That new shirt looks nice on you. Will you go to the gym with me?"
Rewarding	Pre-giving	Giving a reward to someone before making a request.	"Look at this nice pair of shorts I bought for you. Will you go to the gym with me?"
Punishing	Threat	If you do not comply, I will punish you.	"If you don't go to the gym with me, I won't let you watch my videos."
Punishing	Aversive stimulation	Punishing someone until he or she complies.	"You cannot listen to my CDs until you go to the gym with me."
Expertise	Expertise–Positive	If you comply, good things will happen to you.	"If you go to the gym with me, you'll live longer and healthier."
Expertise	Expertise–Negative	If you do not comply, bad things will happen to you.	"If you don't go to the gym with me, you'll be more stressed and less healthy."
Activation of internalized commitments	Moral appeal	Telling someone that he or she is immoral for not complying.	"It's wrong for you to sit here and eat junk food while I go work out."
Activation of internalized commitments	Positive self-feelings	Telling someone that he or she will feel better by complying.	"Think of how good you will feel about yourself if you go to the gym with me."

make audience members think about internalized norms, or their ideas about what they ought to do in a particular situation. These strategies focus on how individuals feel about themselves.

• The final group of techniques, called *activation of interpersonal commitments,* includes the techniques of altruism, negative esteem, debt, and negative altercasting. These techniques cause audience members to consider how others will think about them. They are based on audience members' identification with some reference group. Audience members will comply with a persuader's request because of how they believe others will think about them if they do not comply.

SITUATION

Although Marwell and Schmitt's work is seminal in this area, the researchers provide only a partial picture of how compliance gaining works. Other researchers have examined the role of the situation in the persuader's choice of compliance-gaining strategies (Boster & Stiff, 1984; Cody, Greene, et al., 1986;

Table 14.1 Marwell and Schmitt's Compliance-Gaining Techniques (continued)

General strategy	Technique	Explanation	Example
Activation of internalized commitments	Negative self-feelings	Telling someone that he or she will feel bad for not complying	"Think of how jealous you will be when I go to the gym and get in shape and you do not."
Activation of internalized commitments	Positive altercasting	Telling someone that a "good" person would comply.	"A good roommate would go to the gym."
Activation of internalized commitments	Positive esteem	Telling someone that other people will think better of him or her for complying.	"My friends will think you're a great person if you go to the gym with me."
Activation of interpersonal commitments	Negative altercasting	Telling someone that a "bad" person would not comply.	"Only a bad roommate would sit at home while I go work out."
Activation of interpersonal commitments	Altruism	Telling someone that you are calling upon their good nature.	"I really need you to support my exercise routine."
Activation of interpersonal commitments	Debt	Calling in a past favor in exchange for current compliance.	"The last time your parents came to visit, I cleaned the whole apartment. Will you please go to the gym with me?"
Activation of interpersonal commitments	Negative esteem	Telling someone that other people will think poorly of him or her for not complying.	"My friends won't like you if you don't come along."

Adapted from Marwell and Schmitt (1967, pp. 357–363)

Cody & McLaughlin, 1980; Cody, Woelfel, & Jordan, 1983; Sillars, 1980). To understand how situation influences choice of strategy, we will look at the work of Gerald R. Miller and his colleagues.

Miller and his colleagues (1977) identify four situations in which persuaders might be likely to use compliance-gaining strategies. The first situation they describe is *noninterpersonal, short-term consequences,* meaning that the persuader and the receiver do not have an intimate relationship and the results of the compliance are short-term. For example, you want to trade in your car on a new car and want to persuade the car dealer to give you $1,000 for your old car. As a persuader in this situation, you would be likely to use these strategies:

- *A threat:* "Give me a better deal, or I will go to another dealer."
- *A promise:* "Give me what I'm asking, and I'll sign the paperwork to buy the new car right away."
- *Liking:* "I would really like to give you my business."
- *Positive expertise:* "You know the car is worth more than what you've offered."

It is unlikely that a persuader in this situation would use a moral appeal, telling the car dealer that it's not right to make such a low initial offer.

The second situation type is *noninterpersonal, long-term consequences*. The two parties do not have an intimate relationship, but the consequences of the compliance are long-term. Miller and his colleagues (1977) provide the example of a home owner who tries to persuade a neighbor not to cut down a large, shade-giving tree. Likely strategies in this situation include:

- *Positive expertise:* "Think about how much you'll enjoy the shade if you don't cut down the tree."
- *Negative expertise:* "Without that tree in front of your house, we can see right into your living room."
- *Altruism:* "Be a good neighbor. Don't cut down that tree."
- *Promise:* "I'll help you clean up the leaves each fall if you don't cut the tree down."
- *Liking:* "Remember the good times our kids have had playing in that tree."
- *Debt:* "A few years ago, you didn't want us to put up a fence and we didn't."
- *Positive altercasting:* "Be a good neighbor. Keep the tree."

An unlikely strategy would be aversive stimulation, or threatening to not allow the neighbor to use your snowblower in the winter if he or she cuts down the tree.

The third situation type is *interpersonal, short-term consequences*. In this situation, the two parties have an intimate relationship, but the results of the persuasion are short-term. For example, you have to break a date with your significant other to visit with a close friend who is unexpectedly in town. For this situation, Miller and his colleagues (1977) found these strategies effective:

- *Altruism:* "I know you'll appreciate my position."
- *Positive altercasting:* "I'd really appreciate it if we could reschedule our date."
- *Liking:* "You're the best friend anyone could have."

On the other hand, these strategies were not as likely to be used:

- *Moral appeal:* "It's not right that you are so inflexible."
- *Aversive stimulation:* "I'm not going to help you with your homework until you give in."
- *Negative esteem:* "Imagine what my other friends will think of you if you don't let me see my friend."
- *Threat:* "I'll break up with you if you don't let me go out with my friend."
- *Pre-giving:* "Here is a box of the chocolates that you like. I'm sorry that I have to break our date for tonight."

The fourth situation type is *interpersonal, long-term consequences*. Here, the two parties again know each other, but the consequences of the persuasion are long-term. Miller and his colleagues (1977) illustrate the point by describing a situation in which you want to continue an important relationship with your significant other but also want to take a job in another part of the country. For this situation, these strategies are likely:

- *Threat:* "If you don't agree to move, I'll move on my own."
- *Positive altercasting:* "You know how important this job is to me. I'm sure you'll support my decision."
- *Altruism:* "I really need you to go along with my decision to take the job."
- *Promise:* "If you move with me now, we can talk about marriage."

Several strategies were not likely to be used, including:

- *Negative esteem:* "My family won't think very highly of you if you don't support my decision to take the job."
- *Negative self-feeling:* "Think of how bad you'll feel when I move away and you stay here."
- *Debt:* "Remember last year when I went to see your family, even though I had something better to do."

Miller and his colleagues (1977) explain that certain factors related to the situation account for the choice of compliance-gaining strategy. In a noninterpersonal situation, for instance, logic and argument have a greater chance of success than do threat or reward. When you are buying a car, for instance, punishing the car dealer is not going to be as effective as it might be with your child. Likewise, in interpersonal situations, the persuader has more information about the receiver and is better able to control or predict the outcome of the interaction. In long-term situations, persuaders are more apt to use positive compliance strategies. In short-term situations, the choice of compliance strategies is more varied. Miller and colleagues' study of how the situation calls for certain compliance-gaining strategies gives us additional information about how interpersonal persuaders choose their persuasive strategies.

POWER

Another group of researchers believes that a persuader's power influences his or her choice of compliance-gaining strategy. When communicating with a child, for instance, a parent will likely use compliance-gaining techniques that take advantage of the power relationship they share. Lawrence R. Wheeless, Robert A. Barraclough, and Robert A. Stewart (1983) identify three types of power that characterize persuaders.

Persuaders often have power to *manipulate the consequences* of some action. If the persuader can control the outcome of the situation, he or she is likely to use strategies such as promises, threats, and warnings. A parent might promise a child an increase in allowance if the child takes on additional household responsibilities. Your professor uses the promise of a good grade to get you to study.

Persuaders can also use their *relational position* as a source of power. The persuader uses the relationship to bring about the desired behavior in the receiver. You might convince your significant other to dress up before meeting your parents by arguing that your family will like him or her better. Persuaders

Figure 14.1   Given what you know about compliance gaining and situational constraints, what kind of compliance-gaining strategies do you think the father used in this case?

who use their relational position use strategies such as positive and negative esteem, moral appeal, and liking.

Finally, persuaders who are in a position to *define values and norms* have power. The persuader defines what is good and valuable by engaging in a particular kind of action, and the receiver reciprocates. Returning a favor that had been previously offered is an example because it marks a course for future interaction. Giving a birthday present to a new friend is likely to lead to your receiving a gift on your birthday. Considering these variables, which compliance-gaining strategies would a father use to persuade his daughter to do household chores (Figure 14.1)?

COMPLIANCE GAINING IN THE MEDIA AGE

The study of compliance gaining has moved from a discussion of general strategies to a complex description of how situational and source characteristics interact to determine choice of compliance strategies. Researchers have not yet studied how the nature of the medium affects compliance choice, but let's discuss two tentative hypotheses here.

First, media may make it more likely for persuaders to view a compliance-gaining situation as less personal than a face-to-face interaction. Sending an e-mail message to someone or calling the person on the telephone results in a less direct threat to both parties' self-image. Thus, the persuader may be more likely to use negative or threatening compliance strategies when using these media. This may be especially true if the persuader does not have an intimate relationship with the receiver. When e-mailing your boss, you might be more likely to assert your request for a raise more forcefully than you would in a face-to-face interaction. Of course, the recipient of your e-mail may be someone with whom you have an intimate relationship. In that case, you probably wouldn't use negative strategies.

Second, power is often obscured when two parties interact through a medium. Unless I include specific identifiers, such as "Dr.," in an e-mail message to my students, they may perceive me as less powerful than I would appear to be in the classroom. Thus, my demands or use of negative strategies may be less effective in the electronic medium than in a face-to-face interaction. On the other hand, a persuader can also appear more powerful when communicating through a medium. A younger colleague on my campus is often mistaken for a student because of his youthful appearance. In a face-to-face interaction with another faculty member, he may lack the power to support a compliance-gaining request. In an e-mail interaction, my colleague can hide his youthfulness and increase his power.

Compliance-gaining research has answered many questions about how persuaders bring about behavioral change in their audiences. Factors including situation and power influence a persuader's choice of persuasive strategy. As research in this area expands, scholars will no doubt explore the influence of medium on compliance strategy. As we turn our attention to personal selling and negotiation, watch for ways that persuaders in those contexts use compliance-gaining strategies. First, however, we will look at another theory about how persuaders make requests of their audience members.

Sequential-Request Strategies

Researchers have also addressed how persuaders structure their request messages to gain receivers' acceptance. These approaches generally focus on ways to make initial requests in order to gain acceptance of an ultimate request. These approaches are called **sequential-request strategies.** Let's look at two techniques persuaders use: the foot-in-the-door technique and the door-in-the-face technique.

FOOT IN DOOR

The **foot-in-the-door technique** (FITD) uses a small initial request, followed by a larger second request. The technique works on the premise that the receiver will accept the initial request and then accept the later request as well. James Price Dillard (1991) explains that the receiver, upon acceptance of the initial request, forms a favorable impression of himself or herself, which enhances attitude change toward the second request. The classic example of FITD is a door-to-door salesperson who asks to come inside the potential customer's house for a glass of water. When the resident grants the request, the salesperson then proceeds to demonstrate his or her product. The resident, feeling good because he or she is a nice person who provided a drink for the salesperson, then proceeds to purchase the salesperson's product.

In a meta-analysis of FITD studies, Dillard (1991) draws several conclusions about the use of the FITD technique. First, the technique is more successful if the request is pro-social—that is, if it benefits someone other than the

sequential-request strategy
a persuasive approach based on the theory that the way in which a request sequence is structured and the characteristics of the initial request determine the acceptance of the ultimate request

foot-in-the-door technique
a persuasive strategy in which the persuader uses a small initial request, followed by a larger second request

requestor. Fund-raisers for social causes would be more successful with the FITD technique than would a salesperson, for example.

Second, Dillard (1991) argues that one persuader need not make both requests. One person can make the first request, and a second person can make the follow-up request (Fern, Monroe, & Avila, 1986). A telemarketer, for instance, might have you "take part in a short survey" before proceeding to sell you some product. It does not make any difference if the person conducting the survey also makes the sale or if the consumer is transferred to someone else for the sale.

Third, Dillard argues that using an incentive, instead of a request, may reduce the receiver's acceptance of the second request (Dillard, Hunter, & Burgoon, 1984). That is, just because you accepted the soda—an incentive—from the second car salesperson does not mean you will be likely to purchase the car there. Instead of offering you refreshments, the salesperson would have been better off having you complete a short survey. In fact, having the receiver perform some kind of action, such as filling out a survey, may enhance compliance with the second request.

Fourth, it is not clear what effect the size of the initial request has on acceptance of the second request (Dillard, 1991). Research indicates that both too small and too large an initial request inhibit acceptance of the second request. It appears that persuaders must strike a balance between asking for too little and asking for too much. Completing an hour-long survey at the car dealership probably would be too large a request to make of a potential customer. Likewise, simply asking a customer to tell you the time and then trying to sell him or her a car would probably not be enough.

Finally, delay between the initial request and the subsequent request makes no difference in the acceptance of the second request (Dillard, 1991). The salesperson who asks for a drink from a resident might be able to come back later and make a sale. The attempt to make a sale would not have to occur at the time of the initial request.

Although research has not addressed the role of media in the success of the FITD technique, we can survey some ways FITD is used in mediated persuasion. The FITD technique may be an effective way for websites to foster loyalty from their customers. By having the customer complete a short registration process before being allowed to look at the site, the company gets its foot in the door, so to speak, with the customer. The customer may feel like a valued part of the online community and come back to the site in the future.

lowball
a version of the foot-in-the-door technique in which the persuader makes an apparently favorable but misleading initial offer

A specific foot-in-the-door technique is the **lowball,** in which the persuader makes a favorable initial offer to the receiver. The problem is that the lowball offer does not include all the necessary details. When those details are included, the terms of the agreement are not as favorable as they were at first. You might be shopping for an apartment, for instance, and meet with a property manager who gives you a very low rent figure. Make sure that you ask about other charges, including electricity, heat, water, cable television, and trash removal. Often, when these costs are added, the price is much less reasonable.

Robert B. Cialdini and his colleagues (1978) explain that we feel committed to fulfilling the pledge because we agreed to the initial offer, even after we

ETHICAL INSIGHTS

Ethics and Lowballing

The lowball technique is often used unethically by persuaders. This technique often takes the form of bait-and-switch. In the bait-and-switch, consumers see an advertisement that says something like this: "Prices as low as $14.99." Potential customers come to the store expecting to find products at this price. Instead, there are only a few items at that price, there are no items remaining at that price, or perhaps there never were any items marked with that price. When you ask about the low-priced item, the salesperson attempts to sell you a higher-priced item. Sometimes, it may be in the customer's best interest to purchase a higher-priced but higher-quality item, but the potential buyer came to the store expecting to purchase a cheaper version.

The American Association of Advertising Agencies (1990) calls upon its members to not make "price claims that are misleading." Advertised prices should accurately reflect the merchandise available. In some respects, this type of advertising is not misleading if some products were marked with the advertised price. On the other hand, if the advertising gives the impression that much if not all of the merchandise is for sale at the advertised price, then we might say that the advertising is unethical. What do you think?

1. Is it unethical to advertise the lowest price for an item if there are items available at that price? What if there are no items in stock at that price?

2. Is it fair for the salesperson to sell a customer a higher-priced item?

3. What if it is in the customer's best interest to purchase a higher-priced item?

4. How would a salesperson know when it is acceptable to cross this line?

learn the truth about the lowball offer. You might decide to rent the apartment even with the addition of the extra costs, for example. Jerry M. Burger and Richard E. Petty (1981) say that we feel obligated to fulfill the agreement because of our acceptance of the first offer. They explain that lowballing works most effectively when the same person makes both offers.

In many cases, use of the lowball technique is not ethical. Persuaders should be honest and forthright with their customers. As customers, we should make sure to investigate fully the terms of a purchasing agreement before finalizing the sale. In particular, when we conduct transactions online, we must be sure to read all agreements and terms of the sale. Often, users quickly click through agreements without reading them and realizing their consequences. The ethics of lowballing is the subject of Ethical Insights: Ethics and Lowballing.

DOOR IN FACE

A related strategy is the **door-in-the-face technique** (DITF). Here the persuader first asks for a large request that is turned down by the receiver. Then, the persuader makes a smaller request that the receiver is more likely to accept. Dillard (1991) explains that the technique works because the receiver views the retreat as a concession on the part of the persuader and feels the need to reciprocate. The technique creates the impression that the two parties are engaged in a negotiation. In a negotiation, when one side makes a concession, the other side feels compelled to respond by making a concession. Automobile salespeople often use the DITF technique. When you go to purchase a car, the

door-in-the-face technique
a persuasive strategy in which a persuader first asks for a large request that the receiver turns down; then, the persuader makes a smaller request that the receiver is more likely to accept

INTERNET ACTIVITY

Using Sequential Request Techniques

You have just read about sequential request techniques and how advertisers use them to persuade audiences. Read the article at http://www.as.wvu.edu/~sbb/comm221/chapters/twostep.htm. Then, design a scholarship fund-raising pitch aimed at alums of your school that you could use in a telemarketing context. Use your knowledge of persuasive interviews as well. Write a script for the calls you would make. What approach do you use? Why? What limitations might there be to this approach?

first price you are quoted is often much more than you are willing to pay. The dealer then reduces the price, and you accept. Often, the longer the receiver holds out, the lower the price becomes. The first dealer in our opening example in this chapter used the DITF technique.

In the DITF technique, it is important that the persuader be the same in the two requests (Fern, Monroe, & Avila, 1986). When you purchase a car, for instance, you always deal with the same sales representative, even though that person must constantly go back and forth between you and the manager of the dealership. If you were to deal directly with the manager on subsequent offers, the effect of the high initial offer would be nullified.

The difference in size between the initial request and the second request does not have an impact on the receiver's acceptance of the second request (Dillard, 1991; Fern, Monroe, & Avila, 1986). The price of the car you are considering purchasing may go from $20,000 to $18,000 or from $20,000 to $19,500 without changing the effect on your final decision. Thus, the dealership is likely to make only a small concession after its initial offer.

Unlike in the FITD technique, delay between the initial and the subsequent request negatively affects the success of the DITF technique (Dillard, Hunter, & Burgoon, 1984; Fern, Monroe, & Avila, 1986). The sooner the second request is made, the more likely it is that the receiver will accept. Car dealerships often do not want you to leave once the bargaining process starts. They want you to accept their offer on the spot and encourage you to do so by telling you that the offer is good only for a short period of time. Test the research on sequential request techniques by completing the Internet Activity: Using Sequential Request Techniques.

Research has not yet addressed persuaders who use the DITF technique through media, but we can make several hypotheses. The technique may not be successful for selling to customers via e-mail. Because customers can now obtain a great deal of information about the products they purchase, they would be very likely to comparison shop online and find a better deal in a short period of time. Salespeople who sell via e-mail would be wise to make the first price the lowest possible. In addition, because the salesperson in a mediated selling environment cannot control the time factor, a delay between initial request and subsequent offers may adversely affect his or her persuasive success. As consumers turn to mediated shopping environments, persuaders will have to consider the efficacy of their traditional techniques.

How persuaders structure their persuasive messages has an impact on audience response. The FITD technique uses a small initial request, followed by a larger second request. Lowballing works by obscuring the full details of an initial offer. The DITF technique, on the other hand, uses a large initial request followed by a smaller subsequent request. Compliance-gaining and sequential-request strategies are particular ways to understand how interpersonal persuaders achieve their goals. Watch how persuaders use these theories as we discuss three contexts of interpersonal persuasion: personal selling, conflict resolution, and interviewing.

Personal Selling

Sales representatives constantly employ persuasive strategies to achieve their goal of personal selling, selling goods and services to customers. Whether a salesperson sells life insurance to individuals, automotive parts to large corporations, or jewelry to department store customers, persuasion plays a key role in the effectiveness of the salesperson's message. Before we examine some of the specific strategies used in the sales context, let's explore several challenges facing salespeople in the media age.

PERSONAL SELLING IN THE MEDIA AGE

With the advent of new media technology, the challenges of personal selling have changed. Let's look at some of these changes and how they affect interpersonal persuasion.

First, *consumers are more educated* about the products and services they purchase (Anderson, 1995). Individuals have access to a wealth of consumer information from websites and news publications. It is possible to quickly access and read reviews of new products. If you are thinking of purchasing a new car, for instance, it is easy to obtain information from the Web about the cars you are considering. You can learn about gas mileage, cargo capacity, engine size, and a variety of other factors from each manufacturer's website. From there, you can compare the vehicles you are considering. You can also consult *Consumer Reports* to learn which cars are the safest, most efficient, and have the best resale value. Then, when you go to the car dealership to test-drive your choices, you will be better prepared to ask questions of the sales representative. The sales representative, then, must know a great deal of information about all the cars on the market to persuade you to choose one car over another. Sales representatives working with Dotcomguy (Figure 14.2) would be faced with challenges brought about by the media age.

Businesses often use buying committees to make their purchasing decisions. These committees are comprised of purchasing, engineering, finance, and operations managers (Anderson, 1995). Each member of the committee brings a level of expertise to the decision. The sales representative must be able to communicate effectively with each member of the committee to make the sale.

Figure 14.2
Equipped with only a laptop computer and an Internet connection, Dotcomguy set out to live the year 2000 completely online. He purchased food, clothing, and household goods from the Internet. If you were a salesperson, what persuasive strategies would you use to get Dotcomguy to buy your product?

A second implication that the media age has for personal selling is the *variety of media channels* available for reaching customers. In the past, sales representatives went door-to-door to engage in truly personal selling. Even today, a salesperson may try to demonstrate the power of his or her company's vacuum cleaner on your home's carpet. Or you might know someone who sells Avon or Tupperware in a face-to-face setting. Media, however, are quickly replacing door-to-door sales as the means for reaching consumers. Sales representatives use e-mail, for example, to communicate with their clients. Not all of this e-mail is junk mail. For instance, I receive regular updates on new computer products from the sales representative of a local supplier. This information is usually welcome and helpful. Sales representatives also use videoconferencing to demonstrate new products and answer questions from clients.

Finally, sales representatives must understand the *complex nature of contemporary society*. We have discussed this point in earlier chapters, but it's worth repeating here. The United States is no longer a monolithic society with common beliefs, values, and interests. The increasing number of ethnic minorities, for instance, places greater demands on sales representatives to understand and adapt to their clients. Campbell's, for instance, markets different soups to different regions of the country. Being sensitive to the needs and beliefs of many cultures is imperative in today's media age. With these challenges in mind, let's now discuss how selling professionals use technology to meet the information and cultural needs of their clients.

A MODEL OF PERSONAL SELLING

Rolph Anderson (1995) presents a useful seven-stage model of personal selling: prospecting and qualifying, planning the sales call, approaching the prospect, making the sales presentation, negotiating resistance or objections, confirming and closing the sale, and servicing the account. Let's discuss each stage of Anderson's model.

Prospecting and Qualifying   Prospecting and qualifying includes identifying customers who need or want to purchase the products or services you sell. Sometimes the salesperson must demonstrate the product for the client to see its usefulness. In other cases, the salesperson might determine at this stage that the client simply does not need the product. To pursue the sale would be unwise and perhaps unethical. Potential customers must also have the authority to close the sale. In an organizational setting, only certain people have the final authority about what products or services to purchase. Targeting them is important. It is also important to target those individuals who can influence the purchasing agents. Thus, the salesperson must consider persuasive strategies aimed at those who will directly use the product or service. Finally, clients must be screened for their financial resources. It is foolish to try to sell to someone who cannot afford what you sell.

Planning the Sales Call   The next step in Anderson's (1995) model is planning the sales call. Anderson explains that the sales representative must address five specific topics during the planning stage:

- *Establish definite objectives:* A sales call might generate sales, develop a market by educating the client, or protect the market by providing information about competitors. The sales representative needs to be clear about the objectives of the contact.
- *Choose which persuasive strategy to use:* Each goal has a different persuasive strategy. The salesperson might consider using one of the compliance-gaining techniques or the DITF or FITD techniques that we have just explored.
- *Plan for an effective and efficient meeting:* The rep should not waste the time of the potential client.
- *Prepare for the customer's reaction:* The rep should think about how he or she can overcome the objections the client is likely to raise.
- *Develop confidence and professionalism:* Thorough planning can help the rep build confidence and a professional approach. Both are important in the sales interaction.

Approaching the Prospect   The third step in Anderson's (1995) model is approaching the prospect. The best sales approaches, Anderson argues, are those that are well-planned, face-to-face meetings between the sales representative and the prospective client. A firm handshake is a good way to start the meeting. A smiling face and comfortable body posture are also important. In addition, the seller wants to clearly articulate the benefit of the product or service to the customer and perhaps demonstrate the product.

Making the Sales Presentation   The initial approach that we have just examined may lead to the sales presentation. In some cases, the approach period is very brief, followed by a longer sales pitch. We discuss the mechanics of creating a sales presentation in Chapter 15.

Negotiating Resistance or Objections   Before, during, and after the sales presentation, the sales representative must negotiate resistance or objections from the client. Anderson (1995) says that it is important to differentiate valid from invalid objections. Invalid objections are a way for the client to put off making a decision or to avoid saying no. Valid objections are legitimate concerns the client has about the product or service. Anderson presents several strategies for overcoming the client's objections:

- Showing the client an alternative product that the client may prefer instead.
- Explaining that other clients have had similar objections but that once they started using the product or service, their feelings of apprehension went away.
- Comparing the proposed product with another company's product to show the client that the competitor's product has greater disadvantages.
- Confirming the client's objection but turning that objection into an advantage. For instance, an objection to price can be overturned by showing the client how much quality he or she will receive and demonstrating that, in the long run, the client will actually save money.
- Denying the validity of the objection by showing that the client's position is false. The client may hedge on purchasing the product because of some rumor or other inaccuracy. For instance, a rumor that the rep's company is about to declare bankruptcy should be immediately denied.
- Offering proof that the product will work as intended. Demonstrating the usefulness of the product or proposing a trial use of the product are ways of offering proof.

By answering objections, persuaders can convince clients to purchase their products or services. The salesperson must be honest and ethical when addressing the client's objections.

Confirming and Closing the Sale   The sixth stage in the selling model is the close, or confirmation, of the sale (Anderson, 1995). At this point, the sales representative secures the client's commitment. A variety of strategies may be used to close the sale:

- The stimulus-response close uses a series of leading questions to which the client answers "yes" to lead to the final question of purchase. For example: "Wouldn't you like the benefits of this product? Wouldn't you like to use it worry-free for many years? Can I sell you this product?" This technique, although often successful, should be used ethically.

- The choice close offers the client several products from which to make the final purchase. The salesperson might ask, "Would you like the black or the brown pair of shoes?"

- The testimonial close provides written or verbal testimonies from others who have used the product, affirming its quality and value.

- The no-risk close guarantees the client's money back if he or she is not happy with the product.

In some cases, a rep might use manipulative or unethical strategies to close a sale. It is important that sales representatives not manipulate the client's decision and that they make sure the client is able to choose whether to purchase the product or not. An unethical close also jeopardizes the long-term relationship between seller and buyer.

Servicing the Account   The final stage in Anderson's (1995) personal selling model is servicing the account. Anderson argues that it is less expensive to keep customers than to win new customers. With this principle in mind, he suggests that sales representatives do all they can to foster a good relationship with their clients. Review what we have said about relationship marketing in Chapter 13. The sales rep might send the customer a thank-you note or make a follow-up phone call to ensure that the product is working as promised. The sales representative can inform the buyer of new products or upcoming sales or ask the customer how he or she can be of help in the future.

Personal selling involves an important relationship between persuader and audience member. In the media age, this relationship is changing due to more expert buyers, enhanced use of mediated communication, and more diverse audiences. Persuasion lies at the core of the selling process. The seller attempts to identify with the client and to structure persuasive messages in ways that best secure the adoption of the seller's products and services.

Interviewing

Interviewing is another context in which interpersonal persuasion takes place. Forms of interviewing are present in many of our day-to-day activities and in much of the work of professional persuaders. Examples of interviews include the employment interview, the appraisal interview, the complaint resolution interview, and the advocacy interview. In this section, we describe some of the characteristics of an interview, the goals of the interviewer and interviewee, types of interview questions and responses, and several types of interviews. Knowledge of the skills and theories of interviewing can help you be persuasive in this context.

CHARACTERISTICS

interview

a structured interaction
in which questions and
answers are used to
achieve specific
objectives

An **interview** typically involves two people who take turns sending and receiving messages through both verbal and nonverbal channels. Andrews and Baird (2000) identify four additional characteristics of interviews. First, interviews are *purposive;* they are designed to achieve some objective. Usually the purpose is clearly stated and understood by the participants. Second, interviews are more *structured* than are informal discussions. Usually there is an implicit, if not an explicit, agenda for the interaction. Third, the interactants in an interview are more *prepared* than they would be for a casual conversation. Ideally, both individuals have done research about the other and they have thought about what they will ask and answer. Finally, Andrews and Baird note that interviews follow a *predictable sequence.* The interviewer asks questions about specific topics and the interviewee responds. Thus, according to Andrews and Baird, interviews are "prepared, structured interactions between two or more parties in which questions and answers are used to achieve relatively specific and mutually understood purposes" (p. 283). Let's now examine the specific obligations and roles of each participant.

GOALS OF THE PARTICIPANTS

Both interviewer and interviewee attempt to persuade each other during the interview. In a job interview, for instance, the applicant more than likely wants to impress the potential employer, persuading him or her to offer a position. Likewise, the employer, if attracted to the applicant, wants to persuade the applicant to accept the position if it is offered. Because persuasion is central to the interview, let's examine ways in which both participants can improve their persuasiveness.

First, the participants should *establish goals and purposes* for the interview (Neher & Waite, 1993). They should consider what they want to accomplish, what constraints exist that might keep them from achieving this goal, and what topics should be covered. The participants might also consider how they can create a positive impression on the other participant.

William W. Neher and David H. Waite (1993) contend that each participant should *conduct audience analysis* to learn about the other person. In an employment interview, for instance, the interviewer can review the applicant's resume to learn about previous experience, related experience, and other clues about the applicant's qualifications. The applicant can learn about the employer from a number of sources. The World Wide Web, in particular, can be a good place to learn about companies, their products, and their mission.

Third, interview participants should consider the *climate or psychological setting* of the interview (Neher & Waite, 1993). An employment interview can create stress for both participants. Hostility, defensiveness, and anxiety often mark a disciplinary interview or a dismissal interview. Interview participants should consider what type of feelings they will have during the interview and how they can reduce escalation of undesirable feelings, such as defensiveness.

Fourth, participants should determine the *structure* for the interview. Some interviews, such as public opinion polls, are characterized by a high degree of formality. In a polling interview, the questions have to be carefully phrased and ordered to produce reliable results. A problem-solving interview, on the other hand, may progress in a somewhat orderly manner, but without tight controls over question phrasing and structure. In short, interview organization and structure depend on the needs of the participants and the situation (Neher & Waite, 1993).

TYPES OF QUESTIONS

One characteristic of interviews is their use of a series of questions to achieve some goal or objective. Charles J. Stewart and William B. Cash (1997) explain that a question is "any statement or nonverbal act that invites an answer" (p. 62). Thus, a simple head nod, shrug of the shoulders, or verbal statement can be considered a question. Stewart and Cash (1997) explain that any interview question has three characteristics: open or closed, primary or secondary, neutral or leading. Each question type has advantages and disadvantages.

Open questions are broad, giving a great deal of freedom to the respondent. The degree of openness varies, however. Some questions are very broad, such as "Tell me about yourself." Or, open questions can be more narrow, such as "What ideas do you have to improve student recruitment?" Open questions encourage the respondent to talk, in the process revealing what he or she thinks is important. In addition, open questions pose little threat to the respondent and communicate interest and trust in the interviewee's response (Stewart & Cash, 1997). Open questions may, however, lead to a rambling response from the interviewee in which useful information is obscured or withheld.

Closed questions are restrictive, providing limited options for response. Like open questions, closed questions vary in their degree of restrictiveness. Some are moderately closed, such as "What is your major?" Others, such as "Have you completed our official application form yet?" are highly closed, with the answer limited to a yes or a no. Closed questions allow interviewers to control the respondent's answer by asking for specific information (Stewart & Cash, 1997). However, closed questions do not probe the nature of the respondent's attitude and often require additional questions and answers for clarification.

Primary questions begin a new topic of discussion or a new area within a topic (Stewart & Cash, 1997). A question such as "Tell me about your last job" initiates a discussion of the applicant's previous employment history. The question, "Now I'd like to talk about your experiences with public speaking" switches the discussion to a specific area of expertise for a job applicant.

Secondary questions attempt to gain more information from the respondent. They follow primary questions. They may be open or closed and are sometimes called "probing" or "follow-up" questions (Stewart & Cash, 1997). There are several types of secondary questions:

- A nudging probe uses simple phrases or nonverbal behaviors to urge the respondent to continue. The interviewer might nod or say, "I see."

- A clearinghouse probe ensures that the respondent provides all important or available information (Stewart & Cash, 1997). The question, "Are there any other qualifications you have for this position that are not apparent from your resume?" is a clearinghouse probe.

- An informational probe allows the interviewer to get more information from a respondent who is vague or superficial (Stewart & Cash, 1997). An example is the question, "Tell me more about your experiences on the speech and debate team in college."

- A reflective probe is used to clarify information that may be inaccurate or that is ambiguous. The interviewer might say, "You mean to say you graduated in May, not December, is that correct?"

- A mirror or summary probe clarifies the previous exchange between participants. The interviewer might say, "Just to make sure I have this, you graduated in May 2000 with a degree in Communication Studies from Miami University, is that correct?"

Neutral questions allow the respondent to answer without pressure or direction from the interviewer. Our examples so far have been neutral questions. *Leading* questions, however, implicitly or explicitly suggest a response (Stewart & Cash, 1997). For example, an attorney may ask a defendant, "On the evening of the crime, you were not working, is that correct?" There is potential for bias when leading questions are used. Some leading questions are so biased toward a particular answer that they are called loaded questions. The question, "Have you stopped cheating on your exams?" is a loaded question, because it automatically implies that the respondent, at one time at least, cheated on exams. In some cases, leading questions can be valuable to the interviewer. A lobbyist might gain the support of a politician by using the leading question, "I'm sure we can count on you to vote against the governor's oppressive budget proposal, right?"

TYPES OF INTERVIEWS

There are numerous interview situations, each having different goals and using different types of communicative behavior. Two types of interviews are most relevant to our discussion of persuasion: the selection interview and the persuasive interview.

The Selection Interview   Employers use the selection interview to screen potential employees. Despite suggestions that the process is expensive, inefficient, and inaccurate, the selection interview remains a central feature in an organization's hiring process (Stewart & Cash, 1997). In our discussion of the selection interview, we focus on its structure, typical questions, and how the applicant can prepare for it. Thus, we examine the interview from the perspective of both the employer and the applicant.

Stewart and Cash (1997) argue that it is important that the selection interview be structured. A structured interview tends to be more reliable, more useful, and more fair for the applicant. The selection interview begins with a short greeting and a handshake between interviewer and applicant and proceeds to the orientation phase. During the orientation phase, the interviewer tells the applicant how the interview will proceed, how long it will last, and who in the organization is involved in the selection process. Then, the interviewer asks the applicant an open, easy-to-answer question about his or her education, experiences, or background (Stewart & Cash, 1997). The question should not be the typical "Tell me about yourself" inquiry, argue Stewart and Cash. The next few questions should also be open questions, to get the applicant talking and allow the interviewer to learn a great deal of information right away. The interviewer should also provide information to the applicant about the position and the organization. Also, the applicant should be given the opportunity to ask questions of the interviewer. The questions applicants ask often reveal information about them. The interviewer closes the interview by explaining what the applicant can expect next. In some cases, the interviewer may offer a contract on the spot. In other cases, the applicant continues with additional screening interviews. Rejections should be handled carefully to maintain goodwill between the applicant and the organization.

Throughout the interview, interviewers ask a variety of questions of applicants. Questions typically center on the applicant's interest in the organization, work-related experience, education and training, career plans and goals, and job performance. Stewart and Cash (1997) posit that applicants should be asked what they know about the organization to determine if they have done research. Not only does this indicate the applicant's level of interest in the position, but it lets the interviewer know what additional information to provide.

Today, so-called *behavioral interviewing* uses questions in which the applicant is asked to describe a particular type of situation: for example, a failure, a success, or a time when the individual displayed leadership. These type of questions are used to provide "real evidence" of how people will perform (Bellinger, 1998). They are intended to produce a more accurate picture of the applicant (A. Fisher, 1996). Interviewers have found that applicants use impression management techniques (see Chapter 9) to gain the favor of employers. Jim Kennedy (1999) argues that just as with older forms of interview questions, applicants can learn how to answer behavioral questions as well. Interviewers should watch for responses that sound rehearsed and ask secondary questions about specific details of the experience the applicant describes. Interviewers can also ask what the applicant learned from the experience (Kennedy, 1999).

Applicants can prepare for the selection interview by studying the job market, their field of future employment, the organizations to which they are applying, current events, and the interview process (Stewart & Cash, 1997). A variety of resources exist to help applicants learn about the job market, organizations, and positions for which they are applying. Applicants should also read current events magazines so that they can discuss thoughtfully important issues of the day. Stewart and Cash explain that answers to questions should be "succinct, specific, and to the point" (p. 172). Successful applicants also ask open questions that probe the position, the organization, and the interviewer's opinions. Prepare for your next job interview by completing the Internet Activity: Persuasive Interviewing.

The Persuasive Interview   Another type of interview is the persuasive interview, a ubiquitous type of interview that happens whenever two individuals ask

Persuasive Interviewing

Interviews often provide persuasive opportunities. In particular, the selection interview used to hire new employees is an important venue for persuasion. Explore the site http://www.job-interview.net concerning selection interviews. How would you answer some of the questions the articles on the site discuss? What tips do you find useful at this site? What ideas don't seem as useful? As an interviewee, what do you think is the most important aspect about persuading the interviewer in a select interview?

and answer questions with the purpose of changing attitudes. Perhaps you answer your telephone only to have a telemarketer ask you if you would answer a few short questions about a particular subject. You agree, and before long you are listening to a sales pitch for the product or service the telemarketer is selling. If this has happened to you, then you have been a participant in a persuasive interview. At the heart of the persuasive interview is the goal of convincing someone that a product, service, or idea can best fulfill a need that they have. Stewart and Cash (1997) outline nine steps in a persuasive interview. We'll see how these steps can lead to an attitude change on the part of the interviewee. We use the telemarketing interview to exemplify each of the steps, but keep in mind that there are many types of persuasive interviews.

In the first step, *analyze the interviewee*, the interviewer considers the physical and mental characteristics of the respondent, including age, sex, race or ethnic identification, intelligence, and education level. The respondent's socioeconomic background, including group memberships, occupation, and geographic background, should also be analyzed by the interviewer. The interviewer should also consider the respondent's emotions, needs, and values. (In Chapter 11, we considered how persuaders respond to their audience's emotions, needs, and values.) Finally, the interviewer should try to gauge the respondent's likely response to the interviewer and his or her proposal. Telemarketers often neglect this first step of the persuasive interview, failing to take the time to learn about the person they are calling. As a result, they are often unable to persuade the respondent.

Stewart and Cash's (1997) second step is to *assess the relationship* between interviewer and respondent. The researchers contend that relationships range from cooperative to hostile. In particular, the interviewer should assess the degree of inclusion, affection, and control in the relationship. A telemarketer usually faces the obstacle of not knowing the respondent. This lack of intimacy usually harms the interviewer's goal: It is easy for the respondent to hang up on someone he or she does not know.

The third step in a persuasive interview is to *study the situation*. The interviewer should assess the setting and timing of the interview to determine if those factors create any obstacles. Telemarketers who call during the dinner hour or late in the evening are likely to face angry respondents. A call made during the late afternoon or early evening may be received more favorably.

The fourth step of the interview is to *investigate the topic*. Interviewers should be knowledgeable about the product, service, or idea they are trying to sell. It is important that they have information readily available to answer any questions the respondent may pose. Telemarketers who are not familiar with their product are likely to sound uninformed and will have a difficult time convincing the respondent to purchase what they are selling.

The first four steps of the persuasive interview are preliminary work that is done by the interviewer. The fifth step is for the interviewer to *open the interview*. Stewart and Cash (1997) maintain that the interviewer should provide his or her name, organization, and purpose of the interview. It is important not to let this stage go on too long, advise Stewart and Cash. Telemarketers who cannot pronounce the name of the respondent often fail to make a favorable impression. The opening is crucial to building trust and identification between interviewer and interviewee.

The sixth step is to *create a need or desire* in the respondent. The interviewer should develop the main needs or desires one at time, focusing on no more than three or four total. Questions can be used to gather information about the respondent, but also to get the respondent to acknowledge that he or she has certain needs or desires. A telemarketer might ask, "Do you know what the police officers' support league does for your community?" If the respondent knows the answer, then he or she is likely to already support the cause. If the respondent does not know the group's purpose, the interviewer can provide the respondent with details. Agreement questions—"This makes sense, right?"—are used to obtain small concessions prior to the final request. Throughout this step, the interviewer must adapt to the respondent's mood, questions, and level of knowledge about the subject.

The interviewer's next task is to *establish criteria* that show that he or she is attempting to meet the respondent's needs. These criteria are based on earlier discussions with the respondent. A telemarketer might suggest, for example, that the respondent is looking for some way to exercise without spending a lot of money.

Establishing criteria leads to the final step, which is to *present the solution*. The interviewer suggests a solution that meets the criteria previously identified. The telemarketer might suggest that membership in the YMCA is the best way to exercise without spending a lot of money because the Y has reduced memberships for students and families. At this step, the interviewer should be prepared to handle objections from the respondent and minimize any concerns the respondent may have.

Finally, the interviewer must *close the interview*. Closing the interview involves looking for cues that the interviewee is close to making a decision, asking the respondent to agree to a contract, and then carefully concluding the interview to maintain the trust and identification that has developed. The telemarketer may ask if he or she can send the respondent materials or may take the respondent's credit card number over the phone.

Selection interviews and persuasive interviews are two examples of how interpersonal persuaders interact with their audiences. The questioning skills developed through interviewing are also helpful for persuaders as they attempt to resolve conflicts with other people.

Conflict Resolution

conflict
the situation that results when two interdependent individuals or groups have incompatible goals

Conflict is an inevitable result of our interaction with others. Whether you are trying to decide which movie to see with your significant other or trying to resolve a grade with a professor, conflict arises when individuals with incompatible goals communicate with each other. When conflict occurs, persuasion can often be a useful way to reach agreement. By understanding the causes of conflict, the variables involved in conflict, and some ways of resolving conflict, you can be a more effective interpersonal communicator.

CAUSES OF CONFLICT

There are a number of factors that give rise to interpersonal conflicts. First, you may have *different values, philosophy, goals, or objectives* than another person. For instance, your roommate might not share your ideas about the value of a clean apartment. The two of you might disagree about the appropriate level of cleanliness. Or you might disagree with classmates when working on a group paper for a class. They may want to settle for a C, whereas you might want an A.

Differences in perception of the other side account for many disputes. Often, we do not accurately gauge how the other side feels or thinks. You might think that your roommate is mad at you and respond accordingly. But your roommate may not be mad at you at all. Depending on what you may have said to your roommate, a conflict may arise because of your misperception of your roommate's emotional state.

Individuals must often compete for *limited resources*. When there is a finite amount of financial or other resources available, we must compete with others for those resources. One department chair on your campus might have a conflict with another department chair because they both seek the money to hire new faculty, for example.

Conflicts also arise due to *turf* battles. When someone perceives that another is trying to take his or her ground, the individual seeks to preserve that ground. Divisions of large organizations often differ over who is responsible for a given job. Faculty in colleges and universities sometimes disagree about the appropriate person or department to teach a certain course. Conflict arises in these situations when more than one individual or group attempts to use shared resources to carry out the same mission.

A MODEL OF DISPUTE RESOLUTION

Disputes typically involve four variables: actor attributes, conflict issues, relationship variables, and contextual factors (Putnam & Poole, 1987). Understanding how these ideas are related can help individuals settle disputes with others. *Actor attributes* include the needs, personalities, beliefs, and attitudes of those involved in the dispute. The individuals involved in a dispute have certain qualities that influence the conflict resolution process. In a political dispute, politicians often use positions or issues as leverage for getting what they want. Or an extremely argumentative union negotiator will take a firmer stand than will someone who is not as argumentative.

Conflict issues are the root causes of the dispute and the positions of those involved. Knowledge of these issues aids a disputant in presenting arguments to the other side. For instance, a consumer who understands the differences between two similarly priced products has an advantage when negotiating with a salesperson. Or the consumer who knows what other stores charge for a product can effectively negotiate with a salesperson. A community activist who knows the past environmental record of an organization can be effective when arguing in front of the city council. A union negotiator who knows what workers in similar organizations are paid has power when bargaining with the organization's management.

Relationship variables include trust, power, and degree of interdependency. The disputants can be related in several ways. They may be competitive. For example, two sales representatives who offer the same product or service to the same set of customers would be competitive. Power, in this case, resides with the customer, who can choose the salesperson who offers the best price for the product or service. Having more options is a source of power as well. When a citizen watchdog group can write letters to multiple newspapers, advertise on television stations, appeal to the city council, and sue the organization, the group has power. Being legitimate, either formally or informally, can be powerful. Being an effective persuader is another source of power. Persuaders are powerful when they can convincingly state their case and have others see the situation from their perspective.

Contextual factors include climate issues, precedent, and legal-political constraints. The climate in which conflict is managed is important. Read the discussion in Thinking Critically: Climate and Conflict Resolution for a look at how climate—the environment or atmosphere of the disagreement—can influence the conflict resolution process.

A defensive climate usually results in a bitter resolution process. Individuals should avoid a defensive climate, which is characterized by these qualities:

- *Evaluation:* Judging and criticizing the other party or parties. When the union calls the management dishonest, the climate is negative.
- *Control:* Imposing the will of one participant on the others. An academic department on campus that blocks the curriculum development of another department creates a negative conflict climate.
- *Strategy:* Using hidden agendas. A negative climate is created when one or both sides do not state their true reasons for the conflict.
- *Certainty:* Being rigid in one's willingness to listen to others. When one side does not acknowledge the good reasons of the other side, a negative climate ensues.

THINKING CRITICALLY

Climate and Conflict Resolution

Imagine that the chairs of the finance committee and the communications committee of a nonprofit organization are engaged in conflict over the extent of the current advertising campaign. The finance committee chair does not have much faith in the communications committee and its chair's ability to spend the organization's advertising budget wisely. The communications committee chair believes the finance committee is too conservative in its approach to spending. As you think about the kinds of arguments each side might make in this situation, consider what we have said about the climate of a conflict.

The two individuals would not want to make statements that would create a negative climate. Specifically, the two would want to avoid these kinds of statements:

- *Evaluation:* "Your committee has always done a poor job for this organization."
- *Control:* "We will not let you spend what you are requesting."
- *Certainty:* "I fail to see the logic behind anything you are saying."

Instead, the two individuals would seek to use these types of statements:

- *Description:* "We believe that our organization is suffering from an identity crisis. Our research shows that the community does not understand what we do. Therefore, we believe that we must engage in an extensive publicity campaign, and that will be expensive."
- *Problem orientation:* "Let's see what we can do to achieve our goals of publicity and financial security."
- *Empathy:* "I know that you and your committee have always worked to make sure that this organization is successful."

As you think about the types of statements that foster positive and negative climates for conflict resolution, consider conflict in your own interpersonal relationships:

1. What kinds of conflict do you experience?
2. Are you more likely to create a negative or a positive conflict resolution climate? Why?
3. How are most of your conflicts resolved?

Instead, a supportive climate, marked by these traits, should be fostered:

- *Description:* Presenting ideas or opinions. The two sides should attempt to describe their positions and their reasons for their positions.
- *Problem orientation:* Focusing attention on the task. The two sides should avoid attacking each other and should seek to resolve the conflict at hand. They should advocate positions that they believe will help solve the conflict.
- *Empathy:* Understanding another person's thoughts. Efforts should be made to understand the reasons behind the other side's position.

METHODS FOR RESOLVING DISPUTES

A number of methods can be used to resolve disputes. After briefly discussing several methods, we look more closely at the method of negotiation. Often, an *authority* settles a dispute. The college dean, for instance, may settle a dispute between two feuding department chairs. The two parties may simply *avoid* discussion of the issue in question until it goes away or becomes so big that it must be confronted. *Third parties* are often used to resolve disputes, in several different approaches. In mediation, the third party facilitates an agreement between the two sides. In arbitration, the third party makes the final decision. In litigation, the two sides go to court to have a judge or jury make the decision. In a fact-finding investigation, the third party investigates the dispute and writes an opinion, but the opinion is not binding on the parties. An ombudsman is often used to check out the complaints of the two sides and then expedite a solution.

Another method of resolving disputes is negotiation. **Negotiation** is the process in which both sides present their positions to each other, consider these positions, and then reach a compromise based on these original positions. Dan O'Hair, Gustav W. Friedrich, and Lynda Dixon Shaver (1998) identify three dimensions of negotiation: information management, concessions, and positioning. *Information management* refers to how research and information are used during the negotiation process. It also includes gaining information from the other side concerning which issues it perceives to be important. *Concessions* involve exchanging certain bargaining objectives for others. Concessions should never be made unilaterally. That is, the bargainer should never give up something without having the other side give up something as well. Finally, *positioning* refers to how the bargainer focuses attention on its key issues during the negotiation process. It is important that each party keep attention focused on its central issues.

negotiation
the process in which both sides present their positions to each other, consider those positions, and then reach a compromise based on the original positions

In short, conflict arises when two individuals or groups experience interaction, interdependence, and incompatible goals (Putnam & Poole, 1987). Disputes are often based on the actions of one of the parties or occur as a result of one party's perceptions about the other party. The parties may also constrain or interfere with each other's goals, aims, and values (Putnam & Poole, 1987).

Detecting Deception

A great deal of research in the communication discipline has focused on a very important skill for audience members of interpersonal persuasion, detecting deception. When we communicate with someone, whether a car salesperson, local politicians, or a significant other, it is often useful to try to determine if they are deceiving us. In the final section of this chapter, we'll examine some of the current research regarding deception detection and the implications of this research for your interpersonal persuasive encounters.

David Buller and Judy Burgoon, two of the leading deception researchers in the communications discipline, have developed **interpersonal deception theory** (IDT) which outlines a communication perspective toward deception and its detection. Specifically, IDT examines the "unique interpersonal communication constraints and demands" that take place in communication encounters (1994, p. 304). IDT theory states the following premises (Burgoon, Buller, Ebesu, & Rockwell, 1994):

interpersonal deception theory
the theory that examines the interpersonal communication elements of a potentially deceptive encounter

1. Interpersonal deception activates strategic behavior on the part of both sender and receiver. The sender tries to create a credible performance and the receiver attempts to determine the credibility of the sender's communication.

2. As the interaction evolves, both people's behavior changes and influences one another.

3. When communicating, each individual must accomplish multiple communication functions, which may hinder the performance and detection of deception.

4. The process of interacting promotes expectations and familiarity that guide behavior and judgments.

Buller and Burgoon and their colleagues explain that a great deal of deception research focuses on noninteractive encounters, in which the participants of studies do not relate with each other. Instead, a psychological profile of the deceiver becomes the predictor of deception. On the other hand, Buller and Burgoon and their colleagues are interested in how the unique interactive experience of face-to-face interpersonal communication affects the ability to detect deception. A variety of questions, they explain (1994), can be used to detect deception. Unexpected questions are aimed at surprising the deceiver and repeated questions are designed to test the coherence of the deceiver's story. Deceivers may employee strategies such as nonspecific answers, rehearsed responses, and spontaneous responses. In particular, spontaneous responses appear more sincere because they also use spontaneous nonverbal communication as well.

In one study of deception, Burgoon, Buller, Ebesu, and Rockwell (1994) tested how the use of these questions, asked of acquaintances and strangers, aided the deception of detection. The researchers make the following claims:

1. "People conversing face-to-face overattribute honesty to one another, especially, with familiar others, which results in inaccuracy in detecting another's deception" (p. 318). That is, when you communicate with someone you know, you believe them to be more trustworthy than they may be.

2. People who were familiar with each other were also familiar with each other's behaviors, which decreased accuracy in detecting lies.

3. Receivers will leak their suspicions to senders, who will then create more credible deceptions.

4. For receivers who are novice at detecting deception, unexpected questions of acquaintances were the most useful in detecting deception. For expert receivers, using repeated questions were effective in communicating with acquaintances. With strangers, however, repeat questions produced the lowest accuracy for both novices and experts.

Burgoon, Buller, Ebesu, and Rockwell (1994) explain that their study of deception paints a "more complicated, dynamic picture of deception than obtained with previous noninteractive investigations. The results challenge the assumption that successful deception detection lies in identifying a stable profile of sender deception cues. Unmasking deception requires considering multiple sender and receiver factors and the dynamic interplay between the two" (p. 319).

In a different line of research, Hee Sun Park, Timothy R. Levine, Steven A. McCornack, Kelly Morrison, and Merissa Ferrara (2002) argue that communication variables play a small role in the detection of deception. They asked 202 undergraduate students to describe how they detected deception. The most commonly reported methods of detected deception were using third-party information, a combination of methods, or physical evidence. Another popular method was the use of direct, solicited confessions, where the deceiver was confronted about the deception. At-the-time verbal and nonverbal behaviors were used in only 2.1 percent of the cases they studied, but were often used in combination with other methods. However, only 14.9 percent of the lies they studied were discovered at the time the lie was told. Thirty-nine percent of the lies were not discovered until at least a week later. Park and the other researchers believed that their study should cause other deception researchers to reexamine how deception is studied.

Summary

We are all interpersonal persuaders. Whether negotiating a new car purchase or convincing our friends to do one activity over another, we use interpersonal persuasion every day. We might persuade others by using compliance-gaining strategies. When we seek compliance from others, we choose from among 16 or so strategies. Our choice of certain compliance strategies over others depends on a variety of factors, including our relationship with the receiver, the long- and short-term consequences of compliance, and our perception of relational power.

Interpersonal persuaders also structure their message so as to achieve behavioral change in their receiver. The foot-in-the-door technique uses a small initial request, followed by a larger request. The lowballing technique uses a low initial offering, which then increases as negotiations continue. The door-in-the-face technique uses a large initial request, which is followed by a smaller, more reasonable request.

Salespeople use a variety of techniques to sell us their product or service. Personal selling in the media age is a complicated process involving seven processes. Sales representatives qualify their customers, plan their sales call, and then approach the prospect and make the sales presentation. Often sales reps have to overcome resistance before closing the sale. Servicing the account after the sale is important to ensure the long-term success of the relationship.

Interpersonal persuasion occurs in interviews as well. The selection interview is used to screen applicants for a position and make a hiring recommendation. Salespeople, political candidates, teachers, and others use the persuasive interview.

Conflict often arises in interpersonal communication. Persuasion can be used to reduce conflict between individuals. Conflict arises for several reasons, including perceptions, resources, and turf. Effectively resolving conflict requires that participants know how to manage information, climate, and knowledge about the conflict.

Although researchers are not sure about the best way to detect deception, they have suggested several behaviors that you can use to assess the truthfulness of interpersonal persuasion.

Key Terms

WWW: Visit the book's website at http://www.mhhe.com/borchers2 for multiple-choice quizzes, Internet activities, and key terms flashcards.

compliance gaining 387

sequential-request strategy 393

foot-in-the-door technique 393

lowball 394

door-in-the-face technique 395

interview 402

conflict 408

negotiation 411

interpersonal deception theory 411

15

Creating Persuasive Presentations

Learning Objectives

After reading this chapter, you should be able to:

1. Describe the influence of media on persuasive presentations.

2. Understand the various components of a persuasive presentation and the theories and the techniques persuaders use to communicate with audiences.

3. Identify effective techniques of using multimedia presentation aids.

4. Consider the types of strategic decisions persuaders make.

5. Implement techniques for creating mediated persuasive messages.

No matter your profession, you will more than likely have to give a persuasive presentation at some point in your personal or professional life. If you are an attorney, for instance, speaking in public will be an almost daily occurrence. As a sales representative, making the sales presentation will often determine whether you secure the account. As a parent, you may feel compelled to speak at a school board meeting about a proposed policy. In each of these situations, there are some specific guidelines that you can follow in preparing and presenting your ideas. There are also guidelines and theories that are common to all persuasive speaking situations. In this chapter, we take a look at the persuasive presentation apart from the specific contexts we have studied so far.

We'll discuss ways in which you can effectively persuade audiences as a speaker. As in other contexts of persuasion, persuasive speakers use language and visual images to create intimate relationships with audience members. We first discuss how persuaders relate face-to-face to audiences in the media age;

then we explore how changes in our culture are influencing our traditional theory of persuasive speaking. We also look at how to create various forms of mediated persuasive messages. Finally, we address the nature of mediated presentations via videoconferencing or telephone.

Presentations in the Media Age

As we studied in Chapter 14, the media age has influenced how persuaders interact with audiences in face-to-face contexts. In particular, Robert L. Lindstrom (1998) notes three ways in which our mediated environment has influenced the persuader-audience interaction. First, persuaders today seek to *give value* to the information they convey to audiences. Lindstrom observes that information has little value until it can be synthesized and focused to a particular purpose. Persuasive speakers do more than transmit information to audiences today. Instead, they create value for themselves, their organization, and the ideas they have. Lindstrom contends that the value of a presentation is not in the information it contains, which the audience probably has access to, but in the meaning the presenter gives to that information. In essence, persuasive speakers must make clear the value of their information (Lindstrom, 1998). Making a persuasive presentation is similar to other strategies of persuasion that we have discussed, such as branding.

In addition, audiences today are more *interactive*. Persuasive speakers today address audiences who are willing to engage in the coproduction of meaning. Audiences who have access to information do not simply desire to be motivated, but instead attend presentations to "trade in the currency of information" (Lindstrom, 1998). Speakers and audience members come to the presentation to "explore each other's knowledge base and mine information" (p. 1). There is value in what they discover through their interaction.

Finally, persuasive presentations are *ubiquitous*—they are an ever-present part of our activity in the world. In organizations, presentations "are more than tactical solutions to business needs, they are an integral part of the strategic access, flow and dissemination of everything about how we do business" (Lindstrom, 1998, p. 1). In the media age, organizations seek to process raw information into knowledge assets. Presentations are not reserved for a "big event," but instead occur continuously in the day-to-day operations of an organization. Lindstrom argues: "Every direct and indirect interaction is a presentation. Every individual is a presenter" (p. 1). This point makes clear the importance of learning how to effectively present information to audiences so they identify with what is said. In this chapter, we discuss ways in which persuaders can identify with audiences by giving value to the information they present. We'll begin our discussion by examining the nature of the presentation topic.

Describe a memorable persuasive speech. What were some of the qualities that made the speech memorable? Describe the language that was used. How was the speech organized?

Topic and Thesis Statement

Persuaders address three basic types of topics: fact, value, and policy. Knowing the type of topic for your presentation allows you to effectively analyze information related to your topic and to synthesize the information for your audience. Thus, understanding the topic helps you to give value to information, which we have said is crucial in today's world. The words the persuader uses to make the topic known to the audience is called the **thesis statement:** the one sentence in the presentation that sums up the entire speech. The thesis statement should be carefully phrased as a simple, declarative sentence. Let's look at the three types of topics.

thesis statement
a carefully worded declarative sentence that highlights the main idea of a persuasive speech

A speech on a question of *fact* is intended to convince the audience that something is true or false. An attorney persuading a jury that a defendant did not commit a crime is speaking to a question of fact. The corresponding thesis statement might be: "Mr. Smith was on a business trip when the crime for which he is accused took place, and he is, therefore, innocent." A scientist testifying before a congressional committee about the dangers of global warming would be speaking to a question of fact. The scientist's thesis statement might be: "Global warming poses a significant risk to our nation."

A speech on a question of *value* attempts to persuade the audience that something is right or wrong. A speech by a concerned parent to the school board arguing that sex education is an important topic for the school's curriculum is addressing a value. He or she might argue this thesis: "Our school district has a moral responsibility to teach sex education to its students." A lobbyist trying to convince a state legislator that capital punishment is wrong would also be speaking about a value. He or she might state this thesis: "It is morally wrong for our state to execute criminals."

A speech on a question of *policy* attempts to convince the audience that there is some problem in the current system and that some action should be taken to solve this problem because the current system cannot solve the problem without intervention. A presentation to a group of investors to convince them to invest in the organization would be a policy speech. The persuader would say, "Don't miss this opportunity to invest in a new company that promises a high return on your investment." Likewise, a persuader might present an argument to the city council that it should support the development of a performing arts center in town. The advocate might state, "A performing arts center would benefit the community in numerous ways, and the city should support it." Questions of policy inherently involve questions of fact or value. We discuss this interaction later.

Audience Analysis

Understanding the topic and the thesis statement is the first step in formulating a persuasive presentation. Persuaders must also understand the audience to which they will speak. It is important for persuaders to understand their audience so that they can effectively formulate persuasive strategies. No matter your topic, understanding your audience is important. We discussed audience analysis at length in Chapter 5. However, it may not be possible for you to analyze your audience as precisely as a political candidate or a marketing company would. For instance, you may have to present a proposal to an audience of your supervisors. Or you may want to meet with a colleague to persuade him or her to support a project that you are working on. In these cases, you need to use a two-step process of audience analysis. First, you need to decide which audience to target. Second, you want to learn about the audience you have selected.

CREATING THE AUDIENCE

For your presentation to be successful, you need to determine who should be present to hear it. In essence, you create, to some degree, the audience for your presentation. Keep in mind that not everyone in an organization or a community is involved in making decisions. You should focus your efforts on those audience members most critical to the decision-making process. For example, a sales representative seeks to understand who makes purchasing decisions in an organization. Rarely would the sales representative start by speaking to the CEO or the president of the company. Instead, the persuader would identify those individuals who can influence the decision-making process: those who use the product, the managers of those who use the product, or individuals in the business department who authorize purchase orders. Targeting these individuals will be more likely to lead to the final sale. There are several ways that persuaders can identify optimal audience members for a message.

Consulting an organizational chart is one way to determine who is responsible for certain decisions. Many organizations have a chart that identifies the chain of command and lists the duties and responsibilities of each position. The persuader could use the chart to identify who is empowered to make the desired decision and who is not. Persuaders can also ask members of the organization for the names of those who make relevant decisions. Textbook sales representatives frequently ask me the names of faculty members who teach particular courses. Then, the representative can effectively promote a new or revised book to the appropriate individuals.

DIRECT ANALYSIS

Knowing whom to target is not enough. You must also obtain information about them. In Chapter 5, we discussed several methods of audience analysis. Many of these methods are applicable for face-to-face presentations as well. Some persuaders use polling techniques to learn about their audience. For example, Michael Schrage (1999) suggests that CEOs employ polling similar to that used by political candidates. Company presidents, he explains, can use polling to understand how to improve their company's image with disgruntled suppliers or to understand what their customers want. To prepare for a summer retreat on internal communication at my university, the president's office conducted a survey on the perceptions of communication on campus; ways it might be improved; and the communication channels used most frequently by faculty, staff, and students. The survey provided information to speakers at the retreat, who were able to focus their remarks on the specific attitudes on campus toward communication.

When possible, persuaders might informally ask members of the audience questions about their attitudes toward the topic as well. Perhaps the best way sales personnel can learn about their audience is by asking direct questions. I recently purchased a new vehicle. After going to several dealerships and looking at a particular class of automobile, one salesperson finally asked why I was interested in that type of car. I replied that I simply wanted to get as much car as I could for the price. He suggested a sport utility vehicle that was reasonably priced, large, and had the same features as the cars I was considering. The salesperson made the sale because he asked me a question to which the other salespeople assumed they knew the answer.

Persuaders should also research the audience they are addressing. Persuaders should know, for example, how their product fits with the company's way of doing business. The Laurel Grocery Company, which sells products to grocery-store chains, physically scouts each prospective new customer before making the sales pitch. Laurel's sales executives see how a prospective store is laid out and what kind of technology it uses (Cohen, 1996). Using this information, the company can better pitch its products to the store's upper management. In any case, persuaders should attempt to answer specific questions about their audience.

SEGMENTATION

When you can't obtain direct information, you are forced to make inferences about your audience. Audience segmentation techniques may help persuaders make those assumptions. For example, sales personnel must be adept at understanding their audience, even though they often receive limited cues about the audience's needs and motivations. Salespeople often can use past customer history as a way to understand their audience. When you call to order a pizza, for example, the restaurant may review your past ordering history and ask if you would again like to order a pizza with pepperoni and green peppers. Customers might also be categorized by the size of their previous purchases, the length of time they have been using the company's products, or some other segmentation strategy.

To learn more about an organization, persuaders can examine the organization's culture, which includes its attitudes, values, ideals, and practices. Studying the culture, or subcultures, of an organization can give persuaders insight into how the members of the organization may respond to persuasive messages. Printed material, such as mission statements or annual reports, can also provide clues about the attitudes, values, and objectives of the organization's management. Studying these reports can help persuaders identify which arguments may be useful when persuading members of the organization. Formal or informal discussions with workers, supervisors, or others in the organization can also provide information about the organizational culture.

Persuaders often address multiple subaudiences with a single presentation. In an audience composed of several managers, some may be concerned with finances; others, with feasibility. Some may oppose the persuader's idea; some may support it. Crafting the presentation to cater to these multiple positions is important to its success. For a look at one persuader's attempt to address

THINKING CRITICALLY

Speaking to Multiple Audiences

The Ford Motor Company faced public criticism and potential liability in 2000 for its use of what appeared to be defective Firestone tires on its Explorer sport utility vehicles. The tires had been implicated in the deaths of at least 88 people before steps were taken to recall them. Following a great deal of news media attention, Ford CEO Jacques Nassar testified about Ford's role in the incident before a joint hearing by the House Commerce Subcommittee on Telecommunications, Trade, and Consumer Protection and the House Commerce Subcommittee on Oversight and Investigations. Nassar's speech—excerpts of which were aired on nightly news shows—was created for several audiences, including Ford customers, Ford employees, legal authorities, and the general public.

Nassar (2000) addressed Ford employees and customers at the beginning of his speech, saying that "Ford has a distinguished heritage and a bright future—it is an American icon. The strength of Ford has always been its employees and loyal customers." With this statement, Nassar asserted that Ford was a quality company and that its employees had been responsible in the past. He also sought to gain the confidence of the public who purchase Ford vehicles.

Next, Nassar detailed the issue involved: "When did Ford know that there was a problem with the Firestone tires?" Nassar argued that Ford took action when it was finally able to see confidential claims data from Firestone's investigation of its tires' defects. Nassar's arguments in this section of the speech were aimed at authorities who might consider pursuing legal action against Ford.

Nassar ended the speech by reasserting what Ford was planning to do in the future as a result of the defective tires. Nassar attempted to show that Ford was acting responsibly and that, in the future, such events would not take place. Nassar concluded by again asking for the public's faith in the company: "I want you and all the Ford owners to know that we at Ford will not rest until every bad tire is replaced. And I will do everything in my power as President of Ford Motor Company to maintain the confidence and trust of our customers."

1. Do you think Ford CEO Jac Nassar effectively appealed to each of his target audiences?
2. What ethical pressures do persuaders face when they appeal to multiple audiences?
3. What other specific audiences, besides employees, customers, and legal authorities, might Nassar have addressed?

various audiences in one speech, read Thinking Critically: Speaking to Multiple Audiences.

OTHER AUDIENCE ANALYSIS FACTORS

In any type of presentation situation, it is important that the speaker consider the occasion and the physical setting of the presentation. Keep these questions in mind:

• Will the presentation be made around a conference table or in a large lecture hall? A setting such as a conference room allows you to know your audience intimately. It may be possible to have audience members introduce themselves. A large auditorium may require the use of a sound system. Interacting with a large number of people is also more difficult than identifying with a small group. Audience size and presentation location should be considered early in presentation planning.

- Will appropriate technology (such as a computer and projector or an overhead projector) be available? Will the room be dark enough for audience members to see the displayed images? To take full advantage of multimedia presentational aids, you must be certain that your laptop or computer file will work with the equipment available. The projector must also be bright enough to clearly display the images you use. Be sure to test the visuals before the actual speech.

- At what time of day will the presentation occur? It is easier to keep the audience's attention at certain times of the day than at others. In particular, audiences are more alert in the morning than they are right after lunch or in the late afternoon. Also, it is important to plan for breaks if the audience will be listening to multiple presentations over a long period of time.

- What are the audience's time expectations? It is important that persuaders not speak longer than their allotted time. Doing so steals time from other speakers, and the persuader risks bombarding the audience with too much information. On the other hand, persuaders must speak long enough to convince the audience that they have adequately discussed their topic.

How have you used audience analysis in the past? How successful were you? Do speakers you have heard generally understand their audiences?

Analysis of Topic

With a good understanding of their audience and the setting, persuaders must next analyze their topic to identify appropriate arguments and forms of support. In essence, we are considering the concept of invention, which we discussed in Chapter 2. Persuaders can find arguments for their presentation by using one of two analytic frameworks: stasis and the stock issues. The stasis framework is useful for fact or value speeches, whereas stock issues is used for policy topics. These frameworks suggest arguments persuaders can use to overcome audience attitudes that oppose the speaker's message.

Persuasive speeches that seek to prove the existence of a fact or value use the **stasis** method of inventing arguments. Stasis refers to the "stopping points" in an argument. For each fact or value argument, there are three points at which speakers and their opposition clash, or disagree: definition, existence, and quality. First, the parties may disagree on the *definition* of a fact or value. Before they can prove the worth of a value or the validity of a fact, persuaders must identify the essential components of that value or fact. For instance, in a murder case, attorneys must consider legal definitions of what constitutes murder, homicide, manslaughter, and other related charges. Each term has specific criteria that have been established through legal precedent and legislative action. To prove that a defendant committed a "homicide," the prosecuter must first describe the essential characteristics of a homicide, as defined in the law. A persuader arguing that capital punishment is morally wrong must first define what constitutes a moral form of punishment. The persuader would consult readings in philosophy, sociology, and criminal justice to learn how experts have defined moral punishment. The persuader might find an expert who says that moral punishment involves three factors: it is administered fairly, it is effective at deterring future actions, and it is appropriate to the wrong committed.

stasis
the three points at which the two sides in a controversy clash, or disagree: these points are definition, existence, and quality

Once persuaders have defined the fact or value, they must prove *existence.* Proving existence involves showing that the current situation fits (or does not fit) the definition just established. For an act to be considered "homicide," for example, the persuader must show that the suspect in question acted with malice or intent or whatever the law specifies. Using witnesses and physical and circumstantial evidence, the attorney attempts to persuade the jury that the defendant's actions meet the definition of homicide. A persuader opposed to capital punishment must prove through examples, testimony, or statistics that capital punishment is not administered fairly, that it is not effective at deterring future actions, and that it is used inappropriately.

Finally, the persuader must consider the issue of *quality,* or mitigating circumstances that would negate the facts. There may be instances when certain situations exist that outweigh the conclusion drawn from applying the current situations to a definition. For instance, a murder that is committed in self-defense is often not prosecuted. That a murderer was attempting to protect his or her own life outweighs the conclusion that he or she committed homicide. The speaker who supports capital punishment might argue that even though capital punishment does not qualify as moral punishment, there are some cases in which it would be justified, such as in the case of mass murderers. By using these three ideas—definition, existence, and quality—persuaders can identify arguments for fact and value topics.

The stock issues are useful for speeches that address a policy concern. The **stock issues** are common arguments that are useful for contending that the audience should take a particular course of action. In essence, the stock issues help the persuader prove that a new course of action is necessary because there are problems with the current system that cannot be solved without change. Let's explore the stock issues.

The first stock issue is *ill,* which identifies a problem in the present system. The ill can refer to a wide range of issues, including the well-being of individuals, waste and inefficiency, injustice, financial costs, and others. Ill can be measured either quantitatively—how much money is being lost or how many people are affected—or qualitatively—to what degree the problem exists. A persuader urging the city council to build a fine arts center in a community might argue that the city is losing out on concerts, plays, and other performances that are currently being staged in other cities. The speaker might estimate that building a new fine arts center would result in increased tax revenue of $4 million each year. Thus, revenue is being lost because currently the city does not attract these performances.

The second stock issue is *blame,* or the inherent obstacles in the current system that prevent the system from solving its problems. The blame considers the reasons improvement cannot be achieved without action. Blame can take one of three forms: structural, the current system cannot prevent the harms; attitudinal, the present system will not prevent the harms; and philosophical, the present system should not prevent the harms. The persuader in favor of the fine arts center might encounter all three obstacles. Structurally, the city cannot afford to construct a fine arts center within its current tax structure. Attitudinally, members of the city council may not care about a fine arts center. They may be in favor of a new hockey arena instead. Philosophically, the members

stock issues

common arguments used in policy speeches to contend that the audience should take a specific course of action: these issues are ill, blame, cure, and cost of the city council may think that such a building should be constructed with private money, not with public money.

Cure is the plan, or solution, that will overcome the inherent obstacles in the present system and rid the system of its ills. The cure should be both practical and specific. It is important to note that the solution must address the obstacles identified in the blame issue. That is, the solution to building the fine arts center must address the community's tax structure, it must overcome attitudes that favor a new hockey arena instead, and it must overcome attitudes that public money should not be spent on a fine arts center. The persuader would have to devise a new tax system and show that a fine arts center would generate more revenue than a hockey arena, and that public money has been and should be used for such a project because the public will benefit from it.

Finally, *cost* identifies the possible disadvantages to enacting the solution. The benefits of the solution—overcoming the ill—must outweigh any potential harms that might result from implementation of the solution. The persuader in favor of the fine arts center must think about how a new tax system might jeopardize businesses in the city or what other projects, such as the hockey arena, would have to be put on hold to build the center. By acknowledging these disadvantages, the persuader can overcome oppositional attitudes in the audience. With this basic definition, let's consider another example.

The stock issues could be useful to a company president seeking to address problems of morale at the organization. The president would study the problems of poor employee morale, such as increased turnover, low production, and low profits. The president would then isolate the inherent barriers in the current system responsible for the harms. Perhaps the employee cafeteria is expensive and the food is of poor quality. Or the management does not communicate the organization's successes to the employees. Once the inherent barriers are identified, the president can determine solutions. In this case, they might be to overhaul the cafeteria and enhance channels of communication with the employees. Before adopting the reforms, the president would need to address the financial cost of such decisions.

Supporting Ideas

The stasis and the stock issues models focus the persuader's attention on the specific arguments that can help him or her identify with the audience. To support these arguments, the persuader must conduct research on the subject. In this section, we examine types of supporting materials and how persuaders can locate this information.

PREMISES AND EVIDENCE

Persuaders typically look for premises and evidence, which we discussed in Chapter 10. Briefly, to review, *premises* are statements that express beliefs about values or the nature of the world. The speaker who is opposed to capital punishment might rely on the audience's premise that all people are equal. The fine arts center speaker might assume that the city council wants to generate as much revenue for the city as it can. We generally accept premises as true and do not require additional support for them. *Evidence* includes statistics, examples, and testimony. Statistics are numerical representations of data and include averages, correlations, and hypothesis tests. A persuader opposed to capital punishment might correlate the race of convicted murderers with how often they receive a death penalty sentence to show that such punishment is not administered fairly. Examples are descriptions of actual or hypothetical events. The speaker in favor of building a new fine arts center might describe how a similar center has benefited a similar city. Testimony includes the statements of experts or peers who are in a position to interpret information. Using the statements of past customers who are satisfied with a product is an effective use of testimony.

What type of supporting material do you find most persuasive? Why?

LOCATING PREMISES AND EVIDENCE

There are several methods of locating premises and evidence. Ziegelmueller and Kay (1997) identify three ways persuaders can identify either perceptual or value premises. Premises are consciously expressed, implicitly revealed, or community inferred. First, audience members *consciously express* premises. That is, they clearly state them. Organizations often state their perceptual and value premises in the form of a mission statement, which identifies the company's goals, its beliefs about itself and its products, and its beliefs about the value of its employees and customers. A mission statement is a good starting point for someone seeking to understand the premises held by an organization. In addition, focus group interviews reveal, to some degree, the premises held by those interviewed. Political candidates often hold focus group interviews with potential voters to probe their views of certain issues. In focus groups, potential voters may be exposed to some damaging information about the candidate sponsoring the interview to gauge voter reaction. The candidate may wish to find out if past drug use or marital infidelity, for instance, will be liabilities. Focus group participants are encouraged to state their beliefs about whether such characteristics would harm the candidate's chances.

Premises are also *implicitly revealed*. Recall what Rokeach wrote about instrumental and terminal values. Instrumental values guide the means by which we live, and terminal values are goals we have for our lives. By studying how audience members talk about instrumental or terminal values, persuaders can draw inferences about the premises they hold. Surveying audience members gives persuaders the opportunity to ask questions that refer to instrumental or terminal values. From audience members' responses to the question, the persuader can infer their premises. A political candidate may survey potential voters to learn their beliefs about education, welfare, or community improvement. From the audience's responses to the questions, persuaders can begin to understand audience members' core values.

Finally, premises are *inferred through audience analysis*. As we discussed in Chapter 5, audience analysis allows the persuader to understand the demographics, psychographics, and geodemographics of audiences. From demographics, the observable classifications of audience members, persuaders can draw inferences about the beliefs of people who belong to a certain group.

Evaluating Evidence

Evidence consists of examples, statistics, and testimony. Persuaders who use evidence are more persuasive than those who do not, but you must be careful to evaluate the evidence you choose to use. Visit CNN's website at http://www.cnn.com, and use the search feature to look for articles on a topic of your choosing. What statistics are used in the article? Are these statistics reliable? What testimony is offered? Is the testimony reliable? What examples are provided by the article?

Although inferring premises from demographic information isn't completely accurate, persuaders might assume that an audience of mothers would be interested in the issue of child care. Persuaders also make use of psychographics, or the lifestyle choices of audience members, to draw inferences about their premises. People who shop at discount department stores, such as Target, might believe that it is important to save money. Persuaders may also use geodemographics to draw inferences about an audience's belief system. Where and how you live can say much about what you believe. People who live in expensive suburban communities and who drive sport utility vehicles might believe that those who work hard should reward themselves by purchasing expensive consumer goods. There are a variety of ways of determining an audience's premises.

Persuaders also use a variety of strategies to locate evidence. One such approach is to use organization-generated research, such as financial data, customer satisfaction surveys, or advertising effectiveness measures. Large organizations typically employ individuals to generate such data. A speaker addressing a group of potential investors would use previous sales information and future projections. A salesperson would use customer satisfaction survey results to persuade new customers to try a product. This information is usually not available to the public at large.

In other situations, the speaker may have to conduct library research. You are probably most familiar with this type of research, which includes newspaper articles, books, and interviews. Professional speakers make use of the same type of evidence. Once you graduate, however, access to libraries may be more difficult for you than it is now. However, many university libraries offer community memberships to local residents. Public libraries in local communities also offer access to information. Some large organizations have their own research departments to generate this type of research. In addition to the catalogs and databases available at local libraries, persuaders often use commercial services such as Lexis-Nexis for research. The Internet makes it easier for individuals to access a great variety of bookstores, newspapers, and other news services. The Internet Activity: Evaluating Evidence asks you to think carefully about using Internet research. Although plagiarism—the unattributed use of another person's ideas or words—has always existed, the Internet makes it easier for persuaders to use other people's work without giving them credit. Persuaders today have many sources available to them, and it can sometimes be difficult to identify the original author of a source. Plagiarism, however, is unethical and can have serious consequences, as Ethical Insights: Ethics and Plagiarism illustrates.

ETHICAL INSIGHTS

Ethics and Plagiarism

In 1999, Boston University (BU) media professor John Schulz resigned as chair of the department of mass media, advertising, and public relations after he forgot to attribute one sentence in a lecture that he gave to 400 first-year university students ("Department chair," 2000). The professor admitted using the 64-word sentence without attributing the source of the information. His action was revealed by a student who recognized the words and raised questions to the dean of the School of Communications at BU. Schulz explained, "The failure to attribute a source is a serious offense in a university dedicated to the pursuit of truth and in a college that is committed to teaching ethics to future communicators" (quoted in "Department chair," 2000, p. 3).

Plagiarism is a serious offense that persuasive speakers must always consider. You plagiarize when you do not give credit for another person's words in a speech that you present or a paper that you write.

Most schools have policies governing academic dishonesty such as plagiarism. The final statement from the National Communication Association Credo for Ethical Communication (NCA, 1999) addresses the situation: "We accept responsibility for the short- and long-term consequences for our own communication and expect the same of others." Schulz took responsibility for his actions, although some of his colleagues questioned the severity of the self-imposed sentence. As you think about Schulz's actions, consider these questions:

1. Was it necessary for Schulz to resign as department chair for this incident? Why or why not?

2. When should you cite a source in your speech? Is it ever acceptable not to cite a source?

3. What is your school's policy toward plagiarism? Do you think it is too harsh or too lenient, or is it sufficient?

Arrangement

Stasis and the stock issues help persuaders identify the main arguments in their presentations. By locating premises and evidence, persuaders can prove their arguments. Arrangement refers to how those arguments are ordered to have the maximum effect on the audience. There are some elements of arrangement that are common to all persuasive speeches. After discussing them, we examine four methods of arranging persuasive speeches.

ELEMENTS COMMON TO ALL PERSUASIVE SPEECHES

Before introducing the main arguments of the speech, the persuader should start with an *introduction*. The speaker first must get the audience's attention. There are a number of ways to accomplish this:

- *Using a statistic:* "Seventy-five percent of all Americans are not prepared financially for their retirement."

- *Using an example:* "Joe and Betty Smith worked hard all their lives and were able to put away a small nest egg for their retirement. Thinking they had saved enough to live comfortably after retirement, the couple retired from their jobs. They quickly discovered that what they had saved would not be sufficient. Joe and Betty were forced to take on part-time jobs so that they would have enough to live out their retirement. Don't let this happen to you. Invest in our company's mutual fund so that you can live the retirement of your dreams."

- *Using suspense:* "It's lurking in everyone's future. We know it's coming, but seldom take action to prepare for it. I'm talking about retirement planning." Suspense involves not immediately revealing the topic but instead making it clear through a series of ambiguous statements.

- *Asking a rhetorical question:* "How many of you have considered how you will pay for your retirement?" A question such as this may prompt some audience members to raise their hands. However, speakers should be careful of expecting an audience response to questions. Audience members may give you a response you don't anticipate, or they may give you no response at all.

The introduction should also establish a reason for the audience to listen to the presentation. In other words, the speaker should show that the topic is significant to them. The speaker should also identify his or her qualifications to speak on the subject. In Chapter 9, we noted that the speaker's qualifications are one aspect of credibility. The introduction is a good time to establish credibility and rapport with the audience. Finally, the introduction should indicate the thesis statement and forecast the main points of the speech. The speaker might say: "Saving for retirement is not easy, but it's possible if you take action early in your career. Today, we will discuss the significant problems facing Americans because they do not adequately plan for retirement, why they do not plan accurately, and finally, how you can take action now to secure your retirement." By including these elements in the introduction, the speaker can establish rapport with the audience, gain their attention, and convince them that they should listen to the presentation.

The *conclusion* is another element of the speech that is common to all types of persuasive topics. The conclusion comes after the main points have been developed, and it serves four functions. First, the conclusion should signal to the audience that the speech is coming to a close. The speaker may move to a particular location in the room, use wording such as "Finally" or "In conclusion," or take a longer-than-normal pause after finishing the final main point. Second, the conclusion should review the main points of the speech. Just as the speaker began the speech by forecasting its main points, he or she should summarize what was said at the end of the speech. Third, the speaker should restate the thesis statement to again remind the audience of the point of the presentation. Finally, the speaker should leave the audience with some kind of memorable statement. The speaker might again use a quotation, example, statistic, or rhetorical question. Or the speaker might issue a challenge to the audience to act based on what was said. It is important that the speaker leave a positive lasting impression on the audience.

All persuasive speeches should have an introduction—to orient the audience to the speaker and the topic—and a conclusion—to bring closure to the speech and leave a lasting impression on the audience. The arrangement of the body of the speech depends on the type of topic the speaker is addressing. The first two arrangement methods we discuss—criteria-satisfaction and topical—are useful for fact or value speeches. Problem-cause-solution and the motivated sequence arrangements are useful for policy speeches.

ORGANIZATIONAL PATTERNS FOR FACT/VALUE TOPICS

The *criteria-satisfaction* organizational pattern is one way to arrange speeches that concern questions of fact or value. This arrangement method conforms to the stasis framework we discussed previously. The first point of the speech deals with definition, or criteria. In this part of the speech, the speaker presents the definition that has been established using expert authorities. The second point of the speech deals with satisfaction, or existence. In this part of the speech, the speaker applies the current situation to the previously established definition. The speaker opposing capital punishment might use this structure:

I. Moral punishment has three qualities.
    A. It is administered fairly.
    B. It is effective at deterring future actions.
    C. It is appropriate to the crime committed.

II. Capital punishment is immoral.
    A. It is not administered fairly.
    B. It is not effective at deterring future criminal actions.
    C. It is used for children and the insane.

Topical organization simply uses the aspects of the definition as the main points of the speech. Arguments about definition and existence form the subpoints for the speaker's main points. Thus, the previously described speech would instead be organized in this way:

I. Capital punishment is immoral because it is not administered fairly.
    A. Moral punishment is administered fairly.
    B. Capital punishment is not administered fairly.

II. Capital punishment is immoral because it is not effective at deterring future actions.
    A. Moral punishment effectively deters future actions.
    B. Capital punishment does not deter future actions.

III. Capital punishment is immoral because it is not appropriate to the crime committed.
    A. Moral punishment is appropriate for the crime committed.
    B. Capital punishment is used for children and the insane and therefore is not appropriate.

So far, we have discussed organizing the definition and existence issues. However, there is a third issue of the stasis framework: quality. The most effective way of organizing a speech where quality is important is to adopt the topic approach, using the quality arguments as the main points.

ORGANIZATIONAL PATTERNS FOR POLICY TOPICS

The *problem-cause-solution* organizational pattern is useful for persuasive speeches on questions of policy. *Problem, cause,* and *solution* are words that describe three of the four stock issues: ill, blame, and cure. This organizational pattern uses the first three stock issues as main points. The speaker does not present the fourth stock issue, cost. Instead, the speaker considers the cost issue—all the possible disadvantages—and prepares to respond to them in a question-answer period or refutes them in various parts of the speech. Mike Allen (1998) explains, in a meta-analysis of previous research, that two-sided messages, which offer arguments both in favor of a position and against a position, are more persuasive than one-sided messages—which show only one side of the position—*if* the two-sided message refutes opposing arguments. Thus, by showing how the disadvantages do not outweigh the benefits of the solution, persuaders can effectively persuade their audience.

Let's consider an example of a CEO who is arguing that the company conduct its business online. In the final point, the speaker addresses possible disadvantages to the proposed plan.

I.   Our company faces significant risks if we do not conduct business online.
 A. Our competitors have all gone online, and our profits dropped 3 percent in the last quarter.
 B. Our customers want to purchase our products online.

II.   To conduct business online, we must overcome two obstacles.
 A. We must face our own fears about conducting business online.
 B. We must develop an online presence.

III. My proposal will allow us to overcome these barriers and develop a vital online business.
 A. We will borrow from our creditors to develop a company website.
  1. By acquiring debt, we will not have to lay off any of our workers or downsize our current operation.
  2. The increased revenue generated by our online presence will let us pay off the debt within 5 years.
 B. Our Communications Division will develop our online presence, and it will be operational in 3 months.

Another way of organizing policy speeches is the *motivated sequence,* developed by Alan Monroe and his colleagues (see Gronbeck, 1998). The motivated sequence reflects the way in which we process information when we make decisions. It has five stages: attention, need, satisfaction, visualization, and action. Gaining attention is usually part of the introduction. Discussing the ill and blame stock issues develops the need. The satisfaction is the solution to the problem—the cure stock issue. The visualization step uses examples and narratives to illustrate the benefits of the solution and/or the calamities of not solving the problem. The action step is usually part of the conclusion. Let's examine the CEO's speech about an online presence again, this time organized by the motivated sequence.

I.   Attention (and introduction).

II.   Need: Our company needs an online presence to remain viable.
 A. Our company faces significant risks if we do not conduct business online.
 B. To conduct business online, we must overcome two obstacles.

III.   Satisfaction: My proposal will allow us to overcome these barriers and develop a vital online business.
    A. We will borrow from our creditors to develop the company website.
    B. Our Communications Division will develop our online presence, and it will be operational in 3 months.

IV.   Visualization: By going online we can ensure the future of our company.
    A. Imagine the future if we do not use e-commerce.
    B. Imagine the future if we use e-commerce.

V.   Action (conclusion).

By using the motivated sequence, speakers can develop a narrative in the visualization step that will motivate the audience to take action. The problem-cause-solution format is effective in helping the audience analyze the situation along with the speaker. In any case, speakers must choose which organizational pattern will help them most effectively give value to the information they present.

Using Verbal Symbols

Persuaders often use visual images in their presentations to gain the audience's attention, prove a point, or advance a claim. Yet the primary tool used by presenters is language. Recall from Chapter 7 that the language persuaders use is often self-disclosive, personalized, and visual. Persuaders also use language strategically, as we discussed in Chapter 7.

Delivery

Throughout the history of rhetoric, theorists have at times praised delivery and at other times condemned delivery for its ability to sway audiences to accept poorly supported arguments. In the media age, delivery, for better or worse, has become an important aspect of a speaker's effectiveness. Successful politicians, lawyers, and sales representatives are able to communicate in a conversational style to their audiences. As audience members, we expect presenters to look, act, and sound like movie stars. We expect eloquence on the part of persuasive speakers. We first discuss four modes of delivery used by persuaders and then focus on how persuaders can use their voice to move an audience.

MODES OF DELIVERY

Persuaders use four modes of delivery: manuscript, memorized, impromptu, and extemporaneous. When a persuader uses a *manuscript,* he or she reads the speech from a fully written text. The advantages of this method of delivery include knowing exactly what to say, using powerful language, and not having to worry about memory lapses. Disadvantages are that the speaker cannot maintain uninterrupted eye contact with the audience and that the speaker cannot adapt to audience reaction without departing from the script. Persuaders who are testifying in front of a committee or delivering an important speech in which careful word choice is important use manuscript delivery. In some cases, the speaker may read the text of the speech from a TelePrompTer, which allows the persuader to seem as if he or she is looking at the audience.

A *memorized* delivery method requires that the persuader commit a complete manuscript to memory and present the speech without the aid of notes or teleprompting equipment. Speakers use this style when they want to have maximum eye contact with the audience, as well as use specific, carefully selected words or phrases. Speakers who rely on their memory may struggle at times to come up with the right word, or they may lose their place. Political candidates will often use the memorized mode to deliver stump speeches that they have presented many times previously.

An *impromptu* delivery method is used when the speaker has little or no time to prepare the speech. This style is often used during meetings, when a speaker is called on at the last minute to give a presentation. A speaker may use brief notes or no notes at all when speaking impromptu. Impromptu speaking can be effective because the speaker is not tied to a preset text, but the speaker may leave out important points or use less effective language than in a planned speech.

In *extemporaneous* delivery, the speaker presents the speech from a previously prepared outline. Extemporaneous speakers have had time to consider the points, ideas, and language they want to use, but they can also react spontaneously to the audience's response as well as make strong eye contact with them. Speakers in many situations find that the extemporaneous style is the most effective.

Which style of delivery is most comfortable to you? Which style do you think is generally most effective? Why?

VOCAL CUES

Leathers (1997) explains that how we talk communicates meaning. Our voice gives cues to our emotional state, perceived personality characteristics, and our image as a communicator. There are six vocal cues that we use when we communicate: volume, pitch, rate, regularity, articulation, and pronunciation (Leathers, 1997). We'll briefly examine these cues.

In terms of *volume*, loudness communicates power, and soft speaking communicates lack of confidence and apprehension. *Pitch* refers to the musical note the voice produces (Leathers, 1997). A persuader who uses a high pitch conveys excitement, whereas someone using a lower pitch is sad or angry. We tend to associate a high pitch with someone trying to create a false impression. *Rate* is the speed at which we speak. Effective communicators speak somewhat rapidly and without breaks, or disfluencies, in their delivery.

Regularity is the predictability in a person's vocal patterns. Some persuaders consistently use similar patterns of pitch and rate. In some instances, such as in the case of the Reverend Jesse Jackson, this helps the persuader's image. At other times, predictable inflection patterns give the sense that the persuader is overly rehearsed and doesn't mean what he or she is saying. A telemarketer who uses a consistent inflection pattern exemplifies how regularity can damage a persuader's effectiveness. *Articulation* is using the movable parts of the mouth to make correct transitions between sounds and words (Leathers,

1997). Saying a tongue twister is a good way to practice articulation. Persuaders who mumble their words are seen as less credible than those who speak clearly. *Pronunciation* involves saying words in the acceptable way. Persuaders who stress the wrong syllable in a word, for example, endanger their credibility.

Competent communicators project an image of competence by their mastery of these vocal cues. For instance, competent persuaders speak fluently, vary their pitch and volume, and speak at a fast rate. Charles L. Becton (1997) argues that attorneys must use their voices to convince jurors of their sincerity. He explains that attorneys should vary their rate of cadence, pausing, and intonation to persuade juries. Becton recommends that persuaders write prompts on their speaking notes to remind themselves to use appropriate vocal cues at given moments in the speech.

GESTURES AND BODY MOVEMENTS

Persuaders must also master the art of using nonverbal communication, such as gestures and body movements. Hand gestures can add impact to what the speaker says as well as foster identification between the speaker and the audience (Figure 15.1). Speakers who use open gestures, with their palms facing up, invite the audience to identify with what is being said because they are inclusive. Gestures in which the palms face down maintain distance between the speaker and the audience. Speakers may find that moving throughout the audience is a good way of identifying with individual audience members. Elizabeth Dole effectively used movement during her speech at the 1996 Republican National Convention. Movement can be particularly effective when the speaker must identify with audience members who are seated far from the speaker's lectern or podium. In any case, gestures and body movements should be unobtrusive, and they should add to the point the speaker is making, not detract from it.

Sample Persuasive Presentation

We have just discussed the theories and techniques useful in creating a persuasive presentation. To gain a better understanding of how these principles are enacted in persuasive discourse, we'll now apply them to a sample persuasive speech given by former Senator Paul Wellstone. On October 3, 2002, Wellstone made the following speech on the floor of the United States Senate. Wellstone would die in a plane crash three weeks following this speech and for many of his admirers, Wellstone will always be remembered for his strong stand against the Iraqi war. The speech is condensed here, but retains its structure. Let's read the introduction to Wellstone's speech.

I rise to address our policy in Iraq. The situation remains fluid. Administration officials are engaged in negotiations at the United Nations over what approach we ought to take with our allies to disarm the brutal and dictatorial Iraqi regime.

The debate we will have in the Senate today and in the days to follow is critical because the administration seeks our authorization now for military action, includ-

Figure 15.1 Adding emphasis to your verbal delivery and using strong hand gestures can increase credibility with an audience. Is it possible to use hand gestures poorly?

ing possibly unprecedented, preemptive, go-it-alone military action in Iraq, even as it seeks to garner support from our allies on a new U.N. disarmament resolution.

Let me be clear: Saddam Hussein is a brutal, ruthless dictator who has repressed his own people, attacked his neighbors, and he remains an international outlaw. The world would be a much better place if he were gone and the regime in Iraq were changed. That is why the United States should unite the world against Saddam and not allow him to unite forces against us.

A go-it-alone approach, allowing a ground invasion of Iraq without the support of other countries, could give Saddam exactly that chance. A preemptive, go-it-alone strategy toward Iraq is wrong. I oppose it. I support ridding Iraq of weapons of mass destruction through unfettered U.N. inspections which would begin as soon as possible. Only a broad coalition of nations, united to disarm Saddam, while preserving our war on terror, is likely to succeed.

You probably noticed Wellstone's use of powerful language in the second paragraph. Using strong terms to describe Hussein, Wellstone is hoping to show that he feels strongly about the issue and shares Bush's feelings toward the Iraqi leader. The last paragraph of the introduction summarizes Wellstone's position regarding war with Iraq. In particular, his thesis is the sentence: "A preemptive, go-it-alone strategy toward Iraq is wrong." You'll note that his speech addresses a policy topic—going to war with Iraq. However, Wellstone supports the current position toward Iraq—working through the UN—and opposes the policy change proposed by President Bush. Thus, Wellstone is not arguing for a new policy; he is arguing in opposition to a proposed policy and seeking to preserve the status quo. Let's now consider the first main point of Wellstone's speech.

> Our primary focus now must be on Iraq's verifiable disarmament of weapons of mass destruction. This will help maintain international support and could even eventually result in Saddam's loss of power. Of course, I would welcome this, along with most of our allies.
>
> The President has helped to direct intense new multilateral pressure on Saddam Hussein to allow U.N. and International Atomic Energy Agency weapons inspectors back in Iraq to conduct their assessment of Iraq's chemical, biological, and nuclear programs. He clearly has felt that heat. It suggests what can be accomplished through collective action.
>
> I am not naive about this process. Much work lies ahead. But we cannot dismiss out of hand Saddam's late and reluctant commitment to comply with U.N. disarmament arrangements or the agreement struck Tuesday to begin to implement them. We should use the gathering international resolve to collectively confront this regime by building on these efforts.

In his first point, Wellstone is arguing the blame stock issue. You'll recall that for policy topics, such as this, the persuader must address the stock issues of ill, blame, cure, and cost. In the segment of the speech you have just read, Wellstone is arguing that the current policy of working with the UN to disarm Iraq can work. Consequently, unilateral, preemptive action by the United States—which was President Bush's proposed policy change—is not necessary, according to Wellstone's view. In fact, Wellstone argues that much damage would result from Bush's proposed policy. In the second main point, Wellstone addresses the cost stock issue:

> I have supported internationally sanctioned coalition military action in Bosnia, in Kosovo, in Serbia, and in Afghanistan. Even so, in recent weeks, I and others—including major Republican policymakers, such as former Bush National Security Adviser Brent Scowcroft; former Bush Secretary of State James Baker; my colleague on the Senate Foreign Relations Committee, Senator Chuck Hagel; Bush Mid-East envoy General Anthony Zinni; and other leading U.S. military leaders—have raised serious questions about the approach the administration is taking on Iraq.
>
> There have been questions raised about the nature and urgency of Iraq's threat and our response to that threat: What is the best course of action that the United States could take to address this threat? What are the economic, political, and national security consequences of a possible U.S. or allied invasion of Iraq? There have been questions raised about the consequences of our actions abroad, including its effect on the continuing war on terrorism, our ongoing efforts to stabilize and rebuild Afghanistan, and efforts to calm the intensifying Middle East crisis, especially the Israeli-Palestinian conflict.

There have been questions raised about the consequences of our actions here at home. Of gravest concern, obviously, are the questions raised about the possible loss of life that could result from our actions. The United States could post tens of thousands of troops in Iraq and, in so doing, risk countless lives of soldiers and innocent Iraqis.

In the first paragraph of this point, Wellstone used as proof for his claims the fact that others, including some Republicans, held the same position as him. After listing their names, Wellstone discusses some of the possible disadvantages to U.S. war with Iraq: damage to the war on terrorism, the Middle East peace efforts, and the U.S. economy. Wellstone concludes the second point of his speech by reminding his audience of the possible casualties that may result from the war. Finally, Wellstone outlined what he saw as a better solution than the one proposed by President Bush.

The resolution that will be before the Senate explicitly authorizes a go-it-alone approach. I believe an international approach is essential. In my view, our policy should have four key elements.

Wellstone then outlined the four key elements he believed should characterize our policy toward Iraq, which included working with others, through international law, to completely disarm Hussein. Wellstone's conclusion summarizes the main points of his speech:

Our response will be far more effective if Saddam Hussein sees the whole world arrayed against him. We should act forcefully, resolutely, sensibly, with our allies—and not alone—to disarm Saddam Hussein. Authorizing the preemptive go-alone use of force right now, which is what the resolution before us calls for, in the midst of continuing efforts to enlist the world community to back a tough, new disarmament resolution on Iraq, could be a very costly mistake for our country.

Wellstone addressed the stock issues of blame, cost, and cure in his speech. He gave his support to the current policy and argued it would be effective, he identified the costs of going to war, and outlined a solution that he thought would be more effective than that offered by Bush. Wellstone did not specifically address the issue of ill. In fact, he conceded that Hussein was a problem that needed attention in the third paragraph of the speech. His approach in the speech was to show that the policy proposed by Bush was not needed and would be disadvantageous to the United States and to the world. You'll note that Wellstone used a plain, clear style of speaking. His delivery was fiery, energetic, and emphatic. Wellstone effectively created rhythm and pausing to emphasis his points. His delivery in the speech you've read here was no exception. Wellstone's speech provides a good example of how the stock issues are used to discuss public policy.

Making Strategic Decisions

As persuaders create messages for audiences, they make several strategic decisions about their message and how they will present it to an audience. The key questions that persuaders ask themselves as they create their presentation include those listed here:

1. Should I forewarn my audience about my persuasive intent and topic?
2. Should I present arguments in favor of my position only, or should I present the other side's arguments, too?
3. Should I present my best argument first, last, or in the middle?
4. Should I be the first presenter to an audience or the last?
5. How can I prevent my audience from being persuaded by a future speaker?

We'll discuss relevant research findings that help to answer each of these questions.

FOREWARNING

One of the initial decisions you'll have to make as a persuader is when and how to tell your audience of your persuasive intent or topic. Forewarning is a statement made to the audience indicating the speech's persuasive intent and/or topic. The forewarning statement can be made by the speaker or by someone who introduces the speaker. Benoit (1998) found that "when warned to expect a persuasive speech, auditors [audience members] were less persuaded by it than when they were not warned" (p. 145). Benoit cautioned against deceiving the audience about the topic or intent of the speech. Not only would such action be unethical, but it would undermine the persuader's credibility. Instead, Benoit offered several tips for persuaders.

We have previously discussed the thesis statement, which is the sentence in the introduction that explains your topic and position. Benoit (1998) cautioned against being too explicit in the thesis statement. Additionally, if the persuader will be introduced by someone else, the introduction speech could be more implicit in identifying the speaker's topic and purpose.

Of course, there are some cases when the persuader's topic and/or intent is clear to the audience, even before efforts are made to reduce forewarning. In these situations, Benoit (1998) suggest explaining to the audience that the persuader has its best interestes in mind during the speech. Additionally, the speaker should take steps to reduce the presence of bias in his or her speech.

ONE-SIDED AND TWO-SIDED MESSAGES

Persuaders must also choose whether to present only their position on a topic, or to present and refute counterarguments to their position. A one-sided message, as it is called, "consists of a message only presenting arguments in favor of a particular position" (Allen, 1998, p. 87). A two-sided message "is a message that presents the arguments in favor of a proposition but also considers the opposing arguments" (Allen, 1998, p. 87). Allen explains that while Aristotle suggested using two-sided messages, social science research has provided conflicting advice on the topic. Some scholars contend there is no advantage to including two-sided messages, while others believe that two-sided messages help to forewarn the audience of future oppositional arguments or that the persuader's credibility is enhanced by offering two-sided messages.

In a meta-analysis of existing studies, Allen (1998) traces the confusion about using two-sided messages to how those messages are presented. If there is no refutation of the counterarguments, then the two-sided message is likely to be weaker than a one-sided message. However, if the persuader refutes the opposition's argument, a two-sided message is almost always stronger than a one-sided message. Allen warned, "The idea that a person would merely mention a counter position without refutation should be discouraged" (p. 96).

President Bush, in an address to the nation on September 7, 2003, used a two-sided message to appeal for support in the Iraqi war. He said:

> I recognize that not all of our friends agreed with our decision to enforce the Security Council resolutions and remove Saddam Hussein from power. Yet we cannot let past differences interfere with present duties. Terrorists in Iraq have attacked representatives of the civilized world, and opposing them must be the cause of the civilized world. Members of the United Nations now have an opportunity—and the responsibility—to assume a broader role in assuring that Iraq becomes a free and democratic nation.

Bush acknowledged the opposition's disagreement with Bush over the tactics used to remove Hussein from power in Iraq. But, as Allen recommended, Bush also provide refutation for their reservations and argued that they have the duty to take an interest in Iraq.

ORDERING EFFECTS

Another line of research has examined the ordering of arguments in a persuasive presentation. If you have a series of arguments, in other words, should you present the strongest one first or save it for last? Presenting the strongest argument first is called the anticlimax approach; saving it for last is called the climax approach. Putting the strongest argument in the middle is called the pyramidal approach, the least effective of the strategies according to research, although it is still unclear which is most effective.

PRIMACY VERSUS RECENCY EFFECTS

Similarly, researchers have studied whether it is best to be the first of several persuaders to present to an audience, or if it is better to be the last presenter. If you are one of several presenters to make a sales presentation, for instance, you may wonder if it is better to be the first presenter to make the pitch or the last. Early studies conducted on this topic, and studies conducted since, have been inconclusive. Hovland et al. (1957), for instance, explain, "Hence, it is probably premature to postulate a universal law of primacy" (p. 22). They found that many conditions give rise to the persuasive effective of messages and that simply focusing on ordering misses many other aspects of the situation. Perloff (1993) agrees with this early assessment. He explains that a host of contextual factors, such as audience attention, audience familiarity with the issue, and the amount of time between messages, influence message effectiveness. His advice: "order of presentation probably does not make that much of a difference in most persuasion situations" (p. 169).

INOCULATION

inoculation
refutation of a persuasive message before that message has been presented

A final consideration is how much the persuader wishes to undermine the persuasive efforts of subsequent persuaders and their messages. Researchers use the term **inoculation** to refer to the refutation of a persuasive message before that message has been presented. If you think about getting a vaccine, for instance, you can understand how this may work. A vaccine introduces a small amount of a disease into your body so that your body can develop immunity to that disease. In persuasion, inoculation works in a similar way. Michael Pfau, Steve Van Bockern, and Jong Geun Kang (1992) explain that "inoculation employs threat, operationalized as the warning of impending persuasive challenge to attitudes, along with refutational preemption" (p. 214). Not only, then, does inoculation provide refutation and counterarguments, it triggers the "receiver's motivation to strengthen arguments supporting" their own attitudes about a message (p. 214). That is, there is some emotional reason why audience members will resist the coming persuasive message.

Pfau, Van Bockern, and Kang (1992) exposed seventh-grade students to messages about smoking, in order to inoculate them against pressure to smoke. The students were shown videos that included both threatening and refutational messages about smoking. The threat was communicated by cautioning students that they would be pressured to smoke and that no matter how they currently felt, they would question their own views of smoking in coming years. Refutational arguments included that smoking wasn't cool and that even experimental smoking could lead to regular smoking. Inoculation attempts were effective in this experiment, but only for students with low self-esteem. The study also found that video was an effective medium by which to inoculate students about smoking. Despite the limitations of the study, Pfau, Van Bockern, and Kang found general support for the inoculation concept and its application to reduce teenage smoking.

Multimedia Presentation Aids

Another decision persuaders make is whether to use visual aids in their presentation. In Chapter 6, we discussed the powerful role that images play in persuasion today. Technology has allowed persuasive speakers to harness the power of images in their presentations. Especially useful for persuaders are software programs such as Microsoft PowerPoint, Aldus Persuasion, and Corel Presentations, which allow users to create slides containing visual elements such as movies, sounds, pictures, graphs, and animations. By connecting a computer using the software to a projector, the speaker is able to project the slide show on a screen for a large audience to view (Figure 15.2). Visual images, video, and color are

Figure 15.2
Speakers today use multimedia presentation software to enhance their presentations. What are some advantages this persuader gains by using media aids?

powerful tools for influencing audiences. Visit the website for this book for links to some good training sites for the various presentation software applications.

FUNCTIONS

Multimedia presentation aids serve four functions for persuaders: clarity, interest, retention, and simulation. Visuals can help *clarify* for an audience what the speaker is communicating. Charts and graphs are effective ways of presenting numerical information to an audience. Richard E. Mayer and Valerie K. Sims (1994) explain that multimedia animations can be very effective at helping some types of learners see associations between words and meanings. Frank Herrera and Sonia M. Rodriguez (1999) report that visual materials used in legal persuasion can communicate ideas in a more comprehensive and convincing fashion than can testimony and facts alone.

Multimedia presentation aids also help the speaker *keep the audience's interest*. Our minds are captivated by the use of visual images. Thus, audiences stay focused on a presentation longer if the speaker incorporates visual images. In particular, animations that allow words and images to "fly" across the screen are good ways of keeping the audience's interest.

Third, audience members *remember what they see*. One study showed that jurors remember 85 percent of what they both hear and see, as opposed to 15 percent of what they only hear.

Fourth, multimedia presentation aids can *simulate reality* for the audience. Photographs, as we have discussed, are effective ways to represent reality for an audience that did not experience it firsthand. Computer technology can be used to create virtual-reality simulations for audience members so that they can not only see a re-created reality, but feel and hear an experience as well.

Finally, computers can *"structure an experience for the audience"* (Lindstrom, 1998). Quite often, persuaders move sequentially through a previously determined series of slides, using the multimedia presentation simply to reinforce the points they are making. This typical type of multimedia presentation does not promote interaction between audience and persuader, an interaction which we have said is crucial in the media age. Consider, however, another way in which a speaker might use multimedia. Usually, persuaders respond only verbally to audience questions or comments. Lindstrom (1998) sees a time, however, when speakers will use multimedia aids to guide the interaction between themselves and their audience. For instance, by linking their presentation to a website, persuaders can seamlessly move from their scripted presentation to an interactive, dynamic, live exploration of archived resources. The possibilities for this type of interaction between persuader and audience member have been largely unexplored.

DESIGN

With today's computer technology, designing multimedia presentation aids is not as complicated as it once was. Microsoft PowerPoint, for example, provides easy-to-use templates that predetermine the colors, typefaces, and layouts of the multimedia presentation. Persuaders should keep a few design tips in mind when creating their presentations.

Multimedia presentations should make use of *images* because they attract attention and serve as proof for what the persuader is saying. Sources of images include purchasing a collection of stock images, visiting websites that sell images, or using a digital camera or a scanner to digitize your own images. Some organizations, realizing the power of images for their members, have made it easy for them to obtain up-to-date images for multimedia presentations. The Goodyear Tire and Rubber Company uses a company intranet to provide photographs and video to sales personnel, who download the media for use in multimedia presentations. This database allows presenters to create customized packages to reach specific audiences. Visit the website for this book to find links to image databases on the Web.

Likewise, *video* is effectively used by persuaders to document an event, demonstrate a process, or gain the attention of the audience. With the right hardware, any video can be converted into digital format for use in multimedia presentations. Persuaders can also purchase and download video from various stock agencies. Or organizations can provide their speakers with video support, much as Goodyear has done with its intranet.

Persuaders may make use of *audio* in their multimedia presentations (Mason, 1997). Audio can take the form of music or narration. Audio helps the speaker communicate mood, motivate the audience, and keep the audience's attention. Certain music, for example, puts the audience in the desired mood for listening to the presenter's information. Fast, upbeat music communicates one type of mood, whereas slow, somber music creates a different expectation in the audience. Research suggests that audio cues motivate people to take certain actions. In addition, audio keeps the audience's attention. Persuaders should be careful to use audio that enhances the presentation. Many of the audio features in software applications—such as screeching brakes and "laser" effects—detract from a presentation rather than add to it.

Multimedia presentations should make effective use of *color*. Researchers Jew and Peterson (1995) suggest that when people are exposed to visual displays, they focus first on color, followed by pictures, then symbols, and then words. In addition, people can focus on only a small portion of a visual display, not on many words or images at one time. We can sense color, however, even when we are not directly focused on it, say Jew and Peterson. Color attracts 40 percent more attention than black-and-white images, holds the viewer's attention three times as long, and has four times the retention value, write Jew and Peterson. High-contrast colors make it easy to distinguish words from background. Use of certain colors to set off certain types of information can also increase the rate at which audiences comprehend information. In addition, color reduces eye fatigue and increases the accuracy of information retrieval (Mason, 1997).

Presentations should strive to be *simple in their appearance* by limiting the amount of text they contain and avoiding distractions. To limit the use of words in a graphic, use phrases rather than full sentences. A slide should not contain more than six or seven words across and six or seven lines down. Speakers should also guard against using animations that are inappropriate to the situation.

Typefaces should be appropriate, large enough, and easy to read. We have previously discussed how different typefaces communicate different moods or tones. The tone of the typeface should match the tone of the presentation. Type size should be large enough to be seen from far away. Generally, that means a minimum of 18- to 24-point type. Typefaces should also be easy to read. For multimedia presentations, speakers should generally avoid cursive faces and use sans serif faces, such as Helvetica, Chicago, or Arial. Speakers should always test their presentations to make sure that graphics containing text are legible.

Finally, multimedia presentations should *support the persuader's message* (Ackley, 1999). Clip art, pictures, and sounds that do not support the speaker's basic message should be avoided because they distract the audience from focusing on the message. Persuaders should also be careful of using "wizards" or other step-by-step templates because they were created for generic speaking situations and do not always lend themselves to persuader's specific needs. A well-designed multimedia presentation can greatly enhance a persuader's message.

Describe an ineffective PowerPoint presentation you've seen. Why was it ineffective? How might it have been improved?

USE

Speakers use multimedia presentation aids in a variety of situations. We will look at courtroom, sales, and advertising contexts. The challenge for attorneys today, argue Herrera and Rodriguez (1999), is to keep the jury's attention while clearly presenting complicated theories and evidence. This can be accomplished by the use of "virtual evidence"—the charts, graphs, and pictures commonly associated with visual aids. Computer technology has allowed attorneys to go one step further and create virtual-reality demonstrations for jurors. Computer-generated video and animations can help jurors see the crime scene from the perspective of the victim or the suspect. Computers can faithfully reproduce such situations using mathematical formulas. Jurors respond quite favorably to computer-generated visuals in the courtroom, report Herrera and Rodriguez. Use of virtual evidence raises questions about fairness and accessibility, however. Such technology is expensive, and not all parties in the judicial process are able to afford its use. In many jurisdictions, virtual-reality applications have yet to be used, so the legal admissibility of such evidence has not been determined (Herrera & Rodriquez, 1999).

The General Systems Division of the computer company Hewlett-Packard used elaborate computer technology to sell its Unix chip technology. The speakers stood in front of a blank green screen. The 5,000 audience members who viewed the presentation via satellite, however, saw the speakers interacting with computer-generated special effects in much the same way as a weather forecaster on television interacts with a weather map. In essence, the presentation used a virtual set to present information clearly, consistently, motivationally, and with impact (Rasmusson, 1997). Although this type of technology may be out of the price range of many persuaders, it clearly demonstrates the power of technology to present visual images to audiences.

In the 1990s, the Chrysler Corporation wanted to introduce a new subcompact car to the American market. The last time the company had done so was in 1978. Robert Marcell, head of Chrysler's small-car design team, constructed a persuasive message that called upon his team members' emotions by using photographs, complemented by verbal communication. The 15-minute presentation used photographs of Marcell's hometown, a mining town that had died as a result of competition from foreign mining companies. After each slide, Marcell repeated the phrase, "We couldn't compete." Marcell effectively recreated for his employees a setting that was near in time and space and motivated them to design the successful Neon subcompact car (Conger, 1998). Marcell used the same slide show in his pitch to Chrysler CEO Lee Iacocca, and he received the go-ahead to develop and market the Neon.

In any case, multimedia presentation aids should not be the persuader's message. Rather, they should enhance what the speaker says. Persuaders should also be careful not to be tied to the presentation. It can be necessary to deviate from a prepared presentation from time to time as audience members ask questions or if a point needs further development. Consider how you'll use multimedia by completing the Internet Activity: Using Multimedia.

Creating Mediated Persuasive Messages

So far in this chapter, we have discussed how to make a persuasive presentation to a face-to-face audience. While many of the theories we have discussed in this chapter—and throughout the book—hold true for creating mediated persuasive messages, there are elements related specifically to the medium of

INTERNET ACTIVITY

Using Multimedia

We have said that in the media age, audiences are often persuaded by visuals. Today's technology, such as PowerPoint, provides an excellent way to identify with audiences. Visit Presenters University by Proxima at http://www.presentersuniversity.com. Read several articles about multimedia presentations. What useful tips do the articles suggest? Download one of the free templates offered and create a PowerPoint presentation on a topic of your choice. Use another software application if you don't have PowerPoint available. What colors will you use? Why? What design template will you use? Why?

the message that warrant special attention, but that would still require you prove the stock issues of ill, blame, and cure for a topic involving changing someone's actions. A print advertisement, for instance, should prove these three arguments. At the same time, you would need to take into consideration unique aspects of the medium for which you are creating the message. A television advertisement, however, has a limited amount of time to communicate a message and usually relies primarily on images. In this section, we'll explore some of the ways that you can create mediated persuasive messages. Keep in mind that a complete discussion of these topics is beyond the scope of this book and that you should look for other books or classes on your campus that fully cover these topics.

PRINT ADVERTISING

A popular medium for persuasion is called print advertising. Whether designing an advertisement for a newspaper or magazine or simply creating a flyer to hang around campus to promote an event, follow the guidelines here to create a persuasive document. The first part of the advertisement that your reader will notice is the headline. The headline generally uses the largest typeface of the advertisement. Usually it appears at the top of the ad, but often is placed in the middle or at the bottom. Jewler and Drewniany (1998) provide the following tips for creating a headline:

1. Use the headline to capture the attention of the reader. The headline is the first thing the reader usually sees, so it must capture the attention and stop the reader from passing by the advertisement.

2. The headline should lure the readers into the body copy. It may ask a question, appeal to the reader's emotions or demographic profile, or entice the reader in some way.

3. The headline should also make a connection to the reader. It may suggest that the reader will receive some benefit from the product or service advertised, or it may reinforce a brand name with which the reader is familiar.

Persuaders should also consider using a visual in a print advertisement, such as a photograph, drawing, or cartoon. Recall what we discussed in Chapter 6 about visual images. Use visual images to get the audience's attention, prove your arguments, or suggest propositions in an argument. Jewler and Drewniany (1998) also suggest showing the product, showing the product being tested or in use, or showing the unhappy results of the product not being used.

Headlines and visual images can be effective ways of gaining attention for your ad, but the ad copy—the text of the ad—"completes the story" (Jewler & Drewniany, p. 117). The ad copy is where the persuader communicates the cultural, logical, and motivational appeals that we have discussed in previous chapters. Jewler and Drewniany provide several tips for writing ad copy:

1. Write in the second person, using the word *you*. This helps the reader feel as if the ad is written for them, not a generic demographic profile.

2. Be specific by avoiding generalities and vague words. Use words that refer to specific items, colors, or benefits. Use specific descriptions of your topic.

3. Use the present tense and active voice whenever possible. "We try harder," is more persuasive than "We have tried harder."

4. Test your copy by reading it aloud, and rewrite if necessary. Professional advertisers often test their texts on focus groups to determine if the ads are effective.

VIDEO ADVERTISING

As we have seen throughout the book, television is the dominant medium in the United States today. Television is used to advertise products nationally, regionally, or locally. Persuaders who are proficient at using the television medium enhance their chances of identifying with audiences. We'll outline here the basic steps in creating a television commercial, according Jewler and Drewniany (1998).

First, the persuader must determine the benefits of the product or service being advertised. It is important to also consider the audience when determining the benefits. The persuader must next translate the benefit into a story based on visual images. For instance, your college might engage in an advertising campaign to attract new students. The advertisers would have to determine the benefits of the university, such as excellence in the sciences. The story that is told might be that students are actively engaged with faculty at your school in important scientific research. The visuals that would accompany this story would be video, or pictures, of students and faculty working in the school's scientific labs. Perhaps visuals of the people they impact, such as cancer patients, could be used to demonstrate the importance of the research. Once the concept is in place, the story is put into script form.

Then, the persuader must consider the various technical elements, such as camera shots, that will give meaning to the story and message. A long shot covers a broad area and shows a great deal of information. You might open the commercial for your school with a long shot of the campus. A medium shot is tighter than a long shot, focusing on something specific. Typically, a medium shot is of two people, from the waist up. This shot could be used to show the students and faculty working in the labs. A close-up focuses on a single face that fills most of the screen. This shot could be of the cancer patients affected by the research and, at the end, the students, who would be shown smiling and exuding confidence in their decision to attend the school.

The script and the various technical elements are combined in the storyboard, which is a script illustrated with visuals. It includes sound effects, images of the desired video, and directions for the voiceover and on-screen dialogue. The storyboard is used by the commercial's director to film the shots and record the dialogue and sound effects. Following production, the advertiser selects the appropriate channels and time slots for the commercial, so that it reaches its desired audience.

WEBSITES

The Internet has unique characteristics that make it challenging to use as a persuasive medium. Hypertext links allow users to create their own order for the information, or to leave the site whenever they wish. Additionally, the computer screen presents challenges. It is also difficult to read large quantities of information on a screen and to read for a long period of time. Yet the integration of text, color, visual images, and audiovisual information provides unique opportunities to persuaders as well. Let's discuss some of the techniques of creating Web-based persuasive documents.

We have discussed the importance of knowing the audience throughout this book. Web sites can be challenging for persuaders because they attract such a varied audience. Most websites must appeal to multiple audiences, who will have very different reasons for visiting the site. When creating Web-based persuasion, it is important to consider the possible audiences, identify their needs, and create content and structure in a way that will be easy for many audiences to navigate. Using links, for instance, that identify the various audiences can be useful in helping them find the information for which they are looking.

Persuaders should also consider the nature of the computer screen and its effect on message design. Most viewers look at the top of the page before deciding whether to read the page or go to another site. The headline for the page should be placed at the top, preferably on the left. The upper-left hand corner is often seen as the most important part of the Web page. Also, the information should be structured to eliminate the audience from scrolling more than three pages. Appropriate navigation should be provided so that the user can find their way around the site. Too little navigation and the user is likely to get lost and leave the site, frustrated. Navigation links should be placed where they will be easy to find on the page, such as in the left-hand column or at the top or bottom. Color should be used and should help the persuader achieve his or her goal. Consider the symbolism of the colors chosen and make sure that the page is readable. Text color, for instance, should contrast with the background color.

The typeface and layout are also important components of the Web page. Persuaders should use bigger type and plain font faces. Text should be contained in short lines and in table format, if possible. When links are used, only a few key words or phrases should be highlighted to lead to the link. The Web makes it easy to display visual images. However, images should be compressed using JPEG or GIF technologies so that they load quickly on the Web page. To assist audience members who are using a page reader, use an ALT tag to identify the nature of the image. (A page reader speaks the contents of a Web page, or other document, to someone who is listening impaired.)

We have previously described effective techniques for designing the Web page. Web page viewers are not likely to read every word on the page, and they often leave a site after only a few minutes, or seconds. Additionally, the text contained on a website is only a fraction of that which would be included in a speech, book, or brochure. Here, we'll focus on specific writing principles for Web-based persuasion:

1. Consider the headings and hierarchies used on the page. Since websites are arranged hierarchically, it is important that this structure is apparent to the viewer.

2. Use lists, such as that being used here. Lists make it easy for viewers to see what information is offered on the page and help them to recall the information. Lists may be numbered or unnumbered, depending on the type of information communicated.

3. Links should be used to provide supplementary information to what is included on the page. Small amounts of information should be included on the main page, not on a linked page.

4. The text should be scannable, by using boldface type, one-idea paragraphs, and the inverted pyramid style of writing. In the inverted pyramid, the most important information is included first and the least important information is last, so that it can be skipped or excluded.

Presenting via Mediated Channels

Some of the presentations you may make will not occur interpersonally—face-to-face—but instead through mediated channels, such as videoconferencing or by telephone. As technology expands and becomes more readily and economically available, persuaders will use alternative means of communicating with audiences. These alternative media are not necessarily a substitute for face-to-face communication, however. When you must make a presentation through some medium, such as the telephone, consider these factors.

First, understand what verbal and nonverbal cues will be available. If you are speaking on a telephone, you will not be able to use many nonverbal behaviors. It will still be possible to communicate a great deal of emotion and tone with your voice, however. Smiling while you speak communicates energy and enthusiasm for the topic. With videoconferencing, more nonverbal channels are available, but it is important to know the width of the camera angle so you do not move or gesture beyond its range. With some forms of videoconferencing, the audio can be garbled. Be sure to speak slowly and project into the microphone so that you can be heard.

Second, you must be aware of what kinds of multimedia technology you can use. It may be possible—depending on the videoconferencing setup—to use presentation software in your presentation. It may be difficult to do so as well, however. Make sure that the lighting lets your audience read what you are displaying. Some videoconferencing programs have the ability to show the audience an image from your computer. In some cases, you can even control the desktop of those you are conversing with, showing them a website or a file that you have available on your computer.

Finally, keep in mind any time constraints or other barriers posed by the technology. With some interactive television networks, once the time requested has expired, the camera turns off—even if the speaker is in midsentence. Some networks also prohibit the showing of copyrighted materials, such as videotapes, because the information is technically being broadcast. Persuaders will be more likely to use technology in their presentations as it becomes easier to use and more affordable.

Summary

Persuasive presentations require an understanding of the audience, careful attention to arrangement of ideas, thorough investigation of information to support the ideas of the speech, and eloquent delivery. By learning how to use these tools effectively, persuaders can influence the attitudes of audience members.

As do mediated persuaders, the persuasive speaker uses a variety of tools to understand the audience. Direct analysis and segmentation are two broad categories that are used. In the media age, it is particularly important that persuaders give value to the ideas they present because audiences have access to a great deal of information.

After analyzing the audience, the speaker analyzes the topic using stasis—for fact or value topics—or the stock issues—for policy topics. Each framework highlights the important topics speakers must discuss in their speech if they are to prove their thesis.

Research yields information speakers can use to support their ideas. Supporting information can be arranged in a variety of patterns. For fact or value speeches, persuaders use topical or criteria-satisfaction order. For policy speeches, persuaders use the stock issues or the motivated sequence.

Through language, delivery, and nonverbal communication, persuaders bring life to their ideas. They can choose from a variety of techniques to create memorable wording and delivery. They also choose from a variety of strategic options as they consider their message.

Many persuaders today use multimedia visual aids to support their message. These aids should be designed and used carefully by persuaders.

You may be asked to create mediated persuasive messages. Print, video, and Web-based messages make use of their specific medium, but they also consider the additional theories we have discussed in the book.

Key Terms

WWW: Visit the book's website at http://www.mhhe.com/borchers2 for multiple-choice quizzes, Internet activities, and key terms flashcards.

thesis statement 417

stasis 421

stock issues 422

inoculation 438

References

Ackley, T. E. (1999, January–February). Amazing educational possibilities: That's what presentation software provides—for students and teachers alike. *Instructor, 108,* 70–72.

Adams, T. (1991). *Grassroots: Ordinary people changing America.* New York: Citadel Press.

Aden, R. (1994). The enthymeme as postmodern argument form: Condensed, mediated argument. *Argumentation and Advocacy, 31,* 54–63.

Advertising outlook: How the pie will be sliced in '99. (1999). *Broadcasting and Cable, 129,* 26.

Alger, D. (1998). *Megamedia: How giant corporations dominate mass media, distort competition, and endanger democracy.* Lanham, MA: Rowman and Littlefield.

Allen, M. (1998). Comparing the persuasive effectiveness of one- and two-sided messages. In M. Allen & R. W. Preiss (Eds.), *Persuasion: Advances through meta-analysis* (pp. 87–98). Cresskill, NH: Hampton Press.

Alter, J. (2000, August 28). Betting that substance sells: Working his way through "issues" that bore the press, Gore may just win over ordinary voters. *Newsweek,* p. 26.

American Association of Advertising Agencies. (1990). *Standards of practice of the American Association of Advertising Agencies.* (Available from American Association of Advertising Agencies, 405 Lexington Avenue, 18th Floor, New York, NY 10174-1801.)

American Association of Political Consultants. (n.d.). *Code of ethics.* (Available from American Association of Political Consultants, 600 Pennsylvania Avenue, SE, Suite 330, Washington, DC 20003.)

Anderson, R. (1995). *Essentials of personal selling: The new professionalism.* Englewood Cliffs, NJ: Prentice-Hall.

Andrews, P. H., & Baird, J. E. (2000). *Communication for business and the profession* (7th ed.). Boston: McGraw-Hill.

Ang, I. (1991). *Desperately seeking the audience.* London: Routledge.

Anschuetz, N. (1997). Point of view: Building brand popularity: The myth of segmenting to brand success. *Journal of Advertising Research, 37,* 63–66.

Aristotle. (1991). *On rhetoric* (G. A. Kennedy, Trans.). Oxford, England: Oxford University Press.

Asher, H. (1998). *Polling and the public: What every citizen should know* (4th ed.). Washington, DC: Congressional Quarterly Press.

Averill, J. R. (1980a). A constructivist view of emotion. In R. Plutchik & H. Kellerman (Eds.), *Emotion: Theory, research, and experience* (pp. 305–339). New York: Academic Press.

———. (1980b). Emotion and anxiety: Sociocultural, biological, and psychological determinants. In A. O. Rorty (Ed.), *Explaining emotions* (pp. 37–72). Berkeley: University of California Press.

———. (1986). The acquisition of emotions during adulthood. In R. Harre (Ed.), *The social construction of emotions* (pp. 98–119). Oxford: Basil Blackwell.

Babrow, A. (1995). Communication and problematic integration: Milan Kundera's "Lost Letters" in "The Book of Laughter and Forgetting." *Communication Monographs, 62,* 283–300.

Baker, S., & Martinson, D. L. (2001). The TARES test: Five principles for ethical persuasion. *Journal of Mass Media Ethics, 16,* 148–175.

Baldwin, T. F., McVoy, D. S., & Steinfeld, C. (1996). *Convergence: Integrating media, information, and communication.* Thousand Oaks, CA: Sage.

Bandura, A. (1994). Social cognitive theory of mass communication. In J. Bryant & D. Zillmann (Eds.), *Media effects: Advances in theory and research* (pp. 61–90). Hillsdale, NJ: Erlbaum.

Barry, D. (1999, March 28). Ideas & trends: Civil disobedience, negotiated; Arresting choreography. *New York Times,* p. D1.

Baudrillard, J. (1983). *Simulations.* New York: Semiotext(e).

———. (1998). *The consumer society: Myths and structures.* Thousand Oaks, CA: Sage.

Becton, C. L. (1997). Using your voice in closing argument. *Trial, 33,* 68–70.

Beiler, D. (2000). The body politic registers a protest. In M. A. Bailey, R. A. Faucheux, P. S. Herrnson, & C. Wilcox (Eds.), *Campaigns and elections: Contemporary case studies* (pp. 121–136). Washington, DC: CQ Press.

Bell, D. (1973). *The coming of the post industrial society: A venture in social forecasting.* New York: Basic Books.

Bellinger, R. (1998, July 20). In behavioral interviews, you should "tell a story"—Job interviews get more specific. *Electronic Engineering Times,* p. 122.

Bennett, W. L. (1998). *News: The politics of illusion.* (2nd ed.) New York: Longman.

Bennett, W. L. (1992). White noise: The perils of mass mediated democracy. *Communication Monographs, 59,* 401–406.

———. (1996). *News: The politics of illusion* (3rd ed.). New York: Longman.

Benoit, W. (1995). Sears' repair of its auto service image: Image restoration discourse in the corporate sector. *Communication Studies, 46,* 89–105.

Benoit, W. L. (1998). Forewarning and persuasion. In M. Allen & R. W. Preiss (Eds.), *Persuasion: Advances through meta-analysis* (pp. 139–154). Cresskill, NH: Hampton Press.

———. (2000, August 31). Issues and Gore's favorable reaction. E-mail correspondence to CRTNET News. Available: http://lists1.cac.psu.edu/cgi-bin/wa?A2= ind0008&L=crtnet&P=R12240

Benoit, W. L., Blaney, J. R., & Pier, P. M. (1998). *Campaign '96: A functional analysis of acclaiming, attacking, and defending.* Westport, CT: Praeger.

Benoit, W. L., & Brinson, S. L. (1999). Queen Elizabeth's image repair discourse: Insensitive royal or compassionate queen? *Public Relations Review, 25,* 145.

Benoit, W. L., McKinney, M. S., & Holbert, R. L. (2001). Beyond learning and persona: Extending the scope of presidential debate effects. *Communication Monographs, 68,* 259–273.

Berger, A. A. (1984). *Signs in contemporary society.* New York: Longman.

———. (1998). *Seeing is believing: An introduction to visual communication* (2nd ed.). Mountain View, CA: Mayfield.

Berlo, D. K., Lemert, J. B., & Mertz, R. J. (1969). *Public Opinion Quarterly, 33,* 563–576.

Blair, C., Jeppeson, M. S., & Pucci, E. (1991). Public memorializing in postmodernity: The Vietnam Veterans Memorial as prototype. *Quarterly Journal of Speech, 77,* 263–288.

Blitzer, W. (2002, May 22). Skepticism of embedding unfulfilled. Wolf Blitzer Reports. Retrieved on November 2, 2003 from http://www.cnn.com/2003/US/05/22/wbr .embedding/index.html.

Blumer, H. (1969a). Social movements. In B. McLaughlin (Ed.), *Studies in social movements* (pp. 8–29). New York: Free Press.

———. (1969b). *Symbolic interactionism: Perspective and method.* Berkeley: University of California Press.

Blumler, J. G. (1979). The role of theory in uses and gratifications studies. *Communication Research, 6,* 9–36.

Boihem, H., & Emmanouilides, C. (Producer). (1996). *The ad and the ego: Truth and consequences* [Film]. (Available from California Newsreel.)

Boorstin, D. J. (1975). *The image: A guide to pseudo-events in America.* New York: Atheneum.

Borger, G. (1997, June 9). Play it again, Dan. *U.S. News and World Report,* p. 40.

Bormann, E. (1985). *The force of fantasy: Restoring the American dream.* Carbondale: Southern Illinois University.

Boster, F., Cameron, K. A., Campo, S., Liu, W., Lillie, J. K., & Baker, E. M. (2000). The persuasive effects of statistical evidence in the presence of exemplars. *Communication Studies, 51,* 296–306.

Boster, F. J., & Stiff, J. B. (1984). Compliance gaining message selection behavior. *Human Communication Research, 10,* 539–556.

Boulding, K. E. (1956). *The image: Knowledge in life and society.* Ann Arbor: University of Michigan Press.

Bowers, J. W., Ochs, D. J., & Jensen, R. J. (1993). *The rhetoric of agitation and control.* Prospect Heights, IL: Waveland Press.

Branham, R. J., & Pearce, W. B. (1996). The conversational frame in public address. *Communication Quarterly, 44,* 423–439.

Briggs, R., & Hollis, N. (1997). Advertising on the Web: Is there response before click-through? *Journal of Advertising Research, 37,* 33–45.

Bromley, D. B. (1993). *Reputation, image, and impression management.* Chichester, England: Wiley.

Brummett, B. (1994). *Rhetoric in popular culture.* New York: St. Martin's Press.

Brummett, B., & Duncan, M. C. (1994). Twin peeks: Using theory in two analyses of visual pleasure. In B. Brummett (Ed.), *Rhetoric in popular culture* (pp. 179–198). New York: St. Martin's Press.

Buchler, J. (1940). *The philosophy of Peirce: Selected writings.* London: Routledge and Kegan Paul.

Bureau of Justice Statistics. (2000, August). *National crime victimization survey.* Washington, DC: U.S. Department of Justice, Office of Justice Programs.

Burger, J. M., & Petty, R. E. (1981). The low-ball compliance technique: Task or person commitment? *Journal of Personality and Social Psychology, 40,* 492–500.

Burgoon, J. K., Buller, D. B., Ebesu, A. S., & Rockwell, P. (1994). Interpersonal deception: V. Accuracy in deception detection. *Communication Monographs, 61,* 303–325.

Burke, K. (1966). *Language as symbolic action: Essays on life, literature, and method.* Berkeley: University of California Press.

———. (1969a). *A grammar of motives.* Berkeley: University of California Press.

———. (1969b). *A rhetoric of motives.* Berkeley: University of California Press.

———. (1970). *The rhetoric of religion: Studies in logology.* Berkeley: University of California Press.

———. (1972). *Dramatism and development.* Worcester, MA: Clark University Press

———. (1973). *The philosophy of literary form: Studies in symbolic action* (Rev. ed.). Berkeley: University of California Press.

———. (1984). *Attitudes toward history* (rev. ed.). Berkeley: University of California Press.

Burrell, N. A., & Koper, R. J. (1998). The efficacy of powerful/powerless language on attitudes and source credibility. In M. Allen & R. W. Preiss (Eds.), *Persuasion: Advances through meta-analysis* (pp. 203–216). Cresskill, NH: Hampton Press.

Bush, G. W. (2000). New prosperity initiative [On-line]. Available: http://www.georgewbush.com/speeches/ new-prosperity.asp

Bush, George, W. (2003, January 28). State of the Union. Retrieved on Sept. 9, 2003, from http://www.whitehouse.gov/news/releases/2003/01/20030128-19.html.

———. (2003, September 7). Address of the president of the nation. Retrieved Sept. 8, 2003 from http://www.whitehouse.gov.

Buss, D. D. (1998, December). Making your mark in movies and TV. *Nation's Business*, p. 28.

Cacioppo, J. T., & Gardner, W. L. (1999). Emotion. *Annual Review of Psychology, 50,* 191.

Callahan, S. (1988). The role of emotion in ethical decision-making. *Hastings Center Report*, pp. 9–14.

Campbell, D. (2000, August 17). Homeless, once again: Bulldozer runs Fargo man from seven-year dairy truck. *Fargo (ND) Forum*, p. A1.

Campbell, G. (1963). *The philosophy of rhetoric* (L. F. Bitzer, Ed.). Carbondale: Southern Illinois University Press (Original work published 1776).

Campbell, R. (1998). *Media and culture: An introduction to mass communication.* New York: St. Martin's Press.

Carey, J. W. (1988). *Communication as culture: Essays on media and society.* Boston: Unwin Hyman.

Carlson, M. (1999, May 24). Once again on the march: Colin Powell fixed his crusade by working harder and altering his alliances. *Time*, p. 50.

Carter, B. (2000, January 13). CBS is divided over the use of false images in broadcasts. *New York Times*, p. C1.

Caudle, F. M. (1990). Communication and arousal of emotion: Some implications of facial expression research for magazine advertisements. In S. J. Agres, J. A. Edell, & T. M. Dubitsky (Eds.), *Emotion in advertising* (pp. 127–160). New York: Quorum Books.

Census. *See* U.S. Bureau of the Census.

Chapin, B. (1999). Access to electronic information, services, and networks: An interpretation of the Library Bill of Rights. *Teacher Librarian, 26,* 21.

Charatan, F. (2000). Health websites in U.S. propose new ethics code. *British Medical Journal, 320,* 1359.

Chesebro, J., & Bertelsen, D. (1996). *Analyzing media: Communication technologies as symbolic and cognitive systems.* New York: Guilford Press.

Childs, K. (1998). *Washington Post* defends anonymous source policies. *Editor and Publisher, 131,* 9–10.

Cialdini, R. B., Cacioppo, J. T., Bassett, R., & Miller, J. A. (1978). Low-ball procedure for producing compliance: Commitment then cost. *Journal of Personality and Social Psychology, 36,* 463–476.

Clausing, J. (2000, February 7). Report rings alarm bells about privacy on the Internet. *New York Times*, p. C10.

Cody, M. J., Greene, J. O., Marston, P. J., O'Hair, H. D., Baaske, K. T., & Schneider, M. J. (1986). Situation perceptions and message strategy selection. In M. L. McLaughlin (Ed.), *Communication Yearbook 9* (pp. 390–420). Beverly Hills, CA: Sage.

Cody, M. J., & McLaughlin, M. L. (1980). Perceptions of compliance-gaining situations: A dimensional analysis. *Communication Monographs, 47,* 132–138.

Cody, M. J., Woelfel, M. L., & Jordan, W. J. (1983). Dimensions of compliance-gaining situations. *Human Communication Research, 9,* 99–113.

Cohen, A. (1996). Selling to senior executives. *Sales and Marketing Management, 148,* 43–44.

Conger, J. A. (1998). The necessary art of persuasion. *Harvard Business Review, 76,* 84–95.

Cose, E. (1999, August 2). The trouble with virtual grief: The pain that so many people feel for JFK Jr. should not be confused with the actual suffering of family and friends. *Newsweek*, p. n.a.

Cranberg, G. (1999). In reporting on Whitewater, an anonymous source misinformed the press. *Nieman Reports, 53,* 9.

Cruz, M. G. (1998). Explicit and implicit conclusions in persuasive messages. In M. Allen & R. W. Preiss (Eds.), *Persuasion: Advances through meta-analysis* (pp. 217–230). Cresskill, NH: Hampton Press.

Cuprisin, T. (2003, August 20). Satellite TV surpasses 20 million subscribers. Retrieved Sept. 3, 2003, from http://www.jsonline.com/enter/tvradio/aug03/163614.asp.

DeFleur, M. L. & Dennis, E. E. (1998). *Understanding mass communication: A liberal arts perspective.* Boston: Houghton Mifflin.

DeLuca, K. M. (1999). *Image politics: The new rhetoric of environmental activism.* New York: Guilford Press.

Denton, R. E., Jr., & Woodward, G. C. (1990). *Political communication in America.* New York: Praeger.

Department chair steps down over attribution question. (2000). *Quill, 88,* 3.

Derrida, J. (1982). *Margins of philosophy.* Chicago: University of Chicago Press.

Detenber, B. H., & Reeves, B. (1996). A bio-informational theory of emotion: Motion and image size effects on viewers. *Journal of Communication, 46,* 66–83.

Detenber, B. H., Simons, R. F., & Bennett, G. G. (1998). Roll 'em: The effects of picture motion on emotional responses. *Journal of Broadcasting and Electronic Media, 42,* 113–127.

Dillard, J. P. (1991). The current status of research on sequential-request compliance techniques. *Personality and Social Psychology Bulletin, 17,* 283–288.

———. (1993). Persuasion past and present: Attitudes aren't what they used to be. *Communication Monographs, 60,* 90–97.

Dillard, J. P., Hunter, J. E., & Burgoon, M. (1984). Sequential-request persuasive strategies: Meta-analysis of foot-in-the-door and door-in-the-face. *Human Communication Research, 10,* 461–488.

Dondis, D. A. (1973). *A primer of visual literacy.* Cambridge, MA: MIT Press.

Dorch, S. (1994). What's good for the goose may gag the gander. *American Demographics, 16*(5), 15–16.

Douglas, S. J. (1995). *Where the girls are: Growing up female with the mass media.* New York: Random House.

Duffy, M. (1997). High stakes: A fantasy theme analysis of the selling of riverboat gambling in Iowa. *Southern Communication Journal, 62,* 117–132.

Durham, D. (1997). How to get the biggest bang out of your next spokesperson campaign. *Public Relations Quarterly, 42,* 38–41.

Eco, U. (1979). *A theory of semiotics.* Bloomington: Indiana University Press.

Ehninger, D., & Brockriede, W. (1963). *Decision by debate.* New York: Dodd, Mead.

Ehrenberg, A. (1974). Repetitive advertising and the consumer. *Journal of Advertising, 14,* 25–34.

Elliott, M. T., & Speck, P. S. (1998). Consumer perceptions of advertising clutter and its impact across various media. *Journal of Advertising Research, 38,* 29–41.

Faludi, S. (1991). *Backlash: The undeclared war against American women.* New York: Crown.

Fern, E. F., Monroe, K. B., & Avila, R. A. (1986). Effectiveness of multiple request strategies: A synthesis of research results. *Journal of Marketing Research, 23,* 144–152.

Festinger, L. (1957). *A theory of cognitive dissonance.* Stanford, CA: Stanford University Press.

Fishbein, M., & Ajzen, I. (1975). *Belief, attitude, intention and behavior: An introduction to theory and research.* Reading, MA: Addison-Wesley.

Fisher, A. (1996, December 23). Then I called my boss a moron. . . . *Fortune, 134,* 243.

Fisher, W. R. (1987). *Human communication as narration: Toward a philosophy of reason, value, and action.* Columbia: University of South Carolina Press.

Fiske, J. (1987). Television: Polysemy and popularity. *Critical Studies in Mass Communication, 3,* 391–408.

Fiske, J. (1989). *Understanding popular culture.* Boston: Unwin Hyman.

Fitzgerald, M. (1997, April 26). Only on Sunday? Newspaper industry study finds reader loyalty waning on weekdays. *Editor and Publisher, 130,* 38.

Fitzgibbon, J. E., & Seeger, M. W. (2002). Audiences and metaphors of globalization in the DaimlerChryslerAG merger. *Communication Studies, 53,* 40–55.

Flass, R. (1999, September 20). Girl Scouts overhaul "nice" image with PR. *PRWeek, 2.*

Fleetwood, B. (1999). The broken wall. *Washington Monthly, 31,* 40.

Foss, S. K., & Kanengieter, M. R. (1992). Visual communication in the basic course. *Communication Education, 41,* 312–323.

Fotheringham, W. C. (1966). *Perspectives on persuasion.* Boston: Allyn and Bacon.

———. (1990). *The history of sexuality: An introduction.* New York: Vintage Books.

Fournier, S. (1998). Consumers and their brands: Developing relationship theory in consumer research. *Journal of Consumer Research, 24,* 343–373.

Fournier, S., Dobscha, S., & Mick, D. G. (1998). Preventing the premature death of relationship marketing. *Harvard Business Review, 76,* 42–49.

Frey, L. R., Botan, C. H., Friedman, P. G., & Kreps, G. L. (1991). *Investigating communication: An introduction to research methods.* Englewood Cliffs, NJ: Prentice-Hall.

Friedenberg, R. V. (1997). *Communication consultants in political campaigns: Ballot box warriors.* Westport, CT: Praeger.

Gates, B. (2000, September 11). 20/20 vision—A future for small business. Conference at Sydney Star City Casino, Sydney, Australia.

Gauntlett, D., & Hill, A. (1999). *TV living: Television, culture and everyday life.* London: Taylor & Francis.

Geller, L. K. (1998). The Internet: The ultimate relationship marketing tool. *Direct Marketing, 61,* 36–38.

Geracimos, A. (1998). Rules change in the fame game. *Insight on the News, 14,* 40.

Girl Scouts and girl power. (1999, November 20). *Economist, 353,* 35.

Gitlin, T. (1987). *The sixties: Years of hope, days of rage.* New York: Bantam Books.

Goffman, E. (1959). *The presentation of self in everyday life.* Garden City, NY: Doubleday.

Goldstein, M. J. (1959). The relationship between coping and avoiding behavior and response to fear arousing propaganda. *Journal of Abnormal and Social Psychology, 58,* 247–252.

Graber, D., McQuail, D., & Norris, P. (1998). Introduction: Political communication in a democracy. In D. Graber, D. McQuail, & P. Norris (Eds.), *The politics of news: The news of politics* (pp. 1–16). Washington, DC: Congressional Quarterly.

Green, N. (1998, May). Creating the brand experience. *Interiors, 157,* 241.

Greenstein, J. (1999, October). The heart of the matter: A statistical term leads the media astray. *Brill's Content,* p. 40.

Griffin, E. (2000). *A first look at communication theory* (4th ed.). Boston: McGraw-Hill.

Grimm, M. (1993). Swoosh over Europe: Nike goes global. *Brandweek, 34,* 12–13.

Gronbeck, B. E. (1995). Rhetoric, ethics, and telespectacles in the post-everything age. In R. H. Brown (Ed.), *Postmodern representations: Truth, power, and mimesis in the human science and public culture* (pp. 216–238). Urbana: University of Illinois Press.

———. (1998). *Principles of speech communication* (13th brief ed.). New York: Longman.

———. (1999, September 17). Feelingstalk. Presentation at Communication and Theatre Association of Minnesota, Moorhead.

Grumet, T. (1997). When seeing isn't believing. *Popular Mechanics, 174,* 97–99.

Gumpert, G., & Cathcart, R. (1979). Introduction. In G. Gumpert & R. Cathcart (Eds.), *Inter/Media* (pp. 9–16). New York: Oxford University Press.

Gusfield, J. R. (1994). The reflexivity of social movements: Collective behavior and mass society theory revisited. In E. Larana, H. Johnston, & J. R. Gusfield (Eds.), *New social movements: From ideology to identity* (pp. 58–78). Philadelphia: Temple University Press.

Gustke, C. (1997, May 5). The 21st century. *Industry Week, 246,* 48–54.

Ha, L., & Litman, B. R. (1997). Does advertising clutter have diminishing and negative returns? *Journal of Advertising, 26,* 31–42.

Habermas, J. (1973). *Theory and practice.* Boston: Beacon Press.

———. (1979). *Communication and the evolution of society.* Boston: Beacon Press.

Hamilton, M. A., & Hunter, J. E. (1998). The effect of language intensity on receiver evaluations of message, source, and topic. In M. Allen & R. W. Preiss (Eds.), *Persuasion: Advances through meta-analysis* (pp. 99–138). Cresskill, NH: Hampton Press.

Hammond, J., & Morrison, J. (1996). *The stuff Americans are made of: The seven cultural forces that define Americans—A new framework for quality, productivity and profitability.* New York: Macmillan.

Harrison, K., & Cantor, J. (1997). The relationship between media consumption and eating disorders. *Journal of Communication, 47,* 40–67.

Hart, R. P. (1999). *Seducing America: How television charms the modern voter* (Rev. ed.). Thousand Oaks, CA: Sage.

Harvey, M. L., Loomis, R. J., Bell, P. A., & Marino, M. (1998). The influence of museum exhibit design on immersion and psychological flow. *Environment and Behavior, 30,* 601–626.

Hauser, G. A. (1986). *Introduction to rhetorical theory.* Prospect Heights, IL: Waveland Press.

Heath, R. P. (1996). The frontiers of psychographics. *American Demographics, 18*(7), 38–43.

Henderson, P. W. (1998). Guidelines for selecting or modifying logos. *Journal of Marketing, 62,* 14–30.

Herbeck, D. A. (1994). Presidential debate as political ritual: Clinton vs. Bush vs. Perot. In S. A. Smith (Ed.), *Bill Clinton: On stump, state, and stage* (pp. 249–272). Fayetteville: University of Arkansas Press.

Herrera, F., & Rodriguez, S. M. (1999, May). Courtroom technology: Tools for presentation. *Trial, 35,* 66.

Hewgill, M. A., & Miller, G. R. (1966). Source credibility and response to fear-arousing communications. *Speech Monographs, 32,* 95–101.

Hilts, E. (1998, April 25). San Francisco's latest media convergence: The alliance of the Gate, the *Chronicle* papers, and KRON-TV is now challenged by a new alliance of six Knight Ridder newspapers, their Web sites, and KPIX-TV. *Editor and Publisher, 131,* 40–41.

Hirschman, E. C., Scott, L., & Wells, W. B. (1998). A model of product discourse: Linking consumer practice to cultural texts. *Journal of Advertising, 27,* 33–50.

Hofstede, G. (1980). *Culture's consequences: International differences in work-related values.* Beverly Hills, CA: Sage.

Hallien, L. (1999a). Magazines. *Broadcasting and Cable, 129,* 46.

———. (1999b). Newspapers. *Broadcasting and Cable, 129,* 43.

Hovind, M. B. (1999). The melodramatic imperative: Television's model for presidential election coverage. In L. L. Kaid & D. G. Bystrom (Eds.), *The electronic election: Perspectives on the 1996 campaign communication* (pp. 15–28). Mahwah, NJ: Erlbaum.

Hovland, C. I., Mandell, W., Campbell, E. H., Brock, T., Luchins, A. S., & Cohen, A. R. (1957). *The order of presentation in persuasion.* New Haven, CT: Yale University Press.

Huff, D. (1954). *How to lie with statistics.* New York: Norton.

Hunter, J. D. (1991). *Culture wars: The struggle to define America.* New York: Basic Books.

Huus, K. (1998). Two years of living electronically: Covering breaking foreign news for the Internet. *Nieman Reports, 52,* 63.

Hyde, M. J. (1984). Emotion and human communication: A rhetorical, scientific, and philosophical picture. *Communication Quarterly, 32,* 120–132.

Infante, D. A., Rancer, A. S., & Womack, D. F. (1993). *Building communication theory* (2nd ed.). Prospect Heights, IL: Waveland Press.

Jackson, D. S., Park, A., & Thompson, D. (2000, March 13). Katie's crusade: Colon cancer is one of the deadliest and most preventable malignancies. What you need to know about the disease—and the surprisingly painless test that could save your life. *Time,* p. 70.

Jameson, F. (1991). *Postmodernism, or, the cultural logic of late capitalism.* Durham, NC: Duke University Press.

Jamieson, K. H. (1988). *Eloquence in an electronic age.* New York: Oxford University Press.

———. (1992). *Packaging the presidency: A history and criticism of presidential campaign advertising.* New York: Oxford University Press.

———. (2000). *Everything you think you know about politics—and why you're wrong.* New York: Basic Books.

Jamieson, K. H., & Birdsell, D. S. (1988). *Presidential debates: The challenge of creating an informed electorate.* New York: Oxford University Press.

Jamieson, K. H., & Campbell, K. K. (1997). *The interplay of influence: News, advertising, politics, and the mass media* (4th ed.). Belmont, CA: Wadsworth.

Janis, I. L., & Feshbach, S. (1953). Effects of fear-arousing communications. *Journal of Abnormal and Social Psychology, 48,* 78–92.

Jew, R., & Peterson, M. Q. (1995). Envisioning persuasion: Painting the picture for the jury. *Trial, 31,* 74–80.

Jewler, A. J., & Drewniany, B. L. (1998). *Creative strategy in advertising* (6th ed.). Belmont, CA: Wadsworth.

Johannesen, R. L. (1996). *Ethics in human communication* (4th ed.). Prospect Heights, IL: Waveland Press.

Johnson, D. W., & Grefe, E. A. (1997). Ethical political consulting: Oxymoron? *Campaigns and Elections, 18,* 43–44.

Jorgenson, P. F. (1998). Affect, persuasion, and communication processes. In P. A. Andersen & L. K. Guerrero (Eds.), *Handbook of communication and emotion* (pp. 404–423). San Diego: Academic Press.

Kaid, L. L., & Bystrom, D. G. (Eds.). (1999). *The electronic election: Perspectives on the 1996 campaign communication.* Mahwah, NJ: Erlbaum.

Katz, D. (1993). Triumph of the swoosh. *Sports Illustrated, 79,* 54–73.

Katz, E., Blumler, J. G., & Gurevitch, M. (1974). Uses of mass communication by the individual. In W. P. Davison & F. T. C. Yu (Eds.), *Mass communication research: Major issues and future directions* (pp. 11–35). New York: Praeger.

Kay, J. (1994). Lee Iacocca as debater and storyteller: Speeches concerning the problems and future of the automobile industry. In M. W. Seeger (Ed.), *"I gotta tell you:" Speeches of Lee Iacocca* (pp. 119–166). Detroit: Wayne State University Press.

Kennedy, G. (1963). *The art of persuasion in Greece.* Princeton, NJ: Princeton University Press.

Kennedy, J. (1999). What to do when job applicants tell . . . Tales of invented lives. *Training, 36,* 110.

Kerry, J. (2003, 16 May). Affordable health care for all Americans. Retrieved Sept. 9, 2003, from http://www.johnkerry.com/.

Key, W. B. (1981). *Subliminal seduction: Ad media's manipulation of a not so innocent America.* New York: Signet.

Kilbourne, J. (1999). *Deadly persuasion: Why women and girls must fight the addictive power of advertising.* New York: Free Press.

King, M. L. (1963, August 28). I have a dream [Address delivered at the March on Washington for Jobs and Freedom]. Washington, DC.

Klatch, R. E. (1999). *A generation divided: The new left, the new right, and the 1960s.* Berkeley: University of California Press.

Knupp, R. E. (1981). A time for every purpose under heaven: Rhetorical dimensions of protest music. *Southern Speech Communication Journal, 46,* 377–389.

Kohli, C., & LaBahn, D. W. (1997). Creating effective brand names: A study of the naming process. *Journal of Advertising Research, 37,* 67–75.

Kohn, P. M., Goodstadt, M. S., Cook, G. M., Sheppard, M., & Chan, G. (1982). Ineffectiveness of threat appeals about drinking and driving. *Accident Analysis and Prevention, 14,* 457–464.

Kopfman, J. E., & Smith, S. W. (1996). Understanding the audiences of a health communication campaign: A discriminant analysis of potential organ donors based on intent to donate. *Journal of Applied Communication Research, 24,* 33–49.

Korgaonkar, P. K., & Wolin, L. D. (1999). A multivariate analysis of Web usage. *Journal of Advertising Research, 39,* 53.

Kramarae, C. (1981). *Women and men speaking: Frameworks for analysis.* Rowley, MA: Newbury House.

Kuczynski, A. (2000, January 12). On CBS, some of what you see isn't there. *New York Times,* p. A1.

Kupper, J. (1999, April 4). Anatomy of an upset. *Campaigns and Elections, 20,* 38–41.

Labich, K. (1999). Attention shoppers: This man is watching you: Do you breeze by store displays? Avoid narrow aisles? Paco Underhill knows you do, and his methods are changing retail behavior. *Fortune, 140,* 131.

Langer, S. K. (1960). *Philosophy in a new key.* Cambridge, MA: Harvard University Press.

Lavidge, R. J. (1999). "Mass customization" is not an oxymoron. *Journal of Advertising Research, 39,* 70.

Lazarsfeld, P. F., Berelson, B., & Gaudet, H. (1944). *The people's choice: How the voter makes up his mind in a presidential campaign.* New York: Columbia University Press.

Lears, T. J. J. (1983). From salvation to self-realization: Advertising and the therapeutic roots of the consumer culture. In R. W. Fox & T. J. J. Lears (Eds.). *The culture of consumption: Critical essays in American history 1880–1980* (pp. 1–38). New York: Pantheon.

Leathers, D. G. (1997). *Successful nonverbal communication: Principles and applications* (3rd ed.). Boston: Allyn and Bacon.

Leckenby, J. D., & Hong, J. (1998). Using reach/frequency for Web media planning. *Journal of Advertising Research, 38,* 7–18.

Leckenby, J. D., & Kim, H. (1994). How media directors view reach/frequency estimation: Now and a decade ago. *Journal of Advertising Research, 34,* 9–21.

Lester, P. M. (2000). *Visual communication: Images with messages* (2nd ed.). Belmont, CA: Wadsworth Thomson Learning.

Lichter, S. R., Noyes, R. E., & Kaid, L. L. (1999). No news or negative news: How the networks nixed the '96 campaign. In L. L. Kaid & D. G. Bystrom (Eds.), *The electronic election: Perspectives on the 1996 campaign communication* (pp. 3–14). Mahwah, NJ: Erlbaum.

Lieberman, J. (2003, January 13). Senator Joe Lieberman announces candidacy for presidency of the United

States. Retrieved Sept. 9, 2003, from http://www.joe2004.com.

Lieberman, T. (1999, September/October). New drugs: A dose of reality. *Columbia Journalism Review,* pp. 10–11.

Limburg, V. E. (1994). *Electronic media ethics.* Boston: Focal Press.

Linden-Ward, B., & Green, C. H. (1993). *American women in the 1960s: Changing the future.* New York: Twayne.

Lindstrom, R. L. (1998, October). Presentation intelligence. *Sales and Marketing Management,* p. 1.

Ling, D. A. (1970). A pentadic analysis of Senator Edward Kennedy's address to the people of Massachusetts, July 25, 1969. *Central States Speech Journal, 21,* 81–86.

Littlejohn, S. W. (1996). *Theories of human communication.* Belmont, CA: Wadsworth.

Llewellyn, J. T. (1994). Bill Clinton's stump speaking: Persuasion through identification. In S. A. Smith (Ed.), *Bill Clinton: On stump, state, and stage* (pp. 52–72). Fayetteville: University of Arkansas Press.

Lobove, S. (1998). George Orwell, meet John Malone. *Forbes, 161,* 66–68.

Logue, C. M., & Miller, E. F. (1995). Rhetorical status: A study of its origins, functions, and consequences. *Quarterly Journal of Speech, 81,* 20–47.

Lutz, W. (1989). *Doublespeak: From "revenue enhancement" to "terminal living," how government, business, advertisers, and others use language to deceive you.* New York: Harper-Perennial.

Lyotard, J. F. (1984). *The postmodern condition: A report on knowledge.* Minneapolis: University of Minnesota Press.

Mannes, G. (1995, January 13). And now a word from our sponsor. *Entertainment Weekly,* p. 64.

Marschall, R. E. (1999). The century in political cartoons. *Columbia Journalism Review, 38,* 54.

Marshall, C. (1997, November). Classic forget-me-nots. *Management Today,* pp. 136–137.

Martin, E. (1999, May 10). Under extreme pressure, networks cast a wide net. On a mission: Serious erosion and fragmentation force execs to rethink the audience numbers. *Advertising Age,* p. S6.

Marwell, G., & Schmitt, D. R. (1967). Dimensions of compliance-gaining behavior: An empirical analysis. *Sociometry, 30,* 350–364.

Maslow, A. H. (1943). A theory of human motivation. *Psychological Review, 50,* 370–396.

Mason, L. D. (1997, February). Design issues for producing effective multimedia presentations. *Technical Communication, 44,* 65–71.

Matalin, M., & Carville, J. (1994). *All's fair.* New York: Random House.

Mayer, M. A., & Carlin, D. B. (1994). Debates as voter education tools. In D. B. Carlin & M. S. McKinney (Eds.), *The 1992 presidential debates in focus* (pp. 127–138). Westport, CT: Praeger.

Mayer, R. E., & Sims, V. K. (1994). For whom is a picture worth a thousand words? Extensions of a dual-coding theory of multimedia learning. *Journal of Educational Psychology, 86,* 389–401.

McAllister, M. P. (1996). *The commercialization of American culture: New advertising, control and democracy.* Thousand Oaks, CA: Sage.

McBurney, J. H., & Mills, G. E. (1964). *Argumentation and debate: Techniques of a free society.* New York: Macmillan.

McCarthy, J. D. (1994). Activists, authorities, and media framing of drunk driving. In E. Larana, H. Johnston, & J. R. Gusfield (Eds.), *New social movements: From ideology to identity* (pp. 133–167). Philadelphia: Temple University Press.

McCarthy, T. (1978). *The critical theory of Jurgen Habermas.* Cambridge, MA: MIT Press.

McCombs, M. E. (1981). The agenda-setting approach. In D. D. Nimmo & K. R. Sanders (Eds.), *Handbook of political communication* (pp. 121–140). Beverly Hills, CA: Sage.

McElroy, J. H. (1999). *American beliefs: What keeps a big country and a diverse people united.* Chicago: Ivan R. Dee.

McGee, B. R. (1998). Rehabilitating emotion: The troublesome case of the Ku Klux Klan. *Argumentation and Advocacy, 34,* 173–188.

McGee, M. C. (1980). The "ideograph": A link between rhetoric and ideology. *Quarterly Journal of Speech, 66,* 1–16.

———. (1983). Social movement as meaning. *Central States Speech Journal, 34,* 74–77.

———. (1990). Text, context, and the fragmentation of contemporary culture. *Western Journal of Speech Communication, 54,* 274–289.

McLuhan, M. (1964). *Understanding media: The extensions of man.* New York: Signet.

Meggs, P. B. (1997). Mondrian as a marketing tool. In S. Heller & M. Finamore (Eds), *Design culture* (pp. 3–5). New York: Allworth Press.

Merikle, P. M. (2000). Subliminal perception. In A. E. Kazdin (Ed.), *Encyclopedia of psychology* (Vol. 7, pp. 497–499). New York: Oxford University Press.

Messaris, P. (1997). *Visual persuasion: The role of images in advertising.* Thousand Oaks, CA: Sage.

Meurs, L. V. (1998). Zapp! A study on switching behavior during commercial breaks. *Journal of Advertising Research, 38,* 43–53.

Meyer, D. S., & Staggenborg, S. (1996). Movements, countermovements, and the structure of political opportunity. *American Journal of Sociology, 101,* 1628–1651.

Meyrowitz, J. (1985). *No sense of place: The impact of electronic media on social behavior.* New York: Oxford University Press.

Millar, M. G., & Millar, K. U. (1990). Attitude change as a function of attitude type and argument type. *Journal of Personality and Social Psychology, 59,* 217–228.

Miller, G., Boster, F., Roloff, M., & Seibold, D. (1977). Compliance-gaining message strategies: A typology and some findings concerning effects of situational differences. *Communication Monographs, 44,* 37–51.

Miller, K. (1999*). Organizational communication: Approaches and processes.* Belmont, CA: Wadsworth.

Miller, S., & Berry, L. (1998). Brand salience versus brand image: Two theories of advertising effectiveness. *Journal of Advertising Research, 38,* 77–82.

Mills, G. (1964). *Reason in controversy.* Boston: Allyn and Bacon.

Mitchell, A. (1998, July). The one-to-one gap. *Management Today,* pp. 90–91.

Mongeau, P. A. (1998). Another look at fear-arousing persuasive appeals. In M. Allen & R. W. Preiss (Eds.), *Persuasion: Advances through meta-analysis* (pp. 53–68). Cresskill, NH: Hampton Press.

Morello, J. T. (1998). Argument and visual structuring in the 1984 Mondale-Reagan debates: The medium's influence on the perception of clash. *Western Journal of Speech Communication, 52,* 277–290.

Morgan, M., & Signorielli, N. (1990). Cultivation analysis: Conceptualization and methodology. In N. Signorielli & M. Morgan (Eds.), *Cultivation analysis: New directions in media effects research* (pp. 13–34). Newbury Park, CA: Sage.

Morris, D. (1997). *Behind the oval office: Winning the presidency in the nineties.* New York: Random House.

Moseley, M. (1999). Young Americans volunteer but don't vote. *Campaigns and Elections, 20,* 35.

Muir, J. K. (1994). Clinton goes to the town hall. In S. A. Smith (Ed.), *Bill Clinton: On stump, state, and stage* (pp. 341–364). Fayetteville: University of Arkansas Press.

Nabi, R. L. (1998). The effect of disgust-eliciting visuals on attitudes toward animal experimentation. *Communication Quarterly, 46,* 472–486.

Nassar, J. (2000, September 6). *Testimony.* House Commerce Subcommittee on Telecommunications, Trade and Consumer Protection and the House Commerce Subcommittee on Oversight and Investigations. Washington, DC: Government Printing Office.

Natale, R. (1999). The surreal thing. *Los Angeles Magazine, 44,* 42.

National Communication Association (NCA). (1999). *Credo for ethical communication.* (Available from the National Communication Association, 1765 N Street NW, Washington, DC 20036.)

National Press Photographers Association. (n.d.). *Code of ethics.* (Available from the National Press Photographers Association, 3200 Croasdaile Drive, Suite 306, Durham, NC 27705.)

Naylor, L. L. (1998). *American culture: Myth and reality of a culture of diversity.* Westport, CT: Bergin and Garvey.

Neher, W. W., & Waite, D. H. (1993). *The business and professional communicator.* Boston: Allyn and Bacon.

Nesbit, D. D. (1988). *Videostyle in Senate campaigns.* Knoxville: University of Tennessee Press.

Networks given financial incentive for anti-drug messages. (2000, January 14). Associated Press.

Nielsen//NetRatings. (2003). Average Web usage: month of July 2003. Retrieved September 2, 2003, from the World Wide Web: http://www.netratings.com/news.jsp?section=dat to&country=us.

Nimmo, D., & Combs, J. E. (1990). *Mediated political realities.* New York: Longman.

Ogden, C. K., & Richards, I. A. (1923). *The meaning of meaning.* New York: Harcourt, Brace.

O'Hair, D., Friedrich, G. W., & Shaver, L. D. (1998). *Strategic communication in business and the professions* (3rd ed.). Boston: Houghton Mifflin.

Ong, W. J. (1982). *Orality and literacy: The technologizing of the word.* London: Methuen.

Padgett, D., & Allen, D. (1997). Communicating experiences: A narrative approach to creating service brand image. *Journal of Advertising, 26,* 49–62.

Paige, S. (1998, February 9). Talking the talk. *Insight on the News, 14,* 9–14.

Palmer, J. W., & Griffith, D. A. (1998). An emerging model of Web site design for marketing. *Communications of the ACM, 41,* 44–51.

Parenti, M. (1992). *Make-believe media: The politics of entertainment.* New York: St. Martin's Press.

Park, H. S., Levine, T. R., McCornack, S. A., Morrison, K., & Ferrara, M. (2002). How people really detect lies. *Communication Monographs, 69,* 144–157.

Parry-Giles, S. J. (2000). Mediating Hillary Rodham Clinton: Television news practices and image-making in the postmodem age. *Critical Studies in Media Communication, 17,* 205–226.

Parry-Giles, S. J., & Parry-Giles, T. (1999). Meta-imaging, *The War Room,* and the hyperreality of U.S. politics. *Journal of Communication, 49,* 28–45.

Patchen, R. H., & Kolessar, R. S. (1999). Out of the lab and into the field: A pilot test of the personal portable meter. *Journal of Advertising Research, 39,* 55.

Patterson, P., & Wilkins, L. (1998). *Media ethics: Issues, cases.* Boston: McGraw-Hill.

Patterson, T. (1994). *Out of order.* New York: Random House.

Patton, P. (1997). The tyranny of the swoosh. In S. Heller & M. Finamore (Eds.), *Design culture* (pp. 59–62). New York: Allworth Press.

Pax, S. (2003, March 22). Where is Raed? Message posted to http://dearraed.blogspot.com/2003_03_01_dear_raed_archive.html.

Peppers, D., & Rogers, M. (1993). *The one to one future: Building relationships one customer at a time.* New York: Doubleday.

———. (1998). Don't drown customers in choices. *Sales and Marketing Management, 150,* 24.

Perloff, R. M. (1993). *The dynamics of persuasion.* Hillsdale, NJ: Lawrence Erlbaum Associates, Publishers.

Peterson, R. A., & Ross, I. (1972). How to name new brands. *Journal of Advertising, 12,* 29–34.

Petty, R. E., & Cacioppo, J. T. (1986). *Communication and persuasion: Central and peripheral routes to attitude change.* New York: Springer.

Pfau, M., Van Bockern, S., & Kang, J. G. (1992). Use of inoculation to promote resistance to smoking initiation among adolescents. *Communication Monographs, 59,* 213–229.

Pichardo, N. A. (1997). New social movements: A critical review. *Annual Review of Sociology, 23,* 411–430.

Plassman, B. L., et al. (2000). Documented head injury in early adulthood and risk of Alzheimer's disease and other dementias. *Neurology, 55,* 1158–1166.

Poland, D. (1997, September 5). Fact-free speech: Net newsie Matt Drudge piled his dirty dish too high this time. Now he may be taken to the cleaners. *Entertainment Weekly, 395,* 84.

Polgreen, L. (1999). The death of "local radio." *Washington Monthly, 31,* 9.

Porter, R. E., & Samovar, L. A. (1998). Approaches: Understanding intercultural communication. In L. A. Samovar & R. E. Porter (Eds.), *Intercultural communication: A reader* (3rd ed.) (Ch. 1: pp. 5–21). Belmont, CA: Wadsworth.

Posavek, H. D., Posavac, S. S., & Posavac, E. J. (1998). Exposure to media images of female attractiveness and concern with body weight among young women. *Sex Roles: A Journal of Research, 38,* 187–198.

Post, T. (1999, February 22). The convergence gamble. *Forbes, 112,* 1.

Postman, N. (1985). *Amusing ourselves to death: Public discourse in the age of show business.* New York: Penguin Books.

———. (1992). *Technopoly: The surrender of culture to technology.* New York: Vintage.

Postman, N., & Powers, S. (1992). *How to watch TV news.* New York: Penguin Books.

———. (1972). *Dramatism and development.* Worcester, MA: Clark University Press.

Public Relations Society of America. (2000). *Member code of ethics 2000.* (Available from Public Relations Society of America, 33 Irving Place, New York, NY 10003.)

Putnam, L. L., & Poole, M. S. (1987). Conflict and negotiation. In F. M. Jablin, L. L. Putnam, K. H. Roberts, & L. W. Porter (Eds.), *Handbook of organizational communication* (pp. 549–599). Thousand Oaks, CA: Sage.

Ranchhod, A. (1998). Advertising into the next millennium. *International Journal of Advertising, 427,* 1.

Randall, N. (1997, April 22). The new cookie monster. *PC Magazine, 16,* 211–213.

Rasmusson, E. (1997, April). Sales meetings go Hollywood: Multimedia technology livens up the conference room. *Sales and Marketing Management, 149,* 76.

Reese, S. D. (1991). Setting the media's agenda: A power balance perspective. In Anderson, J. A. (Ed.), *Communi-*

cation Yearbook 14 (pp. 309–340). Newbury Park, CA: Sage.

Rein, I. J. (1994). Imaging the image: Reinventing the Clintons. In S. A. Smith (Ed.), *Bill Clinton on stump, state and stage: The rhetorical road to the White House* (pp. 187–200). Fayetteville: University of Arkansas Press.

Revenaugh, M. (2000). Beyond the digital divide: Pathways to equity. *Technology and Learning, 20,* 38.

Rogers, E. M., & Dearing, J. W. (1988). Agenda-setting research: Where has it been going, where is it going? In J. A. Anderson (Ed.), *Communication Yearbook 11* (pp. 555–593). Newbury Park, CA: Sage.

Rokeach, M. (1968). *Beliefs, attitudes, and values: A theory of organization and change.* San Francisco: Jossey-Bass.

———. (1973). *The nature of human values.* New York: Free Press.

———. (1979). From individual to institutional values: With special reference to the values of science. In M. Rokeach (Ed.), *Understanding human emotions* (pp. 47–70). New York: Free Press.

RoperASW. (2003, October 29). *American youth wielding more household buying power . . . but have less cash in their pocket according to RoperASW study.* Retrieved November 10, 2003 from http://www.roperasw.com/newsroom/press/p0310002.html.

Rosen, R. (1986). Soap operas: Search for yesterday. In T. Gitlin, (Ed.), *Watching television (pp. 42–67).* New York: Pantheon.

Rosenberg, S. W., Kahn, S., & Tran, T. (1991). Creating a political image: Shaping appearance and manipulating the vote. *Political Behavior, 13,* 345–367.

Rosenwein, R. (1999, October). The news that dare not speak its name. *Brill's Content, 2,* 76–81.

Rothstein, E. (1996, December 29). Trend-spotting: It's all the rage. *New York Times,* p. H1.

Rowan, J. (1998). Maslow amended. *Journal of Humanistic Psychology, 38,* 81–93.

Rowland, R. C. (1992). Argument fields. In W. L. Benoit, D. Hample, & P. J. Benoit (Eds.), *Readings in argumentation* (pp. 469–504). Berlin: Foris.

Sandel, M. J. (1996, September 2). Easy virtue. *New Republic, 215,* 23.

Savan, L. (2000). Truth in advertising. *Brill's Content, 3,* 62–63, 114.

Schachter, S. (1971). *Emotion, obesity, and crime.* New York: Academic Press.

Schenden, L. (1999, June 8). School's "out" for summer. *Advocate,* p. 63.

Schlenker, J. A. (1998). A feminist analysis of *Seventeen* magazine: Content analysis from 1945 to 1995. *Sex Roles: A Journal of Research, 38,* 135–149.

Schrage, M. (1999). Every Fortune 500 CEO should have his own Dick Morris: Got a strategy? Get a poll! *Fortune, 139,* 162.

Seideman, T. (1996, September 17). Multimedia is the message. *Inc., 18,* 82–83.

Sellnow, D. D. (1996). Rhetorical strategies of continuity and change in the music of popular artists over time. *Communication Studies, 47,* 46–61.

Serwer, A. (2003, July 7). The hole story. *Fortune, 148,* 52–62.

Sharpe, K. (1999, September 13). Web punctures the idea that advertising works: Old tests, like reach, frequency, fail as predictors of ad success. *Advertising Age,* p. 44.

Shepard, A. C. (1997). Webward ho! *American Journalism Review, 19,* 32–37.

Sherrid, P. (1999, September 20). What's up, Dr. Koop? *U.S. News and World Report,* p. 51.

Signorielli, N., & Morgan, M. (1990). Introduction. In N. Signorielli & M. Morgan (Eds.), *Cultivation analysis: New directions in media effects research* (pp. 1–15). Newbury Park, CA: Sage.

Sillars, A. L. (1980). The stranger and the spouse as target persons for compliance-gaining strategies: A subjective expected utility model. *Human Communication Research, 6,* 265–279.

Simon, R. (1999). Backstage at the opening. *U.S. News and World Report, 126,* 20.

Simon, R. W., Eder, D., & Evans, C. (1992). The development of feeling norms underlying romantic love among adolescent females. *Social Psychology Quarterly, 55,* 29–46.

———. (1991). On the rhetoric of social movements, historical movements, and "top down" movements: A commentary. *Communication Studies, 42,* 94–101.

Slater, M. D., & Rouner, D. (2002). Entertainment-education and elaboration likelihood. *Communication Theory, 12,* 173–191.

Slayden, D. (1999). Vicarious realities: Internet discourses and narratives of the future. In D. Slayden & R. K. Whillock (Eds.), *Soundbite culture: The death of discourse in a wired world* (pp. 267–288). Thousand Oaks, CA: Sage.

Smith, C. R., & Hyde, M. J. (1991). Rethinking "the public": The role of emotion in being-with-others. *Quarterly Journal of Speech, 77,* 446–466.

Smith, L. D. (1994). The New York convention: Bill Clinton and "A Place Called Hope." In S. A. Smith (Ed.), *Bill Clinton: On stump, state, and stage* (pp. 201–222). Fayetteville: University of Arkansas Press.

Society of Professional Journalists. (1996). *Code of ethics.* (Available from Society of Professional Journalists, 3909 N. Meridian Street, Indianapolis, IN 46208.)

Sopory, P., & Dillard, J. P. (2002). The persuasive effects of metaphor: A meta-analysis. *Human Communication Research, 28,* 382–419.

Spindler, G., & Spindler, L. (1990). *The American cultural dialogue and its transmission.* London: Falmer Press.

Spring, J. (1992). *Images of American life: A history of ideological management in schools, movies, radio, and television.* Albany: State University of New York Press.

Sproule, J. M. (1988). The new managerial rhetoric and the old criticism. *Quarterly Journal of Speech, 74,* 468–486.

———. (1994). *Channels of propaganda.* Bloomington, IN: ERIC Clearinghouse on Reading, English, and Communication.

Stabiner, K. (1997). *To dance with the devil: The new war on breast cancer.* New York: Delacorte Press.

Steele, E. D., & Redding, W. C. (1962). The American value system: Premises for persuasion. *Western Speech, 26,* 83–91.

Stephens, M. (1998). *The rise of the image, the fall of the word.* New York: Oxford University Press.

Stewart, C. J. (1991). The ego function of protest songs: An application of Gregg's theory of protest rhetoric. *Communication Studies, 42,* 240–253.

Stewart, C. J., & Cash, W. B. (1997). *Interviewing: Principles and practices.* Madison, WI: Brown and Benchmark.

Stewart, C. J., Smith, C. A., & Denton, R. E. (1994). *Persuasion and social movements* (3rd ed.). Prospect Heights, IL: Waveland Press.

Sundar, S. S., Narayan, S., Obregon, R., & Uppal, C. (1998). Does Web advertising work? Memory for print vs. online media. *Journalism and Mass Communication Quarterly, 75,* 822–835.

Tan, A., Fujioka, Y., & Tan, G. (2002). Television use, stereotypes of African Americans, and opinions on affirmative action: An effective model of policy reasoning. *Communication Monographs, 67,* 362–371.

Tedesco, J. C., Miller, J. L., & Spiker, J. A. (1999). Presidential campaigning on the Information Superhighway: An exploration of content and form. In L. L. Kaid & D. G. Bystrom (Eds.), *The electronic election: Perspectives on the 1996 campaign communication* (pp. 51–64). Mahwah, NJ: Erlbaum.

Teinowitz, I. (2000). FTC cracks down on rebate offers: Value America, Office Depot, Buy.com charged with misleading consumers. *Advertising Age, 71,* 29.

Telford, A. (1997, October). Sexism in advertising. *Communication Arts,* pp. 84–91.

Tellis, G. T., & Weiss, D. L. (1995). Does TV advertising really affect sales? The role of measures, models, and data aggregation. *Journal of Advertising, 24,* 1–12.

Templin, C. (1999). Hillary Clinton as threat to gender norms: Cartoon images of the First Lady. *Journal of Communication Inquiry, 23,* 20.

Thomsen, S. R., & Rawson, B. (1998). Purifying a tainted corporate image: Odwalla's response to an *E. coli* poisoning. *Public Relations Quarterly, 43,* 35.

Toulmin, S. E. (1998). *Uses of reasoning.* London: Cambridge University Press.

Treadwell, D. F., & Harrison, T. M. (1994). Conceptualizing and assessing organizational image: Model images, commitment, and communication. *Communication Monographs, 61,* 63–85.

Trujillo, N. (1991). Hegemonic masculinity on the mound: Media representations of Nolan Ryan and American sports culture. *Critical Studies in Mass Communication, 8,* 290–308.

Trujillo, N., & Ekdom, L. R. (1985). Sportswriting and American cultural values: The 1984 Chicago Cubs. *Critical Studies in Mass Communication, 2,* 262–281.

Tumtulty, K. (1998). Caught in the town's most thankless job. *Time, 151,* 68–69.

Twitchell, J. B. (1996). *Adcult USA: The triumph of advertising in American culture.* New York: Columbia University Press.

U. S. Bureau of the Census. (2002). *Statistical abstract of the United States.* Washington, DC: U.S. Government Printing Office.

Waddell, C. (1990). The role of pathos in the decision-making process: A study in the rhetoric of science policy. *Quarterly Journal of Speech, 76,* 381–400.

Walker, G. B., & Bender, M. A. (1994). Is it more than rock and roll? Considering music video as argument. *Argumentation and Advocacy, 31,* 64–79.

Walton, D. (1992). *The place of emotion in argument.* University Park: Pennsylvania State University Press.

Wanta, W., & Hu, Y. (1994). The effects of credibility, reliance, and exposure on media agenda-setting: A path analysis model. *Journalism Quarterly, 71,* 90–98.

Warnick, B. (1989). Judgment, probability, and Aristotle's *Rhetoric. Quarterly Journal of Speech, 75,* 299–311.

Warnick, B., & Inch, E. S. (1994). *Critical thinking and communication: The use of reason in argument* (2nd ed.) New York: Macmillan.

Weissman, R. X. (1999a). Broadcasters mine the gold. *American Demographics, 21*(6), 35–37.

———. (1999b). Gay market power. *American Demographics, 21*(6), 32–34.

Wheeless, L. R., Barraclough, R., & Stewart, R. (1983). Compliance-gaining and power in persuasion. In R. Bostrom (Ed.), *Communication Yearbook 7* (pp. 105–145). Beverly Hills, CA: Sage.

Wheildon, C. (1995). *Type and layout: How typography and design can get your message across—or get in the way.* Berkeley, CA: Strathmoor Press.

Whereatt, R. (2000, March 2). Minnesota poll: Ventura's job approval drops, but only slightly, in new poll. http://www.startribune.com [online].

Whillock, R. K. (1998). Digital democracy: The '96 presidential campaign on-line. In R. E. Denton Jr. (Ed.), *The 1996 presidential election* (pp. 179–198). Westport, CT: Praeger.

Whitcover, J. (1998). Where we went wrong. *Columbia Journalism Review, 36,* 18–25.

White, R. (1999). What can advertising really do for brands? *International Journal of Advertising, 18,* 3.

Who's spinning who? (1999, September 20). *PRWeek,* 14–15.

Williams, R. (1977). *Marxism and literature.* Oxford, England: Oxford University Press.

Williams, R. M. (1979). Change and stability in values and value systems: A sociological perspective. In M. Rokeach (Ed.), *Understanding human emotions* (pp. 15–46). New York: Free Press.

Wilson, B. J., & Smith, S. L. (1998). Children's responses to emotional portrayals on television. In P. A. Anderson & L. K. Guerrero (Eds.), *Handbook of communication and emotion: Research, theory, applications, and contexts* (pp. 533–569). San Diego: Academic Press.

Witte, R. S. (1993). *Statistics* (4th ed.). Fort Worth, TX: Harcourt Brace Jovanovich.

Wood, J. (1998). *Gendered lives: Communication, gender, and culture* (2nd ed.). Belmont, CA: Wadsworth.

Wood, L. (1998). Internet ad buys—What reach and frequency do they deliver? *Journal of Advertising Research, 38,* 21–28.

Woodward, G. C. (2003). *The idea of identification.* Albany, NY: State University of New York Press.

Workman, N. V. (1996). From Victorian to Victoria's Secret: The foundations of modern erotic wear. *Journal of Popular Culture, 30,* 61–73.

Zanna, M. P., & Rempel, J. K. (1988). Attitudes: A new look at an old concept. In D. Bar-Tal & A. W. Kruglanski (Eds.), *The social psychology of knowledge* (pp. 315–334). Cambridge, England: Cambridge University Press.

Ziegelmueller, G. W., & Kay, J. (1997). *Argumentation: Inquiry and advocacy.* Boston: Allyn and Bacon.

Zollo, P. (1999). *Wise up to teens: Insights into marketing and advertising to teenagers* (2nd ed.). Ithaca, NY: New Strategist Publications.

Credits

TEXT AND ILLUSTRATIONS

p. 81, Copyright © 2001 National Press Photographers Association. Reprinted courtesy of the National Press Photographers Association; **p. 83,** Courtesy of the American Association of Political Consultants; **p. 84,** Copyright © 1990 American Association of Advertising Agencies. Used by permission; **p. 85,** Reproduced with permission from The Public Relations Society of America (www.prsa.org); **p. 87,** Copyright © 1996 Society of Professional Journalists; **p. 117,** MSNBC screen shot reprinted by permission from Microsoft Corporation; **p. 123,** Reprinted with permission from the Fargo Forum; **p. 133,** Reprinted with permission from Omaha.com; **p. 378,** Copyright © 2001 iVillage Inc. All rights reserved. Reproduced with permission.

PHOTOS AND ADVERTISEMENTS

p. 99, © Gail Mooney/CORBIS; **p. 141,** Courtesy Ford Motor Corporation; **p. 158,** © Alan Schein Photography/CORBIS; **p. 161,** Courtesy of Marvin Windows and Doors; **p. 162,** Courtesy Ford Motor Company; **p. 166,** © Wally McNamee/CORBIS; **p. 173,** Image courtesy of www.adbusters.org; **p. 174,** Chico's Media, Inc.; **p. 176,** © Reuters NewMedia Inc./CORBIS; **p. 181,** © Wally McNamee/CORBIS; **p. 206,** AP/Wide World Photos; **p. 237,** Image courtesy of www.adbusters.org; **p. 247,** © Matthew Mendelsohn/CORBIS; **p. 260,** © AFP/CORBIS; **p. 265,** AP/Wide World Photos; **p. 273,** © Reuters New Media Inc./CORBIS; **p. 289,** © Reuters NewMedia Inc./CORBIS; **p. 330,** © Owen Franken/CORBIS; **p. 333,** © Wally McNamee/CORBIS; **p. 334,** © Reuters NewMedia Inc./CORBIS; **p. 392,** © Brian Leng/CORBIS; **p. 398,** © Reuters NewMedia Inc./CORBIS; **p. 433,** © AFP/CORBIS; **p. 439,** © Ed Young/CORBIS

Index

ABC, 98, 103, 131, 228, 366
ABC World News Tonight, 336
Abercrombie and Fitch, 95
Ability, 50
Abraham, Spencer, 253
Acceptance speeches, 344
Access, 67–68
Access to news, 124
"AccuWeather" forecasts, 98
Achievement, 226
Achievers (VALS survey), 146
Ackley, T. E., 441
Act (Burkean pentad), 197
Actor attributes, 409
Ad and the Ego, The, 238
Ad hominem fallacy, 299
Ad populum fallacy, 300
Ad verecundiam fallacy, 299
Adams, T., 328
Adbusters, 80, 172, 236–237, *fig. 8.1*
Adcult, 381
Aden, Roger, 38, 273, 276, 286–287
Adequate sampling test, 295
Adjustment, 352
Advertising, 357–382
  challenges, 364–368
    audience demographics, 365–366
    environment, 366–368
    media-user behavior, 364–365
  challenges, responding to, 368–380
    branding, 369–371
    cross-promotion, 371–373
    internet advertising, 377–380, *fig. 13.1*
    product placement, 373–375
    relationship marketing, 375–377
  effects of, 380–381
  ethics and, 83–85
  in media age, 358–360
  media selection for, 361–364
    direct mail, 364
    Internet, 364

magazines, 363
newspapers, 362
out-of-home advertising, 363–364
radio, 363
television, 362
  political campaigns and, 341–343
  research for, 360–361
    measuring audiences, 361
    targeting audiences, 360–361
Advocacy ads, 342
Advocates, 103
Affective/emotional information, 136
African Americans, 69, 73, 79, 81, 113, 127, 190, 218, 236, 262, 295
Agassi, Andre, 374
Age demographics, 144
Agency (Burkean pentad), 197, 205
Agenda-setting theory, 58–60
Agent (Burkean pentad), 197
Agent Orange, 351
Agitation, 351
Agreement, method of, 282
AIDS, 193
AIDS quilt, 331–332
"Air Jordan," 180
Aish Ha Torah, 235
Ajzen, Icek, 134
Aldus Persuasion, 438
Alexa toolbar, 63–64
Alger, Dean, 97
Allen, D., 369
Allen, Mike, 429, 436–437
Alliteration, 189, 205
Alter, Jonathan, 339
Altoids, 149
Alzheimer's disease, 279
Amazon.com, 63, 69–70, 133, 235, 376
Ambiguity, 48
Ambiguous images, 249, 251
Ambivalence, 48
American Association of Advertising Agencies, 84–85, 259, 283, 395

American Association of Political Consultants, 83
American Bureau of Circulation, 362
American Communists, 350
American Dream, 223, 292
American Express, 221, 374
American Gothic, 172
American Library Association (ALA), 68
American Revolution, 225
America's Promise, 246
AmeriCorps, 224
Amplified voices, 372
Analogy, 281–282
Anderson, Rolph, 397, 399–401
Andre Agassi Tennis, 374
Andrews, Patricia Hayes, 385–386, 402
Ang, I., 139
Angelou, Maya, 240
Announcement speeches, 333
Anonymity of audiences, 132
Anonymous sources, 125
ANOVAs, 279
Anschuetz, Ned, 371
Anti-Semitism, 235
Antithesis, 189
AOL Time Warner Inc., 97
Apparent movement, 164
Apple Computers, 50–51, 187, 373
Appropriate statistical unit test, 295–296
Appropriate time period test, 296–297
Arbitron ratings, 154–155, 362
Architecture, 182–183
Argument
  by analogy, 281–282
  by causal correlation, 282
  by causal generalization, 284–285
  by example, 281
  by sign, 285
Argument fields, 297–298
Argumentation, 21–22

Aristotle, 9–10, 16–17, 36–39, *table 2.3,* 40, 61, 243, 249, 287, 303, 308–309, *table 11.1*
Arrangement, 40
Articulation, 431–432
Asher, Herbert B., 143
Asian Americans, 79, 218
Assertiveness, 262–263
Associated Press, 107
Associating, 18
Asymmetrical balance, 161–162
AT&T, 251
Atlantic Recording, 97
Attack ads, 342–343
Attitude, 134, 194
Attitude formation, 134–138, *fig. 5.2*
  affective/emotional information, 136
  cognitive information and, 135–136
  past behaviors, 136
Attracting attention, 171–172
Attraction, 385–386
Audience measurement methods, 293–294
Audience-oriented theories, 44–51
  cognitive dissonance theory, 45–46, 52
  elaboration likelihood model (ELM), *fig. 2.2,* 48–51, 52
  problematic integration theory (PI), 46–48, *table 2.6*
Audiences, 129–156
  advertising and, 360–361, 365–366
  analysis of, 138–139, 402, 417–421, 424
  attitudes and, 134–138
    attitude formation and, 134–137
    changing of, 137–138
    defining, 134
  empowerment of, 125–126
  ethics and, 89–90
  in media age, 22, 100–101, 130–133, *fig. 5.1*
  polling and, 140–143
  ratings and, 152–155
  segmentation of, 144–152
    demographics, 144–145
    geodemographics, 149
    Internet audiences, 149–150
    psychographics, 145–149
  tests of premises and, 293–294
Audio, 440–441
Audit Bureau of Circulation (ABC), 154–155
Authenticity, 89
Authority, 410
Authority beliefs, 135

Averages, 278
Averill, J. R., 305–306
Avila, R. A., 396
Avoidance, 352, 353
Avowals, 77–78
Axial balance, 161–162

Babrow, Austin, 46–48
Bachelor, The, 56, 219
Backing, 286
Backstage, 265–266
Bai, M., 252
Baird, John E., 385–386, 402
Baker, S., 88–89
Baldwin, T. F., 116
Bandura, A., 321
Barbie, 369
BarnesandNoble.com, 235
Barraclough, Robert A., 391
Barry, Dan, 208
Baudrillard, Jean, 14, 237
Beanie Babies, 219
Beatles, 351
Becton, Charles L., 432
Beetle Bailey cartoons, 249–250, *fig. 9.2*
Begging the question fallacy, 298
Behavioral interviewing, 405
Beiler, D., 252
Beliefs, 135–136
Believable images, 249, 250
Believers (VALS survey), 146–147
Belittling, 200
Bell, D., 15
Bellinger, R., 405
Bender, Melinda A., 275
Benedetto, R., 3
Bennett, Gary G., Jr., 320
Bennett, W. Lance, 120–123, 128, 179, 253, 255, 270, 335, 339
Benoit, William, 266–268, *table 9.1,* 335, 339, 346, 436
Bentsen, Lloyd, 345–346
Berelson, Bernard, 55
Berger, Arthur Asa, 43, 161–162, 165–168
Berger, Peter L., 51
Berlin Wall, 381
Berlo, David K., 245–248
Berry, Lisette, 369
Bertelsen, D., 8–10, 12, 132
Bertolli, 371
Bessette, Lauren, 124–125
Better Business Bureau, 83
Better Homes and Gardens, 303
Beverly Hills 90210, 269

Biases, 125
Birdsell, David S., 345
Birkenstocks, 44
Blair, C., 183
Blair, Jayson, 86
Blair Witch Project, 167
Blame (stock issue), 422–423, 429, 434–435
Blaney, J. R., 335
Blitzer, Wolf, 70
Bloggers, 4–5
Bloomberg Information Radio, 157
Blumenthal, Sidney, 98
Blumer, Herbert, 51, 348
Blumler, J. G., 56
BMW, 374
Body movement, 262–263, 432–433
Boihem, H., 238
Bolstering, 268
Bookspan, 97
Boorstin, Daniel, 206–207, 249–251
Borger, Gloria, 253
Bormann, Ernest, 51, 53, 204, 307
Boster, F., 279, 388
Boston Red Sox, 169
Boston University, 426
Boulding, Kenneth, 248, 252, 270
Bowers, John W., 329, 350–353
Boy, Gerald, 86
Bragg, Rick, 87
BrainReserve, 220
Brand, 369
Brand image, 369–370
Brand salience, 369
Branding, 369–371
Branham, Robert James, 264
Brauer, D., 252
Bravo, 127
Breaking news, 125
Briggs, Rex, 379–380
Brightness, 159
Brill's Content, 140, 154, 295
Brinson, Susan L., 268
Broadcasting, 131
Broadcasting and Cable, 170
Brockriede, W., 294, 298
Bromley, D. B., 264, 266
Bruce Almighty, 370
Brummett, Barry, 43, 179, 215, 231
Buchler, J., 42
Buddhism, 354
Budweiser, 369
Buller, David, 411–413
Burger, Jerry M., 395
Burger King, 371–372
Burgoon, Judy, 411–413

Burgoon, M., 394, 396
Burke, Kenneth, 17–19, 51, 119, 192–200, 205
Burrell, Nancy A., 188
Bush, George H. W., 246, 253, 342–344, 346
Bush, George W., 3, 19, 39, 67–68, 187–188, 196, 201, 206, *fig. 7.3*, 209, 211, 224, 228, 246, 264–265, *fig. 9.4*, 277, 288–289, *fig. 10.4*, 291, 312, 329, 333, 343, 346, 433–435, *fig. 15.1*, 437
Buss, D. D., 374
Bustamante, Cruz, 326
Buy.com, 75
Buzz, 219–220
Bystrom, D. G., 336

Cable television, 111
Cacioppo, John T., 48–51, 61, 305
California Closets, 232
California HealthCare Foundation, 151
Callahan, Sidney, 304
Calvin Klein, 74
Camera angle, 165–167, *fig. 6.5*, 172
Campaign, 326
Campaigns, persuasive, 325–335
    media and, 326–329
    political, 335–347
    visual images and, 331–335
Campbell, G., 304
Campbell, Karlyn Kohrs, 97, 100, 102, 124, 130, 132
Campbell, Richard, 107, 116, 118, 123
Campbell's, 398
Canadian Association of Broadcasters, 75
Canadian Broadcast Standards Council, 75
Canon, 374
Cantor, J., 308
Capitulation, 352, 353
Carey, James W., 12
Carlin, D. B., 346
Carlson, Margaret, 246
Carrier Corporation, 142
Carter, B., 170
Carter, Jimmy, 329, 345
Carville, James, 338, 342
Cash, William B., 403–407
Castle Rock Entertainment, 97
Cathcart, Robert, 384
Caudle, Fairfid M., 319
Causal correlation, 282–283
Causal generalization, 284–285
Cause, 428–429

CBS, 81, 98, 120, 131, 169, 175, 366
CBS Evening News, 170
CD Universe, 151
Celebrex, 70
Census (2000), 152
Central-route processing, 49–50
Certainty, 409–410
Channels, media, 103, 106–119
Chapin, Betty, 68
Characterological coherence, 290
Charatan, F., 373
Chaucer, 240
Chesebro, J., 8–10, 12, 132
Chevrolet, 205
Chicago Hope, 269
Chico's, 172–174, *fig. 6.7*
Childs, K., 270
Choice, 65, 229
Christian Internet Broadcasting Network, 7
Christian Science, 354
Christianity, 109, 224
Chrysler Corporation, 38, 115, 257, 291–292, 442
Chung, Connie, 98
Cialdini, Robert B., 394
Cicero, 36, 61, 245
Circle, 160–163
Circular reasoning, 298
Civil War, 191–192, *fig. 7.1*, 348
Claims, 274–276
Claritin, 251
Clausing, J., 151
Climate issues, 409
Clinton, Bill, 59, 60, 83, 98, 100, 117, 142, 175, 236, 246, 250, 252, 254, 260–261, 266, 269, 293, 299, 331, 334, 338–340, 342–344
Clinton, Hillary Rodham, 118, 200, 207, 234, 254
Clooney, George, 199
Closed questions, 403
Clutter, 366–368
CNN, 3–4, 68, 70, 97, 336
CNN Headline News, 100
CNN Interactive, 97
CNN.com, 169, 425
Coca-Cola, 27, 106, 157, 170, 180, 205, 251, 303, 369–370, 374, 380
Cocooning, 220–221
Code confusion, 43
Codes, 43
Codes of ethics, 71, 81–88
Cody, M. J., 388–389
Coercion, 65

Cognitive dissonance theory, 45–46, *table 2.5,* 52
Cognitive effects of television, 112
Cognitive information, 135–136
Cohen, A., 419
Cohen, Joseph, 280
Coleman, Gary, 326
Coleman, Norm, 293–294
Collages, 149
Color, 159–160, 441
Combs, J. E., 102, 336
Comedy Central, 131
Comic purification, 200
Commission on Presidential Debates, 68
Committed viewers, 153
Committee on Public Information, 55
Commoditization, 27
Common ground, 18
Communities, Internet, 378–379, *fig. 13.1*
Community, 297–298
Compaq, 284
Comparable units test, 297
"Compassionate Conservatism," 224
Competition, 124
Competitiveness, 366–367
Compliance gaining, 387–393, *fig. 14.1*
    in media age, 394–395
    power, 391–392
    situation, 388–391
    techniques, 387–388, *table 14.1*
Computer.com, 357–358
Computer-generated images, 168–169
Concept, 42
Concept mapping, 148
Concessions, 411
Conclusions, 427–428
Concomitant variation, 282
Concrete images, 249, 251
Confederate flag, 191–192, *fig. 7.1*
Conflict, 408
Conflict, cultural, 218–219
Conflict issues, 409
Conflict of interest, 69–70
Conflict resolution, 408–411
    causes of, 408
    methods of, 410–411
    model of, 408–410
Conger, Darva, 250
Connecting, 18
Connotation, 42
Consciousness, media and, 7–12, *table 1.1*
    electronic media, 10–11
    hypermedia, 11–12

Consciousness, media and *(continued)*
  literacy, 9–10
  orality, 8–9
Consequence, 291
Consistency, 291
Consolidation, 109–110
Constatives, 77–78
Consultants; *see* Political consultants
Consumer culture, 237–238
Consumer Reports, 397
Contested meanings, 191–193
Context, 295
Contrast, 164
Contrast ads, 343
Control, 352, 409–410
Convergence, 115–119
Conversational style, 202–203, 264
Cookies, 150
Coors, 374
Copernicus, 293
Coproduction of meaning, 17
Corel Presentations, 438
Corrective action, 267–268
Correlation, 57, 278
Cose, Ellis, 252
Cost (stock issue), 422–423, 434–435
Costs of news, 124
Countermovements, 348
Couric, Katie, 99, 259–261, *fig. 9.3*
Covert persuasion, 268–270
Cranberg, G., 270
Crawford, Cindy, 175
Creating audiences, 418
Credibility, 37, 244–248, 249
  ethos and, 245–246
  source of, 246–248
Credo for Ethical Communication
  (NCA), 29, 59, 66, 87–88, 115,
  151, 235, 308, 327, 426
Critical thinking, 90
Crossley, Archibald, 141
Cross-promotion, 371–373
Cruise, Tom, 374
Cruz, Michael G., 275
Cultivation analysis, 57–58
Cultivation theory, 127
Cultural Indicators research project, 57
Cultural products, 216
Cultural transmission, 57
Cultural values, 216–218, 226–228,
  314–315
Culture, 12–15, 214–241
  behaviors, 216–218, 228–230
  beliefs, 216–218, 221–226
    conflicts and, 218–219
    frontier, 223–224

    on human nature, 225–226
    immigrant, 222–223
    political, 225
    primary, 222
    religious and moral, 224
    social, 224–225
  defining, 215–219
    mainstream, 217–218
  maintaining, 230–235
    hegemony, 231–233
    patriarchy, 233–235
  media and knowledge, 13–15
  postindustrial culture, 15
  transforming, 236–240
    consumer culture, 237–238
    multiculturalism, 239–240
  trends, 219–221
    buzz, 219–220
    scanning, 220–221
    values, 216–218, 226–228
Culture scanning, 220–221
Cuprisin, T., 111
Cure (stock issue), 422–423, 429,
  434–435
Curiosity, 56
Curves, 161–163
Custom Foot, 375
Customization, 376
Cut, 167

Daimler Chrysler, 191
Dannon, 81, 283
Data, 276–280
  evidence as, 277–280
  premises as, 276
  tests of, 292–293
Dateline NBC, 70
Davis, Eric, 260
Davis, Gray, 325–326
Days of Our Lives, 336
DBS (direct-broadcast satellite)
  systems, 111
Deadlines, 124
Dean, Howard, 176, *fig. 6.8,* 220, 327,
  331, 340–341, *fig. 12.4*
Dean, James, 351
Dearing, James W., 59
Deception, 66–67
Decision making, 70–73
Deductive reasoning, 38, 281, *table*
  10.2, 283–285
  argument by causal generalization,
    284–285
  argument by sign, 285
Defeasability, 268
Definition, 421

DeFleur, M. L., 108, 110–111
Deliberative speeches, 36
Delivery, 40, 264, 430–432
  gestures and body movements, 432
  modes of, 430–431
  vocal cues, 431–432
Dell Computer, 375
Dellinger, Dave, 353
DeLuca, Kevin Michael, 332–333, 347
Democratic National Conventions,
  202, 331, 339–340, 343–344, 350,
  352–353
Democrats, 109, 175, 200, 220, 236,
  246, 292, 337, 344
Demographics, audience, 144–145,
  365–366
Denial, 266, 268
Dennis, E. E., 108, 110–111
Denotation, 42
Denton, Robert E., 329–330
Derived beliefs, 135–136
Derrida, Jacques, 44
Des Moines Register, 107
Description, 410
Descriptive statistics, 278
Desiron, 127
Detenber, Benjamin H., 320
Diagonal direction, 161–162
Diallo, Amadou, 280
Dialogical perspectives on ethical
  decision making, 73
Diana, Princess of Wales, 243, 266, 268
Diet Pepsi Twist, 5
Differance, 44
Differences, method of, 282–283
Digital divide, 67, 115
Digital television recorders, 111
Digital video, 167
Dillard, James Price, 134, 137,
  190–191, 393–396
Direct eye gaze, 172
Direct mail, 364
Discourse, 78–79, *table 3.2*
Disney, 169
Disneyland, 118
Dissolve, 167
Dissonance, 45; *see also* cognitive
  dissonance theory
Distinguishing between customers, 376
Divergence, 47
Diversion, 57
Dobscha, Susan, 377
Dodge, 298
Dodge Ram, 257
Dole, Bob, 98, 175, 338, 343
Dole, Elizabeth, 264, 432

Dominance, 386
Dondis, Donis A., 159, 161
Door-in-the-face technique (DITF),
    395–397
Dorch, Shannon, 145
Dotcomguy, 397–398, *fig. 14.2*
Dots, 160
Doublespeak, 192–193
Douglas, Susan, 233
Dr. Laura, 74–75
Dramatism, 193
Dramatistic redemption, 198–201
Dramatized news, 121–122
Drewniany, B. L., 163, 443–444
Drkoop.com, 373
Drudge, Matt, 86, 98
Drudge Report, 86, 98
Drug Control Policy office, 269
Duffy, Margaret, 54
Dukakis, Michael, 342
Duke, David, 287–288
Duncan, Margaret Carlisle, 179
Durham, Deborah, 259
DVD players, 376–377
Dynamism, 248

E★Trade.com, 275, 369
Early Show, The, 170
Earnhardt, Dale, 242–243
Ebesu, A. S., 411–413
Eco, Umberto, 43
Economic motivation, 378
Economic Way of the Cross, 207
Eddie Bauer, 179
Eder, Donna, 321
Editing, 175
Edward Jones Investments, 313
Efficiency, 226
Effort, 228
Ehninger, D., 294, 298
Ehrenberg, A., 380
Eisenhower, Dwight D., 329, 351
Ekdom, L. R., 218, 226
Elaboration likelihood model (ELM),
    35, *fig. 2.2,* 48–51, 52
Electronic eloquence, 26–27, 201–208
    conversational style, 202–203
    personification, 201
    self-disclosure, 202
    verbal distillation, 203–205
    visual dramatization, 205–208
Electronic intimacy, 168
Electronic media, 10–11; *see also* Media
Elektra Records, 97
Elizabeth II, Queen, 266, 268
Elliott, Michael T., 366–368

Emmanouilides, C., 238
Emoticons, 385
Emotion, 305
Emotional appeals, 172–173, 305–311,
    table 11.1
    defining, 305–307
    fear as, 308–311
Emotional language, 298
Empathy, 410
Enlightenment, 200
Entertainment Industry Foundation
    (EIF), 260
Entertainment media, 100, 126–127,
    269
Entertainment programming, 100
Entertainment Tonight, 250
Enthymemes, 287–288
Ephemeral media messages, 100
Epideictic speeches, 36–37
Episcopelian Church, 220
Equality, 227
Equity, 89, 370
ER, 198–200, 269, 275
ESPN Sportscenter, 131
Esteem needs, 312–313
Ethical insights
    ethical responsibilities of persuaders
        and audience members, 66
    ethics, advertising, and self-esteem,
        308
    ethics and audience analysis, 151
    ethics and cross-promotion, 373
    ethics and lowballing, 395
    ethics and organizational image, 259
    ethics and plagiarism, 426
    ethics and reasoning, 283
    ethics and spin control, 199
    ethics and the boundaries of
        persuasion, 327
    ethics and the digital divide, 115
    ethics and violent entertainment, 59
    ethics and visual images, 170
    persuasion process and, 29
    protecting the interests of minorities,
        235
Ethics, 63–91
    advertising and, 83–85
    audience members and, 89–90
    challenges of media age, 65–70
        access, 67–68
        conflict of interest, 69–70
        deception, 66–67
        oppression, 68–69
        privacy, 69
    Credo for Ethical Communication
        (NCA) and, 87–88

decision making and, 70–73
    First Amendment, 71–72
    Johannesen on, 72–73
    universal vs. situational, 71
definition, 64
five guiding principles, 88–89
journalism and, 86–87
judgment making and, 73–76
organizational advocacy and, 85–86
political persuasion and, 82–83
public sphere and, 76–81
visual images and, 81–82
Ethics Newsline (Institute for Global
    Ethics), 76
Ethos, 37, 245–246
Evaluative judgments, 47, 134,
    409–410
Evans, Cathy, 321
Evasion of responsibility, 266–268
Evidence, 277
    as data, 277–280
        examples, 277–278
        statistics, 278–279
        testimony, 280
    in persuasive presentations, 423–425
    tests of, 292–297
        context, 295
        recency, 294
        source ability, 294–295
        source identification, 294
        source willingness, 295
Example, 277–278, 281, 426
Existence, 422
Experiencers (VALS survey), 146
Expert testimony, 280
Expertise strategy, 387–388
Expressive movements, 348, 354–355
Extemporaneous delivery, 431
External consistency, 293
Eye movements, 261–262
Eyes Wide Shut, 169

Fact, 291, 417
Factual speeches, 417
Factual testimony, 280
Fact/value topics, organizational
    patterns for, 428
Fairness Doctrine, 108
Fallacies, 298–300
    ad hominem, 299
    ad populum, 300
    ad verecundiam, 299
    begging the question, 298
    non sequitur, 299
    slippery slope, 300
    straw argument, 299–300

Faludi, Susan, 234
Fantasies, 53
Fantasy themes, 53
Fantasy types, 53
Farce, 319
Fargo, 102
Fargo Forum, 123
Farley, Chris, 384
Fear appeals, 308–311, *fig. 11.1*
Federal Communications Commission (FCC), 109
Federal Elections Commission, 75
Federal Trade Commission (FTC), 59, 67, 75, 83–84
"Feelingstalk," 339
Feminist perspectives, 210–212
Ferguson, Marylin, 355
Fern, E. F., 396
Ferrara, Merissa, 413
Feshbach, S., 308
Festinger, Leon, 45–46, 61
Film, 166
Firm, The, 374
First Amendment (U.S. Constitution), 59, 71–72
Fishbein, Martin, 134
Fisher, A., 405
Fisher, Walter, 51, 250, 289–292
Fiske, John, 126, 215–216
Fitzgerald, Mark, 107
Fitzgibbon, J. E., 191
Five canons of rhetoric, 39–41, *table 2.4*
Flass, R., 253
Fleetwood, Blake, 87
Fleetwood Mac, 331
Flexible stability of attitudes, 134
Focus groups, 148–149
Fogle, Jared S., 67
Food Network, 131, 362
Foot-in-the-door technique (FITD), 393–395
Ford, Gerald, 346
Ford Excursion, 313
Ford Motor Company, 115, 161–162, *fig. 6.3*, 187, 205, 375, 420
Forensic speeches, 36
Forewarning, 436
Form, 160–162, *figs. 6.2-4*
Fortune, 141, 370
48 Hours, 120
Foss, Sonja K., 14, 183–185
Fotheringham, Wallace C., 17
Foucault, Michel, 210
Fournier, Susan, 370–371, 377
Fox, 154, 367

Fox Sports, 374
Fragmented news, 122
Fragmented society, 365–366
Framing, 165, 167, 197–198
Frank, Reuven, 121
Franklin, Benjamin, 224
Franz, Dennis, 260
Freedom, 227
Frequency, 361
Frequency distributions, 278–279, *table 10.1*
Frey, L. R., 278
Friedenberg, Robert, 337
Friedman, Steve, 170
Friedrich, Gustav W., 411
Friends, 12, 142, 231–233
Frontier beliefs, 223–224
Fujioka, Y., 127

G. D. Searle, 70
Gallup, George, 141
Gallup Polls, 3, 144, 223
Gandhi faction, 351
Gannett Corporation, 108
Gap, 27, 95, 237–238
Gardner, W. L., 305
Garlikov, Rick, 287
Gatekeepers, 103
Gates, Bill, 118, 249
Gateway Computers, 375
Gaudet, Hazel, 55
Gauntlett, D., 127
Gay Financial Network, 145
Gay.com, 145
Geller, L. K., 376
General Electric, 97
General Semanticists, 42
Geodemographics, 149
Geracimos, Ann, 244
Gerbner, George, 57
Gestures, 432–433, *fig. 15.1*
Get Out the Vote (GOTV) strategy, 304
Gilbey's London Dry Gin, 106
Giles, Robert, 37
Gingrich, Newt, 175
Girl Scouts of the USA, 253
Gitlin, Todd, 350, 353
Giuliani, Rudy, 74
GLAAD (Gay and Lesbian Alliance against Defamation), 75
Goals, 354
Goffman, Erving, 264–265
Gold Card viewers, 153
Goldstein, M. J., 308
Golf Channel, 131

Gone with the Wind, 231
Goodyear Tire and Rubber Company, 440
Gore, Al, 67, 202, 211, 332, 338–340, 342–343, 346
Gore, Tipper, 332
"Got milk?," 77–79, 172, 205
Graber, Doris, 119–120, 123
Gramm, Phil, 341
Graphic movement, 164
Green, Nancye, 182–183
Green Party, 225, 337
Greene, J. O., 388
Greenpeace, 327, 333
Greenstein, J., 296
Grefe, Edward P., 82
Grenada military action, 292
Griffin, E., 34–35
Griffith, D. A., 377
Grimm, M., 180
Gronbeck, Bruce, 14, 327–328, 339–340, 429
Gross, Larry, 57
Ground Zero, 264–265, *fig. 9.4*
Grumet, T., 81
Guerrilla faction, 351
Guilt, 195, 198–200
Gumpert, Gary, 384
Gusfield, J. R., 328
Gustke, C., 220–221

Ha, Louisa, 366, 368
Habermas, Jurgen, 76–80, 328
Habitat for Humanity, 223
Hamilton, Mark A., 187–188
Hammond, Joshua, 228–230
Hand gestures, 432–433, *fig. 15.1*
Happy Meal, 372
Harmonic Convergence, 355
Harmony, 164
Harrison, K., 308
Harrison, Teresa M., 257–258
Harrison, William Henry, 338
Hart, Roderick P., 337
Harvey, M. L., 182–183
Hauser, Gerard A., 307
Hawk, Tony, 51
Hayden, Tom, 353
HBO, 97
HDTV (high-definition television), 111
Heath, R. P., 146, 148–149
Hegemony, 231–232
Henderson, Florence, 5
Henderson, P. W., 158, 179–182
Herbeck, Dale, 345

Herrera, Frank, 439, 441–442
Hewgill, M. A., 308
Hewlett-Packard, 205, 442
Heyward, Andrew, 170
Hierarchy, 194
Hill, A., 127
Hilton Hotels, 142
Hilts, Elizabeth, 118
Hinduism, 354
Hirschman, Elizabeth C., 370
Hispanics, 109, 218, 239
Hitler, Adolf, 196, 209
Hofstede, Geert, 239–240
Holbert, R. L., 346
Hollie, 362–363
Hollis, Nigel, 379–380
Holocaust, 196
Home and Garden Television, 362
Homer, 9
Homestead Act, 222
Hong, J., 361
Horizontal direction, 161
Horse race, political campaign as, 336
Horton, Willie, 342
Hovind, Mark B., 336
Hovland, C. I., 437
How to Lose a Guy in Ten Days, 370
Hu, Yu-Wei, 59
Hue, 159
Huff, D., 278
Huffington, Arianna, 326
Human nature, beliefs on, 225–226
Human-nature perspective on ethical
   decision making, 73
Humor, 319
Humphrey, Hubert, 352
Humphrey, Hubert, III ("Skip"),
   293–294
Hunter, James Davison, 218–219
Hunter, John E., 187–188, 394, 396
Hunt's, 371
Hussein, Saddam, 3–4, 19, 24, 187,
   272, *fig. 10.1*, 433–435, 437
Huus, Kari, 114, 117–118, 120, 132
Hyde, Michael J., 305–307, 317–318
Hypermedia, 11–12
Hypothesis tests, 279

"I Have a Dream" (King), 189–190
Iacocca, Lee, 291–292, 442
IBM, 221, 251
IBM Lotus, 226
Iconic signs, 42
Ideal speech situation, 79–80
Identification, 18, 173, 195, 376
Ideographs, 209

Ideology, 209, 354
Iliad (Homer), 9
Ill (stock issue), 422, 429, 434–435
Image, 248; *see also* Visual images
   choosing meanings for, 255
   creating, 253–254
   evaluating, 255–256
   organizational, 258
   in political campaigns, 338–339
   repair of, 266–268, *table 9.1*
Image events, 332–335, *fig. 12.2*
Immigrant beliefs, 222–223
Impersonal media sources, 97
Impersonated voices, 372
Implied movement, 164
Impression management, 264–266
Impressions, 372
Impromptu delivery, 431
Imus, Don, 363
Inch, E. S., 273
Incongruity, 200
Inconsequential beliefs, 136
Indexical signs, 42
Individual persuaders, 261–266
   delivery and, 264
   impression management and,
      264–266
   nonverbal communication and,
      261–264
Individual values, 314–315
Individualism, 227, 240
Inductive reasoning, 38, 281–283, *table
   10.2*
   argument by analogy, 281–282
   argument by causal correlation,
      282–283
   argument by example, 281
Industrial Revolution, 16
Infante, Dominic A., 34
Inferential statistics, 278–279
Information management, 411
Information motivation, 377
Information overload, 28, 66
Innovators (VALS survey), 146
Inoculation, 438
Inside Politics, 336
Instantaneous media messages, 100
Institute of Public Opinion, 141
Institutional sources, 97, 256–261
   image and, 258–259
   spokespeople and, 258–261
Instrumental values, 315–316, *table
   11.2*
Intel, 38
Interaction, 76, 376
Interactive audiences, 416

Interactive control motivation, 377
Interactive multimedia, 169–170
Intermedia Advertising Group, 5
Internal consistency, 292–293
Internalized commitments, activation
   of, 387–389
International identification, 20
International Monetary Fund, 207
Internet
   advertising and, 364, 377–380, *fig.
      13.1*
   audience segmentation on, 149–150
   gay and lesbian market and, 145
   hypermedia and, 11–12
   as media channel, 113–115, *table 4.3*
   media content and, 100
   newspapers on, 108
   political campaigns and, 220,
      340–341
   polling and, 142
   ratings, 155
   relationship marketing and, 375
   safety needs and, 312
   Starr Report and, 100, 114
   visual images and, 104–105
Internet activity
   analyzing media convergence, 119
   appealing to values, 318
   assessing a poll, 143
   culture scanning, 221
   describing images, 252
   evaluating evidence, 425
   evaluating photographs, 167
   exploring Internet advertising, 380
   exploring Internet communities,
      379
   fulfilling safety needs, 312
   gender, power, and cyberspace, 212
   identifying claims in political
      cartoons, 179
   identifying media influence, 104
   international identification, 20
   judging credibility, 249
   managing power in *The Simpsons*,
      233
   persuasion on Internet, 27
   persuasive interviews, 406
   presidential eloquence, 208
   presidential persuasion, 39
   protecting privacy online, 70
   reasoning in everyday life, 287
   resolving ethical issues, 76
   sequential-request strategies, 396
   setting Internet news agenda, 60
   understanding media frames, 350
   using multimedia, 443

Internet activity *(continued)*
  VALS survey, 147
  watching debates, 347
Internet advertising, 377–380
Internet communities, 378–379,
  fig. 13.1
Internet radio, 109, 363
Interpersonal, long-term consequences,
  390–391
Interpersonal, short-term
  consequences, 390
Interpersonal commitments, activation
  of, 388–389
Interpersonal deception theory (IDT),
  411
Interpersonal persuasion, 383–414
  compliance gaining and, 387–393,
    table 14.1
    in media age, 392–393
    power, 391–392
    situation, 388–391, *fig. 14.1*
    techniques, 387–388
  conflict resolution and, 408–411
  detecting deception and, 411–413
  interviewing, 401–408
    characteristics of, 402
    goals of participants in, 402–403
    questions for, 403–404
    types of, 404–408
  in media age, 384–385
  personal selling and, 397–401
    in media age, 397–398
    model of, 399–401
  sequential-request strategies and,
    393–397
    door-in-the-face technique
      (DITF), 395–397
    foot-in-the-door technique
      (FITD), 393–395
  variables of, 385–387
    attraction, 385–386
    dominance, 386
    involvement, 386
    situation, 386–387
Interpretation, news as, 336–337
Interviewing, 401–408
  characteristics of, 402
  goals of participants in, 402–403
  questions for, 403–404
  types of, 404–408
    persuasive, 405–408
    selection, 404–405
Introductions, 426–428
Intrusiveness, 367
Invention, 39
Invisible persuasion, 24–25

Invisible technologies, 15, 21
Involvement, 386
iQVC.com, 375
Iran-Contra hearings, 166, *fig. 6.5*
Iraq war, 4–5, 70, 206, 272–273, *fig.
  10.1,* 333, 432–435, 437
Island Hideaways, Inc., 169
Issues, 339
*It's Elementary: Talking About Gay Issues
  in School,* 236
iVillage.com, 378–379, *fig. 13.1*
Ivory soap, 250

Jackson, Bo, 181
Jackson, D. S., 260
Jackson, Jesse, 207, 431
Jackson, Michael, 275
Jameson, 1991, 16
Jamieson, Kathleen Hall, 14, 26–27, 40,
  97, 100, 102, 124, 130, 132, 158,
  183, 201–206, 208, 211, 255, 264,
  273–274, 277, 280, 289, 292, 338,
  340, 342–343, 345–346
Janis, I. L., 308
Janos, James, 252
Jefferson, Thomas, 224
Jensen, Richard J., 329, 350–353
Jeppeson, M. S., 183
Jessell, Harry, 170
Jesus Christ, 193
Jew, Rodney, 160, 189, 441
Jewler, A. J., 163, 443–444
Jews, 196, 209, 235
Johannesen, Richard L., 64–65, 72–73
John Paul II, Pope, 209
Johnson, Dennis W., 82
Johnson, Lyndon B., 329, 351, 353
Johnson, Michael, 181, *fig. 6.11*
Jordan, Michael, 180–181
Jordan, W. J., 389
Jorgenson, P. F., 303, 317
Journalism, 86–87
Judge Judy, 260
Judgments, ethical, 73–76, 90

Kahn, Shulamit, 262–264
Kaid, L. L., 336–337
Kanengieter, Marla R., 14, 183–185
Kang, Jong Geun, 438
Kant, Immanuel, 71
Katz, D., 180–181
Katz, Elihu, 56
Kay, Jack, 276, 280–283, 291–292,
  294, 297, 299, 424
Kazdin, A. E., 106
Keller, Ed, 144

Kemp, Jack, 98
Kennedy, Carolyn Bessette, 124–125
Kennedy, Edward M., 197–198
Kennedy, G., 39
Kennedy, Jim, 405
Kennedy, John F., 168, 338, 346, 351
Kennedy, John F., Jr., 124–125, 243, 252
Kennedy, Robert F., 352
Kenneth Cole, 374
Kerry, John, 37–38, 227
Key, Wilson Bryant, 106
Kilbourne, Jean, 68
Kim, Heejin, 361
King, Martin Luther, Jr., 189–190
Kinney, Michael, 87
Kmart, 237, 372
Knowledge, 13–15
Knupp, Ralph E., 330–331
Kohli, C., 369
Kohn, P. M., 309
Kolessar, R. S., 154
Kopechne, Mary Jo, 197
Koper, Randal J., 188
Kopfman, Jennifer E., 151
Korgaonkar, Pradeep K., 377–378
Kramarae, Cheris, 210–212
Krispy Kreme, 370
Ku Klux Klan, 287–288
Kucynski, A., 170
Kupper, J., 332

LaBahn, D. W., 369
Labich, K., 182
Landers, Ann, 253
Langer, Suzanne, 42
Language and persuasion, 186–213
  contested meanings, 191–193
  electronic eloquence, 201–208
    conversational style, 202–203
    personification, 201
    self-disclosure, 202
    verbal distillation, 203–205
    visual dramatization, 205–208
  power and, 188, 208–212
    feminist perspective, 210–212
    ideology, 209
  social reality, construction of,
    193–201
    dramatistic redemption, 198–201
    framing, 197–198
    naming, 196
    symbol use, 194–196
  using language strategically, 187–191
    language and imagery, 188–189
    language intensity, 187–188
    metaphors, 190–191

powerful language, 188
  rhetorical figures, 189–190
Language intensity, 187–188
Lauer, Matt, 99, 254
Laurel Grocery Company, 419
Lavidge, Robert J., 360–361
Law and Order, 367
Laybourne, Gerry, 116
Lazarsfeld, Paul, 55
Lazio, Rick, 118
Leading questions, 404
Leaks, 270
Learned attitudes, 134
Lears, T. J. Jackson, 237
Leathers, Dale G., 261–264, 431
Leckenby, John D., 361
Lemert, James B., 245–248
Lester, Paul Martin, 159–161, 164, 169
Letterman, David, 200
Levine, Timothy R., 413
Levi's, 371
Lewinsky, Monica, 98, 254
Lexis-Nexis, 425
Lexus, 205
Lichter, S. R., 336–337
Lieberman, Joe, 18–19
Lieberman, T., 70
Lifestyle rhetorical visions, 53
Liking vs. nonliking, 262–263
Limbaugh, Rush, 108–109, 363
Limburg, V. E., 64
Lincoln, Abraham, 193, 230
Lincoln Navigator, 140
Lindstrom, Robert L., 416, 440
Lines, 160
Ling, David, 197–198
Literacy, 9–10
Litman, Barry R., 366, 368
Little, Brown & Co., 97
Llewellyn, John T., 344
Lobo, Rebecca, 253
Lobove, Seth, 375
Logos, 179–182, *fig. 6.11*
Logos (logical proof), 38
Logue, Cal M., 246
Los Angeles Times, 15
Love needs, 312
Lowball, 394–395
Low-power FM stations (LPFMs), 109–110
Lucent Technologies, 227, 251
Luckmann, Thomas, 51
Lutz, William, 192–193
Lycos, 379
Lynch, Jessica, 272
Lyotard, J. F., 16

MacDowell, Andie, 77–78
Macerana, 219
Macintosh, 373
MacLaine, Shirley, 355
Madden NFL, 374
Magazines, 363
Magical advertising, 359
Mainstream culture, 217–218
Makers (VALS survey), 147
"Man in the Mirror" (Jackson), 275
Mannes, G., 374
MANOVAs, 279
Manuscripts, 430–431
Marcell, Robert, 442
March on Washington, 72
Marlboro Company, 214
Marschall, R. E., 178
Marshall, Caroline, 204
Martha Stewart Living Omnimedia, Inc., 257
Martin, Ed, 131
Martinson, D. L., 88–89
Marvin Windows, 161–162, *fig. 6.2*
Marwell, Gerald, 387–389, *table 14.1*
Masculinity, 240
Maslow, Abraham, 311–314, 319
Mason, L. D., 440–441
Mass customization, 118
Matalin, Mary, 338, 342
Material coherence, 290
Maxus, 151
Mayer, Richard E., 346, 439
Mazda, 66–67, 75
McAllister, Matthew P., 364–367, 371–372
McBurney, J. H., 292, 294
McCain, John, 121, 255, 333–334, *fig. 12.3*
McCarthy, Eugene, 352
McCarthy, J. D., 328, 348–350
McCarthy, Joseph, 350
McCarthy, Thomas A., 79
McCombs, Maxwell E., 58
McCornack, Steven A., 413
McCurry, Mike, 260–261
McDonald's, 27, 249, 251, 369, 371–372
McElroy, John Harmon, 221–225, 228
McGee, B. R., 305
McGee, Michael Calvin, 16, 17, 24, 204, 209, 215, 347
McKinney, M. S., 346
McLaughlin, M. L., 389
McLuhan, Marshall, 13, 103
McQuail, Denis, 119–120, 123

McVoy, D. S., 116
Mead, George Herbert, 51
Mean, 278
Meaning, 181
Measures of central tendency, 278
Media, 101
  advertising and, 358–381
  compliance gaining and, 392–393
  interpersonal persuasion in, 384–385
    compliance gaining and, 392–393
    personal selling and, 397–398
  knowledge and, 13–15
  motivational appeal and, 320
  persuasion in, 6, 22–25, *fig. 1.2*
    movements and campaigns, 326–329
    sources of, 243–244
  persuasive presentations in, 416
  political campaigns and, 335–337
    campaign as horse race, 336
    news as interpretation, 336–337
    news as melodrama, 336
  reasoning process in, 273–274
  source images and, 254
  Toulmin's model of reasoning in, 286–289
Media agenda, 59–60
Media audience, 100–101
Media channel, 99
Media content, 99–100
Media framing, 348–350
Media influences on persuasion, 95–128
  assumptions about, 101–102
  channels, 106–119
    Internet, 113–115
    newspapers, 106–108
    radio, 108–110
    television, 110–113
  defining, 96–101
    media audiences, 100–101
    media channels, 99
    media content, 99–100
    media sources, 96–99
  entertainment media, 126–127
  how media persuades, 103
  media channels, 115–119
  news, 119–126
    audience empowerment, 125–126
    decisions about, 123–125
    definition of, 120–123
    presentation of, 125
  sensory experience of, 104–106
    music and auditory symbols, 1(
    subliminal persuasion, 105–1′
    visual symbols, 104–105

Media influences on visual images, 164–170
  computer-generated images, 168–169
  interactive multimedia, 169–170
  motion pictures, 166–168
  photography, 165–166
  television, 168
  typography, 164–165
Media sources, 96–99
Media theories, 54–60
  agenda setting, 58–60
  cultivation analysis, 57–58
  one-shot model, 55
  two-step flow of information, 55–56
  uses and gratifications research, 56–57, *table 2.7*
Median, 278
Mediated persuasive messages, 442–446
  print advertising, 443–444
  video advertising, 444–445
  websites, 445–446
Mediated reality, 6, 102, 168
Medicare, 168
Medium, 99
Meggs, P. B., 164
Mein Kampf (Hitler), 196
Melodrama, news as, 336
Memorized delivery, 431
Memory, 40
Mercury Sable, 313
Merikle, P. M., 106
Mertz, Robert J., 245–248
Message composition, 253
Message credibility, 253
Message salience, 253
Messaris, Paul, 104, 171–175, 177, 331
Metaethical discourse, 79
Metaphors, 39, 172, 190–191
Metatheoretical discourse, 79
Metro News, 97, 124
Metropolitan Transportation Authority, 149
Meurs, Lex van, 365
Meyer, D. S., 348
Meyrowitz, Joshua, 10, 12, 112
Mfume, Kweisi, 207
  ⋯⋯ Glen, 377
  ⋯⋯ tion, 372
  ⋯⋯ 3, 7, 168, 438,

Millar, Murray G., 137
Miller, Eugene F., 246
Miller, Gerald R., 309, 389–391
Miller, Jerry L., 341
Miller, K., 85
Miller, Stephen, 369
Million Man March, 355
Million Mom March, 72
Mills, G. E., 292, 294
Mislabeling, 176
Miss Saigon, 158
Mitchell, Alan, 375, 376
Mitsubishi, 374
Mod Squad, The, 371
Mode, 278
Mondale, Walter, 168
Mongeau, Paul A., 308–309, 322
Monroe, Alan, 429
Monroe, K. B., 396
Montage, 167
Moral beliefs, 224
Morello, John T., 168
Morgan, Michael, 57–58, 112, 122
Mormon Trail, 223
Morris, Dick, 83, 343
Morrison, James, 228–230
Morrison, Kelly, 413
Mortification, 266–267
Moseley, M., 224
Mothers Against Drunk Driving (MADD), 349–350
Motion pictures, 166–168
Motivation, 50
Motivational appeals, 302–322
  emotion and, 305–311
    defining, 305–307
    fear, 308–311
  nature of, 317–320
    humor, 319
    media, 320
    narrative form, 318
    visual communication, 319
  needs and, 311–314
  power of, 303–305
  social construction of affect, 320–321
  values and, 314–317
Movement, 163–164
Movements, persuasive, 325–335, 347–355
  expressive movements, 354–355
  media and, 326–329
  media framing and, 348–350
  outcomes, 352–354
  types of, 348
  understanding, 350–352

  verbal symbols and, 329–331
  visual images and, 331–335
Moveon.org, 220
MSNBC, 114, 116–119, *fig. 4.2*, 132
MTV, 5, 98, 175
Muir, Janette Kenner, 333–334, 345
Multiculturalism, 239–240
Multilevel commercial function, 372
Multimedia presentation aids, 438–442, *fig. 15.2*
Multiplaced commercial function, 372
"Murphy Brown" speech, 294
"Must See TV," 129–130
MyYahoo.com, 150, 375

Nabi, Robin L., 319
Nader, Ralph, 349
Naming, 196
Naperville North (Illinois) High School, 80
Narrative fidelity, 290–291
Narrative probability, 290
Narratives, 289–292
  evaluating, 290–291
  motivational appeal and, 318
  using, 291–292
Narrowcasting, 131
Nassar, Jacques, 420
Natale, R., 374
National Advertising Division (NAD), 83
National Communication Association (NCA), 29, 59, 66, 87–88, 115, 151, 170, 235, 259, 283, 308, 327, 373, 426
National Flood Insurance Program, 52
National Fluid Milk Processor Promotion Board, 205
National Press Photographers Association, 81–82
National Public Radio (NPR), 125–126
National Rifle Association (NRA), 299–300
Native Americans, 79, 192, 218
NATO, 255, 293
Naylor, L. L., 226
Nazis, 196, 209
NBC, 57, 67, 70, 97, 98, 111, 116, 121, 129–131, 170, 254, 259, 366, 374
Needs, 311–314
Negative, 194
Negotiation, 400, 411
Neher, William W., 402–403
Nesbit, D. D., 201, 244

Neurology, 279
Neutral questions, 404
New Age movement, 348, 354–355
New England Journal of Medicine, 296
New Line Cinema, 97
New Prosperity Initiative, 291
New social movement (NSM) theory, 354–355
New York Times, 15, 86–87, 107, 125, 208, 362
New Yorkers, 149
News, 99, 119–126
  audience empowerment, 125–126
  decisions about, 123–125
  definition of, 120–123
    dramatized, 121–122
    exceptions, 122–123
    fragmented, 122
    normalized, 122
    personalized, 121
    presentation of, 125
News decisions, 123–125
News media, 99
  propaganda in, 269–270
Newspapers, 106–108, *table 4.1,* 362
Newsweek, 175, 339
Nielsen ratings, 142, 153–154, 295, 362
Nielsen//NetRatings, 155
Nightline, 342
Nike, 26–27, 180–184, *fig. 6.11,* 187, 205, 273–274, 359, 374
NikeTown store, 183
Nimmo, D., 102, 336
Nixon, Richard M., 168, 329
Nokia, 229
Non sequitur fallacy, 299
Nonpersonal, long-term consequences, 390
Nonpersonal, short-term consequences, 389–390
Nonstop voices, 373
Nontransactional privacy concerns, 378
Nonverbal communication, 261–264
Nonviolent resistance, 351, 353
Normalized news, 122
Norris, Pippa, 119–120, 123
North, Oliver, 166, *fig. 6.5*
Nosticism, 354
Noyes, R. E., 336–337
NPR (National Public Radio), 125–126
NSM (new social movement) theory, 354–355
NYPD Blue, 153

Ochs, Donovan J., 329, 350–353
O'Donnell, Rosie, 372
Odwalla Fruit Juice Company, 266, 268
Odyssey (Homer), 9
Offensiveness, reduction of, 267
Office Depot, 75
Ogas, Ogi, 269
Ogden, C. K., 41–42, 191
O'Hair, S. Dan, 411
Oklahoma City bombing, 53–54
Old Navy, 95–96
Olympics, 359
Olympus, 205
Omaha World Herald, 133, *fig. 5.1*
One-shot media model, 55
One-sided messages, 436–437
Ong, Walter, 7–10, 30, 112, 127
OnStar, 161–163, *fig. 6.4*
Open questions, 403
Open-mindedness, 90
Operation Rescue, 331
Opinion leaders, 56
Oppression, 68–69
Oprah, 336
Optimism, 228
Orality, 8–9
Order, 198–200
Oregon Trail, 223
Organization, 85
Organizational advocacy, 85–86
Organizational images, 258–259
Organizational patterns
  for fact/value topics, 428
  for policy topics, 428–430
Osbourne, Ozzy, 4–5, 24
Osmond, Donny, 5
Osmond, Marie, 5
Outcomes of persuasive movements, 352–354
Out-of-home advertising, 363–364
Overdetermined effects, 22–24
Oxygen Media, 116, 119

Padgett, D., 369
Paige, S., 109
Palmer, J. W., 377
Parallelism, 189
Parallelogram, 160
Parenti, M., 126
ParentSoup, 379
Park, A., 260
Park, Hee Sun, 413
Parry-Giles, Shawn J., 250, 254
Parry-Giles, Trevor, 250
Participants, 355

Password, 269
Past behaviors, 136
Pastene, 371
Patchen, R. H., 154
Pathos, 37
Patriarchy, 233–235
Patterson, Thomas E., 64, 120–121, 336
Patton, Phil, 180–182
Pauley, Jane, 116
Paulsen, Lisa, 260
PBS (Public Broadcasting System), 236
Pearce, W. Barnett, 264
Pederson, Sally, 332
Peirce, Charles Sanders, 42–43, 159, 171
Pentad, Burkean, 197–198
People for the Ethical Treatment of Animals (PETA), 333, *fig. 12.2*
People magazine, 97
People's Advocate, 325
People's Choice, The (Lazarsfeld et al.), 55
Peppers, Don, 376
Pepsi, 160, 299
Pepsi Twist, 4–5, 24
Perceptual premises, 276
Perfection, 195
Peripheral-route processing, 49–50
Perloff, R. M., 437–438
Persian Gulf War (1991), 238
Personal identity, 57
Personal rewards, 386
Personal selling, 397–401
  in media age, 397–398
  model of, 399–401
    approaching prospect, 399–400
    closing sale, 400–401
    making presentation, 400
    negotiating, 400
    planning sales call, 399
    prospecting and qualifying, 399
    servicing account, 401
Personalized news, 121
Personification, 148, 201
Persuasion, 3–30
  audience and, 27–30
  culture and, 12–15, 214–241
    media and knowledge, 13–15
    postindustrial culture, 15
  definition, 16–22, *fig. 1.1*
  interpersonal, 383–414
  in media age, 6, 22–25, *fig. 1.2*

Persuasion (continued)
. media and consciousness, 7–12
electronic media, 10–11
hypermedia, 11–12
literacy, 9–10
orality, 8–9
objectives for, 25–26, table 1.3
commoditization, 27
electronic eloquence, 26–27
forming relationships, 26
repetition, 26
postmodern condition and, 16
visual images and, 171–178
as argumentative claim, 177–178
as proof, 173–176
as representation of reality,
171–173
Persuasion, sources of, 242–271
defining credibility, 244–248
ethos and, 245–246
source credibility and, 246–248
image and, 248–256
characteristics of, 249–251
choosing meanings for, 255
creating, 253–254
effects on audiences, 251–252
evaluating, 255–256
media and, 254
image repair, 266–268
individual persuaders, 261–266
delivery and, 264
impression management and,
264–266
nonverbal communication and,
261–264
institutional sources, 256–261
organizational images, 258
spokespeople, 258–261
in media age, 243–244
propaganda, 268–270
in entertainment media, 269
in news media, 269–270
Persuasion, theories of, 31–62,
tables 2.1,2
audience-oriented theories,
44–51
cognitive dissonance theory,
45–46, 52
elaboration likelihood model,
fig. 2.2
elaboration likelihood model
(ELM), 48–51, 52
problematic integration theory
(PI), 46–48, table 2.6
early rhetorical theory, 35–41
Aristotle, 36–39

five canons of rhetoric, 39–41,
table 2.4
function of theories, 34–35
media theories, 54–60
agenda setting theory, 58–60
cultivation analysis, 57–58
one-shot model, 55
two-step flow of information,
55–56
uses and gratifications research,
56–57, table 2.7
nature of theory, 32–34
semiotics, 41–44
social construction of reality, 51–54
symbolic convergence theory,
53–54
Persuasive campaigns; see Campaigns,
persuasive
Persuasive interviews, 405–408
Persuasive movements; see Movements,
persuasive
Persuasive prefaces, 298
Peterson, Martin Q., 160, 189, 441
Peterson, R. A., 369
Petition, 351, 353
Petsmart.com, 275
Petty, Richard E., 48–51, 61, 395
Pfau, Michael, 438
Phantom of the Opera, 158
Philip Morris Company, 259
Philosophy of Literary Form, The
(Burke), 194
Photography, 165–166
Physical appearance, 263–264
Physical attractiveness, 385
Physical environment, 386
Physical proximity, 385
Physiological needs, 311
Pichardo, Nelson A., 354–355
Pier, P. M., 335
Pizza Hut, 364–368
Plagiarism, 425–426
Plassman, B. L., 279
Plato, 9, 245–246
Playboy magazine, 245, 295
Pokemon, 371–372
Poland, D., 98
Polarization, 351, 353
Polgreen, L., 109
Policy agenda, 60
Policy speeches, 417
Policy topics, organizational patterns
for, 428–430
Political beliefs, 225
Political campaigns, 335–347
consultants and, 337–338

media and, 335–337
campaign as horse race, 336
news as interpretation, 336–337
news as melodrama, 336
message and, 338–347
advertising management and,
341–343
convention management and,
343–344
debate management and, 345–347
images, 338–339
Internet management and,
340–341, fig. 12.4
issues, 339
motivating voters, 339–340
stump speech management and,
344–345
Political cartoons, 177–179, fig. 6.10
Political consultants, 337–338
Political conventions, 343–344
Political debates, 345–347
Political perspective on ethical decision
making, 72–73
Political persuasion, 82–83
Polling, 140–143
Poole, M. S., 408, 411
Popcorn, Faith, 220–221
Popular culture, 216
Porter, R. E., 217, 305, 307
Posavac, E. J., 308
Posavac, S. S., 308
Posavek, H. D., 308
Pose, 166–167
Positioning, 370–371, 411
Positive affective reactions, 181
Positive nonverbal indicators, 262–263
Post, T., 116
Postindustrial culture, 15
Postman, Neil, 13–15, 21, 26, 40, 80,
118, 120, 127, 193, 244, 248, 277
Postmodern condition, 16
Pottery Barn, 231–232, 303
Powell, Colin, 3–5, 20, 24, 37,
246–247, fig. 9.1, 249
Power, 76
The Simpsons and, 233
compliance gaining and, 391–392
language and, 188, 208–212
nonverbal communication and,
262–263
Power distance, 239
Powerlessness, 262–263
PowerPoint, 3, 7, 168, 438, 440, 443
Powers, S., 120
PPM (personal portable meter), 154
Practical discourse, 77–78

Practicality, 226
Predispositions, 134
Premises, 276, 423–425
Presentation of news, 125
Presentations, persuasive, 415–448
    analysis of topic, 421–423
    arrangement, 426–430
        common elements of, 426–428
        organizational patterns for
            fact/value topics, 428
        organizational patterns for policy
            topics, 428–430
    audience analysis, 417–421
        creating audiences, 418
        direct analysis of, 418–419
        segmentation, 419–420
    delivery, 430–432
        gestures and body movements,
            432
        modes of, 430–431
        vocal cues, 431–432
    in media age, 416
    mediated channels and, 446–447
    mediated persuasive messages and,
        443–446
        print advertising, 443–444
        video advertising, 444–445
        websites, 445–446
    multimedia presentation aids,
        438–442
        design of, 440–441
        functions of, 439–440
        use of, 441–442
    presentational speaking, 442
    samples of, 432–435
    strategic decisions about, 435–438
        forewarning, 436
        inoculation, 438
        one-sided and two-sided
            messages, 436–437
        ordering effects, 437–438
    supporting ideas, 423–425
        premises and evidence, 423–425
    topic and thesis statement, 416–417
    using verbal symbols, 430
Previews, 39
Price, 11
Priceline.com, 363
Primacy effects, 437–438
Primary audiences, 131
Primary beliefs, 222
Primary motivation (VALS survey),
    146
Primary questions, 403
Primetime Live, 103
Primitive beliefs, 135

Print advertising, 443–444
Print media ratings, 154–155
Privacy, 69, 377–378
Probabilistic judgment, 47
Problem, 428–429
Problem orientation, 410
Problematic integration theory (PI),
    46–48, *table 2.6*
Proctor and Gamble, 75
Product placement, 373–375
Profane advertising, 359
Profit, Elizabeth Claire, 355
Progress, 227
Promulgation, 351
Pronunciation, 432
Propaganda, 268–270
    in entertainment media, 269
    in news media, 269–270
Protocols of the Elders of Zion, The, 235
PRWeek/Business Wire poll, 198
Pseudoevents, 206–208, *fig. 7.3*
Psychographics, 145–149
Public agenda, 60
Public Relations Society of America,
    85–86, 151, 259, 373
Public sphere, 76–81
Pucci, E., 183
Puffery, 84
Punishing activity, 387–388
Puns, 319
Purification, 198–200
Purpose (Burkean pentad), 197
Purposes, 387
Putnam, L. L., 408, 411

Qualification, 247–248
Qualifier, 285
Quality, 366, 422
Quayle, Dan, 248, 253–254, 294,
    345–346
Queer Eye for the Straight Guy, 127, 220
Quintilian, 245–246

Race demographics, 145
Radio, 108–110, 154, 363
Raed (blogger), 4–5
Raines, Howell, 86
Ramos family, 277
Rancer, Andrew S., 34
Ranchhod, Ashok, 379
Randall, Neil, 150
Rasmusson, E., 442
Rate, 431
Rather, Dan, 170
Ratings, 152–155
    Internet, 155

    print media, 154–155
    radio, 154
    television, 153–154
Ratio (Burkean pentad), 197
Rawson, Bret, 268
Reach, 361
Reaction shot, 167
Reagan, Ronald, 203, 205–206, 211,
    292, 338, 344–345
Real World, 175
Reasoning, 273
Reasoning process, 272–301
    evaluating, 292–300
        argument fields, 297–298
        fallacies, 298–300
        tests of evidence, 292–297
    in media age, 273–274
    narratives and, 289–292
        evaluating, 290–291
        using, 291–292
    Toulmin's model of reasoning,
        274–289
        additional components of,
            285–286
        claims, 274–276
        data, 276–280
        in media age, 286–289
        warrant, 280–285
Rebel without a Cause, 351
Rebuttal, 285
Recall, 181
Recency, 294, 437–438
Recognition, 181
Red Stripe beer, 374
Redding, W. C., 226–228
Redemption, 198–200
Reduction of offensiveness, 267
Reece, Gabrielle, 283
Reese, Stephen D., 59
Reeves, Byron, 320
Referent class, 218
Reflexive variables of persuasion, 25
Reform movements, 348
Reform Party, 225
Regularity, 431
Regulatives, 77–78
Rein, I. J., 249
Relationship marketing, 361, 375–377
Relationship variables, 409
Relationships with audience, 25–26
Relative frequency distributions,
    278–279, *table 10.1*
Relevancy, 291, 293
Religious beliefs, 224
Remove Intoxicated Drivers-USA
    (RID), 349

Rempel, J. K., 134, 136
Repetition, 26, 189–190
Replay TV, 100–101
Republican National Conventions, 432
Republicans, 175, 196, 236, 246, 253,
    292, 297, 337
Resources (VALS survey), 146
Respect, 89
Responsibility, evasion of, 266–268
Restaurant, The, 374
Reuters, 107
Revenaugh, M., 115
Revere Ware, 371
Reverse zoom, 167
Reviews, 39
Revolutionary movements, 348
Rewarding activity, 387–388
Rhetoric, 17
Rhetoric, The (Aristotle), 36
Rhetoric of Agitation and Control, 350
"Rhetoric of Hitler's Battle, The"
    (Burke), 196
Rhetoric of Motives, A (Burke), 17
Rhetorica ad Herennium, 36, 39, 61
Rhetorical figures, 189–190
Rhetorical questions, 427
Rhetorical visions, 53
Rhythm, 164
Richards, Ann, 264
Richards, I. A., 41–42, 191
RJR/Nabisco, 221
Rockwell, P., 411–413
Rocky, 230
Rodriguez, Sonia M., 439, 441–442
Rogers, Everett M., 59
Rogers, Martha, 376
Rokeach, Milton, 135–136, 216–217,
    226, 276, 314–316, *table 11.2*
Roker, Al, 99, *fig. 4.1*
Rolling Stone, 140
Roper, Elmo, 141
Roper Poll, 144
Roper Youth Report, 144
Rosen, R., 126
Rosenberg, Shawn, 262–264
Rosenwein, Rifka, 98
Ross, I., 369
Rothstein, Edward, 219
Rouner, D., 126
Rove, Karl, 338
Rowan, John, 313
Ryan, Nolan, 233

Sábado Gigante, 131
Safety, source credibility and, 246
Safety needs, 312

Salinger, J. D., 351
Samovar, L. A., 217, 305, 307
Sampras, Pete, 283
San Diego Padres, 374
San Jose Mercury News, 87
Sandel, M. J., 236
Sanders, Deion, 181
Sarandon, Susan, 207
Satellite radio, 109, 363
Satire, 319
Saturation, 159
Saturday Night Live, 384
Savan, L., 84
Scene (Burkean pentad), 197
Schachter, S., 305
Schenden, L., 236
Schlenker, Jennifer A., 234
Schlesinger, Laura, 74–75
Schmitt, David R., 387–389, *table 14.1*
Schnell, Tony, 118
Schrage, Michael, 418
Schulz, John, 426
Schwarzenegger, Arnold, 326
Scott, Linda, 370
Sears, 243, 251
Seattle protests, 238
Secondary audiences, 131
Secondary questions, 403–404
Sedalia (Missouri) *Democrat, The,* 87
Seeger, M. W., 191
Segal, Ken, 342
Segmentation, audience, 144–152,
    419–420
  demographics of, 144–145
  geodemographics of, 149
  of Internet audiences, 149–150
  other methods of, 150–152
  persuasive presentations and,
    419–420
  psychographics of, 145–149
Seideman, T., 169–170
Selection interviews, 404–405
Selective representations of reality, 176
Self-actualization, 313–314
Self-concept, 29–30
Self-disclosure, 202
Sellnow, Deanna, 105
Semantic triangle, 41–42, *fig. 2.1*
Semiotics, 41–44
Sequential-request strategies, 393–397
  door-in-the-face technique (DITF),
    395–397
  foot-in-the-door technique (FITD),
    393–395
Serbia, bombing of, 255
Servicing accounts, 401

Serwer, Andy, 370
Sesame Street, 127
Seven Days, 170, 374
Seventeen magazine, 234
Sex demographics, 145
Sexual appearances, 173
Sexual orientation demographics, 145
Shakespeare, William, 240
Shapes, 160–162, *figs. 6.2-4*
Sharpe, K., 361
Shaver, Lynda Dixon, 411
Sheehan, Michael, 338
Shepard, Alicia C., 116
Sherrid, P., 373
ShopForChange.com, 316
Sign, 41, 42, 285
Signorielli, Nancy, 57–58, 112, 122
Signposts, 39
Sigrid Olsen, 177, *fig. 6.9,* 184
Sillars, A. L., 389
Silver Slider viewers, 153
Similarity, 386
Simon, Bill, 326
Simon, R., 338
Simon, Robin W., 321, 326
Simons, Robert F., 320
Simplified images, 249, 251
Simpson, O. J., 175–176
Simpsons, The, 233
"*The Simpsons* as a Critique of
    Consumer Culture" (Tingleff),
    233
Sims, Valerie K., 439
Situation, 386–387
Situational ethics, 71
Sixties, The (Gitlin), 350
Slater, M. D., 126
Slavery, 191–192, *fig. 7.1*
Slayden, David, 24, 381
Slippery slope fallacy, 300
Slogans, 204–205, 329–330, *fig. 12.1*
Small indulgences, 221
Smith, C. A., 329–330
Smith, C. R., 305–307, 317–318
Smith, L. D., 343–344
Smith, Matt, 342
Smith, S. L., 320–321
Smith, Sandi W., 151
Social beliefs, 224–225
Social environment, 386–387
Social escapism motivation, 377
Social influences of television, 112–113
Social reality, construction of, 51–54,
    193–201
  symbolic convergence theory, 53–54
Social responsibility, 89

Social roles, 306
Social Security numbers, 151
Socialization motivation, 378
Society of Professional Journalists
    (SPJ), 80, 87, 170
Socioeconomic variables, 55–56
Solidification, 351
Solution, 428–429
Songs, 330–331
Sophists, 245
Sopory, P., 190–191
Sopranos, The, 370
Source ability, 294–295
Source credibility, 246–248
Source identification, 294
Source willingness, 295
Sources of persuasion; *see* Persuasion,
    sources of
Space for news, 124
Spatiality, 163
Speck, Paul Surgi, 366–368
Speech acts, 77–79, *tables 3.1,2*
Spiker, Julia A., 341
Spin, 198
Spin control, 198–199
Spindler, George, 216–218, 226
Spindler, Louise, 216–218, 226
Spokespeople, 258–261
Sports Illustrated, 97, 363
Spring, Joel, 216
Sprint, 111
Sproule, J. Michael, 41, 269
SRI Consulting Business Intelligence,
    146
Staggenborg, Suzanne, 348
Staging, 175
Stallone, Sylvester, 230
Starbuck's Coffee, 238
Starr Report, 100, 114
Stasis, 421
State Farm, 309–311, *fig. 11.1*
State of the Union speeches, 19, 203
Statistical evidence, 278–279, 295–297
Statistics, 278, 426
Status, 386
Steele, E. D., 226–228
Steinfeld, C., 116
Stephens, Mitchell, 158
Stern, Howard, 363
Stewart, Charles J., 329–330, 403–407
Stewart, Martha, 256–257, 372
Stewart, Robert A., 391
Stiff, J. B., 388
Stock issues, 422, 429, 434–435
StopDrLaura. com, 75
Stossel, John, 228

Straight Talk Express, 255
Strategy, 409
Straw argument fallacy, 299–300
Strivers (VALS survey), 147
Structural coherence, 290
Structure, 355
Student Nonviolent Coordinating
    Committee (SNCC), 351
Students for a Democratic Society
    (SDS), 351, 353
Stump speeches, 344–345
Stuttering Foundation of America,
    228
Style, 39, 40
Subjective familiarity, 182
Subliminal persuasion, 105–106
Subliminal Seduction (Key), 106
Subway, 67
Success, 226
Sun Safety Alliance, 47
Sundar, S. Shyam, 379
Sunset Boulevard, 158
Super Bowl, 4–5, 100–101, 131, 275,
    357–358, 369, 381
Superiority, look of, 172
Suppression, 352, 353
Survivor, 56, 175
Survivors (VALS survey), 147
Suspense, 426–427
Syllogism, 284
Symbiotic advertising, 359
Symbol, 19, 42; *see also* Visual images
Symbol use, 194–196
Symbolic convergence theory, 53–54
Symbolic signs, 43
Syndromes, 306
Synecdoche, 204
Synoptic phrases, 201, 204
Synthetic images, 249–250

t tests, 279
Taco Bell, 158, 372
Tactics, 354
Taft, William Howard, 203–204
Talk radio, 108–109
Tan, A., 127
Tan, G., 127
Taoism, 354
TARES, 88–89
Tasks, 387
TBS, 97
Technological advances in television,
    110–112
Tedesco, John C., 341
Telecommunications Act (1996), 109
TelePrompTers, 40, 431

Television, 110–113, *table 4.2*
    advertising and, 362
    cognitive effects, 112
    ratings, 153–154
    social influences, 112–113
    technological advances, 110–112
    visual images and, 168
Telford, Anne, 234
Tellis, G. T., 380
Templin, Charlotte, 234
Ten Commandments, 224
Terminal values, 315–316, *table 11.2*
Terms for Order, 198–200
Testimony, 280
Tests of evidence, 292–297
Texaco, 69
Thehealthchannel.com, 312
Theoretic discourse, 78
Theory, 34; *see also* Persuasion,
    theories of
    functions of, 34–35
    nature of, 32–34
Thesis statement, 417
Thinkers (VALS survey), 146
Thinking critically
    adapting to audiences, 140
    alternative voting methods, 337
    analyzing a news article, 123
    climate and conflict resolution, 410
    creating the Krispy Kreme brand,
        370
    defining persuasion, 21
    ethics and ideal speech situation, 80
    evaluating images of status, 184
    evaluating web pages, 296
    hegemony and advertising, 232
    Martha Stewart's image, 257
    memorable slogans, 205
    processing persuasive messages, 52
    speaking to multiple audiences, 420
    values and business presentations,
        317
Third parties, 410
Third World debt, 207
This Old House magazine, 52
Thompson, D., 260
Thomsen, Steven R., 268
Tiffany's, 87
Time and Again, 116
Time for news, 124
Time magazine, 97, 106, 175–176
Time-Life, 97
Times Square, 157–158, *fig. 6.1,* 170
Tingleff, Sam, 233
Titanic, 169
TNT, 97

Today show, 70, 98–99, *fig. 4.1,* 254, 259, 370
Tommy Hilfinger, 237, *fig. 8.1*
Topic, 416–417, 421–423
    for fact/value, 428
    for policy, 428–430
Topoi, 38
Toulmin, Stephen, 274–275, 297
Toulmin's model of reasoning, 274–289, *figs. 10.2,3*
    additional components of, 285–286
    claims, 274–276
    data, 276–280
        evidence as, 277–280
        premises as, 276
    in media age, 286–289
    warrant, 280–285
        deductive reasoning, 283–285
        inductive reasoning, 281–283
Town hall meetings, 333–334, *fig. 12.3*
Toy Story 2, 371
Toyota Tacoma, 140
Toys "R" Us, 75
Trading Spaces, 131, 227
Tragic purification, 200
Tran, Thuy, 262–264
Transaction-based security, 377
Transcendence, 268
Transcendent issue, 291
Transitions, 39
Treadwell, D. F., 257–258
TrendBank, 220
Trends, 219–221
Triangle, 160, 162
Tron, 169
Trujillo, Nick, 218, 226, 233
Trujillo, Stephen, 292
TRUSTe, 69
Trustworthiness, 246
Truthfulness, 89
Tumtulty, K., 260
Turner New Media, 97
Turner Pictures, 97
20/20, 103, 228
Twitchell, James B., 358–361, 380–381
Two-sided messages, 436–437
Two-step flow of information, 55–56
Typeface, 164–165, *table 6.1,* 441
Typography, 164–165

Ubiquitous persuasion, 24–25, 359, 416
Ueberoth, Peter, 326
Uncertainty avoidance, 239
Uncle Sam, 172
Underhill, Paco, 182

United Airlines, 75
United Nations Security Council, 3–4
Universal ethics, 71
Universal pragmatics, 76–81
University of Nebraska, 43
University of Wisconsin–Madison, 81
Unix, 442
Unstated claims, 24
UPN, 170, 374
U.S. Congress, 175, 291–292, 420, 432
U.S. Constitution, 225, 229
U.S. Department of Commerce, 115
U.S. Department of Defense, 70
U.S. Department of Homeland Security, 312
U.S. Postal Service, 103, 118
U.S. Supreme Court, 220
USA Today, 3, 10, 112
Uses and gratifications research, 56–57, *table 2.7*

VALS survey, 146–148, 298
Value, 217; *see also* Cultural values
Value America, 75
Value premises, 276
Value speeches, 417
Values, 314–317, *table 11.2*
Van Bockern, Steve, 438
VCRs, 110–111, 365
Ventura, Jesse, 18, 238, 245, 252, 293, 295, 328
Verbal distillation, 203–205
Verbal symbols, 329–331
    in persuasive presentations, 430
    slogans, 329–330
    songs, 330–331
Vertical direction, 161–162
Vicary, James, 105–106
Victoria's Secret, 234–235
Video, 166–167, 440
Video advertising, 444–445
Vietnam War Memorial (Washington, D.C.), 183
Vietnam War protestors, 329, *fig. 12.1,* 351–353
Viewer's Guide to Watching Debates, 347
Viewers Lite, 153
Vilsack, Tom, 332
Violation of reality, 171
Violence, 65
Virtual evidence, 441–442
Virtual reality, 169
Visual communication, 319
Visual dramatization, 205–208

Visual images, 157–185
    applications for communication of, 178–183
        architecture, 182–183
        logos, 179–182
        visual spectacles, 179
    attributes of, 158–164
        color, 159–160
        form, 160–162, *figs. 6.2-4*
        lighting, 162–163
        movement, 163–164
        spatiality, 163
    ethics and, 81–82
    evaluation of, 183–185
    language and, 188–189
    media influences on, 164–170
        computer-generated images, 168–169
        interactive multimedia, 169–170
        motion pictures, 166–168
        photography, 165–166
        television, 168
        typography, 164–165
    as multimedia presentation aids, 440
    persuasion and, 171–178
        as argumentative claim, 177–178
        movements and campaigns, 331–335
        as proof, 173–176
        as representation of reality, 171–173
    sensory experience of media and, 104–105
Visual parodies, 172–173, *fig. 6.6*
Visual spectacles, 179
Vivid images, 249, 251
Vlasic, 148
Vocal cues, 431–432
Voice control in cross-promotion, 372
Volume, 431
Voter motivation, 339–340

Waddell, Craig, 304
Waite, David H., 402–403
Walker, Gregg B., 275
Wall Street Journal, 70, 125
Walton, Douglas N., 305
Wanta, Wayne, 59
War Room, 342–343
War Room, The, 250
Warner Brothers, 97, 359
Warner/Chappell Music, 97
Warnick, B., 273, 305
Warrant, 280–285
    deductive reasoning, 283–285
    inductive reasoning, 281–283

Washington, George, 193, 206
Washington Monument, 206
Websites, 4, 7, 116–117, *fig. 4.2,*
    132–133, *fig. 5.1,* 150, 268–269,
    296, 445–446
Weiss, D. L., 380
Weissman, R. X., 145, 153
Wells, William B., 370
Wellstone, Paul, 432–435
Wendy's, 204
Wheeless, Lawrence R., 391
Wheildon, Colin, 165
Whereatt, R., 245
Whigs, 338
Whillock, R. K., 341
Whitcover, Jules, 108
White, R., 380
White space, 163
Who Wants to Be a Millionaire?, 131,
    204, 362
Wilkins, L., 64

Will and Grace, 370
Williams, Raymond, 215, 218, 230
Williams, Robin M., 217, 314–315
Wilson, B. J., 320–321
Wilson, Woodrow, 55
Winfrey, Oprah, 31, 34, 219
Wipe, 167
Witte, R. S., 278
Woelfel, M. L., 389
Wolin, Lori D., 377–378
Womack, Deanna F., 34
Women's World Cup (1999), 153
Wood, Grant, 172
Wood, Julia, 121, 233
Wood, L., 361
Woodland Hills Church (St. Paul,
    Minn.), 7
Woods, Tiger, 359
Woodward, Gary C., 18–19, 105
Word, 42
Work, 76

Working Assets, 316
Workman, Nancy V., 234–235
World Bank protestors, 329
World Trade Organization protests, 238
World Wide Web, 96, 98, 113, 169,
    296, 402

Xerox, 75

Y2K disaster, 178, *fig. 6.10*
Yahoo!, 115, 150, 252, 375, 379
YMCA, 407
Youth Council (NAACP), 351
Yugoslavia, bombing of, 293

Zanna, M. P., 134, 136
Zapping, 365
Ziegelmueller, George, 276, 280–283,
    292, 294, 297, 299, 424
Zollo, P., 108
Zoom, 167